# Foundations of Family Resource Management

*Foundations of Family Resource Management* uses the lenses of consumer science, management, and economics, and beyond to help students make intelligent decisions about resources, time, and energies at the individual and family level. It has a strong interdisciplinary, global, and multicultural focus.

This sixth edition brings in new material on millennials, delayed marriage, household composition, neuroscience, behavioral economics, sustainable consumption, technology, and handling crises. It has been updated in line with the latest census data and academic literature.

The text contains lots of features to support student learning, including chapter summaries, "Did You Know?" questions, glossary of key terms, examples and cases, critical thinking activities, and review questions for discussion and reflection. Lecture slides and an instructor manual are available as digital supplements.

This textbook meets the standards and criteria for the Certified Family Life Educator (CFLE) designation of the National Council on Family Relations (NCFR) and will be suitable for resource management courses in family and consumer science, human ecology, and human environmental science programs.

**Elizabeth B. Goldsmith** is a Professor Emerita in the College of Health and Human Sciences at Florida State University and Research Affiliated Faculty in the College of Liberal Arts and Human Sciences at Virginia Tech University, USA. She is a Fulbright Scholar, has been awarded grants from Stanford University, the Smithsonian, and Duke University, and has served as Domestic Policy Advisor for the White House and as an advisor on bankruptcy education for the U.S. Dept. of Justice.

# Foundations of Family Resource Management

**Sixth Edition**

Elizabeth B. Goldsmith

Routledge
Taylor & Francis Group

LONDON AND NEW YORK

Sixth edition published 2023
by Routledge
2 Park Square, Milton Park, Abingdon, Oxon, OX14 4RN

and by Routledge
605 Third Avenue, New York, NY 10158

*Routledge is an imprint of the Taylor & Francis Group, an informa business*

First edition published by Wadsworth Publishing Co Inc, 1995
Fifth edition published by Pearson 2013
This book was previously published by Pearson Education, Inc.

*British Library Cataloguing-in-Publication Data*
A catalogue record for this book is available from the British Library

*Library of Congress Cataloging-in-Publication Data*
Names: Goldsmith, Elizabeth B., author.
Title: Foundations of family resource management / Elizabeth B. Goldsmith.
Other titles: Resource management for individuals and families.
Description: Sixth edition. | Abingdon, Oxon; New York, NY: Routledge, 2022. |
Earlier editions published as: Resource management for individuals and families. |
Includes bibliographical references and index.
Subjects: LCSH: Life skills. | Lifestyles. | Resource allocation. |
Stress management. | Time management. | Work and family.
Classification: LCC HQ2037 .G65 2022 (print) |
LCC HQ2037 (ebook) | DDC 646.7—dc23/eng/20211013
LC record available at https://lccn.loc.gov/2021048879
LC ebook record available at https://lccn.loc.gov/2021048880

ISBN: 978-0-367-76384-8 (hbk)
ISBN: 978-1-003-16674-0 (ebk)

DOI: 10.4324/9781003166740

Typeset in Bembo
by codeMantra

Access the Support Material: https://www.routledge.com/9780367763848

# Contents

# Preface

The world is constantly changing and with it the way we live and find meaning. It is with this in mind that *Foundations of Family Resource Management, Sixth Edition* is launched building on the previous five editions under the title *Resource Management for Individuals and Families* and my graduate education at Michigan State University. Moreover, I served as a policy advisor to the White House and as a professor at Florida State University where I am Professor Emerita, and at Virginia Tech University, the University of Alabama, the University of Wyoming, and New Mexico State University.

The sixth edition brings in new material on work from home (WFH), Gen Z, millennials, delayed marriage and childbirth, household composition, behavioral economics, sustainability, technology, and handling crises. It has been updated in line with the latest census data and academic literature and topics such as economic insecurity and mindfulness. This definitive textbook introduces students to management principles and models about time including original material on time bursts, relationships, decision making, personal and family finance, planning, and responsibilities.

Combining systems theory and practice, students are introduced to the fundamentals of family resource management and how to function better and to get organized. The future is also addressed.

Many chapters contain Suggested Activities with ideas for class or group discussion or individual reflection.

Highlights in this edition include:

- Chapter one adds neuroscience to the list of interdisciplinary influences on the study of resource management and cites it throughout the book, such as in the Chapter 5 section entitled "The Brain and Steps in Decision Making."

- Network Theory.

- The Model of Social Influence original to the author.

- New Critical Thinking Projects and Case Studies such as one on Dr. Jane Goodall, a famous scientist and conservationist, to encourage students to develop their critical thinking skills and to examine unique ways of living and contributing.

- New terms too numerous to list here, in the work world reskilling, entrepreneurship, and the gig economy.

- Expanded coverage on artificial intelligence and well-being.
- A companion website with powerpoints and presentation materials for each chapter.

This textbook is suitable for students studying family resource management—what works, what doesn't, and how individuals and families are changing. The road is often rocky; achieving the right work and personal balance is complex. Recent events have made this truer than ever before as homes and lifestyles are being redefined.

# Acknowledgments

With thanks and appreciation to the editorial and production team members including Michelle Gallagher, Emily Kindleysides, Matthew Twigg, Assunta Petrone, Natalie Tomlinson, and Helena Parkinson of Routledge for their hard work and determination. My thanks also extend to the reviewers of the present edition and to the previous ones. I am pleased to add that I am the author of *Consumer Economics: Issues and Behavior*, fourth edition, also with Routledge.

Many thanks to my students and colleagues around the world, the National Council on Family Relations (NCFR), Voice of America (VOA), and to the J. William Fulbright Scholarship Board (CIES) and the Bureau of Educational and Cultural Affairs of the U.S. Department of State, the University of the West Indies, the University of Malta, my academic home, Florida State University (FSU), and to my family for their love and support.

Chapter **1**

# Management Today

**DID YOU KNOW THAT...?**

… By 2050, the world's population is estimated to be 9.3 billion.
… More than half of U.S. households are headed by someone 50 years of age or over.

DOI: 10.4324/9781003166740-1

… The median age at first marriage in the United States is 30.5 for men and 28.1 for women up from ages 23.7 and 20.5, respectively, in 1947. Current median ages are higher in Nordic countries and Western Europe. Lower in India especially in rural areas.

… In the United States, in 2020, 58 percent of adults aged 18 to 24 lived in parental homes up from 55 percent in 2019.

## What Is Family Resource Management?

**Resource management** is the process of planning, scheduling, and allocating resources to maximize satisfaction, well-being, and efficiency. It can be applied to many realms of life with the emphasis in this book on individuals, families, and households.

In this digital age, life is propelling us forward in paths we would never have imagined Nearly everyone is involved in building careers, updating their homes and healthy practices, and changing lives, theirs and others This book honors that effort which may require **grit**—the combination of passion and perseverance extolled in a book by Angela Duckworth who studied West Point cadets—those who succeeded and those who dropped out. She next studied the rejection-filled career field of sales which challenges people in a different way but nonetheless requires strength and fortitude. Grit requires **futuristic thinking skills**—the ability to predict future events and trends that will affect you. One must be energized by change—creative and adaptable.

Juggling personal life, family, technology, and work is critical to understanding contemporary management. To explain further, the study of resource management is about how individuals and families decide, plan, and act to progress, fulfill their needs, and accomplish goals in an increasingly complex, technological society. The word "management," whether applied to business or the family, implies working together. Management fulfills this task in a family by enabling families to engage in collective decision-making and by providing a framework that supports and maximizes the benefits to family members. The National Council on Family Relations (NCFR) sums it up this way:

Family resource management is an understanding of the decisions individuals and families make about developing and allocating resources including time, money, material assets, energy, friends, neighbors, and space, to meet their goals.

Individual and family resource management raises a lot of questions about how life is managed, such as: How can I find a fulfilling career?

Where should I live?

Should I go to graduate school? What should I be doing with my life? How can I succeed?

Where do I fit in?

In using technology, am I sacrificing privacy for more convenience?

Surely you would have asked yourself at least some of these questions. This book is about time management, thinking and planning, and making decisions and choices as an individual and as a member of a family or group. Much of our planning is a sorting-out process, which leads to automatic actions like removing spam from email or more complicated life decisions such as choosing where to live, whom to marry, and if and when to have children. When you choose, you are accountable for the resources used and the paths selected such as applying to a school or for an award. Your time and what you choose to do with it are gold.

**Resiliency** (defined as the ability to adapt) is needed to meet individual and family goals. All individuals and families encounter difficult and complex issues. A case in point is the worldwide pandemic that individuals, families, governments, health organizations, and employers faced in 2020 and 2021, and beyond (Gates, 2020). Issues surrounded solving the pandemic, administering vaccines, and keeping Covid-19 from happening again—the second has long-term consequences for everyone including managers and leaders. Risk is inherent in how people dealt with the pandemic and with the privacy, security, and surveillance example in the critical thinking box. Risk can be a good thing (propelling us forward such as space travel) but risks must be weighed.

### CRITICAL THINKING

**Privacy, Security, and Surveillance**

In recent years, societies are moving toward a state of constant surveillance with motion detectors in homes, cameras in homes, schools, businesses, and on streets, Google Homes and Amazon Echoes—we as humans allow them to listen in and/or film our daily lives. Household technology has changed with hundreds of millions of smart-home devices in more than 40 million U.S. homes and that number is expected to double in 2021 (Source: Amazon.com founder Jeffrey P. Bezos who owns *The Washington Post*). Questions arise as to the wisdom of collecting this information and the amount needed. When will it crest or morph into different forms?

**Choice** is the act of selecting among alternatives. For example, according to the polling company Nielsen, "Younger generations are growing up with more choices at their fingertips" (Levin, 2018, p. D1). This includes changes in television viewing habits. Peter Katsingris, senior vice president of audience insights at Nielsen, says younger generations "'don't know that you had to watch at 3 o'clock on a Wednesday if you wanted to see a show.' For them, dependency on a network schedule is 'like looking at a typewriter.'" A broad definition of television viewing includes streaming through any device connected to a TV. Of course, websites and mobile apps open this definition further.

Mindsets are changing, time use is changing, and there is a renewed emphasis on healthy and affordable lifestyles. When we choose, we rely on what we have or what we can most easily access. For example, there is no sense in searching for a $300-a-month apartment or an entry-level job that pays $120,000 a year, because they don't exist.

Risk, as mentioned earlier, is a factor in the choice. **Risk** is the possibility or perception of harm, suffering, danger, or loss. Let's say a new housing development is being built in your town. The roads haven't even been put in yet, but people buy lots at a certain price based strictly on maps they are shown and their knowledge of the area, developer, and potential services. They are taking a huge risk. The purchase contract may include a time factor: Perhaps the lots will have to be built on within three years or sold back to the developer at the original purchase price, thus limiting the time in which the purchaser's investment can increase. The development may or may not grow in three years and as we have seen in recent years, the real estate market could be in turmoil. Buying an existing house at a low price rather than building a new one in a proposed development may stretch money further.

A basic principle in management is that *where there is risk, there is opportunity*. In the aforementioned housing development example, it is possible that it could be a good opportunity given location and other factors. Some people are more risk-averse (or the flip side, risk attracted) than others, so another factor in management is your personality. Decisions are not made in a vacuum; environment and time play roles, too. For example, physical stores are part of our environment and store layouts affect how quickly people can shop and how enjoyable they find the experience (Skogster et al., 2008). Have you ever been in a confusing store where nothing seemed to be in its logical place? With online stores, shoppers have little patience with ill-designed websites.

People's lives can also seem in confusion, lacking logic or organization. As Syd McGee, interior design company co-owner, noted "I grew up the youngest of six kids. My family lived with a certain level of constant chaos" (2020, p 15). Can you relate to his statement?

## CASE STUDY

### So Much to Choose From

In 2019, Coca-Cola introduced Orange-Vanilla Coke, its first new flavor in more than a decade. There is no question that this flavor was selected after extensive data analysis. "We wanted to bring back positive memories of carefree summer days," Cola-Cola brand director Kate Carpenter said on the company's blog. "'That's why we leaned into the orange-vanilla flavor combination – which is reminiscent of the creamy orange popsicles we grew up loving, but in a classically Coke way.'" (Ziati, 2019). This introduction of a new flavor came at a time when many people are questioning the role of soda in a healthy diet and when municipalities around the country were passing so-called soda taxes. According to consulting company Beverage Marketing, Americans buy more bottled water than carbonated beverages (Meyer, 2019). Because beverage preferences are changing so rapidly, companies like Starbucks offer temporary flavors such as Cherry Mocha around Valentine's Day (February 14th) and in November and December offer a special holiday red and green cup. Each year the design changes.

Through our choices, we define our lives and influence other people's lives and the world in which we live. "Our most meaningful and significant thoughts, feelings, and behaviors in our everyday lives occur in relation to the things we value and strive for, and much of our action is in the service of the attainment of valued goals" (Grant & Gelety, 2009, p. 78). No decision is made in total isolation; we are constantly being influenced and influencing others. According to Stephen Covey, author of *The Seven Habits of Highly Effective People*, "Our basic nature is to act, and not be acted upon. As well as enabling us to choose our response to particular circumstances, this empowers us to create circumstances" (1989, p. 75). A modern example is the Marie Kondo movement based on her book *The Life-Changing Magic of Tidying Up* (2011 in Japan, 2014 in the United States) which swept the world with its message of organization and reducing clutter, known as the Kon Mari method. On Netflix, Marie Kondo spread her message that your household items and clothes (including folding and storage techniques) should spark joy. Her emphasis is on minimalism.

The study of management explores how human beings react to change and how they cause change to happen. It has been said that the only thing humans can rely on is that things will change. Family life and household functioning, for example, have undergone enormous changes in the last 50 years. More women are working outside the home than ever before and are more highly educated. Fifty-three percent of the new Ph.D.s in the United States are granted to women (*USA Today*, November. 11, 2018, D1).

Here is an example of massive choice from Japan: Beverage makers there, trying to keep pace with Japan's fad-driven culture, launch more than a thousand new drinks each year, many claiming to boost energy or provide other health benefits (Terhune & Kahn, 2003). Vending machines provide easy access to the many beverages, but does anyone really need a thousand more beverage choices a year? How are decisions made in this frenzied atmosphere? One explanation is as follows:

Riho Yamanaka, a 29-year-old Tokyo hotel manager, consumes up to four drinks a day and says she switches brands all the time. "When the new drinks come out, I probably try them at least once or so," says Ms. Yamanaka. "But I don't go for one particular brand" (Terhune & Kahn, 2003, p. B4).

## Introduction to Family, Lifestyle, and Household Trends

The United States is growing older, more suburban, more diverse, with more multi-generations living under one roof, with more single-headed households, and with more Hispanics and Asians. As an example of the aging population, the 85-plus population nearly doubled from 1990 to today. Another example was in the chapter's Did You Know That …? According to the Joint Center for Housing Studies of Harvard University, more than half of U.S. households are now headed by someone 50 or over (2018). The number of Hispanics surpassed the number of blacks in 2003. Once driven by immigration, the Hispanic growth is more fueled now by births. This group has increased to 43 percent since 2000. The majority of blacks live in the south and the trend is upward as many return south in retirement, and as young professionals, they seek jobs in the urban centers of the south. A growing number of Americans are claiming to be more than one race. Census.gov provides further information on these trends and others are to be discussed in this chapter. For example, on their website, they have a report that said, "as we gear up for the 2020 Census, the U.S. Census Bureau recognizes the unique challenges associated with conducting the census as accurately as possible in American Indian and Alaska Native areas." One challenge to getting an accurate count is the presence of remote villages and communities and because of seasonal movements for fishing and hunting or for warm-weather jobs. As of the writing of this chapter, the 2020 Census collection was done (99.98 percent of all housing units and addresses nationwide were accounted for) and analyses were underway.

A household consists of all the people who occupy a housing unit (a house, apartment, group of rooms or a single room is considered a housing unit if occupied) according to the U.S. Census Bureau. The trend is

Multigeneration family gathering.

toward a higher number of households in the United States from 1960 to now. Particularly relevant to the study of family resource management is that less than 25 percent of households have a mother, a father, and children living at home, yet the nation's–housing stock is geared to this family constellation. The percentage of U.S. babies born outside of marriage continues to rise, according to government statistics. The age at first marriage also continues to rise, as noted in the "Did You Know That" statements introducing the chapter: the median age in the United States for first marriage is 30.5 for men and 28.1 for women.

The biggest change over five decades has been the decline in married households, down to 44 percent, and the rise of the householder living alone (20 percent) or with a partner (8 percent). There are 122.8 million (and the number is growing) households, with most classified as family households (see Table 1.1). There

Table 1.1 Example of U.S. Household Growth

|  | Family Households | Nonfamily Households | Total Number |
|---|---|---|---|
| 1990 | 64.5 million | 27.4 million | 91.9 million |
| 2000 | 71.8 million | 33.7 million | 105.5 million |
| 2010 | 79.95 million | 33.46 million | 113.4 million |
| 2020 | 83.67 million | 44.77 million | 128.4 million |

Source: U.S. Census Bureau (census.gov) Since a new census is taken every ten years the next one to be collected and reported is in 2030, for that data and the information gathering leading up to it go to the U.S. Census Bureau. In between the ten-year reports data are collected, for example, a 2017 study showed the number of married couples increased but this may be just a reflection of growth in the U.S. population.

## CASE STUDY

### The New Royals

Of course, the lives of royals are atypical but the May 19, 2018, marriage of Britain's Prince Harry and Meghan Markle, a divorced mixed-race American actress received international attention. She became the Duchess of Sussex upon her marriage to Prince Harry. Royal followers know that decades earlier the marriage of the Prince of Monaco to American actress Grace Kelly also received a lot of press and good wishes. These are highly public families and thus a subject we can all share and observe. As this book went to press, Harry and Meghan were living in California with their son, Archie, and daughter Lili.

To discuss further, Prince Harry's older brother William did things differently than his father by picking someone older, Kate Middleton (though only six months), who went to the same university, and whom he dated for a long time. Kate is not of royal blood and was not brought up around royals. Her parents own a party store business and her mother used to be a flight attendant. She may become the first English queen with a university degree. Some say the marriage of William and Kate is more a marriage of equals, and the couple represents changes in marriages overall. In the Western world, brides and grooms tend to be older and more similar in socioeconomic and educational levels than 25 or 50 years ago.

are fewer people per household and part of this increase is due to an aging population besides the postponing of marriage for reasons such as money and attaining further education. Divorce levels are leveling off, with more couples likely to reach their ten-year wedding anniversary. Divorce rates peaked in the United States in the 1980s. According to the 2020 Census, more couples are cohabitating.

More important than memorizing the percentages and the numbers is to reflect on what it all means. How are people living and managing their lives, not just in North America but around the world? Accelerated changes in families and households are happening in Asia, Australia, South America, Europe, and Africa.

Analyses take place for many years after the data are collected. The goal of the Census is to count everyone once, only once, and in the right place.

## Happiness

Given the changes already made in—and still to come to—marriages, sustainability, the Internet, biology, medicine, social values, demographics, the environment, and international relations, what kind of world is emerging? *Will people be happier and healthier in the future?*

**Happiness** is not so easily defined, but most would agree that it is the degree of happiness with which one judges the overall quality of his or her life as favorable. In the United Kingdom, the Office for National Statistics said that societal and personal well-being is beyond what is produced. Using different scales and measures such as the Community Life Survey they found average ratings of life satisfaction and happiness are at their highest levels.

France's president suggested that France's gross domestic product measure include subjective aspects such as happiness levels.

A key question in the regularly conducted General Social Surveys (GSS) of the United States is:

Taken all together, how would you say things are these days—would you say that you are very happy, pretty happy, or not too happy?

---

**CRITICAL THINKING**

### Does Happiness Equal Progress?

Read the following and comment if you agree or disagree.

> *I was reading that the number one secret to happiness isn't fame, money, or freedom. It's progress. Progress=happiness. Happiness comes from setting a goal, and moving towards it, step by step. People with fitness goals succeed because they know where they're going. We should all strive for progress, not perfection. Some quit because they feel progress is too slow, never really grasping the fact that slow progress is still progress! Be proud of every step you take toward your goal.*

> (Source: Matt Moinar, September 29, 2020, Focus on progress and laugh along the way. *Tallahassee Democrat*, p. 2C.)

How would you answer that question? When Americans answer this question, the top choice is "pretty happy," followed by "very happy," and then "not too happy." Psychologists draw a distinction between overall happiness and well-being as this question measures reactions to specific events or single areas of life such as an individual's financial life (Blanchflower & Oswald, 2004). Daniel Gilbert, the author of *Stumbling on Happiness*, says that money itself doesn't make you happy but what makes people happy is what they do with the money. He says that experiences such as travel produce more satisfaction than durable goods. What do you think of that?

## Population Shifts

Population shifts affect management patterns. It is important to know where humans are living now and where they will be living. The worldwide trend is for populations to become increasingly urban and mobile. Today, about half of the people on Earth live in or around cities. In the United States, there are over 330 million people and going up every day with 83.7 percent of the population living in urban areas. The world population is 7.8 billion and rapidly going up. The latest population numbers can be found on Google or at census.gov. By 2050, the world population according to the United Nations is projected to be 9.3 billion. The U.S. population alone will be over 500 million. An estimated 75 percent of the world's population will be urban dwellers. This switch will have enormous implications for the environment, employment, and transportation like electric cars, and other factors affecting the quality of daily life. For example, the median age of the U.S. population is about 37.9 years and rising. States with the oldest (meaning median age) populations are Maine, New Hampshire, and Vermont.

## Management as a Process

**Management** is the *process* of using resources to achieve goals. In other words, management is the process of using what one has to get what one wants. The process includes the functioning, actions, thinking, and events that occur over time. Although situations change, the basic principles integral to management remain the same. How does this apply to families? One study found emerging adults with lower income and less education often delayed family formation decisions because of the strong link between finances and family formation decisions (Kelley et al., 2020).

CRITICAL THINKING

**Increased Urbanization**

Pick one of these implications (environment, employment, or transportation) and explain how you think increased urbanization will impact how families function.

Populations throughout the world are aging, too. By 2025, according to estimates made by the U.S. Census Bureau's International Database on Aging, more than half of Japan's population will be over the age of 50. Table 1.2 shows the most populous countries currently and projected for 2050.

Table 1.2 World's Most Populous Countries and 2050 Projections

| | Countries |
|---|---|
| Current | 2050 (estimated) |
| China | India |
| India | China |
| United States | United States |
| Indonesia | Nigeria |
| Brazil | Indonesia |
| Pakistan | Pakistan |
| Nigeria | Brazil |
| Bangladesh | Bangladesh |
| Russia | Mexico |
| Mexico | Russia |

Sources: U.S. Census Bureau and the United Nations Population Department.

This chapter introduces the fundamentals of management as they relate to individuals, families, and households. It begins by asking, "What is management?" Some answers will emerge as we examine the management process and see how management can be put into action. Other important questions to be explored include "Why manage?" and "Who manages?" Management styles are influenced by several factors, and the study of management draws upon a number of other disciplines. Of necessity, life management must be both versatile and dynamic, for it applies to single adults as well as to families and must adapt to the changing composition of families.

Let's briefly talk about young single adults. Some of their life choices are moving to a city or suburb, hunting for an apartment, townhouse, or small house, and joining friends for dinner, but what happens when the job opportunity is in a small town or rural area?

*Working in the suburbs can rule out the use of public transportation to get around, possibly forcing you to incur the costs of buying a car, gasoline and car insurance and paying for parking. When Rochelle Kleter, 24 years old, accepted a position as an analyst at Citibank's Short Hills, N.J., branch, she traded her 15-minute commute to the bank's Manhattan office for a 1½ hour drive, for which she had to buy a car.*

*(Mattioli, 2008, p. B8)*

She also noticed that she was the youngest person in her office; colleagues ran home to families. On the plus side of a smaller office and a smaller place, you don't get lost in the shuffle. Ms. Kleter says, "In New York, you get lost in the crowd because there are so many people and it's harder for upper managers to get to know you." Her story might have changed in 2020 when working from home for millions changed commuting behaviors. A male NYC financial company employee (office on 32nd floor) in his 20s was told to stay home from April 2020 until he was called back to the office which was then estimated to be January 2021 and still until the writing of this chapter has been extended indefinitely. He is still working from home in the suburbs and loving it. He got to open windows in his home office, ride his bike, and get outside.

This chapter will examine some of these life changes and show how the study of management has adapted to them. As with all chapters, this chapter concludes with a Summary, Key Terms, Review Questions, and References.

Management includes both thought and action. The importance of knowledge management, the "thought" part, cannot be underestimated. We all struggle to learn from past experiences, especially mistakes and failures, and we struggle even more to apply the knowledge gained to new situations. Thus, we face several challenges when trying to initiate knowledge management; among them are

Arrogance (the feeling that there is nothing new to learn)

Previous failed attempts (why try again?)

Lack of commitment, drive, and awareness (why should I?)

Lack of empathy, support, energy, or enthusiasm (who cares?)

These and other challenges, concepts, and themes recur throughout the book. They are reflected in the titles of the first seven chapters: values, attitudes, goals, resources, decision-making, problem solving, planning, implementing, evaluating, and communication. Chapters 8–14 then apply these concepts to the specifics of managing human needs, time, work and family, stress, fatigue, environmental resources, and finances. Central to the discussion in each chapter is the way different personalities and situations affect how choices are made and acted upon.

The **management process** involves thinking, action, and results. Because it is results-oriented, management is considered an applied social science. Management specialists evaluate the knowledge obtained through the study of management in terms of its ability to make an individual's or family's management practice more effective. People need results. It is inherently satisfying to commit to and work toward a goal.

Although management is practical, it is not necessarily simplistic. It becomes complex because individuals' and families' choices are constrained by limited resources. How people handle these constraints is what makes the study of management so stimulating. If everyone had equal resources and abilities, the same dreams and wishes, and the same drive and ambition, then there would not be much to discuss. Everyone would lead identical lives. How boring that would be! In actuality, each individual has his or her own set of resource mix—attitudes, talents, and skills that are brought to bear in situations. Additionally, individuals vary in the way they respond to external and internal forces. Internal forces are the personal drive behind our actions. External forces include the ups and downs of the economy, the condition of the environment, and the rules and laws of society. Consequently, we must view management within the context of the greater environment, which changes constantly, as does the individual or group attempting to manage life within that environment.

The purpose of this chapter is to provide an overview of the management process; each aspect of the process will be examined in depth later in the book. Figure 1.1 provides a model of the management process and indicates the chapters in which each step is discussed. Each part of the model plays a critical role in the reinforcing circle, or loop, of the management process.

The process begins with a problem, need, want, or goal. The person initiating the management process identifies a problem or something that he or she desires. **Problems** are questions, dilemmas, or situations that require solving, such as "Should I buy or rent a home?" **Needs** are what we need to survive or sustain life, such as food and shelter. **Wants** are things that we desire, such as an expensive sports car, but that is not necessary for us to survive. In general conversation, the words *needs* and *wants* are sometimes used interchangeably, but in management, they are viewed as distinct. Needs can include the need for wellness, social interaction, financial support, and information. Regarding the latter, we want to know what is going on around us, what is in the news, and what the weather will be like so we can plan our actions. We have a need to satisfy intellectual curiosity, which is why you are reading this book, and to engage in cognitive activity. For example, people need food, air, water, and shelter to survive. Wants are more specific; they are things or activities that make people feel comfortable and satisfied. Thus, a person may be hungry (a need) but may want to satisfy that hunger with a specific food, such as a burrito or a slice of pizza.

**Goals** are end results that require action for their fulfillment. Goals connect individuals to situations, providing a sense of meaning and control over events and environments. A college diploma is a goal of most college students. Passing courses and applying for graduation are the actions required to reach that goal. In the greater scheme of life, goals are arranged in a hierarchy from fairly ordinary to extraordinary.

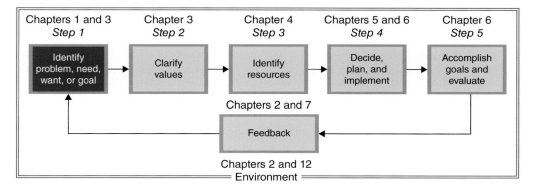

Figure 1.1 **The management process.**

Once individuals or families have identified the problem, need, want, or goal, they move to the next step, which is the clarification of values. What do they really want, and does it fit into their value system? **Values** are principles that guide behavior, such as honesty or loyalty. **Clarification** means to make it clear, to make it easier to understand, or to elaborate. As they move through the management process, people need to clearly identify what they want to achieve and to ensure that their goal-seeking behavior is compatible with their values. For example, an individual may desire more money, but robbing a bank probably doesn't fit the person's or society's value system. Management is based on values and goal-seeking behavior; without these, the process would be aimless and misdirected. Behavior has consequences.

The next step in Figure 1.1 involves identifying resources: finding out what one has to work with. **Resources** are whatever is available to be used, such as information, time, skills, human and mechanical energy, Internet access, and money. Consider the situation described by writer Ruth Davis Konigsberg in the case study:

### CASE STUDY

#### Time Problems

If there was one time in my marriage when life felt the most unfair, it was during the witching hour. When our children were young and I was working from home, I would relieve our babysitter at 5 P.M. and start to feed and bathe our three-year-old and six-month-old and begin various pre-bedtime rituals. By 6 P.M., this thought would be running through my head: If my husband doesn't come home from the office soon to help, I'm going to be losing my mind. By 7 P.M., my panic turned to anger: Do I have to do *everything*? Each minute before his arrival seemed like an eternity, my task much more onerous than the pressure he was facing to make daily deadlines. Was our parenting arrangement altering my perception of time…

Can you relate to the family situation in the Time Problems case study or can you project that this may be a problem in your future?

The quantitative and/or qualitative *criteria* that reconcile resources with demands are known as **standards**. Standards are set by individuals and families for themselves; they are also set by friends, employers, schools, and governments. For example, governments establish speed limits (a standard) as part of their traffic management in order to preserve life and property, and schools and businesses establish appearance or dress codes for their students and employees. During the management process, standards may have to be adjusted such as moving mealtimes around based on changed schedules. The standard setting is dynamic, meaning that it is subject to change, and flexibility is key. What is acceptable one year may not be acceptable the next. For example, a school may set school uniforms as the standard one year and do away with the practice the next.

The next step in the process has three aspects: deciding, planning, and implementing. *Decision-making* refers to choosing between two or more alternatives. *Planning* requires making a series of decisions that lead to action, and *implementing* means putting plans into action. Plans give focus and direction to the pursuit of wants, needs, and goals. In working through this step, a manager evaluates and adjusts decisions and plans as needed. For example, an individual planning a trip may select a new route or time of arrival as circumstances change.

## CASE STUDY

### Standards or Rules in a Planned Community

This is a true story told to the author, to protect anonymity location and specific details are not mentioned.

Homeowner associations (HOAs) have rules and regulations. You may be aware of them if you have lived in such a community or neighborhood. One of the rules has to do with political signs. In this case, a homeowner did not put a political sign in their front yard (this was against the subdivision's rules) but put a political candidate sign in their backyard visible to a public walking path. An HOA person got off the path and walked on the homeowner's lawn to take a picture of the sign and the homeowner called the police. Is this trespassing? Should the HOA person have walked on his land? What are the HOA rules? What are the homeowner's rights?

## CRITICAL THINKING

### School Uniforms

Do you think school uniforms are a good or bad idea? Explain why. Did you or anyone you know wear school uniforms? What were the pros and cons of wearing uniforms from the students' and parents' points of view? Consider factors like conformity, cost, and time.

The last step of the management process sees goals accomplished or fulfilled and the process as a whole evaluated. Individuals are pleased when they achieve their hard-sought goals, but they often overlook evaluation, which in many ways is the most important step in the process.

Was the problem solved?

What was learned?

Which decisions or plans worked and which ones failed?

What adjustments should have been made?

The answers to these questions are part of the **feedback** (information that returns to the system) that enables the individual's overall management knowledge and ability to grow.

The management process is never stagnant. One learns from and grows with each decision. New situations provide opportunities for advancement and self-learning. By evaluating past experiences, people learn how to approach the world and discover where their skills and talents lie. In many ways, the study of management is a discovery of self and of how others relate to the world.

So far, we've looked at the management process primarily as an internally driven system (people's problems, wants, needs, and goals motivate them to act), but in fact the process takes place in the larger context of the external environment. For example, a person at a busy fitness center may want to use the treadmill but will have to wait if someone else is using it. The environment, therefore, can present limitations or barriers to an individual's or family's course of action. As previously noted, the rules and laws of society also affect how wants and needs are fulfilled and what goals are feasible. Thus, the management process must be viewed within an environmental context as Figure 1.1 indicates. Environment refers to everything outside the individual.

Let's note two other features of the management process. First, in certain situations and decisions (especially hurried ones), the steps may not progress in exactly the order shown in Figure 1.1; sometimes several steps may occur simultaneously. Second, although understanding the individual components of the process is important, the management process is far more than a set of concepts.

The essence of the process is that the concepts are interrelated. The process may start with a problem or a need and end with a solution, but the critical element is what happens in between. From the first step to the last, management knowledge, skills, and tools are used.

**Management tools** are measuring devices, techniques, or instruments that are used to arrive at decisions and plans of action; examples include clocks, lists, forms, calendars, budgets, and timetables. Are you a list maker? Are you very conscious of what time it is? Did you know that the mechanical clock was invented in the 14th century? Before that, people did not think of time in fixed units, but more as a progression, a cycle based on nature. Of course, nature is not linear; it ebbs and flows in an inexact way. For example, depending on where you live, the first day of spring (March 21) may find the ground covered with snow. The calendar says it is spring; nature says it is not. In this case, using weather as a time measure may be more appropriate than using a calendar.

## Successful Plans: Putting Management into Action

Planning is the operationalization of choices; often, it means making a list of steps to be taken. This is the stage when people ask, "Okay, we know what we want; now how are we going to get there?" So a particularly critical management skill is the ability to create and execute an effective plan. Planning helps individuals to

Highlight important problems and opportunities

Invest resources in the right tasks

Encourage the development of goals

Make decision-making more efficient and effective

Motivate and coordinate efforts

Provide a feeling of growth and accomplishment

Involve others

How much planning is necessary? The answer depends on the situation and individual's goals, resources, levels of motivation, and abilities. One fundamental management principle is that planning skill increases with knowledge, practice, and effort. The more individuals plan, listen to feedback, and evaluate their decisions, the stronger their management skills become.

To be successful, a plan needs to be realistic, clear, flexible, well-thought-out, and executed. The experience of job hunting provides a good example of how planning works and how feedback can help individuals make adjustments to their plans. Most college students want to graduate and get a good job that uses their skills, education, and training. Beyond this generalization, an individual student's career goals become more specific. For example, Jennifer's goal is to be employed in a government job in human services or human resources (HR) when she graduates. Her Bachelor of Science degree and senior-year internship provide her with knowledge, skills, contacts, and a platform based on tools. She knows how to analyze data and reports. In terms of values, she wants to serve people in a meaningful and caring way, and she especially likes working with children. As part of her career plan, she wants a job that will start soon after her graduation in May. In January she begins filling out applications, sending out résumés, including an online portfolio, and interviewing. But many of her letters and applications go unnoticed, and she receives very few responses. By April she begins adjusting her plan to include more than government jobs. She applies for jobs in nearby states, in the human resources departments at various companies, and at other places through the career services center on campus. At Jennifer's first interview, the interviewer tells her (provides feedback) that she should rewrite her résumé so that it highlights her past work experiences more clearly. So Jennifer rewrites it and has three more interviews. In June she is hired and begins work in July. Her job is not what she had envisioned, but it does use her skills and provides the potential for growth. She is pleased to be working with families and children, and in hindsight she is glad she has had two months off between graduation and the start of her new job. Jennifer feels that managing this first professional job search has taught her skills, such as the need to be flexible and listen to interviewers' feedback that will help her the next time she looks for a job.

## CRITICAL THINKING

### Gap Year

Increasingly in the United States, students are taking a gap year between high school and college or between college and going to full-time professional employment or to graduate school, law school, or medical school. Malia Obama, daughter of former President Barack Obama and former First Lady Michelle Obama took a gap year between high school and attending Harvard University. A Virginia Tech University student majoring in Human Development asked the writer of this book whether she should take a gap year before going on to a Master's program. She wanted to travel (this was before the Covid-19 pandemic) and figure out if that is really what she wanted to do. What do you think about the purpose of the Gap Year? Will more graduating high school or college students take it?

## Why Manage?

The answer to the question, "Why manage?" is that people have no other choice. Certainly, life involves nonmanaged actions such as everyday activities that do not require a lot of thought or planning (getting up in the morning and brushing one's teeth), but the bigger things that most people want, such as a job and a family life, require management skills. Essentially, management takes people from where they are to where they want to go. Having a future to work toward is integral to people's sense of well-being. Humans need to feel in control of their lives. But being in control is only one of the many benefits management offers. Management also provides new ways of critiquing life situations and offers new perspectives on the nature of change. When people are frustrated or confused, management supplies constructive order, reduces chaos, and suggests steps to follow. For example, familiarity with the management process helped Jennifer plan, make adjustments, and overcome discouragement in her job search.

As a field of study, management is exciting and challenging because it is

Change oriented

Economically, culturally, and socially significant

Dynamic, intriguing, and complex

Personally and professionally rewarding

Integral to developing leadership and teamwork skills and receptive to community involvement

Furthermore, the study of management provides a great deal of insight into a major area of human behavior—the decisions people make and the actions taken based on those decisions. Knowledge of management will help students of human behavior to better understand themselves and the actions of those around them.

Few subjects are more positive and more encouraging than management, or more appropriate for college students who are about to embark on new life paths. Most college students at some time in their lives will be in a position of managing others or working in teams, so studying management while in school is a skill-building asset. Management applies to all stages of life. The ever-changing environment, coupled with their own changing needs, impels individuals to constantly search for new courses of action, goals, and solutions to problems. It is important to realize that despite difficulties, new ideas do spread and new options open up all the time.

## Who Manages?

The answer to the question "Who manages?" should be obvious by now: Everyone does. Management is such a natural and normal part of life that few people stop to think about how they do it. The management process should be employed every time someone makes a decision involving school, career, or personal life. Using this process, individuals consider their needs and wants, their resources, their preferences, the situation, the other people involved, and so on. Then they create a plan of action and implement it. The decision-making of the individual lies at the heart of the management experience.

As Figure 1.1 illustrates, however, management is much more than decision-making; it is a multifaceted process involving many concepts, actions, and reactions. Besides those already mentioned, management includes organizing, scheduling, synthesizing, analyzing, resolving tension, negotiating, reaching an agreement, mediating, problem solving, and communicating. In other words, although management is fundamental to human life, it is often a difficult process.

### CRITICAL THINKING

#### Staying or Moving?

Jason has graduated but doesn't have a job and is living with his parents while he searches for a job. Should he continue to stay at home after he finds a job and build his savings, or should he rent an apartment and try to make it on his own even though the rent will take nearly all of his income and savings? If he decides to live with his parents, should he stay for a year? Two years? What factors should Jason consider besides money in making his decision? What other options does he have?

Throughout this book, most examples will involve individuals, households, and families, but the basic principles apply to all walks of life. As we've seen, however, management is particularly applicable to career situations. Being on time, organizing and finishing work, and scheduling appointments are behaviors that take place in the office as well as at home.

## Influences on Management Styles

Whether at home or at work, people are constantly searching for ways to do things more efficiently and effectively. Commuters try to find routes that will cut ten minutes off their travel time, and retirees try to find ways to stretch their dollars further. Although everyone manages, each person has his or her own **management style**, or characteristic way of making decisions and acting.

Five factors influence management styles:

History influences the way a person makes decisions and the options he or she considers. "History" can apply to individuals, families, and societies.

Biology dictates basic physiological needs such as food, shelter, air, and water.

Culture provides a systematic way to fulfill needs. As social beings, people care about each other.

Personality is the sum total of individual characteristics, enduring traits, and ways of interacting. For example, personality affects how a person interacts with the environment.

Technology applies methods and materials to the achievement of objectives. Technology includes laws, techniques, tools, material objects, and processes that help people get what they want.

### *Maslow's Hierarchy of Needs*

Of these factors, the most fundamental is biology. According to psychologist Abraham Maslow (1908–1970), physiological needs must be met before higher-order needs are considered. He hypothesized that each individual has a series of needs ranging from low-order needs to higher-order needs (see Figure 1.2).

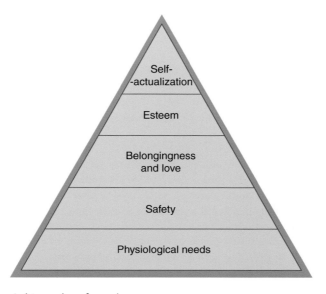

Figure 1.2 Maslow's hierarchy of needs.

In Maslow's hierarchy of needs, physiological needs (e.g., thirst, hunger) must be at least partially met before higher-order needs such as safety and love (Maslow, 1954).

The highest level of need, self-actualization, is the fulfillment of one's highest potential. Self-actualizers fully integrate the components of their personality or self. In other words, they attain self-realization, the process by which individuals have the opportunity to invest their talents in activities that they find meaningful.

Of the other factors influencing management style, history, culture, and personality help define human needs and aspirations. Technology provides the means by which humanity progresses.

## Technology

Although we will look at technology in more detail later in the book, it's important to consider it here because it plays a significant role in the management and will play an even larger role in the future. It's important to study technology because it is playing an increasingly larger role in our daily lives in forms ranging from cell phones to email to e-commerce. We are so used to searching for information on the Internet that it is difficult to imagine life before Google.

Technology differs from the other influences on management style (i.e., history, culture, and personality) in that it is usually visible; technological advances are easily observed and measured. For example, one television set per household used to be the norm and now several would be more typical.

The number of mobile devices keeps rising to the point there are more cellphones than there are people in the United States. How is this possible? Most people have more than one wireless device, which includes smartphones, tablets, and wireless cards. Jon, a stockbroker, has two phones—one for work and one for personal use and he carries both every day and says it can be confusing. To report actual numbers would outdate immediately so suffice it to say mobile devices and services cost money and take up time in their use and updating. Smartphones and service charges constitute one of the fastest-growing expenditure categories. Updated figures are kept by the U.S. Department of Commerce and the Consumer Electronics Association. Smartphone use varies by age group; the younger the age, the more likely the person will have multiple devices. And this is not an American phenomenon. Japan and most of Europe are well ahead of the United States in Smartphone use.

Cellphones are both time-savers and time-users. Before the invention of the cell phone, how did people reach each other, and how did they spend the time now spent on the phone? In addition, email, text messaging, and the Internet have added new dimensions to communication. Most American households have personal computers and Internet access. The average American spends over ten hours a day on media of various sorts.

The use of technology determines its worth. The most documented house in the United States, the White House, provides some examples of this phenomenon. In 1879, President Rutherford B. Hayes had the first telephone installed in the White House, but it was rarely used because hardly anyone else in Washington had a telephone, so there was no one to call or to call in; thus telephone is an obvious example of shared technology. When the typewriter was introduced to the White House in 1880, it was put to more immediate use. Previously, all presidential correspondence had to be handwritten by a clerk, so the typewriter was clearly a useful innovation. In 1891, during Benjamin Harrison's administration, electric lights were installed in the White House. The president was afraid of getting a shock, however, so he refused to operate the electric lights and summoned servants to turn them on or off. To show the progression of technology, over a hundred years later during the Bill Clinton administration, the White House was rewired so that computers could be used more readily and television interviews could take place in a variety of locations without the necessity of dragging around long, heavy cables. Subsequent presidents added even more technology.

When microwave ovens were introduced in the 20th century, many people were not sure that they were really safe and useful. Today, microwave ovens are pervasive. Technology is more than a system of machines; it can refer to ideas or ways of doing things. Today's technologies crisscross many fields so that an invention in one industry, such as computers, can revolutionize another, such as retail. It is becoming increasingly important, then, to be knowledgeable in a variety of fields and to keep up with developments in other disciplines.

## Interdisciplinary Foundation

As the previous section explained, various factors (e.g., history, biology, culture, personality, and technology) influence individuals' management styles. But the field of resource management is even broader than these factors suggest. Although the discussion here will be limited to the connections between management and some of the social and biological sciences, neuroscience, anthropology, psychology, sociology, economics and other disciplines have also contributed to the development of the field. These include geography, political science, agriculture, philosophy, organizational behavior, marketing, biology, chemistry, engineering, and physics. For example, philosophy contributes to our understanding of values, marketing to the consumption decisions made by individuals and families, and engineering to the mechanics and functioning of the home. Geography tracks regions, landscapes, and other spatial units. The distribution of people, resources, and culture is a driving force in geography. Connections to political science may seem obscure, but public policy affects individual and family life through services offered, taxes, and the ultimate control of resources.

## Neuroscience

*Neuroscience* is a growing field dedicated to the scientific study of the nervous system. Within it, there are subfields such as the study of decision-making and neuroeconomics focusing on the use of money and consumer behavior. Neuroscience is itself an interdisciplinary field combining math, psychology, physiology, communication, molecular biology, and anatomy (especially the study of the brain and the spinal cord and how they function). Although the documented study of the brain has its origins in ancient Egypt, it became more organized as a distinct field of study in the latter half of the 20th century and with advances in technology in the current century has moved even further into our understanding of neurons (nerve cells) and the effect on the body. We can learn a lot from this area, especially about memory, addiction, reward behaviors, emotions, learning, wellness, and perception relevant to resource management.

## Anthropology

The word *anthropology* comes from the Greek *anthropo* (man) and *logy* (science). Simply defined, anthropology is the science of human beings. Anthropologists seek to study and interpret the characteristics of a particular population or activity in its place in time. This includes communities, subcultures, and entire societies. Of anthropology's many subfields, cultural anthropology is the most relevant to management. Culture affects what people learn and how they behave. Culture applies to management on two distinct levels: as a set of general attributes of people in a society or group and as material culture, or the objects and tools individuals, groups, and families use. (Because the family is the social group of interest in this book, discussions of material culture will focus on objects associated with the family and home use.) Occasionally a new group is found. In 2011, for example, a Brazilian tribe with 200 individuals was discovered.

The White House is often first in the United States to have new technology.

Culture also refers to patterns. Those who study management are interested in repetitive patterns of living. The characteristic way, or pattern, in which an individual conducts her or his life is called **lifestyle**. Needs, wants, tastes, styles, and preferences all contribute to lifestyles.

## Psychology

The word *psychology* is formed by combining *psyche* (the mind) and *logy* (science). Psychology focuses on how the individual thinks and behaves. Communication of meaning is a driving force in psychology. Social psychology and cognitive psychology are particularly relevant to the study of management. Two of the main constructs in social psychology are goals and attitudes both of which figure strongly in the study of management. Social psychology is the study of individual behavior within a group; it examines attitudes, problem solving, social influences, leaders and followers, and communication. These topics will be discussed in depth in future chapters.

**Cognitive psychology** is the scientific study of the mind that explains the nature of human intelligence and how people think. It is dominated by the *information-processing* approach, which analyzes thinking processes as a sequence of ordered stages. Values, attitudes, and decision-making are integral to cognitive psychology as well as to management. Studies are conducted on judgment, perception, memory, attention, and memory.

## Sociology

Whereas psychology focuses on the individual or the individual operating in groups, sociology emphasizes the collective behavior of social groups, including organizations and communities. *Sociology* comes from the Latin *socius* (companion or associate) and *logy* (science).

Sociology applies the scientific method to the study of human society. It explores why some groups function the way they do. For example, sociological studies investigate the norms and roles of retired workers, schoolchildren, and employed women. Because the family is a societal group, sociology coupled with family relations contributes much to our understanding of family managerial behavior. Families usually share common goals or purposes and interact in pursuit of these objectives. Each member of the family is perceived by others as a member, and all members are bound together by traditions and networks. Sociologists study customs, structures, and institutions, as well as how individuals function in groups and organizations. Sociologists research the connections between work and family. They are particularly interested in conflict (social disorder) and cohesion (social order) as driving forces.

### Economics

*Economics* is the social science concerned with the production, development, and management of material wealth at different levels: households, businesses, or nations. It tracks markets, industries, and economies as key units of study. The driving forces of change are economic value, worth, and scarcity (constraints).

Harvard economists Alberto Alesina and Paolo Giuliano say that strong family ties imply more reliance on the family as an economic unit and that household production is important versus over-reliance on government or the marketplace (2007). They stress the role of the family as an economic unit.

Economists study human behavior within the context of the relationship between desired end results and scarcity. Specifically, it covers human resource planning, labor market changes, cost–benefit analyses, and resources such as land, natural resources, and capital (human-made resources). For the purposes of resource management, the most relevant topics are those related to human resource planning, financial management, households, and specifically microeconomics, which focuses on the behavior of individual consumers. The most basic economic problem is how individuals decide how to allocate scarce resources to achieve the results they desire.

In conclusion, management works in tandem with other disciplines—the interdisciplinary influences are noted in Table 1.3. It deals with people, their values, and their growth and development; and in so doing, it concerns itself with the social structure and the community.

Concepts and skills integral to management, such as attitudes, decision-making, and planning, are also integral to other disciplines. Knowledge from neuroscience, anthropology, psychology, sociology, economics, and other disciplines provides direction and strength to management research and theory. The next section shows how these theoretical aspects of management can be applied to contemporary problems.

## Life Management for Individuals and Families

Although management principles can be applied to individuals, families, groups, organizations, governments, and businesses, this book focuses on individual, family, and household management—on what can be called life management. This section discusses life management and provides definitions of several key families and household terms.

**Life management** encompasses all the decisions a person or family will make and the way values, goals, and resource use affect decision-making. It refers to more than just specific goal achievement. In life management, people are seen as possessing a "self," which helps regulate their actions. They **self-monitor**, which means assess or alter their actions, language, and reactions according to those around them. Someone engaging in road rage, telling off others in surrounding cars or chasing them, is someone with low self-monitoring. Thus, life management includes all the events (the good, the bad, and the ugly), situations, and decisions that make up a lifestyle. Life management is a holistic approach that looks at management as a process that evolves over a life span. The process takes place in a social context as part of the environment that surrounds individuals and families.

Table 1.3 The Interdisciplinary Influences on the Study of Resource Management

| Discipline | Units of Analysis | Focus/Drive[a] |
|---|---|---|
| Neurosciences | Individuals | Decision-making, cognitive processes, health and wellness |
| Anthropology | Dominant Cultures<br>Subcultures<br>Societies | Culture |
| Psychology | Individuals | Communication, self-knowledge, goals, attitudes |
| Sociology | Social groups | Conflict and cohesion |
| | Organizations | |
| | Communities | |
| | Families | |
| Economics | Households | Value, worth, scarcity |
| | Markets | |
| | Industries | |
| | Economies | |

[a]All these disciplines share an interest in understanding human behavior.

## Managing the Second Half of Life

Designer Michael Kors says, "I think the older I get, the more I realize that the ultimate luxury is time." The second half of life requires a reshaping of time use and goals. One choice may be seeking early retirement from a main career. The **FIRE** (Financially Independent, Retire Early) **Movement** is catching on with Millennials and Gen Zs—the goal is to intentionally increase an individual's or family's savings rate by increasing income and decreasing expenses resulting in passive or accumulated income enough to retire earlier than the conventional retirement age. It is controversial. Some disagree that early retirement should be a goal. The FIRE Movement leads to questions about motivation and lifestyle adjustments and how early to retire and what to do in the second half of life, past the young adult and middle age stages.

Should the image and concept of retirement be reinvented? "Longer lifespans, shifts to self-funded retirement, market volatility, and lifestyle changes have reshaped retirement into a significant life stage that requires thoughtful long-term planning and diligent preparation (Sharpe, 2020, p. 54). To summarize, the second half of life presents its own unique challenges and opportunities in the following areas:

Health

Living arrangements

Finances

Social and personal growth

Functional abilities

Identity/Purpose

Nearly a third of U.S. households age 65 or older (9.7 million) pay at least 30 percent of their income for housing, and more than half of these pay over 50 percent (Housing America's Older Adults, 2018).

For example, a 62-year-old woman tries to swim from Cuba to the United States to attempt to set a new record, and a 55-year-old attorney decides he would rather teach elementary school than be a lawyer so he goes back for an education degree and a year later is teaching fifth graders. A 42-year-old female lawyer changes direction and gets her nursing degrees and finishes out her career in the health field. Commitment to a newly defined goal or desired future has an energizing effect. Patterns (personal, family, work, leisure) established in the first half of life may no longer suffice. Children grow up and leave; some grownup children return home after a failed marriage or a financial loss; jobs prove less challenging; an expected promotion does not come through; or an early retirement buyout package is offered.

Examples of changes or new goals in midlife include the following:

A seasoned runner decides to run in a marathon.

A college graduate now 60 years old decides to contact her college friends through Facebook.

An educator takes accounting classes with the idea of starting a side business.

You have probably heard of the midlife crisis. It has long been thought of as something that afflicts men, but research indicates that many women also go through a midlife crisis, which usually entails a substantial reexamination of their lives leading to changed outcomes. Sometimes this reexamination comes from a reaction to another office shakeup. When companies reorganize way too much it puts a strain on men and women employees (Shellenbarger, 2019).

About early retirement buyout packages, one man in his 50s took advantage of a generous buyout package from a car company and started his own scrap metal business with two friends from the same industry. They knew there was a market, they knew where the sources of scrap metal were, and they put their expertise together. Although they are no longer in the car industry per se, they are in a related industry in which they travel the world buying up the metal and transporting it to car factories. As owners of a new, smaller company, they are enjoying the freedom of working closely together. Often the most successful career transitions are made this way, by finding a new way to use old skills, knowledge, and relationships. As another example, four friends formed a partnership and bought land on the side of a mountain where they are selling off property and building retirement homes for themselves and their families.

## *Improving Skills*

Individuals may find themselves having spent their first 25 years getting educated and the next 25–30 years on the job, and then facing the prospect of 30–40 years of retirement. How they react to this scenario has a great deal to do with their personality and the details of the actual situation, such as finances and health. Even if they remain employed, work may be redefined by the workers themselves or by the demands of the workplace. Baby boomers, born between 1946 and 1964, are a generation known for re-invention. They may be filled with worry and doubt and desperately seek a change not only for themselves but also for their children. A Florida couple moved after retiring from state employment and teaching after 30 years back to their home state of Montana. They knew they would miss their friends but their children had grown and left and they felt the need to start over. Another Florida couple moved to Virginia to be near their daughter's family and a new granddaughter.

Many people question the nature of their work at midlife; many do not want to stay in the same job for 30 years, others hang on for the income and retirement benefits. In any event, upcoming retirement will require a new plan formation. Unless they manage options or find new opportunities, they may deteriorate, become bored, "retire on the job," lose all joy in work and in life, and become a burden to themselves and those around them (Drucker, 1999, pp. 188–189). Some refuse to retire or to accept society's definition of aging. When federal judge Milton Pollack—at 96 years old, the third oldest federal judge in the United States—was asked about retirement, he said, "Having a daily occupation keeps me active and I have no plans to leave the bench" (Davis & Smith, 2003, p. C1).

Guitarist Joe Perry of Aerosmith, a member of 1970s rock 'n' roll band that still performs, says,

> *Society programs you to be a couch potato, and you don't have to be. This isn't about rock 'n' roll: it's about getting out there and living life instead of just watching it go by I don't think of myself as being 52; I just think of myself as being.*

> *(Umminger, 2003, p. 4D)*

Another member of the band, bassist Tom Hamilton, says, "You have to make sacrifices. You can't open a bag of potato chips whenever you want." Joe responds, "You can but you can't eat it" (Umminger, 2003, p. 4D). The band members said they have to watch what they eat and work out in gyms because fans don't want to see a fat rocker. With aging and growth come compromises; staying active is not easy. For those of us in less public professions than rock stars, possible solutions to workplace ennui include

Enriching the present job by taking advantage of training opportunities or travel; teaming up with colleagues on projects. A higher percentage of women than men want to travel when they retire.

Starting a second or a different career or moving to another organization or locale. As an example of the twists and turns this can take, a woman sold her large urban interior design firm after 20 years and downscaled to a corner of a fabric store in a small city. In a few years, that store moved and joined forces with a leading furniture store, which led to more work (and money) for the interior designer than ever before, but in an environment shared with more people, a situation she enjoyed. Her overhead was low because her rent was low, and the only person she had to pay for was herself. She set her own hours, decided how many clients to take, and used the furniture store to display her skills. Another interior designer chose to work entirely out of her home thus saving any overhead or travel costs except to client's homes.

Developing a parallel or extra job or career (called being part of the **gig economy**): keeping the basic job, but adding another track such as a part-time job, possibly an outgrowth of a hobby or interest area. Women want to pursue hobbies more than they have in the recent past and you may have noticed the subsequent growth in hobby and special interest stores or areas of stores to meet these needs and to go further, many women are starting small businesses in a variety of ways as part of the growing field of **entrepreneurship** involving men and women nationally and internationally. Other options include being a delivery driver or Uber/Lyft driver or working part-time for the Census Bureau or state government or helping with elections.

Joining in a nonprofit activity such as community service, politics, school boards, or neighborhood associations. Jennifer at age 60 and anticipating retirement joined two community clubs, one economics-based, the other political, to see if she would like them for when she had more leisure time and as a way to stay connected. As a people person, she knows she needs a lot of contacts and likes to follow issues.

In addition to the obvious changes that may occur during the second half of life in families, health, or jobs, more subtle changes may take place, such as redefining success or determining what is important. People of all ages need to feel that they have a purpose and are making a contribution at home, at the workplace, or in the community. Are they growing or stalling?

## CASE STUDY

### Amber, 45, Is Wondering, What Next?

There is no timetable to denote second half of life, but in the mid-40s or around age 50, one may wonder what is coming next. A case in point is Amber who says I have a husband, a job, a house, a dog, all the things I thought I needed. Yet, I feel there is something else out there. Should it be going back to school to retrain, a new place to live or work, a promotion, new friends, a hobby, a side gig? I find myself wondering, is this all there is?

As more workers become knowledge workers, the need to retire has become less evident than it was when most people were manual laborers, and the physical limitations of age prevented continued employment. Now that work is less physically defined and people are living longer, and as more people work from their homes (using computers and broadband connections), a societal redefinition of retirement is under way.

## Singles, Households, Nonfamily Households, and Families

Living solo continues to grow in the United States, up from 25 percent in 1990 to 27 percent in 2010 to 30 percent in 2020. There are fewer married households and more adults living alone. The share of adults living without children is climbing. More single men and women are buying houses.

In many Western European countries, the percentage is higher with more than 33 percent of households consisting of one person. In Paris, "the city of love," there are more singles than married couples.

Traditionally, the study of management has focused primarily on the family, but the growing number of single adults means that the field must pay equal attention to their lifestyles and needs. The number of single adults is increasing for several reasons. Populations are aging resulting in more empty-nest households and elderly singles. In addition, because the age at first marriage is rising, there are many more young adult singles and more singles between marriages. Delaying marriage is related to delaying childbirth.

In the United States, there are more multigenerational households with adult children returning home after college or military service or failed marriages or sometimes with a spouse and children. Under one roof, there are more blended families with stepparents or stepchildren and extended families including cousins, great-aunts, and grandparents. A wide variety of nonrelated people are living together—unmarried partner couples, friends, and roommates sharing expenses. As an example, 26-year-old John, who was restarting his life after being in the military, found he could rent a room in a three-bedroom house for $500. He would rather do that than spend $1,000 for his own apartment while he was going back to school.

In 1900, the average life expectancy in the United States was 47, and only 3 percent of the population lived past 65. Now the average life expectancy is 78.69 years. Of course, many live well into their 90s and some into their 100s. By 2043 Americans age 65 and older will be 20 percent of the population. As had been said before, *we are an aging population*, and this is true for most of the developed world.

As mentioned before, the delay of marriage until a later age for both males and females is a significant demographic change. Fewer people are getting married besides delaying marriage. According to the National Center for Health Statistics, the average age of first-time moms keeps climbing in the United States Far later than the age at which her great-grandmother had her first child. Delayed childbearing is becoming more the norm and being unmarried and giving birth is also becoming more typical.

To return to the subject of the single lifestyle, there is no doubt that from a management point of view it has both pluses and minuses. For example, on the positive side, single adults enjoy increased freedom of action, privacy, and solitude, whereas on the negative side they may experience more loneliness. *Solitude* connotes a sense of enjoyment in being alone. Most of us enjoy periods of peaceful, uninterrupted reading or time on the Internet. Solitude offers the advantage of being restful and life-restoring. On the other hand, singles may feel burdened by their inability to share responsibilities; single people have to take care of everything by themselves such as grocery shopping and running errands. Generalizing about singles is difficult, however, because many singles have children or live with friends or family members, have pets, and enjoy the support of co-workers and neighbors.

Cohabitation has increased in the United States. Most are heterosexual couples, but there are also same-sex couples. Same-sex marriage ceremonies are available in some states and under consideration in others.

Many popular images of singles are incorrect or confused. Consider the common belief that elderly singles choose to retire primarily in the Sunbelt states, especially Florida. Actually, Nevada's elderly population grew by more than 70 percent during the 1990s and the early 2000s, whereas Florida's grew only by 18.5 percent. Las Vegas, Nevada, was one of the fastest-growing cities in the United States during the decade of the 2000s. Census data indicate that elders are flocking to Maine, North Carolina, South Carolina, Georgia, Alaska, Arizona, New Mexico, Hawaii, Utah, and Colorado. The greatest rise in elderly population growth is taking place in the suburbs going along with a national trend toward more living in the suburbs and fewer in rural areas. Rural residents constitute approximately 19 percent of the U.S. population vs. 20 percent in 1990.

Besides the suburbs, singles, young and old, are attracted to the towns and cities with colleges and universities such as State College, Pennsylvania; Iowa City, Iowa; Bloomington, Indiana; Madison, Wisconsin;

Austin, Texas; and Chapel Hill and Raleigh-Durham, North Carolina. Large numbers of elderly live in small towns or rural New England and in the rural Midwest. The phrase *aging in place* refers to the phenomenon of people staying where they were brought up or spent most of their working years—for example, in the Midwest or in the suburbs. More senior communities are forming outside cities so people stay near families including grandchildren, friends, co-workers, and services and stores they are used to versus starting all over again with relationships and interests. Eileen, age 50, moved her parents close to her in a southern state, but after three years her parents moved back north to be with friends and family. Much as they liked the warmer weather it was too difficult to adjust.

Census data reveal that working-age singles tend to cluster in cities (and surrounding suburbs) such as New York, Tampa/St. Petersburg, Washington, Miami, Houston, Atlanta, Orlando, Austin, Denver, Seattle, Boston, and San Francisco. If trends hold true, more elders, along with the rest of the population, will migrate West and South in the future.

It is also not an unusual pattern to see active elders retire to warm-weather states and then when they become older and frailer move back to the areas from which they migrated or move closer to grownup children or suburbs with services like doctors and grocery stores. Multigenerational houses are springing up. Taxes, safety, caregiving, and expenses are factors. As an example, Rodney and Ann in their early 70s sold their large organic farming business and built a special aging in place home complete with a caregiver suite on an acre lot in a suburb with more services. Likewise, Christy and Al, retired educators, built an aging in place home closer in for the same reasons, with more services nearby and less driving required. Both couples figured new construction and less land would mean less maintenance.

This definition combines some practical and objective criteria with a more social-psychological sense of family identity.

A narrower definition is provided by the Census Bureau, which says that the word **family** refers to a group of two or more persons related by birth, marriage, or adoption and residing together in a household. Child development and family experts try to find out how changes in the family affect children. One study reported that "Research in the United States has shown that children growing up in 2-parent households do better in school than children from single-parent households" (Heveline, Yang, & Timberlake, 2010, p. 1362).

A free-form definition would indicate that the family is whatever an individual says it is. The definition of immediate family used by the American Red Cross Disaster Services Program includes mother, father, spouse, dependent children, dependent grandchild/grandchildren, dependent stepchild/stepchildren, regularly financially supported significant others, fiancés, housemates, and/or other family members. They use this definition to determine who qualifies for aid in a disaster. Setting parameters is important because when money is involved, anyone may claim to be a fiancé or a long-lost relative: What happens, for instance, when three women say they were fiancées of the same man? The American Red Cross asks for verification before aid is disbursed. Examples of acceptable forms of verification include

## CRITICAL THINKING

### Changes

As you read these descriptions of singles and families, what do they tell you about how families and households are changing and what might happen in the future? What sorts of housing designs fit different groups?

The definition of a household is broader than the definition of a family. People's lifestyles are categorized by housing units rather than by marital status. According to the Census Bureau, a **household** comprises all persons who occupy a "housing unit"—that is, a house, an apartment or a cluster of rooms, or a single room that constitutes "separate living quarters." A household includes related family members and all the unrelated persons, if any, such as lodgers, foster children, wards, or employees who share the housing unit. A person living alone or a group of unrelated persons sharing the same housing unit is also counted as a household. Household change generally parallels population change. The smallest gains in the number of new households were in slow-growing states, mainly in the Northeast. A nonfamily household is defined as those who live alone or with nonrelatives.

Cohabitation, discussed earlier, contributes to the rising number of nonfamily households. It is estimated that a quarter of the time, one cohabiting partner wants to marry, while the other doesn't. Although most people think of cohabitants as young adults, they may be older. The majority of people who have experienced a divorce will try cohabitation before remarrying, but the trial run may be quite short.

No universal definition of the family exists; however, a number of definitions are considered appropriate. According to Lamanna, Riedmann, and Stewart (2018, p. 4), the family involves relationships in which people are usually related by ancestry, marriage, or adoption:

form an economic unit or otherwise practical unit and care for children or other dependents,

consider their identity to be significantly attached to the group, and

commit to maintaining that group over time.

Current joint ownership of a home

Current joint rental/lease agreement

Current joint bank account or credit cards

Current joint ownership or holding of investments

Current utility bill with both names

Joint obligation on a current loan

Current joint renter's or homeowner's insurance policy

Registration with a state or a local domestic partnership registry or certification of a union celebrated overseas. Immediately following September 11, 2001, disasters in Washington, DC, and New York City, the American Red Cross assisted families of the 3,333 deceased or seriously injured, opened 55,370 cases, and made 131,185 disaster health contacts and 236,498 disaster mental-health contacts. The American Red Cross is allied with the International Red Cross and other groups who share a common goal of relieving suffering. The organization's definition of a family is considered more inclusive than the U.S. Census Bureau's definition. Besides nonprofit organizations like the International Red Cross, businesses seek to define "family" for their benefits programs. Who should be covered in a family health plan? Most Fortune 500 companies offer domestic-partner benefits, as do several states.

From the Census Bureau's point of view and for those who rely on census data, consistent definitions of "family" and "household" are important because comparisons can be made from decade to decade. A family includes among its members the householder. According to the Census Bureau, the **householder** is the person (or one of the persons) in whose name the home is owned or rented. If a home is owned or rented jointly by a married couple, either the husband or the wife may be listed first. Prior to 1980, the husband was always considered the household head (householder) in married-couple households. The American Red Cross has another definition of household. It says that a household is defined as a family or other group of individuals who live together and act jointly in conducting most or all domestic activities, or an individual who lives alone or lives with others but acts alone in conducting most or all domestic activities.

To summarize much that has been covered in this chapter, according to the Census Bureau, since 1980 the percentage of traditional family households has declined but the number of non-traditional households has increased, and the percentage of people living alone has risen. Included in this count of people living alone are the over 2 million Americans who are in prison.

## Changes in Family and Household Composition

To conclude, the term "family" refers to relationships, usually by marriage or through children, shared commitment, or shared resources over time, or to genetic relationships; and the term "household" refers to housing units and the occupants who share the residence. Households and families have fewer people on average with one of the notable exceptions of Hispanics as discussed earlier. Hispanic fertility is 2.9 births per woman compared to the national average of 2.1. Perhaps this content about families and households can seem confusing but the point is that people are redefining what constitutes a family or a household. They are not less committed to the concept of family and television shows such as *Modern Family* portray diverse family forms and everyone has to live somewhere. Issues about parent-adolescent dyads of recent Latino immigrants were addressed in a 2020 NCFR/Reuben Hill award-winning study using a longitudinal design and the Family Stress Model (Lorenzo-Blanco et al., 2019).

Statistics indicate significant changes in the composition and size of families. According to the last census, in the United States:

In the nation's rural counties many are losing population especially in the Midwest and Northeast, some experiencing higher death rates than birth rates.

Ethnic and racial growth is uneven. Since 2000, Asians, although a small share of the population, grew at a faster rate than African-Americans.

The percentage of households with children younger than 18 is declining but this varies greatly by region and by group. Twenty-three states and Washington, DC, lost 10 percent or more of their child population since 2000.

The trend is toward more mixed marriages with one in seven new marriages of spouses of different racial or ethnic backgrounds.

Life expectancy is up with men making more gains than women (14 to 4 percent) explained by better heart treatments and heart disease prevention and less smoking, the less easily measured aspect of stress may also be a factor.

If you take all this information together a picture starts forming of today's lifestyles. For a woman, she may be single during her twenties, marry for a few years, have a child, divorce, remarry, and then be widowed. When high school classes convene for their fortieth reunion, it is not unusual to find several people who have been married three or four times.

Although the statistics given so far describe mostly conditions in the United States, changes in the composition of families are a global trend. Timeworn traditions concerning the proper age for marriage and to have children are being questioned.

Regardless of family stage or type, the main difference between individual and family decision-making is that decisions are more complex when made by two or more persons. The bigger the family, the more complicated the decision-making process, because more people's needs are considered and resources stretch further. Family decision-making is an important area of study because the family provides the setting in which essential resources are created, transformed, and transferred. In conclusion, managing life, whether as an individual or as a member of a family, within the context of the mounting pressures and stresses of everyday existence, is not an easy task. As we have seen, not only families but also the society in which they live and the economy are undergoing dramatic changes. People try to adapt to and influence these changing situations through the choices they make. For example, from 2007 to 2011 during a recession and immediately after in the United States people became thriftier, spending less, reducing debt load, and saving more. They revamped household budgets and focused on what they really needed. Following this period, the Covid-19 pandemic brought another wave of change greatly affecting children, adults, consumers, and family behavior (Chen et al., 2022). Whatever the year or circumstances, financial management, an aspect of the umbrella subject of resource management, provides opportunities to shape future outcomes for the benefit of individuals, families, and communities. Resiliency and grit, introduced at the beginning of this chapter, are continually challenged.

## CRITICAL THINKING

### Savings Rate is Up

Have you or members of your family cut back on spending? If so, in what ways? Before the recession Americans saved less than 2 percent of disposable income and this went up to 5.7 percent in 2019 and higher in 2022 a time of recovery (Source: U.S. Bureau of Economic Analysis) Have you or members of your family tried to save more? A related question is what are Americans saving for? According to a SunTrust Financial Confidence Index survey reported in the United States TODAY November 12, 2018. p. D1 of 2,500 adults, 45 percent of Americans say they save money for travel, more than any other reason. Is the ability to travel a high priority for you in the long run? Perhaps saving for a house is more important.

## What Lies Ahead?

This book is divided into four parts. Part 1 includes the present chapter and the next one on management history and theories. These two introductory chapters provide a framework for interpreting the management concepts and applications to come in subsequent chapters. Part 2 covers management concepts and principles; values, attitudes, and goals; resources; decision-making; planning, implementing, and evaluating; and communication. Each chapter in Part 2 will elucidate the steps in the management process model presented in Figure 1.1. Part 3 on management applications has chapters on managing human needs, time, work and family, stress and fatigue, environmental resources, and finances. The book concludes in Part 4 with a chapter on future challenges. Each chapter begins with the chapter outline, a "Did You Know?" section, an epigraph, and concludes with a Summary, Key Terms, Review Questions, and References. At the end of the book is a Glossary and an Index.

## SUMMARY

Are you creative and adaptive? Do you have grit? Are you managing your resources efficiently in our increasingly digital era? There is no doubt, the landscape is changing. Change in television viewing was one example given in this chapter, about 40 percent of homes led by millennials don't subscribe to cable or satellite services (Levin, 2018, p. D2). Indications are that Zoomers (Gen Z) are following suit. Studying individual and family resource management provides a perspective, a way of thinking, and acting. It is motivated by curiosity and the desire to understand human behavior and, in particular, changes in family and household behavior. This chapter addressed the following questions:

What is management?

Why manage?

Who manages?

Management is the process of using resources to achieve goals. Besides resources and goals, management involves many interacting elements, including problems, needs, wants, values, decision-making, planning, implementing, communication, and feedback, all operating within an environmental and entrepreneurial context.

The unique contribution of management is the insight it provides into decision-making and decision implementing. Management is necessary because it provides a sense of direction and purpose. Everyone manages, some with more skill than others. Many of the principles of management are timeless, but the application of management to everyday life is constantly changing.

Examples of change include the dramatic increase in the number of single adults and the trend toward marrying at a later age. We are an aging population with more diverse families. Many Americans are burdened by rising housing costs. Different definitions of "family" and "household" were presented, with a recognition that there are various configurations.

The evolving nature of society and technology has made management an increasingly necessary and far more complex subject. Given the health, environmental, economic, and social problems in the world today, the need for skilled managers at all levels has never been greater. Many challenges lie ahead for the thinker and the planner in all of us.

## KEY TERMS

| | | |
|---|---|---|
| choice | grit | planning |
| clarification | happiness | problems |
| cognitive psychology | household(er) | resiliency |
| decision-making | implementing | resource management |
| entrepreneurship | life management | resources |
| family | lifestyle management | risk |
| feedback | management process | self-monitoring |
| Fire Movement | management style | standards |
| futuristic thinking skills | management tools | values |
| gig economy | needs | wants |
| goals | neuroscience | |

## REVIEW QUESTIONS

1. How is the field of neuroscience related to family resource management? Define neuroscience and build from there.

2. Why does Daniel Gilbert, author of *Stumbling on Happiness*, say that experiences might bring more satisfaction than durable goods? Do you agree or disagree? What would Marie Kondo say about managing household goods?

3. Harvard economists Alberto Alesina and Paolo Giuliano say that strong family ties imply more reliance on the family as an economic unit that provides goods and services and less on outside institutions such as those found in the marketplace and government. Why does household production (doing things together or making things within the home) activity have such an impact on family ties? Can you give an example from your own family?

4. How does technology influence management style? Give an example of a technological change in the 21st century and explain how individual or family lifestyles were impacted.

5. Sociologists Lamanna, Reidmann, and Stewart in their book give a definition of family which includes a list of common characteristics including economic unit, identity & attachment, and commitment. Does your family fit these or would you add something to the list or take something away? Explain your answer.

## REFERENCES

Alesina, A., & Giuliano, P. (2007). The power of the family. *NBER Reporter*, No. 4, p. 36.

Blanchflower, D., & Oswald, A. (2004). Money, sex and happiness: An empirical study. *Scandinavian Journal of Economics, 106*(3), 393–415.

Chen, C. Y. C., Byrne, E., Velez, T. (2022). Impact of the 2020 pandemic of COVID-19 on families with school-aged children in the United States: Roles of income level and race. *Journal of Family Issues, 43*(3), 719–740.

Covey, S. R. (1989). *The seven habits of highly effective people.* New York: Simon & Schuster.

Davis, A., & Smith, R. (2003, July 3). Judge Pollack's investor-lectures. *The Wall Street Journal*, p. C1.

Drucker, P. F. (1999). *Management challenges for the 21st century.* New York: HarperCollins.

Duckworth, A. (2016). *Grit.* New York: Scribner.

Gates, B. (April 30, 2020). Responding to Covid-19—a once-in-a-century pandemic? *New England Journal of Medicine, 382*, 1677–1679.

Gilbert, D. (2006). *Stumbling on happiness.* New York: Alfred A. Knopf.

Grant, H., & Gelety, L. (2009). Goal content theories: Why differences in what we are striving for matter. In G. B. Moskowitz & H. Grant (Eds.), *The Psychology of Goals* (pp. 77–97). New York: Guilford.

Heveline, P., Yang, H., & Timberlake, J. (2010). It takes a-village (perhaps a nation): Families, states and educational achievement. *Journal of Marriage and Family, 72*, 1362–1376.

*Housing America's Older Adults* (2018). Report of the Joint Center for Housing Studies of Harvard University.

Kelley, H., LeBaron, A., & Hill, E. J. (2020). Family matters: Decade review from Journal of Family and Economic Issues. *Journal of Family and Economic Issues*, p. 472.

Kondo, M. (2011). *The life changing magic of tidying up.* Berkeley, CA: The Ten Speed Press.

Konigsberg, R. D. (2011, August 8). Chore wars. *Time*, 45–49.

Lamanna, M., Riedmann, A., & Stewart, S. (2018). *Marriages, families and relationships: Making choices in a diverse society* (13th ed.). Boston, MA: Cengage Learning.

Levin, G. (2018, November 12). Young viewers bailing on TV at sharper rate. *USA Today Life*, D1–D2.

Lorenzo-Blanco, E., Meca, A., Pina-Watson, B., Zamboanga, B., Szapocnik, J., Cano, M., Cordova, D., Unger, J. (2019). Examining the temporal order of ethnic identity and perceived discrimination among Hispanic immigrant adolescents. *Developmental Psychology, 54*(5), 929–937.

Abstract. Romero, A., Des Rosiers, S., Soto, D., Villamar, J., Pattarroyo, M., Lizzi, K., & Schwartz, S. (2019). Longitudinal trajectories of family functioning among recent immigrant adolescents and parents: Links with adolescent and parent cultural stress, emotional well-being, and behavioral health. *Child Development.*

Maslow, A. (1954). *Motivation and personality.* New York: Harper & Row.

Mattioli, D. (2008, February 19). For some, suburban jobs prove subpar. *The Wall Street Journal*, p. B8.

McGee, S. (2020). *Make life beautiful*. New York: Harper Horizon.

Sharpe, D. (2020). Reinventing retirement. *Journal of Family and Economic Issues*, p. 54.

Shellenbarger, S. (2019, January 14). How to navigate yet another office shakeup. *The Wall Street Journal*, p. D1.

Skogster, P., Uotila, V., & Ojala, L. (2008). From mornings to-evenings: Is there variation in shopping behavior between-different hours of the day? *International Journal of Consumer Studies, 32*, 65–74.

Terhune, C., & Kahn, G. (2003, September 8). Coke lures Japanese customers with cellphone come-ons. *The Wall Street Journal*, p. B4.

Umminger, A. (2003, August 18). They walk their way. *USA Today*, p. 4D.

Ziati, M. (2019, February 8). Coca cola debuts orange vanilla, its first new flavor in more than a decade. *USA Today*.

Chapter **2**

# Management History and Theories

DOI: 10.4324/9781003166740-2

Human Ecology and Ecosystems

Economic Theory

Optimization and Satisficing

Risk Aversion

## DID YOU KNOW THAT...?

… Americans eat an estimated 386 billion ready-to-eat snack foods a year and that number is rising. According to the U.S. Bureau of Statistics not only are the numbers up but also the price of snacks in recent years has risen faster than most other food categories.

… When boomerang children return home most live in their childhood bedroom and the main reasons they return are for a romance on the rocks or for economic or health reasons.

What people eat and when has changed radically in the last few years, and these are just one part of daily life management. Personal, work, and family lives have changed greatly, and our homes and how we use them reflect these changes.

Besides reading diaries, advertising, newspaper accounts, and conducting research studies, we can find out a great deal about daily life from the past from ongoing archaeological digs. To understand how far families and homes have come, read this advertising copy depicting the olden days:

> *When America was young—a patchwork of small towns connected by dusty roads and wagon trails—it was the general store that stood at the heart of the community and provided simple necessities for family life, work, and home. It was a place for the whole family to gather, to take time out to reach for their dreams—a jar of penny candy for the children, a pretty dress for big sister, a new set of dishes for Grandmother's dining room table. Early Americans were steadied by their practicality, ingenuity, values, and warm sense of humor. They were sustained by their dreams for a better life for themselves and their family.*
> (JCPenney, AmericanLiving.com, 2008)

## CASE STUDY

### Meals and Snacking Behavior

"There's a changed definition of what a meal is," said David Porta Latin, NPD's National food and beverage analyst. Today I might have a piece of fruit and trail mix and call that lunch. In the past, we would've thought of that as exclusively snacks." The blurred line between snacks and the traditional trio of breakfast, lunch and dinner impacts what Americans choose to munch on, too. For example, breakfast sandwiches can be eaten as meals or snacks despite the first word in the name. A granola bar, dried cranberries and yogurt are often a meal for 27-year-old Shamika Johnson of Akron, Ohio. She says, "I work. I'm busy. Sometimes it is easier to get snacks." She adds that snacks were fun and now they are a reality.

*Source: Ziati Meyer (2019, February 4). Do you love snacks? Here's Why you're not alone. USA Today, Section B, p. 1.*

Of course, this quote glamorizes America's past, but there is no doubt that all of us, regardless of country, have some nostalgia for when times were simple, and everything seemed possible. Today, convenience and home delivery or curb side pick-up often win out over charm. Practical, time-saving methods outweigh sentiment. As a case in point, when the first edition of this book came out in the '90s it was only available in print in hard cover and sold at campus bookstores. Since then, it is also available electronically in several forms including Kindle and from online sources. Book publishing has moved on as have families, homes, workplaces, and traditions but as the opening quote by Ansel Adams illustrates the world is still a beautiful place for us to wonder at and explore.

This chapter opens with descriptions of changes in homes which serve as the environmental and support sides of our daily lives, the place we come home to. This chapter then explains the theoretical underpinnings of the study of family resource management, including discussions of social exchange and economic theories. In so doing, this chapter lays the foundation for what is to come in the rest of the book, such as in-depth explorations of attitudes, values, and decision making. Throughout the book, management serves as a roadmap or guide. Although many of the examples will be from the United States, other countries could be substituted. No doubt the past generations struggled, but the family remains strong and we still have our dreams of a better future for ourselves and our children and grandchildren.

We need to study the various theories that have been formulated about managerial behavior to help us understand how and why people plan, decide, and act the way they do. This chapter explores the nature of theory and its application to management. Worldwide, there has been a revival of interest in green, or environmentally friendly, ways of doing things such as ecotourism and a revisiting of traditional ways of managing a home and the environment surrounding it.

Some people collect household goods such as furnishings and appliances from the past or reproductions. Here is an example regarding vacuum cleaners:

> Store owners from Virginia to Oregon say they can barely keep them in stock. "As soon as I get one, it just flies out the door," says Istikar Ahmed, who runs a vacuum store in the Washington suburbs Joe De Maria, for instance, has shelled out more than $900 for
> vacuums during the past four years—he's got four—and each one has fallen short. Not only do they break down but he says they don't pick up the dirt left by his children and two hairy dogs. "The attachments are so short, you can't get under the couch," the Miami homeowner complains. What's his dream machine now? "My mother's old metal Kirby, which you could bang into the furniture, or throw down the stairs," he says.
>
> (Fletcher, 2002, p. W9)

Common household objects such as vacuum cleaners are part of the larger picture of how people live; although keeping a clean house may not be everyone's number one concern, it is something everyone has to deal with to some degree. As noted in the first chapter, the subject of household organization has been reinvigorated by a Japanese author, public speaker, and Netflix personality Marie Kondo (2011).

Knowledge of the evolution of management theory (the ways and whys of doing things) provides a useful background for understanding the management process diagrammed in Figure 1.1, which is repeated here as Figure 2.1. This chapter specifically addresses the feedback and environmental components of the model.

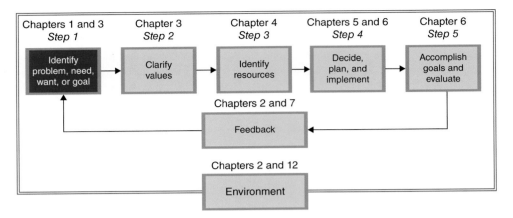

Figure 2.1  The management process model.

## History of Management

### The Early Years of Management

Although managers and management have existed since the beginning of organized civilization, the earliest records of management are found on the walls of cave dwellings in Western Europe, most notably France. These cave drawings indicate which members of the societal unit hunted, gathered food, and reared children. Over time, around the globe, village centers sprang up as people went from subsisting on wild resources to farming. This more settled approach led to larger towns. Populations grew and with them the need for more advanced systems of food storage and freshwater access. Homes lasted longer, and attention was paid to pottery and other forms of food display and storage and to stone carving and other forms of decoration.

Moving up in time, we come to ancient Greece and Rome where home management became the subject of philosophical discussions. Several Biblical verses refer to the importance of keeping an orderly home. Since the Middle Ages, numerous books about household management have been published. A contemporary book summarizes the household accounts of an estate in medieval England (Woolgar, 1993). Diaries and memoirs describe what it was like to live in previous eras.

Much of what we know about these human ancestors and their households come from archaeological digs that reveal the kinds of settlements people lived in, the cooking pots used, foods eaten, and ornamentation. For example, in North Florida half of the area was covered by pine forests and the early native people used pine for canoes, utensils, sculptures, and bowls. When the colonial Europeans came, they harvested pine for timber and used it in shipbuilding. Later, pine was used for tar, pitch, rosin, turpentine, and paper pulp. Each culture saw the same resource, pine trees, but used it differently.

In the 18th and 19th centuries, in the United States, standards of hygiene were undergoing a transformation. After trying out her new shower in 1799, a Philadelphia woman named Elizabeth Drinker noted in her diary that she tolerated the new experience "better than expected, not having been wet for 28 years" (Crossen, 2002).

In rural areas, pioneer homes were often single-room (also called "single pen") log cabins with a fireplace. This was followed by a "dogtrot" structure consisting of two rooms joined by a breezeway for ventilation in warm climates and an enclosed hall in cooler climates. A more upscale home might be a "four-square" with four rooms joined by an enclosed central hallway and stairs leading up to an attic, loft, or bedrooms

**Standards of Personal Care**

How many showers or baths would be normal where you live? Daily? Weekly? Does it vary by age or income group? Why do you think standards of hygiene change?

Simple beginnings, a log one-room house with loft or attic above.

and stairs leading down to a basement. In the Midwest, there were "I-houses," so named for the states Iowa, Indiana, and Illinois, which were typically two-story versions of the dogtrot, four rooms down and four rooms up (Haase, 1992). Some of these early homes were modest, whereas others became quite grand when they added a porch out front supported by pillars. The pillars might be made of brick and finished with plaster and white paint. For further reading consult *A Field Guide to American Houses: A Definitive Guide to Identifying and Understanding America's Domestic Architecture* by Virginia Savage McAlester (2015). The author's drawings and explanations center on homes one would find in neighborhoods and small towns since she says many books had been written about monumental homes and she wanted to document everyday life and purposely chose the title a field guide.

In the early years, cooking may have been done in the house, or the kitchen may have been behind the house in a separate building. Drinking and bathing water was brought in buckets from streams and lakes, then wells, and later pumped from outside near the back door. The most welcome addition to homes was running water usually in the form of a kitchen sink with cold water. Can you imagine what a life-altering experience it must have been going from hauling water to being able to turn a spigot to get water? And, then later on, to add hot water from the spigot that didn't have to be heated on a stove for baths or whatever?

Ben Franklin (1706–1790), inventor of the Franklin stove, bifocals, and the lightning rod, popularized the adage "time is money." He was also deputy postmaster in charge of the mails in the northern colonies. By 1792, the U.S. post office had a regular mail delivery schedule. In the United States, today we have mail delivery once a day Monday through Saturday, but in cities in colonial times, in the United States and also in England, twice a day service, morning and afternoon, was not unusual. In the United States, there are discussions about taking away Saturday delivery or to reducing delivery to three days a week in order to save money and in response to changes in how people communicate. At the same time, home delivery of packages by for-profit services has gone way up.

In the 19th century, middle-class households commonly owned clocks, whereas in the previous century only the wealthy had clocks. The stopwatch, a timepiece that can be instantly started and stopped by the press of a button, was invented in the 1880s. New inventions were altering the way homes functioned and looked. The first vacuum cleaners were hand-pumped models of wood and canvas almost as big as coffee tables.

Home management, or domestic management, emerged as a formal subject of study in the United States in the 19th century. High school and college courses covered a wide range of management topics. These courses and the home care books written for the general public offered advice for healthful living; among other things, they extolled the virtues of early rising, cleanliness, sunshine, and fresh air.

The first textbook to mention household management in the title was Maria Parloa's *First Principles of Household Management and Cookery,* published in 1879. Parloa advised that "a bed that has been made up a week or more is not fit to sleep in; as moisture gathers, which often proves fatal to persons sleeping in one" (Parloa, 1879, p. 7).

Ellen H. Richards, an American chemist and founder of the home economics movement, is credited with forming the bridge between scientific analysis and household management through guiding the discussions at the Lake Placid Conferences, held in New York from 1899 to 1908.

During these years, the economy was growing, and the nation was prosperous; yet many Americans lived on farms, and life was hard. The labor force participation rate for men age 65 and over was 80 percent: "People literally worked until they died or until they couldn't work any more, retirement was a privilege of the well to do" (Willis & Young, 2003, p. 84).

Authors Lillian Gilbreth and Christine Frederick toured the United States and Europe on the lecture circuit spreading the word about the new scientific methods of efficient home management and house-hold production (Frederick, 1918; Gilbreth, 1927). Frederick, based in New York and married to an advertising executive, designed a model kitchen in her home that is on display at the Smithsonian's National Museum of American History and testified before Congress about the important role that women play as consumers. Gilbreth saw the home as a workplace and the homemaker as both worker and manager. She and her husband, Frank, a factory efficiency expert, had 12 children. Their lives were portrayed in his book, *Cheaper by the Dozen*, which formed the basis of two movies. When Frank died in 1924, Lillian took up his cause and applied work-saving methods to the home. She designed the Gilbreth management desk that was displayed at the 1933 World's Fair. Her goal was to increase pro-ductivity, reduce drudgery, and accumulate "happiness minutes," which she thought of as time spent in leisure or creative pursuits (Smithsonian, 2000). She redesigned kitchens based on photographs of operations in the room and, in later life, applied her knowledge to bettering living conditions for the disabled.

Nationwide, government- and industry-sponsored experimental kitchens and college residential laborato-ries (more commonly known as home management houses) were set up to record the time required and the human and mechanical energy used to perform household tasks. Two of the earliest colleges with residence courses were Stout Institute in Wisconsin (now the University of Wisconsin, Stout) and the University of Illinois. Florida State University was unique in being the first college to build a house specifically for home management. The usual way it worked was like this: During students' senior year they moved into the home management house or residence for a semester, where they experienced living on a budget, record keeping, time and meal management, and other forms of efficient home management. They shared rooms and simulated family and household conditions. Some campuses offered multiple houses or apartments and different levels of living conditions and budgets. With changes in college life and professional training, the need for this type of experience lessened, and by the 1970s and 1980s most campuses transformed the houses and put them to other uses such as childcare centers or faculty offices or removed them to make way for parking lots or classroom buildings.

When management practitioners such as Frederick and Gilbreth applied techniques that were being used in the workplace to the home, they were emulating the work of Frederick Taylor (1856–1915), among others. Known as the father of scientific management, Taylor was famous for his time and motion studies. He proposed scientific management principles designed to maximize production efficiency. By carefully studying the most efficient ways assembly line jobs could be performed and implementing changes to increase efficiency, he was able to achieve significant productivity improvements (Taylor, 1911). Taylor revolutionized assembly lines. He was not afraid of work. He was so willing to pitch in that when confronted with a blocked drain in a factory, he put on overalls, tied shoes to his elbows and knees, and crawled through the muck to remove the obstruction (Wooldridge, 2000). He believed in the carrot (reward) and stick (punishment) approach. Taylor promoted time clocks, synchronization, and anything that would speed up work. Some workers thought he went too far and criticized him for depersonalizing the workplace. His influence went beyond business: His scientific management principles were applied to nonprofit organizations and government agencies and facilities, including the Watertown Arsenal of the U.S. Army. Others, observing his work, applied the same principles to the home by redesigning floor plans, standardizing and updating equipment, and suggesting better work methods (e.g., saving steps and using less time and human energy in such tasks as keeping household accounts, making beds, washing dishes, and cooking). These improved work methods in the home, known as **work simplification**, became an integral part of the study of management.

American homes were changing rapidly. Of course, regional and individual variations existed, but in general, the time period between 1900 and the present can be divided into three eras: premodern, modern, and postmodern.

Tables 2.1–2.3 summarize the main characteristics of household production and consumption patterns in representative decades. Notice that in 1900 most houses did not have indoor plumbing. Although Thomas Edison had invented the incandescent lightbulb in 1879, only 8 percent of U.S. homes had electricity by 1907 (Cowan, 1983). In 1909, even the houses that had electricity did not have the number of wall outlets we are used to today, so wires and cords for appliances had to be screwed into a central light fixture or lightbulb socket.

## Household Production/Consumption System I: Premodern (Early 1900s)

In the early 1900s, people were collectors more than decorators. Kitchen and laundry equipment were primitive in the premodern era, and housework was backbreaking labor. Furthermore, it increasingly had to be done by the sole adult woman in the household because, by this time, servants were disappearing: They could find more lucrative employment in the growing number of factories, offices, and shops. American families were also experiencing a radical change in the way things were bought and made. According to historian Susan Strasser, the period from 1885 to 1915 was a time of "massive transformation": "During this period there was a transformation in the factory and in the distribution process. All

**Table 2.1** Household Production/Consumption System I: Premodern (Early 1900s)

Typical families in the early 1900s made most of their own clothes, food, and household cleaning products. They were likely to buy such basics as soap, flour, and baking powder.

- *Household work:* Hands-on, arduous, specific, repetitive.

- *Kitchen/laundry equipment:* Inside sink (probably only cold water), stove, washtub or wringer washer, possibly an icebox.

- *Bathroom equipment:* Outdoor privy, indoor slop buckets, bathtubs, or buckets for washing filled with water heated on the stove; the rich and/or city dwellers might have indoor plumbing.

- *Servants:* One servant for every 15 households.[a]

- *Shopping:* Home delivery is common—doctors, peddlers, and tailors come to the home; groceries, ice, baked goods, and dairy products are all delivered. At stores, shop owners take products off the shelf and hand them to the customer. Catalog shopping becomes popular; catalogs offer everything from medicines to whole houses. Beginning of exposure to media advertising and brands.

- *Electricity:* Newly introduced, rare in homes except those of the rich, particularly those who live in cities. Mostly used for lighting.

- *Lighting:* Kerosene (mostly lower and working class, rural), gas (upper, middle class, urban), candles, and some electricity.

[a]Cowan, R. S. (1983). *More Work for Mother* (pp. 99, 240). New York: Basic Books.

the really major innovations came in during this time" (Goldsmith, 1993, p. 47). The introduction of the automobile created a veritable revolution in transportation, which led to great changes in the marketplace and consumer demand. There were about 8,000 cars (horseless carriages) in 1900 and less than 10 miles of concrete road in the United States. By 1910 the automobile had changed everything, including what was inside homes as well as the actual location of homes: Living in the suburbs now made more sense. The gap between rural and urban life began to narrow, and this trend would continue through the 1920s and 1930s. Some families returned to the farm in 1929 and up (during the Depression years) in order to feed their families.

One of the primary changes affecting the home was the switch from making most goods at home to purchasing mass-produced items at the store. Things that used to take all day to make (e.g., soap and bread)

**Table 2.2** Household Production/Consumption System II: Modern (1950s)

Typical families in the mid-20th century bought most of their clothing, food, and household cleaning products from stores.

- *Household work:* Hands-on and machine-aided, somewhat arduous, specific, repetitive.

- *Kitchen/laundry equipment:* Sink (with hot and cold water), stove, refrigerator, washing machine, perhaps a dryer and a dishwasher.

- *Bathroom equipment:* Sink, toilet, bathtub/shower (one or two bathrooms in the average new home).

- *Servants:* One to every 42 households.*

- *Shopping:* Home delivery less common than in the early 1900s. Customers serve themselves at stores. Moderate exposure to media advertising and brands. Shopping centers begin.

- *Electricity:* In over 80 percent of homes.[a]

- *Lighting:* Electricity most common; kerosene still used in some rural areas.

[a]*Historical Statistics of the United States* (1975). Washington, DC: U.S. Government Printing Office.

could now be bought in minutes. A time revolution, as well as an economic, social, and technological one, was taking place. The value of light, air, and sunshine was revisited.

Heavy draperies were replaced with pulled-back, lighter curtains. Homes were redesigned. A popular style introduced in the Midwest, especially around the Chicago area, and throughout the South was the bungalow with its more horizontal lines and one or one and a half stories:

> It incorporated a number of progressive ideals of the early 1900s—the straightforward use of materials, an informal way of living, and accessibility to outdoors. The first Bungalow owners were interested in affordable homes that would both simplify their lives and allow them to enjoy the outdoors as part of their daily routines. Most were middle-class families who felt secure enough about their social standing that they didn't need to use shelter as an outward display of their worth.
>
> (Connolly & Wasserman, 2002, p. 8)

In 1900, the economy was strong and prices were low. It was a good time to be a consumer. Sanitation and health improved. Books and collectibles were kept clean behind glass doors. By the 1920s chrome, metal, and glass infiltrated homes—what was sleek, modern, and curved were preferred. Pianos provided entertainment in the home, as did record players and radios in later years. Outside the home, movie theaters sprang up. Hollywood lifestyles portrayed on the screen and in the press brought a new level of glamor and sophistication to rural areas. By the 1930s central air-conditioning added comfort to high-rise buildings.

**Table 2.3** Household Production/Consumption System III: Postmodern (21st century)

One of the most substantial changes in 2020 and beyond in response to the pandemic was more home delivery of foods and other goods. Typical families in the 21st-century order and sell more products over the Internet and receive more home deliveries. They also rely heavily on stores and online delivery services for gifts, clothing, diapers, toys, and household cleaning supplies and on restaurants especially takeout restaurants and drive-thru windows for food and drinks such as specialty coffees. Purchase of prepared deli and frozen food is common and food preferences keep changing

- *Household work:* Hands-on and machine-aided, somewhat arduous, specific, repetitive. Some products and household tools have made it easier and less hands-on.

- *Kitchen/laundry equipment:* Sink, stove, dishwasher, microwave oven, refrigerator, washing machine, dryer.

- *Bathroom equipment:* Sink, toilet, bathtub/shower (multiple bathrooms and sinks common in an average new home; also whirlpool baths and separate showers widely available).

- *Servants:* Rare, partially replaced by childcare centers and cleaning services.

- *Shopping:* Home delivery expands with toll-free catalog shopping by phone and the use of Internet shopping using computers. Stores with customer self-service usual. Multipurpose superstores common. Malls reducing or closing or re-purposing into offices, schools, and fitness gyms. Pervasive exposure to media advertising and brands through traditional and electronic/digital methods.

- *Electricity:* In nearly all homes.[a]

- *Lighting:* Electricity most common.

[a]98 percent of all Americans have phones, electricity, and a flush toilet.

From 1910 to 1940, the United States and other industrialized nations saw a great expansion of high school education. Students were encouraged to graduate from high school. After graduation, they went to work in towns and in factories.

In the 1930s and 1940s, daily chores in middle–class homes included shoveling coal into the furnace, washing, and drying dishes, carrying laundry out to be hung on clotheslines, canning fruits and vegetables, and mending clothes. Books of the time still carried very specific instructions on the "right way to live." For example, *The Settlement Cookbook* (1948 edition) begins with the proper way to run a household, including how to air out a room by lowering the upper sash of one window and raising the lower sash of the opposite window.

There were even sections on the proper feeding of infants and invalids, including this piece of advice: "Use the daintiest dishes in the house. Place a clean napkin on the tray and, if possible, a fresh flower." Small children were to have cooked cereal at seven o'clock and diluted orange juice at nine o'clock. When looking back, some people cringe at the idea of this much routine, while others revel in it. "The notion of a domestic life that purrs along, with routines and order and carefully delineated standards, is endlessly appealing to me. It is also quite foreign, because I am not a housewife. I am an 'at-home mother,' and the difference between the two is vast," says contemporary writer Caitlin Flanagan (2003, p. 141). Flanagan says that being an at-home mother today has less to do with the house itself and much more to do with the fact that the home is where the children happen to be.

## Household Production/Consumption System II: Modern (1950s–1990s)

The end of World War II brought an all-time high in housing demand. Color, frills, and the latest appliances became important after the austere war years. By the 1950s, most houses had indoor plumbing, electricity, a modern kitchen, and laundry equipment. New ranch-style homes sported large picture windows in the front. The sole television in the home drew the family from the kitchen into the living room. In 1954, the first Swanson TV Dinner, which had turkey with cornbread dressing and gravy, sweet potatoes, and buttered peas, was cooked in 25 minutes in a 425°C oven and sold for about $1.00. As shopping centers began to spring up, home delivery became less common, and families drove to the store to shop. The American family was being redefined. The TV dinner allowed them to eat in a modular way rather than taking portions from bowls and platters that were passed around the table.

In the 1960s, the casual lifestyle came into vogue in the form of fondue pots, shag rugs, conversation pits in living rooms, and barbecue pits outside. Gold and avocado green invaded kitchens and the rest of the house. By the end of the decade, psychedelic colors and lively prints came into vogue. Color televisions replaced the old black and white.

The 1970s and 1980s saw a return of interest in country-style décor, quilts, and collectibles, leading to an eclecticism or mix of styles popular through the 1990s. The decade of the 1990s was a transition point in-home design because of the introduction of computer technology to electronics and appliances and changes in the way people spent their time. It was also an economic boom, so homes grew bigger.

## Household Production/Consumption System III: Postmodern (21st Century)

By 2019, the average new American home was 2,687 square feet with three or four bedrooms and three bathrooms. Homes are considerably larger than the 1950s average square footage of 983. The state of the economy affected new housing sizes, so during the recession that hit the bottom in 2009, houses were smaller, and the Tiny House Movement caught on in subsequent years. As this book went to press, the U.S. economy was in a stage called recovery, and hence, the housing sizes were increasing, and at the same time people started pondering how much square footage they really needed and could afford. Low mortgage rates in 2020 and 2021 along with other factors drove up the numbers of homes bought. There was a surge in remodeling and demand for home offices.

Computers, cell phones, and Wi-Fi have changed how families live and communicate.

Household equipment have become more sophisticated, and shopping easier, but individuals and families still devote many hours each week to household tasks and food purchase and preparation.

In the 21st century, home design continues to reshape to suit the ongoing desire for newness, spending less on utilities and being greener, and meet the changing needs of the families and their pocketbooks. Active family members want to be together while doing different activities; thus, kitchens, dining areas, and living spaces are combined into one large room without walls or minimal walls. This large room which may be called a family room or great room is multifunctional usually with the flat-screen television(s) in full view. Family members are within eyeshot or earshot of each other in such a space. It harkens back to the early pioneer one-room houses with the exception that in modern homes family members can retreat to their own bedrooms and bathrooms. Two or three children are not piled into one bed to save space and to keep warm (as in the depression of the 1930s or even earlier as evidenced in Jane Austen's novel *Pride and Prejudice*) but more and more in middle-class homes, a child has his or her own bed, bedroom, and bathroom or shared bathroom. Style-wise contemporary and sleek lines are back in favor.

The microwave oven is standard, along with a stove, refrigerator, and dishwasher. Wealthier homes may have multiples: two kitchen sinks, two dishwashers, wall ovens, and two or three laundries. Energy- and water-saving appliances are appealing as part of the green movement, to help the environment and also to reduce utility bills.

These household and consumption changes have been accompanied by changes in the field of management, which has expanded beyond its initial emphasis on efficiency and economy in the home to include much more. No longer is management primarily concerned with household tasks and the streamlining of work methods in the home, although it should be noted that the home continues to be central to people's lives. Even during a recession when most people cannot afford a large new home, they can still afford a shower curtain or a small appliance. Inexpensive home products and repairs tend to be recession-proof.

Shelter will always be at the forefront of human endeavor. When asked which one or two of a dozen items say the most about you, *Americans rank home as number one*, ahead of their jobs, hobbies, and the like. As people age, they place more value on their homes. So, the importance of home is not ignored in this book and it is one of the subjects that sets family resource management apart, but we will move on to encompass a greater life view of management which includes a myriad of individual, family, and societal concerns ranging from balancing work and family life to elder care. In other words, currently, the discipline is defined more as family resource management or life management than as home management. Accordingly, it is referred to as resource management or, simply, as management.

As a way to provide a perspective on how times have changed, the Cato Institute in Washington, DC, lists the following comparisons between American life now and a century ago:

- Four times as many adults are getting their high school diplomas.

- Six times as many women now have bachelor's degrees.

- More than 70 percent of Americans have at least one automobile, a microwave oven, an air conditioner, and a washer and dryer.

- Accidental deaths have dropped by 61 percent, despite all the additional cars and airplanes, and the millions of people using them. In 2008, when gasoline prices soared, fewer people drove and the number of traffic deaths went down considerably. In 2020, people drove less and traffic deaths went down again. Evidence of how the state of public health and the economy and prices affect consumer behavior.

Although not every social, educational, and housing change can be documented here, there can be no doubt that life in the United States has changed in a way that most people would define as progress. In the last few years, a resurgence of interest in the home has been evidenced by television channels and programs devoted entirely to home remodeling and repair, interior design, and cooking. It is also evidenced by media stories about the ups and downs in the financial and real estate markets and by the proliferation of giant home supply stores.

Kitchens have increased in size considerably, even though the size of families has dropped.

There are more fire pits, outdoor kitchens, and garages. The percentage of two-car garages in U.S. households went up from 48 percent in 1973 to 64 percent in 2001; and 18 percent of households had three-car garages in 2001. Organizational and storage units and specially made garage refrigerators and freezers have made their way into the marketplace.

> In a national survey of homeowners, Whirlpool found that the garage basically functions as America's junkroom, holding all the items the house won't—or can't Whirlpool sees the garage as the next master bath—a room just waiting to be "accessorized": But don't use that term around men, its target market. Whirlpool calls the new line "Gladiator," and nearly every item features a rugged design made of steel. The devices range from a small, portable fridge that basically functions as a beer box to an interlocking "gear wall" designed to replace Pegboard.
>
> (Hallinan, 2002, p. B1)

It's clear that changes in the interplay between homes and the people who live in them are not lost on designers, retailers, and researchers. Ted Selker, an associate professor at the Massachusetts Institute of Technology, says,

> The kitchen of the future for me is about creating a value and having relationships mesh with how we work in the home to make cooking for four at home more fun than having takeout or more fun than going to a fancy restaurant.
>
> (Sessa, 2000, p. R20)

However, it depends on whether you feel cooking is fun. Many of my students say they were raised on takeout food and they like home delivery from grocery stores and restaurants or subscribe to meals in box services. Some singles and couples do not bother having a kitchen table. Formal dining rooms are being repurposed.

To summarize, the proliferation of cellphones, laptops, and smart watches where family members gather is being shaken up. One way this is playing out is that many families watch television, read, eat snacks and meals, and go online with a laptop at the same time—going back and forth between these activities and having conversations. Another design idea incorporates crafting or quilting in this combined area. Harnessing technology and creating multipurpose rooms are not new endeavors; what is new is the number and types of combinations being explored.

A list of landmark books and other references is provided at the end of this chapter as an aid to further study and as a way for you to appreciate the research and theoretical work that forms the basis for your studies in this field.

## Four Eras of Management

To help describe management's development in the 20th and 21st centuries, several theorists organized its history into chronological categories. For example, Gross, Crandall, and Knoll (1980) conceptualized home management as having six stages of development, and Berger (1984) used these stages as a framework for

A three-story Victorian-style house with a basement. Note the trim and detailed work. The eye is drawn upward with a vertical design.

reviewing management research between 1909 and 1984. Carole Vickers introduced a simpler version that divided family/home management history into four principal eras:

1. *Era one (c. 1900 to 1930s):* Health, sanitation, hygiene, and the importance of household production as a legitimate form of economic production. Ellen Richards, discussed earlier in the chapter, was one of the pioneers of this era and the ones to come.

2. *Era two (c. 1940s to early 1950s):* Household equipment, efficiency, step saving, task simplification, and standardized work units. World War II influences household consumption and production.

3. *Era three (c. 1950s to 1960s):* Family values, goals, standards, resources, decision making, organization and process, optimization of families, gradual swing away from work performance in the home. The corporate world grows and with it an emphasis on business management.

4. *Era four (c. 1970s to 1980s):* Development of a systems framework emphasizing the interconnections among family, home, and the greater society. Leading theorists Ruth Deacon and Francille Firebaugh (1988) showed how systems theory could be applied to individual and family management problems. Some would say a more sociological approach to studying the family took hold versus a more hands-on efficiency emphasis.

To extend the eras delineated by Vickers to today, *a systems framework still dominates* the study of management–emphasizing interconnections and processes. From the practical standpoint of home design, it can be said "Embrace the process" and build by learning from one experience at a time (McGee, 2020, p. 35).

Twenty-first-century theorists are increasingly aware of developments in psychology (for example the influence of positive psychology founded by Martin Seligman), neuroscience, anthropology, sociology, and

**Boomeranging and the Increase in Multigenerational Households**

According to data from real estate website Homes.com, a romance on the rocks (divorce or break-up) is the main reason young adults aged 26–40 move back in with their parents usually to their childhood bedroom. Another reason is to save money for a home or other purchase. "'It's a fairly large portion,' says Grant Simmons, vice president of search marketing at Homes. com, noting that this love-lorn population has contributed to an overall increase in multigenerational households."

*Source: Adam Bonislawski (2010, February 14). The broken-hearted head home.* The Wall Street Journal, *M5.*

economics and how they play significant roles in explaining motivations and management behavior and the choices such as boomeranging made by individuals and families. Later sections of this chapter will examine the contributions of systems and economic theory to management in more detail.

## Legislation, Policy, and Research

The evolution of management in the 20th and 21st centuries has been affected by the legislation, policy, and research as well as by technological, economic, and societal changes. In 1914, Congress passed the Smith–Lever Act to improve life in rural America by providing funds for extension programs through the U.S. Department of Agriculture (USDA). The Smith–Hughes Act, passed in 1917, provided funding for the training of primary and secondary school teachers in what was then called "home economics." In 1925, the Purnell Act extended the Smith–Lever Act and provided funds for economic and sociological investigations to develop and improve rural home life. The grants were administered by the U.S. Bureau of Home Economics, then part of the USDA. Currently, the USDA, as well as many other government agencies in the United States and in other countries, associations, and private foundations, fund management research for both urban and rural populations. Employment opportunities in resource management exist in government at the county, state, and federal levels in the Cooperative Extension Service administered through the USDA.

The 1920s saw a great deal of discussion about the nature of management from a variety of sources, including business, government, and education. For example, attendees of the first worldwide Management Congress held in Prague in 1922 concluded that management principles were universal and could be applied to a variety of business and nonbusiness situations (Drucker, 1999). Since then numerous other conferences, acts, and policies have had an impact on individuals and families, and many of these will be discussed throughout this book. Interest in improving human rights surged worldwide in the period from the 1970s to the 1990s. And, certainly, consumer protection legislation improved greatly over the last century and improvement is still underway with concerns about food safety and quality in particular.

The field of resource management emphasizes raising living standards, quality of life, and well-being through a variety of means, including improvements in health and nutrition, welfare, child labor laws, education, and work-leave policies. A topic such as welfare reform encompasses many factors critical to its success, such as prevention of human trafficking, child abuse and neglect; financial support for children; childcare;

availability of transportation, education, and employment; use of social indicators for evaluation and policy analysis; and community- based planning. Each of these requires research to determine human needs and the best ways of addressing them.

Research is the collection, processing, and analysis of information. Because management falls within the realm of applied social science, the results of research studies should be useful and made available to citizens and policy makers. Collection methods include survey, observation, mechanical measurement, focus groups, archival research, physiological measures, diaries or records, and laboratory and field experiments.

A combination of methods is often used to cross-check results, and interviews are often part of the process. For example, *Newsweek* real estate writer Daniel McGinn, author of *House Lust: America's Obsession with Our Homes*, interviewed homeowners, real estate agents, architects, researchers, and others. He found that housing size increased as homeowners started owning more cars, clothes, and other possessions.

In a study conducted by Merillat (a cabinet manufacturer) with 1,252 interviews in an online survey, it was found that regarding kitchens, respondents fell into four segments:

1.  *Luxury leaders:* affluent with a large home, highly educated, older, enjoy the latest products, the kitchen is the "star" of the home.

2.  *Domestic dwellers:* live in a comfortable home that is nice but not ostentatious, enjoy quiet evenings at home and outings with the family, use the kitchen for homework, pay bills and read, prefer low maintenance.

3.  *Busy bees:* similar to domestic dwellers but busier, eat out a lot, the kitchen often disorganized and cluttered, need more storage and organizational solutions.

4.  *Career builders:* most likely first-time homebuyers trying to move up the ladder, kitchen not so important, little emotional attachment, consider resale value, the island is the landing zone for laptops, newspapers, and mail (Quintana & Grossman, 2007).

---

### CRITICAL THINKING

#### Kitchen Size

Kitchens, considered the most important and most expensive room in the house, is more than what they seem. Why do you think they have become bigger at the same time that families have become smaller? Which of the four segments fits the household you grew up in the best? Is it one segment or a combination? Or, would you add a fifth category?

---

*What topics besides homes are covered in management research? Most management research falls into one of two categories: (1) financial or economic resources and (2) family or household resources. Specific topics include financial planning, environmental impacts, retirement planning, credit card and debt reduction, family and financial decision making, control issues, bankruptcy and debt reduction, stress, division of household work, time use, and balancing work and family. One of the most-studied topics has been time use. Researchers have explored time spent on housework, home-based paid work, and child care; who does what and when; and how factors such as employment, income, and size of family affect time use, demands, and household production and consumption. A study revealed that for 21-year-olds, telecommunications, television, and the Internet are so ubiquitous in their lives that they bounce seamlessly from one to another, sometimes consuming several media simultaneously. MTV found evidence of this when it recently asked 18- to 24-year-olds how many hours a day they spend surfing the Web, downloading music and emailing friends. The company's researchers were shocked when they added up the hours and found that the average time totaled more than 24 hours a day. "Young people manage to squeeze 31 hours into a 24-hour period," says Betsy Franck, executive vice president of research and planning for MTV Networks, in New York. "They're the masters of multitasking."*

*(Weiss, 2003, pp. 31–32)*

An offshoot of time management is the subject of the division of household labor—who does what in the home? Research studies focus on one of the following approaches or subjects:

1. Time availability

2. Psychological differences between men and women.

3. Environments such as type of housing unit and external resources

4. Task preferences

5. Number of children and their ages, older dependents, individuals with disabilities

6. Employment outside the home, impact of shift work

7. Impact of education level

8. Number of years of marriage, previous marriages

9. The handling of family finances and problems thereof (Durband & Law, 2019)

Researchers also commonly investigate issues of satisfaction and well-being. They are interested in measuring not only how people are spending their time, energy, and money but how they feel about their resource allocation and life in general.

## Theory Overview

Recall from Chapter 1 that family resource management is an applied social science. "Good science begins with good construct definition and conceptualization" (Elliot & Niesta, 2009, p. 56). For example, goals are individually defined and conceptualized but a class of a hundred students in family resource management may share some similar goals. The study of management is a combination of theory, concepts, technique, research, and practice. There is not one management theory or framework, but several. Management is an interdisciplinary field that borrows concepts and theories from related disciplines (see Chapter 1).

**Theory** is an organized system of ideas or beliefs that can be measured; it is a system of assumptions or principles. The word "theory" comes from the Greek verb *theorein* (to behold or contemplate). We form theories, for example, when we wonder why a couple has decided to marry or divorce. We look for clues to the outcome—why is the couple compatible or not compatible? A theory summarizes what is known about a phenomenon and permits the formation of **hypotheses**, or predictions about future occurrences.

Theories are useful because they reduce wastage of time and effort and provide ways of structuring one's thoughts and knowledge about behaviors. A fundamental theory is that past behavior is an indicator or strong predictor of future behavior. This explains why people go back to the same vacation spot year after year or buy a second home. Many choose to ignore the latest hotels or restaurants. An innovator such as Elon Musk (the richest man in the world), on the other hand, wants to try something new, take risks. Thus, the well-thought-out marketing campaign for an established resort or cruise ship considers the needs of returnees and also seeks to entice new customers with uniqueness and novelty such as a rock-climbing wall or a clear water tube that encircles the top deck of the ship. Likewise, families and households must roll with the tides, keeping up with changing needs and wants. A wedding brings in new family members, as do the birth of babies and adoptions.

## Functions of Theory

The primary function of theory is to organize observations and other information so that individuals can make sense of the events that occur around them. For example, researchers can observe the way people behave in situations requiring the allocation of resources, planning, and the implementation and evaluation of decisions. A theory of management not only attempts to explain the observed behavior of people in general but also seeks to provide an understanding of a single individual's or family's behavior. People are constantly making predictions about their own and others' behavior. For example, perhaps we assume we will like or dislike oysters based on a past experience of eating them. Most predictions are so automatic that we don't even think about them. When we look at a restaurant menu, we unconsciously skip over the salad section if we never eat salads. However, when an unconscious prediction turns out differently than expected (e.g., a friend who is always late shows up ahead of time), we realize that we had made a prediction and that the prediction was wrong. In the case of the early-arriving friend, we are pleasantly surprised.

Theory of behavior has many aspects. Predicting behavior is one aspect; controlling behavior is another. "The vast majority of meaningful human behavior is purposeful or willed or controlled (though not necessarily consciously so)—it is employed toward some end. It is the events, or goals, that direct, energize, and sustain purposeful behavior over time" (Moskowitz & Grant, 2009, p. 2). Although the word "control" sometimes has a negative connotation, as in brainwashing or mind control, in management it has a more prosaic meaning. **Controlling** refers to the things people do to check their course of action. For example, you may be concerned over whether you have enough money in your bank account to cover your credit cards or whether you can get a better grade on the next test. These concerns involve both predictions and possible alterations of behavior. As a final comment on the function of theory, consider Kurt Lewin's statement that "there is nothing so practical as a good theory." Theories provide a useful way to organize information. Without theories, the prediction of future events would be nearly impossible.

## Theories Ahead

Before a new theory can be promoted, the theorist must first develop definitions of key terms, formulate statements or assumptions, and then test the theory. One of the problems in developing and explaining theories is that they are abstract. But once a theory is put into action and the subsequent behavior can be observed, the thought processes behind the behavior become more understandable. Because so many studies and books have used systems theory, most of this chapter will now focus on its components and applications. The remainder of this chapter will examine the application of economic theory—specifically, optimization, satisficing, and risk aversion—to the study of management. Other theories specific to resource exchange, time, stress, and fatigue will be covered in subsequent chapters.

## Systems Theory

The dynamic and ongoing nature of systems theory makes it particularly applicable to managerial thought and behavior. One of the reasons why systems theory has endured is its versatility—it fits nearly all situations. The principle underlying systems theory is that the whole is greater than the sum of its parts. This emphasis on the whole and the interconnectedness of its different parts is appropriate for the eclectic, interdisciplinary field of management. Also, as individuals and families are part of larger behavioral and environmental systems, it makes sense to view them as parts of a whole rather than as isolated units.

**Systems theory** is a way of viewing interactions. Theories emphasize not only interconnectedness but also interactions among different systems. It focuses on the behavior of feedback and its complexity. The circle in the drawing above represents the circular nature of systems and of feedback.

A **system** is an integrated set of parts that function together for some end purpose or result.

Systems may be composed of living or nonliving things.

Because management focuses on human behavior, the emphasis in this book is on living systems in the context of environments—in particular, the home, work, and community environments. **Domi** is the plural of domus which is the Latin term meaning house or home. In ancient Rome and in Roman territories the domus was a type of house occupied by the upper classes. In current parlance, domi has evolved to the word domesticity or more broadly to describe a gathering place. In the author's home city there is Domi Station, a building near a train station which serves as a community gathering place for entrepreneurs.

A system as a whole has characteristics that set it apart from other systems. For example, a family is a system. Families have things in common with other entities, such as streets, neighborhoods, or schools, but at the same time, they have distinct traditions, ways of celebrating and living, and consumption patterns. The place or point where independent systems or diverse groups interact is called an **interface**. A doctor's office may serve as the interface between a patient's home and medical services. **Telemedicine** also called telehealth is a modern interface (electronic contact and sharing of information) between doctor and patient.

**Boundaries** are the limits or borders between systems. They separate one domain from another. Everyone has personal and family boundaries. Boundaries may be visible, as in fences and doors, or invisible, as in rules of behavior or unmarked borderlines between properties. For example, young children learn early in life where their yard stops and their neighbor's begins.

They carry this lesson about boundaries into adulthood. Thus, boundaries maintain functions and influence human behavior. It can be referred to as **boundary management** meaning the establishment of and maintenance of boundaries.

Homes and workplaces are filled with visible and invisible boundaries. One of the survival skills necessary for any new employee is to learn where the boundaries are—who talks to whom, how flexible lunch breaks are, and which doors are kept open and which remain closed. In a home situation, consider how quickly visiting relatives learn house rules and behavior, such as when breakfast will be ready, who gets the bathroom first, and how loud and how long the television can be played. The boundaries of a system determine what is allowed and what is not.

## Open and Closed Families

Some families are more open to the outside environment than other families; in other words, they more freely exchange information and materials with outside influences. To use systems terminology, families can be categorized as mostly morphogenic or morphostatic. **Morphogenic systems** are adaptive to change and are relatively open. In an open system, matter and energy are freely exchanged between the system and its environment. Its boundaries are permeable.

In contrast, **morphostatic systems** are resistant to change. They are stable and relatively closed.

A relatively open family may have neighborhood children in and out of the house much of the day, chat with neighbors often, spend a lot of time on the telephone, entertain often, and leave the blinds open. A relatively closed family may not even know neighbors' names while keeping the blinds shut and staying to themselves. Even without meeting the new family on the block, neighbors may be able to surmise something about their relative openness by the changes they make to the yard or the exterior appearance of the house. At the same time, a quick prediction based only on appearances may turn out to be wrong. For example, a seven-foot-high fence may be a sign that a family is closed or may simply indicate the presence of a large dog.

Although a family's overall style will be "open" or "closed," variations exist within families, and boundaries can exist between family members. For example, one member of a family may not speak to another. Some family members may be very open and gregarious, whereas others may be more private and take a more contemplative approach to life. Within families, each member sets her or his own boundaries of space and privacy. Conflict can occur when boundaries are not respected. Think how often the plots of television shows and movies revolve around a violation of privacy, such as parents reading a teenager's diary or one family member's overhearing of another's supposedly private conversation or reading another's emails.

In addition, situations (such as the Covid-19 pandemic) can alter the way a family interacts with others and their environment. For example, a family crisis can turn a relatively open family into a closed family, at least temporarily. Closure may be a protective mechanism until an adjustment period has passed. Systems theory emphasizes the adaptive nature of families.

## Subsystems and System Elements

A **subsystem** is a part of a larger system. Individuals and families are subsystems of communities. Communities are subsystems of counties, which are subsystems of states, and so on. Each system at each level has a reason for existing. This interconnectedness of systems is the reason why management is no longer limited to the infrastructure of the home; theorists realize that decisions made at home ultimately affect the community, the country, and the world and vice versa. For example, families and economic institutions have always been closely related. Families supply work, and society supplies wages that families use to buy goods and services and pay taxes. Thus, each subsystem affects other systems. This emphasis on how the interaction of parts affects the whole is the essence of systems theory.

### Inputs, Throughputs, and Outputs

Management has borrowed several system terms from computer terminology and applied them to the individual and the family. Three of these terms—inputs, throughputs, and outputs—form the basic elements in systems theory as it is applied to management. The term **"inputs"** refers to whatever is brought into the system (i.e., things, ideas, information). The processing of inputs is called **throughput,** or transformation. **"Transformations"** refers to transitions from one system to another. The term **outputs** refers to the end results, or products, leftovers, and waste. Figure 2.2 presents a managerial-action model showing

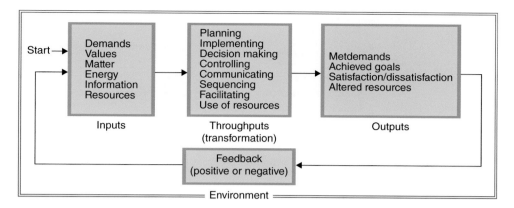

Figure 2.2 Managerial action using the systems approach.

the interaction of inputs, throughputs, and outputs. In the model, inputs such as resources and demands are transformed through planning, decision making, facilitating, and other throughputs into outputs such as met demands, altered resources, and satisfaction/dissatisfaction. **Demands** are events or goals that require action for their fulfillment. For example, if a landlord demands that rent be paid on time, tenants need to respond to this demand. "Facilitating" means to make something easier. Facilitation helps move the managerial process along.

**Sequencing** occurs when one thing follows another, as in a series of events. For example, scenes in a play follow a sequence. In resource management, events occur in sequence to ensure a successful outcome. Before writing a check to the landlord, tenants determine whether they have enough money in their checking accounts to cover the rent. This process is facilitated if the tenants have kept their accounts balanced and their records up to date.

Calculating whether they have enough money in the account *after* they have written checks for the rent would be placing events out of sequence.

Sharpe and Winter (1991) applied inputs, throughputs (transformations), and outputs to the concept of managerial effectiveness. They hypothesized that effective management leads to satisfactory outcomes, but that there are many potential ways to be a more effective manager. For example, they hypothesized, managerial effectiveness increases when the goals (inputs) are clear, actionable, and verifiable and when the manager generates workable alternatives (transformations). Increased efficiency in the use of time and evaluation are two output-related hypotheses. These hypotheses illustrate how input, throughput, and output can be applied to management.

## Feedback

Feedback occurs when part of the output is returned to the input in the form of information. The term "feedback" was introduced in Chapter 1 as part of the management process diagrammed in Figure 1.1, which also appeared earlier in this chapter in Figure 2.1. Figure 2.3 is a model that focuses specifically on the feedback loop. This model begins with the current assessment of the performance or situation and then proceeds to the establishment of objectives and goals. Think about it. There are many ways to achieve the same goal. As in most management models, an evaluation component leads to further feedback. Was the right way chosen? The feedback loop is important because it reinforces the concept that feedback affects future decisions and the allocation of resources. The model in Figure 2.3 also demonstrates that feedback is not an end in itself, but a process or operation.

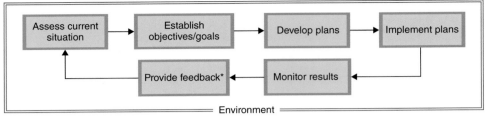

*Feedback is the return of information about the result of monogeneral action.

Figure 2.3 Model of the feedback loop in management.

Feedback can be positive or negative. In general conversation, the words "positive" and "negative" connote good and bad, but in systems terminology, the words are used differently. **Positive feedback** is information put into the system that anticipates and promotes change; thus, it indicates that a new course of action is needed. **Negative feedback** is information put into the system that indicates that the system is deviating from its normal course and that corrective measures may be necessary if the desired steady state is to be maintained. Individuals and families use feedback to make future decisions. For example, negative feedback may reinforce a previous decision as being correct and emphasize that no further change is needed.

To illustrate positive feedback, consider the situation of John, a college student, who receives a B+ on a midterm exam in a course where the grade is based on the midterm and the final exam. As John wants to get an A in the course, his midterm grade indicates that he will have to study harder for the final to earn an A in the course. Therefore, the B+ grade (although it is a disappointment) gives John positive feedback. As he enjoys the class and thinks he is capable of getting an A, he plans to study harder to improve his grade. Kevin, another student sitting next to John, also gets a B+ on the midterm, but he decides to put his energies elsewhere and is prepared to settle for a B in the course. Thus, the test grade gives Kevin negative feedback; he chooses to maintain the system by studying at his current pace rather than by intensifying his work.

Feedback serves an important function. People use feedback to learn whether they are doing and saying the right things. Their future decisions hinge on the type of feedback they receive and how they act on that feedback. Are they reaching their goals? The concept of feedback will be covered more extensively in the chapter on communication.

## Entropy and Equilibrium

According to systems theory, each system has a tendency to run down and possibly misfunction as its energy flow ebbs and becomes less structured. This tendency toward disorder or randomness is called **entropy.** It is more likely to occur in a closed system than in an open system. For example, an executive who works 60-hour weeks and eventually wears down and needs a vacation is experiencing entropy. The vacation revitalizes the executive, and she returns with renewed energy and vigor. In a system, entropy can refer to a lack of energy as well as a lack of information. Entropy unchecked leads to disorganization and disruption; order is destroyed.

A system also seeks **equilibrium** which means feedback causes it to readjust itself with a tendency toward wanting to put things back the way they were. Children may not want family traditions changed, and if the parents are divorcing, they usually want them back together again. Students may want the same favorite professor repeatedly for different classes. They are comfortable with that professor, know what to expect and how they will perform in terms of grades. Changes in the external environment will move individuals and families toward equilibrium-seeking behaviors especially if they were content with things as they were.

## Murphy's Law and Systems Theory

Plenty of attention is paid to various rules and laws that influence our lives. Murphy's Law is named after an Air Force captain who noticed during rocket-sled deceleration tests that a crucial gauge had been wired wrong and summarized: "If there's more than one way to do a job and one of those will end in disaster, then somebody will do it that way" (Edwards, 2002, p. 72). Even a simple toy, such as roller skates, left at the top of the stairs can spell disaster. As our homes become more complex technologically and as this technology becomes more interlocking, the chances for something going wrong increase. A poorly wired doorbell can cause home fires.

**Murphy's Law**, most simply stated, is, "if something can go wrong, it will." It implies that "in complex systems even the tiniest flaw can cause a cascade of failures" (Edwards, 2002, p. 72).

## Homeostasis

Even though things can easily go wrong in a system, there is also a general tendency for the system to try to remain balanced. This tendency to maintain balance, called **"homeostasis,"** works as a control device. When something gets out of control, tension is created, and the system becomes unbalanced, triggering the homeostasis mechanism. For example, people who have a Monday-through-Friday workweek use the weekend to renew their sense of balance and get their home and family life back in order. They run errands, go to the grocery store, answer mail, wash clothes, mow their lawns, and spend time with their families and friends. By Sunday night, they hope they will have achieved a feeling of homeostasis—a sense that things are back under control and in order for the week ahead.

## Equifinality and Multifinality

The concepts of equifinality and multifinality are also important in systems theory. **Equifinality** refers to the phenomenon in which different circumstances and opportunities may lead to similar outcomes. The goals are the same but as said before there are lots of ways to get there. **Multifinality** refers to the phenomenon in which the same initial circumstances or conditions may lead to different conclusions or outcomes. For example, consider the situation of two friends, Brett and Nick, who are high school seniors deciding which college to attend. Although they have been accepted by the same colleges and have the same backgrounds and career goals, Brett chooses to stay at home and attend a community college, and Nick chooses to go away to a four-year college. These different outcomes, given the same initial conditions, are an example of multifinality. Now consider the situation of Megan and Tia, two students who have never met. Even though they have totally different backgrounds and ambitions, they end up choosing the same college—an example of equifinality, similar outcomes arrive even when given different initial conditions.

Equifinality and multifinality are useful concepts because they illustrate the complex nature of management. Different outcomes given the same initial surface factors may indicate that other factors are at work—not apparent to the outside observer. For example, individual tastes, preferences, and attitudes play a large part in decisions and outcomes. Nick might be ready for a four-year college away from home, but Brett may not. The expense might be another consideration in their decisions. Megan and Tia may have more in common than is readily apparent, or both may be attracted to the same feature of a particular college.

## The Personal System

The goal of personal systems management is to recognize and to make productive the specific strengths and abilities of each individual. Respect for the uniqueness of the qualities of each individual is a critical part of management. Each person is a system composed of many subsystems, including (1) biological/physiological, (2) behavioral, (3) psychological, and (4) social subsystems. Each subsystem in turn has many components.

For example, values and ethics are part of the psychological subsystem; they provide integrity and direction to decisions, guiding individuals through the many moral dilemmas they encounter each day.

Each individual's personal system exists within a greater system of relationships, friendships, and family. Inputs to the personal system include other people, the environment, heredity, and past experiences, all of which help shape the individual's personal management style.

Owing to the dynamic nature of systems, the individual is always changing and always interpreting feedback. An example of feedback is the story of what happened to Lucky, the dog.

George Blooston who writes for *AARP magazine* wrote:

> One of my jobs at this magazine is encouraging AARP members to be careful with their money. Really, folks, put away whatever you can. Spend only on necessities. But what is a necessity? Last fall Lucky bolted across the street toward a friend and was hit by a speeding SUV. In 12 days we spent $20,000 to save him. Yes, there went a semester at college, or a new car, or years off the mortgage. There went the emergency fund. But I have no regrets. We could find the money. In good conscience we couldn't not spend it.
>
> *(2008, p. 49)*

"Lucky" was indeed lucky to have such a devoted family, and the story shows that management takes into account human emotions; it is not all steps-to-follow or rationality (meaning, based on reason). Besides management researchers, industry and government are interested in how people's attitudes change. The Gallup organization regularly monitors people's attitudes on a variety of subjects, including conditions in the United States and in their personal lives. In one survey, respondents reported that they were more satisfied with their personal lives than with the way things were going overall in the United States.

## Family Systems Theory and Management

The goal of family systems management is to recognize and to make productive the specific strengths and abilities of each family. As discussed earlier, systems have a tendency toward equilibrium. In family dynamics, the tendency toward equilibrium puts pressure on a changing family member to revert to his or her original behavior within the family system (Lamanna et al., 2018).

In family systems, boundaries change over time as families change. The permeability of boundaries alters as family members age and move on to other life stages. **Boundary ambiguity** is common in blended families in which members are unsure where the lines are; how daily life should be arranged; and who should be invited to what family/holiday events.

## Application of Systems Theory to Households

In the previous two sections, we have focused on the management of personal and family lives. Systems theory and terminology can also apply to homes. For example, the concepts of inputs, throughputs, outputs, and feedback can be applied to both simple and complex household operations.

An example of a simple household operation is doing the laundry. Water, detergent, and clothes are inputs for the washing machine. The throughput is the cleansing, rinsing, and spinning action, and the outputs are dirty wastewater and clean clothes. If the clothes are not clean, this signals (provides feedback) that something is wrong with the system, and a change is needed.

**CASE STUDY**

### The Rubio Family

In the Rubio family, divorced Linda married divorced Andrew, whose ex-wife Emma, also remarried, lives down the street. Linda and Andrew have five children between the ages of 15 and 25 from their first marriages. Emma comes to their house unin-vited, even walks in the door (the door is usually unlocked so that the children can come and go) and opens the refrigerator, and takes out a drink. Sometimes Linda has wandered into the kitchen for her morning coffee and been surprised to find Emma sitting there. Has Emma crossed boundaries? What should Linda and Andrew say or do? Explain your answer.

As the Rubio case study illustrates, interactions within families are qualitatively and quantitatively different from interactions among other groups. Family systems theory has come to be one of the leading theories in clinical and programmatic work with families. It is useful, for example, in helping a family who has undergone a trau-matic event. Anyone studying to be a marriage and family therapist would learn family systems theory. In prac-tice, the focus may be on a particular subsystem such as the marital (or couple), parental, or sibling subsystem.

Family systems theory assumes that families share goals and work together to achieve them. A constant is to try and be good parents spending time with children and ensuring they do well in life. This involves not just time but quality time. An example of a family goal would be that each of the children goes to college. To reach this goal all family members may work extra jobs or put in overtime or make financial invest-ments to accumulate enough money; in addition, the children may study extra hard in school to get good grades and/or excel in athletics or music, or other activities leading to better scholarships and financial aid.

In short,

> *Family systems theory allows one to understand the organizational complexity of families, as well as the interactive patterns that guide family interactions. One of the central premises of family systems theory is that family systems organize themselves to carry out the daily challenges and tasks of life, as well as adjusting to the developmental needs of its members*
>
> *(Fleming, 2003, p. 643)*

Another important aspect of family systems theory is that families are dynamic in nature and have patterns of rules and strategies that affect the interactions that take place. Rules would include such things as meal-times and bedtimes. According to an Impulse Research poll, 67 percent of American families have assigned or "usual" seats at the table. What happens when someone upsets this rule and sits in someone else's chair?

Families are resilient; they respond to change by readjusting patterns of interaction and resource use. They have the ability to recover from misfortune such as losing a house to foreclosure or suffering through a family trauma. Family systems theory also emphasizes the importance of family history, a psychological perspective introduced by Murray Bowen in the 1970s and further explored by Monica McGoldrick in *You Can Go Home Again*.

McGoldrick emphasizes that people and their problems do not exist in a vacuum but are part of a broad family system. She says that

*The "family" comprises the entire emotional system of at least three and increasingly four generations, who move through life together, even though they often live in different places. As a family, we share a common past and an anticipated future. The patterns of the family life cycle are changing dramatically so that there is less continuity than ever before between the demands on current families and the patterns of past generations. Thus it is easy to lose all sense of connection with what has come before in your family, and this can be a serious loss.*

*(McGoldrick, 1995, p. 30)*

Further, McGoldrick says,

*While each family is unique in its particular history, all families are alike in their underlying patterns. Famous families may, because they are in the spotlight, have certain responses to their notoriety, but all families have basic ways they deal with love, pain, and conflict; make sense of life and death; cross time, class, and cultural barriers. All families must find ways of dealing with loss and of integrating new members.*

*(1995, p. 30)*

More complex household operations include preparing meals, establishing schedules, and caring for children. For example, meal preparation involves deciding what to eat, shopping (the average grocery store offers more than 50,000 different products), preparing food, serving, eating, and cleaning up. Setting schedules requires communication and the coordination of activities, people, and time. Childcare involves innumerable decisions, tasks, and responsibilities in addition to emotional factors. Family economists have tried to put a dollar value on household work, which has been used in determining life insurance and other financial implications and in resolving court cases involving divorce, or the injury or death of a stay-at-home spouse or parent. Estimates run anywhere from $50,000 and up to replacing a main caregiver. Clearly, household work and in-home childcare and eldercare have value. Raising a child from birth to 18 (not counting college or private or charter school fees) is estimated at $230,000. These figures are often constructed from the U.S. Bureau of Labor Statistics averages for a variety of expenses and occupations, such as maid and chauffeur. To calculate the value, wages and

How we live today. Modern house exterior.

the number of hours the service typically takes are determined; other factors, such as the age of the children, are also taken into account. Critics of this approach say that, realistically, if a wife and mother, for example, is the victim of a car accident, her family will not replace her with a team comprising a bookkeeper, a cook, and so on. Furthermore, the emotional loss is not added into these types of calculations.

Much more goes into household systems than the work input of an at-home parent. All members contribute to household production and consumption. Inputs may be rented, leased, provided by the community, or owned. Raw materials, market goods and services, durables, labor, knowledge, and management skills are inputs to the household system. An example of household production would be the preparation of a meal. This activity contributes to household well-being and the desired end result (output, goal) of improved human resources. Household production/consumption does more than satisfy immediate needs—it provides for an increased human capability, a provision for the future.

## Human Ecology and Ecosystems

Conditions in the greater environment have an important influence on how households and families function. The study of how living things relate to their natural environment is called **ecology**. Adding the word "human" produces the term **human ecology**, which simply means humans interacting with their environment. A more comprehensive definition of human ecology says that it is the study of how humans—as social, physical, and biological beings—interact with each other and with their physical, sociocultural, aesthetic, and biological environments as well as with the material and human resources of these environments (Bubolz & Sontag, 1988).

Human ecology views humans and their near environments as integrated wholes, influencing each other (Bubolz & Sontag, 1988). The **environment** is the all-encompassing external conditions influencing the life of an organism or population. In this book, the emphasis in considering the environment is on the quality-of-life conditions for individuals and families. Environment is essentially everything that surrounds humans; but because this concept is so broad, theorists have divided environment into microenvironment and macroenvironment. **Microenvironment** (also called microhabitat or near environment) is the environment that closely surrounds individuals and families. Apartments, sorority and fraternity houses, classrooms, libraries, and dormitory rooms are part of a college student's microenvironment. **Macroenvironment** (also called macrohabitat or far environment) surrounds and encompasses the microenvironment. Sky, trees, and oceans are part of the macroenvironment.

### Family Ecosystem

**Family ecosystem** is the subsystem of human ecology that emphasizes the interactions between families and environments. According to Paolucci et al. (1977), family ecosystem has three basic elements:

1. *Organisms:* These are the family members.

2. *Environments:* Both the natural and human-built environments are included.

3. *Family organization:* This functions to transform energy in the form of information into family decisions and actions.

The ecosystem approach is useful because it emphasizes the interaction between families and the conditions that surround them. A change in a single component of the family ecosystem has an impact on the other parts. For example, if one family member has an alcohol or drug abuse problem, it will affect everyone else in the family. This interaction could be illustrated as

Individual Family Member ↔ Family

Many management situations involve individuals or families interacting with factors in their environment. This exchange can be illustrated most simply as

Individual/Family ↔ Environment

Notice that in these illustrations, the arrows point both ways; the environment impacts the individual or family and vice versa. The nature of systems is the emphasis on linkages and complexity of situations. A related theory is **social exchange theory**, which focuses on individual resources and the trading or bartering of these resources, often related to power in families. Exchanging gifts at holiday time or for birthdays is an example of social exchange. Another example would be a father limiting his child's access to the Internet.

### Global Ecosystems

Global ecosystems encompass all the family ecosystems and are regulated by interactive physical, social, political, economic, chemical, and biological processes. To begin to understand the global ecosystem, one must understand the dynamics of family ecosystems. For instance, each family contributes to the greater society and is a microcosm of the larger social system in which it exists. Each patch in a quilt adds a special nuance of color, pattern, strength, utility, and texture to the finished product. Collectively, the sum of all the parts is infinitely more interesting than the individual pieces. Each extended family and each nation benefits from the combined strength of its various people and cultures.

Millions of family ecosystems combine to form national ecosystems that in turn make up the global ecosystem. Human ecology emphasizes the global interdependence of individuals, families, and communities, and the resources of natural, constructed, and behavioral environments, for the purpose of wise decision making and use of resources essential for human development and to improve the quality of life and the environment (Bubolz & Sontag, 1988).

In homes, family ecosystems interact with the systems that supply food, heat, healthcare, information, water, gas, electricity, clothing, and transportation. These same systems operate in the global ecosystem on a much larger scale. The welfare of nations depends on these life-support systems. For example, maintaining an adequate food supply is a concern at the household level, the national level, and the global level.

International environmental issues continue to dominate the global policy agenda. Long-range solutions to environmental problems require planning and cooperation among nations. As planning is a fundamental part of management, this field will play an increasingly vital role in encouraging the conservation of resources and the promotion of informed and sound health and environmental attitudes and practices at the individual, family, and household levels.

## Economic Theory

Although systems theory has been the dominant influence on management over the last few decades, the application of economic theory to management has attracted renewed attention. Economics is about how people choose. It is based on eight guideposts (Gwartney et al., 2018):

1. The use of scarce resources is costly; trade-offs must always be made.

2. Individuals choose purposefully, trying to get the most from their limited resources.

3. Incentives matter.

4. Individuals focus on the difference in the costs and benefits between alternatives.

5. Information can be scarce and is costly to acquire.

6. Actions may generate second effects; in other words, decisions have both immediate effects and spin-off, or later, effects.

7. Preferences vary between individuals. A ticket to the ballet may be worth $100 to one person and absolutely nothing to another. Value is subjective.

8. Theory is useful in making predictions. The focus in economics is on the behavior of a large number of individuals.

According to Sherman Hanna of Ohio State University, the most obvious application of economic theory to family resource management is in terms of the maximization of satisfaction or utility subject to resource constraints (1989, 1997).

Economic theory assumes that individuals seek to maximize satisfaction from the decisions they make. It also assumes that individuals are rational (use reason in making decisions) and will act in their own self-interest. Economic theory focuses on the interaction between buyers and sellers. Economists are basically concerned with the nature of the exchange—for example, what a thing costs and what is gained in return. If you are really thirsty a drink will mean more to you than a friend who is not thirsty. You will be more appreciative of who gives you a drink.

Please read the following and answer the end questions;

*These are interesting times. In many ways, they are characterized by uncertainties, paradoxes, and contradictions. Technology has dramatically increased the speed and reduced the cost of information, communication, and transportation. But, has this improved our well-being or merely turned our lives into meaningless rat races? Why do people feel so insecure even though their incomes are at historic highs?*

## CRITICAL THINKING

### Economic Insecurity

Please read the following and answer the end questions;

*These are interesting times. In many ways, they are characterized by uncertainties, paradoxes, and contradictions. Technology has dramatically increased the speed and reduced the cost of information, communication, and transportation. But, has this improved our well-being or merely turned our lives into meaningless rat races? Why do people feel so insecure even though their incomes are at historic highs?*

Source: Gwartney, Stroup, Sobel, & Macpherson (2018). *Economics: Private and Public Choice*, 16th edition, Boston, MA: Cengage, p. xxi.

## Optimization and Satisficing

Economic theory includes many subtheories. **Optimization** means obtaining the best result, such as maximizing profit for a business or maximizing satisfaction for a household (Hanna, 1989, 1997). Optimization refers to the effective use of resources to gain the maximum satisfaction.

Holly Hunts and Ramona Marotz-Baden of Montana State University wrote that

> *Optimizing means that all assessment tools are considered in the search for the best choice. An optimizing search is thorough, and the choice that meets the assessment tool standards of high quality while considering cost is the choice made. An example might be choosing a wedding dress. A young woman may search tirelessly for months for the perfect dress—looking at patterns, looking at magazines, attending bridal shows, and searching the Internet. Optimizing is possible when time is not limited and when true quality can be measured.*
>
> *(2003, p. 5)*

Although in theory individuals and families will seek to optimize their resources, in reality they often do not behave in optimizing ways. For example, they may not buy the low-cost generic product in a grocery store even though it has the same quality as a more expensive brand name product. Or they may not buy the lowest-cost airplane ticket because they don't want to fly at an inconvenient time or plan far enough ahead to get the lowest price. Comparison shopping can save money, but some people may feel that it is not worth the aggravation, time, energy, and patience required. An optimization approach to consumption-related problem solving may include:

1. An examination of utility or objective

2. A consideration of the desired consumption levels of different goods and services

3. An analysis of constraints or limitations

Much of what is consumed today has evolved, sometimes rapidly, as a result of cultural and technological changes that occurred in the late 19th century and the 20th. In addition, the massive migration from rural to urban areas as well as the massive immigration into the country has had an enormous impact on the overall economy as well as on economic theory and application. Similar conclusions can be drawn worldwide (e.g., the trend of migrating from rural to urban is global), although each nation has its own timetable and we don't want to lose cultural identity and responsiveness to issues like food sovereignty in the rush to urbanize.

Intensive information seeking is an important aspect of optimization theory. As economic theory emphasizes the measurable and the rational, information seeking is heralded as a logical course of action. Theorists reason that the more people know the more informed (better) their decisions will be. This makes intuitive sense, but not everyone does what is reasonable and logical all the time. Besides, even the best-informed decisions can go wrong. For example, Randall and Elaine spent months researching which car to buy. They read articles about new cars, checked the recommendations of *Consumer Reports* magazine, and then went out and bought the worst car of their married life. Apparently, the marketplace is less than perfect (e.g., a particular car could be poorly manufactured even though the model is highly recommended).

Furthermore, people must consider the possible outcomes in deciding how much planning and implementing effort is optimal. Expending considerable effort to obtain information about a choice that will have a little long-term effect on the family may not be a wise use of time and other resources. Decisions may fail

CRITICAL THINKING

## Montana Indian Education for All Act

Holly Hunts and Jioanna Carjuzaa of Montana State University had this to say in an Abstract about thinking outside discipline boundaries. After reading, please react and apply culturally responsive concepts to where you live.

> *The Montana Indian Education for All (IEFA) Act is an unprecedented reform effort 40 years in the making. In this paper we summarize the IEFA professional development opportunities provided to faculty at a land grant university in the western United States while highlighting a faculty member's personal efforts to integrate IEFA in a culturally responsive manner. We explain how, instead of limiting the transmission of ideas, expanding discipline boundaries has opened a flood-gate to new information and other 'ways of knowing' for the faculty member and her students.*
>
> Source: Jioanna Carjuzaa and Holly Hunts (2013). Thinking outside discipline boundaries to integrate Indian education for all across the curriculum, Vol 6. *Learning without Boundaries?*

because of lack of access to information, inability to process information, or the lack of time to gather or process information. Not everyone has equal access to the Internet, for example, although schools and communities are working to make the distribution of this technology more equitable.

Attempts have been made to integrate economic and social systems theories. For example, mate selection is an intriguing example of a decision that is not based entirely on reason. Gary S. Becker (1930–2014), and winner of the Nobel Prize in economics, posited that the economic forces that influence people to get married and have children are as powerful as the forces that govern decisions to buy a new car or change jobs. Others disagree. They argue that selecting a mate, having children, and other highly personal choices are more emotional than rational. Less controversial is the use of optimization theory by household and business managers. Decisions that are largely objective, such as which refrigerator or laser printer to purchase, may be well suited to a short information search and a rational decision. Thus, optimization may be most useful in simple, straightforward situations involving a short information search and little emotion. Whether it is applicable in decision situations such as mate selection, as suggested by Becker, is open to debate. But as the basic point of optimization is the maximization of satisfaction through obtaining the best result, the theory should be applicable to a variety of situations.

**Satisficing** refers to picking the first good alternative that presents itself so that an individual stops searching once it appears that an initial choice will suffice. This strategy makes sense when time and choices are limited. Someone with a flat tire who is late to work may not want to take the time to comparison shop for tires. She will probably buy a tire as quickly as possible so that she can proceed on her way. Hunts and Marotz–Baden describe satisficing in the following way:

> *For example, if a husband is searching for a car and the minimum assessment standards include that it started when the key was turned and that it cost less than $10,000, then the first car that met those minimum standards would be chosen. In goods and services where it is difficult to determine true quality until the good or service is consumed, consumers often satisfice. Childcare is an example. The first childcare*

*center that is a reasonable distance from work and home, is within the family budget, and looks inviting might be the one chosen, simply because it met minimum assessment tool standards.*

*(2003, p. 5)*

Applying economic theory to personal consumption is complicated because "values other than efficiency are important for many people, including satisfaction derived from the process rather than the end product, and creation of unique products not available from the market" (Hanna, 1989, 1997). Thus, shopping in and of itself is an enjoyable activity for many individuals, and this should be considered in discussions of rational economic behavior. The fastest choice may not be the best choice if shopping itself creates satisfaction. Furthermore, according to Hanna, "in the business world, firms that do not adopt more efficient ways of doing things will not survive in the long run, but households can just muddle along using inefficient techniques" (1989, 1997).

*This statement makes one wonder how efficient households have to be to exist and function.*

Are they really "small factories" as Gary Becker said? How much of economic theory, with its emphasis on rationality and logic, can be applied to households and families? Questions such as these fuel management research.

## Risk Aversion

The possibility of experiencing harm, suffering, danger, or loss is known as **risk.** Although we tend to associate risk with physical danger, it can also involve such things as losing money, energy, time, or reputation. In the last section, car buyers Randall and Elaine experienced consumer risk, but risk can also take other forms including health and safety risk, educational risk, relationship risk, occupational risk, and financial risk. Foxall, Goldsmith, and Brown (1998) have identified several types of perceived risk that affect decision making:

- *Functional or performance risk:* The possibility that a choice may not turn out as desired or have the expected benefits.

- *Financial risk:* The possibility that substantial amounts of money may be lost.

- *Physical risk:* The possibility that harm may come from a choice.

- *Psychological risk:* The possibility that a choice may damage a person's image of self or self-esteem.

- *Social risk:* The possibility that a choice may not be approved by others or may cause social embarrassment or rejection.

- *Time risk:* The possibility that the ability to satisfy wants will decline over time. In economics, it is assumed that a consumer would nearly always prefer to receive a good or service now rather than later.

To summarize, not all risks are bad, and risk carries with it many characteristics.

A person may be risk-averse, risk-loving, or risk-neutral. Changing jobs or spouses involves risk. Traveling or moving involves risk. Indeed, *people like a certain amount of risk; otherwise, games, gambling, quiz shows, and competitions would not exist.* Risk provides a little excitement and a release from tedium. One person may dream of winning the lottery and quitting his boring job. Another may take up skydiving to spice up her life. As these examples suggest, risk is not absolute. The perception of risk varies from person to person. One individual may think riding down the Grand Canyon on the back of a mule is an exciting adventure, whereas another may view it as foolhardy.

Trying to avoid the dire outcomes associated with risk is a rational course of behavior. In economic theory, the avoidance of risk is called **risk aversion**. Risk-averse individuals and families seek to minimize problems and maximize satisfaction by avoiding risk. For example, a risk-averse individual who dislikes heights and enclosed spaces would avoid riding elevators to the top of tall buildings. Just as different people perceive risk differently, the amount of risk aversion varies from person to person, family to family, and situation to situation.

Although some people feel comfortable betting on horse races or playing slot machines, others would never dream of spending money on gambling. The amount of risk a person is likely to take also varies by the stage in the life cycle. A person who is 18 years old is likely to take more risks than someone who is 84. People's resources also affect the amount of risk they are likely to assume. *What constitutes a risk depends on the individual*. The greater the resources, the more confident an individual will feel about taking a risk. If the decision fails, the individual will not feel the loss as keenly as someone with fewer remaining resources.

Yet even people with substantial resources may be wary of risk or feel uncertain in new situations. The decision maker estimates how much risk the situation involves and tries to turn an uncertain outcome to his or her advantage. Understanding the principles of perceived risk and being sensitive to the presence of risk can help the decision maker use risk-reduction strategies (e.g., gathering more information or following safe procedures) more effectively (Foxall et al., 1998). Chapter 5 discusses the relationship of risk and uncertainty to decision making in more detail.

A tenet of economics is that humans try to get maximum benefit for the least amount of effort, including the use of resources that will give them an acceptable level of the benefit desired (Hunts & Marotz-Baden, 2003). Risk aversion is part of the equation. It provides insight into the study of management. The fundamental principle of the maximization of satisfaction through the avoidance of risk provides plausible explanations for many types of decisions.

## SUMMARY

The study of management as taught and practiced today has its roots in the 19th century. As it has adjusted to technological, social, scientific, and economic changes in the 20th and 21st centuries, the field has necessarily become far more complex than it was originally. One particularly significant change in the 20th century was the transformation of the home from being primarily a producer to primarily a consumer of goods and services. Not only has the amount of household production declined, but the types of products it does produce and consume have also changed significantly. Who stays at home has changed as well. In the first half of the 20th century most adult women stayed at home, but today less than 13 percent of U.S. households include a stay-at-home spouse (meaning not working for pay or income from a source outside the home).

The integrative nature of management relies heavily on systems theory and with it the concept of boundary management introduced in this chapter. In general systems theory, each part contributes to the behavior of the whole, but the whole is greater than the sum of its parts. Feedback can be positive or negative; it is modeled as a loop (Figure 2.3). Family systems theory emphasizes the ways families organize themselves to carry out daily tasks and face challenges. Because the parts of a system are interrelated, systems are especially vulnerable to Murphy's Law (if something can go wrong, it will go wrong), and the tiniest flaw can cause damage. But, for the most part, systems try to balance themselves.

Polls show that Americans tend to be more satisfied with their personal affairs than with overall conditions in the United States, which is part of the greater environment. Families and environments are interdependent within the global ecosystem. Environments, near and far, provide the setting for human interactions, although individuals and families vary in the degree to which they are open or closed to the environment.

Economic theories play a role in management. According to optimization theory, the individual increases her or his chance for satisfaction and minimizes problems in a rational way by searching for information. Satisficing refers to situations where individuals choose the first good option that presents itself. Risk aversion holds that the goal is to maximize satisfaction by avoiding risks, although some people are risk lovers or neutral about risk.

Underlying family systems theory, social exchange theory, and economic theory is the belief that behavior is not random and occurs for some reason or reasons. In resource management, most behavior is rational, although individual preferences and situations play a great part in behavior.

Theories provide useful ways to organize information, allowing for predicting future behavior. They do not explain everything but provide valuable starting points and frameworks. The next chapter goes on to explore how values affect decision making and how goals drive managerial behavior.

## KEY TERMS

| | | |
|---|---|---|
| boundaries | homeostasis | positive feedback |
| boundary ambiguity | human ecology | risk |
| boundary management | hypotheses | risk aversion |
| controlling | inputs | satisficing |
| data analytics | interface | sequencing |
| demands | macroenvironment | social exchange theory |
| domi (plural domus) | microenvironment | subsystem |
| ecology | morphogenic systems | system |
| entropy | morphostatic systems | systems theory |
| environment | Murphy's law | telemedicine theory |
| equifinality | negative feedback | throughputs |
| equilibrium | optimization | transformation |
| family ecosystem | outputs | work simplification |

## REVIEW QUESTIONS

1. The *Human Ecology Review*, a journal of the Australian National University Press published a special issue addressing the Great Indoors – A Transdisciplinary Conversation. You have just read the current chapter which documents changes in the United States. Given the information in the chapter, compare and contrast typical homes and household tasks in 1900, in 1950, and today.

2. "There is nothing so practical as a good theory," says Kurt Lewin. Explain how theory is useful. Also, discuss the deep and rich theoretical heritage of family resource management. Name two of the most used theories.

3. According to the chapter content, what is the difference between positive and negative feedback?

4. How is a family a system? How do families cope with change? Give an example.

5. Economist Gary Becker says a household can be regarded as a "small factory." What does he mean by that? What is produced in households?

## REFERENCES

Berger, P. S. (1984). Home management research: State of the art 1909–1984. *Family and Consumer Sciences Research Journal, 12*(3), 252–264.

Blooston, G. (2008, August). Because you know money can buy some happiness. Retrieved from www.AARPMagazine.org. p. 49.

Bubolz, M., & Sontag, S. (1988). Integration in home economics and human ecology. *Journal of Consumer Studies and Home Economics, 12*, 1–14.

Connolly, M., & Wasserman, L. (2002). *Updating classic American bungalows.* Newtown, CT: Taunton Press.

Cowan, R. (1983). *More work for mother.* New York: Basic Books.

Crossen, C. (2002, December 11). Buying home spigots, water was never taken for granted. *The Wall Street Journal.*

Deacon, R. E., & Firebaugh, F. M. (1988). *Family resource management: Principles and applications* (2nd ed.). Boston, MA: Allyn & Bacon.

Drucker, P. (1999). *Management challenges for the 21st century.* New York: Harper Business.

Durband, D., & Ryan Law (2019). *Financial counseling.* Switzerland Springer.

Edwards, O. (2002, October 7). Mores. *Forbes.*

Elliott & Niesta (2009), p. 56 in Chapter 2 in Moskowiz, F. and H. Grant. *The Psychology of Goals.* New York: Guilford.

Flanagan, C. (2003, September). Housewife confidential. *Atlantic Monthly*, 141–142.

Fleming, W. (2003). Family systems theory. In J. J. Ponzetti, Jr. (Ed.), *International encyclopedia of marriage and family* (2nd ed., Vol. 2). New York: Macmillan.

Fletcher, J. (2002, August 1). Out with the new, in with the old. *The Wall Street Journal*, p. W9.

Foxall, G., Goldsmith, R., & Brown, S. (1998). *Consumer psychology for marketing.* London: Routledge.

Frederick, C. (1918). *The new housekeeping.* New York: Doubleday.

Gilbreth, L. (1927). *The homemaker and her job.* New York: Appleton.

Goldsmith, E. (1993). Home economics: The discovered discipline. *Journal of Home Economics, 85*(4), 45–48.

Gross, I. H., Crandall, E. W., & Knoll, M. M. (1980). *Management for modern families* (4th ed.). Englewood Cliffs, NJ: Prentice-Hall.

Gwartney, J., Stroup, R., Sobel, R., & Macpherson, D. (2018). *Economics: Private & public choice* (16th ed.). New York: Cengage Learning.

Haase, R. (1992). *Classic cracker: Florida's wood frame vernacular architecture.* Sarasota, FL: Pineapple Press.

Hallinan, J. (2002, August 12). Help for hopeless garages. *The Wall Street Journal*, p. B1.

Hanna, S. (1989, 1997). Optimization for family resource management. *Proceedings, Southeastern Regional Family Economics/Home Management Association.*

Hunts, H., & Marotz-Baden, R. (2003). Family systems theory, a new look at an old friend. *Consumer Interests Annual, 49*, 1–13.

Kondo, M. (2011). *The life changing magic of tidying up.* Berkeley, CA: The Ten Speed Press.

Lamanna, M., Riedmann, A., & Stewart, S. (2018). *Marriages, families, and relationships* (13th ed.). New York: Cengage.

McAlester, V. S. (2015). *A field guide to American homes.* New York: Knopf.

McGee, S. (2000). *Make life beautiful.* New York: Harper Horizon.

McGinn, D. (2007). *House lust: America's obsession with our homes.* New York: Currency.

McGoldrick, M. (1995). *You can go home again.* New York: Norton.

Moskowitz, G., & Grant, H. (2009). *The psychology of goals.* New York: Guilford.

Paolucci, B., Hall, O., & Axinn, N. (1977). *Family decision making: An ecosystem approach.* New York: Wiley.

Parloa, M. (1879). *First principles of household management and cookery*. Boston, MA: Houghton, Osgood.

Quintana, M., & Grossman, R. (2007, May). *Merillat's third phase of research*. Adrian, MI. Retrieved from www.merillat.com.

Seligman, M. (2018). *The hope circuit: A psychologist's journey from helplessness to optimism*. New York: Hachette Book Group.

Sessa, D. (2000, November 13). Have dinner. *The Wall Street Journal*, p. R20.

Sharpe, D. L., & Winter, M. (1991). Toward working hypotheses of effective management: Conditions, thought processes and behaviors. *Lifestyles: Family and Economic Issues, 12*(4), 303– 323.

Smithsonian. (2000). *National museum of American history, on time exhibit*. Washington, DC.

Taylor, F. W. (1911). *Principles of scientific management*. New York: Harper & Row.

Weiss, M. (2003, September). To be about to be. *American Demographics*, pp. 29–36.

Weston, L. P. (2003, June 14). What's a homemaker worth?

Willis, G., & Young, L. (2003, April). Retire happy. *Smart Money*, p. 84.

Wooldridge, A. (2000, April 28–29). Where business profs walk tall. *The Wall Street Journal Europe*.

Woolgar, C. (1993). *Household accounts from medieval England*. Oxford: Oxford University Press.

## FURTHER READING*

Andrews, B. R. (1935). *Economics of the household*. New York: Macmillan.

Becker, G. S. (1981). *A treatise on the family*. Cambridge, MA: Harvard University Press.

Beecher, C. (1841). *Treatise on domestic economy*. Boston, MA: Marsh, Capen, Lyon, & Webb.

Bonde, R. L. (1944). *Management in daily living*. New York: Macmillan.

Bratton, E. C. (1971). *Home management is*. Boston, MA: Ginn.

Cushman, E. M. (1945). *Management in homes*. New York: Macmillan.

Fitzsimmons, C., & Williams, F. (1973). *The family economy, nature and management of resources*. Ann Arbor, MI: Edwards Brothers.

Gilbreth, L., Thomas, O. M., & Clymer, E. (1955). *Management in the home*. New York: Dodd, Mead.

Goodyear, M. R., & Klohr, M. C. (1965). *Managing for effective living* (2nd ed.). New York: Wiley.

Kyrk, H. (1933). *Economic problems of the family*. New York: Harper & Row.

Kyrk, H. (1953). *The family in the American economy*. Chicago: University of Chicago Press.

Lamanna, M., & Riedmann, A. (2009). *Marriages and families* (10th ed.). Belmont, CA: Thomson Wadsworth.

Liston, M. (1993). *History of family economics research: 1862–1962*. Ames, IA: University Publications, Iowa State University.

Magrabi, F. M., Chung, Y. S., Cha, S. S., & Yang, S. (1991). *The economics of household consumption*. New York: Praeger.

May, E. E., Waggoner, N. R., & Boethke, E. M. (1974). *Independent living for the handicapped and the elderly*. Boston, MA: Houghton Mifflin.

Oppenheim, I. (1976). *Management of the modern home* (2nd ed.). New York: Macmillan.

Reid, M. G. (1934). *Economics of household production*. New York: Wiley.

Rice, A. S., & Tucker, S. M. (1986). *Family life management* (6th ed.). New York: Macmillan.

Richards, E. H. (1900). *The cost of living as modified by sanitary science*. New York: Wiley.

Stage, S., & Vincent, V. (1997). *Rethinking home economics*. Ithaca, NY: Cornell University.

Starr, M. C. (1968). *Management for better living*. Lexington, MA: Heath.

Steidl, R. E., & Bratton, E. C. (1968). *Work in the home*. New York: Wiley.

Swanson, B. B. (1981). *Introduction to home management*. New York: Macmillan.

Talbot, M., & Breckinridge, S. (1919). *The modern household*. Boston, MA: Whitcomb & Barrows.

Walker, K. E., & Woods, M. E. (1976). *Time use: A measure of household production of family goods and services*. Washington, DC: American Home Economics Association.

## NOTES

\* When a book has appeared in several editions, the newest is cited. This list of seminal works (textbooks, popular books, and reference books) is intended to supplement those already cited in the reference list; it is not meant to be comprehensive. In addition, management articles can be found in the *International Journal of Home Economics*, *Human Ecology Review*, *International Journal of Consumer Studies*, *Journal of Family and Consumer Sciences* (formerly the *Journal of Home Economics*), *Family and Consumer Sciences Research Journal* (formerly the *Home Economics Research Journal*), *Journal of Marriage and Family*, *Journal of Consumer Affairs*, *Journal of Family and Economic Issues*, *Journal of Family Issues*, *Journal of Consumer Education*, *Kappa Omicron Nu Forum*, and in the journals of allied fields. Other sources of management theory, research, and applications include theses and dissertations, Agricultural Experiment Station Bulletins, the *Family Economics Review* and other government publications, and conference proceedings.

Chapter **3**

# Values, Attitudes, Goals, and Motivation

## MAIN TOPICS

Values and Attitudes

Types of Values

Values, Lifestyles, and Consumption

Societal and Cultural Values

Families, Values, Standards, and Households Value Chains

Attitudes

Goals and Motivation

Goals versus Habits

Goal Attributes

Categories of Goals

Goals and Performance, Creativity, and Learning

Setting Goals

Disengaging from Goals

College Students' Values, Goals, and Life Outcomes

Motivation

DOI: 10.4324/9781003166740-3

… The number of people with Masters and Ph.D. degrees doubled since 2000 in the United States
… Motivation (intrinsic and extrinsic) drives much of behavior including consumer behavior.

Do you agree with Erika Jenkins that so much of success is self-defined? What is success? Is it about fame, family, accumulating wealth, climbing up the ladder at work, friends, and happiness? How would you describe a perfect life? Don't limit yourself, paint in broad, bold strokes. Some say the best way to predict the future is to create it.

What is a compelling vision? A **vision** is a statement that serves as an inspirational guide for the future. It sets a course of action. For example, the President of the United States on his first day in office usually outlines a vision discussed with the Chief of Staff and top aides (as explained by Bradley Blakeman, of the George W. Bush administration, on January 7, 2021, in a White House History Association webinar on Presidential Transitions). The vision can be for the first hundred days in office or the next four years. In your case, once you have the description of the vision, what should you do next? Decide what you really care about and move forward. Think about the amount of time to commit to the vision, maybe a semester, maybe a year. Ask yourself:

## CASE STUDY

### Success Is Not Easily Achieved

Erika Jenkins, age 22, kept losing. She would apply again and again for awards that she was nominated for, but she couldn't seem to win. At the beginning of her junior year, she resolved never to apply again and to focus on her classes, graduating, and getting a job. Her advisor and the Director of Student Achievement, Walt McCormick, at the university wouldn't let up because everything in her record and past experiences indicated she could win. Walt called Erika in September and said, "you have to apply for this new award." She said no and he called her again.

Walt said, "Applying is a process, you have to apply over and over again, that is how it works." And, he added he would coach her and read her essay. He also tried to encourage her through the ups and downs by quoting the famous opening lines to Charles Dickens' *A Tale of Two Cities*:

It was the best of times, It was the worst of times, It was the age of wisdom,
It was the age of foolishness, It was the epoch of belief,
It was the epoch of incredulity, It was the season of light,
It was the season of darkness, It was the spring of hope,
It was the winter of despair, We had everything before us, We had nothing before us…

Walt said, "Dickens wrote compelling stories, he had tremendous powers of persuasion. He knew what people value, what they care about, and how to tap into emotions. You have to try again." Erika did and she won a year abroad teaching children in a wonderful country. She sparkled as she told her success story at a student awards banquet. Her message was to never give up and to listen to people who believe in you.

- What resources are needed to ensure success?

- What steps should I take?

- What are measurable results or outcomes?

- What will a successful plan look like?

David Lloyd George says, "Don't be afraid to take a big step if one is indicated; you can't cross a chasm in two small jumps." Let's begin with an examination of your values, attitudes, and goals that underlie choices such as whom to live with, where to live, what to consume, and which career path to follow.

The opening quote by Winston Churchill said that one's general attitude or approach to life, being a pessimist or optimist, affects how we approach opportunities or obstacles (Goldsmith, 2015). A number of studies have found that people who report being happy when they are 20 years old report being equally happy when they are 70. Conversely, 20-year-olds who report being unhappy at 20 will still be unhappy at age 70. Fulfilling goals brings happiness through a sense of accomplishment. Happiness falls into three categories:

> *There's a pleasant life with lots of richly positive emotions in the past, present, and future. The second type of happy life is one in which you are totally absorbed and immersed in what you do. It is feeling positive about knowing you are using your highest strengths and virtues in love, work, and play. The third type of meaningful, happy life is using your highest strengths in service to others, for something larger.*
>
> *(Condor, 2002, p. 4D)*

This chapter explores these and related concepts. Why does happiness matter? How often have you heard someone say, "I just want you to be happy" or express that sentiment regarding someone else? For example, on the occasion of the second marriage of Nikki, her closest friend Lisa said to acquaintances, "I just want her to be happy this time."

As noted in Chapter 1, management is the process of using resources to achieve goals. "Goals are of central importance to the study of motivation. Goals represent the hub of self-regulation" (Elliot & Niesta, 2009, p. 56). The goals people seek and the way they perceive and use resources are affected by their values and attitudes. Setting goals is a necessary first step because, after all, you can't get what you want until you have a clear idea of what it is that you want. This chapter focuses on step 1 (identifying problem, need, want, or goal) and step 2 (clarifying values) in the management process model (see Figure 3.1).

The chapter begins with a discussion of values and attitudes and then proceeds to goals. The values and goals of college students in particular are examined. As the successful achievement of goals is closely linked to

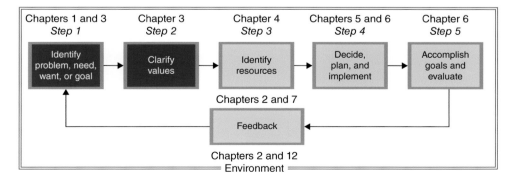

Figure 3.1 The management process model.

Charles Lindbergh with his plane, the Spirit of St. Louis, was ready to start on his attempt to cross the Atlantic.

Source: Library of Congress.

motivation, it plays an important part in this chapter. Consider the motivation and achievement of Charles Lindbergh, the first aviator to fly nonstop across the Atlantic Ocean from the United States to Europe. Discussing his flight in an article in the *New York Times* on May 13, 1927, he said:

> *We (that's my ship and I) took off rather suddenly. We had a report somewhere around four o'clock in the afternoon before the weather would be fine, so we thought we would try it.*

In the same article, F. Scott Fitzgerald, the renowned novelist, described the flight of the *Spirit of Saint Louis* more eloquently:

> *In the spring of '27 something bright and alien flashed across the sky.*
> *A young Minnesotan [Lindbergh] who seemed to have had nothing to do with his generation did a heroic thing, and for a moment people set down their glasses in country clubs and speakeasies and thought of their old best dreams.*

## CRITICAL THINKING

Has the spirit of invention and adventure epitomized by Lindbergh's solo flight across the Atlantic evaporated? Can you think of current-day inventors, entrepreneurs, and adventurers? What sort of activities do they do? What goals have they set?

There is no denying that the 20th century brought an incredible amount of innovation and progress to the world and that the 21st century continues this tradition with incredible upgrades in batteries, energy, mobile phones, transportation such as autonomous cars, and information collection. Business keeps changing rapidly to keep up with the demand for better, faster, and more efficient devices. The industrial revolution of the 19th century was about saving muscle power, having machines do what people used to do. The current revolution, called either the digital or the information revolution, is more about organizing data and enhancing technology for rapid information retrieval and exchange. Japan is leading in the invention of versatile robots.

With any revolution or innovation, many unwanted or misguided steps are taken along the way, think of product recalls encouraging the reader to think about the issues surrounding goals and personal and societal values, to set priorities, to not be discouraged, to seize opportunities, and to progress are the behavioral goals of this chapter.

## Values and Attitudes

**Values** are principles that guide behavior. For example, a person who values honesty will try to act in honest ways. Values are deep-seated psychological constructs that direct individual preferences and strategies for goal achievement. They form the foundation for behavior, including goal-seeking behavior. An example of a value is wisdom, which is the accumulated philosophic or scientific learning and also the ability to discern inner qualities and relationships. A person with wisdom listens and has insight, knowledge, and good sense.

> ### CRITICAL THINKING
>
> Socrates said, "Wisdom begins in wonder." Another saying by Naguib Mahfouz is, "You can tell whether a man is clever by his answers. You can tell whether a man is wise by his questions." Do you ask questions in your classes? Or, can you recall what you would consider to be a good question asked by another?

If wisdom is a value you hold, then how does one go about gaining wisdom beyond the usual context of college classes and assignments? Here are a few steps to follow:

1. Wisdom gathering isn't confined to books but can be *experienced* through travel and listening to speakers, by shadowing a professional in his or her daily work life, or in a number of other ways.

2. Seek the *connections*, the patterns, and connect the dots between different realms of life. Figure out how one subject intersects another.

3. Wisdom implies *deep thinking*, going beyond the surface. Why is someone saying what he or she is saying? What is the background to a comment or action? Often there is a lesson to be learned not only by what you experience but by observing what others experience.

Wisdom is part of a person's internally integrated value system called **value orientation**, which is expressed in part in the way he or she makes judgments. A person's judgments are based on the value meanings derived from his or her feelings (the **affective domain**) and thinking (the **cognitive domain**) about events, situations, groups of people, and things. Both the affective and the cognitive domains are based on previous experience. Thus, valuing is an ongoing, never-ending process that forms an integral part of an individual's personality and behavioral systems. Different generations may hold slightly different values.

**Mindfulness** is a way of thinking or philosophical stance using new techniques in time and stress management. It stems from concerns of too busy lives and too much information.

**Behavior** is what people actually do. The word "behavior" implies action. Often a gap exists between values (the ideal) and behavior (the actual). For example, a man may say that he is on a strict weight-reducing diet yet stuff his grocery cart with candy bars. Another person may say that she thinks a speed limit of 55 mph is a good idea, yet habitually drive much faster. Knowing the gap between values and behavior, researchers are careful to ask survey questions not only about values and attitudes but also about actual behavior.

> ## CRITICAL THINKING
>
> Yoga and the Art of Mindfulness In recent years, there has been an upswing in yoga and other exercise methods that reduce stress. Along with more attention to being mindful, based on the premise that being in the present and taking a step back from pressure are helpful to the individual. Why do you think more people are practicing yoga (or a related exercise or movement program) and trying to be more mindful?

Consider shopping online while at work and the possible conflict of values with employers. Research shows that online shopping surges in the middle of the workday (10 A.M. to 2 P.M. which includes the lunch hour) and falls off in the evening and on weekends. Rick Dalmazzi, president of Certicom, an encryption company based in Hayward, California, doesn't get upset about his employees shopping online with company computers "within reason" because they all work more than 40 hours a week: "We have a philosophy around here that people should be comfortable at work and if they're comfortable at work, they'll work harder." Mr. Dalmazzi says, "I'm totally fine with these areas where business life and personal life mix" (de Lisser, 2002, p. A8). Online shopping behavior keeps changing along with the attitude of employers about how employees spend their time.

Environment plays a role in behavior. For example, maybe it is more difficult to maintain an average weight today because of the plenitude and easy availability of food. Twenty years ago, the typical restaurant plate was 10 inches in diameter; now it is 12 inches. The fastest-growing food chains market themselves as upscale, organic, or nutritious as well as convenient. **Attitudes** are outlooks or opinions that may express values, serve as a means of evaluation, or demonstrate feeling regarding some idea, person, object, event, situation, or relationship. They are states of mind or feelings, likes and dislikes about some matter, such as liking or disliking Subway, Chipolte, or Starbucks. Additional examples of objects of attitudes are:

- People
- Images
- Smells or scents
- Food or cuisine
- Environments
- Pictures or art
- Colors

- Countries or regions

- Music

- Sounds

- Animals

- Words

- Colleges or universities

- Sports teams

Memory plays a significant part in determining attitudes. Everyone has her or his own unique set of attitudes, but the number of attitudes varies from person to person. One person may have attitudes on everything and everybody, whereas another may have few attitudes. Talk shows would be dull if hosts or interviewers, guests, and the audience had no attitudes or opinions. Attitudes can range from the significant to the petty.

Sometimes values and attitudes are confused. They do share the characteristic that both are abstract. In addition, both can be either explicit, meaning that they are held at the conscious level and are readily verbalized, or implicit, meaning that they are held subconsciously and can only be identified by behavior. But values and attitudes also differ in several respects. Whereas values are fairly constant (as deep-seated psychological constructs), attitudes are more transitory and subject to change. Values represent broad tendencies and highly prized beliefs (e.g., helpfulness, courage, and ambition), whereas attitudes are narrower predispositions (e.g., having a particular attitude about a clothing style, rap music, or modern art). Advertising plays on both values and attitudes by appealing to people's feelings about cleanliness, youthfulness, power, and prestige.

## CRITICAL THINKING

### No Children Allowed

Jamie received a wedding invitation that said no children under eight were allowed at the wedding or reception. Along a similar vein, a restaurant said no children under ten were allowed or that a certain area of the restaurant would be child-free. Some first-class sections of airplanes are also not allowing young children. Catering to child-free environments may be good for business but is it good for parents and children or society in general? What do you think about the wedding invitation, the restaurant, and the airplane company policies?

Goals are end results, the purpose toward which much behavior is directed. Goals are linked to deadlines, accomplishments, completion, or achievement. They are most likely to be attained if they are specific and stated in measurable terms. For example, rather than merely hoping to finish a race, an experienced runner is likely to set a goal of cutting X number of seconds off his or her best recorded time.

Goals give shape, meaning, and direction to people's lives. A life without goals would be aimless. Samuel Johnson (1709–1784), a noted author and critic who lived in England, said, "You become successful the moment you start moving toward a worthwhile goal." What goals are you moving toward?

A survey of 1,000 people conducted by Market Facts TeleNation found the top priorities to be

1. Physical and spiritual well-being

2. Financial stability

3. Relationships

4. Personal or professional development

5. Work and career happiness

6. Service to others

Every day people make complex decisions that reflect their attitudes, values, and goals. If students value good grades, they decide to spend time studying. Attitudes often occupy a middle ground between values and goals. Students who hate studying (an attitude) are going to have difficulty reconciling their value of wisdom and their goal of attaining good grades.

## Types of Values

Because the world is filled with an almost infinite array of different stimuli, one of the most basic human functions is to classify concepts, objects, and events into clusters or groups. In so doing, people simplify their world and lay the groundwork for interpretation and action. For example, values can be classified in four different ways:

1. Absolute and relative

2. Intrinsic and extrinsic

3. Traditional, personal, and professional

4. Instrumental and terminal

Each of these will be discussed in the following sections.

### Absolute and Relative Values

**Absolute values** are extreme and definitive; such values can be described in black and white terms, as in the phrase "honesty is the best policy." People who hold honesty as an absolute value would say that honesty is right in all situations. **Relative values** are interpreted based on the context. They can be visualized as shades of gray that depend on the situation for definition. A person who holds honesty as a relative value will usually be honest, but in certain situations will put friendship, politeness, or consideration first. For example, if a friend gets a terrible haircut and asks how it looks, Person X, who has absolute values, will respond that the haircut is awful. Person Y, who has relative values, will simply say that her friend's hair might be a little short. In this situation, Person Y is placing the values of friendship and sensitivity over the value of total honesty.

People with more relative values tend to seek additional information about an event or situation. They want more details or knowledge before expressing an opinion or taking action.

### Intrinsic and Extrinsic Values

Values can also be classified as **intrinsic values**, which are ends in themselves (internally driven), or **extrinsic values**, which derive their worth or meaning from someone or something else. A couple finding their own way around a foreign city might find that experience intrinsically rewarding; they are demonstrating the values of independence and self-reliance. On the other hand, winning an Academy Award has extrinsic value because in this case, a group of people has rewarded an individual for professional excellence.

The concepts of intrinsic and extrinsic can be applied to leadership.

> *Internal leadership skills reflect intrinsic values such as honesty, integrity, respecting others, professional ethics, and developing vision. External leadership is demonstrated with actions such as taking risks, sharing a vision, fostering collaboration, giving power away, being a role model, communicating well, and celebrating success.*

> *(Buck, 2003, pp. 8, 9)*

## Traditional, Personal, and Professional Values

Traditional values are those commonly held by the predominant society in which one lives. A traditional value or societal standard widely held in the United States and Canada is that children should begin going to school around the age of five or six. Another value of these two nations is that education is important and a key to future success.

Weddings are value-laden traditional events. The wedding veil has evolved over the centuries. It symbolizes youth, innocence, modesty, and mystery. In the United States, the color is white. In Japan, many brides still wear the traditional tsuno-kakushi—a white hood that symbolizes hiding the horns of jealousy. A Finnish bride may wear a gold crown, which she places on the head of a bridesmaid during the reception dance to signal that the bridesmaid may be the next to marry. The American tradition is for brides to toss the bouquet to a group of unmarried women. The tradition of wearing something old stands for continuity and the wearing of something new for the future. A borrowed object refers to happiness, and blue stands for fidelity, purity, good fortune, and love. In the past, in the United States, another tradition was for the bride to wear a penny in her shoe (or in England a sixpence) symbolizing good fortune or luck. The significance of the train on the wedding dress originated in the Middle Ages when train length indicated rank in court: The longer the train, the higher the prestige. If you have seen images of Princess Diana's wedding gown, you'll remember the extreme length of the train.

Values are focal points for discussion and policy making. For example, government campaigns encourage families to eat together more often. These campaigns exist in part because of evidence showing that when families eat together, there is less likelihood of criminal or juvenile problems, as well as there are higher degrees of interaction, higher grades, and better nutrition. The traditional family meal is under threat as more people eat alone.

According to a report compiled by FFP Complete, a market research department of Taylor Nelson Sofres, nearly one in two meals consumed in Britain are eaten by solitary diners and convenience food is becoming more popular. This British report also indicated that many people appear to be eating separately at different times even though they live together. In the United States, Sara and Jack, a married couple in their early 50s with grown-up children, told the author of this book that they eat their dinners on trays in front of the television every night. He is exhausted from his day at work as a golf pro dealing with the public, and she from her job in real estate, likewise dealing with the public. This is the second marriage for both, and Sara says they fell into this pattern quickly and both are happy with it. Their situation raises the interesting question: Should the government be involved in trying to change people's eating patterns at home or at school?

Each person must separate out societal values or messages from what she or he truly believes. When someone finds himself or herself thinking "I should be a better friend" or "I should be thinner" or "I should have a house that reflects my stature in the community," he or she should stop and ask, "Says who?" These thoughts often reflect extrinsic messages that you have internalized, but are they really you? Personal values are those that individuals hold for themselves, such as courage (standing up for one's beliefs), forgiveness (the ability to pardon others), and the right to pursue happiness. Perhaps you value solitude, health, and frugality more than others in your community do. People pride themselves on their personal values.

---

**CRITICAL THINKING**

**Your Values**

Circle the word in these pairs that you value more: Independence or teamwork? Thriftiness or generosity? Responsibility or freedom? These words are not exact opposites. They are called forced choices. In a statement say why you chose the words that you did. If you selected independence what does that say about you and the types of activities that you enjoy most?

---

Personal values affect consumption patterns. The under-30 group is spending less on clothes, cars, and entertainment, and more on food, home furnishings, and homes including renting for longer periods of time, according to the Bureau of Labor Statistics:

Examples of personal values are:

- Giving the gift of time
- Putting someone else's feelings first
- Forgiving a wrong
- Expressing gratitude
- Mentoring another student or a fellow employee
- Serving the community

Professional values are related to jobs and careers; examples include being ambitious, capable, or logical. The same value can fall into all three categories. For example, a society, an individual, and a profession may all hold politeness as a value. Conversely, societal, personal, and professional values may be in conflict.

---

**Suggested Activity**

List the parts of your life that are most important to you, ways you look after yourself, and personal characteristics you value in yourself and in others. Do your relationships nurture these types of values? Does your current lifestyle match your values? Is there a disconnect? Where? Perhaps cleanliness and orderliness are important to you, but your apartment, house, or dorm room is a mess—is that a temporary or permanent state?

Employees who place a high value on honesty and integrity may become whistle-blowers, exposing the wrongdoing in a company or government agency. Their values are in conflict with the values of their employer or at least with those of particular other employees.

One of the goals of a job interview is to determine whether there is an appropriate fit between the prospective employee's values and those of the organization. To help determine this, many organizations give psychological tests to applicants including forced choice questions as in the preceding critical thinking exercise.

## Instrumental and Terminal Values

Milton Rokeach, one of the most respected authorities on values, divided values into two types: terminal values and instrumental values (see Table 3.1). Terminal values are preferences for end states of existence, such as equality, freedom, or comfortable life. Instrumental values are preferences for general modes of conduct, such as being helpful, loving, or intellectual. An individual taking the Rokeach Value Survey is asked to rank the values in each list from 1 (most important) to 18 (least important). Of particular significance are the top three values—these tend to be consistent over time.

Rokeach defined values as global beliefs that guide actions and judgments across a variety of situations. He concluded that values are individual attributes that affect attitudes, motivation, needs, and perceptions (Rokeach, 1973).

## Values, Lifestyles, and Consumption

Henry David Thoreau said, "My life is like a stroll upon the beach, as near the ocean's edge as I can go." Values, lifestyles, and goals are shaped by experiences and are influenced by many sources, including parents, siblings, friends, teachers, religions, organizations, cultures, and the media.

Shopping behaviors provide examples of values in action. A person who compares shops has different values (and perhaps resources) than a person who buys the first thing she or he sees. Remember in the previous chapter on the economic theory we talked about optimization (trying to get the most for your money by comparison shopping) versus satisficing (satisfying a need by buying the first thing that fits). Choosing what to buy and where to shop are examples of consumption decisions based on values and lifestyle. Consider the differences between the consumption styles of college students Chelsea, Anthea, and work intern Zoey. Chelsea usually shops at The Gap, but if she does not have much money to spend, she goes to Old Navy or another less expensive store. She goes shopping for clothes every week. Anthea prefers department stores and tries to find what she needs as quickly as possible so that she can leave. She sees shopping as a chore, so she goes only a few times a year and has turned to shopping over the Inter-net. Zoey goes a totally different route. In her new internship with the government, the work dress code required a structured jacket or blazer daily and hard closed-toed shoes. She went to Goodwill and bought six tailored jackets in dark colors for under $50 and was pleased with herself.

## Societal and Cultural Values

Although values are enduring and measurable, they are not static. An individual's and society's values can change through an evolutionary process. They may be influenced by all of the following:

- Family or societal upset
- Technological, economic, and cultural changes

Table 3.1  Terminal and Instrumental Values

| Terminal Values (End States of Existence) | Instrumental Values (Modes of Conduct) |
|---|---|
| A comfortable life (a prosperous life) | Ambitious (hardworking, aspiring) |
| An exciting life (a stimulating, active life) | Broadminded (open-minded) |
| A sense of accomplishment (lasting contribution) | Capable (competent, effective) |
| A world at peace (free of war and conflict) | Cheerful (lighthearted, joyful) |
| A world of beauty (nature and the arts) | Clean (neat, tidy) |
| Equality (brotherhood, equal opportunity) | Courageous (standing up for your beliefs) |
| Family security (taking care of loved ones) | Forgiving (willing to pardon others) |
| Freedom (independence, free choice) | Helpful (working for others' welfare) |
| Happiness (contentedness) | Honest (sincere, truthful) |
| Inner harmony (freedom from inner conflict) | Imaginative (daring, creative) |
| Mature love (sexual and spiritual intimacy) | Independent (self-reliant, self-sufficient) |
| National security (protection from attack) | Intellectual (intelligent, reflective) |
| Pleasure (an enjoyable, leisurely life) | Logical (consistent, rational) |
| Salvation (saved, eternal life) | Loving (affectionate, tender) |
| Self-respect (self-esteem) | Obedient (dutiful, respectful) |
| Social recognition (respect, admiration) | Polite (courteous, well-mannered) |
| True friendship (close companionship) | Responsible (dependable, reliable) |
| Wisdom (a mature understanding of life) | Self-controlled (restrained, self-disciplined) |

Source: M. Rokeach (1968, Winter). The role of values in public opinion research. *Public Opinion Quarterly, 32,* 554, by permission of Oxford University Press.

- Dramatic events such as war, famine, or disease

- Environmental threats

The Great Depression, which began in October 1929, and lasted through the 1930s, influenced an entire generation to be cautious spenders. Thrift and security remained especially important values to these people well after the Depression was over. The 2009 recession brought renewed attention to economic problems and behaviors.

In regard to environmental safety (a value), people are now more aware than ever before of the dangers of environmental threats, such as unclaimed floating barges laden with garbage, oil spills, and polluted air and water. Corresponding behaviors range from personal accountability (e.g., recycling or joining cleanup crews) to national accountability (e.g., the promotion of environmental legislation and more vigorous government enforcement of environmental regulations).

**Suggested Activity**

Review Table 3.1 and circle your top three terminal values and your top three instrumental values. Discuss in class why these are important to you.

Families Share Values.

We are all part of cultures and subcultures (Sternquist & Goldsmith, 2018). Values are the cornerstones of a society's culture. They stand for what is worthwhile, preferred, and consistent. **Cultural values** are generally held conceptualizations of what is right or wrong in a culture or what is preferred. Customs, manners, and gestures are indicators of cultural values. For example, bowing in deference to one's superiors or elders is customary in South Korea but would be unusual in the United States. Bowing is the outward behavior that reflects the underlying value of deference or respect. The deeper the bow, the more the respect shown. In the United States, respect for the elderly would more likely be displayed by use of formal names ("Mr. Smith," not "Joe") and by giving up seats on trains and buses as well as by offering other forms of aid.

Although as discussed in the previous chapter, snacking is going up internationally, most people in Western cultures, such as Canada, the United States, Australia, and most countries in Western Europe, customarily eat three meals a day, whereas eating five meals a day is customary in East and Southeast Asian cultures. Even the meaning of gestures (a behavior) varies by culture. For example, the hand sign for "okay" in the United States is considered an obscene gesture in some Latin American countries.

Understanding cultural differences can be helpful in a variety of contexts, including management and planning of workplaces, transportation systems, and homes. For instance, supervisors who keep a close watch on their workers may be viewed as caring in some cultures but overbearing and belittling in others. Cultures also vary in the types of mass transit they prefer, and the amount of crowding people will tolerate in subways and trains. Typical cultural values and standards of comfort, function, and beauty influence floor plans of homes and interior designs.

For example, consider the differences between values in the United States, in Europe, and in Japan. These areas of the world are called "the rich economies of the Triad," which have enjoyed rapid growth in the past and are mature economies with aging populations (Kono & Lynn, 2007). Historically, the Japanese tend to be more concerned with consensus and are group-oriented. Consequently, Japanese businesses offer their employees more security and longer-term employment than most American businesses. This generalization is shifting, and in Japan, there is a value system emerging which gives more importance to self-fulfillment and self-assertion (Kono & Lynn, 2007). As contacts between the countries increase through mass media, travel, and trade, the value gap is narrowing. This trend provokes criticism from some observers and is in evidence in other countries including the rapidly changing cultures of China, India, and Korea, and consider the following about the continent of Africa.

"African economies are some of the fastest growing in the world today. They are mostly underserved in retail, and the media term **Africa Rising** is sometimes used referring to the growing middle class, the rapid spread of technology, and rising incomes Economic reform, stable government better health, and extended availability of mobile phones and the internet will keep Africa rising" (Sternquist & Goldsmith, 2018, pp. 281 and 283).

One does not have to cross national borders to find cultural differences in values, attitudes, and behavior. They exist everywhere within countries. Regional food preferences are a good example. The food in northern Italy is quite different from that in southern Italy. In the United States, grits are a favorite food in the South but are rarely eaten elsewhere. People from different regions of the United States perceive and use time differently.

## Families, Values, Standards, and Households

All families have values and value orientations, and the way they maintain their homes is an expression of those values. As Chapter 1 explained, standards are the quantitative and/or qualitative criteria used to measure values and goals, and to reconcile resources with demands. Different family members may have different standards for time and household work. What is "on time" to one family member may not be "on time" to another. And a teenager's standard of a clean bedroom may not be the same as his parents'. Standards also vary greatly between households. Dennis, a 13-year-old, told his parents about the variations he had observed in the cleaning standards of the households of three of his friends:

> We don't like going to Daryl's house because it is sterile. It is so clean it is spooky, like nobody lives there and we are afraid to touch anything. They even clean the driveway. The only things in Daryl's room are a bed, a dresser, and a desk. Steve's house is a mess because they have that awful dog tearing up everything. Brent's house is about like ours, somewhere in the middle. So we usually end up at our house, sometimes at Brent's.

The physical and emotional qualities of home and family life have been a subject of debate across time and across cultures. National surveys about family values and patterns of behavior indicate that people in the United States think the family is falling apart everywhere but in their own homes. This paradox is called the "I'm OK, but you're not" syndrome.

A study compared attitudes about engagement rings over a 15-year period. It was found that the 200 new brides who said YES and 54 percent who said NO to the question, "Would you ever consider trading in your engagement ring for a bigger, better diamond?" had different marital outcomes when polled later. Of the 46 percent who said YES, 81 percent were divorced. Of the more sentimental type who said NO, 78

**Suggested Activity**

Make a list of your family's values and give an example of each. The example could be an action, a memory, an activity, or a saying that demonstrates the value.

*Couples may or may not have compatible values:*

*Daniel Caine, president of Split-Up.com, a financial-planning firm for divorcing couples, says that divorce is rooted in five areas: insecurity, money, communication, clash of values, and insufficient separation from family. He recommends asking a few questions: Are you comfortable with my religious observance? My family? My urge for wealth? "Opposites attract, but that doesn't mean they stay together," he warns.*

*(Zaslow, 2003, p. D1)*

percent were still married. The psychiatrist who monitored the study, Francisco Montalvo, said the results suggest that people who are "hardwired" to upgrade rings may also be driven to upgrade houses, cars, and even spouses (Zaslow, 2003).

## Value Formation and Socialization

Values are shared by most members of a society and are passed on to younger members by senior members. Families, especially parents, play a fundamental role in forming children's values. The ability to cope with and adjust to life problems and demands is based on the psychological foundations of early family experience. Parents perceive that within their society certain competencies and values are important for their child's growth and development. For example, parents influence their children's dress and grooming standards, manners and speech, and educational motivation. Thus, the culture's child-rearing patterns reflect the parents' and the greater society's values and the environmental context in which the parents live. As society changes, so do the values parents impart to their children. If the immediate society has high expectations so do the parents. This can be evidenced anywhere but is especially obvious in high-end school districts and neighborhoods.

The process by which children learn the rules and values of a society is called **socialization**. Although the family is the primary socializer of children, parents are not the only influence. Values are affected by a host of variables, conditions, and sources, such as the media, friends, and extended family. Furthermore, to imply that socialization is only a childhood experience would be misleading. Although socialization starts in infancy, it is a lifelong process influenced by many sources.

A subsystem of socialization is called "consumer socialization"; through this process, people acquire the skills, attitudes, and information necessary to function in the marketplace. Children initially learn much of their consumption behavior from accompanying their parents on shopping trips or watching them shop online. By adolescence, children are likely to shop with friends. In fact, going shopping with friends has become such a popular teen activity that some stores and malls in the United States limit teen shopping hours. This practice raises an interesting question of societal values and ethics: Should stores be able to restrict who shops in them? The pandemic put a new spin on this by limiting for health reasons how many patrons could be in a store at a single time.

## Traditionalism and Nontraditionalism

Dominant social and cultural trends are often counterbalanced by other trends. For example, the value of traditionalism (going back to basics) appears to recur in cycles. It is estimated that 29 percent of Americans can be called "heartlanders," or *traditionalists*. They hold traditional views, specifically believing in the value of small-town and country life (Ray, 1997). More recent studies by the Pew Research Center put this percentage lower but it varies so much by what is defined as traditional. It can be said that traditionalists are a smaller group within the U.S. population than *modernists* (47 percent), who place a high value on personal success, consumerism, materialism, and technological rationality. The other main group consists of the *cultural creatures* (24 percent), who put a strong emphasis on having new and unique experiences and are attuned to global issues and social causes. There are discussions of differences on all of this among Baby Boomers, Gen X, Millennials, and Gen Z. Most of the readers of this edition are Gen Zers also called **Zoomers** (born mid-to-late 1990s and into 2010s). Zoomers have a strong digital presence.

Newspapers, books, and television and radio shows also take value stances; some would say biases. For example, many magazines and newspapers will not publish cigarette advertisements. The renewed interest in traditionalism is not the exclusive domain of any magazine. Clothing and home furnishing retailers have noticed a renewed interest in traditional patterns, styles, and fabrics. The new traditionalists put the well-being of families and children ahead of ostentatious consumption. A car advertisement directed to the new traditionalists would emphasize the car's safety (e.g., airbags, low accident rate) over its speed.

A swing toward nontraditional behavior is evidenced in large numbers of Asians delaying or rejecting marriage. Marriage ages have risen all over the world but the mean age of marriage in Japan, Hong Kong, South Korea, and Taiwan has risen sharply in the last few decades to over 29–30 for women and 31–33 for men. There are a number of factors involved such as women being more financially independent and having more education. In East Asia, fertility rates have fallen from 5.3 children per woman in the late 1960s to 1.6 now. Family life is being redefined and governments are re-examining divorce laws, pensions, maternal and paternal leave, and subsidies for childcare.

## Value Chains

One of the basics of individual and family resource management is that we borrow or are influenced by other disciplines. In the business world, **value chains** are the glue that holds any business together. "Value chains" refers to a series of events or activities that take place in a specific time and space. According to Peter Senge et al.'s book *The Necessary Revolution: How Individuals and Organizations Are Working Together to Create a Sustainable Future* (2008), employees comprehensively work together to create a place that is ecologically, economically, and socially relevant. He writes that to initiate change there must be a compelling case for change and the time to initiate the changes needed. There must be **systems thinking**, emphasizing how the parts interact. In business, the ultimate goal is maximizing profit or value creation while minimizing costs.

Businesses seek solutions to underlying problems. Their values form a connectedness throughout the organization. For example, the value of Eco consciousness (concern for the environment, the search for safe and renewable resources) can be espoused by companies or by individuals and families.

Thus, *the concept of value chains can fit families* who build a shared commitment over time, agree on choices, and position, strategize, or plan for the future, such as parents saving for the college education of their children. Families are all about sustainability, value creation and retention, and innovation. Shared activities, traditions, or events hold them together and provide a sense of identity.

Shared mealtime reinforces family values.

Source: Getty Images—Stockbyte.

## Attitudes

As noted earlier in this chapter, *attitudes* are favorable or unfavorable feelings or ideas about some matter. They are expressions of likes and dislikes. People have attitudes about other people, objects, and issues. Examples of attitudes are prejudice about racial or cultural issues, notions about the characteristics of rich people versus poor people, and ideas about war, space exploration, or politics. Blogs, talk shows, and letters to the editor in newspapers are filled with attitudes and opinions.

Attitudes are learned and have a basis in memories. Just as with values, children learn their attitudes primarily from their families, but with time those attitudes are also shaped by other environmental influences. As they develop into adults, men and women shape their attitudes about parenting and managing a home. Child rearing and household management practices (ways of planning and doing work in the home, standards of cleanliness, and assigning tasks) are learned first in childhood. Adults choose to accept, reject, or modify the household management practices they learned in their youth.

Once learned, attitudes influence behavior. Two experts on the effects of attitudes on behavior, Icek Ajzen and Martin Fishbein (1980), developed a theory of reasoned action, which assumes that human beings are usually quite rational and make systematic use of the information available to them. This theory is heavily used today in consumer and household behavior research. Ajzen and Fishbein posit that individuals consider the implications of their actions before they decide to engage in a behavior. In their theory, a person's intention to perform (or not to perform) a behavior is the immediate determinant of the action. The individual's positive or negative evaluation of performing a behavior is her or his attitude toward the behavior. The second factor in the intention to act is called the subjective norm. This refers to the person's perception of the social pressures put on him or her to perform or not perform the behavior in question. Ease or difficulty of behavior is also a factor.

Thus, intention to behave a certain way will be affected by whether the person evaluates the behavior as positive, by what other people think, and by whether the action is perceived as easy or difficult. Beliefs shape attitudes and subjective norms, which in turn lead to intention and then actual behavior.

Because attitudes are not directly observable, they must be determined by research or by observation of behavior; however, care should be taken in inferring attitudes and values based solely on behavior. For example, the distance between two people talking to each other may be indicative of their attitudes (likes and dislikes) toward each other, but it may also reflect cultural standards of behavior (see Chapter 7). As another example, work behavior is often easy to observe: Is the person a loner? Or a team player? Is a person always late? Or early? Reliable? Or unreliable? Is the person's work neat? Or sloppy? Attitudes about creativity, time, independence, control, obedience to authority, and conformity to rules all affect work behavior.

## Goals and Motivation

Some attitudes and values are held more strongly than others. Likewise, some goals are pursued more strongly than others. If goals are to be achieved, they must be specific and realistic. Some find it helpful to write down goals and monitor their process as part of journaling and making **vision boards** (collages of images, drawings, pictures, quotations, inspirations). A new year whether a school year or calendar year might signal the need for a journal update or goal reassessment.

Goals are different from attitudes and values because they are deliberately chosen often after weighing the pros and the cons, all the options that are possible.

Figure 3.2 shows the relationship between values and goals. Once a goal has been identified, values provide the impetus—the start—toward its attainment. A person fulfills a desire or a need by engaging in goal-seeking behavior—leading, one hopes, to goal achievement. The seeking of goals requires energy, commitment, and motivation. As the figure shows, not all goals are reached; some have to be reformulated or dropped. Not all goals or opportunities are worthy of the effort. Goals should be desired end states. Accordingly, flexibility is one of the most important characteristics of goal setting. Knowing when to let go of unrealistic or unattainable goals is an important step in the management process. Goals should be constantly re-evaluated and updated. If goals are not fully committed to (and are not exciting and compelling), they have little chance of being attained. Here are some pointers to remember when you set goals:

- What benefits will this goal if attained bring to my life?
- What will I be able to do once this goal is achieved?
- How will this goal benefit others?
- How will I feel when I achieve this goal?

**Habits** are repetitive, often unconscious, patterns of behavior like brushing one's teeth. This action is related to the goals of better dental health and having an attractive appearance. Confucius said that "the nature of men is always the same; it is their habits that separate them." In other words, habits are unique to the individual. They can be either good or bad. Whining and overeating are bad habits. Treating others

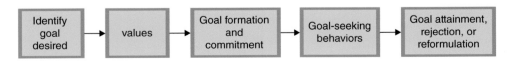

Figure 3.2 Interactive values–goals model.

**Goal-Seeking Behavior**

A colleague suggested that 45-year-old Monica apply for a government board and sent her the information about it. Monica researched it and thought "Why not?" and put in her application to a pool of about 100. She and 10 others were selected to serve two-year terms. Was this goal achievement intrinsic or extrinsic or both?

with respect and being courteous are good habits. Goals encompass more than just the fulfillment of immediate wants and needs. For example, graduating from law school is a goal, but eating a hamburger is not—it is the fulfillment of a need, hunger. In schools, they are teaching the difference between needs and wants as early as second grade.

## Goals Versus Habits

Goals are things people are trying to accomplish. Not all behaviors are goal-directed or goal activated; some are simply basic survival behaviors or habits. Goals can be intrinsic (coming from inside), or they can be extrinsic (coming from outside).

## Goal Attributes

Not all goals are created equal; each has certain characteristics or attributes.

For example, goals vary in

- *Intensity:* Commitment, how much the goal is desired
- *Complexity:* Interrelationships, how many other goals are related to this goal
- *Priority:* How important the goal is and how attainable is it
- *Resource Use:* How much the goal is going to cost (energy, money) and how many resources will be put into this goal versus other pursuits
- *Timing:* How long it will take to attain the goal

These goal attributes are demonstrated by the behaviors of Roger and Stephanie. Roger, a 24-year-old, worked for ten years during high school, college, and post-college and saved every penny to buy a Tesla. Stephanie, also 24 years old, made finding the best job her top priority during her senior year in college and put that goal before everything else. Roger and Stephanie directed their attention, developed strategies, mobilized effort, and persisted until they reached their goals. Both were highly goal-driven. When goals are highly prized, people are more inclined to hang on and not let go,

Goals provide a sense of purpose and direct behavior toward a positive end result (e.g., a Tesla, a job). Although goals are generally regarded as positive, problems can surface when goal conflict occurs in families or other groups. Conflict develops when goals compete with or subvert each other. If a family's goal is to eat a leisurely Sunday dinner together, conflict may arise if the teenage children would rather skip dinner and spend the afternoon with their friends.

Striving for goals has often been compared to climbing a mountain.

## Categories of Goals

For purposes of discussion, it is useful to categorize goals. Goals can be categorized in the following ways:

- *By time:* short-term, intermediate, or long-term
- *By role:* personal, professional, societal, or familial
- *By type:* primary or secondary

Each category will be discussed in the following sections.

### Goals and Time

In terms of time required for attaining, goals can be separated into short-term, intermediate, and long-term goals.

- Short-term goals usually take less than three months to accomplish.
- Intermediate goals can usually be achieved in three months to one year.
- Long-range goals usually take more than one year to achieve.

---

**CRITICAL THINKING**

List the goals you are striving for arranged by time and by priority (put the main one first in each category): Short-term (less than three months):

1.
2.
3.

Intermediate (three months to a year):

1.

2.

3.

Long-range (more than a year):

1.

2.

3.

A fall-semester college junior may have a short-term goal of finishing current coursework, an intermediate goal of finishing the year, and a long-term goal of graduating. College students are assumed to be long-term planners. For example, job recruiters typically ask college interviewees, "What do you plan to be doing five years from now?" With this question, the recruiter finds out whether the student has thought ahead, is a realistic planner, and is ambitious.

For some, goal setting is a luxury reserved for the wealthy and the better educated. Certainly, setting long-term goals implies a secure future or at least one partially under control. Low-income families do not always have the resource base to think beyond fulfilling daily needs and short-term goals. In terms of Maslow's hierarchy of needs, they are concerned with the physiological and safety levels of the hierarchy. For them, planning six months in advance would be a luxury. At the other extreme are celebrities who may have managers or agents, who plan their schedules five years or more in advance.

## Goals and Performance, Creativity, and Learning

Another way to categorize or group goals is by performance, creativity, or learning. **Performance goals** emphasize outcomes or actions, things that can be seen such as at a sporting event with scores or measurements. Examples would be how fast a runner goes or how many basketballs go through the hoop. In sports, we even see the word "goal" used as in goal post or goal line or in hockey a goalie. There are other kinds of performance such as in dance, in music, or in public speaking or debate. **Creativity goals** are unique in that they are characterized by someone wanting to do new things or to be original, not just to master skills. A person would be striving to be ingenious or innovative, a founder or an originator of a movement, style, or school of thought or action. **Learning goals** emphasize the gaining of competence such as learning to be a better reader, understanding more vocabulary, or knowing more about an author or a subject (such as management) or an idea. Both performing and learning goals are about building knowledge, ability, and experience and the two types of goals often intertwine. Creativity goals are about pushing the levels even further, beyond those previously imagined.

Think of the role of teachers and coaches including career coaches in helping children and adults toward achieving performance and learning goals and encouraging creativity. This leads to our next discussion.

## *Goals and Roles*

Another way to categorize goals is by role. In this typology, goals can be personal, professional, societal, or familial. Personal goals include such things as learning how to dance, ski, skydive, or ride a horse. In first grade, the main goal is to learn how to read. Achieving personal goals provides a *positive affect such as pride and satisfaction (and maybe make us scream with delight). The goal is the essence of all we think of what it means to be human. It is to have purpose that directs how we think and act....*

*(Moskowitz & Grant, 2009, p. 1)*

Professional goals are related to one's job or career; they might include improving skills like using computers, writing a contract, or conducting an interview. You achieve career success when you reach the goals you have set for yourself. Because the goals are individually defined, they vary among individuals. For some, success is defined by titles, awards, frequent promotions, or salary increases; for others, these are less important, and success is defined by completion of difficult projects, for example. One way to envision success is to pay attention to the winners in a field—who they are and what they do—with a special focus on those with continued success rather than a singular moment of glory.

Societal goals are commonly held by the greater society; they include such goals as having a full-time job by a certain age, marrying, having children, and retiring. Familial goals are related to being a son, daughter, sibling, parent, or other family members. At any one time, a person might be achieving personal and professional goals while considering or reacting to societal or familial goals.

An individual can have one or two goals or dozens. People who are professionally oriented may have many career goals and may ignore personal goals. Other people may have no professional or career goals (their job is simply something they do to earn money, so they go home at five o'clock and forget about it) and are interested only in personal or family goals. Management comes into play because goals must be prioritized and strategies developed.

What is most important? How do people go about getting what they want? Sergei, aged 50, who wanted to open a Greek restaurant saved money for years, and when the right location became available he went for it.

### Goals by Category: Primary and Secondary Goals

Goals can also be categorized as primary and secondary. For example, if a person's primary goal is to attain a college degree, then his or her secondary goals would include being accepted into a college, passing courses, and completing graduation requirements. Secondary goals are smaller; they motivate and collectively add up to the primary goals.

### Setting Goals

The beneficial effect of goal setting on task performance is one of the most validated concepts in psychology. Simply stated, people accomplish more when they set goals. Studies of survivors of concentration camps found that those who had a purpose for living and well-defined goals were better able to withstand deprivation, including starvation and torture, than those without goals. Many of the survivors said that their main goal was to see their family again.

To be helpful, goals should have certain characteristics. First, goals must be reasonable, attainable, and within the resources of the goal setter. For example, a person who wants to buy a house must have the resources to make a down payment and meet the monthly payments. Saying that goals should be realistic and attainable does not mean that they should be easy to accomplish. Indeed, goals should present some challenges for the goal setter.

Goals should also be clearly formed. When asked about his formula for success, J. Paul Getty, one of the richest men in the world, said, "Rise early. Work late. Strike oil." The importance of having clear, specific goals cannot be overemphasized. The goal of buying a new car is too vague because it cannot be visualized. The goal of buying a certain type of car in one year is effective, however, because it allows the mind to form a specific picture of the car and focuses attention on actions and a time frame for achieving the goal. When the person sees advertisements for that particular car or passes one in a parking lot, her decision to try to buy that car will be reinforced. Of course, during the year she may decide on another model, but at least initially, visualizing a specific car can be helpful. Goals provide an avenue for freedom, a sense of control, and, as noted before, a sense of direction and purpose.

## Optimism, Goals, and Well-Being

In *Authentic Happiness* Martin Seligman, a past president of the American Psychological Association and professor of psychology at the University of Pennsylvania, says that happiness and optimism are essential for a good and successful life. He is a leader in the positive psychology movement, which looks at what is right with people rather than at what is wrong. **Optimism** is a tendency or a disposition to expect the best outcome or to think hopefully about a situation. The belief that things will get better is called the **optimism bias.** Children express it when they say, "When I grow up I will . . ." and you express it when you say, "When I graduate I will " To learn about Seligman's rise as the leader of the optimism movement read *The Hope Circuit: A Psychologist's Journey from Helplessness to Optimism* (2018).

### CRITICAL THINKING

#### How Rational?

"We like to think of ourselves as rational creatures. We watch our backs, weight the odds, pack an umbrella. But both neuroscience and social science suggest that we are more optimistic than realistic. On average, we expect things to turn out better than they wind up being. People hugely underestimate their chances of getting divorced, losing their job or being diagnosed with cancer; expect their children to be extraordinarily gifted; envision themselves achieving more than their peers; and overestimate their likely life span (sometimes by 20 years or more)" (Sharot, 2011, p. 38). Why does optimism bias hold forth in every race, region, and socio-economic group even though there are illnesses, hurricanes, floods, tornadoes, and high unemployment?

Researchers are accumulating evidence that our brains aren't just conjuring up the past but rather are constantly being shaped by imagining the future. Some call this mental time travel. We see ourselves in this new setting, happy and fulfilled. Maybe this explains the popularity of wedding movies and television shows.

Optimists work longer hours and tend to make more money and save more money which makes sense; they are saving for the future. When Americans are asked if they will live up to 100 years, about 10 percent say yes but in reality, less than 2 percent will live that long. A study by scientists at the Mayo Clinic in Rochester, Minnesota, revealed that optimists had 19 percent greater longevity, in terms of their expected life span, than did pessimists (Danner et al., 2001).

So what are we to make of this as management experts? Perhaps a more measured view comes from Martin Seligman who promotes flexible optimism—optimism with its eyes open rather than the total rose-colored glasses variety. He says that people are not stuck with their pasts, but they can learn from them. We should be knowledgeable and hopeful, for example, try to stay healthy but get health insurance, too. The kinds of phrases associated with optimism include a person saying or thinking

- "I'm usually lucky."
- "I'm talented."
- "My dog is better than any other at the obedience class."
- "My rival is no good."
- "I'm smart."
- "I'm good at lots of things."
- "I give everything my best shot."
- "I have a lot to look forward to."
- "I drive better than other people."
- "I look better than my friends."

In pursuit of understanding the linkages between health and illness, other researchers have explored the relationship between optimism and general well-being. *An optimist is more likely to think that goals are reachable.* A Harris poll revealed that Americans are happier and more optimistic about their future than are most Europeans. Gallup polls also measure optimism by country. In one poll, respondents from Germany and the Mediterranean countries indicated that they were less happy and optimistic than Northern Europeans (Taylor, 2003). A more recent poll found that Malta, an island nation in the Mediterranean Sea, is the happiest of the European nations. These poll results are merely indicators and not all evidence comes from surveys. In anecdotal evidence, curators at a New York retrospective exhibition of works by Matisse and Picasso noted that the colorful, cheerful works of Matisse drew far more visitors than did Picasso's (Goodale, 2003).

### Importance of Challenge

If we had no sense of challenge we would never try to change our appearance; notice the new fashions, weather, or the news; or try to get better at anything. A drive to achieve leads to goal pursuit. The novelist F. Scott Fitzgerald said, "Vitality shows in not only the ability to persist but the ability to start over." Starting over is a challenge. Goals need to be reset. How does a person choose the goals to pursue? The study of management assumes that if someone devotes the required resources, plans well, and makes the sacrifices necessary, almost anything is achievable. Consequently, people should aim high and set goals that force them to do their best. By creating a challenge, goals affect performance by directing attention, mobilizing effort, increasing persistence, and motivating strategy development.

Anthony, who is single and 25, listed his goals for the next five years as follows:

- *Career/work:* Own a fitness center
- *Home:* Have a nice apartment
- *Personal:* Date someone seriously, have lots of friends
- *Leisure:* Work out every day

Do Anthony's goals seem realistic for someone who works full-time in a gym and has a college degree in exercise science? How much does it cost to open a fitness center? To rent an apartment? What secondary goals does he need to accomplish to reach his primary goal of owning a fitness center? Anthony's goal of owning a fitness center has created a very real challenge for him and forced him to develop strategies to achieve it. Anthony's strategies include learning all he can from the gym where he now works before opening his own fitness center and fulfilling his secondary goals of paying off his college loans and credit cards and saving money.

## Plans for Attaining Goals

Once goals are set, a plan for achieving them must be developed. Planning includes all managerial activities that determine results and the appropriate means to achieve those results. It involves the following five steps:

1. Set specific goals and prioritize them; weigh options.

2. State the goals clearly and positively. For example, "I will be a nonsmoker by January 1"—not "I will stop smoking." "I will lose five pounds"—not "I will lose weight."

3. Forecast possible future events and the resources that will be needed. This entails determining both the level of material resources that will be needed and the amount of effort that will be required.

4. Implement the plan by following through with the goal-directed activity. In other words, don't just plan, do something. A lot of people get stuck in the planning phase.

5. Be aware of discrepancies between what is and what is desired by detecting what doesn't fit forward progress; make adjustments; be flexible which means redefining goals when necessary.

Note that the planning process begins with prioritizing goals. Prioritizing involves ranking goals by the degree of commitment to them. Commitment is the sense of obligation one feels toward the goal. If a goal is not enticing or inspiring, something is wrong, and the goal will not serve its function of motivating the person to put in greater effort. Prioritizing forces people to decide what they really want and how they are going to get it. Step five involves critical thinking, self-reflection, and being ready and able to read outside clues.

We reset goals all the time. A common one is a New Year's Eve resolution. People fail to keep their resolutions because their willpower is not enough, they haven't chosen realistic resolutions, and they fail to devise a plan to work on them every day. Even the smallest step makes a difference in the long run. Doing ten morning pushups is better than not doing pushups at all.

## Obstacles to Goal Achievement

Many forces such as family or health crises pull us away from goals. All the goal setting in the world cannot stop unplanned events from altering the course of resource use. Obstacles to achieving goals include, but are not limited to, the following: time, parents, family, rules, peers, social customs, demands, imagination, money, health, and natural disasters.

---

### Suggested Activity

Keep a journal. Each week write down your goals (short-term, intermediate, and/or long-term). For one month do not look back at the previous entries; then read all of them at once. Do you see a pattern? Were any of the goals accomplished? Or was significant progress made on any of them? If yes, keep on, or else, perhaps goals need to be re-evaluated.

Obstacles alone do not determine the fate of human goal-seeking behavior. Instead, the way people perceive and react to obstacles will determine whether they will reach their goals. One way to overcome obstacles is to divide larger goals into smaller ones, which allows a person to make progress a little at a time. It also helps to find a trusted, nonjudgmental friend who is willing to discuss one's goals and periodically check on how projects are going.

Monitoring one's progress by marking deadlines on a calendar is useful as well. Everyone should also be aware of when roadblocks are likely to occur. Is it at the start of projects? In the middle? At the end?

**Resilience** is defined as the ability to overcome obstacles and to achieve positive outcomes even after experiencing extreme difficulties. Individual traits associated with resilience include intelligence, competence, a good-natured temperament, internal locus of control, and self-esteem. Researchers also note that relationships can help protect a person from stress and promote positive growth. In other words, resilience—although an inner ability (involving courage and fortitude)—is helped and accentuated by strong, encouraging relationships. Parents play an important role in helping children learn how to be resilient.

### Needs for Achievement: the N Ach Factor

People can make themselves miserable trying to set impossible goals such as earning a million dollars in a year or insisting that everyone be happy every minute of a family vacation. A dad said he expects each child in the family to have a meltdown (crying, screaming, fit) once a day while at Disney World and when they don't he is pleased. Healthy goals are a little out of reach, but they are not impossible dreams. Compromise and flexibility rule the day.

In a classic study, David McClelland, a Harvard psychologist, stressed that individuals vary in their need for achievement, which he called "n Ach" (McClelland, 1961). He found that each individual has a different level of motivation for overcoming obstacles, desiring success, and expending effort to seek out difficult tasks and do them well as quickly as possible. He emphasized that the achievement motive can be expressed as a desire to perform in terms of a standard of excellence or to be successful in competitive situations. *You can choose to act in ways that help you achieve goals.*

A person possessing high n Ach takes moderate risks, not high risks as one might assume. This phenomenon can be demonstrated by the ring-toss game. Low achievers will stand very near the peg and drop the rings over it or stand far away and wildly throw the ring. High achievers will calculate the exact distance from the peg that will challenge their abilities yet will give them a chance for success. Thus, low achievers take a low or high risk, and high achievers take moderate risk. Research indicates that this pattern holds true in most walks of life and for children as well as for adults.

---

**CRITICAL THINKING**

#### Being Able to Bounce Back

Joel Haber, author of *Bullyproof Your Child for Life*, says that a resilient child knows how to handle letdowns. To boost resilience, he says, first show you understand the child's feelings and then ask what he or she has done to rebound. Brainstorm together how to deal with situations and setbacks. Do you remember any negative situations or disappointments that you or your friends experienced? What steps were taken to bounce back? How long did it take?

Renee Spencer (2000) found studies indicating that one supportive adult can provide good outcomes for children coping with poverty, problems at school, malnutrition, separation from a parent, marital discord at home, divorcing parents, and mental illness of parents. David Elkind, a Tufts University professor emeritus and author of *The Hurried Child*, says that teens experience what he calls "an imaginary audience," a feeling that others are watching and evaluating them. There are so many changes going on in teens' lives that they tend to over-magnify other peoples' judging of them. They are often sensitive and self-absorbed during these years. He believes that parents can help during those trying times when their children are making transitions to the next stage. The reason why this is especially important is that the teens are laying the groundwork for how they will deal with future life transitions when they are on uncertain social ground.

Finally, goals need to be re-evaluated. Resistance to goals may mean that it is time to change them or to take a break. Pursuing goals requires energy.

## Disengaging from Goals

So much of goal study is about setting and reaching goals and although in step five we talked about re-adjusting goals we need to go more in-depth about letting go. It turns out that this is a hard thing to do, to let go of, for example, the dream of being married to a certain person or being a star athlete. In the financial world, people have an easier time buying stocks than selling them especially at a loss. They have a hard time facing they made the wrong decision even though circumstances beyond their control have changed. **Goal disengagement** over time means some goals have to be let go or sharply redefined. Different types of disengagement include:

1. Behavioral (switching to new activities)

2. Affective (a change in feelings)

3. Motivational (changing motives, the seeds of actions)

Consider the case study of Brad and Sue and determine if they were disengaged for behavioral, affective, and/or motivational reasons.

---

**CASE STUDY**

### Brad and Sue

Brad and Sue, both professionals with careers, were married for 23 years and then got divorced because of irreconcilable differences. They just did not get along in their later years the way they did when newly married and starting careers and their family. Their college-age son and daughter hoped they would get back together. After living apart for five years Brad and Sue started dating and decided to remarry. They bought a townhouse. Within a year they were separated again. Sue said, "We never should have gotten remarried, we do fine living apart but our differences come out when we live together." A few years passed and Sue married James and moved to another town.

---

Brad stayed single and said he liked it that way. James died. Sue started a new single life.

## *Lifestyles, Goals, and Feedback*

Each person has a basic notion of what he or she wants in the way of food, shelter, and companionship; these basic needs evolve into a more complicated set of needs, which combine to form a lifestyle. Likewise, goals often start simple and evolve into more complicated notions. A recent college graduate might want a job, any job, to get started and then, as time goes by, develop a more specific definition of what a good job is.

Goals don't have to be selfish. They can be altruistic like starting a new club or helping friends move or volunteering. Goals provide meaning and direction. They involve persistence and initiative.

---

## CRITICAL THINKING

### Persistence

A college club which was allied with a subject was losing membership and did not have a faculty advisor. The rule at the university was that student clubs had to have a faculty advisor assigned to them or the club would be dissolved. The department chairman sent out an email asking for a faculty member to be an advisor and also to reinvigorate the club. No one responded, so he sent out one final memo and said unless someone volunteers to be an advisor we will let the club go. A nearly retired professor responded and said, "I'll do it." And, true to his word he did and the club grew. What does this story say about resilience and goal disengagement? What does this say about persistence? What does it say about individual character, goals, and thinking of others?

---

Forming short-term goals is a way to conserve the time and energy needed to reach long-term goals. Short-term goals have the advantage that they can be completed fairly rapidly, giving a sense of accomplishment. An author, for example, might write newspaper and magazine articles during the same time period she is writing a novel so that she always has something in the process or in print.

Individuals and families need feedback to determine whether their goals are viable or need to be changed. Goals are generally thought of as positives in life, but they can be self-defeating if they are too difficult. Goals can also have a negative effect if they cause people to be so single-minded that they do not see other possible goals or courses of action that might be better. Both depression over failure to be an overnight success and single-minded focus on today without a thought of the future can be self-defeating. Vision boards discussed earlier in the chapter can have a down effect if nothing happens. Listening to others and getting feedback helps keep goals realistic and on track.

## College Students' Values, Goals, and Life Outcomes

Psychologists conducted a study of college yearbook photos. They compared the actual life outcomes of women students whose photos showed a genuine smile, called the "Duchenne smile" (named after its discoverer Guillaume Duchenne), with those of women whose photos showed an inauthentic smile, called the Pan American smile. In the Duchenne smile the corners of the mouth turn up, and the skin around the corners of the eyes crinkles (like crow's feet). The muscles that control these functions are connected, and it is difficult to voluntarily control them. The Pan Am smile is a fake smile named after flight attendants posing in advertisements for a now-defunct airline.

Dacher Kelter and LeeAnne Harker (2001) of the University of California, Berkeley, found that the women with a Duchenne smile were more likely to be married, to stay married, and to experience more personal well-being over a 30-year period. Others questioned whether the results had more to do with good looks than with the smile itself, so the investigators went back and rated how pretty each of the women seemed. They found that looks had nothing to do with good marriages or life satisfaction. It turns out that a genuinely smiling woman was simply more likely to be well-wed and happy (Seligman, 2002).

College students' values, goals, and life outcomes have been the subject of many studies. Researchers have found that, overall, college men and women have similar goals and value orientations. For many students, the college years serve as a transition stage between living at home with parents and living on their own—a physical and emotional bridge between childhood and adulthood. Studies have shown that a close family relationship leads to more successful adjustments to college life for students.

Because college is a transitory stage, goal instability is not unusual during the college years. For example, students may change their majors and career choices many times. Thus, goal instability is common for college students and can even be helpful, but it can also be uncomfortable for the individual experiencing it. Nearly one-third of college freshmen do not return for their sophomore year and the numbers on this are much higher for community colleges than for four-year colleges. The main reasons they do not return are job opportunities, financial circumstances, poor grades, and personal situations.

## CASE STUDY

### Doug

Doug's parents went to college so he thought he would, too. He was an excellent band member in high school so he thought he would major in music. By the second semester, he knew college was not for him so he joined the armed forces, where he played in a number of bands mostly in the Washington, DC, area but he also got to travel. After a few years, he got married and was reassigned elsewhere. Not too long after that the marriage went sour and he decided to leave the military and regroup. By age 26 he had experienced a lot of changes and was now ready for school. He wasn't sure whether it should be a four-year college or community college or some other form of training such as becoming a firefighter. But, he was happy and enthused and felt he was rejoining life where he left off in the same college town that he started in.

Although college students have the same array of values as the general population, the media and social scientists over the years have attempted to categorize the general typology of college students by decade or by generation. For example, students of the 1950s have been described as conservative and conforming, as holders of traditional values who had only slight concern for societal problems. After graduation, a typical student from these years went on to become the join organizations and businesses grew incredibly. Many obeyed the laws and fulfilled obligations, as they strove to get ahead. In this decade, significant advances occurred in civil rights.

The late 1960s and the early 1970s are considered years of unrest and change, characterized by the advent of the peace movement, the women's liberation movement, and other societal causes. College students challenged traditional ways of doing things, questioned material gain, and extolled the virtues of individual rights and freedom. Values changed on campuses, exemplified by the widespread introduction of coeducational dormitories and the end of dress codes and curfews.

In the 1980s, the college culture moved back to material goals; students flooded business schools and became more egocentric and less committed to broad sociopolitical change. The students of the 1980s grew up during the downsizing of certain businesses; they saw or experienced social and personal insecurities. As a result, they became more savvy and more skeptical (Stoneman, 1998). A shift that occurred in the 1980s is that since 1982 more women than men have received bachelor's degrees and this trend continues today.

Students of the 1990s enjoyed the benefits of a strong economy and a thriving labor market. They had more money than their predecessors. Colleges realized that standard dormitory style living was becoming less attractive to students.

In the 21st century, Zoomers and earlier cohorts increased their digital ability. Many colleges in the United States and other countries built or renovated dormitories to allow for more single rooms with bathrooms or shared suites with fewer students per suite; others allowed privatized on-campus apartments. The ups and downs of the economy affected the amount of choice in the job market, although, as always, some majors led to more job opportunities than others. Health-related careers surged. As noted at the beginning of the chapter, the U.S. Census reports more students going on for advanced degrees.

## CRITICAL THINKING

### College Students and Social Engagement

How will current students compare with those of previous generations? One trend is more interest in public health. Another is how to spread prosperity to more. Another is the growing concern over crime in the greater society. Some studies report a return to social engagement and involvement by college students. What do you think? Are college students becoming more socially engaged? Do they have lots of friends? Do they do a lot of volunteer or service work? Or, less? What factors influence trends of interest and activities?

Through intensive orientation programs (virtual or in-person), parents' weekends, and other such activities, campuses are trying to build a sense of community and purpose that meets students' needs. It appears that the happiest people (college students or anyone else) "surround themselves with family and friends, don't care about keeping up with the Joneses next door, lose themselves in daily activities, and most important, forgive easily" (Elias, 2002, p. A1).

The next section on motivation has enormous implications for college students. How do they stay in college and keep studying so that they reach their goal of a college degree? Motivation is a combination of individual qualities and parental and society's reaction or support.

## Motivation

"The biggest human temptation is …to settle for too little," says Thomas Merton, an American monk and a spiritual writer. Thomas Edison and his staff tried 3,000 ways to perfect a lightbulb before they found one that worked. A motivated person takes risks and overcomes obstacles to achieve goals. The word "motivation" comes from the Latin word *movere* (to move). In management, **motivation** refers to the movement toward goals or other desired outcomes and to vigor, drive, persistence, creativity, direction, and sustained energy. One of the goals of nurturing children is to build each child's strengths and virtues as well as helping them find a niche where their positive traits can develop to the fullest. For example, in the 2008 Olympics, the parents of one of the gold medal winners in gymnastics mortgaged their house three times to pay for her coaching. They were motivated, as was their daughter.

Motivated individuals work hard. Motivation is shown through tasks, in mastery, in practice, and in public performances, such as piano recitals, debates, or sports events. Motivated individuals develop exceptional qualities usually through an investment of time, staying in the field as long as it takes to build expertise. They keep going despite setbacks. How they do this is one of the puzzles in the study of human excellence.

**Expertise** is "the characteristics, skills, and knowledge that distinguish experts from novices and less experienced people. In some domains, there are objective criteria for finding experts, who are consistently able to exhibit superior performance for representative tasks in a domain. For example, chess masters will almost always win chess games against recreational chess player in chess tournaments, medical specialists are far more likely to diagnose a disease correctly than advanced medical students, and professional musicians can perform pieces of music in a manner that is unattainable for less skilled musicians" (Ericsson et al., 2006, p. 3).

### CRITICAL THINKING

**Are You Motivated?**

Can you remember a time when you were very motivated? When you succeeded in a public performance or in a competition? What steps led you to that performance or outcome? How many months or years of training or studying did it take?

Another way to approach motivation is to say one's eagerness to pursue goals matters. Motivation is not just a personal or family construct; it is the driving force behind companies and organizations (Goldsmith, 2016). Car salespeople try to sell a certain number of cars per month to reach a quota. Real estate salespeople try to sell enough houses in a year to be on the "million dollar seller list." Girl Scouts try to sell enough boxes of cookies to go camping. Goal setting's potential for improving productivity is so well established that it is rarely questioned as a management technique.

*Motivation is a process* rather than an end state. The process begins with an unsatisfied need that creates tension. This tension drives a person to undertake a search for resources or information. Hence, the person does not feel satisfied until her or his need is fulfilled or the goal attained. Internal and external factors contribute to the motivation to achieve goals.

We have intrinsic and extrinsic motivations that affect our behavior including consumer behavior (Oliveria et al., 2021). **Intrinsic motivation** involves the underlying causes and the internal need for competence and self-determination. It can increase or decrease. If someone enjoys performing a task such as distance running it is likely they will pursue it more—it is intrinsically satisfying. It refers to the pleasure or value a person derives from the content of work or activity. If a student works hard in school, the satisfaction he or she derives from learning and mastering a subject provides the intrinsic motivation to keep learning. **Extrinsic motivation** involves forces external to the individual—environmental factors such as titles, raises, preferred offices, promotions, and other forms of rewards including forming meaningful relationships. For a student, extrinsic motivators include "A" grades, the honor roll, the Dean's List, the President's List, the honor society, scholarships, and other forms of recognition for academic performance. A waiter is a member of a cycling club so that on weekends he goes on hundred-mile bike rides with a group of men and women ages 20–58 and his extrinsic motivation is having them with him versus cycling alone. They usually stop and have a drink mid-route and talk about the route and next events. If anyone falls or if equipment fails, they help each other. Famous weight loss organizations and television programs place great emphasis on extrinsic motivation.

Both intrinsic and extrinsic motivations are important for goal achievement. Children need to experience both types. They should feel good about learning (intrinsic), and they should also feel that their efforts are recognized by others (extrinsic). In the home, the family members who do housework should feel good about living in a clean house and about having their cleaning efforts noticed and appreciated by other family members.

One of the unsolved mysteries of life is why some people have more intrinsic motivation than others. These people work hard regardless of the number and quality of external rewards. Are the answers in genetics? In early childhood experiences? In work experiences? In temperament? Psychologists and others are searching for the answers to these questions. Often the intrinsically motivated individual values mastery, or values the learning process over achievement of outcomes. The tennis champion Monica Seles described her intrinsic motivation:

> *I really never enjoyed playing matches, even as a youngster. I just love to practice and drill and that stuff. I just hate the whole thought that one [player] is better than the other. It drives me nuts.*
>
> *(Vecsey, 1999, p. D1)*

Far more is known about the working of extrinsic motivation than about intrinsic motivation. For example, extrinsic rewards are most effective if

- They are specific.
- They are given immediately after a good work performance.
- They are valued by the receiver.
- They are equitable.

What one person perceives as a reward may not be perceived as desirable by another. For example, a trip at the company's expense to a convention might be valued by one employee, but considered a burden by another. As another example, a child who does not like candy will not view a candy bar as a reward. Rewards should be appropriate to the individual and at the same time be perceived as equitable by the family or organization.

This is a key chapter in the book because values, attitudes, motivation, and goals are four of the most important concepts in the management process. Values are principles that guide behavior. They stand for what is worthwhile, preferred, and consistent. Values are tested in times of stress or trouble. A value chain is a glue that holds families together, in time and in space. Value chain analysis is borrowed from business and refers to organizations that have a shared vision and value set and use systems thinking. A vision of the future is important to move plans forward.

Families play a fundamental role in the formation and transmission of values. Parents, as the primary socializers of children, greatly influence their children's values. Goals are end results, the things people are working toward.

We are intrinsically and extrinsically motivated. Motivation and optimism are important elements in achieving goals. Researchers study motivation in many fields from consumer behavior to sports to chess and are interested in what drives individuals to purchase and to perform at high levels. Is it intrinsic (inward, desire for fame or achievement) versus extrinsic (outside rewards, praise, recognition, advertising) motivation or a combination of both? The answers drive economies and societies/organizations.

Attitudes are states of mind or feelings, likes, and dislikes, about some matter. They often occupy a middle ground between values and goals.

A value or goal change recently evidenced is the growing number of people in their 20s, married or not, buying houses, a sign of settling down and establishing roots. This trend may be a symbol of optimism, an area studied by many psychologists including Martin Seligman.

When two people date or become close friends, they try to find out about each other's values, attitudes, and goals, especially the ones they have in common. Do they enjoy the same activities? Do they have similar or compatible views about leisure, work, spirituality, and politics? Do they have similar reactions to situations and people?

Selecting one's life goals is a complex task, which is easier for people who have been raised in a supportive environment or as the opening case study shows mentors can be found on college campuses and other realms in life. To be achievable, goals should be clear, realistic, and challenging, but not overwhelming. Long-term goals take grit (determination).

Most importantly, goals should be flexible. The motivation process starts with an unsatisfied need or unmet demand that creates tension and results in a satisfied need and reduced tension. Goals give direction to life, and values serve as a guide. Different ways to group or categorize goals were given and the concepts of performance, creativity, and learning goals were introduced. Goals are activated, behaviors ensue, steps are taken, evaluations are made. A person can disengage from goals and change course, set new goals or targets. Some success will lead to more success. Goals cannot be set without consideration of resource availability. Resources are the subject of the next chapter.

## KEY TERMS

absolute values
affective domain
Africa Rising
attitudes
behavior
cognitive domain
creativity goals
cultural values
expertise
extrinsic motivation

extrinsic values
goal disengagement
habits
intrinsic motivation
intrinsic values
learning goals
mindfulness
motivation
optimism
optimism bias

performance goals
relative values
resilience
socialization
systems thinking
value chains
value orientation
vision
vision boards
Zoomers (Gen Z)

## REVIEW QUESTIONS

1. Poet Robert Frost wrote, "Home is the place where, when you have to go there, they have to take you in." Does that family value still hold true? Why would a grown person decide it is time to move back home?

2. Businesses and organizations form value chains, a shared commitment to goals built around time and space. Likewise, families form multigenerational value chains. Describe a shared value or tradition in your family that has endured over time.

3. The number of Americans with Masters and Ph.D. degrees has doubled since 2000. Why do you think this is?

4. What does Henry David Thoreau mean when he says, "My life is like a stroll upon the beach, as near the ocean's edge as I can go." How does this statement relate to the ideas in the chapter?

5. Why does Martin Seligman, the founder of positive psychology, say that optimism is essential for achieving goals?

## REFERENCES

Ajzen, I., & Fishbein, M. (1980). *Understanding attitudes and predicting social behavior.* Englewood Cliffs, NJ: Prentice Hall.

Buck, S. (2003). Building capacity through leadership development programs. *Journal of Family and Consumer Sciences, 95*(3), 8–11.

Condor, B. (2002, September 3). Find your strengths, then your happiness. *Tallahassee Democrat,* p. 4D.

Consumer demand. (2003). Retrieved September 3, 2003, from http://www.sric-bi.com/consulting/ConsumerDmd.shtml.

Danner, D., Snowdon, D., & Friesen, W. (2001). Positive emotions in early life and longevity: Findings from the nun study. *Journal of Personality and Social Psychology, 80,* 804–813.

de Lisser, E. (2002, September 24). One-click commerce: What people do now to goof off at work. *The Wall Street Journal,* pp. A1, A8.

Elias, M. (2002, December 9). What makes people happy. *USA Today,* p. A1.

Elkind, D. (1988). *The hurried child.* Reading, MA: Addison-Wesley.

Elliot, A., & Niesta, D. (2009). Goals in the context of the hierarchical model of approach-avoidance motivation. In G. Moskowitz & H. Grant (Eds.), *The Psychology of Goals* (Chapter 2, p. 56). New York: The Guilford Press.

Ericsson, K. A., Charness, N., Feltovich, P., & Hoffman, R. (2006). *The Cambridge handbook of expertise and expert performance.* New York: Cambridge University Press.

Goldsmith, E. B. (2015). *Social influence and sustainable consumption.* Switzerland: Springer.

Goldsmith, E. B. (2016). *Consumer economics: Issues and behaviors, 3rd edition.* Oxford: Routledge.
Goodale, G. (2003, July 3). Sunny side up. *Christian Science Monitor.* Retrieved from www.csmonitor.com.

Haber, J. (2007). *Bullyproof your child for life.* New York: Penguin.

Kelter, D., & Harker, L. (2001). Expressions of positive emotion in women's college yearbook pictures and their relationship to personality and life outcomes across adulthood. *Journal of Personality and Social Psychology, 80,* 112–124.

Kono, T., & Lynn, L. (2007). *Strategic new product development for the global economy.* New York: Palgrave Macmillan.

McClelland, D. (1961). *The achieving society.* New York: Van Nostrand Reinhold.

Moskowitz, G., & Grant, H. (2009). *The psychology of goals.* New York: The Guilford Press.

Oliveria, T., Barbeitos, I., & Calado, A. (January, 4, 2021). The role of intrinsic and extrinsic motivations in sharing economy post-adoption. *Information Technology and People.* Ahead of print No: https://dol.org/10.1108/ITP-01-2020–0007.

Ray, P. (1997). The emerging culture. *American Demographics, 19,* 29–34, 56.

Rokeach, M. J. (1973). *The nature of human values.* New York: Free Press.

Seligman, M. (2018). *The hope circuit: A psychologist's journey from helplessness to optimism.* New York: Hatchett Book Group.

Seligman, M. (2002). *Authentic happiness.* New York: Free Press.

Senge, P., Smith, B., Kruschwitz, N., Laur, J., & Schley, S. (2008). *The necessary revolution: How individuals and organizations are working together to create a sustainable future.* New York: Doubleday.

Sharot, T. (2011, June 6). *The optimism bias.* New York: TIME.

Shaslota, M. (2019, February 23–24). The true confessions of a serial houseplant killer. *The Wall Street Journal,* D10.

Spencer, R. (2000). *A comparison of national psychologies.* Project Report, No. 5. Wellesley, MA: Stone Center.

Sternquist, B., & Goldsmith, E. B. (2018). *International retailing, 3rd edition.* New York: Bloomsbury.

Stoneman, B. (1998, December 4). Beyond rocking the ages: An interview with J. Walter Smith. *American Demographics,* 1–7.

Taylor, H. (2003, May 21). *Americans are far more optimistic and have much higher life satisfactions than Europeans.* Retrieved March 22, 2004, from http://www.harrisinteractive.com.

Vecsey, G. (1999, September 3). Seles feels windy blast from past. *New York Times,* p. D1.

Zaslow, J. (2003, February 6). Ready to pop the question? Hold off until you've done the interrogation. *The Wall Street Journal,* p. D1.

Chapter **4**

# Resources

DOI: 10.4324/9781003166740-4

Resources, Families, and Households

   Resource Forecasting

   Strategy and the Conservation of Resources Theory

**DID YOU KNOW THAT …?**

… More women are now bosses, doctors, and politicians.
… There are over 20 million college students in the United States.

Resources, what they are, who has them, who doesn't, and how to use them wisely in good and bad situations including traumatic events are the subjects of this chapter. The ways to examine resources are endless. Not everyone has equal access to resources as shown in the case study.

**CASE STUDY**

Sandra Stirling, a teacher, was driving by a Subway restaurant in Florida, when she saw a teenage boy with a laptop sitting outside the building. "I turned around and went back," Starling wrote in a Facebook post that went viral. "I asked if he was trying to do schoolwork. He answered 'yes,' because he 'doesn't want to get behind.'" The student was using the restaurant's free Wi-Fi because he said he didn't want to get behind. He said his dad did concrete work in Jacksonville and he was afraid of losing his job, "so home internet wasn't a high priority." Starling concluded that "school is only a small part of some students' struggle" and that not everyone has internet access. (Source: Emily Bloch, May 5, 2020, "Mama is tired": After school closures, some families burn out on online classes, others thrive. *Florida Times-Union.*)

Resource recognition, creation, and exchange are included in this chapter. As a review, resource management in this book is applied to individuals and families, and environments such as home and work environments. A key concept is **sustainability** as in establishing systems and processes that will support human life, enabling individuals and families to continue and thrive. Sometimes you must take a step back to examine what you want or what you should do to go forward.

In the allied field of human resource management (HRM) which is the term more used in business, sustainability is defined as the ability of a company to survive and exceed in a dynamic environment based on an approach to organizational decision-making (Noe et al., 2019). Adjacent sub-disciplines of management include studies of project-based work and strategic and innovation management (Samimi & Sydow, 2020).

Exchanging resources facilitates the pursuit of human satisfaction or happiness. Learning new skills and getting an education are examples of resource creation. Individuals, families, and communities are constantly moving in new directions, seeking new ways to trade and network, and live. For example, Detroit once had 1.85 million inhabitants and now it has close to 675,000. Other U.S. cities dropping considerably in population include St. Louis and Cleveland. Abroad, other cities losing size are Leipzig in Germany and Liverpool in England. Often the cause is a shift in the location of jobs connected to technology, industry, and manufacturing. Cities can make a comeback if they re-invent themselves by attracting new industries and innovating in health and education. Human resources are challenged every day.

From the individual's standpoint, effectively using what you have (resources) to get what you want is a lifelong challenge.

Resources are needed to survive, to feel fulfilled or purposeful, and to execute tasks or projects. They are mobile, complex, and interconnected. Examples of resources are expertise, integrity, time, people, technology, tools, attitude, space, money, materials, objects, food, intelligence, and energy. Let us take integrity, for example. Peterson and Seligman (2004, p. 25) define **integrity** (the practice of being honest and consistent in principles, beliefs, and values) in behavioral terms as

- A *regular pattern of behavior* that is consistent with espoused values (you practice what you preach).

- Public acknowledgment of moral convictions, even if those convictions are not popular.

- Treatment of others with care, as demonstrated by helping those in need, sensitivity to the needs of others.

So, integrity is more than a value; it is a resource, a cluster of behavioral characteristics. Integrity is a fundamental way of behaving in which a person is genuine and sincere and has a strong moral compass. If you have a family name that is well thought of in a community, that name is a resource.

Resources may be exchanged internally within the family or externally between the family and the greater environment, such as a retail, political, or real estate environment. The household is an organized behavior system. One model of resource exchange in a household would suggest that households would select internal exchange when they have the expertise, time, and **resource capacity** to indulge in an internal exchange; but when these are lacking, a search for outside or external exchange will ensue. An example would be homeowners deciding to paint a bedroom themselves rather than hire a painter. Another example would be 25-year-old newlyweds deciding to have a reception at their parents' house rather than reserving a reception hall at a hotel, church, or club.

External exchange is usually necessary for auto repair or other tasks requiring expertise beyond the typical individual's capacity. Wise competitors and service providers use advertising to show what they can provide and how they can make life easier.

*The worth of internal exchanges tends to be undervalued in our society*, and one of the goals of this book is to extol the virtues of building one's human capacity. Companies that combine do-it-yourself products or customization along with free instruction are providing for both internal and external exchange; these types of products/activities will be increasingly popular in the future because they provide satisfying experience with a personal touch. According to Zuboff and Maxmin,

> *The new individuals seek meaning, not just material security and comfort. They enjoy their things but place an even higher value on the quality of the lives they lead, in which those possessions play a part. They insist on self-expression, participation, and influence because they share the certain knowledge that the singularity of their own lives cannot be deduced from the general case. No longer born to a biography, their identities must be invented as they go—cobbled together from personal initiative and private judgment.*

> *(2002, p. 93)*

Another fundamental principle is that resource use changes over time. We no longer go down to the stream and wash clothes. We use washers and dryers, detergent and softeners, electricity, and piped-in water to get clothes clean. Or we may choose to drop clothes at a laundry or dry cleaner and exchange money for human time and energy. Although a comment on this, some cultures prefer to air dry clothing on clothes

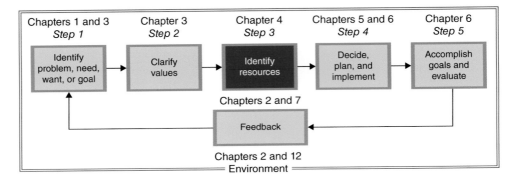

Figure 4.1 **The management process model.**

lines outside on rooftops and balconies or in backyards rather than use dryers inside which take up room and use electricity which costs money. With the right breezy climate, this can be a home management practice that works well.

Many management activities have been transformed from simple but labor-intensive actions to complex processes requiring investment of time, human and mechanical energy, and money. As another example, the resource use of college students has changed considerably. Grandparents and parents remember themselves as cash-strapped, existing for weeks on peanut butter sandwiches, and living in run-down dormitories and apartments; but today's college students have more cash, credit, and digital possessions.

The college market is growing. In 2021, there were over 20 million undergraduate students enrolled in U.S. institutions of higher education. College graduates have higher-than-average lifetime earnings (compared to the general population), and they spend more money on virtually everything. Money is just one of the resources used by college students; time, energy, relationships, and space are others.

This chapter explores the subject of resources from a variety of theoretical and applied viewpoints. Resource theory analyzes, predicts, and explains the nature of resources as well as their perception, exchange, and use. During the economic recession in the United States from 2007 to 2010, stretching resources, such as having enough money for food, house payments, and gasoline, was a practical concern. The following years of recovery and pandemic response required creative use of resources. Evaluation and feedback are integral parts of the management process as Figure 4.1 shows.

## Resources Defined, Concepts, and Applications

*Resources* are what is available to be used. They are assets—anything with a real or perceived value used to attain or satisfy some need. They can be replenished or conserved. We have listed resources before in this book, but it is helpful to fit them into these categories:

- material
- family
- work
- social
- education

- technological

- health

*A resource is any entity, tangible or intangible, which contributes to the ability of an individual or family to produce valued outputs.* Some of the valued outputs may have value only for the individual or the family; other outputs may have market value.

## CASE STUDY

### Frustrated Mothers

The following was a media release received on February 6, 2021, from Ashley Bernardi at Nardi Media LLC: "I'm not fit to be a mother."

"I'm so sick of my kids!"

"All I hear all day is MOM MOM MOM MOM!"

*After almost one year spent at home, there is no question that moms are struggling mentally more than anyone else. From winter blues to navigating kids at home and attempting to work, The New York Times has even created a Primal Scream Line for mothers to call in and express (and scream in) their emotions. In fact, 69% of mothers say they've experienced adverse health effects due to worry and stress from the pandemic.*

A question for readers to ask: How will this change when the "cooping up" period is over with, and children go back to regular school hours and parents back to the office (or not). In 2030, how will time be spent and how will moms feel?

## CASE STUDY

### Issac

Should college student Issac, deep into studying for an exam, take a break?

*Just what he does during that break will determine how helpful that pause will be, a growing body of research shows. A stroll in the park could do wonders, for instance, while downing coffee could leave him just as stressed and depleted as before the break. And, sometimes, forcing oneself to simply power through mental fatigue can be more effective than pausing. Like a muscle, our brains appear to get fatigued after working for sustained periods of time, particularly if we have to concentrate intensely or deal with a repetitive task, says Michael Posner, an emeritus professor at the University of Oregon who studies attention. Taking in the sights and sounds of nature appears to be especially beneficial for our minds, researchers say.*

*Source: Wang, S. (2011, August 30). Coffee break? Walk in the park? Why unwinding is hard to do. The Wall Street Journal, p. D1.*

Not all resource use is directed toward long-term goals; some resources are used to provide for more immediate wants and needs. For example, a librarian spending twenty dollars on lunch is satisfying hunger, an immediate need. The cost of buying lunch is weighed against the time and expense involved in making and bringing a lunch to the library.

In management, time, energy, and money usually receive the most attention, and these resources will be referred to throughout this chapter and in the rest of the book. Replenishing human energy is an issue all college students and young parents face.

Resources take many forms. A sense of humor or a pleasant personality is a resource. Knowledge is a resource. A high school diploma is a resource. Everyone has a unique set of resources and uses those resources differently. Our homes are resources as well. Author David McCullough says:

> We're shaped by the buildings we live in and work in. The rooms in which things happen shape what happens in those rooms—the size of the room, the way the light falls through the windows, the prospect outside the windows. All of that bears on how people feel and how they act.
>
> (Kovach, 2003, p. 226)

**Resourcefulness** is the ability to recognize and use resources effectively. A resourceful person skillfully uses resources to cope with daily challenges. When resourceful people encounter a problem, they solve it or find a way around it, rather than be defeated by it. Resourcefulness is learned in families, schools, work situations, and social organizations. For example, children observe how their parents cope and substitute alternative sources of energy and light when the electrical power fails at home. In an office or school, if the printer breaks, the employees substitute alternative resources (e.g., use the machine in another office or go to a copy center or go digital). To balance work and family, a lot of adjustments are made as the following story shows.

Along with families, schools, and community youth organizations, such as sports teams, Scouts, 4-H, and the YMCA, encourage the development of resourcefulness in children. An individual or a family can act in

## CASE STUDY

### Double Shift

Katie Dyer Buss, of Batavia, Illinois, will be working a double shift Thursday on her seasonal job, answering consumers' cooking questions on Butterball's "Turkey Talk Line." Because she and her husband, Andrew, will miss their family's Thanksgiving Day feast at an uncle's house, they will have their own smaller holiday dinner at home after her second shift ends. Then next weekend they will gather for two separate "mini Thanksgivings" with different branches of the family. "Among all of us, we will eat a Thanksgiving dinner three times," she says. She hopes to work for Butterball, Garner, North Carolina, on Christmas Eve and Christmas Day, too, to raise cash for her and her husband's new home and other needs. About two-fifths of Americans work nontraditional hours…"

*Source: Shellenbarger, S. (2010, November 24). Remaking traditions to fit the new job. The Wall Street Journal, p. D2. Note: Shellenbarger wrote The Wall Street Journal's Work & Family Column for many years. On January 1, 2020, she answered questions on family leave, resumes, and quitting a job too soon.*

such a way as to replenish (add to) resources. An individual may also be a resource creator; learning new skills and furthering one's education are examples of resource creation according to resource-advantage theory, which will be discussed later in this chapter.

One of the most basic concepts in management is that material resources are limited and many of them get out of date, so decisions should be made about their allocation. By helping individuals learn to be more resourceful, resource management can contribute significantly to their quality of life. It is not enough to win millions of dollars, as lottery winners who have lost all their money will attest; more important to one's lifestyle in the long run is what one does with the money to retain it and make it grow.

A newspaper shut down its 1970s-era printing presses and decided to use printers in a neighboring city. Certain economies drove this decision such as lower payroll costs and cheaper production costs through economies of scale. The trade-offs were the time and energy used in transporting the newspapers to their hometown. Space at the newspaper was saved and could be rented out. Within a few months, the company that owned the newspaper office building sold it with plans to move reporters and editors into a much smaller and more economical space. Can you think of how homes are being re-shaped to go with changing family needs? Can you give examples of outdated household technologies? What are the costs and benefits of getting rid of or recycling old technologies?

## Types of Resources

Resources can be classified in several ways. One way is to categorize them as intangible or tangible. **Intangible resources** cannot be touched; examples include software, integrity, confidence, and literacy. For example, project management software used by businesses provides a level of visibility and access by other employees. **Tangible resources** are real, touchable, or capable of being appraised; some examples are offices, homes, laptops, jewelry, land, and other forms of property. Tangible resources are easier to observe and measure than intangible ones. With advances in technology, the move is toward more intangibles than tangibles. Humans will go about their daily lives surrounded by invisible technologies that record their time use, steps walked, groceries to be ordered, and so forth.

### CASE STUDY

#### Children and Teeth Brushing

Technologies exist that enable mirrors to count how much teeth brushing children do in the morning and evening and tell the children they are done. Next, that information is sent to the digital grocery list that more toothpaste should be bought and when. All of this is without visible machines or added on devices. Likewise, televisions are built into mirrors or walls and do not have to be freestanding on a shelf or stand or attached to the wall. So, the trend is for us to lead deviceless lives. What do you think of this? When you walk out of your office building or campus classroom building you can say or think now that it is your personal time and switch off certain monitors and devices as you walk or drive home or go to lunch. Would you like that?

Resources can also be classified as human or material. **Human resources** are the skills, talents, and abilities that people possess. Such resources increase through use. For example, the more a person rides a bicycle, the better bicycle rider he or she becomes. Other examples of human resources are emotion and caring.

Friendships are interesting human resources that change over time, some lasting more than others. Consider the story of nine sorority friends, who graduated from the University of Illinois and were determined to remain friends forever. Two years after they graduated, they met again.

> *They were idealistic young working women, talking excitedly about love, men and each other. They reminisced about sorority days, and vowed to remain central to each other's lives because, as one of them insisted, 'You can have the career, the family—and keep your old girlfriends, too'.*
>
> *(Zaslow, 2003, June 24, p. D1)*

What happened to them? As they turned 40, eight were still friends. All were in their first marriage. Altogether, the friends had 19 children (including three sets of twins). Five worked part-time, and six lived in the suburbs of Chicago; in fact, two lived across the street from each other.

---

### Suggested Activity

*Describe a goal you would like to accomplish in the next two weeks. Name the human and material resources you will need to achieve this goal. Say how you are going to use these resources to achieve your goal.*

---

Karen Roberto, director of the Center for Gerontology at Virginia Polytechnic Institute and State University, says, "If women are friends at 40, there's a strong likelihood they'll be life-long friends" (Zaslow, 2003, June 24, p. D1). The most likely time for women's friendships to fall off is between the ages of 25 and 40 because women are busy marrying, raising children, and establishing careers during those years. The way the former sorority sisters kept up was by scheduling play dates with their children, going on family vacations together, sending emails, calling, and celebrating one another's birthdays. What about males and friendship patterns?

> *Men tend to build friendships until about age 30, but there's often a steady fall-off after that Male friendships are more likely to be hurt by geographical moves, lifestyle changes, or differences in career trajectories. And many men turn to wives, girlfriends, sisters, or platonic female friends to share emotional issues, assuming male friends will be of little help.*
>
> *(Zaslow, 2003, June 24, p. D1)*

There are always exceptions. Jack Patton and Mike McNamara met on the first day in high school 59 years ago. They went on divergent career paths but kept up with one another and now meet several times a week for breakfast. "It really isn't the things we have in common that holds us together," says Mike, "It's the friendship we have" (Ansberry, 2019, p. A14).

Men and women often re-establish friendships or make new friendships near the retirement years because as one gets older having other people around makes him or her feel more connected. Older people may travel or do volunteer or paid work or join clubs such as garden clubs, investment clubs, golf groups, or bowling leagues. There is more time for others, for leisure, for doing part-time or seasonal work, and for learning when child-rearing and career responsibilities diminish.

Considering that time is short, how does one disentangle oneself from friendships that are no longer desirable? Studies show that only 15 percent of people say they can end a friendship, and women have a harder time with ailing relationships than do men. Moving helps, as do changing jobs and other tactics:

> *Ms. Blieszner, a Virginia Tech professor, employed what researchers call "the fade out." She limited contact with her glum friend. "I drifted away, and it worked," she says If possible, winding down a friendship by feigning a busy calendar is preferable to a dramatic confrontation, says sociologist Jan Yager. (It lessens the likelihood of a vendetta.) If the person doesn't get the message, step up the frankness of your hints.*
>
> *(Zaslow, 2003, March 6, p. D1)*

The sum total of human resources, all the capabilities, and traits that people use to achieve goals and other resources, is called **human capital**. Investing in human capital is a lifelong personal goal for many people and a professional goal for those employed in the helping professions (e.g., counseling, education, and social work). Government also invests in human capital through such programs as art and science museum programs, free school lunches, Pre-K, and Head Start. For example, the European Union (a political and economic union of member states) supports countless economic, education, and social programs and initiatives. As another example, employers and employees create value, based not only on some unit of labor in the current moment but also on their entire store of knowledge and experience— their human capital.

> *It's said that a tourist once spotted Pablo Picasso sketching in a Paris cafe and asked if he would sketch her, offering to pay him fair value. In a matter of minutes, Picasso was finished. When she asked what she owed him, Picasso told her 5,000 francs.*
> *"But it only took you a few minutes," the tourist said.*
> *"No," said Picasso, "it took me all my life."*
>
> *(Kay, 1999)*

Our knowledge-based economy is full of Picassos. What goes into a personal or professional decision is not just the time immediately absorbed. The years of experience and education a person has accrued are applied to the situation at hand.

One of the goals of education is to increase human capital. By going to college, students invest in their human capital development. When parents pay tuition fees and alumni provide scholarships, they are also investing in students' human capital.

Although everyone has human capital and the potential for growth and development, only a small percentage of this is used. Of course, no one knows exactly what this percentage is. Scientists have a long way to go before they will completely understand the boundaries and potentials of human capital.

**Material resources** include natural phenomena, such as fertile soil, petroleum, and rivers, and human-made items, such as buildings, money, and computers. Material resources decrease through use; for example, buildings deteriorate (a university building architect told the author of this book that they build new campus buildings with the expectation that they will last 40 to 50 years), money is spent, and computers break down or become outdated. Lifestyles are based on a combination of human and material resources.

**Resource stock** is the sum of readily available resources an individual possesses.

Each individual has a resource stock that she or he draws on, to make and implement decisions.

Sharing material resources, improving everyday lives.

---

### Suggested Activity

*TV psychologist and author Dr. Phillip C. McGraw (Dr. Phil) recommends doing a 10–7–5 exercise in which you write down the 10 defining moments of your life (these are experiences that helped mold you into who you are today), the 7 critical choices you have made, and the 5 pivotal people who have influenced you. Try it.*

See if any patterns emerge about your resource stock.

---

## Economics and Resources

Effective resource use can lead to enhanced chances for success. Economics is related to the creation of new products and the encouragement of entrepreneurship, investment, innovation, and invention. Leading economists emphasize the importance of private and public choice. They say an increase in the economy's resource base would expand one's ability to produce goods and services. If we had more and better resources, we could produce a greater amount of all goods and lead better lives (Gwartney et al., 2019).

Resources have the power to satisfy wants and enhance lives. Individuals use resources differently at different times in their life span. For example, parents have a difficult time understanding why their children "waste money" on candy and poor-quality toys, because the parents would make different choices. In childhood, much resource use is directed to the satisfaction of immediate personal wants and needs; thus, candy is a good purchase in the mind of a five-year-old.

This book is primarily about management, not economics. Nevertheless, most decisions are affected by economic realities. For example, many people would like to go on a trip abroad, but how many can afford to go on the spur of the moment? Everyone is a consumer, if not of trips, then of food, of shelter, and of gasoline.

Patterns in food consumption are an intriguing case in point. Over the last decade, the levels of eating out and bringing prepared foods into the home rose including more home delivery than ever before.

## CRITICAL THINKING

Would you say one out of three of your meals per day is commercially prepared? Or, would you say more? What is the typical pattern of college students when it comes to food preparation and consumption?

As Chapter 1 explained, *economics* refers to the production, development, and management of material wealth.

It is also concerned with distribution and consumption. Any economic system must address four questions:

1. What are the goods and services going to be produced?

2. How are the goods and services produced?

3. Where are goods and services produced?

4. Who will get these goods and services?

What is produced can range from ice cream to health care. The "how" includes types of factories, equipment, materials, labor, and regulations. Where things are produced is getting more complicated. Maytag dishwashers, for example, have Chinese motors and Mexican wiring but are put together in U.S. factories (Aeppel, 2003). This three-tiered, or triad, approach is increasingly used in manufacturing to keep costs down. It used to be that bulky appliances for the U.S. market were all made indigenously because they were so expensive to transport. But, as the labor and production costs became sharply lower in other countries, the expenses involved in importing parts were offset. In addition, totally produced and assembled appliances are being sold worldwide from China, South Korea, and New Zealand. The "who" can be young or old consumers, highly educated or less educated, poor or rich, housebound or frequent travelers, employed or unemployed, parents or singles with or without children or grandparents.

In economics, a central concept is **scarcity**, which means a shortage or an insufficient amount of supply. Scarcity lies at the heart of production and consumption. In the 1980s, toy stores experienced a run on Cabbage Patch dolls for Christmas. Evening news programs showed parents fighting over dolls and told of the disappointment of children who did not receive one. In this instance, the demand far outweighed the supply, creating a shortage. A year later, stores had an oversupply of the same dolls, which were no longer in great demand. In the 1990s, a similar run on another set of toys, Beanie Babies, happened with the same problems of overdemand and undersupply. In more recent years the main "toy" fights have been over electronic games and gadgets. Scarce goods are economic goods. Food, clothing, and shelter are examples of economic goods. So are parks, trees, and clean air. Scarcity can be experienced in good times and bad. Individuals and families can have abundance in one aspect of their lives and be lacking in another. Leisure is an economic good because most people feel they do not have enough leisure time.

> *Juliet Schor, author of The Overworked American, writes,*
> *When surveyed, Americans report that they have only sixteen and a half hours of leisure a week, after the obligations of job and household are taken care of. Working hours are already longer than they were forty years ago. If present trends continue, by the end of the century Americans will be spending as much time at their jobs as they did back in the nineteen twenties U.S. manufacturing employees currently work 320 more hours—the equivalent of over two months—than their counterparts in West Germany or France.*
> *(1991, pp. 1–2)*

Although this quote from Schor's book reflects the scenario years ago, it still holds true that Americans spend more time in employed work than do most Europeans, who have longer vacations and holidays. Experiments with employed time continue nationwide and worldwide. For example, the state of Utah experimented with a four-day workweek (Monday–Thursday from 7 A.M. to 6 P.M.) for state workers. This schedule was initiated for cost-saving purposes and was popular with the employees but not with the public, who wanted services on Fridays. In the fall of 2011, the state went back to a conventional five-day workweek.

Economic thinking recognizes that obtaining any scarce good involves a cost, which leads individuals and families to economizing behavior and goal setting. People use their skills, energy, and ingenuity to produce economic goods. They struggle constantly to reduce scarcity and better provide for their needs. No society has enough economic goods or resources to satisfy everyone's wants and desires, nor does any individual have enough income or wealth to satisfy her or his every want or desire. Scarcity exists when people cannot purchase everything at zero price. Theoretically even the richest person as well as the poorest in the world experience scarcity. Each person defines for himself or herself what constitutes scarcity.

## CASE STUDY

### White Noise

Sound is a resource. Nikki finds she cannot go to sleep without her soundtrack of water flowing and wind blowing in the trees, and she wonders if it would be helpful to use to relax her during the day as well. The soothing sounds of white noise once mostly for bedtime are finding a place in daytime activities.

> *When played through headphones, the sounds help people tune out chatty co-workers, pounding jackhammers and the dentist's drill. Janet Berkman, a 51 year-old retired project manager, in Toronto prefers the sounds of storms, wind, rain and running water when she is on the subway or trying to read in busy surroundings. Ms. Berkman started listening to the sounds late last year after she realized it helped her focus and concentrate. 'Life is getting noisier,' she says, and listening to these sounds 'kind of empties out my brain.' To make the soothing sounds, developers take computer-generated sounds or sounds recorded in nature and make an audio file that usually is 'looped,' or repeated.*
>
> *Source: Mir, A. (2011, August 31). To tune out distracting noises.*
> *The Wall Street Journal, p. D1.*

## Choice and Opportunity Costs

Scarcity forces people to make choices and decisions about the allocation of resources. Should a person buy a new car, or keep the old one and invest in a prepaid tuition plan? Each decision involves a cost; for example, saving for a car means, that money cannot be spent on something else. Economics assumes that people will make choices that will improve their lives. Management offers a guide for making the best choices about how to use and allocate resources such as time and money. The end goal of these choices is maximizing satisfaction.

Opportunity refers to a hoped-for favorable outcome, a chance for progress, winning, fulfillment, advancement, or action leading to the desired goal. Economics assumes one will try to maximize satisfaction by pursuing opportunities. Every choice made means that something else was given up. The highest-valued alternative that must be sacrificed to satisfy a want or attain something is called **opportunity cost**. When someone quits a paid job to stay home with children, he or she is experiencing opportunity costs. Another example is Matt Damon, star of the *Bourne Identity* and other movies, dropping out of Harvard to pursue his acting career. One way to conceptualize opportunity costs is to think of them as trade-offs. Life is full of trade-offs; choosing one activity over another involves a trade-off. For example, choosing to buy one product over another may involve a trade-off between quality and cost. To get a desired good or outcome, it is necessary to trade-off some other desired good or outcome—for example, time with friends versus time with family. Trade-offs, thus, require sacrifice—something must be given up to gain something else.

## Household Activities: Trade-Offs and Time

The basic activities of any household include many examples of resource trade-offs.

In each household, the manager (or managers) must decide how the family resources of time, labor, and money will be allocated. Among other things, the manager must decide which aspects of household production should be carried out by the unpaid work of household members or obtained through market goods and services. A restaurant meal could replace a home-cooked dinner, for example, or a gardener could be hired to care for the lawn and a housekeeper to care for the house. Often a household's trade-offs are between time and money. Obtaining goods or services from outside is usually costlier than producing them within the household.

Buying frozen pre-prepared meals at the store costs more than cooking at home and sending clothes to the laundry costs more than washing them at home. But as time becomes an increasingly scarce commodity, more families are choosing time-saving options and relying on time-saving equipment such as microwave ovens and dishwashers.

In a nationwide survey, women, 18 years or older, were polled about how they felt about cooking at home. Almost 44 percent said they "enjoy it very much," and another 35 percent said they "liked it somewhat"—that amounts to four out of five women who like to cook for themselves or their families. How often do they cook at home? A third said every day, and almost half said four to six days a week (Weber, 2000).

In recent years. the average American adult eats four or five commercially prepared meals a week and there has been an increase in prepared boxes of fresh food (to be cooked) sent to homes. The "meal box" companies are competing for subscribers, and it is yet to be seen how this will play out. "Home cooking" is being re-defined. Kitchens in suburban homes and villages occupied by families are expanding, whereas in cities, kitchens—especially those in apartments occupied by singles—are growing smaller (called small space dwellers) as a reflection of the need for less cooking:

*Like many food-obsessed New Yorkers, Tom Piscitello has grand plans for his kitchen. No, he's not installing zillions of dollars of commercial equipment. He's putting in a guest bedroom. "The room is just the perfect size for a double bed," says Mr. Piscitello, a 42-year-old bachelor who hasn't cooked on his stove in six years. A kitchen, he says, is a waste of space and money: "It's just cheaper to eat out."*

*(Bernstein, 2001, p. D1)*

A paradox is no matter how much food is prepared or how many loads of laundry you do there is still more to do. How often do you wash your underwear? How often do you wash your jeans? Many would say never about the jeans. So, doing laundry is another example of the trade-offs between time and human energy:

*The suburban home shared by Beth Sunderman, her husband, three sons, two dogs and two school-science-fair rats runs on a tight schedule. The boys are home from school at 3, in the car by 5 for baseball practice, and back home at 8:30 for showers, snacks, schoolwork and bedtime. In the background, "there is always a hum," says Ms. Sunderman. "You get sick of listening to it." It's her washer and dryer. Ms. Sunderman has figured out how to do nearly every household chore more efficiently—by microwaving dinner, for example, or having the boys unload the dishwasher. But she can't escape the 15 hours of laundry she does each week.*

*(Nelson, 2002, p. A1)*

As the family example shows, the size of the family, number and type of pets, and activity level affect load size and time spent in housework.

Procter & Gamble (consumer goods manufacturer founded in 1837) provides the following information:

- 35 billion loads of laundry are done in the United States each year.
- 1,100 loads of laundry are started every second in the United States.
- In the United States each person generates one-fourth ton of dirty clothes per year.
- *The average American woman spends 7–9 hours a week on laundry.*

The results of a 2018 Average Time Use Survey conducted by the Bureau of Labor Statistics and reported by Wayzata Home Laundry and Dry Cleaners of Minnesota found that:

- Women spend 119 minutes a week doing laundry (just 60 seconds shy of 2 hours)
- Men spend 28 minutes a week doing laundry

So, what you see here is some discrepancy over hours spent on laundry and this varies by year, data collection methods, and source. How much time do you spend a week? For some, laundry is a chore, others find it relaxing or neutral and mix it in with other household activities. Regardless of the source and despite talk of household work equality, laundry is still primarily a female chore but there is a rise in more men doing the laundry, in particular their own laundry. Newer washers use fewer gallons of water, but as washers can last 25 years, the overall change in water use will occur gradually. Tougher energy-use standards were instigated to meet U.S. federal rules. Regarding technique, L. D. Metcalfe, director of strategic global alliances at Whirlpool Corporation, says, "Their mother taught them. It's handed down like folklore from generation to generation" (Nelson, 2002, p. A1).

## Laws of Supply and Demand

Scarcity affects the price or worth of a resource. According to the law of demand, as the price of a good or service rises, the quantity demanded of that good or service falls. Conversely, as the price falls, the quantity demanded will rise. The supply and demand curve is shown in Figure 4.2.

The law of supply is the law of demand in reverse. According to the law of supply, as the supply of a good or service goes up, the price goes down. Conversely, as the supply goes down, the price goes up. Aren't more people likely to apply for a job that pays $50 an hour than for one that pays $12.00 an hour? Isn't a one-of-a-kind Louis XV desk more valuable than a mass-produced desk from a discount store? Thus, the price paid for goods and services is influenced by supply and demand. In economic theory, the right price is reached when supply and demand are equal.

When prices change radically, they are probably reacting to real or perceived changes in supply or demand. For example, if the weather is too wet and the peanut crop is destroyed, the price of peanut butter will sky-rocket. Grocery shoppers will watch for sales on peanut butter and stock up or substitute another sandwich ingredient for the high-priced peanut butter.

## Economic Well-Being

There is a large literature on wellness and sub-types of well-being (Kihm & McGregor, 2020). **Economic well–being** is the degree to which individuals and families have economic adequacy and security. It refers

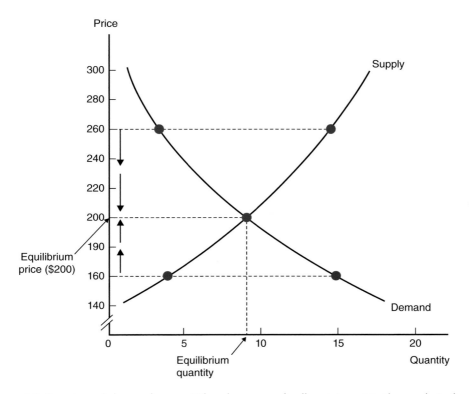

Figure 4.2 Supply and demand curve. When buyers and sellers interact in the market, the equilibrium price is at the point of intersection of the supply and demand curves.

to the desire for or extent of protection against economic risks, such as loss of employment, illness, bankruptcy, bank failures, poverty, and destitution in old age (McGregor & Goldsmith, 1998).

It is a function of many variables in combination, including monetary income, financial assets, human capital, durable goods and services, time, ability to manage, control over financial affairs and resources, values, job security, retirement plans, ability to adjust to changes, and lifestyle decisions. Economic well-being includes **economic security** referring to having a stable income or resources to support a level of living. Families and individuals define what constitutes economic security for them. The goal of reaching individual and family economic security is universal. Pulitzer Prize winning author Isabel Wilkerson points out that:

> *Human beings across time and continents are more alike than they are different. The central question about human behavior is not why do those people do this or act in that way, now or in ages past, but what is it that human beings do when faced with a given circumstance?.*
>
> *(Wilkerson, 2020, p. 387)*

## Allocation, Leveling, and Recognition of Resources

Management is the process of using resources to attain goals through planning and taking the steps necessary to meet goals. A crucial part of the management process is the allocation of resources to appropriate goals. As explained in the previous chapter, goals can be prioritized and divided into short-term, intermediate, and long-term goals. **Resource allocation** helps you get the most from available resources to tackle tasks and reach goals. In business and the field of engineering, project managers often submit resource allocation reports to higher-ups. These reports provide data on how on-schedule projects are and what they are costing in time and money. Are they within budget? In theory, resources should be allocated to meet the most important goals first; but in practice, resources are often diverted to more immediate needs or demands.

Everyone has different types and amounts of resources and different life demands. As explained in the previous chapter, many people who live from day to day do not have the luxury of allocating resources toward long-term goals. Their resources have to go to basic survival needs.

**Resource leveling** is about the techniques used to discover underuse (like clothes lying at the bottom of a closet) or inefficiency (like crock pots or backyard trampolines that have not been used in ten years) which may lead to re-use or a sense of discovery or a call to Goodwill or the Salvation Army Thrift Store. Leveling implies a sense of balance, trying to make sense of resources already owned or in place. In a business or in a non-profit organization it may mean shifting staff or employees around to where they are better suited or sending them for training to meet the changing mission of the company or organization. As an example, Emma was told her government office was shutting down and she could be sent to another city in the same state (which she loved) with a larger office or she could look elsewhere. She chose to take their offer and re-locate and continue her government job and in the long run was happy with that decision.

**Resource recognition** is the realization of the skills, talents, and materials in one's possession. Lack of resource recognition is often a problem with teenagers. As they develop their adult identity, they become more aware and more confident about their resources and how to allocate them. One of the goals of education is to help students become aware of their strengths and how to capitalize on them.

Imagine you are a creative writer in an ad agency. An example of leveling would be to have your work done in-house with a design team (writers and graphic artists) or the owner of the agency could decide to go outside for part or all of the project. In-house would save the agency time and money but draws employees away from other projects. List two situations in your experience wherein teams were discussed vs. working solo (this could be a term paper or a project in school or in an organization or in the employed world):

1.

2.

Describe the outcomes for both. Would you rather work by yourself or as part of a team?

Who should control resources? Many conflicts, from family feuds to full-scale wars, have occurred over this question. How should resources be divided? Which resources should be publicly held? Which ones should be privately held?

### Regulation of Resources

**Private resources** are owned and/or controlled by an individual, a family, or a group. **Public resources** are owned and used by all the people in a locality or country; a national park and a county-owned swimming pool are examples.

In 1776, Adam Smith published *An Inquiry into the Nature and Causes of the Wealth of Nations,* which advanced a theory justifying capitalism. He argued that with economic freedom individuals will follow their own self-interest to fulfill the needs of themselves and their families, thereby benefiting society as a whole. Smith used the term *laissez-faire* to suggest that government should leave business alone. According to him, the "invisible hand" of competition would guide the marketplace. To a certain extent, society still adheres to much of Smith's *laissez-faire* theory, but societal and economic developments in the 20th (the Depression, World Wars) and 21st centuries led many people to believe that government needs to serve as a regulator of the economy, at least to a certain degree. How much governmental regulation is desirable in such areas as health care, environmental, and welfare reform is a topic of continuing public debate.

Economic resources refer to wealth in any form, including credit, money, benefits, and stocks and bonds. Household equipment, cars, savings, property, and investments are forms of wealth, whereas commissions, wages, interest, dividends, bonuses, pensions, and royalties are forms of money income.

Wealth is a measure of what has been accumulated, whereas income is money earned or given to the recipient (e.g., child support, alimony, and government transfer payments such as welfare payments). Employee benefits are goods and services that are part of an individual's or family's resource base. When determining personal and family assets, the value of benefits should be estimated along with income and wealth. Typical employee benefits are health insurance, life insurance, paid vacations and sick leave, and retirement programs. Many employers offer cafeteria plans, which allow employees to choose the benefits they want. For example, employees may add a dental plan or a childcare assistance plan to their basic benefits package.

## Resource Attributes and a Model

In a household, someone decides what will be done; by whom it will be done; when, where, and how it will be done; and which resources will be required. The person (or persons) who do this is the manager. He or she makes decisions about how money is spent, initiates goals, sets objectives, makes plans, keeps records and timetables, makes doctor and dentist appointments, and performs a host of other tasks. The manager may be one person, or management responsibilities may be split among several people. As children grow older and more independent, they take on more responsibility for scheduling their own time, money, and work.

The characteristic way an individual or family manages resources is shaped by six forces:

1. Psychological/personality forces (including value orientations) that shape individual choices and preferences
2. Economic forces that regulate the exchange of money, energy, materials, services, and information
3. Technological forces that generate problem-solving inventions, tools, and methods
4. Sociocultural forces that regulate mores, norms, and customs
5. Political–legal forces that allocate power and provide constraining and protecting laws and regulations.
6. Health including public health services.

These forces constantly interact with each other; any decision about resource allocation will be affected by several or all of the forces. Regarding the last point, health, Lee et al. (2021) point out that a family with a child with Down syndrome has to address quality of life issues for the whole family and interact with health services (illustrated in Figure 4.3 Foa & Foa Resource Model).

Household resources can be classified as human (time, skills, and energy of members) or physical. Resources also have certain other characteristics or attributes such as their interdependence, and, sometimes, their suitability to be stored or exchanged. Examples of resources include the ability to think critically and tangible objects like books, furniture, and clothes.

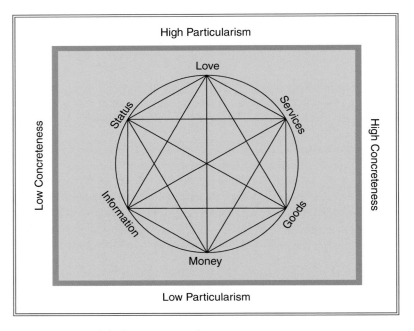

Figure 4.3 Foa & Foa Model of resource exchange.

Source: Foa, U., Converse, J., Tornblom, K., & Foa, E. (Eds.). (1993). *Resource theory: Explorations and applications*. San Diego, CA: Academic Press. Reprinted with permission of Elsevier.

Resources can also be characterized by their affective, cognitive, and psychomotor attributes. Affective attributes refer to feelings about or expressions of resource use. Expressions of love, gratitude, and caring are examples of affective attributes. Decisions regarding which resources are shared and with whom are affected by feelings. Someone is more likely to share private information with a friend, for example, than with a stranger.

Cognitive attributes refer to the knowledge aspects of resource use. Existing knowledge based on past learning and experiences is applied to new situations. The ability to synthesize (bring together information and knowledge), analyze, and evaluate new situations is a crucial part of the cognitive attribute. A resourceful person has a high degree of cognitive ability.

Psychomotor attributes refer to physical reactions to mental stimuli, such as the capacity to respond to threats or to perform work. Being able to respond quickly and appropriately to physical and mental demands is also a part of being resourceful.

Learning and teaching require all three attributes. For example, teaching others to use computers requires good hand–eye coordination (psychomotor ability), knowledge (cognitive ability), and the ability to communicate in an interesting way (affective ability). Most jobs require all three attributes (e.g., surgeon, nurse, and dentist).

Anything that can be used is a resource, but to think of resources in this way makes the concept too expansive to be very helpful. Resources can be examined in a meaningful and systematic way if they are arranged in an interactive model. *One such classic model is the Foa & Foa Resource Model, which illustrates the interdependence of resources* (Figure 4.3). Resource theory was first promulgated by Uriel Foa in 1971 and explained further in 1974 in *Social Structures of the Mind,* which he published with Edna Foa. The theory provides a framework for understanding social interactions and relationships. These relationships provide how the individuals can obtain needed resources—love, services, goods, money, information, and status—from others.

In the model, the resources at the top of the circle (love, status, and services) are more particularistic than the ones at the bottom (information, money, and goods). In other words, people are more selective when exchanging love (only with family and friends) than when exchanging money (with nearly everyone, including store clerks and bank tellers). In the model, resources close to each other on the circle are more likely to be exchanged than those opposite to each other. For example, a mother who loves her baby provides care by feeding or diapering the baby (a service). Note that love and money are directly opposite to each other.

## Resource-Advantage Theory

As mentioned earlier in the book, many disciplines have affected the study of resource management as it relates to individuals and families. When it comes to resource use, many insights can be gained from developments in marketing. This section will describe the **resource–advantage theory**, which applies entrepreneurship and leveraging to resource management.

Entrepreneurship is defined as innovative business ventures; an **entrepreneur** is a person who organizes, operates, and successfully manages a new enterprise. An entrepreneur takes advantage of opportunities and pursues the needs and wants of present and potential customers. He or she is aware that needs, wants, and circumstances change over time.

This is such a broad definition that it applies to human services or human sciences as well as to marketing and artificial intelligence. Indeed, many family and consumer scientists (or human scientists or human

ecologists) are entrepreneurs or innovators. The field is being asked to be more enterprising, to reach more people, and to be more entrepreneurial in the way family and community needs are met. Many people trained in human sciences are business owners (for example, Airbnbs or event planners such as wedding or catering businesses). They may be estate managers, owners of elder care service provider businesses, realtors or investors in real estate, and public speakers or writers—or they engage in some other form of commerce. An estate manager, for example, "can earn between $80,000 and $150,000 a year supervising household staff and financial matters for mansions of 20,000 square feet or more" or for managing multiple homes, according to Mary Starkey, president and founder of Starkey International Institute for Household Management, a Denver-based training, and placement firm (Maher, 2002, p. B8). She says her business "fields between 30 and 40 calls per week from individuals or families interested in hiring estate managers." Her business now in its 40th year is still going strong. When it comes to positions such as private estate manager, there are many people who have started in another job and had a hobby or interest that developed into a business or vocation; they are opening themselves up to more creative ways to apply the basic principles learned in management. There are temporary jobs in these estates involving light nursing activities and fill-ins that pay very well and provide housing found in estates in Europe, Asia, the United States, Canada, and the Caribbean.

Being more enterprising, more open to resource potential is a way to not only survive but also thrive. Enterprising students find out about job opportunities and internships, contact companies directly, use the career services center on campus, go on the Internet, and approach speakers at trade fairs or other industry or campus events. Jacie, a senior, told the author of this book she went to every career campus event she could. At last count, she went to eight and landed the job she wanted in the location she wanted and received a sizable signing bonus.

**Leveraging** means, most simply, doing more with less. It has to do with being more effective in the use of resources. To succeed, businesses exploit underutilized resources and skills and use creative means to contract, barter, borrow, share, rent, buy, sell, and outsource. Leveraging means to go beyond mere efficient use of resources into more creative realms where managers are not constrained by their current resource base. Through leveraging, managers do the following (Morris et al., 2002, p. 8):

- Stretch resources
- Use resources in novel ways

- Use other's people or other firms' resources

- Complement one resource with another—bringing a higher value

- Use certain resources to obtain other resources

For example, smaller businesses lack resources which larger businesses have, so smaller ones make up for the differential to compete. They could offer more personalized or unique services or products. Covel and Flandez found that

> Sales teams at small companies often are outmanned and outspent by large competitors. Whether it's perks like box seats at a professional sporting event or simply more staff and newer technology, big businesses seem to have an advantage when it comes to wooing potential clients to sign on the dotted line. But small companies often find creative ways to level the playing field.
>
> *(2008, May 29, p. B6)*

The leader in resource-advantage (R-A) theory is Shelby Hunt, an organizational theorist and professor of marketing at Texas Tech University. Hunt says that enduring research is time-consuming and programmatic in nature versus focusing on one study or article (Hunt, 2021). He and others developed the R-A theory as a knowledge discovery process central to success (Arnett et al., 2021, Hunt, 2000, 2003, 2010; Hunt & Morgan, 1996, 1997). Hunt says that R-A theory is significantly broader than, but not inconsistent with, the way we view family resource management (personal communication, April 9, 2003). He says one idea would be to consider the resource of "family competence" or "household competence"—that is, some households are superior to other households in doing things that produce valued outputs. In R-A theory,

> Competition is in an ongoing struggle among firms to achieve a comparative advantage in the marketplace. The source of advantage derives from innovation, which is viewed as endogenous to competition. Specifically, superior financial returns flow to those firms that are able either to create value more efficiently or to efficiently create more value for customers; this represents the link to entrepreneurial behavior. Entrepreneurship is the means by which firms discover, create, or assemble resource assortments that allow them to produce valued market offerings.
>
> … R-A theory defines resources broadly to include such phenomena as organizational culture, knowledge, competencies, and argues that many of these noneconomic resources are replicable rather than scarce.
>
> *(Morris et al., 2002, p. 9)*

There is no denying that the word "competition" has some negative connotations. Margaret Wheatley in *Leadership and the New Science* says,

> I crave companions, not competitors. I want people to sail with me through this puzzling and frightening world. I expect to fail at moments on this journey, to get lost—how could I not? And I expect that you too will fail. Even our voyage is cyclical—we can't help but move from old to new to old. To stay the course, we need patience, compassion, and forgiveness.
>
> *(1999, p. 174)*

Resource-advantage theory has been widely used by organizations around the world, specifically in companies in Japan and Europe (including Germany) as well as in the United States. Hunt (2003) notes that the factors affecting competition to the firm include

- Reinvestment

- Knowing self

- Adaptation

- Proactivity (moving ahead positively). And the factors external to the firm are

- Consumers (who constantly change, may not like a firm's products)

- Government actions (fair or not, more visibly successful firms are often a target)

- Competitor actions (including acquisitions, imitation of resources, substitution of resources, and major innovations in resources).

What can applied social scientists, such as students of family resource management, glean from this? For one thing, we can gain awareness, especially to stimulate thinking: Do families and households compete for scarce resources? Is the idea of "keeping up with the Joneses" an example of this? Why are neighbors often at odds with each other over property lines? Perhaps a more positive way is to ask, are families and households proactive in their approach to resource use? Are they as effective in their resource use as they can be? To take it a step further, *are some households superior to other households in doing things that produce valued outputs,* as Hunt suggests? Much of the study of resource management from the social side is about knowing self, knowing how to organize, strategize, and plan successfully—all advantages. Some people may find the competitive aspects of R–A theory objectionable, but it is presented here as a way of looking at resource management—the idea of resource creation is important as we explore the many ways individuals and families cope and how entrepreneurs act.

## Other Resource Allocation Factors: Utility and Accessibility

A basic concept in management is that resources are not useful unless they are perceived as useful. **Resource utilization** is the amount of resource capacity that tasks or jobs take. **Utility** is the value, worth, applicability, productiveness, or, simply, usefulness of a resource. Utility is in the eye of the beholder. For example, a papier-mâché castle made by a 10-year-old boy may not have any market value, but to him, it has great value and is useful in play!

Newspaper surveys have found that their readers look for news they can trust and that has utility (Ridder, 2003). If they read the local newspaper (in print or digital) and do not find anything they can use, they turn to other news sources.

---

### Suggested Activity: Stranded on a Deserted Island

If you were stranded on a deserted island (all alone) but had the following: fresh air and water, plenty of food, a cave for shelter, the clothes on your back, what five other things would you want? Your goal is to survive and be rescued.

1.

2.

3.

4.

5.

Of these five, which resource has the most utility?

Economists and anthropologists recognize different kinds of utility, such as time, place, form, and diminishing utility, and observe that various cultures view resources and utility differently. The concept of utility is learned and subjective. Time utility refers to the availability of a resource when it is needed. Arriving at a closed store with a fistful of dollars is a frustrating and useless activity. Place utility refers to a location. Form utility means that the resource is in an accessible and usable form. Diminishing utility refers to the concept that the first use is more desirable than a later use. Drinking beer is a classic example. The first sip is tastier and more satisfying than subsequent sips, and if too much is drunk, there is an undesirable negative effect.

To be useful, a resource is accessible. Cell phones make messages more accessible. As another example, money locked up in a bank vault overnight is not useful; with the invention of the automatic teller machine, however, money is accessible day and night. The advent of 24-hour grocery stores and digital shopping has also expanded accessibility. *The trend is toward greater accessibility of resources*.

## Decision-Making and Resources

In making any decision, an individual considers accessibility and other resource attributes. By finding out all the information possible about a person, place, or situation before making decisions, some potential problems can be avoided. In deciding which college to attend, for example, a student considers location, the school's reputation, tuition costs, housing options, and availability of courses.

Decision-making uses up a vital resource, however: time. A basic economic principle is that the total cost of an item is equal to its monetary cost plus its time cost.

To save time, consumers rely on established shopping behaviors (e.g., going to the same stores or online sources, buying the same brands, and going to the same barber). Archie, a single 37-year-old project manager, gets a Whole Foods delivery once a week and says that is all he needs. Consumers like Archie are open to change when they have the time, when they perceive the need for a change, or when they realize there is a disparity between what they want and what they are getting. When the motivation for change is present, new alternatives are considered. From an economic standpoint, the best alternative is the one providing the most benefit for the least cost in time, energy, and money.

## Knowledge, Education, and Health: Vital Resources

Have you ever heard the phrase "without your health you have nothing"? For centuries, scholars have debated the question of what our greatest resource is. Is it money, possessions, land, health, capacity to love, or something else? Peter Drucker (1999) says that our primary resource is knowledge, and that the leading social groups will be knowledge workers. Knowledge is gained through experience or study. Are you a born wanderer? Do you need to explore and have adventures?

E. F. Schumacher, author of *Small Is Beautiful,* says that education is the most vital of all resources. He states that "all history as well as all current experience points to the fact that it is man, not nature, who provides the primary resource: that the key factor of all economic development comes out of the mind of man" (1973, p. 79). Schumacher suggests that the development of nations should not start with goods, but with people and their education, organization, and discipline. An educated population leads to economic development through expanded work opportunities and better planning skills. Schumacher says, therefore, that investing in human capital should come before other types of investment.

## Cultural Perceptions of Resources

**Culture** is the sum of all socially transmitted behavior patterns, beliefs, arts, expectations, institutions, and all other products of human work and thought characteristic of a group, community, or population. Language, ideas, customs, taboos, codes, tools, techniques, music, rituals, and ceremonies are all part of the culture. In families, culture is transmitted from one generation to another. Members of cultural groups share common interests and goals.

Margaret Mead, Anthropologist and author of *Coming of Age in Samoa,* said,

> *Each primitive people has selected one set of human gifts, one set of human values, and fashioned for themselves an art, a social organization, a religion, which is their unique contribution to the history of the human spirit. Samoa is only one of these diverse and gracious patterns, but as the traveler who has been once from home is wiser than he who has never left his own doorstep, so a knowledge of one culture should sharpen our ability to scrutinize more steadily, to appreciate more lovingly, our own.*
>
> *(1928, p. 131)*

As explained in the previous chapter, cultural values are generally held concepts of right or wrong that are shared by members of cultural groups.

Cultures have the following six attributes:

1. They develop over time.

2. They supply boundaries or limits of acceptable behavior.

3. They provide a sense of belonging, identity, and security. Saying "I am an African American," or "I am Catholic," or "I am a member of the Smith family" implies an identification with a cultural group.

4. They are so pervasive that they are often taken for granted. Familiar traditions, such as turkey at Thanksgiving or a decorated tree at Christmas, are expressions of culture and provide a sense of continuity and identity to individual and family life.

5. They can be constrictive. In a teenage clique or gang, members may feel forced to act, dress, and think alike. Conformity to the group may take precedence over the identity of the individual.

6. They can be enriching or expressive. Culture can provide a style or a format for intellectual, social, or artistic expression.

### Suggested Activity

*Identify a shopping situation where you want to respond in a more resourceful way, where you want to change from your usual way of shopping. Create a vision of yourself in the situation. How are you responding to the products offered? What do you see? How do you feel as you make choices? What are the return policies?*

Attributes 5 and 6 may seem contradictory, but they demonstrate that culture can be many things. Culture can mold people and at the same time provide a means for individual expression. The boundaries cultures set are called **norms**. Norms, which are based on cultural values, are rules that specify, delineate, encourage, or prohibit certain behaviors in certain situations. One norm of the classroom is for students to sit in chairs at desks. Standing on the desks would go against the norm. Norms are useful because they guide behavior, letting people know how to act in given situations. Manners and etiquette are other types of norms.

Studies indicate that human **cognition** (the mental process or faculty by which knowledge is acquired) is not the same everywhere. Humans come to know things through perception, experience, reasoning, and intuition.

No one is sure why differences exist, although clues may be found in child-rearing and social practices. Richard Nisbett, in *The Geography of Thought: How Asians and Westerners Think Differently … and Why*, says that the characteristic thought processes of Asians and Westerners differ greatly (Begley, 2003). For example, if you ask which of the following two go together—a panda, a monkey, and a banana—a Japanese man is more likely to select the monkey and the banana and a British man, the panda and the monkey. Westerners are more likely to see categories (animals), whereas Asians are more likely to see relationships (monkeys eat bananas). Why is this important to know? Understanding such differences is important for cultural exchange, education, global business, and political relations. For example, Westerners may believe a deal is a deal, and Easterners may be more inclined to change agreements as conditions change: They see relationships between things. Americans are more likely to predict a rise in life quality (an optimism), whereas the Easterners realize that upward trends could very well reverse (Begley, 2003). None of this is set in stone, and many more studies are under way including more by Nisbett (Na et al., 2019).

Usually, a single dominant culture has a major influence on behavior. Citizens of a certain nation share a common language, customs, and history. Subcultures, or subsystems of the dominant culture, may have a strong influence also. These subcultures may have a religious, ethnic, political, racial, social, or economic base. Individuals can belong to a dominant culture and several subcultures at the same time.

Culture is transmitted through a variety of channels, including parents, schools, community organizations, churches, employers, and government. An individual may live and travel in many different cultures. Individuals may change their language, form of dress, or way of acting as they move between different cultural systems. They may dress and act a certain way at work and dress and act quite differently at home.

## Resources, Families, and Households

Cultural expectations of families and households may have changed more rapidly than actual behaviors. In other words, there may be a disconnect between what people are thinking is happening and what is really happening. It helps to provide evidence and watch the numbers. As the chapter opener Did You Know? shows more American women are doctors, politicians, and bosses according to the U.S. Census Bureau and this is a worldwide trend.

When sociologists and family specialists study families, they find discrepancies between ideals and behaviors when it comes to household work and child-rearing.

Many women and men in 21st-century America feel conflicts related to the "stalled revolution"—the uneven changes that have occurred in gender ideologies and the structures of work and family institutions (Gerson, 2002). Ideals about men's and women's proper roles in paid work and family life have shifted over the past half-century toward more gender-neutral, egalitarian views alongside the massive movement of women, especially mothers, into the paid labor force (Brewster & Padavic, 2000). In contrast to mothers' greater investments in market work, fathers' complementary behavior in family caregiving has not changed as quickly. Although fathers' involvement in housework and child-rearing has increased, it remains limited (Robinson & Godbey, 1999). The Covid-19 pandemic led to far more men and women **working from home (WFH)** and this led to changes in time allocation, use of space, and division of labor in homes.

To summarize, most people think things are more egalitarian, but studies show that women still do most of the household tasks and home tutoring. Child-rearing is difficult to study because it involves many aspects that are hard to measure, such as nurturing and disciplining activities. The amount of interaction time is often used as a quantitative measure.

There is no doubt that during the past 50 years, families and households have undergone vast changes. The principal developments include increased labor force participation by women, smaller households but more of them, more single-parent families, an aging population, internationalization of the economy, changes in prevailing values and attitudes, and technological innovations, especially in communications, information, and transportation.

Nearly every social and economic institution has been altered. For example, there is evidence that men are spending more time with their children. The Changing Workforce survey of 2,877 workers showed that fathers were spending a half-hour more each workday, and one more hour each day off, caring for and doing things with their children than they did in 1977 (Shellenbarger, 1998). The ongoing American Time Use Surveys conducted by the Bureau of Labor Statistics and the latest Census reveal more changes in time use.

Some solutions to family problems lie in changes in family and work policies in the private and public sectors. The Family and Medical Leave Act, enacted in 1993, is one example of a public policy designed to strengthen families. Through this act, companies with more than 50 employees must allow them (male or female) to take up to three months of unpaid leave for the birth or adoption of a child or the care of a critically ill family member. Essentially, workers will not have to choose between their job security and their family's well-being during times of family crises, emergencies, or upheaval. Besides public policies, employers, schools, friends, extended family, and community and religious organizations can also help support families. Chapter 8 discusses specific human resource problems of families, and Chapter 10 has more details about the Family and Medical Leave Act.

## Resource Forecasting

**Resource forecasting** allows for the predicting of future resource use affecting populations and countries. In 2011, China overtook the United States in terms of resource use. Over 400 million people are moving to cities in China and the strain on resources (such as increased pollution) is apparent. Of course, being the largest country in the world population-wise adds to the increased consumer demand for goods. China is a top country to watch for future developments in manufacturing and trade.

Food preferences have changed considerably with more meat in the typical Chinese diet than ever before, and meat production takes more resources than grain production.

By way of background, in the 19th century, both Canada and the United States practiced "cut and get out" forestry (Aley et al., 1999). The 20th century saw more sensitivity to the environment, but new building booms brought construction too close to shorelines, which affected barrier dunes and floodplains.

## CASE STUDY

### Tourism

For Starwood Hotels & Resorts Worldwide, growth prospects in China dwarf those in the United States, with 90 hotels slated for China compared to 33 in the United States. Starwood had the first Western-style hotel that opened in 1985, the Sheraton Great Wall in Beijing. It was built for Western travelers. The only Chinese were hotel staff.

That has all changed. CEO Frits Van Paasscjem says,

> "Today 60% of our guests are identifiably native Chinese. The next wave is Chinese travelers going to destinations outside of China ... One of the things we've had to continue to work on is adapting [to] expectations about service levels. In countries [such as China] where wages tend to be lower there tends to be. among high-end travelers a greater expectation of service. With Aloft Beijing we have room service and laundry and a greeter at the front door, typically things that an Aloft in the U.S. wouldn't have."

> Source: Berzon, A. (2011, June 6). Starwood CEO heads to China to grow brand. The Wall Street Journal, p. B6.

Cities in desert areas and even areas previously filled with brimming lakes in the United States grew beyond the capacity of the environment to sustain them. Dust bowls and soil loss resulted, as did more strain on water sources. To **consume** means to destroy, use, or expend. In the 21st century, the sustainability of our natural resources is an important issue requiring a renewed look at (1) policy, (2) conditions, (3) planning, (4) household impact, and the (5) management of ecosystems.

If this course of consumerism continues, waste management will become an increasingly difficult problem worldwide. Although some waste generation cannot be helped, much of the packaging and many of the products themselves are unnecessary. Plastic straws are being banned in some U.S. states and restaurants and school cafeterias are trying to go plastic-free. For a time, a U.S. appliance manufacturer sold $25 lamps that were designed to be discarded when the bulbs burned out. Lighters, razors, and disposable cameras are made to be used once and then thrown away. Convenience has come to be valued over cost per use and sensitivity to the environment.

From the perspective of resource conservation, is the use of disposables a good thing? Obviously, not, many people are beginning to question or reject the notion of the throwaway society as evidenced by a widespread acceptance of recycling and the increased purchasing of products made from recycled materials. Around the world there is an interest in ecotourism, more natural golf courses, and local environment-friendly residential and commercial landscaping.

## Strategy and the Conservation of Resources Theory

Underlying much of management is the concept of strategy. A **strategy** is a plan of action, a way of conducting and following through on operations. Strategy implies careful thinking out of details and consideration of outcomes. Usually, the word "strategy" is associated with military or business management operations, yet it has many applications for individual, household, and family management as well. The strategy revolves around the following questions:

- What do I want to accomplish? Or, what do I want to create?

- What is important?

- How will a plan contribute to goal achievement?

A successful resource strategy incorporates planning what is owned versus what is desired. If a couple wants to buy a new house, they save for the down payment. A person who wants to lose weight should re-evaluate eating and exercise habits to form a weight-loss strategy and then set a timetable and a goal for weight reduction. Similar plans of action or strategy could be set up to reduce household waste, unnecessary spending, or stress. Professor Stevan Hobfoll (1989, 2002) developed a new way of conceptualizing stress which he called the **Conservation of Resources Theory** although he applied this mostly to stress it can be more widely used. He speculated about how people used their resources to resist stress and increase their well-being. In his resource-oriented model, he proposed that people "strive to retain, protect, and build resources and that what is threatening to them is the potential or actual loss of these valued resources" (1989, p. 513). As a strategy, someone may invest their time and energy, two important resources to obtain the highly prized resources of power and money. Factors that will weigh in this pursuit are objects, conditions, personal characteristics such as ambition and drive, and social networks. Resources can be valued in their own right such as health or they can be a means to a goal such as gaining more social support (for a politician this would be votes), money, or position/title.

## SUMMARY

Many new terms were introduced in this chapter to provide a deeper understanding of various aspects of resource management from resource leveling to forecasting. Risk, scarcity, opportunity costs, satisfaction, and attributes of resources were covered in this chapter. Resources are central to the management process and to the pursuit of human satisfaction and happiness. They can be restored and replenished. Without human and material resources, there would be nothing to manage. We would not exist. For individuals, families, and communities, resources are the essential means of exchange (internal and external). Resources are used to attain goals and meet demands. We vary in our resource capacity and our reaction to what we have. An individual may feel his or her life is abundant whereas another person with the same set of resources might feel deprived.

For families and households, resource use provides a living space and a lifestyle around which individual and family needs are met. Knowledge, integrity, education, and health are vital resources, especially during times of turmoil, doubt, and fear.

The Foa & Foa Resource Model illustrates the interchangeability of resources including services that are vital for families. From the fields of marketing and organizational behavior, resource-advantage theory explores the benefits of entrepreneurship and leveraging (doing more with less) and adds to our understanding of resource creation.

Resources can be looked at from many viewpoints, as resource use underlies all human endeavors. Owing to the scarcity of resources, an individual tries to make choices that maximize benefits and minimize costs. The way a person goes about doing so is culturally defined. Studies indicate that human cognition is not the same everywhere: cultural differences in thought processes or perceptions exist. An ongoing issue is the division of labor in the home for both housework and child-rearing.

Management provides a way of looking at problems in an organized, rational, and yet compassionate manner. Material goods and wealth are not the sole determinants of happiness. Wealth and goods can help assure an easier life, but not necessarily a happy one. The elusive nature of happiness and the search to find the right life balance underlie the study of management.

Individuals make decisions purposefully, always seeking to better their circumstances. This constant striving drives people to seek better solutions and explains the "why" behind much of human behavior.

The next chapter takes the resource knowledge and puts it together in the decision-making process. Later in the book, the resource concepts covered in the present chapter will be applied to specific environmental and time and stress management problems. As introduced in this chapter, Professor Stevan Hobfoll created a stress model called the model of conservation of resources. This model is based on the supposition that people try to retain and protect valued resources from perceived loss.

## KEY TERMS

cognition
Conservation of Resources
  Theory
consume
economic security (and
  insecurity)
economic well-being
entrepreneurs
human capital
human resources
intangible resources

integrity
leveraging material
  resources
norms
opportunity cost
private resources
public resources
resource allocation
Resource-Advantage
  Theory
resource capacity

resource leveling
resource forecasting
resourcefulness
resource stock
scarcity
social entrepreneurship
strategy
sustainability
tangible resources
utility
working from home (WFH)

## REVIEW QUESTIONS

1. Economic security is an issue of family, community, and societal concern. How does economic security fit into the general category of well-being?

2. Regarding friendships as a human resource, how many friends do you have? How long have you had them? Do you think certain friendships will continue over the next five years? Which ones and why?

3. What does the story about Picasso and the tourist illustrate about the nature of human capital? Name one skill, talent, or ability that you have built up over the years.

4. What does the Foa & Foa Model illustrate?

5. What role does strategy play in resource management? A college senior, Alison, figures that she will need a minimum starting salary of $45,000 to live in Charleston, South Carolina, based on a budget she has developed. She wants to live in Charleston because she has friends there, but she is having trouble finding a job because she goes to school 500 miles away. Alison's main expense will be at least $1,000 a month for rent. If you were Alison, what would you do next? In other words, what would your strategy be?

## REFERENCES

Aeppel, T. (2003, October 6). Three countries, one dishwasher. *The Wall Street Journal*, p. B1.
Aley, J., Burch, W., Conover, B., & Field, D. (1999). *Ecosystem management*. Philadelphia, PA: Taylor & Francis.

Ansberry, C. (March 21, 2019). Deep, long lasting friendships are more common among women than men. *The Wall Street Journal*, A14.

Arnett, D., Dass, M., & Bhoumik, K. (January 29, 2021). Re-examining market structures: Resource-Advantage theory and the market offering ecosystem perspective. *Journal of Global Scholars of Marketing Science*. Published online.

Begley, S. (2003, March 28). East vs. west: One sees the big picture, the other is focused. *The Wall Street Journal*, p. D1.

Behnke, A., MacDermid, S., Anderson, J., & Weiss, H. (2010). Ethnic variations in the connection between work- induced family separation and turn over intent. *Journal of Family Issues, 31*(5), 626–655.

Bernstein, E. (2001, January 12). The disappearing kitchen. *The Wall Street Journal*, p. D1.

Brewster, K., & Padavic, I. (2000). Change in gender ideology, 1977–1996: The contributions of intracohort change and population turnover. *Journal of Marriage and the Family, 62*, 477–487.

Covel, S., & Flandez, R. (2008, May 29). Three strategies to get customers to say "Yes." *The Wall Street Journal*, p. B6.

Drucker, P. (1999). *Management challenges for the 21st century*. New York: Harper.

Foa, U. (1971). Interpersonal and economic resources. *Science, 171*, 347.

Foa, U., Converse, J., Tornblom, K., & Foa, E. (Eds.). (1993). *Resource theory: Explorations and applications*. San Diego, CA: Academic Press.

Foa, U., & Foa, E. (1974). *Societal structures of the mind*. Springfield, IL: Charles C. Thomas.

Gerson, K. (2002). Moral dilemmas, moral strategies, and the transformation of gender: Lessons from two generations of work and family change. *Gender & Society, 16*, 8–28.

Gwartney, J., Strup, R., Sobel, R., & Macpherson, D. (2019). *Macroeconomics: Private and public* (16th ed.). Ohio: Cengage.

Hobfoll, S. (1989). Conservation of resources: A new attempt at conceptualizing stress. *The American Psychologist, 44*, 513–524.

Hobfoll, S. (2002). Social and psychological resources and adaptation. *Review of General Psychology, 6*, 307–324.

Hunt, S. D. (2000). *A general theory of competition*. Thousand Oaks, CA: Sage.

Hunt, S. D. (2003). *Resource-advantage theory: Toward a general theory of marketing*. Presentation at Association of Marketing Theory and Practice Annual Meeting, Hilton Head, SC.

Hunt, S. (2010). *Marketing theory: Foundations, controversy, strategy, resource-advantage theory*. Armonk, NY: M.E. Sharpe, Inc.

Hunt, S. (January 28, 2021). The nature and origins of impactful research in marketing. *Journal of Global Scholars of Marketing Science*. Published online.

Hunt, S. D., & Morgan, R. (1996). The resource-advantage theory of competition: Dynamics, path dependencies and evolutionary dimensions. *Journal of Marketing, 60*(4), 107–113.

Hunt, S. D., & Morgan, R. (1997). Resource-advantage theory: A snake swallowing its tail or a general theory of competition. *Journal of Marketing, 61*(4), 74–82.

Kay, I. (1999, January 18). Don't devalue human capital. *The Wall Street Journal*.

Kihm, H., & McGregor, S. (2020). Wellness and well-being: A decade review of AAFCS journals (2009–2019). *Journal of Family and Consumer Science, 112*(3), 11–22.

Kovach, R. (2003). Conversation with David McCullough. In E. Abbe (Ed.), *The writer's handbook*. Boston, MA: Writer.

Lee, A., Knafl, K., & Van Riper, M. (2021). Family variables and quality of life in children with down syndrome: A scoping review. *International Journal of Environmental Research and Public Health, 18*(2), 419.

Maher, K. (2002, August 27). The jungle: Focus on retirement, pay and getting ahead. *The Wall Street Journal*, p. B8.

McGregor, S., & Goldsmith, E. (1998, Summer). Expanding our understanding of quality of life, standard of living, and well-being. *Journal of Family and Consumer Science, 22*, 2–6.

Mead, M. (1928). *Coming of age in Samoa*. New York: Blue Ribbon Books.

Morris, M., Schindehutte, M., & LaForge, R. (2002). Entrepreneurial marketing: A construct for integrating emerging entrepreneurship and marketing perspectives. *Journal of Marketing Theory and Practice, 10*(2), 1–19.

Na, J., Grossmann, I., Varnum, M., Karaswa, M., Cho, Y., Kitayama, S., & Nisbett, R. (First published December 23, 2019). Culture and personality revisited: Behavioral profiles and within-person stability in interdependent (vs. independent) social orientation and holistic (vs. analytic) cognitive style. *Journal of Personality*. Published online.

Nelson, E. (2002, May 16). In doing laundry, Americans cling to outmoded ways. *The Wall Street Journal*, pp. A1, A10.

Noe, R.A., Hollenbeck, J.R., Gerhart, B., and P. M. Wright (2019) *Human resource management: Gaining a competitive advantage*. Hoboken, NJ: Pearson.

Peterson, C., & Seligman, M. (2004). *Character strengths and virtues: A handbook and classification.* Oxford: Oxford University Press.

Ridder, P. A. (2003, October 7). *Newspapers Today.* Speech at Florida State University, College of Business Speaker Series.

Robinson, J., & Godbey, G. (1999). *Time for life: The surprising ways Americans use their time.* University Park, PA: Pennsylvania State University Press.

Samimi, E., & Sydow, J. (July 2, 2020). Human resource management in project-based organizations: Revisiting the permanency assumption. *The International Journal of Human Resource Management, 32*(1), 49–83.

Schor, J. B. (1991). *The overworked American: The unexpected decline of leisure.* New York: Basic Books.

Schumacher, E. F. (1973). *Small is beautiful.* New York: Harper & Row.

Shellenbarger, S. (1998, April 15). Researchers are amazed: Men are helping more. *The Wall Street Journal*, p. B1.

Smith, A. (1973). *An inquiry into the nature and causes of the wealth of nations.* New York: Modern Library (Original work published 1776.)

Wayzatalaundry (April 4, 2018). *By the numbers: How much time we spend doing the laundry.* Minnesota: Published online.

Weber, N. (2000, July 27). Who's in the kitchen? It's mom as always. *The Wall Street Journal*, p. A23.

Wheatley, M. (1999). *Leadership and the new science: Discovering order in a chaotic world* (2nd ed.). San Francisco, CA: Berrett-Koehler.

Wilkerson, I. (2020). *Caste: The origins of our discontents.* New York: Random House.

Zaslow, J. (2003, June 24). Staying in touch: One more thing that women are better at than men. *The Wall Street Journal*, p. D1.

Zaslow, J. (2003, March 6). Making friends isn't so hard—it's getting rid of them that's tough. *The Wall Street Journal*, p. D1.

Zuboff, S., & Maxmin, J. (2002). *The support economy.* New York: Viking.

Chapter **5**

# Decision-Making and Problem Solving

DOI: 10.4324/9781003166740-5

... Over 35 million Americans move every year.

... Over ¾ of American small businesses operate out of a home and have a sole employee.

**CASE STUDY**

### Google Founders: Decision Makers

Rapid decisions moved Google founders, Sergey Brin and Larry Page, from pursuing their Ph.D.s in computer science at Stanford University to being listed in the top 20 of U.S. billionaires by 2005. They left Stanford in 1998 to form Google. Along the way, early employees became rich as well. Susan Wojcicki is best known for renting out her Menlo Park, California, garage to them when they were just getting started. She became their 18th employee and now is senior vice president at the search engine company. She oversees all their advertising, which means nearly all their revenue. Talk about opportunity, talk about getting in on the ground floor, the world of technology is filled with such stories. Larry's father was a computer science professor at Michigan State University, so there is a family story in here as well.

On a more conventional level than the Google founders' case study, consider the managing technology situation at the Person household.

> *Trevor Person of Alexandria, VA, has what he calls a "squeaky clean" inbox: He keeps just 10 to 25 emails in it at a time. His wife has about 16,000 emails in her inbox. Many people consider crowded inboxes to be status symbols, says Mr. Person. But he suspects that his wife's hoarding of emails actually exacerbates his compulsion to be an inbox neatnick. He has reached a realization: His wife feels "validated" by a jammed inbox. He feels validated by an empty one.*
>
> *(Zaslow, 2006, p. D1)*

How do you manage your inbox? Are you more like Mr. Person or Mrs. Person? Or, somewhere in between? Making decisions and solving problems are the subjects of this chapter. Mrs. Person does not see her 16,000 emails as a problem, but Mr. Person does. If hoarding is a problem, here are some tips for paring down inboxes:

- Send less email (the theory is that less will be returned)

- Have a system for deleting emails, such as deleting all emails over a month old. Some companies and government agencies have this as a rule; emails more than a month old are automatically deleted.

- Old emails may be kept for sentimental reasons (old lovers, former friends) or to keep a track record of work correspondence. It is up to you to decide when it is time to let go.

Managing inboxes is mostly an individual decision, but here is an example of family decision-making:

> *Imagine volunteering for a lifestyle that forces you to give up nearly half your household income, sell your toys, forgo vacations of the kind your friends enjoy, and work as if three or four lives depended on*

*your next paycheck. That's the world of many solo-breadwinner dads. Bo Rogers, Mesa, Ariz., sold his motorcycle and gave up his gym membership, workouts and racquetball games after he and his wife Melanie had the first of their two children, so she could quit her job. Now, Bo, who is paid solely on commission as a heating and airconditioning salesman, feels pressured and stressed.*

(Shellenbarger, 2003, p. D1)

These are the kinds of decisions that young families make. Reversing a trend of nearly a quarter of a century, more families are opting to have a stay-at-home mother. According to the Bureau of Labor Statistics, the number of such families is increasing from a low of 35.2 percent in 1994. It is too early to declare it a lasting trend, but the numbers seem to indicate a move toward more stay-at-home moms or dads at least when their children are small.

The work from home trend (WFH) mentioned in the last chapter certainly fits here as well. As of this writing, most CEOs in New York City were telling their high-rise office building employees to work from home until September 2021 and at that time the policy would be re-evaluated. Readers of this book will have the advantage of hindsight about WFH trends and the work-family decisions therein.

Here is a way one young mother handles her work and family situation: As a hairdresser, she stays home Sunday–Wednesday to take care of her two-year-old son. She works at the salon Thursday–Saturday. On Thursdays, her sister takes care of the boy, on Fridays her in-laws take over, and on Saturdays, her husband is home from his accounting job and takes care of their son. This is an example of patching together child-care and work arrangements, which is very common.

This combining of care or blurring of the work and personal worlds is not just a social trend but also a response to technological change. Computers and the Internet have made it more difficult to determine who is employed for pay "outside the home" and who is not, because so much can be done from any location. So, it is difficult to know whether the stay-at-home mothers are completely unemployed or are working part-time from home, although in the case of the hairdresser, she goes to a salon to meet her clients and also enjoys the camaraderie of being there during the busiest days. As in the Did You Know? at the start of the chapter, three-fourths of American small businesses are in the home and have one employee according to the U.S. Census Bureau. One woman was told by her doctor to stay in bed for the last three months of her pregnancy. At that time, she was writing her dissertation, so her husband, a librarian, brought her books and articles for her research and she typed away happily, and the baby was fine.

Not everyone is choosing to have children—another trend to consider that may seem to contradict the one just described:

*Anne Hare and her husband made a momentous decision three years ago: They would not have children. It's not that they don't like kids, she says. They simply don't want to alter the lifestyle they enjoy. "With kids, especially young kids, infants and toddlers, you really can't do the active stuff we like to do," said Hare, 43, a fitness-program coordinator from Gainesville, Ga. Hare is among 26.7 million women ages 15 to 44 who are childless, according to new Census Bureau data. The number of women forgoing or putting off mother-hood—nearly 44 percent—has grown nearly 10 percent since 1990, when 24.3 million were in that class.*

(Armas, 2003, p. 8A)

Besides personal choice, some influences on this trend include more women going to college and entering the workforce, then delaying motherhood or deciding not to have children; more families choosing adoption; changes in societal attitudes; more reliable forms of birth control and health and economic factors.

Decision-making was defined in Chapter one as choosing between two or more alternatives. One of the hardest decisions to make is whether to move or stay put. Good decisions meet several criteria. As the previous examples show, they should be acceptable to the persons most involved. Acceptance signifies that the key players in the decision acknowledge that it is reasonable and workable. Decisions also should include *quality*, *flexibility*, and *clarity*.

---

### CRITICAL THINKING

**Moving**

Relocating for work or school is a major life change. According to the U.S. Census Bureau, over 35 million Americans move each year. This involves:

- Time
- Expense
- Planning
- Emotions

Describe a recent move you made or that your family made and address the four points above: time, expense, planning, and emotions. How many people were involved with the move and what were their roles? Did anyone have a truck?

---

Quality means that the decision meets some standard, objective, or goal. If the decision does not do so, or if someone involved in the decision does not accept it, then the decision is likely to be ineffective. Thus, family decisions are more likely to succeed if they have the support of family members and are linked to an agreed-upon standard, objective, or goal. In other words, in families, as in other groups, decisions that are co-created have a better chance of success than those that are individually created.

Flexibility means that the decision should not only be appropriate to the situation but also be adjustable if the situation changes. For example, becoming engaged to be married may seem like a good decision under certain circumstances, but when attitudes or circumstances change (e.g., compatibility wanes, expectations change, another love interest comes into the picture), the couple may choose to break the engagement or wait a while.

Clarity refers to how clear the decision is. Vague decisions do not work because they lack definition and commitment.

Regarding fathers working and mothers staying at home (or vice versa), David Stevenson, an art director for a New York publishing house, who works so that his wife, Noreen, a former media buyer, can stay home with their two small children, says,

> You both commit not just to the marriage, but to this structure that you've set up—this notion that she will stay at home, I'll work, and we're in it together. You gain a certain strength from that—the stamina to press on when things get crazy.

> (Shellenbarger, 2003, p. D1)

He adds that they remind themselves that the rough spots are only temporary and try to laugh about the problems, knowing they will pass. Another employed dad says, "If they want me to work longer hours, I work longer hours. If they want me to travel, I travel" (Shellenbarger, 2003, p. D1).

## Decisions Defined and Explored

**Decisions** are conclusions or judgments about some issue or matter. Management recognizes the influence of values on decisions and the role of goals in providing direction to decisions. The decision process begins when a thing or a change is desired. **Decision-making**, the process of making a choice between two or more alternatives, is an integral part of the overall management process (see Figure 5.1). In systems terminology, decision-making is part of the transformation process that incorporates various inputs and culminates in outputs. Sometimes the process involves negotiation or bargaining with others. The previous chapters on values, attitudes, goals, and resources have laid the groundwork for a full discussion of the decision-making process.

This chapter begins by explaining the relationship between decision-making and management, and then describes the steps in decision-making. Decision models and rules are examined, along with their application to individuals and families. The chapter explains the difference between decision-making and problem solving and explores the concepts of risk and uncertainty.

### Decision-Making as Part of Management

Why do we spend so much of our time being active? Why don't we just lie in bed and watch the world go by? *Because when it comes to living, we are programmed as humans to be active, to accomplish things, and to find out what is going on. We want to make an impact.* An active life requires decisions and effort. We want smooth relationships. People want to have something they do not have, and they are drawn to make decisions and plans to bridge the gap between what is and what could be. Decisions are not all cold and analytical, emotions like **anticipation** (expectations, anxieties) play a part.

Decision-making is essential to maintaining and improving life conditions, including home design. Values guide decisions. A decision maker values an issue or a life condition enough to spend time thinking about it. Values also influence decision makers because they realize that the choices they make will have positive or negative consequences. For example, "design decisions influence how comfortably we live and how much it costs us to attain the lifestyle we aspire to, and thus deserve extraordinary consideration" (Chiras, 2000, p. 2).

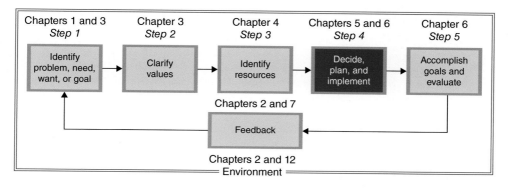

Figure 5.1  The management process.

Decisions vary in intensity and importance. The purpose and content of decisions are related to other aspects of the management process, such as planning, implementing, and cost–benefit analysis. For example, each decision entails a cost in time and energy and sometimes money. Decision makers try to minimize the costs and maximize the benefits of a decision.

This desire to maximize positive outcomes and to minimize mistakes motivates individuals to make the best decisions that they can. Curiously, the plots of many movies, books, and television shows feature individuals who do just the opposite. These characters make decisions that minimize positive outcomes and maximize mistakes. Watching the characters disentangle themselves from their mistakes and put their lives back in order can be interesting and enlightening. Observing how others make decisions and solve problems on television, especially on dating, game, and reality shows like *Survivor*, can help sharpen an individual's own decision-making and problem-solving skills.

Decision situations present both problems and opportunities. In analyzing decision situations, individuals appraise alternatives and identify useful information and resources. An important resource is time. An individual or family can save time by eliminating alternatives that do not fit their values. Why waste time considering an alternative that is morally or ethically unacceptable? Ralph Keeney (1988), a values expert, suggests that if "we begin with values," then "we might not even think of situations as decision problems, but rather as decision opportunities": "Periodically, we might examine achievement on the basis of our values and ask, 'can we do better?'" (p. 466).

As it is value-based, decision-making is highly personalized. An individual's personality and usual modes of thinking and acting influence the way he or she makes decisions. Mood affects decision-making ability and styles. There is one's personal way of reacting to moods and we can "catch" the mood of others. If someone is upset at work and yelling, then others can pick up on the mood or situation and the whole workplace can operate under a shadow or a cloud. Each person's decision-making also tends to follow a pattern, with successful decisions being repeated. The characteristic way that a person makes decisions is called his or her **decision-making style.** Thus, decision-making styles are affected by individuals' values, knowledge, ability, and motivation. The types of decisions made, the speed at which decisions are made, and the amount of information gathered before making a decision are all part of a person's decision-making style. For example, some individuals are quick deciders; others are more deliberate. Differences in style are also evident in the evaluation phase at the end of the decision-making process. Some individuals look back and agonize over every thought and action, whereas others think about past decisions only for a few minutes and then go on.

Some decision styles are irritating. Suppose you go to a meeting, and the boss asks for your opinion. You invest time and effort and present an opinion only to find out that the decision had already been made. How would you feel? Similarly, in a family how would children feel after being asked for their opinion if they find out that their parents had already made the decision?

> It has been said that deciders suffer alone, but those who avoid decisions make others also suffer.
> It's easier to extract a wisdom tooth than a decision from some managers—even if there aren't any wisdom teeth to pull. When David Turnley was a technical writer for a financial-data software company, his boss made so few decisions that no one ever knew what she wanted. Yet, she had to be involved in every decision that she never made. Mr. Turnley himself had some direct reports, and rather than try to explain what he thought she might want done, he frequently let them work directly with her, he says. Her indecision stemmed from a fear of being viewed in a poor light from above. But it was contagious and nerve-racking to those below.
>
> (Sandberg, 2008, p. B1)

**CRITICAL THINKING**

Have you ever been in a similar situation as Mr. Turnley, working with an indecisive boss? Do you think indecision in an employment situation can stem from being viewed in a poor light? In a home setting, a couple or family may never entertain because they feel their house or entertaining skills are not good enough. Would that be understood or not by their friends?

## The Brain and Steps in Decision-Making

Thinking, planning, and deciding are some of the most advanced functions of human (and presumably many others) brains. Although people sometimes react in stereotyped ways to the environment, the human brain has an astonishing capacity to respond flexibly and to anticipate the outcome of behavior.

(Purvis et al., 2019)

Decision-making involves a series of steps that result in the choice of an alternative. The process can be long or short. This section will discuss the parts of a decision plan which involve several steps. However, research shows that the brain appears to make up its mind 10 seconds before a person becomes conscious of a decision.

> *"We think our decisions are conscious," said neuroscientist John-Dylan Haynes at the Bernstein Center for Computational Neuroscience in Berlin, who is pioneering this research. "But these data show that consciousness is just the tip of the iceberg. This doesn't rule out free will but it does make it implausible."…*
> *In ways we are only beginning to understand, the synapses and neurons in the human nervous system work in concert to perceive the world around them, to learn from their perceptions.*
>
> *(Hotz, 2008, p. A9)*

Dr. Haynes and other scientists have found that regions involved in decision-making become active up to 10 seconds before subjects in experiments consciously chose a button to press. This was done with brain scans. About 70 percent of the time the researchers could tell ahead of time what button would be pushed. Dr. Haynes says, "It's quite eerie."

When the process is long and complicated and includes a sequence of intentions, it constitutes a **decision plan**. Decision plans can be specific or general. For example, Zak's plan to buy his favorite cereal and milk at the grocery store this afternoon is a specific decision plan. Jen's plan to buy a car next year is a general decision plan because she does not know what kind of car she wants or exactly when she will buy it. Because decision-making is a transformation process, the inputs, such as how much money and time Zak and Jen have, will affect the decisions.

Decision makers use different strategies for different situations. The strategy selected will depend on (1) the decision involved, (2) the characteristics of the decision task, and (3) the decision-making style of the decider. In general, though, most people follow six steps in making decisions. The acronym DECIDE (also called the DECIDE Model) provides an easy way to remember these steps (Malhotra, 1991).

- **D**efine the decision (distill and define the issue).

- **E**stimate resources.

- Consider alternatives.

- Imagine (visualize) the consequences of alternative courses of action.

- Develop an action plan and implement it.

- Evaluate the decision.

These steps are discussed in detail in the next paragraphs.

**Step 1: Define the Decision**. In defining the decision, the individual takes into account the purpose of the needed behavior, and the relevant background information—what information is needed, and how it will be used in decision-making. In so doing, the layers of a potential decision are peeled back to reveal the core of the situation. Once the decision has been defined, the decision maker can move on to the next step.

**Step 2: Estimate the Resources Needed**. The decision maker decides what resources will be needed. As discussed in the previous chapter, resources include time, energy, money, information, and anything else that is useful to the decision and subsequent planning and action. The number of possible alternatives is limited by the resources possessed or anticipated in the future. A ski vacation in Utah is out of the question if a person has only a hundred dollars to spend.

**Step 3: Consider Alternatives**. What we are looking for in this step is compatibility or congruency. Given the limitations on their resources, individuals seldom consider all alternatives. For example, test-driving every car on the market before choosing one would be impractical. Instead, a prospective buyer would eliminate many models because of their cost, accessibility, features, and style or because they did not suit her tastes and preferences; then she would test-drive just a few cars. Narrowing down the possibilities to one or two acceptable alternatives is an important part of the decision process.

**Step 4: Imagine the Consequences of Alternative Courses of Action**. Imagining or thinking through the most likely alternatives is the next step. Envisioning what will happen if a certain decision is made is so enjoyable or distasteful that some people get stuck on this step. For example, in consumer decision-making, this step involves **prepurchase expectations**, which are beliefs about the anticipated performance of a product or service. Before buying, people usually try to imagine how much pleasure or pain they will get from the purchase.

**Step 5: Develop an Action Plan and Implement It**. Once an alternative is selected, a course of action, a strategy, must be developed. Putting the decision into action is called *implementation*. During this step, the decision maker monitors the progress made and evaluates how well implementation is proceeding. Are things going as planned? On schedule? Are adjustments to the plan necessary?

**Step 6: Evaluate the Decision**. After the process has been completed, the decision maker looks back to judge how successful the decision was. "Did I make the right decision?" "Should I have done something else?" In consumer decision-making, this step involves **postpurchase dissonance**. After a major purchase, such as a car, the buyer is likely to seek some reinforcement for the decision by talking to other owners of the same model or reading advertisements or news stories about the car. Being assured that the right decision was made reduces doubt or anxiety. The right decision will also be reinforced if, for example, the bag boy or girl at the grocery store says, "hey, cool car!" when loading groceries in the car's trunk.

### Caitlin's Dilemma

Caitlin is a senior at Celia K. Ward High School. She is finding it difficult to decide what to do after graduation. Two of her choices are going to the nearby community college or finding a full-time job. Her friends have told her about jobs in local businesses or she can stay working at the yogurt shop if she wants to and eventually move up to Assistant Manager. Her mother would like her to go to college and feels it is a mistake if she falls out of the habit of studying. If she goes to college she will have to stay at home because she cannot afford her own apartment unless she takes on a lot more hours at the yogurt shop or elsewhere. What values are Caitlin and her mother expressing? What alternatives should she explore further? What decision would you make if you were Caitlin?

## How could the DECIDE model help her?

The chances of post purchase dissonance, at least the doubt about whether one made the right decision or not, are reduced if there were no or few alternatives to start with. Let us say someone moves to a town, and there is only one house for sale. The person will buy it and not look back, because there were no other choices at that time. However, if confronted with dozens of choices, that homebuyer is more likely to wonder whether he or she made the best decision.

## Self-Doubt, Self-Ambivalence, and Decision-Making

Every now and then we do not feel like doing much. We are simply not inspired. A soccer team member and college senior named Anna said by March she was tired of school and just wanted to graduate and get on with it. She had accepted a good job in a location she wanted.

### Suggested Activity

*Boredom or Blocked?*

Anna was expressing boredom. A friend of hers named Jake said he felt blocked, He could not seem to get ahead and get the job he wanted. Have you ever felt bored or blocked? What changes did you make to get re-energized? Explain the circumstances or life stage you were in.

In a connected realm, self-perceptions including self-doubt and self-ambivalence affect decision–making. *Self-doubt* can cloud the ability to make decisions or to accept decisions once made. Some people have no choice but to make fast decisions.

> *Presidents and parents, after all, are expected to make crucial decisions on a dime. Doctors are being asked to save lives, and graduate students to know how Aristotle's conception of virtue differed from Acquinas's conception of—uh-oh. Who's kidding whom?*
>
> *(Carey, 2008, p. D5)*

Social psychologists have studied the imposter phenomenon since the 1970s when they found that high-achieving women often suspected that they really weren't as capable as others thought, that they had fooled everybody, and that their success was owing to some kind of luck rather than achievement. Since other studies have documented the same effect in adolescents and adults, male and female, of all ages. Perhaps this is a reflection of being an anxious or self-critical person or a societal stereotype, or it could be the phenomenon that limits them or affects their future goals.

Questionnaires to determine self-doubt and feeling like an imposter may ask respondents to react to the following types of statements:

- If I receive a promotion or award, I am hesitant to tell others.

- I give the impression that I am more competent than I am.

- Sometimes I feel my success hinges more on luck than anything else.

Respondents indicate whether they would strongly agree or disagree with these statements, or whether they would fit somewhere in the middle. In a Wake Forest University survey, psychologists investigating students' test-taking behavior found that students who scored high on an imposter scale would tell the experimenter that they would do poorly on the upcoming test of intellectual and social skills: "Sure enough, the self-styled imposters predicted that they would do poorly" (Carey, 2008, p. D5). They went in with a mindset of self-doubt. But, when they were asked privately—anonymously, as they were told—how they thought they did on the test, the same people rated themselves higher. This shows that what other people think—in this case, the experimenters—affects this "I am an imposter" response. It would seem all this is rather negative and holding people back, but other studies have shown that it appears not to be paralyzing. In one study, college women who scored high on anxiety level and imposter feelings as they approached academic goals also scored high on a desire to show others that they could do better. In other words, they had the competitive spirit and tried harder (Carey, 2008). So, self-doubt is a factor to consider in decision-making, but it does not appear to hold individuals back, and emotionally well-adapted people also feel self-doubt some of the time.

Self-ambivalence has not been as thoroughly researched as self-doubt but what **self-ambivalence** refers to is uncertainty or indecisiveness as to what course to follow (e.g., what to purchase) because of a conflicted attitude toward the self. A self-ambivalent person may report that they are torn between different parts of their personality and thus this interferes with decision-making. It may exist because there are conflicting thoughts or feelings about a person, an object, a product, or an idea. Someone would be said to be ambivalent and self-ambivalence may be linked to low self-esteem (Riketta & Ziegler, 2006). In the workplace, an employee could feel ambivalent about a boss or a coworker or they could feel ambivalent about themselves.

## Models, Rules, and Utility

Although change is a necessary part of life, many individuals are reluctant to change and continue to follow existing patterns of behavior. Adhering to established goals and objectives and the plans, strategies, and tactics devised for attaining those goals is referred to as "maintaining the status quo." According to Silver and Mitchell (1990), when faced with uncertain alternatives, most people tend to stay with the status quo. But if a person, family, or organization wants to change or to understand the mechanisms of decision-making, they may find decision-making models useful. These models assume that rational decision makers will evaluate alternatives and then make the best possible choice.

As decision-making is an abstract concept, decision-making models are useful because they provide a way to visualize how the elements of a decision interact. Figure 5.2 shows examples of the central-satellite and

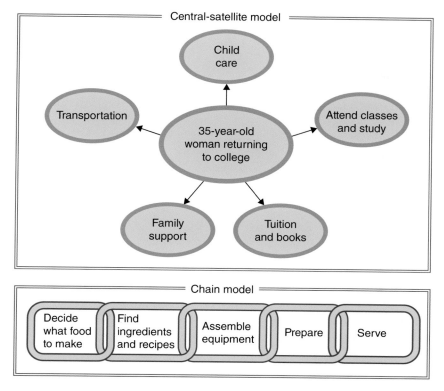

Figure 5.2 Examples of decision situations using the central-satellite and chain models.

chain models. In the central-satellite model, a central decision is surrounded by decisions that are offshoots of the central decision. In the chain model, each decision builds on the previous one, forming a sequence of decisions, such as the steps involved in preparing a meal. The chain model is appropriate for smaller, systematic decisions, whereas the central-satellite model is suitable for larger, more complicated situations. Businesses such as catering services or conference- and wedding-planning services use both models to organize receptions, banquets, meetings, and events.

## Suggested Activity

Put one example of your own decisions in each of the central-satellite and chain models. Remember that the chain model is sequential, and the other has a large decision in the middle surrounded by smaller decisions or categories of decisions.

As illustrated in Figure 5.3, values lie at the base of decisions. Two other concepts in management, resources and goals, also play important roles. Decision trees are not only used in business strategy sessions but they can also be used by individuals in personal and professional decision-making. The model shows that people select alternatives based on their goals and perception of available resources and those values underlie decisions. A more usual method used by many individuals in choosing between alternatives (e.g., whether to move to one locale or another, which job offer to select) is to make a pros-and-cons list.

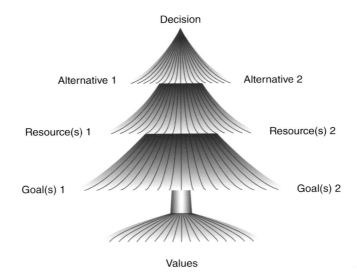

Figure 5.3 A decision tree: Values lie at the root of all decisions.

### Decision Rules

Models operate on certain principles or rules of logic. **Decision rules** are principles that guide decision-making. One decision rule is that decision makers will seek the best outcomes. Another decision rule is that individuals will try to use their time to their best advantage, wasting as little as possible. However, this varies by situation and by culture. A study of Chinese students found that they were not very time-conscious, but they were quite price- and quality-conscious (Fan & Xiao, 1998). In a variety of fields, algorithms, models, and scales have been developed to measure improvement in decision rules (Zabinski & Zielosko, 2021).

### Utility and Bounded Rationality

One of the most important decision rules is the necessity to optimize the utility, or the usefulness, of decisions. The concept of utility underlies much of the study of economics and is strongly associated with the study of management. A starting point is a purely rational model (*homo economicus*) that optimizes the exchange of resources for goods (Goldsmith, 2017).

Rational decision makers are assumed to seek the maximum utility (satisfaction) from the decisions they make. Furthermore, the utility concept focuses on how choices are made and on how that process can be improved. Herbert Simon (1955) proposed the concept of **bounded rationality** meaning that individuals seek to make rational decisions but are faced with limitations such as:

- Limited attention
- Limited interest
- Limited energy
- Limited information
- Limited time

These limitations may be internal or external, they can lessen or stall a person's ability to make decisions.

For example, consumers may have limited information; they may not be aware of all the alternatives that exist. The next section on reference groups provides one explanation of why individuals may have only partial knowledge.

## Reference Groups

Decisions have histories. For example, Allison orders pepperoni pizza because she knows from experience that she likes it. Besides past experiences, past and present relationships affect an individual's decision-making. If Allison begins dating Trae, who is a vegetarian, and he prefers pizza with cheese, green peppers, olives, and onions, they have several options: They can order two pizzas, or they can order a pizza that is half pepperoni and half vegetarian, or Allison can learn to skip the pepperoni. This simple joint decision-making situation illustrates how many choices exist and how individual tastes and relationships affect those choices.

The people who influence an individual or provide guidance or advice are members of that person's **reference groups**. Trae and Allison are members of each other's reference groups. Figure 5.4 illustrates a typical college student's reference group. An individual does not have to be present in person or geographically close to being a member of a reference group. A person is considered part of a reference group if the memory of his or her values and attitudes affect someone's decision-making. For example, Rob, a newspaper editor, has not seen his high school journalism teacher for many years, but she is still a member of Rob's reference group because he thinks of her often and when he makes decisions about his paper, he remembers what she taught him.

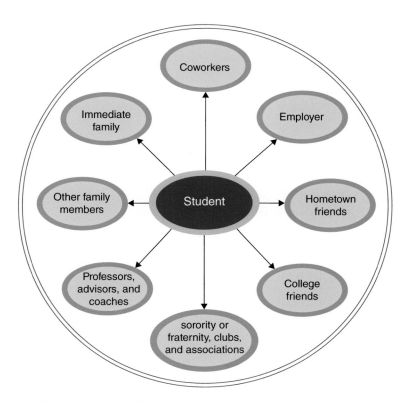

Figure 5.4  A college student's reference groups.

Reference groups can be divided into two types, primary and secondary, depending on the amount of contact the individual has with a person or group. An individual has regular contact with the people in primary reference groups; family, coworkers, and close friends fall into this category. Secondary reference groups include those individuals and groups with whom contact is infrequent, such as distant relatives, organizations, and professional associations. The influence of reference groups on decision-making and behavior cannot be overestimated.

## Personal Decision-Making

Although all decisions—from which car to buy to whether to smoke—are influenced by others, *ultimately the individual is responsible for his or her own decisions*. Individuals begin to learn decision-making at an early age.

During the socialization process, children are given the opportunity to make choices and to learn from decision situations. By the time they become adults, most people assume themselves to be competent decision makers. In reality, this assumption may fall short if there is a difference between the actual and perceived quality of decisions. The actual quality of decisions refers to what is truly happening. The perceived quality of decisions refers to what an individual thinks is happening in the decision process. Potentially, then, people can deceive themselves into thinking that a poor decision is a good one or at least an acceptable one. Experience and improved decision-making skills can narrow the gap between the perceived and the actual.

Decision-making style is affected not only by an individual's socialization, knowledge, ability, and motivation, but also by his or her personality traits such as compulsiveness, open-mindedness, innovativeness, self-confidence, and courage.

Another factor that can affect decision-making style is self-esteem. Low self-esteem often results in indecisiveness. In other words, someone who is unsure of his or her ability to make sound decisions is likely to be indecisive. Indecisiveness can be a major problem for individuals, families, and organizations. Possible causes of indecisiveness are

- Stress
- Ill health, depression
- Fear of the unknown
- Procrastination
- Fear of making a wrong decision or mistake
- Fear of acting on one's own
- Lack of "good judgment"
- Feeling overwhelmed
- Fear of taking responsibility or standing alone on an issue
- Overdependency on other people's opinions

### Indecisiveness and the Peter Principle

Some individuals always seem to be indecisive; others are indecisive only in certain situations. Lawrence J. Peter and Raymond Hall (1969) proposed an explanation for indecisive behavior. They suggested that people may reach a point in their work at which they can no longer successfully function.

Specifically, Peter and Hall said that people tend to be promoted until they reach a level beyond their competence—a point at which they can no longer make and implement effective decisions. They called this phenomenon the **Peter Principle**. Even though the Peter Principle is pervasive, it can be avoided by fitting the right person to the right job and by making performance expectations clear from the outset. Examples of this principle can be found in a variety of organizations and settings, including the home and the community.

## Avoiding Decisions

Being indecisive is linked to another decision-making phenomenon—avoidance. Passing the decision-making buck is a way individuals avoid decisions.

Avoidance typically results in statements such as the following:

- "I thought you were going to settle this."
- "That's not my job."
- "You're the boss. Don't ask me what I think, just tell me what to do."
- "Why is it up to me?"

Failure to assign clear responsibility for tasks in the home or at the office may lead to some of these remarks. When chores are not assigned and the dishes are not done or the garbage is not taken out, family members may all say, "That's not my job." Parents and children need to have a clear understanding of who will do what in the home. At the same time, tasks, chores, and duties are not static. Nonperformance may also result because goals and priorities have changed; there are no longer commonly held beliefs about how to act. There is a fundamental difference between compliance and commitment. Complying means going along with some idea or action. Commitment signifies belief in an idea or action. High-commitment workplaces and households are more productive and are more comfortable places to be.

## Decidophobia

Not making decisions is also a decision. **Decidophobia** is the fear of making decisions, specifically the fear of failure. Sometimes the problem stems from being overwhelmed with choices. Sherwin Williams has over 1,400 different colors of paint; how could a decidophobic choose given that array of choices?

Here is another example of consumer overload: In one year U.S. manufacturers came up with 150 new deodorant and antiperspirant products, whereas a few years earlier the number was only 20 (Forelle, 2003). Think of all the kinds of toothpaste and other personal care products there are.

A person with decidophobia is frozen and cannot choose an alternative or form a plan of action. Decido-phobics see decisions as problems, not as opportunities.

Here are a few ways decidophobics can break out of the nondecisive mode:

- Use the decision-making models and the DECIDE acronym, which divide decisions into parts. Often it is easier to break a big decision into smaller parts and make those decisions first.
- Moderate expectations.
- Start each day with the single most important task and complete it. If you are a list maker, do not have more than five items on the list; that way you are more likely to get everything done and feel a greater sense of accomplishment and control.

- Step back from the decision; sleep on it overnight; give it some time. You might even think about a vacation or a change of scene to get perspective.

- Talk it over with caring friends or family members, go online to explore houses in a new location. Perhaps there is a fresh approach, an avenue you have not considered, or perhaps researching or talking about it will at least offer the chance to clarify what you really want. Mark Twain said, "I can teach anybody how to get what they want out of life. The problem is that I can't find anybody who can tell me what they want."

Decidophobia is a learned behavior; it is a type of helplessness (dependency on others), and it is a form of perfectionism. So that they do not establish this pattern, young children should be given the opportunity to experience decision-making (e.g., choosing the red shirt or the blue one, the apple or the orange) in order to develop decision-making skills. Setting up a variety of activity areas or learning centers in preschools or kindergartens is an excellent way to provide children with early decision-making experiences. During free time, the children can choose the activity they want to engage in, whom they want to be with, and what they want to accomplish—all useful life preparation skills.

### Intuition

Intuition plays a role in decision-making. One way to increase decision-making acumen is to trust feelings and instincts (Kaye, 1996). A multistep approach, like the one mentioned earlier in the chapter, is not always necessary to select a course of action.

Sometimes decisions are influenced by **intuition**, or the sense of knowing what to do without going through rational processes. For example, Brad accompanies Kirsten, his wife, to two out-of-state interviews. Brad likes one state but cannot stand the other, although he cannot give specific reasons for his feelings. Fortunately, Kirsten gets offers from both employers, and she and Brad choose the state they both feel good about.

As it is difficult to measure, intuition is one of the least scientific aspects of decision-making, but it is still recognized as a factor. As another example, when making an offer on a house, should you pay the suggested price of $350,000 or should you offer $340,000 or $365,000 (going higher anticipating a bidding war)? What does your research of house prices in the area (price per square foot and so forth) tell you? What does your intuition tell you? Should you go lower and hope the homeowner takes the offer, but be ready to renegotiate if necessary? Or should you offer the suggested price? Sizing up situations involves rational decision-making and information seeking as well as intuition.

## Family Decision-Making, Including Division of Household Work

The main difference between personal and family decision-making is that the latter is more complex. The more people involved in making a decision or potentially affected by a decision, the more complex the decision process is likely to be. Consider, for example, how difficult it can be for five coworkers to decide where to go to lunch or for a group of friends to decide which movie to see and when to meet. Similar difficulties can arise in a family setting, depending on how many family members are involved in each decision. In a simple situation, only one family member makes a decision and everyone else simply accepts whatever that person decides. For example, one person may suggest going to the school basketball game, and the entire family agrees and accepts the decision. In a more complex situation, each family member may suggest a different course of action. Instead of agreeing to go to the basketball game together, the family members go off in different directions: The teenage son goes to the basketball game, the mother to a Parent Teachers Association (PTA) meeting, the daughter to a friend's house, and the father to a club meeting. If the family has only one car, this is going to be a difficult situation to manage. These examples illustrate two of the questions raised by family decision-making: Will the manager alone make most of the decisions, or does each family member have a say? Are most decisions made smoothly, or is conflict more usual?

Homes and families can provide a base for cooperation, coordination, and negotiation. Family members bring to this base their own needs and wants, but sometimes one family member's needs and wants conflict with another's. When conflict rather than harmony is characteristic of the home or family, the decision-making process becomes more complicated.

A practical example of a family decision-making situation is who does what in the home. Women are more likely to do the laundry, prepare meals, shop for groceries, clean the house, care for children, buy gifts, make decisions about furniture and decoration, and wash dishes. Men are more likely to do yard work, grill food outside, make minor home repairs, and keep the car in good condition. Although this is changing in recent years, with men doing more than in the past in childcare and food preparation, according to American Time Use Surveys conducted by the Bureau of Labor Statistics women still spend more time in housework than men (more details in the next section). Men do more housework when they live alone but spend fewer hours on it when they live with their parents (Baxter et al., 2010, p. 1523). A fundamental question in marriage and family research is whether cohabitating before marriage affects or leads to more equalitarian housework arrangements. The answer is yes. Equal division of labor is well established before marriage in previously cohabitating couples (Baxter et al., 2010, p. 1506).

## CASE STUDY

### The Beckers

*With three kids and a home business, and a disabled mother living with her, Kristen Becker often lets the dishes and laundry pile up. 'I am very comfortable with chaos,' she says. Her husband isn't. He organizes his clothing by type, color and pattern, alphabetizes his CD collection and keeps rubber gloves in his car for unexpected spills, she says. He sometimes goads his wife into being neater by making only his half of their king-size bed, heaping the magazines and bills splayed across the kitchen counter into teetering stacks, or moving his wife's mound of laundry across the room. Mrs. Becker retaliates by letting her messes pile up even higher.*

*Source: Bernstein, E. (2009, November 17). When Mr. Clean meets Ms. Messy. The Wall Street Journal, p. D1.*

Coltrane (1989) concluded: "Generally, mothers were more likely than fathers to act as managers for cooking, cleaning, and childcare, but over half of the couples showed responsibility in all areas" (p. 480).

For information on time use in the home please refer to the American Time Use Survey taken by the Bureau of Labor Statistics. The Survey measures the amount of time people spend doing various activities, such as paid work, childcare, eldercare, volunteering, and socializing. Here are some of the results:

- Less time continues to be spent overall on housework. *(American households spent 30 percent less time on household chores than in 1965.)*

- More husband participation, with fathers tripling their domestic work since 1965.

- More shared responsibility in the home. To break this down further,

- In 1965, married women spent an average of 33.9 hours per week on housework; in 1995, the number was 19.4. In the latest American Time Use Survey, mothers with full-time jobs and young children have the largest total workload, logging five more hours a week than dads.

- For married men, the average weekly housework hours in 1965 were 4.7 compared to 10.4 in 1995 (Bianchi et al., 2000).

- 16 percent of the U.S. population or 40.4 million, provide unpaid eldercare. On a given day, 26 percent of eldercare providers spend an average of 3.4 hours in eldercare activities.

---

## CRITICAL THINKING

### What do you think of the following passage?

*Like Betty Friedan's unhappy housewife, today's working dad may be suffering from gender idealization, which pressures him to be both breadwinner and involved father. "There are many reasons to be concerned about men," says Ellen Galinksy of the Families and Work Institute, which just released a report concluding that long hours at work and the blurring of boundaries between the office and home are to blame. That study and other new research show how much dads are feeling squeezed.*

In a survey by the Families and Work Institute at Boston College, 57 percent of men agreed with this statement "in the past three months, I have not been able to get everything done each day because of my job."

Source: Konigsberg, R. D. (2011, April 8). Chore Wars. *TIME*, p. 48.

---

## CRITICAL THINKING

### Food for Thought

In recent times in the United States more men are cooking inside the home (according to one survey, fathers participate in nearly one-third of the time that a family spends cooking) and more women are joining the ranks of professional chefs, historically a male domain. The White House chef under the George W. Bush and Barack Obama administrations is a woman following on many previous administrations with male chefs. Why are more men cooking at home and more women becoming chefs? Any thoughts? Could it be as cultural theorists surmise that Americans are making more and better food choices whether they dine in or dine out and that there is a higher interest in food quality and preparation regardless of gender or place?

Source: Baksian, A., Jr. (2011, May 21–22). Guys and dollops.
*The Wall Street Journal*, p. C7.

In more and more households, partners share activities such as childcare and grocery shopping. For example, one study revealed that in 14 percent of the households men and women share grocery-shopping duties. In response to this and the research finding that men are more likely to buy whatever they see, Audrey Guskey, a marketing professor at Duquesne University, says that stores court men with end-of-aisle displays of chips, beer, and soft drinks— items men commonly buy on impulse (Meyer, 1997). Who shops and who does what in the home continue to be contested terrains. Household members need to have clean living quarters, food to eat, and clean clothes to wear; and if there are children, they need to be cared for. Homes that are clean and neat seem calmer, roomier, and healthier. The critical thinking exercise brings up the point that men are cooking more in the home and this surge is part of a more balanced division of labor in most households.

Individuals who live together decide on a standard of living, a comfort zone they can live with. Possible solutions to getting the housework done more efficiently and more pleasantly include

- Trying teamwork: picking a half hour or an hour a week to clean together, perhaps Saturday morning, and concentrating on tasks like mopping floors and cleaning bathrooms.

- Keeping communication lines open, renegotiating tasks.

- Not wearing shoes in the house and having a place or box near each entry door where shoes can be kept; or at least having outside mats to rub shoes on before entering the house.

- Having a chart or checklist; rewards for completion of tasks.

- Buying the latest equipment and products to make the tasks easier. For a two-story house, putting cleaning supplies and vacuum cleaners on each floor; in a multi-bathroom house, putting cleaning supplies in each bathroom.

- Multitasking by listening to music while cleaning; folding laundry while watching television.

- Using time fragments, cleaning for short periods of time, and taking a break.

- Cleaning from the top down. As the dust settles, starting at the top of a bookshelf or ceiling fan and working downward.

- Using space fragments, dividing a room into areas, and cleaning one area at a time.

- Attacking the area that is most visually bothersome first.

- Reading labels, making sure the products are being used correctly. If the label says to leave the product on for ten minutes for best results, do it.

- Hiring help, outsourcing. At what point does doing so make financial sense, figuring in satisfaction and pleasure?

Economists are looking at household production in a fresh way. A finding of the Bureau of Labor Statistics in its 2003 Survey was that if a person's income is more than $44,000 a year, it makes more financial sense to hire a lawn service than do it oneself (assuming the person dislikes this task). Tasks can be divided into two categories: consumption, which is enjoyable, and production, which feels more like work. Take gardening, for example. Is that work or leisure? If a person hates it, then hiring someone to do it makes sense.

## Families, Environment, and the Elbing Model

According to Marshall (1991), "the future of American families is not predetermined, but depends heavily on the choices made by families, employers and especially public institutions" (p. 5). Consequently,

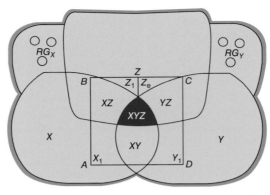

ABCD: Family decision situation
X: Family member
Y: Family member
Z: Environment
RG$_X$: Reference group for member X
RG$_Y$: Reference group for member Y
XZ: Alternatives perceived by X
  and acceptable in existing
  environment
YZ: Alternatives perceived by Y
  and acceptable in existing
  environment

XY: Alternatives perceived by both
  X and Y but not acceptable in
  the environment
X$_1$ and Y$_1$: Alternatives perceived by one
  member but not acceptable in
  the environment
Z$_1$ and Z$_e$: Acceptable alternatives not
  perceived by family members
Solution
  XYZ: Alternatives perceived by both
  family members and acceptable
  in the environment

Figure 5.5 The Elbing model for viewing alternatives in a family decision situation.

Source: A. Elbing (1978). *Behavioral decision organisations* (1st ed.) © 1978. Electronically reproduced by permission of Pearson Education, Inc., Upper Saddle River, NJ.

family decision-making is strongly influenced by families' awareness of what is feasible and acceptable in the environment in which they live. Alvar Elbing developed a model (see Figure 5.5) to illustrate how two individuals in a family make decisions given their reference groups, perceived and acceptable alternatives, and environmental constraints. The Elbing model demonstrates that decisions are influenced by many factors and considerations. The *XYZ* section in the center of the model represents the solution because alternatives in this section are perceived by both individuals and are acceptable in the environment.

### Accommodation, Consensual Decision-Making, and De Facto Decision-Making

There are three types or styles of family decision-making: accommodation, consensual, and de facto. In **accommodation**, the family reaches an agreement by accepting the point of view of the dominant person. Power is a critical factor in accommodation. In **consensual decision-making**, the family reaches an agreement equally acceptable to all individuals involved. De **facto decision-making** is characterized by a lack of dissent rather than by active assent. It usually occurs when no one really cares about the outcome of the decision. For instance, no one in a family may have strong feelings about which television show to watch.

Families in which husband and wife share equally in making most of the decisions are **syncratic**. Families can also be **autonomic**, which means that an equal number of decisions are made independently by each spouse. Thus, in syncratic families, the decisions are shared, whereas in autonomic families the spouses make an equal number of separate decisions. Usually, the partner who commands the greater amount of material resources will achieve greater power in spousal decision-making.

Studies suggest that decision-making power in couples is also related to their emotional interdependence, and ability to control each other and influence the ultimate degree of consensus. Godwin and Scanzoni (1989) theorized that the more modern the gender role preference of the wife, the less control her husband had. Their study of 188 married couples revealed that socio-emotional factors affected both coerciveness and control. Specifically, emotional bonding contributes to spouses' influence over each other and to whether they reach a consensus.

> Spouses who reached higher levels of consensus included husbands who had patterns of previous coopera-
> tiveness during conflict situations, more equitable economic resources of the spouses, wives whose commu-
> nication styles were less coercive, and spouses who demonstrated greater control (p. 943).

Further, husbands who were committed to the marital relationship were more likely to respond positively to their wives' suggestions, ideas, and directives.

In conclusion, it appears that explaining decision-making power (who decides what and to what extent) in couples is more complicated than simply looking at who contributes the greater amount of resources. Other important factors include how close to each other the husband and wife are, the degree of cooperativeness and communication between them, and their levels of education. For example, a study in India revealed that literate women participated to a greater extent in decisions related to health and size of the family, their children's education, and the family's investments and savings than did illiterate women (Mohanty, 1996).

The types of decision-making discussed so far have involved couple-centered families in which most decisions are made by the spouses. An alternate scenario is child-centered families in which the children make or affect most of the decisions of the whole family, including the choice of foods, television shows, and activities. The difference between couple-centered and child-centered families is not absolute, for children affect decisions in every family. Nevertheless, children do have more influence in some families than in others. The next section will discuss family and couple consumer decision-making and show how children influence parents' buying behaviors.

## Consumer Decision-Making in Families

Scottish professors Monika Schroder and Sabine McKinnon (2007), researching the learning of good judgment in key consumer skills, found that the family in its primary role as creator of values was considered the most important agent in the consumer education process. Why? Because, according to the subjects in the study, the family establishes a routine pattern of decision-making. The researchers say that families are value transmitters. Other sources of consumer skill development were the support from social networks in the wider community and real-life experience through trial and error.

Consumer decision-making in the marketplace provides an excellent illustration of family decision-making. How one family spends money may not seem that important, but, collectively, family spending amounts to billions of dollars when multiplied across all families. For this reason, manufacturers and advertisers spend enormous amounts of money on consumer research to determine who decides what in a family and why. In short, consumer decision-making is big business and the driving force behind the well-being of national economies.

Complicating this interaction between consumers and the marketplace is a level of distrust. After interviewing people of several nationalities Schroder and McKinnon said:

> *Respondents made it clear that the balance between consumer and producer power was not entirely satisfactory. It emerged that the motives of marketers are still viewed with suspicion. Respondents spoke of "being manipulated" (Danish female; Polish male), "ripped off" (French female), "falling into traps" (Spanish female), "don't believe all you see on TV" (Spanish female).*
>
> (Schroder & McKinnon, 2007, p. 158)

Families must decide (1) what to buy, (2) where to shop, (3) how much to pay, (4) when to buy, and (5) who should buy. The first decision is the most important families have to decide whether they want to buy something. This decision leads to the other four. Deciding what to buy is more difficult when there are countless brands to consider. For example, 34 new food products are launched each day in the United States (Mogelonsky, 1998). Let us consider the "when-to-buy" decision.

*There are life change points that radically affect consumption.* Examples are marriage, having children, moving, getting a job, getting a dog, buying a house, empty nesting, and retiring. Newlyweds are the ultimate consumers, buying more in the first six months of marriage than a settled household does in five years (Ellison & Tejada, 2003). The publisher of *Bride's* and *Modern Bride* magazines estimates that U.S. newlyweds spend $70 billion establishing their households. In many instances, life changes stimulate gift buying as well as buying for one's own consumption. A growing number of couples register for gifts and some ask for gift cards. One couple who were remodeling their house and with the wife-to-be aged 43 asked for Home Depot gift cards and received nearly $3,500, enough for plenty of remodeling supplies and a few appliances (Shellenbarger, 2011, p. D2). Jason, a 24-year-old recent college graduate, explained it this way:

> *All my friends are getting married. So my girlfriend and I are buying wedding gifts every couple of months and we've never done this before. We try to find something that fits what they like to do, like cooking, keeping in mind what their style is—contemporary or traditional.*
>
> Cueing into life changes has not escaped marketers:
>
> Corporate marketers say certain points in life make consumers especially vulnerable to sales pitches, with the soon-to-be-married often being the most susceptible.
>
> It's a time when they aren't just choosing a marriage partner, but also are making brand decisions about toothpaste, detergent, and appliances that could last even longer. Unless a couple has been living together for years, weddings represent a moment when two sets of habits and brand preferences meet and usually only one survives.
>
> (Ellison & Tejada, 2003, p. B1)

The family decision-making process involves eight distinct roles (see Table 5.1). These roles provide a way of conceptualizing how family members make decisions—some family members are buyers, others are users, still others influencers, and so on. For example, a mother or father buys disposable diapers, the baby uses them, and the parent who changes the diaper disposes of it.

Purchases based on family decision-making can involve conflict. For example, a couple may differ about the amount of money to spend, the brand or type of good to buy, the stores to shop in, or who should do the purchasing. Conflict will decrease if the couple agrees on which goals are desirable.

Purchasing decisions may be influenced by a number of variables, including reference groups, work life, leisure pursuits, culture, subculture, social class, stage in the life cycle, mobility, geographical

**Table 5.1** Eight Roles in Family Decision-Making

There are eight distinct roles in the family decision-making process. A look at these provides further insight into how family members interact in their various consumption-related roles:

1. *Influencers:* Family member(s) who provide information to other members about a product or service

2. *Gatekeepers:* Family member(s) who control the flow of information about a product or service into the family

3. *Deciders:* Family member(s) with the power to determine unilaterally or jointly whether or not to purchase a specific product or service

4. *Buyers:* Family member(s) who make the actual purchase of a particular product or service

5. *Preparers:* Family member(s) who transform the product into a form suitable for consumption by other family members

6. *Users:* Family member(s) who use or consume a particular product or service

7. *Maintainers:* Family member(s) who service or repair the product so that it will provide continued satisfaction

8. *Disposers:* Family member(s) who initiate or carry out the disposal or discontinuation of a particular product or service. The number and identity of the family members who fill these roles vary from family to family and product to product.

Source: Leon G. Schiffman & Leslie Lazar Kanuk, *Consumer behavior,* 4th ed. © 1991 Pearson Education (Englewood Cliffs, NJ: Prentice-Hall, 1991), p. 341. Note: Newer editions cover similar material. Adapted with permission of Pearson Education.

location, and children. For instance, young families with preschool children have different buying decisions to make than do retired couples. Joint decision-making is most common among the middle class, whereas autonomous decision-making is most likely in the upper and lower classes (Loudon & Della Bitta, 1988).

Children have a significant influence on their parents' buying habits. A study by Infocus Environmental of Princeton, New Jersey, found that one-third of parents changed their shopping habits because of environmental information their children gave them. When questioned about their information source, the children said they learned about the environment in school. The study reported in *Marketing News* (Schlossberg, 1992) indicated that children affect their parents' buying and shopping habits by encouraging them to purchase items in recyclable packaging (24 percent) and to avoid products in containers that are not recyclable or biodegradable (17 percent). The study concluded that children are influencing far more than the foods their parents purchase and that they are having a significant impact on their parents' environmental consciousness.

## Getting Out of the House

This section will discuss ways to get out of the house including nearby places to visit all the way to camping and the great outdoors as in the critical thinking exercise.

## CRITICAL THINKING

### Camping Requires Planning

Read the following and react. Have you ever gone camping? What are the pros and cons?

*Coronavirus has wreaked havoc over the past year, infecting 106.8 million people and killing 2.3 million worldwide – with 27.1 million of those cases and 466,000 of the deaths coming from the United States. By any measure things have been disrupted. How COVID-19 will ultimately affect 2021 is unknown. But a few things are evident. Corona fatigue is real. People are ready to get out and on the move. And for more than 50 million Americans, that likely means a camping trip. Camping – be it via a tent in the backcountry or a hard-sided camper parked in full-facility campsite that mirrors many comforts of home is a relatively pandemic friendly activity…Plan early and reserve a camping spot as soon as possible…'Summer holiday weekends are the busiest and we encourage folks to make reservations as soon as possible to secure their spot,' said Scott Simpson, division director for South Dakota state parks and recreation.*

Source: Gary Garth (2021, February 10). "Planning to go camping this spring or summer? Think about booking your spot now." *USA Today*. Published online.

Much of the previous coverage in this chapter has been on children, consumption, and household responsibilities, joint decision-making, and so on. It is also important to note that before the pandemic a surprising number of Americans were less home-focused: They were getting out of the house—going to gyms, parties, restaurants, clubs, and bookstores—and the critical thinking exercise shows they are ready to get out of the house again.

**Hatching** is a term that refers to local-area nesting, finding other places outside of the work or the home where one can spend time. Hatching has also been called "the third space" and is epitomized by television shows like *Cheers* and *Friends* and *How I Met Your Mother*.

People are looking for ways to reconnect through discussion groups, book clubs, investment clubs, and running or biking groups. They may purposely move to planned urban developments (PUDs) with built-in activities and town centers with shops and restaurants, join bird-watching groups, or take up gardening, hiking, photography, golfing, and boating. Some of these activities are free and some are costly. For individuals returning to outdoor activities, a whole range of equipment, clothing, and accessories is necessary. Thinking about what to buy is part of the anticipation, the build-up, and makes participants happy.

### Suggested Activity

*Is there a life change point in your immediate future? If so, how will it affect your consumption patterns?*

*Getting out there is not cheap:*

> *"My husband would have a stroke if he knew the price," says Jackie Menefee, who put together a quick weekend getaway to get out for a change. The couple made a two-hour drive from their Chesapeake, Va., home to an ocean resort for two nights of pampering and a Champagne tasting. They had a good time, but she wasn't prepared for a $600 tab. "It was very upscale," she says.*

*(Daspin, 2003, p. W9)*

That is not a lot of money compared to $30,000 a night for a deluxe suite in Dubai or in Abu Dhabi. On a more modest scale, one homeowner drives to Home Depot or Lowe's, home supply stores, every Saturday morning and looks around and drinks a cup of coffee. Others go to flea markets, garage sales, or antiquing with friends.

> *Carol Ann Band says she's just happy to get out. Between growing her own vegetables for home-made baby food to weekly Sunday dinner with relatives, all the time spent in the house is wearing thin. Now the 37-yearold in Fresno, Calif. has hit on a way to relieve the stress: she joined a women's tennis league and is playing a couple times a week. "I'm a better mom for the hours I take away," she says.*

*(Daspin, 2003, p. W9)*

As we know from systems theory, activities wax, and wane. There is a cyclical, or wavelike, effect, and the nesting instinct is not immune from it. It goes in and out of fashion. In the early 1980s the term "cocooning" caught on big as people retreated from the dirt and crime of the streets into their safe and warm homes. Baby boomers were buying their first homes and filling them up with oversized furniture and children's equipment. The phrase "couch potato" emerged. September 11, 2001, brought another wave of nesting behavior as families drew closer in the wake of the terrorist attacks and the uncertainty that followed. National, international, and business travel slowed. Huge sectional sofas began to sell as well as home theaters costing $100,000 or more. At the same time, sociologists noticed a countermovement of people looking for companionship and connectedness outside the home. Church attendance and library use went up for a while. Perhaps there is a limit to how much home and family time is possible. "You can only cocoon with your family for so long," says Erik Gordon, a professor who studies consumer trends at the University of Florida. "Even if they don't drive you nuts, they bore you" (Daspin, 2003, p. W1). In 2011, when people were isolated in their homes without power because of Hurricane Irene and other storms they longed to get outside and reconnect with the rest of the world. Similar trapped feelings occurred again in 2020 and 2021.

The search for the right balance of time inside and outside the family/home continues, and much of it is driven by a person's life stage as well as by environmental, health, and economic conditions. Much of what this book is about is that search and the factors that play into it.

## Problem Solving

*Problems* are questions or situations that present uncertainty, risk, perplexity, or difficulty. **Problem solving** involves making many decisions that lead to a resolution of the problem. Life is full of problems that need solving. One needs to engage in **creative thinking** by devising a novel solution to problems.

In some disciplines, the terms "decision-making" and "problem solving" are used interchangeably, but in family resource management they are used differently. Decision-making encompasses all sorts of situations (many of them routine), needs, and wants, whereas problem solving implies that a certain degree of difficulty or risk is involved. An example of a decision is whether to wear a blue shirt or a green shirt. A problem is more complicated than that— there are more factors, more variety. As noted earlier, the greater number of people involved in a decision, the more complex the decision process. Thus, family problem solving is usually more complex than individual problem solving.

Because problems arise from difficulty or crises, they put even more strain on families than routine decision-making. If any family member has hidden agendas or demands, problem definition or analysis can be extremely difficult. Skilled family managers can often spot potential problem areas and try to resolve them before they become full-blown problems involving intense family conflict.

An example of a problem situation for families is who to invite to a wedding and another is how to deal with childcare or elder care emergencies. Put yourself in the role of decades long family arguments with marriages and remarriages. Or the situation of working at a job and receiving a call from the day care center that your child is running a temperature and you need to come right away to take the child home, or the nursing home calls and says that your dad fell down and has been taken to the hospital. Another situation is that your grandma is in an independent living community and your family gets the call that grandma can no longer function because of Alzheimer's disease. On her own, she can no longer find her apartment or the dining room. She crossed a four-lane highway by herself and wandered down the street and had to be brought back. The facility is asking your family to remove grandma and find a more appropriate place with more personalized services.

> While child-care problems get more attention in the workplace, the emergencies that beset the aged—a fall, a stroke, the errant behavior of dementia—tend to be more disruptive, forcing working caregivers to drop everything and rush to the scene. But how do you lay the groundwork at work for a crisis you can't foresee? From consultants, coaches and caregivers, here are some ideas: Work as if you're leaving tomorrow for vacation. "Get your backlog as close to zero as you can, and keep it there," says David Allen, a productivity coach. Create an understandable system to track projects and documents.
>
> (Shellenbarger, 2008, p. B1)

Dealing with unpredictable long-term caregiving like elder care is different from short-term emergencies like the one or two stay-home days for a child. Experts also suggest marshaling resources (know your employer's time-off policies, your rights under the federal Family and Medical Leave Act), gathering medical information, and making arrangements. "When caring for her late parents, Diana Abouchar, Northbrook, Ill., made a habit of working long hours and finishing projects promptly. When a crisis called her away, she says, 'I left no trace' of undone work" (Shellenbarger, 2008, p. B1).

---

**CRITICAL THINKING**

How do you plan for the unplannable? If you were a manager and an employee needed to rush to the hospital 30 minutes away to check on an injured family member, how would you deal with that situation? Who would fill in for the employee? How would you help the distressed employee who had to leave suddenly?

---

## Definition, Analysis/Timing, and Plan of Action

Usually, people do not spontaneously become aware of a problem and then suddenly decide to search for and analyze relevant information (Fay & Wallace, 1987). Instead, the person or family is motivated by dissatisfaction with the current state of things. As motivated processes, problem awareness and analysis are subject to five levels of motivation influences:

1. Needs, motives, and goals of the problem solver;

2. Perceptions and beliefs of the problem solver;

3. Values of the problem solver;

4. Resources of the problem solver;

5. Learning, background, and previous experience of the problem solver.

These influences affect the way a person defines a problem and makes decisions to solve the problem.

## Problem Definition

Problem recognition or definition is the first step in problem solving. The person has to recognize the problem as such before engaging in purposeful behavior to resolve the situation. Problem definition is a creative process requiring the individual to see common threads and sense important cause–effect relationships. For example, the person needs to uncover the underlying symptoms that have caused the problem. How does one go about this?

Complicated problems demand more energy and attention because their cause (or causes) may be hidden or multifaceted. Once the problem is defined, the individual can move on to the next step in problem solving—problem analysis. As a practical example, the next sections will show how Michelle engages in problem solving after her boss tells her that she has been denied a promotion because she lacks administrative experience.

## Problem Analysis/Timing

Depending on the type of problem and the individuals involved, problems can be viewed as messes or as experiences that simply require a logical and reasonable response. For example, after being denied a promotion, Michelle

could respond or act in many ways. She knows she has a problem (the problem is clearly defined); now she has to decide what she is going to do about it.

No two problems are the same because each involves its own unique timing, individuals, and circumstances, and stems from a specific situation. To solve complicated problems, the individual needs to systematically follow the decision steps discussed earlier in this chapter. Taking shortcuts in the decision process will only result in incomplete information that will complicate the problem situation further.

As many complex problems involve the interaction of subproblems, one approach is to divide the problem into subproblems and analyze each separately. One of the most difficult aspects of problem solving is timing. Sometimes it is wise to deliberately delay a decision, in case life changes occur or better options turn up. "**Real-options thinking** *puts a high value on flexibility,*" says Glenn Daily, a fee-only life insurance planner in New York (Quinn, 2001). He suggests that you lean toward the choice that keeps more of your options open rather than choosing a single-option path. "Real options" is a catchall phrase referring to *staying open, waiting and watching for the right opportunity*, such as in making financial decisions—planning when to invest, buy insurance, pay off debt, and so forth. Perhaps your parents said to you, "leave your options open" or "there are other fish in the sea." How do you tell the difference between lasting changes (moving in the right direction) and impulsive moves (instability)? Consider these guideposts of lasting change (or real options):

- They are based on your values and goals, something you have thought about for a long time, bringing beliefs to life.

- They are one option among many.

- Embracing a challenge, the change should be challenging but worth the effort. There is the feeling of moving forward rather than fleeing or avoiding.

Henry David Thoreau said:

I learned this, at least by my experiment: that if you advance confidently in the direction of your dreams, and endeavor to live the life which you have imagined, you will meet with a success unexpected in common hours. You will put some things behind, you will pass an invisible boundary.

## Plan of Action

Once the defining and analyzing phases are over, the individual designs a plan of action. Planning involves putting together the activities or steps to follow. The objective of planning is to produce systems or solutions that can provide satisfaction to the problem solver and other stakeholders in the problem. Michelle decides to get administrative experience so that the next time an opening occurs she will be qualified. Her subproblems include whether her current workplace can provide the necessary experience or whether she will have to get experience elsewhere. Perhaps her boss could be more explicit about the work experience she lacks. Michelle also turns to her colleagues, friends, and family for advice. After she considers their advice and her own perception of the problem, she forms a plan of action. Forming a plan makes her feel more in control of things. Resource management as a discipline encourages individuals to gather as much information as possible, objectively examine their problems and options, and form a plan of action that will help get them what they want.

Motivation is a key part of problem solving. The motivation to solve the problem will depend on the extent of discrepancy between the desired and the actual state and the importance of the problem. Most people will not waste inordinate amounts of time on minor daily decisions such as what to wear or what to eat. Routine decisions such as these rarely are problems. They can become problems, however, if the involved person defines them as a problem or if the decision has a far-reaching impact. For example, what to wear to a job interview or what to serve at a banquet for 500 people may become major problems involving substantial amounts of money and a variety of alternative choices and consequences.

Another essential part of problem solving is the search for information. The search leads to the opening up of alternative courses of action and evaluation. Looking within oneself for information for making decisions is called an **internal search**. Michelle did this first. After her boss told her she had been denied the promotion, she went back to her office, shut the door, and thought over the problem. An internal search is easier and more common than an **external search**, which involves gathering information from family, friends, other people, and the media. When Michelle asked others for advice, she engaged in an external search. As part of her external search, she watched a television news report and read magazine articles about how many people around the country were being laid off from their jobs owing to corporate downsizing or were turning to home-based work because they were tired of working for someone else or commuting. This information helped Michelle put in perspective her failure to receive a promotion. She reasoned that at least she had a job she liked, and she felt sure that given time she would get herself promoted through her effort. As in Michelle's case, complex problem solving usually requires both internal and external searches.

As the search proceeds, the problem becomes more narrowly defined and refined. At all times, decisions should be linked to the primary goal sought. If the goal is landing the best job possible, the job seeker continually looks for information, work experience, and contacts leading to that goal. The desired end state is a solution. Michelle would be well advised to spend time getting the training she needs to get ahead, if not at her present job, at another organization.

## Uncertainty, Risk, and Success

The problems associated with career advancement and job hunting are good examples of uncertainty and risk. In both cases, the individual searches for information to reduce the levels of uncertainty and risk. The more an employee or job seeker knows about a company, such as its policies and track record, the more confident he or she will be on the job or at job interviews.

This is why the office grapevine or gossip is useful: Employees need to know what is going on and what is about to happen. Advance knowledge moderates individuals' perceptions of uncertainty and risk and gives them time to adjust/strategize.

The concepts of risk and uncertainty were introduced in Chapter 2 in the discussion of risk aversion theory. This theory says that rational people will try to reduce or avoid risk, and that risk is subjective because individuals define the level of risk and uncertainty they can handle. For example, a blind date is a risk. To reduce the amount of risk and uncertainty, the couple will try to find out as much as possible about each other before going out on the date.

**Uncertainty** is the state or feeling of being in doubt. *Risk* is the possibility of pain, harm, or loss from a decision. Risk is subjective; that is, each person defines what risk is. A person weighing uncertainty and risk is judging the **probability**, or likelihood, of a good or bad outcome. Shopping, particularly catalog or Internet shopping, involves risks and the consideration of probable outcomes.

## CRITICAL THINKING

### Outcomes

Describe a problem you are trying to solve. Consider possible outcomes to your problem.

| Positive Outcomes | Negative Outcomes |
|---|---|
| _____ | _____ |
| _____ | _____ |
| _____ | _____ |

As you look at these outcomes, what strikes you as the best way to solve this problem?

**Success** is the achievement of something desirable. It can be specific such as milestones reached, money earned, and honors won, or it may be a desired state, such as happiness, contentment, fame, or prosperity, often expressed as a successful outcome. It may be the result of a planned activity or, on rare occasions, chance. True success is defined by the individuals themselves, not by parents, friends, employers, society, or the media. The reason success is included in this discussion is that often success involves risk and uncertainty. Success involves being open to every possibility, realizing that one may experience success in unexpected ways, and being ready for success when it comes. Success is complex.

The first step in job seeking is being aware and researching. The second step is to apply.

*For example, success is presumed to be rewarding for all individuals, but for some this experience becomes closely linked to joy and pride in many achievement situations over time, whereas for others it does not become linked to joy and pride across achievement situations in this manner.*

*(Elliot & Neista, 2009, p. 62)*

---

### CRITICAL THINKING

#### Focusing on Growth Over Glory

Consider the writings of psychologist Heidi Halvorson who says,

*when you find something relatively easy to do, it's very motivating to focus on giving the best possible performance and validating your goodness, and it will probably pay off for you. A very different picture emerges, however, when the road gets rockier—when people are dealing with unfamiliar, complex, or difficult tasks, with obstacles, or with setbacks. That's where the advantages of focusing on growth over glory become clear.*

What does she mean by focusing on growth over glory? Can you give an example of this?

Source: Halvorson, H. (2011). *Succeed: How we can reach our goals* (p. 64).
New York: Hudson Street Press.

---

A town manager of a small community was very surprised when the town's employees, from groundskeepers to the police, threw her an appreciation party. She was not near retirement and the party was not to denote a landmark year of service. It was strictly a "thanks for your effort" party—just to say we appreciate you and want you to know it. Before, during, and after that party, she felt very successful because she had found the right fit between her talents and place of employment. She cares so much that on her morning jogging route she carries a plastic bag to pick up any trash she sees, and when she drives in and out of work in her pickup truck she throws trash in the back. The town is so small that everyone knows this; it is a genuine effort on her part that has gone on for years. They know someone is watching out for them: Isn't that what a town manager should do?

An individual's perception of uncertainty leads to the perception of risk. For example, John, a recent college graduate, may be uncertain whether to wear shorts and a T-shirt or a sports shirt and slacks to his first company picnic. He may also be uncertain about the weather on the day of the picnic. If he thinks it may rain, he might try to reduce his risk of getting wet by taking a hat and a jacket. Although deciding what to wear to a picnic is not a high-risk venture, John wants to dress appropriately so that he will fit in. In contrast, Sam, one of John's coworkers, has not even given a thought to what he will wear to the picnic. His perception of risk in this problem situation is minimal; in fact, he does not even think of dressing for the picnic as a problem situation.

At the picnic, Sam is the only person wearing shorts, and for the next two months, he must endure gentle ribbing about his "bony knees" and plaid shorts. Risk can be perceived as occurring before, during, or after a decision.

## *Types of Risks*

As discussed in Chapter 2, six types of risk affect decision-making: functional or performance risk, financial risk, physical risk, psychological risk, social risk, and time risk. In the last example, John was seeking to reduce physical, psychological, financial, and social risks. If he worries about the best time to arrive at the picnic, then he would add time risk to his list of concerns.

To reduce risk, people search for information or behave in ways that will decrease their uncertainty, such as asking others for advice or repeating behaviors that have worked for them in the past. Saving for retirement involves big risk: Increasingly, workers have to make decisions about saving and investing for retirement, and in uncertain economies, doing so is becoming more and more difficult. Many of life's most important decisions concern the management of financial resources. Figure 5.6 provides a decision-making chart of tasks or decisions ranging from minor (for example, selecting a snack) to major (buying a car) with varying degrees of risk.

| Relatively Minor Decisions | Relatively Major Decisions |
|---|---|
| Only minor impact on life course | Major impact |
| Little information needed | More information needed |
| Reliance on memory for information | External sources of information sought |
| Requires little thought | Requires more thought |
| Minor evaluation of consequences | Major evaluation of consequences |
| Situation or criteria not very important | Situation or criteria critical |
| Low or no risk from poor decision | High risk from poor decision |

Figure 5.6 A decision-making chart.

## At-Risk Children

Certainly, many individual, family, and societal problems are far more difficult than what to wear to an event. A disturbing societal problem is at-risk children. One example is the number of children and families at risk due to deportation.

> Children born in the United States to foreign-born parents comprise approximately 27% of the U.S. population. Approximately 5.7 million U.S.-born children live with parents without legal residency documentation, and nearly 500,000 children had at least one parent detained or deported over a 2-year period. There is a high risk for negative child and family outcomes associated with parental deportation.
>
> (Rayburn et al., 2021)

According to Dryfoos (1991), at-risk children are likely to be low achievers, drug abusers, or premature parents; they are also likely to be in trouble with the law. Many of these children live in high-stress family situations and have little parental support and supervision. Intervention may be needed for the children to succeed academically.

Questions have been raised about what schools can do to help at-risk children (Katz, Dalton, & Giacquinta, 1994). A consensus is forming that school programs as they currently exist cannot solve the rapidly rising incidence of depression and stress, emerging from dysfunctional families. New types of school-based support programs and curricula are suggested as a means for dealing with educational, health, and life issues of at-risk populations.

In New York State, the Home and Career Skills (HCS) curriculum concentrates on developing the critical thinking skills of students so that they can make rational decisions and prepare to meet their responsibilities as consumers, home managers, wage earners, and members of families (Katz et al., 1994). Similar curricula are being used in other states under various names, including Life Management Skills or in Hospitality programs (learning how to work in various occupations such as food service with the goal of owning a restaurant or becoming a chef, or to work in hotel management). In addition, families, both nuclear and extended, community groups, and health organizations need to do all they can to reduce the number of at-risk children and give all children the best possible start in life. Helping children learn to make responsible decisions at an early age is a good starting point, to be followed by continued attention and support through the later years.

### Suggested Activity

*Describe success for yourself. What end state or activity would be a sign of success? What attitudes, decisions, and behaviors would you need to be successful?*

*Name three successful people and explain why you think they are successful. What qualities (e.g., courage, generosity, care for others, self-confidence) made them successful?*

For those in the helping professions, the emphasis when working with families should be on assisting them in making their own decisions and solving their own problems, not imposing the professional's own decisions or solutions. Expressing gratitude to others, mentoring troubled youths, fostering parenting, giving the gift of time, forgiving a wrong, and serving in the community are all positive steps toward reducing the number and severity of at-risk children.

## The GO Model: Visualization of a Problem-Solving Process

Professors Holly Hunts and Ramona Marotz-Baden of Montana State University developed the GO model of problem solving because they believed that teaching problem-solving processes may well be one of the most important tasks of family economists/management specialists. GO stands for "goal-oriented."

The purpose of the GO model (see Figure 5.7) is twofold:

1. To further the theory about problem solving into a goal-oriented model that can help students understand how individuals and families make choices that help them reach goals.

2. To bring about a new method for teaching students about problem solving and goal–oriented strategies. Family systems theory and pedagogical strategies (different learning and teaching styles) serve as its base.

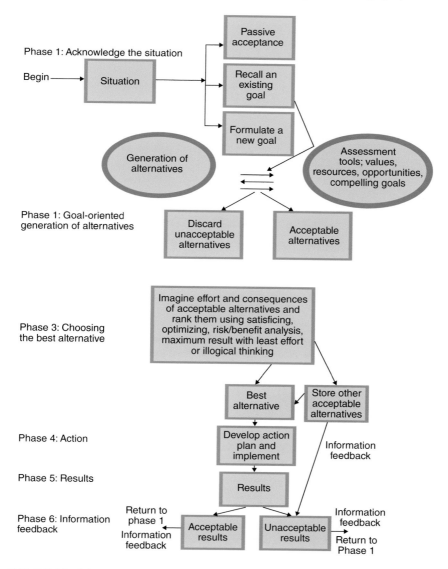

Figure 5.7  GO Model.

## Suggested Activity

The GO model works best on current problems you are facing. Start at the top of the model; enter a situation and work through the process. An example that Hunts and Marotz-Baden have used in their classes is, "Describe the goals and boundaries of the ideal marriage for you. Using the GO model, discuss how feasible your ideal is if you were to marry the person you care most about now" (Hunts & Marotz-Baden, 2003, p. 11). Another example they have used is to imagine the situation in which two roommates or housemates are arguing over bills left unpaid by a third person who moved out suddenly.

Within the model, the situation requiring action is defined, alternatives are ranked, leading to the best alternative and then to a course of action and implementation that leads ultimately to results in Phase 5. Phase 6 provides information feedback that may be acceptable or unacceptable.

The feedback provides information as the process starts all over again in Phase 1, thereby affecting future situations.

> *In a goal-oriented approach, problems are barriers to be overcome if goals are to be achieved. In other words, the emphasis in the goal-oriented approach is on increasing the probability of goal attainment by using problem solving to overcome these barriers.*
>
> *(Hunts & Marotz-Baden, 2004)*

## SUMMARY

In our daily lives, we are surrounded by problems to solve and decisions to make. We aim toward goal completion and a feeling of success. Success is complex and as active, busy people, we use creative thinking to make decisions and solve problems. We try to choose the best alternatives from the choices available; in so doing, we seek to reduce uncertainty and risk and increase the probability of good outcomes.

A decision plan is central to the management process. The acronym DECIDE is an easy way to remember the six steps of decision-making. However, it was pointed out that new research shows that we should not overthink a decision; many are made in less than ten seconds and unconsciously. Brain regions involved in making choices activate before people are consciously aware that they've made a choice. More research is underway about how we make decisions and whether quick ones can work.

The family is critical to the development of decision-making skill. The Elbing model of family decision-making demonstrates that each decision has a history and is influenced by members of reference groups. The central-satellite and chain models of decision-making show the interrelationships among decisions. The decision tree illustrates that values underlie decisions and that resources and goals affect the alternatives considered. Decision-making involves rules and rational patterns of thought as well as intuition.

Decision-making is an art or skill that can be improved through reasoning and practice rather than avoidance. Decidophobia is the fear of making decisions, specifically the fear of failure. Much of a person's success depends upon his or her ability to identify the causes of problems and to develop workable solutions for resolving them. Personality comes into play. Self-ambivalence refers to the co-presence of positive and negative evaluations making it difficult to make decisions. The person is torn by different sides of their personality.

Problem solving differs from decision-making in that problem solving involves difficulty, perplexity, risk, and uncertainty, whereas decision-making refers to all sorts of situations, needs, and wants (some problematic, others not). The GO (goal-oriented) model of problem solving ranks alternatives to help choose the best one, so that a course of action can be implemented, leading to the desired result; feedback assists in making future decisions.

To be effective, decisions need to be implemented, evaluated, and communicated. Planning, implementing, and evaluating are the subjects of the next chapter, and communication will be discussed in Chapter 7.

## KEY TERMS

| | | |
|---|---|---|
| accommodation | decision plan | prepurchase |
| anticipation | decision rules |   expectations |
| autonomic | decisions | probability |
| bounded rationality | de facto decision-making | problem solving |
| consensual decision making | external search | real-options thinking |
| creative thinking | hatching | reference groups |
| decidophobia | intuition | self-ambivalence |
| decision-making | peter principle | success |
| decision-making style | post purchase dissonance | syncratic thinking |

## REVIEW QUESTIONS

1. How rational are decisions? What is bounded rationality? What are the limitations to making decisions (refer to the decision continuum in Figure 5.6)? Describe one of your recent decisions that had limitations or emotions like anticipation.

2. What is the Peter Principle? How is it related to decision-making?

3. The German poet and playwright Johann Wolfgang von Goethe said, "I have come to the frightening conclusion that I am the decisive element. It is my personal approach that creates the climate. It is my daily mood that makes the weather. I possess tremendous power to make life miserable or joyous." Do you agree or disagree? Explain your answer.

4. What does the Elbing model illustrate?

5. What is the difference between decision-making and problem solving? Describe a problem you are trying to solve.

## REFERENCES

Armas, G. (2003, October 25). Number of childless women hits record high. *Tallahassee Democrat*, p. 8A

Baxter, J., Haynes, M., & Hewitt, B. (2010). Pathways into marriage, cohabitation and the domestic division of labor. *Journal of Family Issues, 31*(11), 1507–1529.

Bianchi, S., Milkie, M., Sayer, L., & Robinson, J. (2000). Is anyone doing the housework? Trends in the gender division of household labor. *Social Forces, 79*(1), 191–228.

Carey, B. (2008, February 5). Feel like a fraud? At times, maybe you should. *The New York Times*, p. D5.

Chiras, D. (2000). *The natural house*. White River Junction, VT: Chelsea Green.

Coltrane, S. (1989). Household labor and the routine production of gender. *Social Problems, 36*(5), 473–490.

Daspin, E. (2003, May 16). The end of nesting. *The Wall Street Journal*, pp. W1, W9.

Dryfoos, J. G. (1991). School-based social and health services for at-risk students. *Urban Education*, 26(1), 118– 137.

Elliot, A., & Neista, D. (2009). Goals in the context of the hierarchical model of approach—avoidance motivation. In G. Moskowiz & H. Grant (Eds.), *The Psychology of Goals* (p. 62). New York: Guilford Press.

Ellison, S., & Tejada, C. (2003, January 30). Mr., Mrs., meet Mr. Clean. *The Wall Street Journal*, pp. B1, B3.

Fan, J., & Xiao, J. (1998). Consumer decision-making styles of young adult consumers. *Journal of Consumer Affairs*, 32(2), 273–292.

Fay, C. H., & Wallace, M. J. (1987). *Research based decisions*. New York: Random House.

Forelle, C. (2003, June 16). Deodorant makers sniff out ways to sell in a stagnant market. *The Wall Street Journal*, p. A1.

Godwin, D. D., & Scanzoni, J. (1989). Couple consensus during marital joint decision making: A context, process, outcome model. *Journal of Marriage and the Family*, 5, 943–956.

Goldsmith, R. (2017). Rational choice and bounded rationality. In Gerard Emilien, Rolf Weitkunat, & Frank Ludicke (Eds.), *Consumer Perception of Product Risks and Benefits*. Berlin: Springer Verlag.

Halvorson, H. G. (2011). *Succeed: How we can reach our goals*. New York: Hudson Street Press.

Hotz, R. (2008, June 27). Get out of your own way. *The Wall Street Journal*, p. A9.

Hunts, H., & Marotz-Baden, R. (2003). Family systems theory: A new look at an old friend. *Consumer Interests Annual*, 49, 1–13.

Hunts, H., & Marotz-Baden, R. (2004). The GO model: A new way of teaching problem solving in context. *Journal of Teaching in Marriage and Family*, 4(1), 27–57.

Katz, E., Dalton, S., & Giacquinta, J. (1994). Status risk taking and receptivity of home economics teachers to a statewide curriculum innovation. *Home Economics Research Journal*, 22(4), 401–421.

Kaye, H. (1996). *Decision power*. Englewood Cliffs, NJ: Prentice-Hall.

Keeney, R. L. (1988). Value-focused thinking and the study of values. In D. E. Beal, H. Raiffe, & A. Tuersky (Eds.), *Decision Making* (p. 466). Cambridge: Cambridge University Press.

Loudon, D., & Della Bitta, A. J. (1988). *Consumer behavior: Concepts and applications*. New York: McGraw-Hill.

Malhotra, N. K. (1991). Mnemonics in marketing: A pedagogical tool. *Journal of the Academy of Marketing Science*, 19(2), 141–149.

Marshall, R. (1991). *The state of families, 3: Losing direction*. Milwaukee, WI: Family Service America.

Meyer, M. (1997, August). The grocery gender gap. *Good Housekeeping*, 147.

Mogelonsky, M. (1998, August). Product overload? *American Demographics*, 5–12.

Mohanty, M. (1996, Spring). Women in India: The relationship of literacy and participation in household decision making. *Journal of Family and Consumer Sciences*, 42–43.

Peter, L. J., & Hall, R. (1969). *The Peter principle*. New York: William Morrow.

Purvis, D., Augustine, G., Fitzpatrick, D., Hall, W. Lamantia, S., Mooney, R., Platt, M. L., & White, L. E. (2019). *Neuroscience, international sixth edition*. Oxford: Oxford University Press.

Quinn, J. B. (2001, May 22). The best investing choice is to keep your options open. *Tallahassee Democrat*, Business Section.

Rayburn, A., McWey, L., & Gonzales-Backen, M. (2021). *Family relations*. https://doi.org/10.1111/fare.12534.

Riketta, M., & Ziegler, R. (2006, Fall). Self-ambivalence and self-esteem. *Current Psychology*, 25(3), 192–211.

Sandberg, J. (2008, November 8). Deciders suffer alone: Nondeciders make everyone else suffer. *The Wall Street Journal*, p. B1.

Schiffman, L. G., & Kanuk, L. L. (1991). *Consumer behavior* (4th ed.). Englewood Cliffs, NJ: Prentice-Hall.

Schlossberg, A. (1992, March 2). Kids teach parents how to change their buying habits. *Marketing News*, p. 8.

Schroder, M., & McKinnon, S. (2007). Learning good judgement: Young Europeans' perceptions of key consumer skills. *International Journal of Consumer Studies, 31*, 152–159.

Shellenbarger, S. (2003, October 16). The sole breadwinner's lament: Having mom at home isn't as great as it sounds. *The Wall Street Journal,* p. D1.

Shellenbarger, S. (2008, September 10). Parental pull: How to prepare for an elder emergency. *The Wall Street Journal*, p. D1.

Shellenbarger, S. (2011, June 8). The gifts on every wedding list. *The Wall Street Journal*, p. D1–D2.

Silver, W. S., & Mitchell, T. R. (1990). The status quo tendency in decision making. *Organizational Dynamics, 18*, 34–46.

Simon, H. (1955). A behavioral model of rational choice. *Quarterly Journal of Economics, 69*(1), 99–118.

Zabinski, K., & Zielosko, B. (2021). Decision rules construction: Algorithm based on EAV Model. *Entropy, 23*(1), 1–18.

Zaslow, J. (2006, September 7). Hoarders vs. deleters, revised: Readers share competing email strategies. *The Wall Street Journal*, p. D1.

Chapter **6**

# Planning, Implementing, and Evaluating

**DID YOU KNOW THAT...?**

… Most adults say that they have purchased or would be willing to purchase containers, furniture, file systems, or similar products to help them get organized.

DOI: 10.4324/9781003166740-6

… There are over 6 billion Internet-connected products in the European Union and over 25 billion worldwide.

CASE STUDY

## Planning

When it comes to planning a lifestyle it is hard to beat this.

> *Best selling writer Stuart Woods likes to control his environment in a way that minimizes external fluctuations. Since he feels best at a temperature of around 70 degrees, he owns three homes for different seasons: a co-op in New York, where he spends spring and fall; a home on Mount Desert Island, in Maine, for summer; and a residence in Key West, Fla for winter. He has decorated each one nearly identically, attiring them almost exclusively in Ralph Lauren furnishings, including leather chairs, tweed curtains, sofas and beds. Each one of the four yellow labs he's owned has been named Fred, each replaced by a new Fred upon death. 'You get into certain grooves. I have certain requirements,' said Mr. Woods, 73, best known for his Stone Barrington series of novels.*

> *Source: Keates, N. (2011, July 22). One home, three locations. The Wall Street Journal, D. 7.*

Stuart Wood's case study is an extreme example of someone who likes to control his lifestyle and has the means to do it. The story goes on to explain that his desk area, in particular, is exactly the same in each residence. He sits down and goes straight to work. The problem is the outside world sometimes intrudes on his routine. Recently his favorite restaurant within easy walking distance of his Park Avenue, New York City, co-op closed, one he went to for decades to meet with fellow writers. This was enough of a change for him to question whether he wanted to keep that particular apartment.

*Planning* was defined in the first chapter as making a series of decisions that lead to action. In the last chapter, questions were raised about how do you plan for the unplannable? For example, a tornado or a canyon brush fire in the middle of the night does not allow for much planning. But, with some forethought, a family might have discussed ahead about emergency situations and what they would do, where they would seek shelter, or where they would go. Forethought (asking the "what if" questions) and strategizing are parts of planning.

Many of us make lists, mental and physical, in our personal lives and professionally as teachers or event planners Lists form the core of daily and weekly planning. Do you make lists? Do you use a calendar or daybook (digital or in print) to schedule appointments and to write down test dates? The problem with these is that they are only useful if the individual consults them enough. Especially with the digital forms, individuals may enjoy inputting information but forget to retrieve on a regular basis so they miss events and appointments.

Online lists can be a lot of fun or a lot of work depending on how you use them. Some users find them addictive because they allow for a listing of every trip you have ever taken or book you have read, past fashions and fads you were part of, and so on. Then you use them for planning by adding things you want to do, books you want to read, and places you want to go. According to a reporter:

*This week, I tested a new Web site called Mesophere.com that encourages users to check off lists related to topics ranging from cars they owned to former hairstyles to countries they visited. When the answers from these lists are compiled, they create a mesosphere (emphasis on "me"), or an overall glance at one's life history. Mesophere.com by Mesophere LLC was launched in March as a way to catalog details about yourself or someone else, led a Web-based memory book. It offers some 2,500 lists, and new lists are added daily by users and site managers One of the funniest lists I filled in was titled Fads You've Done, Bought or Worn; it walked me down memory lane as I read the items and checked off Leg Warmers, Electric Slide Dance and Jelly shoes. Another list that made me laugh out loud was Hairstyles You've Worn—ah, the '80s.*

*(Boehret, 2007, p. D6)*

Planning is more than about what was past or even what is to come; it also has to do with the present and your typical behavioral patterns. For example, do you **multitask** (do several things at once)? In our sped-up world, more of us are multitasking—sometimes it works, and sometimes it doesn't, a subject to be discussed in this chapter. One wonders whether we are accomplishing more or less!

To put planning in the context of the overall topic of this book resource management enables better utilization of planning. It helps make planning and management more transparent to avoid losing objects, papers, and data and lessen misunderstandings. In short, planning is an important part of the resource management flow.

Research indicates we waste a lot of time in ordinary activities. For example, an average adult spends about four minutes a day searching for lost keys, remote controls, cell phones, and so forth. Not having enough time is the biggest excuse most people use for not being organized.

*They spend so much time looking after their stuff and getting places that they don't have time to plan and organize; all their time is taken up just keeping up. About 10 percent of Americans categorize themselves as extremely organized.*

*(Fetto, 2003)*

Do you fall into this category?

*Regardless of one's level of organization, however, 89 percent of Americans say they could use help tidying up some corner of their life there are scores of Americans who would be willing to take action and even pay for some help*

*(Fetto, 2003, p. 11)*

These findings in the early 21st century set the stage for the widespread success of the KonMari method detailed in Marie Kondo's best-seller *The Life-Changing Magic of Tidying Up* (published in 2011 in Japan and in 2014 in the U.S.). She says,

*When you put your house in order, you put your affairs and your past in order, too. As a result, you can see quite clearly what you need in life and what you don't, and what you should and shouldn't do. (p. 4).*

One of her key phrases is "Does it (meaning an object or possession) spark joy?"

Planning, implementing, and evaluating are the subjects of this chapter. Examples of plans are college plans, financial plans, lunch plans, weekend plans, wedding plans, child custody plans, national health care plans, and affirmative action plans. Ginger Gentile, Director of Erasing Family says that shared custody agreements help children and parents maintain a sense of stability after divorce (Hibbs, 2021). As the list indicates, plans can range from the mundane to the significant, but all plans are important to the individuals and societies involved. Without plans there would be no birthday cakes or gifts under Christmas trees, nor would there be any roads or businesses. In short, life as we know it would not exist.

In fact, planning is so crucial to human existence that it has been the subject of sayings and fables since ancient times. Think how often you have heard someone say, "If you fail to plan, you are planning to fail." Countless generations of children have heard the story of the industrious ant that planned ahead and stored food for the winter while the foolish grasshopper frolicked in the sun. Of course, when winter came, the grasshopper's failure to think ahead proved fatal.

As the "ant and the grasshopper" story indicates, planning is prevention—a good plan is a management tool that can save countless hours in revising, restructuring, and other ineffective actions. The amount of planning needed varies, however, from situation to situation and from individual to individual.

Planning needs also change over the life cycle. For example, the oldest members of the baby boom generation are entering retirement or are already there and must plan for reduced incomes, in most cases, as well as for more leisure time and potential health problems. Many may be questioning their life purpose without the social involvement and financial rewards that paid work provides.

Like individuals, families make plans, and their plans involve the same type of considerations (i.e., time, energy, personnel, cost, schedules) as do other plans. For example, family tasks and responsibilities are planned and assigned.

A family's plan may include driving the children to school, picking up or ordering groceries for dinner, taking the garbage out, and so on—with a family member performing each task. Yet, despite the amount of planning that families do, how often do they sit down and really think about all they do and evaluate the effectiveness of their planning?

This chapter addresses several questions: How are plans made? How can they be more effective? What forces drive planning behavior? As social and economic conditions worldwide transform, these questions are becoming more and more critical. The world's growing population is straining its resources, increasing the necessity for better planning. In the consumer area, life is moving so fast that individuals are having trouble devising enough plans to handle all the choices and changes that confront them. Several years ago, the *Wall Street Journal* highlighted this problem:

> Mr. Cialdini, the psychologist, believes that consumers are resorting increasingly to what he calls "click whir" behavior. Life has become so complex that consumers can't possibly analyze the merits of all of their decisions, he says. So they are more susceptible to certain cues and symbols like "discount" or "last day of sale" and take less time to analyze fundamental questions like need or cost. When we react to symbols instead of information, then what we do doesn't make sense anymore, he says.
>
> (Morris, 1987, August 4)

## CRITICAL THINKING

What corner of your life could use some tidying up? Have you let some assignment or studying slip? Or car repair? What action should you take?

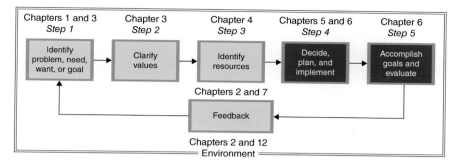

Figure 6.1 The management process model.

As this chapter will show, situations, events, and other factors affect planning, implementing, and evaluating. Besides exploring the complex nature of planning and implementing, the chapter also examines the motivating forces behind these processes.

Why do people plan? What are they trying to accomplish? How successful are their plans? Key topics include the influence of personality and style, as well as of social contexts and environments, on planning. Examples of planning, implementing, and evaluating will be given, providing a blend of theory and **best practices** (methods and techniques to ensure quality). With real-world examples, this chapter is intended to be an important learning resource for students of individual and family management.

This chapter also contributes to the understanding of the management process model first presented in Chapter 1 and repeated here in Figure 6.1. Planning is a process (a subsystem) within the larger process (system) of management. Step 4 in the model is "decide, plan, and implement," and step 5 is concerned with accomplishing goals and evaluation. Thus, this chapter explains the culmination of the management process.

## What Is Planning?

There has been a lot of coverage in this book on goal pursuit. The goal of finding a job requires a plan from applying to interviewing to accepting. Along the way, the applicant and the employer are monitoring progress and evaluating. Planning is a process involving a series of decisions leading to need or goal fulfillment. A **plan** is a detailed schema, program, strategy, or method worked out beforehand for the accomplishment of the desired result. For example, students planning to graduate in May or June follow a plan of action that entails completing required courses and filling out the paperwork necessary to ensure graduation. As the graduation date nears, they may rent or buy a cap and gown. Graduation plans, among others, require a systematic approach to problem solving and goal attainment.

Planning or organizing tools include containers, furniture, files, or similar products used to get organized and also online or digital organizers; an example is Microsoft Outlook which is a personal information manager with a number of applications (Apps) like calendars and email. Their website says, "connect, organize, get things done." In the last few centuries, we have gone from harnessing steam power to our modern world of smart products and software.

A survey showed that 54 percent of American adults say they have purchased or would be willing to purchase these types of things (Fetto, 2003). According to the same source, an *American Demographics*/Harris interactive survey revealed that among the kinds of things Americans would need

Keeping up with financial news is part of this woman's plan to succeed.

to organize are finances, books, collections, kitchens, and games. You could add to that list organizing digital photographs.

When it comes to objects, some people like their shoes all neatly lined up in a closet; others just toss their shoes in; and still others do not use closets and leave their shoes all over the house. A 30-year-old single man living alone had two master closets, so he put his suits and work clothes in one, along with the matching shoes; and he put casual clothes and athletic shoes in the other. Everything was organized by color and season. Only 12 percent of the population alphabetize their spices, according to the New England Professional Organizers. Maybe it is more remarkable that 12 percent do this than that 88 percent do not. What do you think about alphabetizing spices, lining up shoes, and organizing clothes by season, color, and function?

The need to organize is a cultural phenomenon, according to Dean McFarlin, a professor of management at the University of Dayton. He says, "We are a culture that embraces a monochromic view of time. We believe time is a commodity and it can all be lost" (Matchan, 2002, p. 6F).

## The Planning Process and Task

This chapter follows the chapter on decision-making because planning is a more complex process than decision-making. A **process** is a system of operations that work together to produce the desired result. The word "process" implies movement or change. Something is happening. Steps are being taken such as buying a house.

Charles and Emily Borg are both college professors living in a small college town with limited housing options with high prices. Over the course of two years, they looked at 50 houses before choosing one that met their needs. They enjoyed the process of looking although there were days when they tired of it. Their one child was grown so they did not feel in a hurry to choose and eventually settled on a new subdivision where they could customize their house.

*Planning* is a thinking and information-gathering process involving a series of decisions. It is a process because formulating plans requires several steps, such as information gathering, sorting, and prioritizing; then, based on this information, the planner must decide which plan is most likely to succeed.

New house, new beginnings.

The decisions and steps are not random but proceed in an orderly, logical sequence. For example, after living in a dormitory for a semester, a college student may decide to move into an apartment the next semester, but she will not move out of the dormitory without doing some planning. She must decide how much rent she can afford, whether she will look for roommates or live alone, and in what parts of town she would like to live. Before finally selecting an apartment, she will probably talk with several friends and look at several apartments.

To help understand the role of planning in management behavior, researchers have constructed models that depict the various stages of the planning process. The principal aim of such models is to predict future behavior: How does a person normally plan? Will the plan be repeated?

Figure 6.2 shows one such model of the planning process. In the model, the first step is awareness—an individual becomes aware that a plan is needed. In the next step, the person gathers and analyzes information. In the third step, the information is put into the context of the situation, including consideration of others,

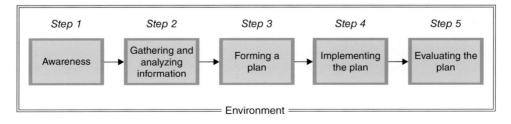

Figure 6.2 The planning process model.

and a plan is formed. The plan is a series of decisions, including decisions about resource allocation. Finally, in the fourth and fifth steps, the plan is implemented and evaluated. As the model shows, plans are made within an environmental context—the person considers what is possible within his or her environment. A beach party is not a practical plan in Minneapolis in the winter, for example, nor is a sit-down dinner with five courses a good choice for a four-year-old's birthday party.

When individuals and families plan, their main task is to figure out what needs to be done and how to go about doing it. In a competitive world where there are many demands on people's time, energy, money, and ability, survival and growth require accurate knowledge, decisions, and implementation. How should people act? Where should they go? How can they prioritize among conflicting activities and responsibilities? How do they choose between work and family duties?

A plan should have a purpose; it should be going somewhere. What does the planner hope to achieve? Management theory stresses the necessity of planning if an individual or a family hopes to achieve the goals that have been set. One of the reasons individuals and families engage in planning activity is that it helps them visualize what may or may not happen. Among the questions, they may consider the following:

- Will others cooperate?
- Is there enough money?
- Is there enough time?
- Is there enough information?
- Does the technology work?

By reviewing these questions, the planner is trying to anticipate problems before they arise. Answers to these questions may lead directly to the implementation of the plan or to more planning and different courses of action.

## Need Fulfillment

Generally, people arrive at their needs through a complex subjective assessment based on their inherent motivations and their perceptions of the external world (Foxall et al., 1998). For example, if a new product is to succeed, consumers must perceive that it will satisfy some need or combination of needs. Likewise, in management theory, if a plan is to succeed, individuals must perceive that the plan and its implementation will be useful and will satisfy some need or combination of needs.

## Time, Stress, and Planning

Planning takes time and motivation when both may be in short supply. Individuals, families, and organizations may become so caught up in everyday activities and crises that they have no time to plan. In that case, they are victims of **Gresham's law of planning,** which comes from the better-known Gresham's law (Simon, 1993). Thomas Gresham, a financial adviser to Queen Elizabeth I, observed that "bad money drives out good," so that "if two coins have the same nominal value but are made from metals of unequal value, the cheaper will tend to drive the other out of circulation" (*Encyclopedia Britannica*, 1989, vol. 5, p. 489). Applying Gresham's law of planning to management, Herbert Simon observed that "short-term concerns create priorities and deadlines that absorb managerial attention and energy at the expense of long-range concerns" (1993, p. 139).

> ### CRITICAL THINKING
>
> ### Winging It Does Not Always Work
>
> *Do a quick Google search of 'planning quotes' and you will be up to your ears in examples of famous politicians, writers, business leaders, and Founding Fathers who have sung the praises of making a good plan. Management consultant David Allen, in his highly acclaimed book* Getting Things Done, *writes that one of the key objectives of the organizational techniques he teaches is 'disciplining yourself to make front-end decisions about all the 'inputs' you let into your life so that you will always have a plan for 'next actions.' In fact, you'd be hard-pressed to find a public figure advising anyone in earnest that the road to success lies in 'just winging it.'*
>
> *(Halvorson, 2011, p. 171)*

What do you think of this quote? Try Googling planning quotes and see what you find.

There are indicators to the fact that families have less and less time that they can devote to planning. One of the ways they are coping with time stress now is to plan further ahead than ever before. Families today live months and years ahead of themselves:

> *They rent next year's summer home before Thanksgiving; buy Christmas concert tickets in the summer; apply to favorite schools for next year, even before this year's class has had a chance to warm the seats In Chicago, Robin Cohn has her children's after-school activities planned for the next eight months; all that is in question is whether her son, a third-grader, will play soccer or basketball this spring. "And we'll decide that in a week or two," she says*
>
> *(Kronholz, 1997, p. A1)*

Part of the reason why individuals and families plan so far ahead is that many of them are competing for the same activities or spaces whether it is camping spaces, conference rooms, churches, or botanical gardens for weddings. They have found that planning is necessary if they are to get what they want when they want it. They have learned that many organizations schedule around the egalitarian principle of first-come, first-served, so the "first" come earlier and earlier. As another example of this, a professor found that she needed to book a New York City room one year in advance at her university-owned townhouse. Staying there will cost her less than $100 a night in a good location! No wonder it is popular with faculty, students, and alumni. Another university offered something similar (during off times) in London near the British Museum.

*The drawback of advance planning is the lack of spontaneity. The paradox of planning is that it can create stress and also relieve stress.* Stress is relieved when people are more relaxed once a decision is made—for example, once the cruise ship tickets are bought the trip is expected to go on as scheduled. But what happens when the cruise, for which tickets were bought six months ahead, is canceled when a hurricane hits right where the ship is going or when there is a pandemic?

Stress can arise from feeling too boxed in, too committed, or too rigid so that changes or new opportunities cannot be readily taken advantage of. This is one of the major plot lines of many television series including the syndicated television shows *Sex and the City* and *The Big Bang Theory*.

Certainly, people who live entirely for the moment haven't got it right, says Chicago's Mr. Csikszent-mihalyi. But those who spend their lives planning their lives don't either. "You end up finding that you have squandered opportunities for really living in order to prepare yourself for living in the future," he says (Kronholz, 1997, p. A1).

Thus, planning is affected by time constraints, stress, and the choice between living in the moment and thinking long-term. But there are other factors that affect planning, such as situational aspects and personality characteristics, including motivation. These will be discussed next.

### Situational Factors

Situational factors, including environmental context, shape wants, needs, and goals. These factors can include a specific precipitating circumstance, such as a broken computer. Until the computer broke down, the owner had no need to consider how to fix or replace it, but now she must either have the computer repaired or buy a new one. Individuals and families continually respond to such changes in situations or circumstances. A problem, need, want, or goal motivates them to plan and act. For example, they may drive up to a restaurant and find it closed. They then must formulate a new plan for where to go and what to eat. Among the situational influences to be considered in making plans are the following:

- *Physical surroundings:* Location, decor, lighting, cleanliness, sound, heat, or cold

- *Social surroundings:* Other people, crowding, and relationships

- *Time:* Time of the day, month, year, and season

- *Task:* The reason the person is there. What needs to be done?

**Task saturation** occurs when people (co-workers, family members, political campaign workers) are so busy doing things that they cannot plan or lead effectively. Signs of task saturation are people canceling meetings or showing up late, or constantly complaining about paperwork. One professor said that she was expected to attend five different committee meetings during a one-hour period, so she had to choose the most important one and stay for the entire time or run around and put in a "guest" appearance at two or three. This is an example of task saturation: one person and too many time conflicts. How did she make the final decision? She incorporated the first rule of management, which is to focus on what is important (which committee mattered the most), not on what seemed most urgent or pressing. Looking back, it was obvious that she was serving on too many committees; she quit a couple at the end of the year and waited for the rest of her terms of appointment to run out.

The importance of situational influences cannot be overestimated. At a more immediate level, is our behavior determined more by our internal attributes (personality traits, attitudes, beliefs, values, self-concept) or situational forces? While many people assume their behavior is largely determined by their internal attributes, social psychological research, with its interpersonal orientation, demonstrates that situational factors often have a very powerful effect on what we do. Situational forces are particularly visible in studies of helping in emergencies, conformity, and pressure to comply with orders to behave in hurtful ways.

> *Three general conclusions can be drawn from these studies. First, our behavior is dramatically influenced by what other people do in the same situation; they serve as models and provide information about how to interpret the situation and what the consequences of various behaviors are. Second, most people are genuinely unaware of how strongly their behavior has been influenced by the behavior of others. And third, it is very difficult for the average person to resist the pressures to comply with the wishes of others.*
>
> *(Bingham, 1991, p. 36)*

## Personal Traits and Characteristics

Although situational factors are important, the person making the decision lies at the heart of the planning process. The planning and implementation that will take place will be based on how that individual assesses the situation. Thus, personality and characteristic ways of behaving play crucial roles in planning.

---

**CRITICAL THINKING**

### Organizing to Reduce Pressure

The famous writer Anais Nin in *The Diary of Anais Nin* wrote, "When I cannot bear outer pressures anymore, I begin to put order in my belongings As if unable to organize and control my life, I seek to exert this on the world of objects." Does this technique work for you also?

---

## Introverts and Extroverts

According to Foxall et al. (1998), **personality** refers either to an extensive range of separate behavior traits (honesty, perseverance, and hostility, for instance) or to overall types of character and response (extrovert vs. introvert). **Introverts** tend to think about themselves first; their thoughts are directed inward.

> *Do you know someone who needs hours alone every day? Who loves quiet conversations about feelings or ideas, and can give a dynamite presentation to a big audience, but seems awkward in groups and maladroit at small talk? Who has to be dragged to parties and then needs the rest of the day to recuperate? Who growls or scowls or grunts or winces when accosted with pleasantries by people who are just trying to be nice? If so, do you tell this person he is "too serious," or ask if he is okay? Regard him as aloof, arrogant, rude? Redouble your efforts to draw him out? If you answered YES to these questions, chances are that you have an introvert on your hands.*
>
> (Rauch, 2003, p. 133)

**Extroverts** are less interested in self and more interested in others and in the environment. This was confirmed in a study of smartphone addiction which found that extroverts used phones more for social reasons and introverts more for a process (Rahim et al., 2021).

Extroverts often have a hard time understanding introverts. Extroverts assume that their company and their thoughts are always welcome. They dominate public life in politics, in sports, and in entertainment, so we tend to be more aware of them than we are of introverts.

Introversion and extroversion are orientations. *People are rarely either completely introverted or completely extroverted*, but they do tend to exhibit more traits of one than of the other. Recent studies indicate that people can choose to act more outgoing or assertive and in so doing their outlook on life will improve. Students in those studies who were told to act like extroverts during a group discussion had more fun and enjoyed the group more than the ones told to be passive and shy. William Fleeson and colleagues suggest that personality influences happiness and, thus, we have some control over our personalities. "Individuals may have the potential to contribute directly to their own wellbeing by changing their behavior," says Fleeson.

How does being introverted or extroverted affect planning? One difference is in the way information is gathered and processed. For example, after purchasing a camera, an introverted person might more likely read the instruction booklet or go online or figure out through trial and error how to operate it, whereas an extroverted person would be more inclined to ask for help from the camera store owner or friends, or through a blog.

## Other Personality Factors and Expertise

Many other personality factors also affect planning. For example, is the individual primarily a dreamer or a realist? Consistent or inconsistent? Precise or imprecise? Impatient or patient? Individuals definitely differ in their need for:

- Adventure
- Novelty
- New objects or products
- New experiences

Consider the difference between a homeowner who rearranges furniture often and repaints interior rooms every five years versus someone who has not touched a stick of furniture, picture, or a wall in over 20 years. The author of this book was told by a neighbor that she bought a model house and garage apartment 20 years ago fully furnished including sheets, towels, furniture, curtains, and kitchen appliances and had not changed a single thing. She gave away all her previous home furnishings to her children or sold them in a garage sale.

The person who never travels or goes to the same cabin every summer on the same week is quite different from the individual on an airplane going to various places several times a month.

Besides differing in personality traits, some individuals are simply more expert than others in planning. They have more foresight, organizational and analytical skills, and imagination. They are motivated to change things and do not accept the status quo. Perhaps their families provided more models of planning behavior than did the families of less expert planners. Planning ability varies between professions as well as between individuals. Consider the range of planning skills necessary in daycare centers, hospitals, and urban and regional projects.

> The ability to perform tasks successfully and dependably is called **expertise**.

It increases as the person acquires more detailed knowledge, has more contact with experts, and develops more memory and experience.

> Expertise then refers to the characteristics, skills, and knowledge that distinguish experts from novices and less experienced people. In some domains there are objective criteria for finding experts, who are consistently able to exhibit superior performance for representative tasks in a domain. For example, chess masters will almost always win chess games against recreational chess players in chess tournaments.
>
> (Ericsson et al., 2006, p. 3)

As it often takes ten years or more of practice to become an expert, it naturally follows that young children have less expertise in most subjects and situations than do adults. Notable exceptions would be the 16-year-olds who win gold medals in gymnastics at the Olympics (who may or may not have started practicing before age six) or child geniuses.

Experts recall more information about messages and situations and are more likely to draw conclusions and make comparisons rapidly. Thus, experts not only have more access to information, but they also tend to recall, reorganize, and respond to messages to a greater extent than others do. Expertise affects beliefs and planning style, which in turn affect intentions to behave and actual behavior. Experts sustain motivation and effort over long periods of time.

Driver or passenger? Which is your preferred role?

## Planning in Families and Other Groups

In a family, one family member may have more mechanical ability than the others and may therefore be expected to fix things, whereas another may have more planning ability and may therefore manage to organize family events or vacations. Other family members will check with the organizer before scheduling events of their own. It's difficult to associate organizational skills with specific demographic traits:

> *Disorganization appears to be an equal opportunity trait, with equal numbers of Americans across most demographic groups saying that they are organized. What does seem to matter is marital status 61 percent of married adults say they are either "extremely" or "mostly" organized, compared with just 54 percent of never- married singles and 49 percent of divorced, separated or widowed adults.*
>
> (Fetto, 2003, pp. 10–11)

In groups here are possible steps to follow in planning through evaluation:

- Define the goal or problem. Explain what the group needs to accomplish.

- Research, find information, but before going outside for answers, first determine what the group already knows, what contacts they may have, and so forth.

- Brainstorm, which means to generate ideas for accomplishing the goal or fixing the problem. Outlandish or wild ideas should be encouraged at this stage, write all the ideas down (later they can be eliminated or fine-tuned).

- Prototype. Detail your ideas and build on them. In this stage, drawings may be made or steps listed, maps drawn. In this stage you are trying to find what might work, a possible solution or innovation. In the end, ideas should begin to come together.

- Choose. Out of everything discussed, what should be selected? Be prepared to explain the choice.

- Implement. Putting plans into action (more on this later in the chapter).

Learn or evaluate. What did the group (and the individual participating) learn from this process? Any unexpected results or learning?

> ### CRITICAL THINKING
>
> **Plans vs. Reality**
>
> Jamie was appointed to a year-long committee. The committee voted to meet twice a month but in with all the cancellations because of things that came up they only met as a group once a month on average. She had originally proposed that they meet once a month and thought twice was too often for the work that needed to be accomplished. Jamie thought she learned from this experience to relax more and realize that the number of meetings would settle to, in her mind, the right amount. Have you ever been in a similar situation when you thought one way and the group another?

## Motivational Factors

Motivated planning behavior is a thinking activity that is directed toward a particular goal or objective. Achievement-motivated individuals keep goals in mind as they plan and complete tasks. When competing activities come their way, they keep focused on their goals such as writing a book, exercising more, filling out job applications, and so on.

Motivation has four main aspects:

1. The goal or objective must be attractive and desired by the seeker.

2. The goal or objective seeker must be persistent.

3. The seeker becomes discontented if she or he does not reach the goal or objective.

4. The goal is possible given the amount of time.

Persistence refers to a person's staying power; it is the personality trait of not giving up when faced with adversity or danger. Read the following case study.

> ### CASE STUDY
>
> **Addressing Moments of Danger**
>
> Amy Hempel is an award-winning American writer who likes to write short stories about addressing danger. What follows is the beginning of an interview with her.
>
> *On her calf next to a scar left by a motorcycle accident, Amy Hempel has the words "sing to it" written in Arabic. She got the tattoo after completing a short story of the same name. It is also the title for her latest collection out on Tuesday, her first in over a decade. Inspiration for the 15 stories came from the Arab proverb "when danger approaches, sing to it." To varying degrees, all of the stories in "Sing to It" are about addressing moments of danger. "I'm very interested in how a person might choose to face something that is threatening, or a person who is threatening," Ms. Hempel says.*
>
> Source: Grey, T. (2019, March 25). "'Sing to It' Keeps Things Short." The Wall Street Journal, A 13.

Figure 6.3 **Motivated planning behavior: Model and example.**

Psychological factors, such as depression, may affect motivation and persistence—in a job search, for example (Smith & Price, 1992). According to Maslow's theory of the hierarchy of needs, which was introduced in Chapter 1, a person attempts to satisfy a more basic need (such as shelter) before directing behavior to higher needs (Maslow, 1954).

Maslow proposed that the typical adult satisfies about 85 percent of physiological needs; 70 percent of safety and security needs; 50 percent of belongingness, social, and love needs; 40 percent of esteem needs; and 10 percent of self-actualization needs. In the years since Maslow introduced his theory, many people have criticized his percentages—in particular, the percentage for self-actualization, which they think is too high. It depends on how one thinks of this. If self-actualization means one is always at the top, totally fulfilled, this would indeed be rare but if it means many times or in most ways one's needs are actualized then this is more likely. In any case, Maslow's basic theory—needs motivate human behavior and unsatisfied needs lead to frustration and stress—is still widely accepted.

Applying Maslow's theory to planning, one might say that a person is motivated to plan and act by some state, condition, or situation, perhaps a social drive (the need to be liked or be more popular) or a physiological drive (hunger or thirst). Figure 6.3 provides a model and an example of motivated planning behavior. The example of a hungry person eating to satisfy his or her hunger is a simple one. Achievement motivation can be far more profound.

Think of all the individuals and the steps involved in planning a new museum or a mission to the international space station. Many organizations use flow charts to graphically illustrate how an operation, such as the development of a new car or a community, is progressing.

Some people seem especially oriented toward the achievement of goals. Achievement-motivated people, such as President Joe Biden, innovator Elon Musk, Bill Gates, and Oprah Winfrey continually set new goals and develop new aspirations. They refuse to rest on their laurels. This characteristic explains why individuals who have made millions in a business venture will, upon selling it, immediately look for another venture to invest their energy in. Money is not their primary objective; rather, obtaining it (the process) is the motivator. For such people, the excitement is in the chase; they value each success more for its message "I've succeeded" than as a vehicle for obtaining life's luxuries. Thus, motivation is an internal drive that is fueled by the process of striving for and attaining goals. Planners are motivated; they must want their plans to succeed.

## Standard Setting

Standards are another important part of the planning process. *Standards* were defined in Chapter 1 as quantitative and/or qualitative criteria that reconcile resources with demands and serve as measures of values and goals (DeMerchant, 1993). The procedures, conduct, and rules of individuals, families, and organizations all incorporate standards. For example, an industry may set a certain standard or level of excellence.

A problem is how do we set standards (or levels of excellence) when technology keeps changing the playing field? How smart will smartphones become? As in the Did You Know? at the beginning of the chapter, there are over 6 billion Internet products in the EU and over 25 billion products worldwide. They are handy, they are useful but are we getting more and more dependent on them to the exclusion or lessening of other life activities or interactions? Parents grapple with these questions of time use and devices all the time.

In planning, standards provide the criteria for action. The standards that are set affect the assessment and allocation of resources, leading to the clarification of demands, decisions, plans, and action. It is important that the plan fit the standards of the individual or situation. In business, a poorly conceived management plan will not meet the standards set by the company.

Likewise, a poorly devised personal or family plan of action may not meet the standards of most families. For example, a 14-year-old son with a grade of F in science may not meet the standards for educational achievement set by the family. Standards emanate from the values and the goals of family members. What do they want, and how do they want to go about getting what they want? What makes sense to them?

Standards evolve or develop over time. A newly married couple gradually develops compatible standards and define what constitutes a comfortable life together. They explore what they value and define what they want as individuals and what they want as a couple. Over the course of their married life, they may go from a tiny apartment to a large house, from a small income to a large income, and at the end of their married life back to a small apartment again and a reduced income. Throughout these changes, the couple's standards will adjust to their needs, life stage, and resources.

## Scheduling, Sequencing, and Multitasking

Almost all plans include schedules or sequences of events and activities. "**Scheduling** refers to the specification of sets of time bounded projected activities which are sufficient for the achievement of a desired goal set" (Avery & Stafford, 1991, p. 327).

Written plans with deadlines or end points, diaries, lists, and timetables are all examples of schedules. Consider list making. A list may be a series of activities or appointments, such as 8:00–11:00, go to classes; 11:00 see adviser; 11:30–12:30 lunch; 12:30–5:00 work. Another common type of list is a grocery list. The generally accepted belief that writing a grocery list will eliminate or reduce impulse buying has been challenged by two researchers, Jeffrey Inman of the University of Wisconsin and Russell Winer of the University of California at Berkeley. They found that list makers are just as likely to make spontaneous purchases as those who shop without them (Inman & Winer, 1999). According to a report on their study in *American Demographics,* 59 percent of all supermarket purchases are unplanned.

Scheduling involves the mental process of sequencing. Sequencing is the ordering of activities and resources necessary to achieve goals. One action succeeds another until the need or the goal is fulfilled. Activities or tasks can be independent, dovetailed, interdependent, or overlapped. These four types will be discussed next.

**Independent activities** take place one at a time. They stand alone. For example, a person who first watches television, then does an hour of homework, and then gets ready for bed is engaged in three independent activities. Each activity is independent of the others because the person could choose to go straight to bed and not watch television or do homework. In other words, none of the activities depends on the others.

**Multitasking** (also called **dovetailing**) occurs when two or more activities take place at the same time. Examples are eating popcorn and watching a movie and talking on the phone while making dinner. People often think dovetailing is a desirable way of organizing activity and getting a lot done in a short time, but it can be ineffective if it leads to unacceptable consequences. Sometimes people try to do too many activities at once. Trying to talk on the phone, answer the doorbell, cook dinner, and watch a small child all at the same time can result in a burned dinner and a crying child. As this example suggests, dovetailing is not a panacea, though it can sometimes be a useful time management tool: doing more activities at the same time does not necessarily produce better outcomes. Individuals must decide how many activities they can reasonably handle at once and this may vary by time of day.

Both men and women say they are multitasking more now than ever before; the types of multitasking at work include:

- Reading email or instant messaging while on the phone

- Skimming printed material or sorting junk mail while on the phone

- Shopping or doing research online while on the phone

- Writing personal "to-do" lists or reading notes or talking on cell phones during meetings

> ### CRITICAL THINKING
>
> **Distracting**
>
> The multitasking of others can be distracting. For example, you take a seat at a conference table and your boss is text-messaging during the meeting and reading email and keeps saying "right, right" as if following the conversation taking place around the table, but she is not. What message is the boss giving to her employees? Are they allowed to do likewise?

In many high-pressure occupations, such as air traffic controller or pilot, a successful person has to multitask. "If you saw the movie 'Top Gun' (1986), you'll remember what all you see Tom Cruise doing in the cockpit. He has got to pick and choose when he does what, that is, multitask very carefully. The chance that he will successfully conclude a flight in a fighter jet depends not only on his capabilities and limitations but also on his equipment" (David Meyer quoted in Anderson, 2001, p. 4).

Multitasking takes place during leisure hours, too. Why simply work out on a treadmill when you can read a magazine, watch television, and talk on a phone at the same time? Should we worry about the long-term effects of multitasking?

> *"Not to worry," says Marcel Just, co-head of Carnegie Mellon University's Center for Cognitive Brain Imaging. While overloading the brain causes distress, which has its own physiological hazards, the brain seems to recover with rest.*
>
> *(Shellenbarger, 2003, March 20, p. D1)*

In this quotation lies one of the antidotes to our sped-up lives: getting enough rest to recover and bounce back, a subject to be covered in Chapter 11. In the short run, the warning signs that multitasking is getting out of hand include anxiety about the lack of completion and the following:

- Lapses in attentiveness

- Loss of concentration

- Gaps in short-term memory

- Communication problems

- Stress symptoms such as shortness of breath (Shellenbarger, 2003, February 27).

We can do several things at the same time, but not without a cost. The process of switching back and forth takes time away from the original motivation of multitasking, which is usually to save time—at some point, the brain crashes. To get back into balance, a person can consciously stop and refocus by listening for the important messages, a technique called living in the moment or living in the present. A lot of this depends on the activity itself: something easy and repetitive, like tying shoes, can be done while someone is talking to you, whereas attempting a more complicated set of tasks, like reading a report while someone is talking to you, will be more frustrating. Multitasking is becoming more common, and each individual has to decide how much is effective and at what point it's time for a break. The editors of *Real Simple* magazine said, "We love multitasking (when it makes sense), innovation (when it has a purpose), and a clean home (especially when it can be done quickly)" (2003, April, p. 36). Who can argue with that?

**Overlapping activities** involve a combination of activities that require intermittent and/or concurrent attention. For example, college students with children combine childcare with schoolwork, going back and forth between the activities. Brittany, for example, comes to the state university for her graduate courses during the week and goes home on weekends (a three-hour drive one way) to see her three-year-old daughter who her mother is caring for during the week.

Activities are **interdependent** when one activity must be completed before another can take place. In other words, one activity builds on another and is not effective in isolation. For example, hiring someone before a position exists and allocating money for a salary would be senseless. Similarly, a newspaper article is not complete until the people involved in the story are interviewed or at least contacted for comment. It is not always easy to differentiate among overlapping, dovetailing, and interdependent activities. People may switch back and forth among the three types of activities in a short period of time. Regardless of type, the behavioral goal of scheduling and sequencing is to provide the desired flow of activities.

Sequencing and scheduling preferences are closely associated with the personality or temperament of the planner as well as with the task itself. How many college students have exactly the same class schedule? Even when they have the same class schedule, it is highly unlikely that they will also eat, socialize, and sleep at exactly the same time. In a family, plans should accommodate the different scheduling needs and preferences of the individuals in the household.

## Attributes of Plans

Workable plans have the following attributes: They are clear, flexible, adaptive, realistic, appropriate, and goal directed. Clear plans are understood by everyone. For example, if an advertisement for a concert says that the concert will start at 8:00 P.M., the audience assumes that it will start promptly, and they should plan to get there ahead of time. In this situation, the concertgoer's plans will have to be flexible because traffic and parking conditions are not totally predictable. Is arriving 10–15 minutes ahead of time suitable? If several people are going to the concert together, how will they adjust their schedules to be ready on time? "Adaptive" refers to the ability of the plan to respond to unanticipated events that may occur. If an organization seeks to be adaptive, "it needs to open itself in many ways":

*Especially important is the organization's relationship to information, particularly to that which is new and even disturbing. Information must actively be sought from everywhere, from places and sources people never thought to look before. And then it must circulate freely so that many people can interpret it.*

*(Wheatley, 1999, p. 83)*

"Realistic" implies that the plan is feasible and likely to work. Being appropriate means that the plan is suited to the situation and the people involved.

As has been suggested throughout this chapter, successful plans are goal directed. Specific, challenging goals lead to higher task performance than do specific, unchallenging goals, vague goals, or no goals (Locke et al., 1994).

## Types of Plans

Many different types of plans exist. Plans can be categorized by time as short-term and long-term plans. Plans can also be distinguished by the parties involved: individuals, households, organizations, communities, or nations. This chapter will concentrate on three types of plans (directional, contingency, and strategic) that are commonly associated with individual and family resource management. Given different situations, a manager can pick the best type of plan.

**Directional plans** progress along a linear path to long-term goal fulfillment. A plan to graduate from high school, graduate from college, and then go to law school to become an attorney is an example of a directional plan. Because a certain degree of work experience is a prerequisite for a higher-level position, career planning is usually directional, although less so now than it used to be because people today change jobs more frequently than in the past.

**Contingency plans** are backup or secondary plans to be used in case a plan does not work. The military is known for contingency plans: If one strategy does not work, they have several others ready to be initiated. Similarly, chess players think of several different potential ways to respond to an opponent's move. Organizations often use a contingency approach. The basic idea behind this approach is that there is no single best way to manage: a method that is successful in one situation may not be successful in another. Therefore, a business manager will devise several plans after assessing the characteristics of the individuals and groups involved, the organizational structure, and his or her own leadership style (Ivancevich & Matteson, 1990). If one plan is not successful, the manager will try another. Likewise, in a family, the manager (or managers) sizes up the situation and the family members and others involved, and prepares several plans leading to a solution. Here again, the manager will be prepared to substitute another plan if one plan does not work.

As an example of how an individual uses the contingency approach, consider Shannon, a 22-year-old who applied to eight different graduate schools. Her plan was to apply to three schools known to be hard to get into, two schools that were moderately difficult to get into, and three easy-to-get-into schools. Shannon wanted to be sure that by September she would be accepted by at least one school, and she did everything she could to ensure that result.

As explained in Chapter 4, a strategy is a plan of action, a way of conducting and following through on operations. **Strategic plans** use a directional approach and include both a proactive search for new opportunities and a reactive solution to existing problems (Wheeler & Hunger, 1987).

The terms "proactive" and "reactive" are discussed in detail in the next section, but here they mean simply that the strategic planner utilizes a forward-looking approach while realizing that past business also must be concluded.

Strategic planning focuses attention on the initial stages of the decision-making process—the opportunities and occasions for choice and the design of new action strategies (Simon, 1993). To conclude, strategic plans are not only associated with the military, business, or politics, but they also occur in individual and family life. For example, job hunting involves many strategies, such as résumé writing (making a record of one's past achievements and experience), reading, prioritizing, and responding to job announcements. Financial crises stimulate the need to strategize. Here is the advice of Elizabeth Warren and Amelia Tyagi, the authors of *The Two-Income Trap:*

> *A family facing a financial crisis should think like a family at war. You must concentrate on preserving what matters most, and you must let the other things go.*
>
> *When the trouble comes, ask the central question: Which of your assets do you most want to hold on to? Maybe it's your car, your home, or your health insurance policy. Decide which things you value most, and pay those bills first. Once you are in trouble, you will need to fight—and you should be fighting for the things you care about, not trying to satisfy the loudest or most aggressive creditor.*
>
> *(2003, p. 168)*

### Proactive Versus Reactive

Stephen R. Covey's groundbreaking book *The 7 Habits of Highly Effective People* delineates seven good habits:

- *Habit 1:* Be proactive.
- *Habit 2:* Begin with the end in mind.
- *Habit 3:* Put first things first.
- *Habit 4:* Think win-win.
- *Habit 5:* Seek first to understand, then to be understood.
- *Habit 6:* Synergize.
- *Habit 7:* Sharpen the saw.

The titles of several of these "habits" are self-evident, but a few deserve further explanation. The last one, "sharpening the saw," means pulling it all together, moving along to higher planes of learning, commitment, and activity.

To **synergize** means to produce a third alternative, which is not my way or your way, but a third way that is best, a product of group thinking. This is a systems approach to problem solving: The whole is greater than the sum of its parts. Synergy comes about when two or more people get together and come up with an idea or achieve an effect that would not be possible individually. It is a creative process. According to Covey (1989), "Synergy means that 1 + 1 may equal 8, 16, or even 1,600" (p. 271). "Win/Win is a frame of mind and heart that constantly seeks mutual benefit in all human interactions. Win/Win means that agreements or solutions are mutually beneficial, mutually satisfying" (p. 207). This is a cooperative versus competitive approach to life.

Being **proactive** means taking responsibility for one's own life. It is about freedom and the power to choose. According to Covey (1989), "Our behavior is a function of our decisions, not our conditions. We can subordinate feelings to values. We have the initiative and the responsibility to make things happen" (p. 71). Proactive people accept responsibility for their own actions; they do not blame others or circumstances for their behavior. "Proactive management involves change-oriented planning where the desired

change is conceived by a person or family and the implementation of the change alters the environment" (Dollahite, 1991, p. 374). Thus, in proactive management, the individual or family is actively seeking solutions to problems by forming plans, including strategic plans.

Proactive (and the next type, reactive) can also apply to leadership in groups. Is the leader more:

- Forceful in style, strategic, and directive or

- Advisory in style, expert, referent, and respectful of others, patient and participative? Both of these types want change, but they go about it in different ways.

**Reactive** people are often overly affected by outside forces, such as changes in the weather or a schedule (such as a canceled event), or the bad attitudes of their co-workers. According to Covey (1989), "When people treat them well, they feel well; when people don't, they become defensive or protective. Reactive people build their emotional lives around the behavior of others, empowering the weaknesses of other people to control them" (p. 72). Proactive people also notice the weather or the social conditions around them, but they respond differently than do reactive people. They have more resilience. Values such as honesty and self-respect drive the behaviors of proactive people more than outside forces do. Other people's opinions matter less to proactive people than they do to reactive people. As Eleanor Roosevelt said, "No one can hurt you without your consent." Typical phrases used by proactive and reactive people are listed in Table 6.1. Notice that the reactive person says, "I can't," whereas the proactive person says, "I choose." Proactive people believe their lives are the sum total of the choices they have made. Planners with proactive styles approach life challenges more assertively than reactive people do. Management theorists and neuroscientists support the notion that effective managers and decisionmakers are proactive and goal-oriented (Sharpe & Winter, 1991; Purvis et al., 2019). Proactive management can help a person or family avoid crises or stress through active anticipation of events to come. In proactive management, an "individual or a family actively clarifies values, makes plans, sets goals, organizes activities, and makes changes before experiencing stressors" (Dollahite, 1991, p. 374).

The three types of plans discussed in this section—directional, contingency, and strategic—are not limited to individuals and families. They are potentially applicable to all organizations and situations. For example, Coca-Cola, in a strategic move to market its product worldwide, seized the opportunity to go global rather than being confined to the United States. Airlines are constantly searching for more profitable routes. Fast-food restaurants look for new locations and new products to expand their share of the market. Likewise, individuals and families try to maximize their chances of improving their lives. For example, a proactive,

Table 6.1  Reactive versus Proactive Language

| Reactive Language | Proactive Language |
|---|---|
| There's nothing I can do. | Let's look at our alternatives. |
| That's just the way I am. | |
| They make me so mad. | I can choose a different approach. |
| They won't allow that. | |
| I have to do that. | I control my own feelings. |
| I can't. | I can create an effective presentation. |
| I must. | I will choose an appropriate response. |
| If only. | |
| | I choose. |
| | I prefer. |
| | I will. |

Source: From Covey, S. R. (1898). *The 7 habits of highly effective people*, Free Press, an imprint of Simon & Schuster, New York.

goal-setting foreign-service officer will try to get an appointment overseas in the desired location rather than wait to be assigned anywhere the government decides to send him or her.

The specific planning mode used (directional, contingency, or strategic) reflects the individual's or the family's perceptions of what type of plan will be most suitable. Key decisions flow from the dominant planning mode and the choice of a proactive or reactive approach.

## What Is Implementing?

Remember that planning leads to implementing meaning putting plans into action and controlling that action. All action has a purpose. One of the purposes may be goal fulfillment such as saving up to buy a car. Controlling takes place because once plans are activated, they need to be checked to make sure that they are leading to the desired end state. As everyone knows, it is easier to make plans than to initiate and monitor them. In monitoring, the person asks, "How am I doing?" A letter saying you've been hired, or you've won an award is an example that one is doing well.

Environmental, economic, social, and a variety of other forces and conditions can positively or negatively affect the outcome of even the most carefully prepared plan. For example, planning a dream house and building an affordable house are two different things.

The factors affecting implementing are the same ones that affect planning: situations, personal traits and characteristics, and motivational factors.

Possible blocks to successful implementation include:

- *Distractions.*
- *Environmental constraints.*
- *Other people.* They may not believe in the same plans you do, or they may drag their feet.

- *Costs and other restrictions.*

- *Competition.* Perhaps there are competing plans that are better. For example, 14 architects may be invited to submit plans for a new university building—only one will be selected.

- *Crises.* Long-term plans may be put on hold if resources are required for more immediate needs.

- Procrastination or lack of motivation.

- Closed-mindedness.

Several strategies can be employed to avoid these blocks. The main strategy is to intelligently size up the situations that arise and respond accordingly. In the end, implementing requires a scanning sensibility—monitoring of your actions and the actions of those around you. **Scanning** is an activity in which individuals or families "read the world," looking for signals and clues (i.e., information, messages, feedback) that could have strategic implications. Three of the elements that play into this—actuating, checking, and controlling—are discussed next.

## Actuating

The difficulty here is what action to take, not any action but the right action. **Actuating** refers to putting plans into effect, action, or motion. For example, Mike, a teenager, has been reading car advertisements and talking with friends for months about buying a used car. Finally, he decides he is ready to look at some cars. Mike is transitioning from think mode to action.

Plans can be actuated in stages. A teacher may interview for a job in January that does not start until August. Within the family system, parents might start saving for their child's college education soon after the child's birth and add money to the college fund on each birthday. Positive and negative feedback (discussed in Chapter 2) play a large part in actuating. Feedback from others may prevent a person from actuating a plan—she or he may want to wait until the time seems to be right. Also, if things are going well, an individual may decide not to "rock the boat" and to let things simply evolve for a while; at other times, a more active and controlling approach is necessary.

Being adaptable or flexible is part of the actuating part of the process followed by checking and controlling to be discussed next. Consider the Case Study of Payal Kadakia.

### CASE STUDY

#### Staying Adaptable

In an interview, Payal Kadakia Founder and Chairman of ClassPass (Fitness and yoga studios) said:

> My dad told me that you have to always stay adaptable. At the time, the value of the advice didn't fully sink in. Here's what I realized in reflecting back. We can build a skill, and it can become obsolete. We can build an incredible product, and someone can copy it. We can do everything seemingly right, and the market can change on a whim. We can, however, develop the muscles-in the form of sustainable behaviors -that enable us to quickly recognize and adapt to change.

> Source: C.L.C. (March/April 2019). Payal Kadakia Founder and
> Chairman of class pass. INC, p. 29.

## Checking and Controlling

The most common times people make daily plans are:

- In the morning

- At the start of work

- At the end of work

- At dinner time

- In the evening before bed

Some keep lists or calendars. It is suggested that

> To increase your productivity and clarity both for work and life outside of work, have a plan for the day. That includes knowing the time of your meetings, deciding what projects you will work on, and being clear on when you will do tasks like answering email. You'll also want to have some plan for your evenings in terms of what you would like to get done or simply relax.
>
> (Saunders, 2020)

Once the plan is activated, different situations or personal factors may indicate the need for corrective action. To be successful, plans need to be checked and rechecked. This checking, or **adjusting**, activity is a type of controlling. For example, a person may make a reservation well in advance of an important event and reconfirm the reservation a day or two before the event.

**Checking** is defined in management as determining whether actions comply with standards and sequencing. An individual determines whether plans are unfolding as they should, in the right sequence, and in a timely fashion. If a check reveals that they are not, a correction is necessary.

For example, changes in planning and implementation can occur when an individual goes grocery shopping with a list. The list is a plan of action; but, while shopping (actuating the plan), the shopper may make several changes, such as substituting one product for another or adding several more items to the grocery cart. In this way, the list serves as a guide. Most plans can be envisioned as a guide—a mental plan of action.

If overdone, checking can produce undesirable effects. Too much checking by the planner or by the implementer of the plan can lead to frustration, resentment, or pressure. Consider the potential frustration of a person on a diet who checks his or her weight several times a day. Or consider how employees feel when the boss stands over them when they are trying to complete a task. Or how an interviewer feels when a potential employee keeps calling about the result of an interview. In the latter case, too much checking can ruin the person's chances for employment. The goal is to have a sufficient amount of checking to ensure a positive outcome (e.g., a weight loss, a completed task, or a job), but neither too much nor too little.

Controlling and corrective action take time. Therefore, the implementer has to weigh the costs against the benefits of spending time and energy on checking. *Controlling* is most effective at significant milestones or critical points in a plan. Teachers and professors do this by giving tests or assignments at appropriate intervals of learning; it is their way of checking the learning progress

In the home, controlling devices include those for:

- Lights

- Locks

- Garage doors

- Smartphones

- Refrigerators, dishwashers, and stoves/ovens

- Heating and cooling

- Televisions

- Routers and printers

- Cars

- Vacuum cleaners

- Securing home deliveries

This list names only a few. Of course, these devices interact such as the way Eva's phone can change channels on the television, and in her case, her phone overrides the handheld remote device held by her husband. You can see how this gets complicated and leads to the subject in the next chapter on Communication.

The goal is seamless communication between the user and the device. Homeowners or renters should be empowered to be in control by giving consent to the features and devices that they want. As with so many other aspects of management, the key to successful planning and implementation is a balance between wants, goals, and actions. Particularly in the checking and controlling phase, achieving a balance is essential to obtaining a successful outcome.

## CASE STUDY

### Running the House from Afar

Technology has made it much easier to run homes from afar including second homes remotely.

*En route to their Maryland-shore vacation home, Joel Fein and Vicky Levin, physicians living in suburban Philadelphia, use the house's internet-connected thermostat to get the temperature where they want it. Between visits, that same device enables them to be sure the temperature hasn't fallen dangerously low. An internet-connected security system provides reassurance that the house is safe from intruders – and when a contractor needs access, the owners can remotely turn off the alarm and unlock the doors.*

*Source: Askt, D. (2019, March 25). How to get the most out of a second home. The Wall Street Journal, R2.*

## What Is Evaluating?

The word "evaluation" comes from an Old French verb, *évaluer* (to be worthy or to have value). To evaluate means to determine the worth of an effort. Thus, **evaluation** is a process of judging or examining the cost, value, or worth of a plan or decision based on such criteria as standards, met demands, or goals. It occurs throughout the management process: in setting goals in the first place, and at each step along the way. As discussed earlier, people may encounter obstacles to goal achievement, such as crises and unplanned-for events or something just plain doesn't work.

### CASE STUDY

#### Evaluating Opening and Closing Decisions

Starbucks, an American-based coffee company and coffeehouse chain, has around 30,000 locations worldwide and expanding. When this book author was in Malta in March 2019, the local population and tourists were eagerly anticipating the first Starbucks opening that summer. At around the same time, a Starbucks closed in a U.S. college town because of poor sales. There were other Starbucks in the same town doing very well. The thriving ones had drive-through windows. Like other retailers, Starbucks is sales-driven and ready to close a poor performer in a fairly short time.

What are some of the criteria in the evaluation process? An individual may seek to determine the quantities (was enough money saved?) or qualities involved in an action, or they may look for the satisfaction of family members.

As judgments are subjective, evaluations can turn out to be flawed or biased. To ensure better end results, people engage in assessments. **Assessment** involves the gathering of information about results, the comparison of those results with the results of the past, and the open discussion of the meaning of those results, the ways that they have been gathered, and their implications for the next moves of the family or the individual (Senge et al., 1999).

Since evaluation can be painful (like closing a store, school, or restaurant or ending a failed relationship), people often ignore this step and proceed immediately to the next problem or goal. Nevertheless, looking back and evaluating past decisions are crucial steps in becoming a better manager. In anticipation, start-ups should have an **exit strategy** even before they begin—at what point will they sell or close the business or morph it into something entirely new?

### CASE STUDY

#### Learning Not to Chase Every New Idea

As has been said, evaluation is one of the most difficult parts of management. It is more fun to imagine and plan than to carefully evaluate every new option or idea that comes along. Consider this from an interview with Daniel Lubetzsky, Founder and CEO of Kind (a food company).

"Our longtime president and chief operating officer, John Leahy, joined the company in 2010, when we were selling nine nut bars, employed 30 team members, and generated roughly $20 million in revenue. To put that in context, today Kind offers more than 70 snacks and employs more than 700 full- and part-time team members. John repeatedly told me, 'We can't do everything. Let's prioritize and do a few things really well, rather than a ton of things less well.' As an entrepreneur, Daniel found that hard to hear but knew it was good advice."

*Source: Saporito, B. (2019, March/April). Learning not to chase every shiny idea. INC. p. 29*

What is true in managing businesses is often also true in managing personal lives. Children may be drawn to dozens of sports and organizations and the options are being sorted through. Improving management skills is important because competence in problem solving has been identified as an essential part of healthy marriages and family systems (Rettig & Bubolz, 1983). To build on success, individuals should acknowledge the things that have been accomplished and the ways they have changed or grown. What decisions are you most proud of? Maybe it was trying out for a school play or a team sport. Whether it worked or not, you learned from trying more than what you would have if you had not tried. Most entrepreneurial businesses have a short run or fail. Thomas Edison conducted 50,000 different experiments to find a working storage battery!

When asked if he was frustrated, his reply was "What failures? I now know 50,000 things which do not work." Once the evaluation is over, work on restoring your energy, clearing your calendar, relaxing, and taking care of things that you have been putting off. Are there new priorities? Is there a need for a new plan?

**Storyboarding** is a technique used by advertisers, movie screenwriters, and television scriptwriters to show the main scenes in a commercial, movie, or television show. A storyboard is a comic-strip type presentation complete with pictures, dialogue, and words to describe the action (Levinson, 1999). Storyboarding can be used as a planning technique in other situations to show the consecutive steps that lead to desired outcomes. It allows a person to visualize the steps to be taken. Figure 6.4 shows a storyboard from a commercial. Use the blank spaces provided in Figure 6.5 to create your own storyboard. The last frame should be your desired outcome.

At the end of the management process, a final evaluation takes place. If a goal is achieved, the manager can look back with satisfaction on how things turned out. Other possible outcomes are the achievement of a new or a substitute goal (not the ones initially set), the solution to a problem, the satisfaction of a need or want, or perhaps none of these. Whether the outcomes are effective or whether they are ineffective, the manager should review what went right and what went wrong with the process so that she or he can learn from it for future decisions.

## SUMMARY

This chapter focused on how to plan within the context of societal changes and the rapid adoption of smart technologies. How to control, how to manage them is a central issue going forward. As the opening case study showed, individuals and families plan their lives and lifestyles. Some of us need more control and consistency than others. Resource management theory focuses on conscious decision-making, leading to the formation and implementation of plans to achieve goals. Planning, implementing, and evaluating are the main subjects of this chapter. They represent both mental and physical activity. Planning begins with

SFX: CAR AND FOOT TRAFFIC AMBIENCE
VO: Why did the chicken cross the road?
To open a 7/24 Savings Plan at
Swing + Trust
Because with $500 in savings...

... he can avoid getting henpecked by
monthly charges on a checking account.
What's more, he can access his nest egg
through our huge ATM network...
SFX: BANK AMBIENCE
... and round-the-clock phone service.

VO: And of course, the interest he'll earn on
    savings isn't just chicken feed.
So open a 7/24 Savings Plan at San Diego
Swing + Trust
And give yourself a good reason to...
SFX: COCKA DOODLE DOO

Figure 6.4  A sample storyboard layout.

Source: Reprinted by permission of Wells Fargo Bank.

mentally organizing activities to accomplish the desired end state. It requires vision, energy, motivation to succeed, and enough foresight to avoid chasing every shiny new idea. Implementing includes both actuating and controlling.

Task saturation refers to being so busy doing things that there is no time to plan or lead effectively.

Planning and implementation require the ability to order and sequence steps in a rational manner. Personality, situations, standards, and the environment all affect planning outcomes. Proactive and reactive

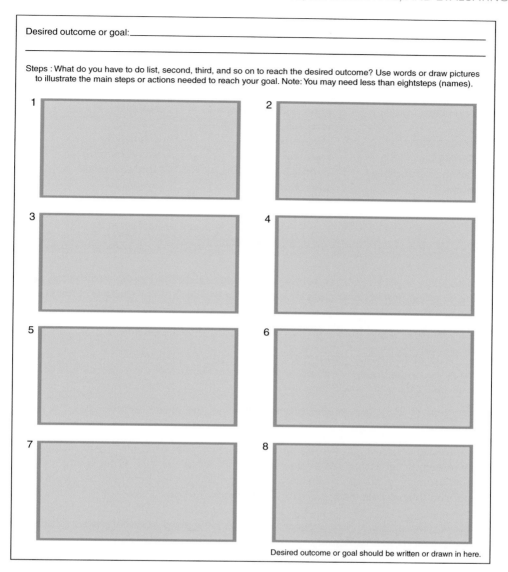

Desired outcome or goal:_____

Steps : What do you have to do list, second, third, and so on to reach the desired outcome? Use words or draw pictures to illustrate the main steps or actions needed to reach your goal. Note: You may need less than eightsteps (names).

1

2

3

4

5

6

7

8

Desired outcome or goal should be written or drawn in here.

Figure 6.5 Storyboarding: A planning technique.

personality types differ in how they approach planning. Their language reflects these differences. Introverts (more internal, more process-oriented) and extroverts (more social) were also discussed. One study showed their use of smartphones differed.

Scanning is an activity in which individuals or families "read the world" by searching for signals or clues that have strategic implications. Assessment involves the gathering of information about results. Storyboarding was introduced as a technique for visualizing the steps in planning leading to the desired outcome.

People vary in their planning expertise. Planning ability can increase with experience and maturity. As Emerson said, "That which we persist in doing becomes easier—not that the nature of the task has changed, but our ability to do has increased."

## KEY TERMS

| | | |
|---|---|---|
| actuating | expertise | plan |
| adjusting | extroverts | proactive |
| assessment | Gresham's law of planning | process |
| best practices | independent activities | reactive |
| checking | interdependent activities | scanning |
| contingency plans | introverts | scheduling |
| directional plans | multitask | storyboarding |
| dovetailing (multitasking) | overlapping activities | strategic plans |
| evaluation | persistence | synergize |
| exit strategy | personality | task saturation |

## REVIEW QUESTIONS

1. Do you know anyone similar to author Stuart Woods described in the introductory story in this chapter? Someone who has several houses or does not like changes in home environments or who names their pets the same name over and over? Explain.

2. What influences affect planning? Include a discussion of Gresham's law of planning in your answer.

3. What is the difference between proactive and reactive styles? Give an example of each in your own life.

4. At the end of Clint Eastwood's *Dirty Harry* movie, the main character says, "A man's gotta know his limitations." What are the limitations to multitasking (or are there any)?

5. The musician John Lennon wrote a song lyric "Life is what happens to you while you're busy making other plans." What do you think he meant by this? What is your opinion about how much of life can be planned and how much just happens? Give an example of something that you planned to do, but "life" got in the way.

## REFERENCES

Anderson, P. (2001, August 6). *Study: Multitasking is counterproductive.* Retrieved March 8, 2004, from http://www.cnn.com/2001/CAREER/trends/08/05/multitasking.study/index.html.

Avery, R., & Stafford, K. (1991). Toward a scheduling congruity theory of family resource management. *Lifestyles: Family and Economic Issues, 12*(4), 325–344.

Bingham, J. (1991). *Social psychology* (2nd ed.). New York: HarperCollins.

Boehret, K. (2007, June 20). Making lists of everything in your life. *The Wall Street Journal,* p. D6.

Covey, S. (1989). *The 7 habits of highly effective people.* New York: Simon & Schuster.

DeMerchant, E. (1993, February). Standards: An analysis of definitions, frameworks and implications. In C. Y. Kratzar (Ed.), *Proceedings of the Southeastern regional home management association of family economics* (pp. 13–22). Roanoke, VA: Virginia Polytechnic Institute.

Dollahite, D. (1991, Winter). Family resource management and family stress theories: Toward conceptualization integration. *Lifestyles: Family and Economic Issues, 12*(4), 361–377.

Editorial note. (2003, April). *Real Simple,* p. 36.

Ericsson, K., Charness, N., Feltovich, P., & Hoffman, R. (Eds.). (2006). *The Cambridge handbook of expertise and expert performance.* New York: Cambridge University Press.

Fetto, R. (2003, April). Get it together. *American Demographics, 24,* 10–11.

Foxall, G., Goldsmith, R., & Brown, S. (1998). *Consumer psychology for marketing.* London: Routledge.

Halvorson, H. (2011). *Succeed: How we can reach our goals.* New York: Hudson Street Press.

Hibbs, S. (February 11, 2021). *Erasing family documentary reveals shared parenting prevents trauma post divorce, backed by two new studies.* Washington, DC: Shirley & McVicker Public Affairs Media Release.

Inman, J., & Winer, R. (1999, May 6). Shoppers are impulsive. *Tallahassee Democrat.*

Ivancevich, J. M., & Matteson, M. T. (1990). *Organizational behavior and management.* Homewood, IL: Irwin.

Keates, N. (2011, July 22). One home, three locations. *The Wall Street Journal,* p. D.7,

Kronholz, J. (1997, November 20). We're all living in future tense—And it's tense indeed. *The Wall Street Journal,* p. A1.

Levinson, J. (1999). *Guerilla advertising.* New York: Houghton Mifflin.

Locke, E., Smith, K., Erez, M., Chah, D., & Schaffer, A. (1994). The effects of intra-individual goal conflict on performance. *Journal of Management, 20*(1), 67–91.

Maslow, A. (1943, July). A theory of human motivation. *Psychological Review, 50,* 370–396.

Matchan, L. (2002, November 16). Declutter your life—professionally. *St. Petersburg Times,* p. 6F.

Morris, B. (1987, August 4). As a favored pastime, shopping ranks high with most Americans. *The Wall Street Journal,* p. D1.

Purvis, D., Augustine, G., Fitzpatrick, D., Hall, W., Lamantia, S., Mooney, R., Platt, M. L., & White, L. E. (2019). *Neuroscience, international sixth edition.* Oxford: Oxford University Press.

Rahim, N., Siah, Y., Tee, X., & Siah, P. (2021). Smartphone Addiction: Its relationships to personality traits and types of smartphone use. *International Journal of Technology in Education and Science, 5*(1), 128–140.

Rauch, J. (2003, March). Caring for your introvert. *Atlantic Monthly, 291,* 133–134.

Rettig, K., & Bubolz, M. (1983). Perceptual indicators of family well-being. *Social Indicators Research, 12,* 417– 438.

Saunders, E. G. (April 8, 2020). How to transition between work time and personal time. *Harvard Business Review.*

Senge, P., Kleiner, A., Roberts, C., Ross, R., Roth, G., & Smith, B. (1999). *The dance of change.* New York: Doubleday.

Sharpe, D., & Winter, M. (1991). Toward working hypotheses of effective management: Conditions, thought processes, and behaviors. *Lifestyles: Family and Economic Issues, 12*(4), 303–323.

Shellenbarger, S. (2003, March 20). Female rats are better multitaskers; with humans, the debate rages on. *The Wall Street Journal,* p. D1.

Simon, H. A. (1993). Strategy and organizational evolution. *Strategic Management Journal, 14,* 131–142.

Smith, S., & Price, S. (1992). Women and plant closings: Unemployment, re-employment, and job training enrollment following dislocation. *Journal of Family and Economic Issues, 13*(1), 45–72.

Warren, E., & Tyagi, A. (2003). *The two-income trap.* New York: Basic Books.

Wheatley, M. (1999). *Leadership and the new science* (2nd ed.). San Francisco, CA: Berrett-Koehler.

Wheeler, T., & Hunger, J. (1987). *Strategic management* (2nd ed.). Reading, MA: Addison-Wesley.

Chapter **7**

# Communication

DOI: 10.4324/9781003166740-7

The Internet and the Human Capacity to Process Information

The Role of the Home and the Individual: Managing Information

## DID YOU KNOW THAT ...?

… We speak about 150 to 200 words a minute.
An artist was paid $35 to design the Nike logo.

## CASE STUDY

### The Australian Open Involving Three Generations

Communication comes in many forms including verbal and nonverbal (e.g., body language). Read the following case and notice both.

*While watching the Australian Open in January, I found it fascinating to witness the interaction of three generations of sensational tennis players, following the stunning win of a young up-and-comer over a teen is great. White-haired John McEnroe interviewed 20-year-old Stefanos Tsitsipas after his four-set win over 37-year-old Roger Federer, who sheepishly walked off the court looking discouraged. Tsisipas was shocked and excited and told McEnroe who he long had admired, "You are my hero." How old is old? A loss of a tennis match led to the speculation, "Will Federer retire from tennis?" McEnroe transitioned his career from professional tennis player to professional tennis announcer. Will we see Federer covering tennis matches in the future?*

*Source: Schrager, J. (2019, March 14). Stepping Down from the Bench Doesn't Have to be the Closing Act for Retiring Judges. ABA Journal. https:outlook.office.com/owa/projection.asox*

Whether in private or professional realms, today's managers must communicate with assertiveness, clarity, and compassion. We are being asked to communicate in new ways. "What's more interactions have become mostly virtual, making everything from internal management to external collaboration to negotiations harder than ever" (Leadership Insights, HBS Executive Education, 2021). According to Adler et al. (2020), communication is:

- process
- Relational (something you do with others, could be words, could be forms of expression like dancing or actors and audiences)
- Symbolic (words or signs as symbols that represent people, things, ideas, and events)

Among the many forms of communication and dialogue to be discussed in this chapter, there are personal interactions as highlighted in the case study, virtual communications (platforms such as Zoom, Teams, and Skype), and commercial interactions such as in the selling of products. The essence of successful advertising is to convince consumers they need a product.

Previously unknown in the United States, energy drinks are now a $3.7 billion category with hundreds of competitors, led by Red Bull. How did that happen? I don't mean in the descriptive sense of a brand's or a product's movement from one group of consumers to another until it becomes familiar to almost everybody. I mean on an individual level. We all have our thirsts —real and metaphorical. How do we decide what will quench them and what won't? How are those decisions affected by the commercial persuasion industry and the billions it spends to influence us? (Walker, 2008, p. xii)

What we drink and how it is marketed (communicated) is a current subject of immense political debate especially when it comes to sugared drinks—sodas, juices—for school-age children.

**Dialogue**, whether commercial, personal, or professional, implies a two-way process, a genuine interaction, reaching out. The objectives are to express interest or concern for the other person and/or their views to be supportive or empathetic. A **monologue** is the opposite of a dialogue. In a monologue, one person speaks and the other listens.

### CRITICAL THINKING

Chad receives an email that he is not accepted into the graduate school he wanted most. As a neighbor and friend, you want to help him. What would you say or do?

How do you talk so people will listen? Instead of allowing our words to mislead, we can learn to communicate more effectively. Conversational skills are the hallmark of management, an integral part of every step of the management process.

*Feedback* connects the steps together, forming a loop, as shown in Figure 7.1. As noted in the opening case study, communication can be verbal and/or nonverbal. Although communication and feedback are normally thought of as verbal, both can be nonverbal as well. For example, a look can often convey more than words.

This chapter will examine both verbal and nonverbal communication. An example of nonverbal communication is Dunkin' Donuts recruiting teenagers to wear temporary tattoos with its brand name on their foreheads. Other topics to be covered include the process of communication, conflict, information overload, keeping the lines of communication open, and the value of listening.

*Encouraging the reader to communicate more effectively is the behavioral goal of this chapter.* Presenting the types, forms, and problems of communication in families, in small groups, and in commercial or professional settings is the informational goal. It is important in the workplace because:

- 40 percent of employees use oral communication face-to-face or one-on-one regularly
- 36 percent of employees regularly attend group meetings
- 30 percent of employees talk on the phone
- 8 percent of employees participate in group conferences (Miller, 2010).

By the chapter's conclusion, readers should be more aware of how they and others communicate. The chapter begins with a discussion of communication as part of the management process.

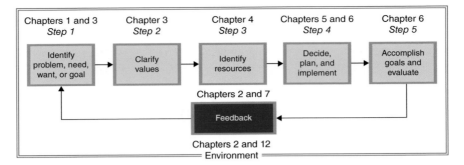

Figure 7.1 **The management process model.**

## Communication as Part of the Management Process

**Communication** is the process of transmitting a message from a sender to a receiver. We connect in various ways including:

- Electronic or digital media, for example, the $129 billion advertising market dominated by Google and Facebook in recent years.

- Networking

- Books

- Newspapers (digital and ink) and magazines

- Multiple TV and radio channels

- Over the phone or the Internet or other forms of social media (Examples: YouTube, Pinterest, Twitter)

- Over the fence, porch, or balcony

- Yelling "It's time for dinner!" or whispering "I love you"

- Through music, dance, and performance

**Market share** refers to how much of the market someone has such as Amazon capturing 50 percent of all online sales in the United States (*Bloomberg*, March 31, 2019). At an airport with an overbooked Sunday night domestic flight, the author of this book (along with the other assigned seat passengers) was offered $1,000 in Amazon gift cards from the airline to give up their seat and leave the next day. Further, the reservationist at the desk said on the overhead announcement that she bought everything from Amazon so what a deal this was. Five people agreed to the offer. Would you?

**Pace** refers to the speed at which you speak or communicate. Since 150–200 words a minute is normal if you speed up it may indicate you are happy, excited, or surprised and if you slow down, it may indicate boredom, talking down to people, or wanting to make a point.

**Interference** is anything that distorts or interrupts messages. Effective communication occurs when the receiver interprets the sender's message in the same way the speaker intended it.

Because information transmission is an integral part of management, to be effective, a manager has to be an effective communicator. In systems terminology, communication is part of the transformation process—transforming inputs into outputs. In transforming information resources (inputs), communication uses up time and energy. The average person spends approximately 70 percent of his or her waking hours in some form of communication—writing, reading, speaking, and listening (Robbins, 1989). In recent years more time is spent on social media and/or digital media. This may be expressed as **screen time** which refers to the amount of time spent on devices such as smartphones, computers, televisions, or video games. On your smartphone, you may get a report such as "Your screen time was down 7% last week, for an average of 3 hours, 27 minutes a day."

Much of a resource manager's time is devoted to goal setting, which also requires effective communication. Goal setting is a sequence that starts with thinking and proceeds to acting, which includes communicating goals to others and engaging their support and interest. As part of this process, managers need to communicate several key decisions, including the following:

1. What goals will be sought?

2. Which goals have the highest priority?

3. How are the goals related?

4. How long will it take to achieve the goals?

5. Who should be accountable for achieving the goals?

The answers to these questions guide the present and future behavior of individuals, families, and other groups.

Effective communication is

- clear

- concise (if you take too long to get to a point, everyone quits listening)

- consistent

- creative

- sensitive to audience and environment

- persuasive (or it explains rather than demands or threatens)

- open to differing opinions

These characteristics are important in both family and professional life. An effective communicator passes along information, giving advance notice of impending changes and plans. Talking through problems and listening carefully to what other family members have to say adds to family cohesiveness. In professional life, communication skills can be crucial to getting ahead. Peter Drucker, an expert in business management, said:

> Your success as an employee—and I'm talking of much more than getting promoted—will depend on your ability to communicate with people and to present your own thoughts and ideas to them so they will both understand what you are driving at and be persuaded.
>
> *(1977, pp. 262–263)*

As Drucker's comments indicate, communication is indeed a process rather than a finished end state; and, as such, it allows individuals to share information, ideas, and feelings. For example, consider the following conversation between Heather and Sam, two college students who have been friends for over a year, but have never dated each other:

**SAM:** I haven't seen you around for weeks. Where have you been?

**HEATHER:** I've been working on two projects, and they've taken all my time. I'm worried about my grades.

**SAM:** Hm. You do look stressed.

**HEATHER:** Yes, I am. But it's almost over—everything is due this week.

**SAM:** You'll do all right. You always worry about your work and then you make A's. Why don't we get together this weekend?

In this exchange, Sam and Heather have communicated information and feelings.

Their remarks show that their relationship has a past, present, and future. Sam puts Heather's concerns into perspective. His comments show that he likes her. If the conversation continues, what are some of the responses Heather might give? Notice that only the verbal communication between Sam and Heather has been presented. Their non-spoken or nonverbal communication is not included. Does Sam smile or grin at Heather? Does he try to show he cares by his tone of voice or stance? Is Heather yawning or looking around?

## Channels, Noise, and Setting

Communication has long been considered part of everything from who gets elected president to who remains married. It is far more than words: It is about relationships, winning and losing, succeeding and not succeeding. It includes channels, noise, and setting. The **channel** is the method by which communication travels from source or sender to receiver. As Figure 7.2 shows, these elements interact to create the total communication environment. Would Sam and Heather's conversation be different if it took place in a crowded cafeteria rather than a deserted hall? A quiet setting allows senders and receivers to concentrate on each other; a noisy setting is full of distractions.

Sometimes the messages are blurred or inaccurate. For example, a man might say "I'm not much of a consumer" right in the middle of a grocery store while he is filling his basket. A consumer columnist says:

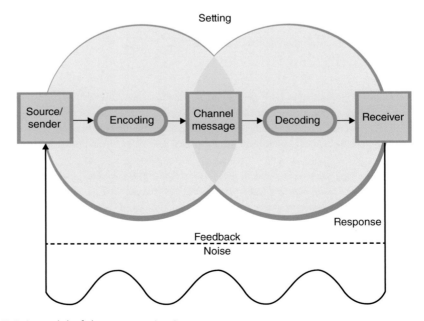

Figure 7.2 A model of the communications process.

*I guess nobody wants to define himself or herself as "a consumer," because it feels a little trivial. Still, once whoever I'm listening to has established the necessary nonconsumer credentials, what usually follows is an opinion about a product or brand that I've written about lately. If it's something that she would not personally buy, then she's amazed anyone would: if it's something that he has personally bought, then he assures me that I failed to capture the real quality or style or excellence of whatever it was. Obviously, we're all consumers. And probably we all think we're better at playing the consumption game than most people.*

(Walker, 2008, p. xix)

**Noise**, defined as an unwanted sound that interferes or distracts, is a barrier to learning and communication. There are two types of noise: external and internal. **External noise** comes from the environment. An airplane overhead, the hot blinding sun, a howling wind, or lightning are all examples of external noise. Notice that in communication theory, noise includes more than just sounds, as the sun and lightning illustrate. **Internal noise** occurs in the sender's and receiver's minds. They may be thinking about something else during the communication—their minds are not on the conversation taking place.

Daydreaming during a class lecture or thinking about a family member at work instead of listening to coworkers discuss the copy machine's breakdown are examples of internal noise. Often internal noise occurs when a word or allusion in the current conversation reminds us of something else.

An interesting experiment revealed how much internal and external noise affects the recall of advertising. Marketing professors Bob Wu and Stephen Newell (2003) found that external noise was not as important as internal noise in affecting subjects' ability to recall advertising (i.e., brand recall and message recall). They suggest that advertisers consider how they advertise during the holidays when consumers are preoccupied with cooking, travel, shopping, and gift buying; maybe this is not the best time to introduce a new product or idea.

Perhaps a better time would be a few months earlier when things are more settled or in January if it is a new diet plan or toothpaste or system of organizing/storage containers. Internal worrying about shocking current news or events may also take away from advertising messages being heard. These findings have implications not just for the marketplace but also for family and household management. Introducing a new way of doing things may go over better during less hectic times.

Noise is any interference in the communication process that prevents the message from being heard correctly, and it can occur at any point in the process. The sender may send out confusing messages, the channel may be distorted, or the receiver may be distracted. There is more noise today than ever before. Because of all the noise, advertisers are having a difficult time getting customers to notice their messages. On the home front, spouses may wonder whether their mates are listening to them when the television is blaring in the background, or the listener is glued to their laptop.

### CRITICAL THINKING

A neighborhood lady noticed that if she gave in-home sales parties for household or kitchen items in September and early October, they were far more successful than if she gave them in the summer. She said women attending were relaxed and buying holiday presents. Another good time for sales was late January and February, but then women were inclined to buy small items for themselves. The saleslady would alter her approach. Do you think season affects the ability to listen to sales pitches and respond by the opening of wallets and purses? Can you give another example? Have you noticed that television advertising changes as it nears holidays?

In today's fast-paced world, too many conflicting messages are vying for everyone's attention. The importance of the setting cannot be overestimated. There are appropriate places and times for discipline, compliments, whispers, shouts, and disputes. Being sensitive to environmental conditions as well as to words is part of being an effective communicator. One way to build a positive environment for communication is for individuals to let others know that they care about them.

Providing a climate of acceptance fosters human functioning and teamwork. For example, children need to know that their parents love them. Likewise, employees need to know that their employers are concerned about their welfare. When there is trust, people feel freer to exchange information, ideas, and feelings. As mentioned in Chapter 2, the greater environment in which individuals and families live has a significant effect on the way they manage. The **setting**, or physical surroundings, is where management messages are communicated. Some settings, such as a church or a boardroom, are more formal than others. Communications should be appropriate for the setting.

Public speakers check out the setting before their speech, so they can match their posture, speaking voice, and microphone volume to the room size and potential audience.

Here is something a little different to consider: **intrapersonal communication** which is communication that occurs within a single person. One way we all communicate is with our inner voice. Pause for a moment in your reading and ask, "What is my inner voice saying right now?" Another way to say this is what are you thinking about?

The design of homes, offices, and campuses communicates to the user the type of relationships that will occur in that setting. A campus with winding walkways, fountains, and botanical gardens has a different atmosphere than a campus consisting of high-rise concrete buildings. Indoor lighting and color affect communication. Warm colors, such as red and orange, and bright lights tend to accelerate talking, whereas cool colors, such as soft blue and green, and low lights tend to subdue communication. Institutional atmospheres are not conducive to quiet personal conversations. When it comes to counseling settings, it is best "to put the client interest first and opt for a blue accent wall or neutral colors for offices" (Law et al., 2019, p. 121). Even clothing is part of the setting. Research has shown that the style of clothing therapists wear will enhance or detract from their relationship with clients (Heitmeyer & Goldsmith, 1990).

## Sending and Receiving

Communication is a two-way process between sender and receiver. **Sending** is saying what one means to say, with an agreement between verbal and nonverbal messages. Modulation is the loudness or pitch of your voice. In good sending, the person must know what she or he wants to say and then say it. The sender should make eye contact with the receiver and speak slowly and distinctly. **Receiving** entails **listening** to the verbal messages and observing the nonverbal messages. If the message is getting through, the receiver will probably show his or her response through facial expressions. A good sender talks with people, not at them, and considers the listener's feelings, personality, and opinions.

Usually, people are receivers and senders at the same time. Communication is not as simple as having one person speak, another listen and then speak, and so on. For instance, more than one listener may be involved. Also, the sending and receiving can be simultaneous.

A sender can also be called a **source**, or communicator. The receiver is the **destination**, or audience. The sender's task is to reach the audience, whether it is one person or a million people. Because of sweeping changes brought on by advances in communications technology and the ease of movement of people (physical and virtual) in today's world, people are communicating and connecting faster than ever before.

The sender and receiver use four communication functions: encoding, decoding, response, and feedback. **Encoding** is the process of putting thoughts, ideas, or information into symbolic form. **Decoding** is the process by which the receiver assigns meaning to the symbols. **Responses** are the individual reactions that follow a message. Feedback is the total response pattern between sender and receiver. An individual's communication style is closely tied to her or his personality, self-concept, the family of origin, and past experiences. Sometimes a message is distorted by a hidden meaning. When a child says, "I hate soccer" after the first week of practice, does he really hate soccer, or is he in an adjustment period and will grow to like it? The parent determines the real message.

## Listening

Whether in the home or office, managers want to be heard by those they manage and also listen to them. Parents want their children to listen. According to Sue Shellenbarger (2003), some of the ways that parents can be more effective in talking with their children include:

- Telling about problems and how they were overcome (not always talking about the wins, mixing in a discussion of the struggles)

- Finding good guys (heroes) and bad guys in stories

- Picking situations that both parents and children really care about

- Including dialogue and details about human nature

Conversely, children want their parents to listen to them. In schools, teachers want their students to listen and learn, retain, and use information. Students want to understand what their teachers are saying. To encourage more listening, the sender should make messages and listening attractive. There are several ways to do this. Sometimes humor works, which is why many speeches begin with a joke or humorous anecdote.

A way advertisers deliver effective messages is to appeal to potential customers' senses. Think of the senses involved in this appeal from General Foods: "Turn a stormy night into a quiet evening with the after-dinner-mint taste of chocolaty Irish Mocha Mint." Listeners as well as senders have a job to do. This is one of the reasons listening is considered active rather than passive.

To be effective, listeners use certain gestures or mannerisms to communicate interest:

- Leaning forward rather than back

- Nodding occasionally to show comprehension

- Smiling

- Looking directly at the speaker and maintaining eye contact

- Making comments such as "I see," "Go on," "Oh," or "Mmm"

- Taking notes or recording, if appropriate.

A good listener summarizes conversations when they end and lets the sender know his or her message was heard by nodding or smiling, or by making some other gesture or response.

## Reflective or Empathetic Listening

Another type of listening is reflective listening. **Reflective listening** or **empathetic listening** involves listening for feelings. **Empathy** is the ability to recognize and identify another's feelings by putting oneself in that person's place. Reflective or empathetic listening is so common that individuals don't examine their skills in this area closely enough. As a reflective listener, the listener's job is to set aside her or his own feelings and enter into the feelings of the person talking. The listener can do this by:

- Identifying the speaker's emotion. Is the person afraid, excited, happy, or frustrated?
- Listening for the details of the story. What is included, and what is left out?
- Paraphrasing or mirroring the speaker's comments to see whether the message is being heard accurately.

Letting the other person work through the problem. Talking out feelings is a way to find solutions.

## Informational and Pleasurable Listening

Listening does not have to be painful, difficult, or critical, nor does it have to involve the use of counseling skills. Much listening is for information or for fun. Informational listening is done to acquire knowledge or instruction. A news program or a college lecture is not only informational but also invokes critical listening.

Pleasurable listening provides enjoyment, relaxation, satisfaction, diversion, amusement, or delight. Tuning the radio or YouTube to a favorite place provides pleasurable listening. Watching a situation comedy show on television provides escape, amusement, and laughter. Other sources of pleasurable listening are available besides the media. Imagine the happiness of a father hearing his child's first word, a high school student learning she has won a college scholarship, or a person overseas receiving a phone call from home. Often the most pleasurable listening comes from unexpected sources or at an unanticipated time.

## Messages

The **message** is the total communication that is sent, listened to, and received. Communication is made up of symbols. **Symbols** are things that suggest something else through association. For example, an engagement ring is a symbol of love and the intention to marry. It communicates a past, present, and future.

Symbols, such as a tattoo or an engagement ring that can be seen are called **visible symbols**. An **abstract symbol** stands for ideas rather than objects. Poor communication often springs from misunderstandings of abstract symbols. For example, Matt tells Suzanne he has an "awesome" apartment. By "awesome" he means that it is close to campus and inexpensive, but Suzanne, hearing the word "awesome," envisions a new, beautifully decorated, spacious apartment. Imagine her surprise when Matt takes her to a crumbling 50-year-old building.

Lasting friendships are built on shared abstract symbols—commonalities of interests or appreciation of each other's differences. In the future, Suzanne will suspect Matt's use of the word "awesome."

Messages can be wanted or unwanted. Consider what happens when the stock market falls deeply, and companies go bankrupt or are bought out by other companies.

> In a stock market that never seems to run out of reasons to go down, you no longer feel like a bull. But that does not necessarily make you a bear. You may, in fact, have become an ostrich. Chances are you didn't leap for the letter opener the last time your investment account statement came in the mail. Nor have you been looking up the value of your portfolio online anywhere near as frequently as you did in the glory days of the summer of 2007 … If history is any guide, your inclination to act like an ostrich is a strong indication that the market is about to turn into a phoenix.
>
> *(Zweig, 2008, p. B1)*

The **Ostrich effect** refers to burying one's head in the sand, not wanting to know what was in the letter or any other form of communication. Behavioral economist George Loewenstein of Carnegie Mellon coined the phrase "ostrich effect" to refer to economic behavior but it can refer to any kind of avoidance of information, hoping it will go away.

## Verbal and Nonverbal Symbols

**Verbal symbols** are words. A **nonverbal symbol** is anything other than words used in communication. Examples of nonverbal symbols include works of art, train whistles, sirens, tone and volume of voice, clothing, eye contact, personal appearance, demeanor, gestures, facial expressions, posture, and yawns. For example, yawns may communicate tiredness or boredom, whereas sirens communicate danger or caution. Conventional scientific wisdom said that the role of gestures was to convey meaning. There is an emerging consensus that gestures serve another function— to help people retrieve elusive words from memory. Regarding art as a communicator, Nike Co-founder Phil Knight met a student named Carolyn Davidson during his last week teaching accounting. Thinking his new sneaker company may need an artist he asked for her number. In 1971, two years late, he paid her $35 to design a logo conveying motion. The result is the famous swoosh (Duong, 2019).

People who gesture a lot may think in spatial terms. "Not everyone talks with their hands. Some people gesture 40 times more than others" (Begley, 1998, p. 69). Communication experts estimate that over 90 percent of the messages sent and received are made up of nonverbal symbols—hence the expression, "It is not what you say, but how you say it."

An ostrich is a 200-pound bird with a 2-ounce brain. The Ostrich Effect refers to avoiding potentially negative information.

Source: Dorling Kindersley Media Library.

According to Joseph DeVito (2009), there are 10 aspects of nonverbal communication including artifacts, proxemics, body language, facial expressions, taste, and even smell. The 10 aspects are listed in Table 7.1. **Artifacts** are the type, placement, or rearrangement of objects around a person as well as clothing and adornment. For example, a student who sits down at a library table and takes 20 minutes to arrange his belongings before settling down to work communicates something different than a person who takes 20 seconds to set up. **Proxemics** is the distance between speakers. Closeness and whispering imply one type of relationship, whereas distance and shouting imply another. Touching behavior includes both touching oneself, such as hair twisting or rubbing one's face, and touching others, such as shaking hands or hugging. A brief kiss on the cheek, for example, conveys something different than a kiss on the lips.

### I-Messages and You-Messages

Verbal messages can be divided into two types: I-messages and You-messages. **I-messages** are statements of fact about how an individual feels or thinks; examples are "I like it when you send me flowers, thanks" and "I feel stupid when you shout at me." **You-messages** are statements that often ascribe blame or judge others, such as "you had better straighten up" or "you had better get it right next time." You-messages can lead to arguments. Family counselors and therapists promote the use of I-messages over the accusatory tone of You-messages to encourage more positive communication in couples and in families. Many You-messages can be rephrased into I-messages as in "I hope things will go better next time" or "this is what I think."

### Message Construction

The structure of a message has a lot to do with its potency. **Message construction** includes the appropriate placement of information in a message to have the maximum impact. The communicator decides whether

**Table 7.1** Ten Aspects of Nonverbal Communication: Channels through Which the Messages Pass

1. Body: movements such as gestures, movements of the face and hands, nodding, general attractiveness

2. Face: happiness, surprise, sadness, disgust, and other emotions exhibited in expressions, worry lines, smiles

3. Eye: eye contact intense or diverted, rolling one's eyes, direction of glance, visual dominance

4. Space: proxemics refers to distances or spatial differences, territory/boundary markers such as armrests in movies and in airplanes, yours and theirs.

5. Artifacts: color, clothing, hair style, tattoos, jewelry, piercings, adornment, decoration, arrangement of objects, space decoration such as your home and office

6. Touch: can communicate positive feelings and intentions, control, helping someone, touch avoidance

7. Paralanguage: how you say something—pitch (high or low), speed, volume (loudness)

8. Silence: allowing time for someone else to speak; time to think; can be a weapon of control or respectful, maybe there's nothing to say or avoidance; maintaining silence so that you don't incriminate yourself.

9. Time: past, present, future; cultural time differences; what is early? What is late?

10. Smell: attraction messages such as use of scent; taste, smell associated with memories and identification.

to place the main point of the comment or speech at the beginning or the end and whether to provide solutions or leave the solutions to the audience.

## Message Content and Complexity

**Message content** refers to the strategies or information that may be used to communicate an idea or policy to receivers. Determining content is the first step in creating a message. Then the communicator must decide on the best way to get the message across to the audience. An example of this is speaking up for a cause.

Many of us have messages or images in our heads about certain individuals and groups. Some of these messages or images are questionable.

*"When you see a 25-year-old woman, you picture her as single, she has a cool job, a cute boyfriend, she's going out at night, has lots of friends, has a college degree. But having interviewed thousands of women, I can tell you that many [young women] have children, are working at some half-baked first job, are not feeling fulfilled, are not in love, might still be living at home, are economically pressed and stressed to the max," says Mary Lou Quinlan, CEO of New York city-based Just Ask a Woman, a division of ad agency BCOM3.*

*(Wellner, 2002, p. 27)*

---

**CRITICAL THINKING**

A children's storybook *Amelia Bedelia* written by Peggy Parish has the main character Amelia Bedelia. One day Mr. and Mrs. Rogers hire Amelia as a maid and leave
her a list of chores. She thinks some are odd like "draw the drapes" and "dress a
chicken," but she sets out to do these chores anyway. She draws a lovely picture on
the drapes and makes a cute outfit for the chicken. When Mrs. Rogers returns, she is
appalled, but Amelia responds, "I did what was asked." Have you ever felt like Mrs.
Rogers? Or, like Amelia? Why do children relate to the character Amelia Bedelia?

---

The Zenlike magazine *Real Simple* offers ageless content on many of the subjects covered in this book,
including time, money, household, lifestyle, and stress management to its mainly 25- to 54-year-old readers. A constant theme is how to make your life easier or better. According to the managing editor, Kristin
van Ogtrop,

> *We all need a friend—a very good one with very good taste—who will come into our house and evaluate
> everything with an objective eye, then firmly suggest we get rid of that horrendous appliance/slipcover/
> light fixture that we've held on to because we're sentimental or lazy.*
>
> (Editor's Note, 2003, p. 37).

To return to the general topic of message content, messages may have humor or even fear, which seems
negative but can be an effective way to point out potential problems in order to reduce risk or achieve
other positive effects. Antidrug public service television spots often use fear as a means of reducing drug
use. Advertisements for property insurance, burglar alarms, and automobiles often include fear messages.

## Channels and Feedback: Model of Social Influence

As mentioned earlier, the channel is the method through which the message travels from sender to receiver.
*Channels may be direct*, as in face-to-face talking, or indirect. In face-to-face channels of communication,
individuals have the advantage of seeing how the other person is reacting to the message, so there is less
chance of miscommunication. This is particularly important in conversations between parents and children.
Age of the child and the subject of conversation are important, too. In a study of American and Northern
Irish children about communication with their parents about war:

> *The results provide support for the presence of developmental differences, with age being a stronger predic-
> tor than gender and country in the frequency and content of parent-child discussions about war. Children
> ages 7 to 11 are more likely than younger children to report talking to their parents about war, and they
> address more topics than do the younger children in their reports of what their parents said about war.*
>
> (O'Malley et al., 2007, p. 1638)

Radio, television, magazines, newspapers, and signs are **indirect channels** of mass communication. How
many newspapers are there in the United States? That is difficult to say because smaller ones go in and out
of business, and some are hardly bigger than newsletters

More newspapers and magazines are offering free sections or versions and relying on advertising revenue,
rather than on subscribers, to pay for labor and paper. Some newspapers are eliminating home delivery
because of the cost of fuel and labor. Most have built up their websites and are trying to get readers to visit
them more often for the latest headlines.

Smartphones provide a channel for more personal communications than do other types of media because the tone of voice is heard, but phone communication is still not as clear as face-to-face conversation. Channels can also be categorized as social channels and advocate or expert channels. **Social channels** include friends, neighbors, and family members. Because of familiarity and proximity, these channels are most likely to involve face-to-face contacts. **Advocate or expert channels** (e.g., experts in a field, salespeople or people with a cause) contact receivers through letters, speeches, or less direct forms of communication.

In systems terminology, *feedback* refers to the return to the input of a part of the output in the form of information. An equally appropriate but simpler definition of feedback is the response process between sender and receiver. Feedback may take a variety of forms. It closes the loop in the communication's flow and lets the sender know how the intended message was decoded and received. Feedback begins when one hears or observes or reads what is being said, stores or responds to the information, and listens for the next message. For example, if Joseph gives Alison a compliment and she says, "thank you," her response provides feedback: Joseph's message was heard accurately and acknowledged.

Feedback provides a control mechanism for the accuracy of communication. By the recipient's response, the sender can tell whether the message was communicated effectively. If Alison bursts into tears, obviously Joseph's compliment was not phrased correctly or received correctly. If he values their relationship, he will restate his comment and try to straighten things out. The advantage of face-to-face conversations is that the feedback is immediate.

**Social influence** is how one person or group affects another's opinions, attitudes, emotions, or behaviors (Goldsmith, 2015). Entrepreneurship, start-ups, and communicating what is new are of interest to all of us as consumers and vital to the growth of local, national, and international economies. To illustrate how this works The **Model of Social Influence** begins with an invention or innovation. A person watching an

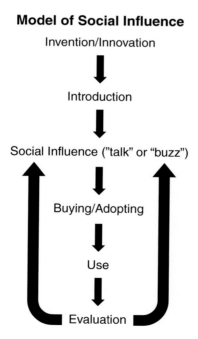

**Model of Social Influence**

Invention/Innovation

Introduction

Social Influence ("talk" or "buzz")

Buying/Adopting

Use

Evaluation

Figure 7.3 Goldsmith Model of Social Influence.

Source: Goldsmith, E. (2015). *Social influence and sustainable consumption.* Switzerland: Springer, p 20.

College graduation.

advertisement or hearing about a new product or service (like an electric car or restaurant opening) may say "Wow, that is new" or "I can use that." The feedback part can be seen in the Model which shows that after the last step evaluation feedback returns to the system in talk or buzz. Let us say a person tries the new restaurant and talks about it online in a review or in person to friends, family members, and coworkers. Then, he or she can decide whether to go back to the restaurant evaluate the results and then start the feedback loop again. Maybe the food was better or worse the second time around and that would be the talk or the buzz.

Anticipation (such as waiting for an event like a wedding or graduation ceremony to start) or speed of adoption are parts of the feedback process, expectations vs. realities.

> *Sometimes invention or technology is ahead of where people want to be. For example, the light bulb was invented in 1879 yet by 1907 only eight percent of American homes had electricity. Why was so clearly a useful invention so slow to be adopted? The answers are primarily habit, comfort with pre-existing means of light, heating, and cooking, availability, and cost.*
>
> (Goldsmith, 2013)

## Communication Conflicts

Many potential communication conflicts and problems can be avoided by applying the general principles already presented on noise, setting, feedback, channels, and messages. But, in addition, certain situations and audiences deserve special attention. This section examines the potential communication conflicts that can occur within families and across cultures.

### In Families

In general, the goal of communication is to provide an understanding that leads to desired actions. In some cases, however, communication fails and conflict results. **Conflict** is a state of disagreement or disharmony.

In poor communication, there is a message struggle or conflict between the sender and the receiver. If survival of the relationship is the goal, this conflict can pose a definite threat.

Negotiations to remedy the conflict are known as **conflict resolution**. The sender, receiver, or another person can initiate conflict resolution. Conflict is particularly common in families because of the intimate, ongoing nature of the relationships. Family members know each other so well that they notice nonverbal communications (e.g., a raised eyebrow, a strained voice) that strangers would be likely to miss. Hence, conflict is more on the surface and less readily hidden in families. The emotional intensity of family relationships is generally much greater than that in other small groups, so family communication problems tend to have more serious and painful implications (Sieburg, 1985).

Although information should flow easily among family members, sometimes it stagnates, and conflict between family members goes on for years. The number of possible interactions also contributes to communication conflicts in families. Addition of a second child to a family increases the number of interactions. As the number of interactions increases, family members may succumb to interaction fatigue. Because the family system is part of the larger environment, interaction fatigue may also develop at work and affect the family at home or develop at home and spill over into work. Kanter (1977) observed that employees who experience interaction fatigue at work may withdraw from personal contact at home.

According to DeVito (2009), several factors will influence your choice of conflict strategies, including

- **Goals**: Longand short–term
- **Emotional State**: Angry, sorry, wanting to make peace
- **Cognitive Assessment of the Situation**: Who is the cause of the conflict?
- **Personality and Communication**: Shy, introverted, extroverted, like to fight actively
- **Family History**: "influences the strategies you use, the topics you choose to fight about, and perhaps your tendencies to obsess or forget about interpersonal conflicts. People often imitate their parents: if your parents argued about money or gave each other the silent treatment when conflict arose, you may repeat these patterns yourself" (p. 260).

What emotions are they exhibiting?

Researchers (Liberman et al., 1980, p. 90) identified several common destructive messages and tactics that characterize ineffective communication within families:

- Ordering turns the interaction into a power struggle between partners or between parents and children. "You do this" and "Stop doing that" are examples of ordering.

- Threatening is similar to ordering, but it goes further. It can lead to passivity or despair.

- Moralizing sends a message of guilt or moral inferiority or suggests that the other person needs guidance or direction. "You should" messages are examples of moralizing.

- Providing solutions occurs when words sound like a question, as in "Why don't you," but really indicate superiority or a kind of parental guidance.

- Lecturing is a more forceful way of providing solutions. You are told what to do or that you always do things wrong.

- Criticizing can mar relationships and lead to dependency and lower self-esteem in the criticized person.

- Ridiculing generates resistance and resentment. It involves biting and hurtful phrases, such as "You're talking like an idiot" or "You're such a mess."

- Analyzing occurs when one person tells another how the latter should think and act. Analyzers are often amateur psychologists who generate anger by invading others' privacy and questioning their motivations with comments like "You think you know what you are doing, but you don't." Often analyzers are wrong, however.

- Interrogating is used to gain information by relentless questioning. "You're not telling the truth, are you?" is an example of an interrogating question.

- Withdrawing is a way to end conversations. The person may say she or he is tired and is going to bed.

Do these messages and tactics sound familiar? They should because they are very common. If they are used too frequently, they can impede effective communication and damage relationships. Being able to recognize these tactics helps the recipient understand the sender better.

Possibly, the message is not conveying the real problem. The real problem may be with the sender or with the relationship between the sender and the receiver. For example, Luciano L'Abate and Tamar Harel suggest that "relationships that cannot become intimate emotionally may make contact with each other through sporadic and sudden ambushes, uproars, upsets, and conflicts over performance and/or production" (1993, p. 243).

Conversely, the Marital Communication Inventory (Bievenue, 1978) has identified behaviors that indicate satisfying marital communication. They include pleasant mealtime conversations, avoidance of the silent treatment, discussions of work and interests with each other, avoiding saying things that irritate each other, and communicating affection and regard. In general, communication between husband and wife is most satisfying when both partners feel they are understood and when they agree on essential points.

## Interpersonal Conflicts

**Interpersonal conflicts** are actions by one person that interfere in some way with the actions of another. **Destructive conflicts** are a specific type of interpersonal conflict involving direct verbal attacks on another individual. Yelling, screaming, abuse, attacks on self-esteem, and words leading to breakups are characteristics of destructive conflicts. On the other hand, **constructive conflicts** focus on the issue or the problem rather than on the other person's deficits.

This type of conflict can reveal issues and lead to deeper relationships, clarification, and a better understanding of the other person. Thus, not all conflicts are negative. Sometimes conflict is necessary to resolve points of difference, clear the air, or relieve tension.

Constructive conflicts can lead to a win–win outcome, which is obviously desirable. A seller of a house may ask $300,000, the buyer offers $290,000, and they settle at $295,000; each one wins, each gets what he or she wanted.

## Gender, Families, Friends, and Communication

### CASE STUDY

#### Kathryn and Lily

*Kathryn and Lily, friends for over sixty years, hadn't seen each other in several weeks. They both felt this was too long, so they arranged to get together. When Kathryn arrived at Lily's home, they sat down and talked. And talked. And talked. They didn't stop, and they didn't get up, until two and a half hours passed. They talked about books they were reading, their significant others, politics, movies, their children, their children's children, and how their bodies and their living situations were changing with age. Later, they exchanged emails. Lily wrote, "That was a wonderful and soul-lifting visit, my dearest old friend..."*

*Source: Tannen, D. (2017). You're the Only One I Can Tell, New York: Random House p. 1.*

In a series of books, Deborah Tannen uncovers the patterns of communication and miscommunication in our lives. Here is an example from Tannen's *You Are Wearing That? Understanding Mothers and Daughters in Conversation* book:

*"Are you going to quarter those tomatoes?" Kathryn heard her mother's voice as she was preparing a salad. Kathryn stiffened, and her pulse quickened. "Well I was," she answered. Her mother responded, "Oh, okay," but the tone of her voice and the look on her face prompted Kathryn to ask, "Is that wrong?" "No, no," her mother replied. "It's just that personally, I would slice them." Kathryn's response was terse: "Fine." But as she cut the tomatoes—in slices—she thought, Can't I do anything without my mother letting me know she thinks I should do it some other way?*

*(2006, p. 11)*

In an earlier book entitled *You Just Don't Understand: Women and Men in Conversation* Tannen took on the topic of male–female communication. She points out that men talk far more than women, especially in public. Men speak more at meetings, in classrooms, and in mixed groups at work. However, overall in a day, women speak about 25,000 words, while men speak only 10,000.

Her book *I Only Say This Because I Love You* explores miscommunication among family members. She suggests that parents should listen more to their teenage children and criticize them less. Couples should talk about assumptions and try to bring hidden messages out in the open. And both sides should learn the art of apology. A win-win solution, where nobody is wrong and a solution is reached, is ideal.

Women tend to question more than men do. Psychiatrist Aaron Beck (1988) points out that wives tend to believe that their marriage is working if they and their husbands are talking about it. On the other hand, men may think the marriage is not working if they talk about it constantly. Generally, women are more comfortable talking about personal matters with family and friends than men are. In the United States, men are more likely than women to use avoidance, for example by walking away (Oggins et al., 1993).

According to Tannen, men and women also differ in the ways they express their troubles and seek out information. Women resent "men's tendency to offer solutions to problems," and men "complain about women's refusal to take action to solve the problems they complain about" (1990, pp. 51–52). Men want to solve problems and move on, whereas women hesitate and seek other people's opinions to gain as much information as they can before moving toward a solution. This is one of the reasons why women make up most of the audience for talk shows. They enjoy considering all the angles to a situation or issue. Men sometimes feel women go to such excess talking over situations that they seem to enjoy wallowing in a problem. Men move to solutions quickly because they derive pleasure from fixing things. Fixing things "reinforces their feeling of being in control, self-sufficient, and able to dominate the world of objects" (1990, p. 70).

Women are more likely than men to ask for directions and accept information from others. The classic example is of men driving around lost rather than stopping and asking directions. Men are also more likely to try to get the "best" parking space in a shopping center. At the root of these behaviors is concern about status, hierarchy, and connections.

According to Tannen, boys as young as age three are using words in their conversations with peers that show they want to be a leader, to be first, and to be best, whereas girls of the same age are more interested in getting along with friends and understanding their feelings and opinions. For example, girls are more likely to say "let's" and "we" in their conversations. Boys' conversations are filled with orders, such as "Get up" or "Give it to me," and ridicule, such as "You're a dope" (Beck, 1988, p. 82). Boys are more inclined than girls to threaten, boast, and argue. Perhaps you disagree. Research studies on gender differences in communication are ongoing.

Tannen contends that men and women have different but equally valid communication styles. Problems arise when men and women talk to each other and expect a certain kind of response. Because of gender differences in conversation, a woman will not always get the response she desires from men and vice versa. Tannen concludes:

> *The biggest mistake people can make is believing there is one right way to listen, to talk, to have a conversation—or a relationship. Nothing hurts more than being told your intentions are bad when you know they are good or being told you are doing something wrong when you know you're doing it your way.*
>
> *(1990, pp. 297–298)*

Tannen's observations have implications for family dynamics and workplace management. As women move into positions of authority, these gender differences in conversation will require greater understanding from both men and women. The solution is not to change styles so that everyone speaks alike, but to understand and appreciate the various forms of communication. In the family, the realistic approach is to "learn how to interpret each other's messages and explain your own in a way your partner can understand and accept" (1990, p. 297).

Shelly Gable, an assistant professor of psychology at the University of California, Los Angeles (UCLA), researches the positive psychology of love and marriage. She encourages messages that amplify the pleasure of a good situation, contributing to an upward spiral of positive emotion. An example would be a partner reacting enthusiastically to a mate's good fortune or a partner getting even more excited and happy about what is happening to his or her mate than the mate does. An enthusiastic partner asks a lot of questions and shows genuine interest. All these responses or reactions are called active/constructive and promote love, commitment, and satisfaction (Seligman, 2003).

Where do most couples meet? At work or school followed by through friends and family, according to the Pew Internet & American Life Project. Others say they met at a social gathering, through the Internet, or in a variety of other ways. As you can see from these responses, proximity, or physical closeness, often plays a role in starting a relationship. The first few hours and days are crucial to establishing a bond. Opportunities for interaction decrease as distances increase and as more people become involved. Colleges and universities have orientations, mixers, and library tours at the beginning of the fall semester to increase interactivity and a sense of ownership of the campus.

**Social Exchange Theory** claims that individuals seek to develop relationships that will maximize the benefits or profits and minimize the costs or deficits. Expectations are communicated in the early stages of relationships and a significant amount of time is spent in dialogue.

## CRITICAL THINKING

Have you spent a long time in conversation face-to-face, over the phone, or on the Internet getting to know another person? Can you recall any movies or series where this was a theme? What would you consider to be a long time?

## Cultures and Subcultures

Culture affects everything we do including communication. The goal of cross-cultural communication is to help minimize surface differences and to build common frameworks for people of different cultures to interact and understand each other. In business and in education, cross-cultural communication is critical to sharing ideas, team building, and negotiations. Knowing the characteristics of our own culture is useful and how distinct we are. For example, Americans are known for being direct in their conversation, so direct that people in other nations sometimes wonder whether Americans aren't a bit naïve or childlike. The author of this book was told by a professor from Finland that people in her country notice that Americans smile a lot and seem so happy, but they wonder if this can be true inside. She asked, "Can anyone be that happy so much of the time?"

The American heritage of being on time, hardy, hardworking, and plain-spoken influences the ways they converse. They also want to get to a point fast; long-winded stories or explanations are turn-offs. Indirectness or hidden agendas make Americans uneasy. As these comments show, cultures have unique ways of communicating, and conflict can arise between cultures with different styles. Misunderstandings may stem from the failure to understand values, decision patterns, symbols, and spoken and nonverbal languages of other cultures. For example, as companies have expanded internationally, many glaring errors have occurred in product names and packaging.

> What is appropriate in one country may not be in another. For example,
> The car slogan "body by Fisher" becomes "corpse by Fisher" in Flemish. "Come alive with Pepsi" comes out "Pepsi brings your ancestors back from the grave" in Chinese and "Come alive out of the grave" in German. The Ford Pinto did not sell in Brazil because Brazilians did not want to be in a car meaning tiny male genitals.

These examples illustrate problems in translating words. Nonverbal differences between cultures are more subtle. A friendly gesture in one culture may be insulting in another. Manners and etiquette vary around the world. Here are some examples of behavior perceived as rude in other cultures:

- Pointing at people, in Japan

- Eating with your left hand, in some Arab countries

- Sitting where people can see the soles of your shoes, in certain cultures

- The "ok" hand gesture in the United States is considered obscene in Germany and Brazil.

Anthropologist Edward T. Hall has studied how people vary across cultures in communicating trust, warmth, and respect. In his book *The Silent Language* he pointed out that "what people do is frequently more important than what they say" (1959, p. 24).

Even the amount of time spent socializing with friends and family varies by culture. The typical American spends 16.3 hours each week socializing compared to 7.5 hours for the typical Japanese (Blinder, 1991).

Also varying is the underlying message. For example, it has been observed that Americans are deal-oriented, impatient, and competitive. But, an advertiser wishing to appeal to a Japanese audience would avoid saying

- "Be the first in your neighborhood to own such and such." Japanese do not like to be out of step with their neighbors.

- "New, free … no strings attached." The average Japanese honors stability rather than "newness" and would be suspicious of something that is given away for free.

Within the United States, a slogan such as "Challenge Everything" used by computer game manufacturer EA Sports was found to offend certain religious and traditional groups who valued harmony and respect versus competition. They did not believe everything should be challenged.

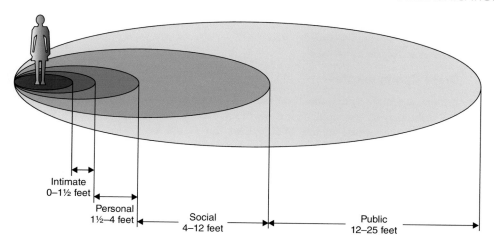

Figure 7.4 The four distance zones.

The correct social space between people also varies across cultures and by relationships within cultures. Figure 7.4 shows the four distance zones common in the United States. Intimate distance in the United States is less than 18 inches; typically, few people enter this space. Personal space is between 1½ and 4 feet. Americans like to have this much of personal space around their bodies; culture dictates that this space should not be invaded by strangers. But in some countries, hugs, slaps on the back, and even spitting on the ground near the feet are meant to convey trust and connection (Adams, 1998). In the United States, business tends to be conducted within the social zone of 4–12 feet. To visualize this distance, think about the distance between salesclerks and their customers (remember that salesclerks often stand behind counters). In Latin America, in Mediterranean countries like Malta, in the Middle East, people tend to get closer. In Malta, it was explained to the author of this book that kissing on both cheeks is mostly a social greeting between people who have met before.

People in Middle Eastern cultures stand closer together when speaking, may kiss each other on the cheek, and men may grasp hands. A businessperson from the United States confronted with this behavior abroad may back away, giving the impression of being cold and unfriendly. According to Hall (1959, p. 209), Latin Americans cannot talk comfortably with one another unless they are at a very close distance that evokes either sexual or hostile feelings in a North American. The public zone in North America is 12–15 feet. In Korea, in a business setting, they may bow first and then shake hands. The Covid-19 pandemic caused people to rethink the business practice of shaking hands (for health reasons) and bowing or elbow bumps or other forms of greeting are being considered.

Besides language and gestures, symbols are interpreted differently across cultures. Colors, flower arrangements, clothing, and numbers all communicate in different ways across cultures. In certain countries, purple is associated with royalty or death and yellow-green, with spring and fertility. However, in Malaysia, green symbolizes the danger and death in the jungle. When a water recreation company in Malaysia used a green corporate symbol, its promotional campaign failed. Red is considered lucky in China and black is considered unlucky in Japan. Flowers can represent death, infidelity, loyalty, or love depending on the type of flower, the occasion, the color, and the country. The number 13 is considered unlucky in the United States and in the United Kingdom—many people will not fly on Friday the 13th, and most hotels do not have a floor numbered 13. In Europe, 13th floors are common. In Japan, the airplanes do not have seat numbers 4 or 9.

CRITICAL THINKING

**Dress Communicates**

An international toy manufacturer based in Southern Europe makes sure they ship the right toys to the right countries. Figures of women or girl children in bikinis would cause outrage in the Middle East but would be perfectly acceptable in Europe. What have you observed about differences in the way people dress and what is acceptable?

As the United States and Canada become more involved in exports, international business, and worldwide communications, and as Europe becomes more unified, an awareness of cultural differences and similarities will become more important. Also, the new focus on the dynamics of family diversity and multiculturalism worldwide has renewed interest in cross-cultural and cross-group communication. Within countries, there are many subcultures as well, and some groups are being underestimated in terms of their influence and buying power. For example, an article in *American Demographics* says that "Black women run their homes, heavily consume media and influence more than $260 billion in spending a year. Still marketers continue to ignore them" (Yin, 2003, September, p. 22). Many new businesses and advertisers are trying to rectify this situation so stay tuned.

*Here is an example from the past:*

*Cynthia Morris is a family woman who has an MBA degree and an executive-level job. By day, she raises funds for national parks programs. By night, the 50-year-old, married African American mother of two writes checks for such things as the tuition for one of her sons' college education and the renovations on the family's 3,500-square-foot house in Potomac, Md. Still, as the chief decision maker in her upper-middle-class household, Morris believes that, to marketers, she is out of sight and out of mind. "It's like a blind spot," she says. "People just don't see us as this influential segment that can make a difference in their market share."*

*(Yin, 2003, September, p. 22)*

Getting the message across in a multicultural business setting.

Statistics reveal that

> *Black women are more likely to be the primary decision maker in their household than white women. Sixty-one percent of African American women make the decisions about major purchases, such as buying a home, compared with just 43 percent of Caucasian women.*
>
> (Yin, 2003, September, p. 23)

College students are another subgroup of potential interest to marketers because of their earning potential. Marketers would like to lock in their brands with college students before they launch into the world of lucrative full-time employment. College students are also trendsetters and early adopters of certain products, such as clothes and cars. But they are a challenge because "Students doubt corporate intentions, they want to be catered to and they don't think companies know what they want. And they are poor: Their idea of a good buy is a bargain" (Yin, 2003, May, p. 20). Free samples work well with this age group because they not only like a bargain but also like to try new things. Does this last statement fit you?

---

### CRITICAL THINKING

#### How Do You Like Yourself Described?

The following is adapted from Adler et al. (2020), Chapter 1. What terms or words do you like for people to use when describing you? Which words would make you cringe or feel put down or misunderstood? Considering this, how might you change how you describe other individuals or groups?

---

## Communication in Small Groups

All groups have in common a shared goal or purpose or a reason for being. Families are a type of small group joined together by ties of affection and kinship. But there are many other kinds of small groups. People get together to solve school, community, work, or environmental problems; for fellowship or support; and for individual and family growth. Once a group has decided on its main goals or purposes, it is ready to proceed. "Small groups," other than families, usually refer to *5–10 people*. Communication can

1. Serve to cement relationships (like church potluck dinners or community picnics)

2. Be used for tasks, like a committee charged with problem solving, or for idea generation such as creating a new project in the workplace or at school

3. Be part of personal growth or information sharing groups such as weight loss groups or political groups or for improving public-speaking groups.

Larger groups may divide into smaller task force groups or committees to solve problems or to take charge of an issue or a fund-raising drive. Groups are too large when some people do not have an opportunity to participate or speak. If this continues to happen, smaller groups are needed. Conversely, groups can become too small or stagnant. When nothing new is contributed time after time, then perhaps a new group should be formed or members added.

### Group Discussions and Cohesion

When a group becomes stagnant or cannot find a project that members consider interesting, then it should try brainstorming. In **brainstorming,** all group members suggest ideas—no matter how seemingly ridiculous or strange. Afterward, the group examines each idea separately to see whether it has merit. Brainstorming is a good way to get the creative juices flowing and introduce some energy into the group. Once a project has been agreed upon, the group should seek out information. Group members should find out how others have initiated similar ideas or programs. Many times a project or program is phrased as a question; for example, how can a group help homeless families in the community? How can a fourth-grade class participate in Earth Day?

After the questions have been discussed, the next stage is to move toward solutions. Groups will discuss and discard many unworkable or unaffordable solutions before they arrive at one or two that group members can agree upon. Next, a plan will be initiated. When necessary, an unworkable plan will be thrown out and a new plan developed. Eventually, the group will have to determine which plans are working and whether the group should move on to other projects.

Several factors contribute to group cohesion: the size of the group, the goal-achievement orientation, the status and resources of the group, the degree to which members depend on the group for need satisfaction, and the demands or pressures under which the members operate. Too large a group will decrease group cohesion. Successfully achieving a goal will spur the group on to new challenges. For example, a successful fund-raising drive for a new town library may lead to another community fund-raising effort.

In summary, communication is the key to whether groups will function smoothly or not. Families and other types of small groups cannot be successfully managed without some degree of open communication. What needs to be done and by whom should be clearly communicated and negotiated. Closed or poor communication will undermine the family's or the group's cohesiveness and future progress.

## Information and Communications Technology

Much of the previous discussion has focused on group dynamics and interpersonal communication problems with a few comments about digital advertising and the upswing in the use of social media. In short, people communicate in a variety of ways using a variety of means or devices. How attentive an individual is to different forms of communication depends on the message, the messenger, and the channel. In addition, different types of media affect different senses. Print media, such as newspapers and magazines, usually affect vision only. The inclusion of perfume samples in magazines affects our sense of smell. Television is multisensory in that it affects both vision and hearing.

### Social Networks and Social Network Sites

One of the greatest technological changes of the 19th and the 20th centuries was the switch from face-to-face conversations to less personal forms of communication. This transformation began in 1876 with the first telephone (patented by a voice teacher, Alexander Graham Bell) and continues today with email and the Internet. **Social Networks** is a broad term used to describe communication connections among individuals and groups. Many disciplines explore social networks, but Family Relations, Sociology, Marketing, Computer or Computational Sciences, and Communications are leaders. **Social network sites** (SNSs) such as LinkedIn (for professionals/careers), MySpace, and Facebook attract billions of users. These users may be referred to as colleagues, friends, contacts, or fans. MySpace became popular with teenagers in 2004 since the site allowed minors. Facebook was originally designed for Harvard University only in early 2004 and spread from there to other campuses and beyond. As web-based services they allow individuals to:

1. Construct a public or semi-public profile within a bounded system,

2. Articulate a list of other users with whom they share a connection, and

3. View and transverse their list of connections and those made by others within the system (Boyd & Ellison, 2007).

In their broadest sense, social networks can be in-person as well as online.

SNSs may offer communication tools like mobile connectivity, blogging, and photo/video-sharing. They allow connections to be made by strangers who otherwise would never have met.

**CRITICAL THINKING**

### Social Networks

Social network sites not only let strangers connect but also allow them to view social networks by showing ties and personal descriptions beyond the original connection. The sites are built on visible profiles that come about usually by answering questions or providing descriptors such as age, location, education, interests, photos, and places of employment. Privacy issues abound especially when it comes to posting photographs, ages, and addresses. To avoid some of these problems, permission can be denied so there is limited access, or a person can choose to "opt out." Have you experienced any problems using social networks? Or, do you know someone who has?

Sometimes relationships are formed between strangers such as Meet-up or dating websites, but research indicates that many people use social networks to enhance or extend existing relationships such as a college connection like a sorority or fraternity or shared living in a college dormitory or later in one's professional life someone met at a conference. A sports bar in Washington, DC says 400 college alumni show up for every university football game to watch the game together and mix. High school reunions have been much easier to arrange since the advent of social networking sites. Researchers Ellison et al. (2007) found that Facebook was used mostly to maintain existing offline relationships or solidify offline connections versus meeting new people. Some people have used social networking sites to build acquaintances in a new location or to help with a new set of circumstances such as the Becka case study shows.

**CASE STUDY**

## Becka

The benefits of social networking sites were experienced by Becka in her late 20s. She lived in a small town and joined a social network with other pregnant women and really enjoyed talking with them about the progress of the pregnancies. The real excitement came when friends on the network started giving birth and she says many of them still "talk" now that their children are school age. Becka says this network "saved her life" by helping her get through the pregnancy because she didn't know anyone in the town she was living in and everyone at work was older and not interested in having children plus she felt free to be herself online and discuss the aches and pains and morning sickness. What she said was really helpful was to talk with women in the same month of pregnancy and to know that what she was feeling was normal.

**CASE STUDY**

## Middle-School Friends

In Deborah Tannen's: *You're the Only One I Can Tell* (2017, p. 1) she gives this example of the importance of middle-school friendships.

Andrea recalls that she and her best friend in middle school, Joelle, walked home together every day. At one point Joelle's family said they might move to another state. The thought of losing her best friend was devastating to Andrea. She thought "If she moves, how will I survive?" Tannen comments that level of feeling (that sense of loss) might be more for parents or life partners but can certainly happen with friends too.

## Information Overload and Habitual Decision Making

As consumers, individuals are constantly bombarded with information. Some of this information is **passively acquired,** such as through billboards on the highway and loudspeakers at discount stores or trade shows, meaning that the consumer does not seek out the information. Other information is **actively acquired**, meaning that the consumer actively looks for it or engages in it such as a social network site or by viewing advertisements in magazines or by reading signs at local stores.

**CASE STUDY**

## 50 Plus

*Christine McCleary is tired of peering at small print when she shops. 'Companies need to redesign things because so much of the population is older,' says the 59-year-old Incline Village, Nevada, resident, after her recent struggles at a local store. And corporate America, believe it or not, is starting to agree: With boomers now turning 65 in huge waves—about 7,000 will turn 65 every day this year—and shoppers 50-plus owning the vast majority of U.S. wealth, retailers are making changes to accommodate their needs. Updates are especially visible in drugstores …*

Source: Ianzito, C. (2011, September). Retail redo. AARP The Magazine, p. 14.

The degree of effort expended on the information search and the amount of exposure to information vary by person, product, and issue. For example, consumers often react to information (e.g., store displays, advertisements) with **low involvement**, meaning that they tend not to think much about it and may find their attention wandering. In **habitual decision making**, choices are made out of habit without any additional information search. Decisions are made with little conscious effort. This allows the consumer to devote real effort and thought to important decisions requiring more careful scrutiny.

**Information overload** refers to that uncomfortable state when individuals are exposed to too much information in too short a time—so much that they cannot process the information. Rather than ignore information as one does in low involvement, the person feels overwhelmed by it. Modern email usage dates to the early Internet which grew out of ARPNET, a network sponsored by the U.S. Department of Defense research agency in the 1960s. There are 3.86 billion users worldwide and 4.3–4.4 billion projected for 2022. Over 270 billion emails are sent each day (Statistia, March 28, 2019).

An offshoot of information overload is **information anxiety**, which is the gap between what individuals think they understand and what they actually do understand. Thus, information anxiety refers to the space between data and knowledge. Richard Wurman, author of *Information Anxiety*, observes that people used to have to make a conscious decision to seek information, but now technology permits information to be transmitted without the desire— or often the permission—of the receiver. Adding to the information explosion is the proliferation of communications technology. To deal with information overload, Wurman advises people to accept that they don't have to know everything about everything. He recommends that they focus on what matters most.

## The Internet and the Human Capacity to Process Information

Information that was once stored in people's heads and in books and file cabinets is now being put into digital form on computers. Once this information is stored in a computer's memory, it can be manipulated and accessed over phone lines, transmitted by satellite, and accessed by many different users.

### CASE STUDY

#### A Wired Mom

*It starts while I'm putting groceries away. My daughter, Ava, 12, tells me I forgot "her" shampoo while my 14-year-old son, Cole, picks through the bags in search of deodorant I didn't buy because he never asked me to. Then Dan, my husband, asks, "Did you get chili powder? I want to make chili on Sunday." (Great, but this is the first I've heard of his plans.) If these requests were to pile up all week, by Friday I'd have a list of errands as long as my arm. So instead, I rely on my laptop, smartphone and Web connection to take care of appeals as they pop up—preserving weekends for sleeping in, gardening and enjoying my family.*

Source: Tynan-Wood, C. (2011, June). Errand-free weekends.
Family Circle, p. 22.

Borrowing computer terminology, the amount of information the human central nervous system can process has been compared to the amount of information a computer can process. It has been estimated that individuals can manage at most seven bits of information (e.g., differentiated sounds, visual stimuli, or recognizable nuances of emotion or thought) at any one time and that the shortest time it takes to discriminate between one set of bits and another is about 1/18 of a second (Csikszentmihalyi, 1990). On the basis of these figures, humans can process at most 126 bits of information per second or 7,560 per minute. In practical terms, this means that an individual cannot process what three people are saying to him or her simultaneously and absorb all the nonverbal cues. These are all estimates, as the exact limit of humans' conscious ability to process information is unknown. Nevertheless, it is known that an individual's interest in the message and the message giver influences how much is processed and retained.

According to University of Chicago researcher Mihaly Csikszentmihalyi,

> *The mark of a person who is in control of consciousness is the ability to focus attention at will, to be oblivious to distractions, to concentrate for as long as it takes to achieve a goal, and not longer. And the person who can do this usually enjoys the normal course of everyday life.*
>
> *(1990, p. 31)*

## The Role of the Home and the Individual: Managing Information

As the preceding quotation illustrates, individuals make choices about what to concentrate on and what to ignore. In part, these are conscious decisions by an individual or family about which technologies they will adopt. In the future, more technology-assisted activities will take place in the home, including shopping, investing, banking, and working. Computers have already made it possible for many people to work from home.

Faith Popcorn, an often-quoted futurist, noted that **cocooning** (the desire to remain at home as a place of coziness, control, peace, insulation, and protection) is being facilitated by such technologies as digital devices, laptops, and microwave ovens. Improved home-based technologies should increase family time. The increase in-home-based technologies is a boon for the elderly, disabled individuals, and others less mobile than the general population.

On the other hand, media specialist Faith Popcorn warns of **emo-surveillance** (emo for emotional) which stands for huge advances in facial recognition and the reading of expressions where our innermost moods can be scanned—perhaps used in the hiring process as well as in commercial ventures i.e. selling products, even homes (Popcorn, 2018). What if realtors watching sensors/cameras remotely could unlock doors and could see the expressions on home viewers' faces as soon as they walked in the door, immediately they would know if the house has a chance of selling or not. All sorts of industries are being revolutionized from banking (called fintech) to real estate by devices and robotics.

Different kinds of costs (pros and cons) of technology are an obvious problem. Financially, new technologies are expensive and may increase the gap between the haves and have-nots in society.

Families should be supportive, expressive, and empathetic to their members and friends. Conversations should take turns. Words should be consistent with gestures, expressions, and other nonverbal messages. Families are inter-dependent and intense, meaning that the actions and words of any one family member may have more impact than reactions or comments by outsiders.

## CRITICAL THINKING

Jealousy among siblings is not unheard of. A sister may win an award and lots of praise and a younger sister may think "she seems to get everything." How does she deal with these feelings of annoyance and say the right thing? Dislikes among siblings can last a lifetime. An employee planning a retirement party for Ms. X was told by Ms. X, "Do not invite my sister under any circumstances." What might you assume from this comment?

Privacy is another issue which has been brought up several times already in this book. It is one of the most important resource management problems going forward. As more information is recorded and exchanged, more is known about an individual's buying habits and personal communications. Legislation is needed to establish ground rules on who will have access to data and under what conditions. Families make decisions as well about access to data and use of technology. Parents decide what technology to adopt and what technology to let children access. Certainly, this is a concern with the Internet. Individuals and families will also have to make decisions about managing information. A way parents handle smartphones is by only allowing them to be used for communication with friends and family. An artificial intelligence professor told the author of this book that his nine-year-old had a smartphone that could only be used this way, other channels were blocked. He said his son only cared about talking with his friends, so it was not a problem.

## SUMMARY

Communication is a process involving relationships and symbols between senders and receivers. As social beings, we want to communicate. Feedback in the form of "talk" or "buzz" was introduced in this chapter in the Model of Social Influence which starts with an innovation or invention. Feedback can be provided online or in-person or through devices like smartphones. Social influence is about how one person or group affects another's opinions, attitudes, emotions, or behaviors.

Social networks such as online reviews have opened the gates of channels of communication (more information is transparent and available). With this expansion comes any issue as well such as how to handle privacy and security of information.

Effective managers are careful communicators. It is impossible to lead or to manage without communicating. Communication serves as a linkage between the various steps in the management process. Dialogues and monologues are opposites.

Communication can be verbal or nonverbal. Ten aspects of nonverbal communication were given in this chapter. An example of a nonverbal symbol conveying motion is the swoosh logo for Nike.

Communication skills can be improved through study and application.

Listening is an important management skill. Hearing other people's needs and being able to express one's own is the basis of human communication.

Communication is satisfying when individuals feel that they are understood and that they understand others.

Five main components make up the total communication environment: message, channels, noise, feedback, and setting. Communication conflicts can arise from any of these components or from a combination of them. Family communication differs from other types in its emotional intensity and ongoing nature. Because of these characteristics, communication conflicts in families can be particularly painful and harmful. Destructive messages and tactics such as ridiculing, ordering, or threatening can be harmful to family relationships.

According to Deborah Tannen and other researchers, men and women have different but equally valid conversational styles.

Communication and communications technology are never stagnant. The modes, the messages, and the means are always changing. Information overload is increasingly a problem. Individuals are constantly being bombarded by messages, some of which are sought (actively acquired information), while others are unanticipated or unwelcome (passively acquired information). There is a limit to how much information humans can consciously process. Future research will provide more insight into the ability to process information and the ways computers can assist further in accessing and storing information. Already computers and other forms of technology and the speed of information have altered the traditional functioning of the home.

As every advance in communications technology has its pluses and minuses, individuals and families must weigh the costs and the benefits before adopting new technology.

## KEY TERMS

| | | |
|---|---|---|
| abstract symbols | external noise | ostrich effect |
| actively acquired information | habitual decision-making | pace |
| advocate or expert | I-messages | passively acquired |
|   channels | indirect channels |   information |
| artifacts | information anxiety | proxemics |
| brainstorming | information overload | receiving |
| channel | interference | reflective listening |
| cocooning | internal noise | responses |
| communication conflict | interpersonal conflicts | screen time |
| conflict resolution | intrapersonal communication | sending |
| constructive conflicts | low involvement | setting |
| critical listening | listening | social channels |
| decoding | market share | Social Exchange Theory |
| destination | message | Social influence |
| destructive conflicts | message construction | social networks |
| dialogue | message content | social network sites source |
| emo-surveillance | Model of Social Influence | symbols |
| empathetic listening | monologue | verbal symbols |
| empathy | noise | visible symbols |
| encoding | nonverbal symbols | You-messages |

## REVIEW QUESTIONS

1. Using the Model of Social Influence, think of an innovation or invention you have experienced in your life and run it through the model steps. Name the innovation or invention, how was it introduced, then did you talk about it, adopt or buy it, use it and evaluate it?

After, did you review it online or tell anyone else about it? Why is it important to be part of the feedback loop?

2. Writer Anne Morrow Lindbergh said, "Good communication is as stimulating as black coffee, and just as hard to sleep after." Do you think that is true? Explain a time when you couldn't get to sleep because of a conversation or something that was said that day. What is your intrapersonal voice saying?

3. Change the following You-messages into I-messages: "You never clean the apartment." "You never put gasoline in the car." "You always leave everything to the last minute. Why don't you do something on time for a change?"

4. List the destructive communication styles or tactics used in families. Which do you think is the biggest problem? Why?

5. There are many forms of nonverbal communication. An art example given in the chapter was the swoosh logo (which conveys motion) for Nike. Name two other famous company symbols. When you see them you know it is that company or brand.

## REFERENCES

Adams, D. (1998, December 23). When holding hands help clinch the deal. *Tallahassee Democrat*, p. 10E.

Adler, R., Rodman, G., & du Pre, A. (2020). *Understanding human communication, 14th edition*. Oxford: Oxford University Press.

Beck, A. (1988). *Love is never enough*. New York: Harper & Row.

Begley, S. (1998, November 2). Living hand to mouth. *Newsweek*, p. 69.

Bievenue, M. (1978). *A counselor's guide to accompany a marital communications inventory*. Saluda, NC: Family Life.

Blinder, A. (1991, July 22). Time is not on America's side. *Business Week*, p. 12.

Boyd, D., & Ellison, N. (2007). Social network sites: Definition, history, and scholarship. *Journal of Computer- Mediated Communication, 13*(1), article 11. http://jcmc.indiana.edu/vol13/issue1/boyd.ellison.html.

Csikszentmihalyi, M. (1990). *Flow: The psychology of optimal experience*. New York: Harper & Row.

DeVito, J. (2009). *Human communication: The basic course, 11th edition*. Boston, MA: Pearson.

Drucker, P. (1977). *People and performance*. New York: Harper College Press. pp. 262–263.

Duong, H. (March 30–31, 2019). The spring off duty 50: Style & vision. *The Wall Street Journal*, D5.

Editor's note. (2003, September). *Real Simple*, p. 37.

Goldsmith, E. (2013). Consumer behavior regarding the storage of perishable foods. *Proceedings of the Cold Chain Management Conference*, University of Bonn: Germany. June 10, 2013.

Goldsmith, E. (2015). *Social influence and sustainable consumption*. Switzerland: Springer.

Hall, E. T. (1959). *The silent language*. Greenwich, CT: Fawcett.

Heitmeyer, J., & Goldsmith, E. (1990). Attire as an influence on the perceptions of counselors' characteristics. *Per- ceptual and Motor Skills, 70*, 923–929.

Kanter, R. (1977). *Work and family in the United States: A critical review and agenda for research and policy*. New York: Russell Sage Foundation.

L'Abate, L., & Harel, T. (1993). Deriving, developing, and expanding competence from resource exchange theory. In U. Foa, J. Converse, K. Tornblom, & E. Foa (Eds.), *Resource Theory: Explorations and Applications* (pp. 223–260). San Diego, CA: Academic Press.

Law, R., Haselwood, C., & Goetz, J. (2019). Key communication and physical environment concepts for financial counselors. In Dorothy B. Durband, Ryan H. Law, and Angela K. Mazzolini (Eds.), *Financial Counseling*. Switzerland: Springer.

Liberman, R., Wheeler, E., de Visser, L., Kuehnel, J., & Kuehnel, T. (1980). *Handbook of marital therapy*. New York: Plenum Press.

Miller, C. (2010, September 15). *Communications in the Workplace: A Collaborative Teacher Student Research Project*, 2003, on the Web September 15, 2010.

Oggins, J., Veroff, J., & Leber, D. (1993, September). Perceptions of marital interaction among black and white newlyweds. *Journal of Personality and Social Psychology, 65*, 494–511.

O'Malley, C., Blankemeyer, M., Walker, K., & Dellmann-Jenkins, M. (2007). Children's reported communication with their parents about war. *Journal of Family Issues, 28*(12), 1638–1661.

Popcorn, F. (January 24, 2018). Five trends for marketers to watch in 2018. *Forbes.*

Robbins, S. P. (1989). *Organizational behavior, 4th edition.* Englewood Cliffs, NJ: Prentice-Hall.

Seligman, M. (2003, September). Love and positive events. *Authentic Happiness Newsletter.* Retrieved March 31, 2004, from http://www.authentichappiness.org/news/news7.html.

Shellenbarger, S. (2003, October 30). Then there was the time I had a typo: What talks of your work can teach kids. *The Wall Street Journal*, p. D1.

Sieburg, E. (1985). *Family communication.* New York: Gardner Press.

Tannen, D. (1990). *You just don't understand.* New York: Ballantine Books.

Tannen, D. (2006). *You're wearing that? Understanding mothers and daughters in conversation.* New York: Random House.

Tannen, D. (2017). *You're the only one I can tell.* New York: Random House.

Walker, R. (2008). *Buying in.* New York: Random House.

Wellner, A. (2002, February). The female persuasion. *American Demographics, 24*, 24–29.

Wu, B., & Newell, S. (2003, Spring). The impact of noise on recall of advertisements. *Journal of Marketing Theory and Practice, 11*(2), 56–65.

Wurman, R. (1990). *Information anxiety.* New York: Doubleday.

Yin, S. (2003, May). Degree of challenge. *American Demographics, 25*, 20–22.

Yin, S. (2003, September). Color bind. *American Demographics, 25*, 22–26.

Zweig, J. (2008, September 13–14). Should you fear the ostrich effect? *The Wall Street Journal*, p. B1.

Chapter **8**

# Managing Human Needs

DOI: 10.4324/9781003166740-8

... About 16.5 percent of the U.S. population is 65 and older, expected to reach 22 percent by 2050.

... 26 percent of the U.S. population (one in four adults) has some type of disability.

Building on the previous chapter on communication, this chapter moves on to other parts of the human experience. People do not live within narrow categories. Saying someone is a teacher is only describing one aspect of his or her life. Understanding this fullness of life and caring for others are the subjects in this chapter. Who is caring for others has become more complicated for a variety of reasons such as issues related to health, finance, divorce and remarriage, and mobility. For example, since most divorced men remarry, their children from the previous marriage will experience a stepmother at some point. Marriage is not only about the integration of people but also about the integration of resources. So, marriage, single-parent families, and blended families will be the topics in this chapter; also adjusting to retirement and financial concerns.

> *Nancy Davis, a 59-year-old senior marketing manager for a law firm in San Diego, had hoped to ease into retirement after her son finishes college in two years. But "I may be 70 before I retire at this point," she said Friday, after watching the markets take their toll on her 401(k). "It's very unnerving". With nest eggs shrinking, housing prices still falling and anxieties about their financial future growing, the oldest members of the babyboom generation are putting the brakes on plans to leave the office.*
>
> *(Greene, 2008, p. A4)*

The United States is a nation of caregivers. The writer and humorist Mark Twain said, "Always do right. This will gratify some people and astonish the rest." Caregiving is very much about doing the right thing.

This chapter explores much more than what is conventionally thought of as caregiving and goes beyond the United States to look at the human resource challenges around the world. It tackles some difficult topics such as the management problems of the homeless and the poor. There are **self-care** (functions and reactions under human control, self-initiated and deliberate) and self-talk methods as well. Consider the critical thinking exercise.

## CRITICAL THINKING

### Self-Talk Approach to Try

Dan Ariely professor and behavioral economist in answer to a question about a job interview and stress, suggests a more effective way to do a pep talk. "Telling ourselves 'I've got this' or

> I'm so ready for this' is a very common strategy for preparing for a challenge, and it makes intuitive sense. But self-talk can actually be more effective if you use the third-person: 'Julia's got this' instead of 'I've got this.' Using the third person creates an emotional separation between ourselves and the stressful event, making it feel more like enthusiastic support from a friend. Research shows that this approach can help people manage stress more effectively."

Try this technique next time you are stressed or preparing for an event and report if it works for you.

Source: Dan Ariely (2021, February 18). "Give yourself better pep talks," *The Wall Street Journal*. Life & Arts section.

# Changes in Population

To discuss managing human needs let us first look at changes in population. In 1900, 1.5 billion people inhabited the earth and most of them lived in large cities in Western Europe. Now, the world population is over 7.7 billion, and the greatest concentrations of people are in Asia with China as the most populous country, followed by India, then the United States, Indonesia, and Brazil. It is estimated that by 2050, India will surpass China as the most populous country.

Half of the world's population is concentrated in cities, and *the trend is toward increasing urbanization* so that by 2050, as noted in Chapter 1, 75 percent of the world's population will live in cities and nearby surrounding areas. This clustering of people will stress natural resources and support systems. Many of the world's cities are called gateway cities because they are located on borders (between countries) or on coastlines. Immigrants often arrive in gateway cities, establish families and businesses, and do not venture further into the interior of countries.

Managing human needs in a finite environment is the focus of this chapter. Resources are used to satisfy needs. As Chapter 4 explained, resources can be classified as human and material. Human resources include all the capabilities (skills, talents, and abilities) that contribute to achieving goals and responding to demands. Health, vitality, and intelligence are examples of human resources. Human resources can be divided into three main categories:

---

**CRITICAL THINKING**

How do you feel about urban vs. small town/suburban vs. rural living? What is your preference and why?

---

1. *Cognitive:* knowledge, intelligence, and reasoning

2. *Affective:* emotions and feelings

3. *Psychomotor:* muscular activity associated with mental processes and the ability to do physical work

Many tasks require skills from two or more of these categories. For example, typing requires cognitive and psychomotor skills. Parenting requires all three types of human resources.

*Human capital* is the sum total of an individual's human resources. Education, training, and practice enhance human resources. Developing human capital in oneself and in others is one of the most important management processes covered in this book. Ultimately, the strength of a nation depends on its stock of human resources—the collective ability of its citizens to solve problems creatively and to meet society's demands.

Today, people find themselves immersed in a tangle of worldwide changes in the economy, society, institutions, education, labor market, and individual lifestyles. Individual concerns must now be viewed in the context of the entire world. The family, as the basic unit of society, has weathered many storms, but many challenges lie ahead.

This chapter goes beyond the theoretical into the realm of population statistics and the practical management problems of certain groups. One important population change in the United States is the rapid increase in the percentage of minority and immigrant groups. About 12 percent of the population of the United States is foreign-born. Most of them come from poorer countries or situations hoping for a better life for their families or sometimes they come for education or work and end up staying. We are becoming a more diverse nation and the same trend applies to many other countries as well.

Another significant trend worldwide is the maturation or aging of society. In the United States, the baby boom generation—children born between 1946 and 1964—has grown up and established family and community roots, cared for teenage children and elderly parents, moved into management positions at work, and bought homes—in fact, probably several homes—over the years. An important aspect of the maturation trend is the growth of the over-65 age group, the "graying of America," although the whole world is aging, the trend being most pronounced in developed countries such as Japan. Elderly people today are healthier, more active, and more affluent than those of previous generations. Eventually, however, there may be caregiving needs, and these will be addressed in this chapter along with adjusting to retirement.

The 21st century has started out being more responsible about the environment and more respectful of individuals' age and cultural differences than the previous century. To express this concept of respect for cultural diversity, Alvin Toffler, author of *Future Shock*, coined the word "demassification," which means breaking away from mass society where everyone must be the same. He says we're moving to a "mosaic society" where diversity is recognized and fostered.

This chapter begins Part 3, the management applications section, of the book. It starts by examining population trends relevant to the study of individuals and families, including an exploration of how these changes take place. Although management concepts are relevant to all individuals and families, the remainder of this chapter focuses on the management needs and concerns of the following populations: two-income families, children, older persons and the elderly, early retirees, the homeless, individuals with disabilities, single parents, stepfamilies or blended families, and poor and low-income families.

Certain human resources, such as trust, love, and care, are difficult to measure, but numbers of people and population shifts can be quantified. The primary source of U.S. population data is the national census, which is taken every 10 years by the Bureau of the Census. The census attempts to count every person living in this country and to collect vital information about family size, and community and housing conditions. Based on this information, the government can determine population shifts and formulate policy.

The first census was taken in 1790 when George Washington was the president. At that time, 3.9 million people were counted. In 2020 there were 329.48 million, most easily rounded up to 330 million. The population change from the previous year (2019) was 1.55 million with the average number of people in a family 3.14 in 128.58 million households.

All statistics in this chapter come from the U.S. Bureau of the Census and the United Nations Population Division unless otherwise noted.

## Population Terms and Trends

**Demography** is the study of the characteristics of human populations—that is, their size, growth, distribution, density, movement, and other vital statistics. **Demographics** are data used to describe populations or subgroups. The study of **family demography** was founded by Paul Glick who wrote the first overview of the field for the *Journal of Marriage and Family* in 1988. Myers (2010) and others have updated this founding work and extended it to include geographic mobility and birth intentions.

Population figures are affected by three main factors: births, deaths, and immigration. The birthrate is technically termed "fertility." The **fertility rate** is the yearly number of births per 1,000 women of childbearing

age. *Countries experiencing a dramatic drop* in the average number of children born per woman from the early 1980s to early 2000s include Brazil, China, India, Indonesia, Mexico, Russia, Thailand, Tunisia, and Turkey. During this same period, the average number of children born per woman increased slightly in the United States, where about two per woman is average. In India three children per woman is average and in Russia it is one per woman. The technical term for death is **mortality**. **Immigration** refers to the number of people who enter and settle in a country where they are not native. Without a decided increase in immigration and birthrate, populations can stagnate or decrease.

Population growth stimulates the need for more products.

The ten most populous states are in this order with California the largest:

1. California
2. Texas
3. Florida
4. New York
5. Illinois
6. Pennsylvania
7. Ohio
8. Michigan
9. Georgia
10. North Carolina

The smallest population state is Wyoming with 567,025. The largest city is New York City followed by Los Angeles.

Another way to look at population is by density which is the average number of residents per square mile in each state, DC (the city in the Washington area), and Puerto Rico. Here are the top five by population density according to the U.S. Census in 2010. The latest census results and analysis (including maps) can be found at data.census.gov.

1. District of Columbia (DC)

2. New Jersey

3. Puerto Rico

4. Rhode Island

5. Massachusetts

The least densely populated state is Alaska.

Even though the population is growing worldwide, in general, fertility rates are plummeting. Today women on average have half the number of children they had in 1972. In 61 countries, fertility rates are now at or below replacement levels. This does not mean that the worldwide population will fall in the immediate future, however, because people are living longer. Globally, the average life span has jumped from 49.5 years in 1972 to 63 years. In addition, as mentioned earlier, the low fertility rate of industrialized nations is offset to some degree by less developed countries, which often have high fertility rates—although this is changing as economies change and birth control methods become more widespread.

Over the years, high unemployment and poor economies have been shown to have a direct impact on fertility rates in industrialized countries. For example, during the Great Depression of the 1930s, the United States had a low fertility rate. Prior to that, especially from 1880 to 1900, the U.S. population growth rose owing to the influx of immigrants from Europe.

The U.S. birthrate rose sharply again after World War II. Unlike earlier population increases, which were caused largely by immigration, this growth was primarily due to the birth of millions of children. This "baby boom," which ended in 1964, was followed by a period of slow growth that did not pick up again until the late 1980s and early 1990s. In 1988, 3.9 million babies were born—the highest number since 1964. Termed the "baby boomlet," these babies were the children of the "baby boomers." A distinct trend has been the rise in the number of women between the ages of 30 and 40 who have given birth for the first time. One-third of the nation's births now are attributed to women over 30. A documented trend is a decrease in teen pregnancies. Since 1990, the teen childbearing rate in the United States has dropped by almost 10 percent.

In families, the birth of a baby brings about many changes in time management and consumption patterns. Parents suddenly find themselves the prime targets of advertisers offering a wide array of baby products. Their grocery carts are filled with products they never purchased before such as diapers, infant formula, baby food, toys, and baby shampoo. The home environment also changes as baby care equipment is added: strollers, cribs, swings, highchairs, and playpens. When children reach the age of two or three then outdoor gym sets grow in popularity.

In response to demographic changes, the marketplace transforms as it tries to keep up with consumer demand. As noted earlier, the baby boomers have reached middle age and the older ones are retired. The number of married couple households without children is rising owing to empty-nest baby boom households and delayed childbearing.

## Population Age and Composition

The United States, Canada and the United Kingdom are growing older. Currently, the U.S. population is the oldest it has ever been. *The median age is 38.2*, up from 32.3 years in 1990. **Median age** is the age that divides a population into two numerically equal groups, half older, half younger.

The number of college students continues to grow. There are over 20 million college students in the United States.

There are more females than males, but the ratio varies across age groups. In the younger years, there are more males than females. For example, between 1994 and 2020 there were more males than females in their 20s. But, among those over age 75, women outnumbered men by nearly two to one.

## Race/Ethnicity

*Race is a categorical description of individuals based on skin color and other inherited visible differences. Race is not based on biology. It is socially constructed, meaning society has placed individuals into categories in which shared assumptions can be made...Socially constructed racial categories include Black, Asian and White.*

(DeGraff and Dillon, 2019, p 52)

Defining race and ethnicity are sensitive issues and individuals and groups can self-define.

*Ethnicity refers to the social, cultural, and sometimes national group of a person, Ethnic descriptions can include assumptions of gender, class, race, religion, or other characteristics of a group of people. Examples of ethnicity include Hispanic, Arab, and Irish. Sometimes, ethnicity and nationality can be the same, as with German nationality describes the political state to which someone belongs*

(DeGraff and Dillon, 2019, p. 52)

"People in mixed families will be continually crossing all racial and ethnic lines in the United States, and their numbers will steadily increase" (Hildago & Bankson, 2011). Related to this is that minority groups are the fastest-growing segment of the U.S. population. As noted in Chapter 1, the skyrocketing growth of Latinos or Hispanics in the United States once driven by immigration is now fueled by high fertility rates especially for Mexicans and Mexican Americans.

## CASE STUDY

### Diana

*The parents of Diana Velasquez, a 22-year-old college student in Chicago, are part of the great contemporary Hispanic migration. They settled in the U.S. in the 1980s and had four children, all first-generation Mexican-Americans. She grew up in an area dominated by large immigrant families but says she doesn't plan to have as many children herself.*

*Source: Jordan, M. (2011, July 25). Births fuel Hispanic growth. The Wall Street Journal, p. 13.*

On average, minority populations are younger than other Americans and therefore have higher birthrates, and their numbers are also increasing owing to immigration. The race categories in the 2020 census included White, Black or African-American, American Indian or Alaska Native, Asian, and Native Hawaiian or Other Pacific Islander. Another choice was Some Other Race. Respondents may report more than one race. For definitions of the categories and percentages and an explanation of the methodology go to census.gov.

There are 574 federally recognized Native American tribes in the United States, including 197 Alaska native village groups. Native Americans number 2.5–4.1 million if you include multiracials—more than 4 in 10 Native Americans consider themselves multiracial. Native Americans are the nation's second wealthiest minority after Asian Americans. Tribes may also be called nations, bands, pueblos, communities, or native villages.

The term "minority" is sometimes a misnomer because a group defined by the Census Bureau as a minority may be a majority group in some parts of the country. For example, in San Antonio, Texas, 52 percent of the residents are Hispanic/Latino. Hispanics/Latinos are the fastest-growing minority group in the United States. Most Hispanics live in Arizona, New Mexico, Florida, Texas, and California. They are most likely to think of family as an extended family (including more relatives than in the nuclear/close family of typical European Americans), and they highly value family (Radina, 2003).

One-third of Blacks or African Americans live in one of the following five states: Georgia, Florida, Texas, California, and New York. The average African-American family has 3.5 members. African Americans typically define family as extended family and kinship groups and place a high value on community (Radina, 2003). Nonrelated friends may be considered members of the family. Mutual support and loyalty are strong values.

Asian Americans constitute 3–4 percent of the nation's population. They are overwhelmingly urban and most likely of all the minority groups to marry outside of race/ethnicity. The Census Bureau's category of Asian and Pacific Islanders covers 17 countries. Most of the Asians entering the United States come from Indochina: Vietnam, Laos, and Kampuchea (formerly Cambodia). There are also sizable groups with Japanese, Korean, Chinese, Taiwanese, and Filipino heritage. They place an emphasis on parent–child relationships and practice filial piety, which means respect for elders and having a moral duty to obey, honor, and assist parents (Radina, 2003). Of the three largest minority groups, Asian Americans are the most highly educated. Full-time college participation rates among young adults are rising for all groups, especially Blacks (Crispell, 1997).

## Households and Families

*The number of households is increasing in the United States, but the number of persons per household is decreasing.* Household change parallels population change. Household growth in the 1990s was fastest in Nevada, especially for 24–35-year-olds. Young adults aged 25–34 living at home were 7.58 million in 2019. The trend is more young adults in this age group living at home.

Four other fast-growing states also saw gains in householders ages 25–34: Arizona, Georgia, Utah, and Delaware. Nearly three in five households have no children, and this trend toward smaller families is expected to continue. One reason for the decline in household size is lower fertility. Another reason is the increase in the number of elderly.

## Marital Status and Rise in Solitary Living

Currently married people number 137.76 million. Currently divorced people as a percentage of people who have ever been married is 14.3 percent, Young people are waiting longer to get married, and the marriage rate itself is decreasing. According to the Census Bureau, men and women are delaying marriage, resulting in the median age of first marriages rising. Historically, 90 percent of Americans married at some time in their lives, but that rate is declining. The highest divorce rate is for couples in their 20s, and divorced people are waiting longer to remarry. At a second marriage, the median age of brides is 32 and the median age of grooms is 34.

One of the biggest changes in the United States is the *extraordinary rise in solitary living*. In 1950, 4 million Americans lived alone making up only 9 percent of households. In former decades, the singles were single men making a living in the open sprawling Western states of Alaska, Montana and Nevada. According to 2011 census data, people who live alone account for nearly 33 million Americans and make up 28 percent of all U.S. households. Put together with childless couples they form the most prominent residential type,

> *more common than the nuclear family, the multigenerational family and the roommate or group home…*
> *They're concentrated in big cities throughout the country, from Seattle to Miami, Minneapolis to New*
> *Orleans….people who live alone compensate by becoming more socially active than those who live with*
> *others and that cities with high numbers of singletons enjoy a thriving public culture*
>
> (Klinenberg, 2019, pp. 60–61)

## CRITICAL THINKING

### Living Alone

React to this: According to Eric Klinenberg, professor sociology at New York University,

> *Living alone allows us to do what we want, when we want, on our own terms. It liberates us from the constraints of a domestic partner's needs and demands and permits us to focus on ourselves. Today, in our age of digital media and ever-expanding social networks, living alone can offer even greater benefits: the time and space for restorative solitude. This means that living alone can help us discover who we are as well as what gives us meaning and purpose. Paradoxically, living alone might be exactly what we need to reconnect.*

Where people are living solo (as a percentage of all households).

(Source: Euromonitor International in Klinenberg, 2019, p. 62.)

Sweden 47 percent

Britain 34 percent

Japan 31 percent

Italy 29 percent

U.S. 28 percent

Canada 27 percent

Russia 25 percent

South Africa 24 percent

Kenya 15 percent

Brazil 10 percent

India 3 percent

## The Nature of Change

Resource managers should now and then step back and evaluate (take stock) and ask: "How am I doing? How is my group, family, or team doing? Are we in good shape? What do we have to do to improve? What should we build on? In *Redefining Diversity*, Roosevelt Thomas Jr. provides an interesting perspective on change within American society. He says that, increasingly, we see America's strength in its diversity—a mixture of colors and creeds bringing their different backgrounds to a common endeavor. Yet, he says, diversity is not confined to race and gender; rather, it applies to intangibles such as ideas, outlooks, and procedures.

Steps in adapting to change may include:

- Re-creating and developing strong relationships

- Collecting and analyzing data to move forward, make a case for change

- Anticipating blocks and conflicts

- Increasing communication among all those impacted

- Framing a crisis as an opportunity to bring about positive transformation and rebuild

- Evaluating plans and first and second steps

**Change** means to cause to be different, to alter, or to transform. Changes can be categorized into two general types: internal and external. **Internal change** originates within the family. Births, marriages, divorces, and deaths are all examples of internal changes. In contrast, **external change** is fostered by society or the outer environment. Tornadoes, hurricanes, and recessions are examples of external changes. An individual or a family may experience internal and external changes at the same time. Consider the following case of scientists coping in the wake of hurricanes.

### CASE STUDY

#### Hurricanes and Adapting

"The work that took us 12 to 15 years to build was destroyed in a couple of hours," says Olga L. Mayol-Bracero, an atmospheric chemist at the University of Puerto Rico, Rio Piedras. Hurricane Maria destroyed her office and one sampling station, another sampling station was almost completely destroyed, and her lab flooded. In total, the damages amount to about $700,000. "When I saw that nothing had survived at my cloud forest station, I was speechless," she explains. "For one or two days, I thought 'What should I do? Should I do something else from now on?"' After the news sank in, Mayol-Bracero decided to rebuild her facilities from the ground up. She's not alone.

*Source: Katie L. Burke (2018, March–April). "Scientists in the Wake of the Hurricanes," American Scientist, p. 69.*

The ability to cope with change is called **adaptability**. Adaptability is an example of a human resource that everyone has but in different quantities. People's temperaments and usual ways of reacting (rapid vs. slow) to new situations affect their response to change. The actual circumstances, such as whether an event is expected or unexpected, will also influence the response.

Because of this personality, behavioral, and situational factors, each person approaches change differently. Consider the following quotation by Winston Churchill, prime minister of England during World War II: "Never, never, never give up." Most changes occur gradually. This transition period can be helpful because it allows individuals to take stock of the situation and consider possible alternatives. Effective managers take advantage of transi-tion time to think through a situation and make plans to deal with it. Changing one's job or residence involves transition time. This is discussed in the next section, which explores "moving" as an example of change.

## Mobility

About one out of four U.S. adults change addresses every year and those in childbearing ages once in every three years. The U.S. population is one of the most mobile in the world. Most of the moves are related to work. Estimates are that Americans change residences about 11–12 times in their adult life, on average, and Europeans move four times (varies greatly by country).

Nearly all individuals and families cope with the problems and decisions associated with moving. One survey found that moving was more traumatic than divorce. The technical term for changing residences (migrating within a population) is **mobility**. Statistics on mobility trends are surprising. According to a survey conducted by the U.S. Census Bureau, the average distance moved is six miles, and renters move more than homeowners do, A similar mobility measure takes place in the European Union with the Euro-barometer survey.

Mobility has several major effects on individual and family behavior. It affects finances. "Research over the past 25 years finds that having a child is one of the most consistent predictors of moving as families adjust to fertility-driven changes in their housing and neighborhood preferences" (Myers, 2010, p. 1623). When peo-ple move, they spend money on household furnishings, moving services, and utility deposits; they may also use the services of realtors and mortgage companies. Second, moving is usually a stressor. Many household services must be changed and rescheduled when relocating—electricity, water, and mail service, to name just a few. Children may have to change schools. Parents may change jobs. Third, moving affects an individual or family morale. Moves may be disruptive or may present opportunities. They may mark the end of val-ued relationships or signify a fresh beginning or do both. In short, moving causes disruption and stimulates adaptation.

### Suggested Activity

Give one example of a time when you or someone you know didn't give up. What were the circumstances and the outcome?

As has been previously stated, the general trend has been movement from rural areas to suburbs and cities. This is evident in China as well as the United States. Certain states have more mobile populations than oth-ers. Nevada has the fewest natives, followed by Florida. At the other end of the spectrum is Pennsylvania, where 80 percent of residents were born in the state.

## Managing Change

As shown in the last section, migration of individuals and families is an increasingly common and complex process. It is only one example of how managing change is inherently messy:

> It is always complicated. It invariably involves a massive array of sharply conflicting demands. Despite the best-laid plans, things never happen in exactly the right order—and in fact, few things rarely turn out exactly right the first time around.... Change means new patterns of power, influence, and control ... and that's why it's so hard. Change is far too important, pervasive, and complicated a phenomenon to be taken for granted. Every manager may be aware of it; that doesn't mean he or she knows how to handle it.
>
> (Nadler, 1998, pp. 3, 5, 11)

Each family and each organization are a complex social system. There are several components that need coordinating (Nadler, 1998), including

- The work or the task

- The people

- The formal organization—the structure, the processes, the systems, and the identity, and

- The informal organization—the collective values, attitudes, beliefs, communication and lines of influence, and accepted standards of behavior.

The challenge is to sustain momentum, to move forward. Sustaining any profound change process requires a fundamental shift in thinking. Participants need to understand the nature of growth processes (forces that aid efforts) and how to catalyze them. But, they also need to understand the forces and challenges that impede progress and to develop workable strategies for dealing with these challenges (Senge, 1999, p. 10). In an article in *Marriage and Family Review*, Kathryn Rettig observed:

> Management is a thoughtful adaptation to the opportunities and demands of life. It involves problem-solving and decision-making, as well as carrying out actions to implement decisions. The consciousness of the deliberations that occur prior to decisions about how to use resources and the controlled implementation of decisions in order to reach valued-goals will distinguish management from other adaptive responses. The need for conscious problem-solving and decision-making is created because of changes that are wanted by individuals and families (proactive management) or because internal and/or environmental changes occur that require different responses (reactive management).
>
> (1993, p. 191)

The management problems and decisions inherent in change must be addressed because households and families are living in an increasingly complex web of internal and external changes. Many functions that were once the domain of households and families, such as meal preparation, are now purchased elsewhere or a food box is delivered to the home.

Before the 1950s, the study of management emphasized internal household processes. Today, management encompasses the interaction of the inside and outside activities and the lives of individuals and families within the greater environment. An employed parent may purchase a precooked dinner at the store and add a salad or a dessert at home. Although this combined effort might seem to involve fewer resource management skills, in actuality these skills are more necessary now than ever before because coordinating inside and outside activities takes time, effort, and planning. As more people, services, and environments become involved and time becomes tighter, more complex problem solving and decision implementation are necessary. The need for coordination within families grows.

# Meeting Individual, Family, and Societal Needs

Along with all the external changes that are occurring, the family itself has become a more diverse institution. Collectively, single-person households, single-parent families, and two-income families outnumber the traditional one-income families with both parents sharing a residence. Even though the family is taking on diverse forms, it remains an important stabilizing force in the rapidly changing, often-chaotic outside world. The word "family" implies a safe harbor, a place to come home to, and people who care.

The remainder of this chapter explores the special management needs of certain populations. This information is based on aggregate data, so specific individuals and families may not fit the generalizations given.

## Rise in Dual-Income Households

### CASE STUDY

#### Cassidy and Liam

Cassidy, age 28, is married to Liam who is a 30-year-old builder. Cassidy works for a university as a sign language interpreter and with students with learning disabilities. She enjoys her job and was offered a 15 percent raise to go to another state doing similar work. It would mean up-rooting her husband (there was no guarantee he would find a job he liked) and she said they had just fixed up a house and wanted to start a family. So, they decided to stay put, but she says it was a tough decision. The timing and location just were not right and the question hanging over their heads was will she get a better offer in the future? What about Liam and his career?

Part of managing changes is managing changing relationships, at home and at the workplace. Perhaps no phenomenon has had a greater effect on the fabric of society worldwide than the increasing number of women in the labor force. The influx of women into the workplace has altered the way families live, the products they buy, and the way they spend their time. The rise in dual-income households in the United States (percent of married couples with children under 18) is well documented by Pew Research Centers as well as by others. About 60 percent of households have dual-income compared to 25 percent in 1960. Those with fathers only employed has declined from 70 percent in 1960 to 31 percent in 2012.

Dual-income households on average have more money than single-earner households; but a book entitled *The Two-Income Trap* says that the money is not stretching as far as it should and that many two-income families are having a hard time. It begins:

> *This book is dedicated to all parents who wake up with hearts thudding over the possibility that buying school shoes and Girl Scout uniforms will mean that there won't be enough left over to pay the mortgage. These people are our neighbors, our brothers and sisters, our friends and coworkers. They travel anonymously among us, but we know them. They went to college, had kids, bought a home, played by the rules—and lost. It is time to rewrite the rules so that these families are winners again.*
>
> *(Warren & Tyagi, 2003, preface)*

What has transpired over the last few decades is that many two-earner families now need both incomes to maintain a minimum standard of living. Senator Elizabeth Warren and Amelia Tyagi, a mother-and-daughter team of writers, question how this came about: How have we come to the point where two incomes are needed to provide what one income used to? Two areas since their book was written that have risen rapidly in cost are gasoline/transportation and health care.

The authors say that mom works to help pay for the housing that puts the family in a good school zone—that the pursuit of safety and education has led to the increased debt load of the average middle-class family. A study in Fresno, California, revealed that the single most important determinant of neighborhood housing prices was school quality (Warren & Tyagi, 2003).

The term "dual income" needs to be distinguished from "dual career." In **dual-career** families, not only do both spouses work outside the home, but in addition, both have made a long-term commitment to a planned series of jobs leading toward an ultimate career goal. Not everyone who is working thinks of himself or herself as a career person.

Dual-earner families usually report that they are happy and satisfied (Runyon & Stewart, 1987). Family resources, such as spousal or partner support and sensitivity, play a key role in the satisfaction levels of dual-earner families (Gilbert, 1993). Tahira Hira (1987) found that satisfied dual-earner families (versus dissatisfied dual-earner families) have more money in their savings accounts, save larger proportions of their annual income, and have smaller monthly debt payments. Such families are also less likely to have an auto loan or outstanding balances on their credit cards. Having two incomes also reduces the fear of unemployment, as the family will have one income to fall back on in case of a recession or company downsizing.

Dual-earner families are also better educated, more mobile, better spenders, and more likely to own their own home than single-earner families (Rubin & Riney, 1994). The lifestyle is not perfect, however. Dual-earner families also report that they have less leisure time and less time for children and friends. Their pace of life is quicker. Jobs requiring extensive travel and numerous transfers increase stress for dual-income families, especially those with children. Spouses may enter into long-distance commuting relations, live halfway between two cities, or relocate for short periods of time to take advantage of a career opportunity (Gilbert, 1993). Dual-earner couples try to adjust their work or vacation schedules to maximize their time together.

Two-income couples may face various management problems, including difficulty in setting priorities and saying "no," budgeting, and making joint financial decisions. Dividing household tasks equitably so that everyone is content may also be a problem. Open communication and dealing with changes before events become overwhelming will help dual-income families keep ahead of their workloads.

The overriding management problem that dual-income families face is how to handle their jobs and their family responsibilities. Lucia Gilbert advises young adults who want to marry and work to plan, which "means thinking about expectations for yourself and a future spouse and communicating these early on in serious relationships" (1993, p. 75). The next three chapters on managing time, work and family, and stress and fatigue will provide additional insight into the management problems of dual-earner families.

## Child Care

*Caregivers are devoted to improving the quality of life for another.* They may be assisting persons with disabilities, children, or elders. The help can be daily or sporadic, temporary, or long-range. This section addresses childcare as a broad issue with numerous ramifications for families and for society in general. Providing financial support for children is a form of childcare. So is providing physical and emotional care. For example, a study of childhood obesity found that parents' practices related to weight management had a significant impact. The family context (stress, parenting style, and emotional climate) cannot be ignored when it comes to helping overweight children who are at risk (Kitzmann et al., 2008).

> *What is childcare?*
>
>    *Policy researchers define* **childcare** *as the full-time care and education of children under age six, care before and after school and during school vacations for older children, and overnight care when employed parents must travel. Childcare may be paid or unpaid and provided by relatives or others, including one of the parents.*
>
>                                        *(Lamanna & Riedmann, 2009, p. 316)*

Childcare is becoming a more critical issue for many families. Families manage childcare in several ways: One parent may stay home, or neighbors, relatives, and friends may provide care. Family day care homes and childcare centers in the community or at the parents' work sites are other options. If children are school age, parents may enroll them in before-school and after-school programs and summer camps. Parents often combine several of these methods.

## CRITICAL THINKING

How were you cared for as a young child? At home, at a childcare center or pre-school, at a relative's or neighbor's house, or another place? Do you have any photos or memories of it? If you have children, what will your preference be for childcare?

Young families with children often have more management problems than do other types of families. For example, studies repeatedly show that families with young children have the maximum time management problems because young children require so many hours of physical and nurturant care. These problems may be exacerbated in young families where parents may be completing their own education or launching their careers when they are having children. Employers, realizing that working parents need support, offer a wide range of childcare options, including resource-and-referral services and on-site childcare.

According to "Pregnancy Over Age 30" by Stanford Children's Health (2019),

> *Many women today are waiting until later in life to have children. In the United States, birth rates for women in their 30s are at the highest levels in three decades. However, an older mother may be at increased risk for miscarriage, birth defects, and pregnancy complications such as twins high blood pressure, gestational diabetes, and difficult labors. Some studies show that while there may be a greater likelihood of pregnancy complications in older women, their babies may not have more problems than babies of younger women.*

Older mothers tend to be highly educated and have established careers. Their careers would be well under way before they have their first child. Furthermore, in such families, many financial arrangements and assignments of household tasks would have been settled before children come along. When the children arrive, the division of labor will have to be renegotiated, but at least initial patterns would have been established.

One controversial aspect of childcare and human capital development is the smaller amount of time American children spend in school compared to children in other countries such as Japan and South Korea. The issue is controversial because some parents and educators believe our schools should continue to be closed in the summer, a tradition that originally was intended to allow children time off to help on the family farm. Less than 2 percent of American families live on farms now, however, and educators and parents think it is time for a change. The relatively low number of days spent in school may have implications for societal well-being if U.S. children are receiving less formal education than children in other industrialized nations. U.S. school districts are experimenting with longer school days and fewer vacation days or split schedules or hybrids—some days in class, other days online.

From the perspective of time management and family relations, the fact that children's school days and vacations often do not coincide with parents' work schedules makes it difficult for families to spend time together or to offer secure home-based childcare. Any changes that are made in the timing and length of children's school days should focus first on what is best for the children and their education given today's global society and future workforce demands.

Parents, whether employed or not, are interested not only in the quantity but also in the quality of time they spend with their children. Enjoying each stage of development, being present for school and sport/music activities, and encouraging children toward independent and fulfilling lives are common parental goals. Former First Lady Barbara Bush spoke at the Wellesley College commencement in 1990 and told the graduates:

> For several years, you've had impressed upon you the importance to your career of dedication and hard work. This is true, but as important as your obligations as a doctor, lawyer or business leader will be, you are a human being first and those human connections—with spouses, with children, with friends—are the most important investments you will ever make. At the end of your life, you will never regret not having passed one more test, not winning one more verdict or not closing one more deal. You will regret time not spent with a husband, a friend, a child or a parent.... Fathers and mothers, if you have children ... they must come first. You must read to your children, you must hug your children, you must love your children. Your success as a family ... our success as a society ... depends not on what happens at the White House, but on what happens inside your house.

Are the needs of this child being met?

Although parenting and family life are rewarding, no matter how hard parents try they often experience problems with children, particularly during the teen years. Drugs, alcohol, child neglect, and abuse are examples of adolescent problems. Child abuse is not limited to young children. Although parental stress is associated with child abuse, it is important to note that most parents do not abuse their children even when experiencing stress. However, stress can lead to other problems such as work or marital problems besides strained parent–child relationships. More on this topic is coming up in the chapter titled "Managing Stress and Fatigue."

### Suggested Activity

*Discuss in class what would be the optimum school schedule considering children's education needs and parental desires. As part of the discussion, include comments and observations about the students' own previous school experiences—were they part of a system with different hours, vacation scheduling, and so on than the norm? What were the pros and the cons? Also, discuss the trend toward reducing high school to three years in accelerated programs versus the more traditional four. Pros and cons?*

Developing better management skills can help parents deal with stress. Well-developed management skills bring a sense of mastery and a feeling of being in control. A parent who has developed these skills will find it easier to form strategies, solve problems, and adjust to change.

An interesting trend related to childcare is the growing number of grown-up children who are staying home with their parents or moving back home after college. Even 30-year-olds are moving back to their parents' home after a divorce or when they are unemployed. Active parenting starts at birth, but it is becoming less clear when active parenting ends. More young adults are living with their parents now than at any time since the Great Depression of the 1930s (Riche, 1990). Through an analysis of the Census Bureau's Survey of Income and Program Participation, demographers found that most people aged 20 or 21 remained in their parents' homes, while most people ages 22 to 24 had left.

Women leave home earlier than men do (Riche, 1990). Demographers also found that many young adults move in and out of their parents' homes and that men are more likely to return after age 25. The main reasons why adult children return to their parents' homes are economic difficulties, marital failure, prolonged education, and job market insecurity. Riche (1990) has called the return of adult children to their parents' homes **boomeranging**; it is regarded as a rational response to changes in the society and economy.

## Caregiving for Older Adults and the Elderly

About 16.5 percent of the U.S. population is 65 or older and this percentage is estimated to rise to 22 percent by 2050. Of course, many older persons are still working full-time and living independently, but there comes a point where some degree of caregiving or extra services may be necessary or a person 65 and up may be the caregiver for someone else.

Caregivers often have a dilemma when it comes to balancing work and the care of an older relative, neighbor, or friend. It is estimated that 70 million Americans care for older relatives or friends. According to the Alzheimer's Association 15 million of those family caregivers are caring for a person with Alzheimer's or another dementia. Most of this is unpaid or volunteer labor so it is hard to track in terms of the general economy and the exact numbers involved plus it could be temporary from a fall, for example. Elder care covers a broad range of services from relatives checking in now and then on an elder to:

- Assisted living

- Adult day care

- Long-term care

- Nursing homes (also called residential care)

- Hospice care

- Home care which can range from a few hours a week to round-the-clock care

We often think that caregiving is about elderly parents, but it can be for a spouse as well.

### CASE STUDY

#### Husband with Alzheimer's

"Even though Roxanne Aune's boss is aware that her 59-year-old husband has early onset Alzheimer's, he'll never know how much it impacts her work. 'I feel I can't say I'm a caregiver because a red flag will go up and my boss will think, 'Oh, there's something wrong with her husband again,' says Aune, 57, of Minneapolis. 'I can't afford to be absent, or start over again, so I don't discuss this part of my life.' Aune, an auditor at a health insurance company, believes she has suffered professionally since her husband's diagnosis last year. 'I feel I get overlooked for projects,' " he says.

*Source: Abrahms, S. (2011, September). The caregiver's dilemma. AARP Bulletin, p. 10.*

Although the need for childcare has been widely discussed, the need for elder care is less acknowledged. The number of available caregivers is dwindling because many adult women are in the workforce and the number of children in families has decreased. "Three out of four caregivers to the disabled elderly (excluding husbands and wives) are daughters, daughters-in-law, or other female relatives and friends (such as nieces or granddaughters)" (Warren & Tyagi, 2003, p. 62).

"When faced with changes in physical health, cognition, and daily functioning, older adults most frequently rely on family members for instrumental support and more intense care activities" (Roberto & Jarrott, 2008, p. 100).

One in four U.S. households is involved in the daily care of an elder. This may involve physical care necessitated owing to a chronic illness or frailty or simply phone calls or email messages to check up on things. As many as 40 percent of Americans who care for their parents also have dependent children. Middle-aged Americans who care for both their children and their elderly parents are called the "sandwich generation." The caregiver role can bring with it a mixture of joy, guilt, service demands, and emotional and financial burdens. The difficulty of the role depends on many factors: the health of the elderly dependent person, the personalities of the elderly person and caregiver, their mutual resources, and the social support they receive from relatives and community groups.

Elder husbands and wives often care for a spouse in need. Most typically this is the wife caring for the husband, but it can be vice versa. "More than 9 out of 10 frail care recipients who are married obtain help from their spouses," themselves often in poor health (Johnson & Wiener, 2006).

Caregiving can take place gradually over several years and may require only a few phone calls or visits, or it can be a 20-year daily commitment to the physical and emotional care of another. From a management viewpoint, the need for caregiving may develop slowly, allowing a family to adjust and plan for it, or it can arise suddenly. A midnight phone call from 1,000 miles away about a stroke or an accident is a crisis that requires an immediate response.

From a management perspective, caregiving for dependent elderly can precipitate numerous resource problems. Time, energy, and money may all be strained in caregiving situations. For example, here is a morning schedule for Bruce Shaw, age 60, who cares full-time for his father, Roger, who is 89.

**6–8 A.M.**

*water/juice salutations/small talk check physical signs*
*physical therapy, twice weekly rotation in bed*

**9–11 A.M.**

*water/juice snack, banana*
*check catheter and output check vital signs breathing treatment*
*pills talk*
*prepare house for the day*

Roger was left paralyzed after receiving the swine flu vaccine 27 years ago. Eight years ago, he lost his sight to glaucoma and lives with Bruce and his wife, Judy. Bruce quit his job as a business consultant, and their home has become a public setting with nurses and health aides passing in and out. Bruce says everybody in the family has had hard days; but caring for his father, he says, "has brought all of us closer together. We share this responsibility" (Ruffenach, 2003, p. D4).

A more recent family case involves a 64-year-old wife providing in-home care for her 73-year-old husband who has advanced Parkinson's -the basics of daily care include food and pill management, fall prevention, dealing with hallucinations, and making doctor appointments. A Monday-Friday helper has been employed since the wife works outside the home.

Caregivers are often exhausted. They need to maintain a sense of humor and be sensitive to the spouse's or elderly person's desire for independence and dignity.

Compounding these needs is the difficulty elderly parents have at letting a child take charge. The adult child may also feel awkward managing her or his parents' affairs and avoid this task until the health or safety of the parent requires it.

Understanding the aging process and the needs of the elderly can help caregivers perform their roles more effectively. The aging process has three aspects: physical or biological, social, and psychological. To date, most gerontological research (**gerontology** is the scientific study of the aging process) has focused on the physical aspects, but the others are important as well. Most elderly people are self-reliant and require little or no caregiving. Many maintain active, independent lives well into their nineties. Health, wealth, and attitude have a lot to do with the

**Table 8.1** Ways to Help Caregivers

Caregivers can easily experience burnout and stress. They neglect their own physical or mental conditions or disabilities when taking care of another person's more urgent needs. Self-care including improved self-talk such as pep talks can help (Ariely, 2021). Caregivers of older loved ones may feel that family and community members are taking for granted their daily responsibilities. Here are some management ideas for how others can help caregivers feel supported.

1. Give the gift of connecting with other caregivers. Many organizations, hospitals, and churches provide a trained leader to facilitate group discussions. Phone calls and informal discussions can help, too. Toll-free elder hotlines provide information about caregiver support.

2. Give the gift of useful information. Learning about Alzheimer's disease, strokes, etc., and what can be expected is enormously helpful. Information about home care agencies, medical equipment suppliers, adult day care services, insurance, and government programs can help. AARP's Tax-Aide program (a free service) assists senior citizens with their IRS returns; however, the scope of help is limited to typical elder concerns, issues of retirees, and lower-income people. Complex returns will require paid professionals.

3. Give the gift of filling in: give the caregiver time off to shop, run errands, or do other forms of self-care. Breaks re-energize and provide perspective.

4. Install equipment in the home that helps with the care, such as special lights for an elder with macular degeneration (a vision problem), and provide communication upgrades, such as smartphones with large visible keys. This is the kind of thing that service providers and grown-up grandchildren can help with. When all generations are involved, benefits accrue.

degree of independence they can maintain. Many more myths about aging will be exposed as scientists learn more about the aging process. Even what constitutes old age is being questioned as researchers learn more about the elderly. Commonly, old age is defined as beginning at age 75 or 80 (some say 65), but this is an arbitrary boundary because chronological age is a poor indicator of a person's social, economic, physical, or mental condition.

## Adjusting to Retirement

The subject of planning for and adjusting to retirement fills whole books and endless advice columns. **Retirement** is the withdrawal from full-time employment or one's position or occupation or main source of income—in short, withdrawing from one's active working life. A person can semi-retire (reduced hours) or retire for a while and go back to work. Retirement is rarely experienced as a full-time forever withdrawal from working whether paid or unpaid. The average age of retirement in the United States is 62 or 63 and in other countries, the range is from 50 to 70. It may be more helpful to divide it into early, intermediate, and late retirement to never retired. Famous actors and politicians say they will never retire. The typical range has to do with personal preference and eligibility ages for public or government old-age benefits and with pension funds or level of personal savings for retirement. The move in the age of the first retirement is upward rather than the other way—people in good health with good jobs are working longer. Less than one-quarter of workers (23 percent) aged 55 and older have savings and investments worth $250,000 or more. By far the largest portion has saved less than $10,000. Even retirees who have been prudent savers and spenders may have a difficult time, so finances are at the forefront and central to their concerns; but there are others as well, such as health—both physical and emotional—and maintaining independence.

> *"We weren't extravagant people. We didn't go on cruises. We didn't buy a Cadillac. And here we are, we thought we could retire, but our savings are just going too fast for us," says Noreen Hilinski, a 67-year-old retiree in Madison, Conn "There's a lot of people who are going to go back to work in my age bracket," Ms. Hilinski says. "More and more of my friends are talking about going back to work."*
>
> (Greene, 2008, p. A4)

One of the most important life changes people make is adjusting to retirement. Regardless of how much workers plan and anticipate this change in role, it can still be difficult because jobs give people a routine, companionship, and a sense of accomplishment. Retired people can feel aimless and useless or directionless especially after the exhilaration and freedom experienced the first year out. It may feel empty. They may find that endless rounds of golf or volunteer work at the hospital gift shop are not fulfilling. Without roles, people feel a sense of loss and a lack of direction, and the loss of work routine can be disconcerting. Declining health exacerbates the problem. To counteract this feeling of loss and provide extra income, many "retirees" take on part-time or seasonal work. If they are self-employed or have a skill like bookkeeping, they may never retire. Someone may say I retired from my main career but now I work for this company or organization.

In many companies, human resource departments assist older employees in the transition period to retirement and help middle-aged workers find home health care for their aged parents. According to an article in *American Demographics*,

> *Home health care is an important concern of middle-aged workers. Most providers help elderly relatives preserve their independence. Helpers are usually women, but men are likely to shop and pay the bills. Out-ofpocket spending accounts for one-third of this $21 billion industry, and caregivers also face a time crunch. As the population ages, employers will offer eldercare benefits to attract and keep good workers.*
>
> (Braus, 1994, p. 38)

In addition, some companies offer retirement planning programs; others allow employees to work part-time to ease into retirement. Many retirees choose to do volunteer work or take on a second career. Others travel or go back to school to finish degrees or take classes or go on field trips. As with all age groups, older adults have varying lifestyles and, therefore, differing management needs. Too much time may be as much a problem as too little time. Other resources that may be affected in the later years include the emotional, health, and financial resources and human energy of both the elders and their caregivers.

As mentioned earlier, making money stretch is a problem for many older persons because income may not keep pace with inflation and increases in health care costs. The elderly most likely to be poor are those who rely solely on Social Security for their sustenance.

Those contemplating early retirement should

- Check on their insurance, pension, and other employer-sponsored retirement plans.
- Contact Social Security.

- Calculate the effects of inflation. If you figure on 3 percent a year, $50,000 today to live on will be worth only $27,189 in 20 years, and it is unlikely that expenses will be cut in half in that time.

- Analyze the condition of your house and car; does anything need fixing or replacing?

- Pay off debt, especially the most expensive such as credit cards, student loans, and car loans.

- Have an emergency fund; emergencies do not stop at retirement.

- Consider lifestyle and interests (as mentioned earlier). Most opt for part-time work in a whole new field to maintain contacts and collect extra income.

Increasingly, aging is considered within the context of total well-being, which requires a careful balance between emotional, spiritual, and physical health. This balance becomes more precarious as we age. Besides reexamining the changing perceptions of aging, people need to enhance their mental and physical vitality by focusing on active strategies that can extend life and improve the quality of life. These management strategies may include

- Deciding what is essential and what is controllable

- Identifying strategies to help prevent health problems or poor quality of life

- Adopting a proactive approach about diet, attitude, and activity levels

- Using practical techniques to incorporate improved lifestyle changes in everyday life.

In addition to valuing independence, older adults value comfort, security, convenience, and a sense of purpose. They want to eliminate problems, receive personal service, and feel good about themselves. Airline and car advertisers appealing to the elder market may emphasize comfort over speed and appearance. As more of our population falls into the elderly category, businesses and service providers will have to adjust their approaches to better meet the needs of older adults.

Exercise energizes and provides perspective.

# The Homeless

*About* 600,000 (number varies by sources and by year) Americans *are experiencing homelessness each year.* They are not easy to count because of their mobility and also because their homelessness may be temporary rather than chronic. The U.S. Department of Housing and Urban Development has data collection instruments and conducts intensive street counts integrating data from shelters, other service providers, and other sources to generate a census of homeless persons and their needs. For example, 65 percent stay in an overnight shelter. The city with the most homeless people is New York City.

Half of all homeless people are in the following states:

1. California (the highest rate of unsheltered people)

2. New York

3. Florida

4. Texas

5. Washington

*A home is the single most expensive purchase for most families*—more than food, more than cars, more than clothes, more than childcare—so when people are homeless, it is a sign of their not being able to support themselves in the most *visible* way through renting or buying a house or finding someone to live with. Although media coverage might imply that homelessness is a new societal problem, it is not. There have been homeless people in the United

States since colonial times and it has been a national issue since the 1870s. What is new is that they are more numerous than ever before and more visible, and counts have become more accurate. Veterans make up one in four homeless people in the United States, although they represent only 11 percent of the general adult population according to the Veterans Affairs Department (November 7, 2007, huffingtonpost.com, pulled March 15, 2008). They can be young veterans from Iraq or Afghanistan service looking for help finding a job or seeking treatment or food.

*The majority of the homeless are single males, although the number of homeless women and children is growing.* For the latest numbers and percentages go to census.gov. Here is an overview:

> *Officials estimate that, on average, single men comprise 51 percent of the homeless population, families with children 30 percent, single women, 17 percent, and unaccompanied youth 2 percent. The homeless population is estimated to be 42 percent African-American, 39 percent white, 13 percent Hispanic, 4 percent Native American and 2 percent Asian-American. An average of 16 percent of homeless people is considered mentally ill; 26 percent are substance abusers. Thirteen percent are employed. Requests for assisted housing by low-income families and individuals increased in 86 percent of the cities during the last year.*
>
> *(NCH Fact Sheet #2, August 2007)*

Often what homeless males and families do is get on a bus and travel to where they think work is or to a city. When they arrive, work is not so readily available and their money runs out or if they have a car, it breaks down and they run out of gas money and sleep in the car.

Chronic homelessness is linked to poverty. However, it is important to distinguish between the homeless and the poor. According to Baum and Burnes (1993),

> Homelessness is more than being poor and without a home; homelessness is a condition of disengagement from ordinary society—from family, friends, neighborhood, church, community. Perhaps most importantly, it is a loss of self. A homeless man we know told us, "The first time, I felt like this is not me. I felt less than a man." Homelessness means being disconnected from all of the support systems that usually provide help in times of crisis; it means being without structure; it means being alone. (p. 23)

Homelessness is a worldwide problem. In 1999, thousands of people were displaced from their homes in Kosovo. In 2008, many people were displaced in Georgia, a country bordered on the north by Russia. In 2011, many families were displaced in Libya, a country in North Africa. These are only three examples of large numbers of people being displaced by internal and border conflicts. They are mentioned here to illustrate that homelessness can affect individuals or families on a wide scale.

The growing rate of poverty, the declining supply of low-income housing, and a rise in drug addiction and alcoholism have all contributed to homelessness (Rubin et al., 1992). An estimated 65–85 percent of all homeless adults in the United States suffer from one or more of the disabling conditions of alcoholism, drug addiction, and mental illness, complicated by serious medical problems (Baum & Burnes, 1993). Other factors affecting the rise in the number of homeless in the United States include cutbacks in public housing, and mental health and social programs. Families become homeless for numerous reasons, including fire, eviction because of failure to pay rent, eviction because of unfit housing, cuts in assistance programs, scarcity of low-income housing, unemployment, and internal strife in countries.

Homelessness can be devastating for children who are suffering a loss of education and security. Naturally, the length of time spent in a homeless condition will affect the severity of these effects. A study reported in the *American Journal of Psychiatry* found that a high level of mental distress is common in all homeless persons and suggests that the focus of treatment should be on empowerment, consumerism, entitlement, community-level interventions, and closer alliances with other advocates for the homeless (Cohen & Thompson, 1992). According to another study, the major cause of family homelessness is the relative inability of heads of homeless families to function independently (Ellickson, 1990).

Community and national efforts are being made to help homeless families. For example, in the United States, the Stewart B. McKinney Homeless Assistance Act guarantees homeless children the right of access to education (Eddowes & Hranitz, 1989). Besides the government enacting legislation, communities, hospitals, and substance abuse treatment centers are working together to find successful ways to help the homeless. As not all homeless persons have the same problems, an effort is being made to tailor programs and alternatives to the needs of the individual and the family.

## Individuals with Disabilities

According to the 2020 U.S. Census, 26.6 percent of the population (one in four adults) has some type of disability. The percentage is lower for those with severe mental or physical disabilities. A large range of issues are associated with care for the disabled and some of the issues are like what was covered earlier about caring for older adults and the elderly. It depends on the disability what is needed, perhaps it is education and job training and independent living facilities. Many countries have legislation to protect and promote the rights of people with a disability

Definitions of disability and handicap differ by governments in various countries, by agencies, by administrations such as the U.S. Social Security Administration, and by legislation such as the United Kingdom's Disability Discrimination Act. Most legislations say that businesses and employers must make reasonable accommodations to avoid direct or indirect discrimination. A classic definition is that a **disability** is a long-term or chronic condition medically defined as a physiological, anatomical, mental, or emotional impairment resulting from disease or illness, inherited or congenital defect, trauma, or other insults (including environmental) to mind or body (Wright, 1980). Often the word "disability" is used as a synonym for "handicap," but the terms are different. A **handicap** is a disadvantage, interference, or barrier to performance, opportunity, or fulfillment in any desired role in life (e.g., social, educational, vocational, familial) imposed upon the individual by limitation in function or by other problems associated with disability and/or personal characteristics in the context of the individual's environment or role (Wright, 1980). Thus, a handicap can occur resulting from a disability, but a disability does not always necessitate a handicap. For example, a deaf person has a hearing disability, but she or he is not handicapped when it comes to sewing because deafness does not affect one's ability to sew.

It is important to understand that disabled individuals may have certain limitations, but they can function wholly and well in many ways. The shift is toward independent living, job training, and accessibility. Individuals with disabilities prefer to be recognized as a person first and only subsequently as a person with a partially disabling condition. Community prejudice and resistance may reduce the opportunities for disabled persons. People with disabilities have been fighting for years to overcome prejudice so that they can have equal access to jobs, schools, and services.

An important aspect of home management is the ability to perform routine tasks. Persons with disabilities may face problems associated with the home, including the loss of mobility, decreased strength, decreased reach, coordination impairment, one-handed use, lack of hand muscles, and visual impairment (Pickett et al., 1990). The hindrance or negative effect in the performance of household tasks or activities is referred to as a **functional limitation**. Wright (1980) offers five examples of functional limitations that may affect task performance:

1. Activity restrictions due to the danger of unexpected unconsciousness

2. Inability to follow rapid or frequent changes in instruction due to slow learning

3. Restrictions in mobility due to neuromuscular impairment

4. Difficulty in interpersonal relationships associated with peculiar behavior

5. Necessity of avoiding respiratory infection or dusty conditions due to hypersensitivity reactions.

As this list suggests, there is a wide range of disabilities. A disability in a family raises several critical questions: Is the disability temporary, such as a broken arm, or long-term? Are family resources adequate to handle the disability? For example, is there enough insurance to cover medical and rehabilitation costs? After an assessment has been made of the severity of the disability and the level of support and resources, a management plan needs to be formulated. A long-term financial plan may include leaving enough assets through a trust fund for disabled heirs. There are lawyers who specialize in working with families with children with disabilities.

**CASE STUDY**

### Special Needs

"Paul Harvey, the father of an adult son with a developmental disability in Orange County, Calif., is brainstorming solutions with a group of other parents. One possibility: a 'qualified personal residence trust,' or QPRT, which lets homeowners stay in a house for years before transferring ownership to an heir at a discount to the current market value. That way, the families can give their homes to a charity or to another family member to manage for the child's lifetime use, Mr. Harvey says. Another option: a 'special needs' trust—a vehicle in which parents can put assets for the child's benefit without endangering government benefits."

*Source: Greene, K. (2011, September 3–4). Taking care of disabled heirs. The Wall Street Journal, p. B8.*

In the case of permanent handicapping conditions, critical changes in the family support system and the home environment may need to be made. Ramps, lower sinks, Braille markings on appliances, easier access to bathrooms and kitchens, and levers instead of doorknobs are examples of possible changes. Specific alterations depend on the needs and desires of the disabled individual.

The nature and timing of the handicapping condition are also important. Was the disabling condition a shock, or did the individual and family have time to make gradual accommodations to the condition? Are adequate social, health, and public services available in the community?

As more baby boomers age and become more at risk for heart disease and other impairments, the ranks of the disabled will grow. In addition, medical advances have kept many more people with disabilities alive longer than in the past. Fortunately, the public today is much more aware of disabilities, including those that are not physically apparent, such as learning problems, and is prepared to adjust to and accommodate the needs of disabled individuals. Every person, disabled or not, needs a safe, functioning environment in which to live and work.

## Single-Parent, Remarriage, and Stepfamilies or Blended Families

As has been noted throughout this text, the composition of the typical American family and household is changing. Nearly half of all brides and grooms walking down the aisle have been married before. These unions start with high hopes; but because about 65 percent of the time children from previous marriages are involved, the new marriages often come with unique management challenges. The divorce rate peaked in the 1980s and now is at its lowest level since the 1970s. Second and third marriages and single-parent and same-sex with children couples have become more usual.

**CASE STUDY**

### Second Marriages

*Every morning, Jacquelyn Beauregard Dillman, stands on her front steps and waves to her husband of 29 years, Bob, as he drives off to work. Every afternoon, the couple has what they call their "lovey-chat," just to check in. Neither*

> ever leaves the house without a kiss goodbye. Both of them were married before. "I love this man with all my heart and being," Ms. Dillman, 72, a retired oncology research nurse in Newport Beach, Calif., says of her husband, a 64-year-old medical oncologist. Is marriage better the second time around? Over-all, second marriages are shorter, with a median length of 14.5 years versus 20.8 years for first marriages, the Census Bureau says.
>
> Source: Bernstein, E. (2011, September 20). Secrets of a second marriage: Beat the 9-year itch. The Wall Street Journal, p. D1.

Single-parent families as well as stepfamilies and remarriages have unique management needs. Raising children is a difficult task in itself but raising children all by oneself can be even more challenging. The single parent finds no relief and has no one to share ideas with or turn to for help with discipline. Insufficient income is another problem most single mothers must face, in part because many fathers fail to make child support payments (Kissman & Allen, 1993). Economic resources and economic well-being usually are higher for married two-biological parent families than for single-parent or stepparent families (Sweeney, 2010). Only about one-third of single mothers receive child support (Goodrich et al., 1989). There are state-by-state provisions for child support and different enforcement divisions or departments. Family income in general drops sharply at the end of a marriage because of the splitting up of resources, maintenance of two households, legal fees, and so forth.

**Stepfamilies or Blended families** are new families that include children from previous relationships. Diversity and complexity of stepfamily structures, consequences of multiple partnerships, and the location turnover for children all have impacts.

> Contemporary marriages are less likely to end with death of a spouse than was true half a century ago and are now considerably more likely to end through a decision to divorce. Marriage itself has become increasingly optional as a context for intimate partnerships and parenthood
>
> (Sweeney, 2010, p. 667)

Educated and wealthy parents are less likely to divorce than low-income parents. A new twist in the location of children following a divorce is for them to stay in the house they were brought up in and the parents move to other housing and switch back and forth living in the original house so that their children are not uprooted.

## CASE STUDY

### Latchkey Parents

When John Marden and Ana Elizabeth decided to split in 2005 after 13 years of marriage, they both moved out of the house they shared in the woods near Santa Cruz, Calif. Their three children, however, stayed put. When it was Elizabeth's turn to look after the kids, she stayed with them. When it was their father's turn, she left and he took over. This arrangement, sometimes known as nesting, has emerged over the past decade as an offshoot of the equalcustody,

> *or co-parenting, trend. It requires what would seem to many splitting couples to be a mind-bogglingly amicable relationship and, usually, a robust pot of marital funds, since the number of homes expands from one to three: his, hers, and the children's.*
>
> When asked about it, Elizabeth, 53, said "I didn't think my kids could deal with the stress of two different houses."
>
> *Source: Luscombe, B. (2011, September 26). Latchkey parents. Time, p. 50.*

*Newsweek* magazine recognized the phenomenon of blended families when it devoted a special issue to the family of the 21st century. An article in the issue on stepfamilies began as follows:

> *The original plot goes like this: first comes love. Then comes marriage. Then comes Mary with a baby carriage. But now there's a sequel: John and Mary break up. John moves in with Sally and her two boys. Mary takes the baby Paul. A year later Mary meets Jack, who is divorced with three children. They get married. Paul, barely 2 years old, now has a mother, a father, a stepmother, a stepfather and five stepbrothers and stepsisters—as well as four sets of grandparents (biological and step) and countless aunts and uncles. And guess what? Mary's pregnant again. This may sound like an unusually complicated family tree. It's not. Some demographers predict that as many as a third of all children born in the 1980s may live with a stepparent before they are 18.*
>
> *(Kantrowitz & Wingert, 1990, p. 24)*

In blended families, stepparents are more likely than biological parents to perceive strains on the marriage from the parenting experience. Studies show that marital satisfaction is significantly lower when both spouses bring children into the marriage. About 60 percent of second unions end in divorce, compared with 50 percent for first marriages. In a study by Valarie King (2007) about adolescents who live with a biological father and have both a resident stepmother and nonresident biological mother she found that:

> *Adolescents vary in their likelihood of having close relationships to resident fathers, resident stepmothers, and non-resident biological mothers, but when they can do so, they appear to benefit. Close relationships with resident fathers and nonresident mothers are associated with fewer adolescent internalizing and externalizing problems. Closeness to resident stepmothers, however, is unrelated to these two outcomes. Results suggest that* fathers play a particularly important role in these families.
>
> *(p. 1178)*

> *The new stepfamily is also complicated by in-laws with long relationships with and concomitant loyalties to the previous spouse, which make it difficult to welcome a new adult in their children's and grandchildren's lives. Furthermore, children in stepfamilies experience biological parents and stepparents very differently. For children, the stepparent may be not another nurturing adult but an intruder who threatens to disrupt their close single-parent-child relationship, thereby influencing yet another loss. Stepparents also place children in a loyalty bind: If I care about mom's new husband, am I betraying my father? Children in first-time families almost always want their original parents to stay together.*
>
> *(Papernow, 1993, pp. 49–50)*

Single-parent and blended families also exhibit special strengths. Blended families succeed if they have a clear understanding of each family member's feelings and needs and if they engage in open communication.

Before remarriage, it is suggested that the adults forming a combined family realize that their commitment to one another will be the base upon which their new family will be built (Kaufman, 1993). During marriage, couples need to nurture their own relationship by supporting each other's interests as well as caring for the children.

In single-parent households, the child may find that having one person make all parenting decisions leads to consistency and stability. If the original marriage involved spousal, substance, or child abuse, being a single parent could be a relief. As circumstances vary widely, each family must be looked at individually to determine its resource management needs. There are many types of single parents, ranging from unwed teenagers to middle-aged men whose wives have left them. Single parenthood can arise from never having married; from being abandoned, widowed, or divorced; or from a single person opting for adoption.

In addition, both single-parent families and blended families must contend with various legal, social, personal, economic, and psychological issues. These family types have to contend with all sorts of small and large indignities because they live in a society built around two-parent first-marriage families. For example, a graduating senior may be allotted only two high school graduation tickets but be from a blended family with two biological parents and two stepparents, and eight grandparents. Who receives the tickets in this case? In a mother-headed household, whom does the son invite to a father–son picnic?

Schools and community organizations are becoming more sensitive to these issues so that fewer children and families are put in awkward positions. Laws and legislation are making it easier for new family forms to function and are providing better protection for family members.

## Poverty and Low-Income Families

World Bank data show that the percentage of people living in households below the poverty line has decreased in each region of the world since 1999, Still, a substantial number live in poverty and it is found even in affluent developed countries. About fi million Americans live in poverty. Approximately 15 percent of Americans live in poverty compared to 11.3 percent in 2000. **Poverty** is the state of deprivation and the inability to provide for basic needs on a consistent basis. **Relative poverty** means having significantly less income and wealth than other members of society.

Poverty is not one of those problems that can be solved overnight.

> Some family problems may not have a complete solution. For example, a family in poverty may have many problems associated with not having enough resources to meet basic family needs. Or a parent may acquire a serious disability that prevents them from fulfilling their roles as spouse and parent. In such circumstances family members may have to accept that some of their goals can not be attained Problem solving can still be used to find ways of making the best of the situation Once a solution is chosen, a detailed implementation plan is needed to specify exactly who will do what and when they will do it. Following through with a solution may be difficult.
>
> (http:family.jrank.org/pages/1337, 2008, March 15)

Overall, the United States has not only a high average income relative to the rest of the world but also a high percentage of what the United Nations Development Program calls human poverty, including many factors, including illiteracy and affordable health care, among industrialized countries (Vo, 1998). Policies are changing and the Affordable Care Act in the United States makes health insurance more affordable for low-income individuals and families.

For families, low income and poverty are defined as a family income less than half the national median. In the United States, often the poverty-stricken family has a mother with children. Government services, early nutrition, health services, reliable transportation, childcare, employment training, and educational programs are positive first steps toward moving a family out of poverty. The families in the worst financial trouble do not always fit the usual stereotypes:

> *They are not the very young, tempted by the freedom of their first credit cards. They are not the elderly, trapped by failing bodies and declining savings accounts. And they are not a random assortment of Americans who lack the self-control to keep their spending in check. Rather, the people who consistently rank in the worst financial trouble are united by one surprising characteristic. They are parents with children at home. Having a child is now the single best predictor that a woman will end up in financial collapse.*
>
> (Warren & Tyagi, 2003, p. 6)

Poverty, like homelessness, is not necessarily a permanent state. There are gradations in income, and income may be low temporarily resulting from sudden unemployment. Low-income families may also experience seasonal variations in income. A family in financial distress may have come into that state because the main breadwinner became injured or ill, was laid off, or a family-owned business failed.

In the United States, from 2008 to 2011 a weak economy was evidenced in such measures as high foreclosure and unemployment rates. This weakening followed on the heels of a strong housing market up to the year 2006 when home prices rose and this happened again in 2021-present, and some people were making money buying and selling or renting houses for a profit. Prior to this, there was a strong national economy in the 1990s which meant that more of the poor were moving out of poverty; they were working and consuming at a higher rate. It should be kept in mind that "low income" is a relative term and that the lifestyles of many of the poor in the United States would be considered middle-class or even high-income in other countries.

The federal government helps low-income families through a variety of programs. **Transfer payments** are monies or services given for which the recipient does not directly pay. To receive these benefits, household income or assets must fall below a specified level. The welfare-to-work laws in the United States have changed many of the traditional ways of supporting the poor. More people are encouraged to work and be less dependent on the government

The terms "poverty" and "low income" are defined not only by the government but also by the families themselves based on previous income levels and lifestyles. The strains that result from the lack of money or assets can have negative effects on family life regardless of the source, which might be unemployment or generally poor economic conditions. Because of the gender gap in earnings, women have a difficult time with the negative impacts of economic hardship on the quality of family life and they are more likely to be taking care of children or grandchildren.

Planning for long-term goals can seem like a luxury. Returning to Maslow's hierarchy of needs in Chapter 1, the emphasis in helping low-income families should be placed on providing for the most basic needs first, such as food, water, and shelter. Low-income families often spend over half of their income on housing. Therefore, securing safe, affordable housing is a particular concern for low-income families and explains why a nonprofit housing organization, such as Habitat for Humanity, is so much needed.

Because of the lack of adequate, affordable housing and other daily-living problems, over time many low-income families become pessimistic about the future. They may feel their lives are out of control, and they give up. They may adopt a perspective called **fatalism,** an attitude that all events are thought to be shaped by fate. A belief in fatalism can lead to low expectations and a sense of hopelessness. Recognizing the possible existence and influence of this phenomenon is helpful in designing appropriate and effective aid for low-income families.

## Suggested Activity

Discuss in groups the types of service activities students have engaged in, such as helping build a house with Habitat for Humanity. What were the activities? What were the feelings or other outcomes associated with being involved in service activities?

## SUMMARY

This chapter examined issues about caring for human needs (including meeting your own needs—self-care) and reported changes and trends and changes such as the increasing median age and the trend toward more solitary living. Societal growth, changes in family structure, mobility, remarriage and stepfamilies, and caregiving were discussed. Through understanding the nature of change, families (and those who help families) may be able to react to it more effectively. As one example, a way of managing post-divorce life may involve the children staying in the home and their parents establishing an elaborate set of rules about what or who is allowed in the shared home, trading off living there to care for the children.

Definitions of poverty and relative poverty (meaning comparing to others) were given. Low income and poverty are experienced in all regions of the world even in the most affluent countries.

China is the world's most populous country followed by India and the United States. The world population is becoming more urban putting strains on resources. The U.S. population is becoming older and more diverse. If the population stays on the predicted course, there will be a larger percentage of minorities, single-parent families, stepfamilies, and the elderly in the future. In summary, the population of the United States and of the world is growing, and consequently, there are more human resource problems to address.

Striving for a certain quality of life is not just a theoretical construct, but a very real day-to-day concern for people. Effectively managing human resources and increasing human capital are a fundamental part of the overall study of resource management. The next chapter explores problems associated with managing time—something we all share.

## KEY TERMS

| | | |
|---|---|---|
| adaptability | external change | mobility |
| boomeranging | family demography | mortality |
| change | fatalism | poverty |
| childcare | fertility rate | relative poverty |
| demographics | functional limitation | retirement |
| demography | gerontology | self-care |
| disability | handicap | step families (or blended |
| dual career | immigration | families) |
| dual-income or dual-earner | internal change | transfer payments |
| households | median age | |

## REVIEW QUESTIONS

1. In *Redefining Diversity*, Roosevelt Thomas says that for a nation diversity is a strength and it means more than race or gender; it is about diversity in ideas, outlooks, and procedures. Do you agree or disagree? Can you give an example of how diversity can be a strength?

2. How has the world population changed since 1900? Where do most people live today, in cities, small towns, or villages? In the United States, what are the *five* largest population states?

3. According to the chapter, managing change is inherently messy. Why is that?

4. What do you think are the benefits and deficits of the 180-day school year for children? Where do you stand on this issue?

5. Choose one of the groups discussed in the section "Meeting Individual, Family, and Societal Needs" and discuss their resource management needs (explain what they have or do not have and what they need).

## REFERENCES

Ariely, D. (February 18, 2021). Give yourself better pep talks. *The Wall Street Journal*, Life and Arts Section, 1.

Baum, A., & Burnes, D. (1993, Spring). Facing the facts about homelessness. *Public Welfare, 51*, 20–27, 46, 48.

Braus, P. (1994, March). When mom needs help. *American Demographics, 16*, 38–46.

Cohen, C., & Thompson, K. (1992). Homeless mentally ill or mentally ill homeless? *American Journal of Psychiatry, 149*(6), 816–823.

Crispell, D. (1997, November). Depending on college. *American Demographics*, p. 39.

DeGraff, A., & Dillon, D. (2019). A systemic approach to understanding diversity in financial counseling. In D. B. Durband et al. (Eds.), *Financial Counseling*. Switzerland: Springer.

Eddowes, E., & Hranitz, J. (1989, October). Educating children of the homeless. *Education Digest*, 15–17.

Ellickson, R. (1990, Spring). The homeless muscle. *Public Interest*, pp. 45–60.

Gilbert, L. (1993). *Two-career/one family*. Newbury Park, CA: Sage.

Glick, P. (1988). Fifty years of family demography: A record of social change. *Journal of Marriage and Family, 50*, 861–873.

Goodrich, T., Rampage, C., & Ellman, B. (1989). The single mother. *Family Therapy Networker, 13*, 55–56.

Greene, K. (2003, November 10). Our picks for the top places to find financial advice, nutrition guides, around-the-world cruises and more. *The Wall Street Journal*, p. R1.

Greene, K. (2008, September 22). Baby boomers delay retirement. *The Wall Street Journal*, p. A4.

Hildago, D., & Bankson, C. (2011). Blurring racial and ethnic boundaries in Asian American families: Asian American Family Patterns, 1980–2005. *Journal of Family Issues, 31*(3), 280–300.

Hira, T. (1987). Satisfaction with money management: Practices among dual-earner households. *Journal of Home Economics, 79*(2), 19–22.

Johnson, R., & Wiener, J. (2006). A profile of frail older Americans and their caregivers. Urban Institute, March 1. Retrieved May 18, 2007, from http://www.urban.org/publications.

Kantrowitz, B., & Wingert, P. (1990, Winter/Spring). Step by step: Who will be? *Newsweek* (Special Issue), 24–34.

Kaufman, T. S. (1993). *The combined family*. New York: Plenum Press.

Kissman, K., & Allen, J. (1993). *Single-parent families*. Newbury Park, CA: Sage.

Kitzmann, K., Dalton, W., & Buscemi, J. (2008). Beyond parenting practices: Family context and the treatment of pediatric obesity. *Family Relations, 57,* 13–23.

Klinenberg, E. (March 12, 2019). Living aline is the new norm. *Time,* pp. 60–61.

Lamanna, M., & Riedmann, A. (2009). *Marriages & families, 10th edition.* Belmont, CA: Thomson.

Myers, S. (2010). Connecting the demographic dots: Geographic mobility and birth intentions. *Journal of Family Issues, 31*(12), 1622–1651.

Nadler, D. (1998). *Champions of change.* San Francisco: Jossey-Bass.

NCH Fact Sheet #2. (August 2007). *How many people experience homelessness?* Published by the National Coalition for the Homeless.

Papernow, P. L. (1993). *Becoming a stepfamily.* San Francisco: Jossey-Bass.

Pickett, M., Arnold, M., & Ketterer, L. (1990). *Household equipment in residential design, 9th edition.* Prospect Heights, IL: Waveland Press.

"Pregnancy Over Age 30," A report by *Stanford Children's Health* (2019).

Radina, M. E. (2003). Cultural values and caregiving. In M. Coleman & L. Ganong (Eds.), *Points & Counterpoints: Controversial Relationship and Family Issues in the 21st Century* (pp. 265–271). Los Angeles, CA: Roxbury.

Rettig, K. (1993). Problem-solving and decision-making as central processes of family life: An ecological frame- work for family relations and family resource management. *Marriage and Family Review, 18*(3/4), 187–222.

Riche, M. (1990, May). Boomerang age. *American Demographics,* pp. 25–30, 52–53.

Roberto, K., & Jarrott, S. (2008, January). Family caregivers of older adults: A life span perspective. *Family Relations, 57,* 100–111.

Rubin, R., & Riney, B. (1994). *Working wives and dualearner families.* Westport, CT: Praeger.

Rubin, B., Wright, J., & Devine, J. (1992). Unhousing the urban poor: The Reagan legacy. Special issue: The Reagan legacy and the American welfare state. *Journal of Sociology and Social Welfare, 19*(1), 111–147.

Ruffenach, G. (2003, November 10). The ties that bind. *The Wall Street Journal,* p. D4.

Runyon, K., & Stewart, D. (1987). *Consumer behavior, 3rd edition.* Columbus, OH: Merrill.

Senge, P. (1999). *The dance of change.* New York: Doubleday.

Sweeney, M. (2010). Remarriage and stepfamilies: Strategic sites for family scholarship in the 21st century. *Journal of Marriage and Family, 72*(3), 667–684.

Toffler, A. (1970). *Future shock.* New York: Random House.

Vo, M. (1998, November 6). A look at the world by the numbers. *Christian Science Monitor,* pp. 8–9.

Warren, E., & Tyagi, A. (2003). *The two-income trap.* New York: Basic Books.

Wright, G. (1980). *Total rehabilitation.* Boston, MA: Little, Brown.

Chapter **9**

# Managing Time

**DID YOU KNOW THAT ...?**

- Tuesday is the most productive day of the week.
- 80 percent of workers spend more than 30 percent of their time writing.

> *Our preoccupation with time induces anxiety, even dread, yet we can't shake it. What gives?*
>
> *(Garfield, 2018)*

DOI: 10.4324/9781003166740-9

**Time management**, defined as the values and systems that guide the conscious decisions made about activities and time use, is the subject of this chapter. Time is managed to fulfill needs, purpose, and goals. For example, a student spending three hours at a university-sponsored job fair hopes to line up internship and job interviews and, more generally, to investigate a variety of employment possibilities. He or she might have gone in with the idea of working for one employer but may be drawn more heavily to another. Exploring options takes time but in this case well worth the investment. The case study of the MacKenzies describes a couple's routine on first coming home from work.

**CASE STUDY**

### The MacKenzies

*Rod MacKenzie was excited to be home from work before his wife. He fed the dog, popped open a Diet Pepsi and settled onto the couch to watch his favorite TV show. Then the phone rang. It was his wife, calling from the car on her commute home. She started telling him how her boss had changed the focus of the project she'd stayed up late to finish. Mr. MacKenzie, 36, kept watching TV, every few minutes murmuring, "uh huh"—and failing to hear her when she asked if he was listening. When he failed to answer, she hung up. Michelle MacKenzie wasn't too happy by the time she walked in the door. Spotting his empty soda can in the kitchen, she asked him, "What have you been doing since you got home?" "You're looking at it." "Have you thought about dinner?" "Why is dinner always my responsibility?"*

*Source: Bernstein, E. (2011, October 4). Putting the Honey Back in Honey, I'm Home. The Wall Street Journal, p. D4.*

Time of day matters and right after-work can be especially stressful for couples as they transition and get ready for the evening. What are the solutions to the MacKenzies' after-work communication problem? One way is to give each other some space to decompress. Another way is to talk about the day but not dump, not go into every detail. More solutions will be discussed throughout the chapter. A first step is often awareness that the transition from a stressful workday to home may often cause friction. This discussion also plays into circadian rhythms, our usual biological patterns, covered in this chapter. A Cornell University study found that on the social media site Twitter the most positive responses were in the morning and became more negative in mid- to late-afternoon, gradually becoming positive again in the evening (Bernstein, 2011). A childcare center worker described four to five o'clock as the crying hour. She said children can be happy and playing all day and suddenly fall apart right when their parents come to get them and she has to explain "the crying hour" phenomenon.

Our employment-centered, high-tech world is putting pressure on people to be more involved and active but what is emerging in most developed nations is increasingly sedentary societies. According to the BBC News, in a survey of the activities of children in 10 nations, British children spent on average 9.4 hours a week playing computer games or watching TV and less than one hour a day being active. Australian children also spent considerable amounts of time playing computer games and watching TV but were more active.

As a general comment, it is acknowledged that the COVID-19 pandemic changed the way we use our time and our homes—maybe forever (Koncius, 2021). This chapter and the next will focus mainly on principles of time use and provide insight into human adaptive behavior. In the home or neighborhood, some of the shifts have been an increase in gardening, outdoor sports, and increased interest in organizational devices and storage. Other areas affected are appliances, furniture (desks, for example), and cleaning methods.

A persistent trend is that American teens eager to be involved, often over-schedule with too many clubs, too many activities. We will have case studies in this chapter on the over-commitment of two high school students which you may relate to or pause to remember. Consider how different college years are timewise compared to high school.

Government agencies, organizations, and companies track how people spend their time because it affects economies, policies, products, services, and sales. The U.S. Bureau of Labor Statistics (BLS) American Time Use Survey (ATUS) measures the amount of time people (ages 18 and up) spend doing various activities, such as paid work, childcare, volunteering, and socializing:

- Household activities: 2.5 hours (women), 1.9 hours (men), more hours spent on weekends than weekdays

- Eating and drinking 1.18 hours

- Leisure and sports 5.24 hours

- Sleeping 8.8 hours

- Caring for and helping household children, parents 1.43 hours

- Working on days worked, employed persons 7.69 hours

Do you see yourself or anyone you know in these time spending categories? The BLS also reports that socializing clocks in at 0.78 hours and that 16 percent of the U.S. population, or 41.3 million people, provide unpaid eldercare.

Sleeping takes up eight hours plus on average across all age groups according to the BLS (see Figure 9.1). The age group 20–24 years sleeps slightly more than this with 8.7 hours for men and 9.1 for women. And, then it goes down for ages 25–34 to 8.4 hours for men and 8.8 hours for women, and then further down for age groups 35–44 and 45– 54, the heavy-working, asset-building, and child-rearing ages. After age 55 the sleeping time may go down for women to less than eight hours.

On average, adults age 75 and overspent 7.7 hours engaged in leisure activities per day—more than any age group. Leisure activities include watching TV, socializing, or exercising.

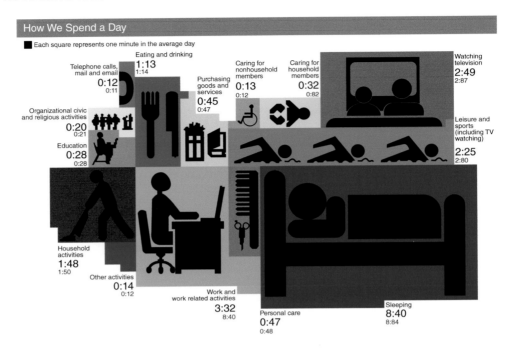

Figure 9.1  How we spend a day.

Source: Bureau of Labor Statistics.

National or international averages are one thing, but more importantly, how do *you* feel about time?

- Do you hate waiting in lines?

- Do you multitask every chance you get?

- Is the Internet connection just too darn slow?

- Do you want everything to happen *now*?

It used to be that when active single adults entered their house after work or a vacation, if there were no messages on their answering machine they would feel left out. People, today, may feel lonely if there are no email or text messages coming in regularly or, on the other hand, they may feel relieved not to have to answer hundreds of messages.

## CRITICAL THINKING

### Time Management

Do you feel overwhelmed with work including schoolwork? Are there too many papers, reports, tests, and classes/meetings? Alexandra, a 22-year-old graduate student, said she was totally overwhelmed and one more thing due would put her over the top. She felt stretched to the limit. Do you ever feel that way and if so, what do you do about it? Do you ever exhaust yourself with nothing to show, no accomplishment toward your goals? How does motivation play in?

**Communication multitasking**, sending, and receiving many messages in a short span of time, is something we accept. Advertisers decide where to advertise—radio, television, Internet, print media, or maybe all four or maybe none of these. The retailer Abercrombie & Fitch prides itself on not advertising, but relying on word of mouth, their established image, and the photos/signage in their stores. An example of communication multitasking is a study that revealed that 100 million U.S. adult Internet users watched TV while they were online—this represents more than two-thirds of the total adult Internet user population (Welcome to the 36-hour day, March 7, 2008). Are television viewing and online surfing time wasters? Do they take you away from concentration and focus? Four-year-old Samantha said she didn't want to go to pre-K because it was too noisy and she couldn't concentrate. Maybe the conflict between distractors and concentration is a life-long challenge.

Not keeping up with messages is a form of procrastination. James, a 31-year-old editor, says that before he left for a two-week vacation to Paris, he spent a whole day cleaning out and answering his email. He tends to procrastinate and needs a crisis or deadline to spur him on to organize it. One of his new solutions is a smartphone that lets him know a deadline is approaching.

## CRITICAL THINKING

### Behaviors

Wanda, a 35-year-old, says this about her email: "I'm quick to open it, read it, and then put it in a folder, but then I never bother to open the folder. So, to put it in the folder means it is essentially gone but I don't want to delete either." Can you relate to Wanda or James, the editor? Do you procrastinate? How do you handle message volume?

Why give so much space in this chapter introduction to email or text message or smartphone management? Organizing clutter is an activity tied to the more general topic of time management. Psychologist Dave Greenfield, the founder of the Center for Internet Behavior, says there are hoarders and deleters, savers and spenders. Essentially,

Because "inboxes are metaphors for our lives," *Dr. Greenfield says, there's no cureall solution to inbox management. We're all too different. But he believes an awareness of our inbox behavior can help us better understand other areas of our lives. "If you have 1,000 emails in your inbox, it may mean you don't want to miss an opportunity, but there are things you can't pull the trigger on," Dr. Greenfield says. "If you have only 10 emails in your inbox, you may be pulling the trigger too fast and missing the richness of life."*

*(Zaslow, 2006, p. D1)*

When cross sections of Americans are asked what is the main problem they are dealing with is, the majority will say they don't have nearly enough time. Futurists and management specialists foresee time poverty as ever-increasing. After all, is life going to become less complicated?

Only 43 percent of families eat together daily and we are talking about one meal or more a day. Parents and children are working and playing harder now than ever before, usually at different times and places. The Internet, 24-hour television, extended stock market hours, and 24-hour toll-free lines have aided in creating this hurry-up, around-the-clock environment. Disc jockeys, airport controllers, police, factory workers, and nurses are used to a 24- hour culture, but now the rest of us are catching up. Want to order something? No problem with the Internet and toll-free lines open 24 hours a day. Time-poor consumers, such as working parents or individuals juggling three jobs, are willing to pay for convenience. Playing into this fast-paced world, an advertisement for CBS MarketWatch.com says it has the "tool to fuel your obsession" by "bringing you the hottest financial stories, market data in real time, and expert analysis you need to stay ahead of the market." The message is that if you wait, you will be left behind. What implications does this high-paced time have for individuals and families, and how are they dealing with it?

### CASE STUDY

## The Importance of Eating Together

*"After my mother passed away and my brother went to study in New Zealand, the first thing that really felt different was the dinner table. My father and I began eating separately. We went out to dinners with our friends, ate sandwiches in front of our computers, delivery pizzas while watching movies. Some days we rarely saw each other at all. Then a few weeks before I was set to leave for university, my father walked downstairs, 'You know, I think we should start eating together even if it's just you and me, He said, 'Your mother would have wanted that.'"* Cody (the writer of this story) concludes that dinner with his dad ended up being one of the happiest times of his day.

*Source: Cody C. Delistraty (2014, July 18). The Importance of Eating Together. HEALTH (theatlantic.com).*

An analysis of time begins with awareness. Waking to the shrill clattering of an alarm clock, checking clocks and watches throughout the day, and going to bed at 11 o'clock are all examples of how our lives are synchronized around time. The hours of the day, weekends, holidays, and seasons provide a rhythm and a framework for people's lives.

One of the recurring themes of this book is how individuals and families make choices. The management of time, a resource that everyone has in equal amount (24 hours a day), affects life choices. Time management at work has been closely examined. When we look at a typical profession's (e.g., management, accounting, engineering) day, about 80 percent of workers spend more than 30 percent of their time writing (Gerson & Gerson, 2012). According to Luciano L'Abate and Tamar Harel,

> To understand how we allocate time and energies from one setting to another we need to invoke the concept of priorities. These priorities stem from definite choices we make about what is important in our lives. How important is a person, an object, or an activity to us?
>
> *(1993, p. 252)*

**Time** is a measured or measurable period. A central management concept is **time displacement**, which is concerned with how time spent in one activity takes away from time spent in another activity (Mutz et al., 1993). For example, choosing to watch television rather than studying will affect the goal of academic achievement. Thus time, as a resource, is related to the fulfillment of wants, needs, and goals. Awareness of time is an important part of human consciousness.

The feeling of losing time or someone wasting your time is undesirable. Activities such as clearing one's credit record after being a victim of identity theft are unpleasant. According to the Federal Trade Commission (FTC), it takes on average 30 hours per person to resolve the problem; and nearly 5 percent of Americans experience identity theft a year. One way to avoid identity theft is to shred all receipts and anything else that contains personal information before discarding them. Another way is to pay cash and guard credit cards closely. In the 2003 Fair Credit Reporting Act revision, more consumer protection was put in place. If consumers suspect their identity has been stolen, they can put a 90-day fraud alert on their credit file by calling one of the three credit reporting bureaus:

- Trans Union 800 680 7289
- Experian 888 397 3742
- Equifax 800 525 6285

The one you call will call the other bureaus. If the problem is not resolved in 90 days, the fraud alert can be extended up to seven years.

Identity theft is an example of a timewaster and the loss of individual control. As mentioned in the introduction, time management is the conscious control of time and activities leading to the fulfillment of needs and goals. The way time is allocated is based on an individual's values, what is important to that person. If a family values a shared dinner hour with a multicourse meal, then family members will set aside time for meal preparation and eating together. If the family values school, work, and community activities more, then those activities will become their time focus, and they will eat meals in shifts. In today's time-pressured societies with so many scheduling and demand conflicts, sit-down family-style dinners are becoming increasingly rare, at least in families with older children. According to Leonard Berry, a retailing expert,

> The Norman Rockwell image of a family seated around a dinner table eating a roast beef lovingly prepared at home no longer accurately reflects America's eating habits. More likely, people are grabbing a quick restaurant meal, buying takeout food, and using the microwave oven. Restaurants now capture more than 40 cents of every dollar spent on food in the United States, up from less than 20 cents in the 1960s. Americans spend about 15 percent of their food dollar on ready-to-eat food prepared for off-premises consumption, according to FIND/SVP of New York City with Americans are spending about $1 billion a year on foods for the microwave.
>
> *(1990, p. 32)*

Note that the Berry quote is given here to provide a sense of the passage of time and to add that now more of the American food dollar is spent on food prepared outside the home. Time is a resource that can be measured in units (e.g., minutes, hours, days) but comprehending it can be difficult because individuals' perceptions and use of time affect the way they think about it.

Time has been the subject of philosophical debate (e.g., "If no one measures time, does it still exist?" and "Has time a beginning or an end?") and the subject of psychological, mathematical, and economic inquiry. In the 5th century C.E., Saint Augustine said, "What then, is time? If no one asks me, I know what it is. If I wish to explain it to him who asks me, I do not know." The best way to measure time remains a subject of debate, with choices ranging from the use of simple time diaries and complex psychographic inventories to consumer focus groups and actual drawings of time (Kaufman & Lane, 1993). Time is thus the most familiar of concepts, yet at the same time the most elusive.

## Time as a Resource

In economic theory, time is considered a resource because it is a scarce commodity. It is saved, spent, and allocated to get something desired. Products and methods that save time are in demand.

As an example, during World War II a way to make juice concentrate was discovered so that the troops could get orange juice in remote locations. Later the frozen juice concentrate was introduced to the American household, and it was estimated that this saved 14,000 hours of drudgery per year (Mintz, 2000). Today, few households buy juice concentrate; more buy it in a carton or plastic container with no mixing, simply pour. Another example of food-related time efficiency is the popularity of prepackaged salad mixes versus buying a head of lettuce.

Not everyone wants to be time-efficient. Back-to-basics enthusiasts enjoy raising chickens, growing their own lettuce, green-cleaning their homes, cutting wood for fireplaces, making scrapbooks, building furniture or canoes, and making food from scratch. A fun question may be: What shall I cultivate or create today?

Some cultures and subcultures challenge the notion of thinking of time in terms of the discrete beats of mechanical linear "clock time." In *The Dance of Change*, Peter Senge states that

> It is important to remember that the mechanical clock was only invented five hundred years ago, in the fourteenth century. Before that, human beings did not think of time in constant, fixed increments that keep adding in a steady linear progression. Today, you can almost hear the machine's wheels grinding relentlessly: sixty minutes to each hour, then another sixty minutes make another hour, then another sixty minutes makes another hour, then another, then another. Nature's time is different.
>
> *(1999, p. 57)*

A resourceful person uses time effectively or imaginatively, especially in difficult situations. President Franklin D. Roosevelt, who dealt with the Depression and World War II, said, "Never before have we had so little time in which to do so much." Notice that unlike money, time is a nonrenewable resource and thus might be considered a more valuable resource. Queen Elizabeth I's last words were, "All my possessions for a moment of time." Money is often traded for time, as when a busy person hires someone to clean the house or take care of the yard or swimming pool.

Companies, organizations, schools, and governments seek to control time when they set opening and closing hours, deadlines, and policies. A prime example of international time management set by governments is *daylight saving time, which exists in some version in 70 countries*. Germany adopted it in 1915. In the United States, only two states as of this writing do not have it (Hawaii and Arizona) and part of the reason it passed into law was that people could stay out later on summer evenings and thus have more leisure time, buy more products, and feel more cheerful.

Farmers and their lobbies opposed it:

To farmers, clock time was irrelevant any time of year. When the sun was overhead, it was noon. Increasingly, however, farmers depended on the railroad for their livelihood. If city folks were buying their milk, the milk had to make the morning train. The farmers lost the battle, and on March 31, 1918,

America turned its clocks ahead one hour. (Crossen, 2003, p. B1)

In 1996, the European Union (EU) standardized an EU-wide summertime period that runs from the last Sunday in March to the last Sunday in October. Attitudes affect how one feels about time. For example, an article in *American Demographics* reported that

Feeling rushed may have more to do with one's attitudes than with one's activities.

People who get more than 15 minutes of exercise a day are only half as likely as others to feel rushed, 22 percent versus 44 percent. People are more likely to feel rushed if they also say they are dissatisfied with themselves, unable to do things as well as others, feel useless, or don't have much to be proud of. (Godbey & Graefe, 1993, pp. 26–27)

## Discretionary Versus Nondiscretionary Time

Time can be categorized as discretionary or nondiscretionary. **Discretionary time** is the free time an individual can use any way she or he wants. How do people spend their free time? *The top preferred leisure pursuit of Americans ages 24–64 years is time with family and friends* followed by reading, television, traveling, gardening, movies, shopping, and exercising (Taylor, 2003). If you look at it by age group, differences emerge so that the preferred leisure activity for individuals ages 65 and over, employed or not, is watching TV followed by reading, according to Bureau of Labor Statistics (BLS) time studies. An average U.S. consumer spends 3 hours and 58 minutes daily watching TV. Younger consumers spend more time on smartphones (used in a variety of ways) and video games than in the recent past.

### Suggested Activity: Chart TV Viewing Time for One Week

Would you say that you watch more or less than 3 hours and 58 minutes a day of TV? One way to find out is to make a chart during an average week.

|           | Morning | Afternoon | Evening |
|-----------|---------|-----------|---------|
| Sunday    |         |           |         |
| Monday    |         |           |         |
| Tuesday   |         |           |         |
| Wednesday |         |           |         |
| Thursday  |         |           |         |
| Friday    |         |           |         |
| Saturday  |         |           |         |

Write down your minutes or hours in each space divided into the categories of morning, afternoon, and evening. In time charting the more often you write it down the more accurate it will be versus recall. Do you notice a pattern? If you watch no TV note that too. Compare with others in the class. Similar charts can be made of food preparation and eating, sleeping, and so on. Note: Later in the chapter, another suggested activity is keeping a complete time log for two weeks.

**Nondiscretionary time** is the time that an individual cannot control totally by himself or herself. For example, class times are nondiscretionary because they are set by the school or college. Opening and closing times of banks, restaurants, post offices, and stores are also nondiscretionary.

Nearly all people have some discretionary time when they can take breaks, use the bathroom, eat meals, and come and go between activities. Evenings and weekends offer the maximum amount of discretionary time. According to the BLS studies, as people age past 55, their average time spent working decreases, and leisure and sleep time increase. Of course, specific individuals might not fit this pattern. These trends are based on millions of people.

## Children, Adolescents, and Time

Children's time use has been measured, and there are some definite differences between countries. What is held in common is that young children usually have more discretionary time (e.g., free time, play time, sports, and recreation time) than adults do, but this situation may be changing.

In *The Hurried Child*, David Elkind makes the point that children today are overcommitted and are growing up too fast and too soon. He argues that they have too little free, unstructured, discretionary time. This lack of free time leads to stress. According to Elkind,

> *Today's child has become the unwilling, unintended victim of overwhelming stress—the stress borne of rapid, bewildering social change and constantly rising expectations. The contemporary parent dwells in a pressurecooker of competing demands, transitions, role changes, personal and professional uncertainties, over which he or she exerts slight direction.*
>
> *(1988, p. 3)*

## CASE STUDY

### Overscheduled High School Sophomore Brooke

*Brooke Ross struggled as a high school sophomore to satisfy competing demands from authority figures she respected. She played on two volleyball teams and studied competitive Irish dance, which she done since age 4, says Ms. Ross, of Hudson, NH. Her daily high school volleyball practices sometimes clashed with dance practice. After school junior-varsity volleyball games three times a week required her to attend freshmen and varsity games as well. That kept her out past 9 p.m., pushing homework time as late as 11:30 p.m., says her mother, Susan.*

Weekends were even busier until Brooke dropped Irish dance.

*Source: Shellenbarger, S. (November 22, 2017). Teaching Teens Time Management, The Wall Street Journal, p. A-11.*

*When the average teen is not in school or doing homework, he or she is most likely to be talking (online or in person),* then, in descending order, viewing TV or being online, performing paid labor or sports, helping with household chores, or participating in clubs or the arts. Jason, a teenager, explains that he feels like he has control over what he does with limits. He says, "Usually I just decide like, oh I really wanna go to this instead, and Mom'll give me the 'oh, oh well if you want to' and then I'll feel bad if I do …" (Ashbourne & Daly, 2010, p. 1429). Family time runs the gamut from the mundane like driving to and from school to special occasions like birthday celebrations and weddings. Some events are obligatory, some open to negotiation.

Adolescents engaging in more than 20 hours a week of paid work are linked to delinquency, drug use, and school misconduct, says Reed Larson, a professor at the University of Illinois (Shellenbarger, 2002). So, more than 20 hours a week of paid work during the school year is to be discouraged.

> *Is there a formula, one exhausted parent asks, for the right mix of clubs, sports, homework and free time? No, but some new guidelines are emerging. For instance, kids who participate in a variety of voluntary sports and clubs tend to work harder in school, studies show. However, too much of any one thing may yield diminishing returns. Part-time jobs carry some risks, researchers say, and family time is an important vaccine against such trouble signs as drug and alcohol use.*
>
> (Shellenbarger, 2002, p. D1)

## CASE STUDY

### Sean's Freshman Year

*Sean Smith, 17, of Kenosha, Wis., overloaded himself in his freshman year by taking five courses, an online Spanish class, band, lacrosse, cross-country and piano lessons and performances. "Since that initial period of awfulness, I've learned to manage my time better," Mr. Smith says. He is still president of two school clubs, a cross-country team member and a piano student, but he has dropped activities that caused conflicts. He also saves time for friends and activities he enjoys.*

*Source: Shellenbarger, S. (November 22, 2017). Teaching Teens Time Management. The Wall Street Journal, A11.*

Adults and Time.

Adults question their busy lives. Time is a moving target and reacts to anxiety and external events such as a decline in the economy. For mostly financial reasons, baby boomers are delaying retirement, reversing the usual behavior of the generations before them.

### Grand Central Station

*Late one evening I sat on a bench in Grand Central Station in the early '90s trying to figure out whether I had the energy or desire to jump on a Metro North Train for the ride home. I reflected on whether I should have ever moved our family from the Rocky Mountains to New York to take on a job that felt bigger than any capabilities I imagined I had. I fretted about whether it was possible to make the changes that my boss wanted and the organization needed. When I looked at my watch I realized that it was 10:00 P.M. and that I had been sitting on the bench for two hours. I knew something had to give. After I managed to lift myself off the bench, board the train and head home, I began thinking about anxieties.*

(DeLong, 2011, Preface)

*Jack Wolfe, a 64-year-old retiree from a natural-gas-pipeline company, moved to a lake between Houston and Dallas last year. Now he's trying to go back to work, "and the closest we are to anything is 60 or 70 miles," he says. "I'm probably going to have to go to work for a few months at a time. What I'd really like to do is inspection work on new pipelines." After nearly a decade in retirement, "I'm trying to go back to work and let our portfolio build back up," he explained. "We've lost such a big amount of money lately, we're going to get to the point where we can't recover."*

(Greene, 2008, p. A4)

Research shows that, regardless of age or phase of the life cycle, adult men and women experience time differently. According to a study by Mattingly and Bianchi (2003), men have more free time; marriage and children exacerbate the gender gap, and market work hours erode men's and women's free time in different ways. As may be expected, the presence of preschool children, employment outside the home, and being married cuts down on women's free time. Within marriage, fathers are spending more time with their children than they did in the past (Bianchi, 2000).

A case can be made that employed adults, male and female, have less discretionary time than before because of the Internet, global business, and availability issues:

*The 24-hour business day started with the Internet, and with international companies kept awake by the fact that every minute, somebody, somewhere is doing business. The whiz kids in the computer world brought their dorm-room hours to work with them, and soon even managers were grinding out work at night. "It starts with technology available to do work all the time. Then as there is more work to do, business speeds up, the market keeps expanding, and there is more of an emphasis on output," says John Challenger, chief executive of the outplacement firm Challenger, Gray & Christmas in Chicago. "Then it becomes doing business all the time, even in the service sector we're seeing formalized first, second, and third shifts." … "I don't think we'll get away from 24/7," Challenger says, "but I do think people will continue to make inroads reclaiming their personal time." (Boss, 2000, p. 16)*

Discretionary time allows the individual to make choices about whom to be with and what to do. These choices are not made in a vacuum, however—an individual's time use and needs must be weighed against what others want and need. Learning time management skills can help individuals maximize their time and use it optimally. The following suggestions can help in managing both discretionary and nondiscretionary time:

- Make a daily "things to do list" or keep a calendar.
- Say "no" to requests for time that keep one from finishing projects already under way.
- Make use of the telephone and the computer whenever possible.
- Delegate.
- Keep a flexible schedule that allows for unexpected events.
- Ask, "Is this the best possible use of my time at this moment?"
- Lessen interruptions, such as unnecessary meetings, visitors, and telephone calls.

For example, regarding lessening interruptions, a family may have a rule that outsiders are discouraged from calling after 9 o'clock at night. In offices, because they are public settings, interruptions are more difficult to manage.

In the 1990s, the average U.S. office worker sent or received 201 messages each day. Most messages were by telephone (50), email (35), or voice mail (22). Other messages were received by postal mail, interoffice mail, pagers, cell phones, express mail, post-it notes, telephone message slips, and couriers or messengers (Clark, 1999). In 2009, the proportion of telephone calls to emails changed so much that some offices took out landline telephones (desktop telephones) to save money saying that workers could use mobile devices to conduct business. Some employees balked at this cost-cutting move insisting that their desk telephones were still useful.

A word about modern households, "nearly one in four US households had a voice-enabled device inside – and about 40 percent of those have more than one" (Felbus, 2019).

Regardless of device or source, the problem (with so many messages and sounds) is that people spend nearly all their time responding to and receiving messages and have little time left to think and plan. Masie said when someone showed up at her front door and rang the bell all hell broke loose. The doorbell made the usual sound and two voice-enabled devices and sound detectors went ballistic in two different rooms so she ended up turning them off before going to the door to greet a friend who she saw on a visual-aided device. The friend was unexpected and the front door was rarely used, otherwise, Maisie said she would have turned off the devices (gifts from her son in the media business) in advance to avoid all the sounds going off.

Nearly half of office workers surveyed said they had difficulty keeping up with their work and were feeling overwhelmed. The director of the study's research team said, "We found that it was very much an interrupt-driven style of work that was emerging For too many people, information is proving to be more of a burden than a re-source" (Clark, 1999, p. R4). Also, a little privacy can boost productivity. According to an advertisement for Steelcase (a manufacturer of desks and office systems),

> While open workplaces invite valuable interaction between people, it's privacy that helps knowledge workers reach their peak state of performance. During the 15 minutes of immersion time needed to reach this

*state of "flow," people are particularly sensitive to interruptions. Once disrupted, most of us require an additional 15 minutes to reach it again.*

*Which is the most productive day of the week? The answer is Tuesday* according to several studies.

> *Mondays get us down. Wednesday is hump day. Thursday is the traditional happy hour day for those still close enough to their youth to remember such things, and Friday, well, Friday speaks for itself. Is it any wonder people aren't getting as much done those days? … many managers schedule meetings and conferences for Monday to give employees an idea of what work needs to be done for the week. Tuesday is really the first day workers have to get moving on that plan.*
>
> (Goforth, 2002, p. 5E)

Which are the happiest days of the week? According to Gallup organization, which conducts nationwide polls, the answer is Saturdays and Sundays (about 58 percent of Americans reporting a lot of happiness and enjoyment) with a decided drop on Mondays. Bad news, of course, can change these attitudes toward day of the week quickly.

How is time spent during the retirement years? Everyone's experience is different, and so much depends on health and circumstances. The first years of retirement are unique, as this case study illustrates:

> *Patricia Breakstone, age 63, remembers her first year of retirement from her 38-year career as a stategovernment analyst in San Diego as a "terrible transition period." Shortly after leaving her job last spring, she started a long-awaited kitchen renovation, which turned her condo upside-down right when she was starting to spend her days at home for the first time in her adult life. Then her dog was struck by kidney disease, and Ms. Breakstone wound up spending $7,000 in veterinary bills over two months as she tried in vain to nurse her pet back to health. As the months wore on, "I didn't want to get up in the morning," she says. Finally a friend goaded her into applying for a part-time job at a bakery near her home, which helped her regain some structure in her days—along with providing a social outlet. "Retirement," she says now, "is a real balancing act."*
>
> (Greene, 2003, p. R1)

Some people clearly enjoy leaving work behind, while others are disoriented. Many discover **drift time**, which refers to enjoying unscheduled time (e.g., the opportunity to have a second cup of coffee and read the whole newspaper in the morning or go online to shop). As the first year of retirement winds down, many find the right pace, a post-work life, that suits them.

"There doesn't seem to be the big hole that I expected after all those years working," says Steve Hold, age 63, who retired from General Electric Co. in Seattle in late 2001, and moved to Tucson, Arizona, the following May. "I was surprised that it was so easy to find things to do and become involved" (Greene, 2003, p. R1). A question that arises is, "What about marital relationships in the first years of retirement?" Ken Schumann, after retiring, came up with several rules, and he says negotiating personal space with your partner is one of the biggest hurdles in the first year. He and a few fellow retirees serving on a panel came up with these recommendations: shell out money for separate phone lines, computers, and email addresses; stake out a space in your home that is yours alone; and negotiate time together and apart (Greene, 2003).

As an addendum to the last quote about Steve, certainly separate cellphones and laptops have made it easier for husbands and wives to keep things private—having their own online spaces, networks, and conversations. So often, technological advances are thought of as for the young but this shows how media and communication advances affect lives at all stages.

**Suggested Activity**

*To find your most productive day of the week, keep a time log or journal for two weeks listing activities. You will become aware of things that are nonproductive time wasters.*

Here is another retirement story. Jim Matheson was always bothered by litter along the side of the road in his town, so when he retired at age 55, he went to the police station to explain his plan to pick up trash. While there, the chief told him they needed help setting up roadside radar signs (the kind that say, "Slow Down, Your Speed is …") and Jim said,

> *"Wait a minute. You're telling me I get to drive the cruiser, right?" … The first time he drove the vehicle on a major highway, "traffic backed up for miles behind me," he says, "What a feeling of power."*
>
> (Greene, 2003, p. R4)

## Modern Tools of Time Management

One hesitates to introduce this topic because next week the tools will change. We love our devices if we think they will save time and enrich our lives. Combined shipments of smartphones and tablets (of various names and manufacturers) have overtaken those of personal computers (PCs) along with voice-enabled devices mentioned earlier. Over the last few decades how we track and record time, schedules, and things to do have changed considerably ranging from

- Relying mostly on watches and clocks, then
- Calendars and schedule books including thick, complicated paper planners to
- Personal organizers that are on computers, cell phones, smart watches or other devices

A graduate student visiting a professor says, "Wait a minute," then pulls out a cell phone and enters the date and time for the next appointment. Her calendar is online, and the idea is that she checks it often to see where she needs to be. What if she does not check often enough? None of these devices, from watches to handhelds, has utility unless the person uses them.

> ### CASE STUDY
>
> ### Louise
>
> Louise, an 85-year-old great-grandmother, had 90 messages on her cell phone because she never checked them and did not intend to, so her son-in-law erased all of them with her permission. The son-in-law was alerted to the situation because another relative said Louise never responded to messages he left. Louise said she only answered the phone if it rang and she was there to get it and that she never had gotten used to the idea of an answering machine. She said she couldn't be bothered with cell phone messages and if it was important, they would call back. The relatives have been told about the situation and updated on the hours when she is most likely to answer and given instructions about what to do in an emergency regarding contacting her.

Around the world, Internet usage is up and so are cell phones, and other handheld and wearable devices. Computers are both savers and wasters of time. Colleen, a 55-year-old college instructor who is married to a teenage daughter, has a rule that she does not open work email on nights and weekends while other instructors use it 24/7 and do not distinguish between work email and personal email. Many people experience withdrawal symptoms when kept away from their electronic devices; others welcome the chance to get away. The average U.S. worker spends more than three hours a day reading, responding to, or disposing of email or text messages. Another metric is when your smartphone says how many hours a day you were on the phone vs. last week.

Reporting numbers has its limitations since usage varies so much by age group, country, occupation, and access. In the case study, Louise spends no time on email, texting, or phone messages. If you did not do any of these how different would your day be?

In the past, the introduction of printing and telephones necessitated adjustments as well, and the computer is no different in this regard. In the 20th century, some people did not get a telephone for many years because they did not like the intrusion or they did not like the cost, so they used the neighbor's phone or went without one. Today, people in a variety of occupations feel overwhelmed by computers, but so did the monks 500 years ago when the Gutenberg printing press brought a 20-fold increase in the number of texts they had to study. As people attempt to fit their lifestyles within the context of the information and technological explosion, experts and entrepreneurs are looking for solutions—applying the very tools that caused the data glut in a mission to help alleviate it. For example, email filtering and message organizing devices are solutions for computers (just as answering machines were for telephones). "Spam walls" destroy spam before it gets to inboxes; other programs flag or give warning messages of possible spam. Spam alerts on phones are useful for screening.

## The ABC Method of Time Control and Goals

The pressures of modern society have led to the publication of many books suggesting ways individuals and families can improve their use of time. One of the best-known classic books is Alan Lakein's *How to Get Control of Your Time and Your Life*, which explains how to set short-term and long-term goals, establish priorities, organize a daily schedule, and achieve better self-understanding. He provided an updated version with an emphasis on results-driven time management in *Give Me a Moment and I'll Change Your Life: Tools for Moment Management*. He is known for the sentiment that time = life.

Lakein encourages the use of the ABC priority method in which the most important activities are designated "A," medium-value activities are "B," and low-value activities are "C." An individual using this method writes down all his or her activities for a given day; rates each activity as A, B, or C; and then tries to accomplish the As first, the Bs next, and the Cs only if there is time.

Figure 9.2 shows how Chris, a 28-year-old doctoral student and teaching assistant, used the ABC method during one busy Thursday. Other authors have suggested low (L), medium (M), and high (H) degrees of importance. The underlying principle is the same whether it is called ABCs or LMHs or apples, oranges, and pears. If you keep a written or mental "to do" list and prioritize the activities by their degree of importance, how strictly do you stick to your priorities?

An important concept in Lakein's book is that daily time use should be directly related to goals. Figure 9.3 shows how Chris describes her life goals and lifestyle goals. Are there connections between Chris's "to do"

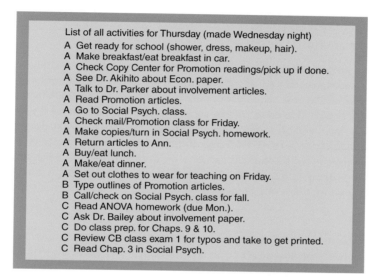

List of all activities for Thursday (made Wednesday night)
A  Get ready for school (shower, dress, makeup, hair).
A  Make breakfast/eat breakfast in car.
A  Check Copy Center for Promotion readings/pick up if done.
A  See Dr. Akihito about Econ. paper.
A  Talk to Dr. Parker about involvement articles.
A  Read Promotion articles.
A  Go to Social Psych. class.
A  Check mail/Promotion class for Friday.
A  Make copies/turn in Social Psych. homework.
A  Return articles to Ann.
A  Buy/eat lunch.
A  Make/eat dinner.
A  Set out clothes to wear for teaching on Friday.
B  Type outlines of Promotion articles.
B  Call/check on Social Psych. class for fall.
C  Read ANOVA homework (due Mon.).
C  Ask Dr. Bailey about involvement paper.
C  Do class prep. for Chaps. 9 & 10.
C  Review CB class exam 1 for typos and take to get printed.
C  Read Chap. 3 in Social Psych.

Figure 9.2  Chris's Thursday schedule.

General Life Goals
My general life goals are (1) to complete my doctorate work and earn a Ph.D., (2) to marry the man of my choice, (3) to obtain a professional position at a large state university, (4) to have at least 2 to 5 articles accepted for publication each year, (5) to be published at least twice in a premier journal, (6) to establish myself as one of the leading academicians in my field, (7) to earn the respect of both my colleagues and my sisters, (8) to earn enough money to take care of my parents and my husband's parents, (9) to truly make a difference in the life of at least one of my students, (10) to establish myself as a consultant, (11) to establish myself as a consumer rights advocate, (12) to get tenure, and (13) to improve my health.

Lifestyle Goals
My lifestyle goals are (1) to live in a new house in an upper-class neighborhood in the suburbs, (2) to live near, but not in, a major city with cultural events, great shopping, and other universities, (3) to drive a Saab or an Alfa Romeo, (4) to be able to buy clothes without worrying about the cost, and (5) to be able to drive to getaway weekends to fun places or visit old friends and family.

Figure 9.3  Chris's general life goals and lifestyle goals.

list for Thursday and her goals? Note also the significance of the practice of writing down activities and goals. A goal strategist, Gene Donohue, says the difference between a goal and a dream is the written word. He says that reviewing goals daily is a crucial part of success and should become part of your routine. How do you do this? The lists and ABCs are one way. Another way is to cut out a photo or map from a brochure or an advertisement of a house, boat, car, vacation destination, or whatever that depicts your goal and put that photo or map on your refrigerator or mirror so that every day you see it and think about it; visualize yourself owning the object or being in the place you want to be. When your goals change or are achieved, remove the visual and replace it with another.

This example uses Lakein's ABC priority method in which A activities are top priority, B activities are less important, and C activities are to be done if there is time.

---

### Suggested Activity

Take the six categories and list a goal or several goals under each one. Be sure to be specific. For example, instead of writing "a house" under the category of Family and Home, write down the size, type, location, view, and acreage. Do you envision a garden, trees, a field, a beach, sidewalks, nearby shops, neighbors, mountains? If you want to get specific, write down what is in the garden. Can you visualize it? What does the air smell like? Put the stated goal into a time frame: When is an achievement (partial or full) likely? Discuss your answers with others. It can also be the case that you have several houses or life situations in mind; feel free to describe several scenarios. Being specific does not mean being limiting, but it does mean trying to focus on a few desired alternatives.

---

Too often people dwell on the past when their time would more productively be spent living in the present and planning the future. Donohue suggests writing down goals in six areas of life:

1. Family and Home (Ask yourself, am I creating an environment conducive to effectiveness?)

2. Financial and Career (Again, ask yourself, am I creating an environment conducive to effectiveness?)

3. Spiritual and Ethical (Are these priorities?)

4. Physical and Health (Are these priorities?)

5. Social and Cultural (Do I need more social contact? Do I need to broaden the scope of what I do and who I know?)

6. Mental and Educational (What places or activities will help with this category?)

You could add more categories like Environment or Friends or figure these fit under the comprehensive or umbrella categories of Family and Home, Physical and Health, and Social and Cultural. These six categories serve as an organizing tool that you can use as a springboard to thinking about your own life. In which of these categories would you like to spend more time?

## Time Perceptions

**Perception** refers to the process whereby sensory stimulation is translated into organized experience. Understanding how time is perceived is necessary because, as noted earlier, time is more than simply clock time; an individual's perception and use of time are also important. Because perception is not observable, researchers have to rely on people's self-reports of their perceptions.

**Time perception** is the awareness of the passage of time. Since 1850, social and behavioral scientists have been trying to determine why people's sense of the length of time can differ from the precise measurement. They have found that many factors come into play in time perception. For example, drug and alcohol consumption alter time perception. Changes in body temperature and lack of exposure to natural daylight have been shown to affect a person's sense of time. Besides these physiological influences, temperament, culture, environment, and absorption in the task at hand may also affect time perception.

## Estimating Duration

Without watches, clocks, newspapers, radio, cell phones, computers, or the television to serve as a guide, people would have to use other means of estimating how much time has passed such as watching the sky and the behavior of other people (are they getting sleepy or hungry?). Several factors influence a person's estimation of time. Being active makes time go faster than being passive. A salesperson in a clothing store usually likes a lot of customers because the time will move more quickly than just standing there. As another example, the driver of a car may think that a trip goes faster than a passenger thinks it does because the driver has something to do other than look passively out the window. An individual who is motivated can concentrate longer on a task and enjoy it more. Time seems to move faster when one is not bored.

Research studies reveal marked differences in individuals' ability to estimate time. Age appears to be one factor. Elderly people tend to find time shorter than younger people. According to Jean Piaget's theory of concrete cognitive operations, children's time estimates become more accurate after the age of seven or eight. This is why younger children irritate their parents on a family vacation by repeatedly asking when they are going to arrive at the destination. Children do not mean to be irritating; they simply do not understand time as an adult does.

## Practical Uses of Time Measurement

Although perceptions and estimations of time vary from person to person, time itself is one of the most accurately measured physical quantities. Indeed, the study of time can be a very practical subject often applied to project management involving planning and scheduling. Time and motion studies are conducted in homes, offices, and factories. The studies evaluate task performance and analyze the time spent in producing a product such as a car or in using home appliances.

As discussed in Chapter 2, the early studies of factory efficiency were closely associated with the work of Frederick Taylor (1911), who is widely considered to be the father of time and motion studies. Taylor's studies later led to the discipline of management as it is taught in business schools today. He introduced the idea of measuring time precisely to examine specific activities with the intent of finding ways to reduce the amount of time they required. These studies aimed at improving efficiency through saving time and human energy. Each job on a factory production line would be divided into different operations, and each operation would then be analyzed in terms of time and energy used. As a result of the findings, assembly line work in factories became more standardized and efficient.

Many of the principles and methods derived from industrial performance studies, such as those conducted by Taylor, were applied to household efficiency studies. Chapter 2 examined some of these studies in the discussion of work simplification. Individuals' and families' use of time and products continues to be studied by manufacturers and marketers of appliances, food, exercise, and household products. They are interested in identifying trends in who does what in the home and learning how many minutes a day are spent in preparing food, eating, cleaning up, and washing clothes so that they can tailor their advertising and their products to fit current household practices and, hence, increase sales by better meeting consumer needs. They are also interested in eating behaviors outside the home. Restaurant chains, grocery stores, and office furniture manufacturers may want to know how workers spend their lunch hours and what they eat. For example, a fast-food chain might use several methods of inquiry, including in-restaurant consumer surveys, focus groups (selected groups of people who are questioned by a discussion leader or moderator about what they think about different topics, in this case, products and services), observations, and self-reports. Companies also rely heavily on point-of-sale information obtained when bar codes from products are entered into a cash register or in data derived from beverage and snack machines, for example

Time measurement also has practical applications in evaluating skills such as word processing (number of words per minute), sales (number of sales per month), and library use (number of books checked out per week). Mall and store hours are determined by the number of customers per hour. On Friday and Saturday nights bars and restaurants stay open later than they do on other nights. During the holiday season, stores remain open longer to meet increased customer traffic and boost sales.

The amount of Social Security retired people receive is based on the number of years they were employed and how much they earned. Divorce settlements account for the number of years of marriage. Daily, people try to determine whether they will be on time for work, school, or appointments; whether they will have enough time to eat lunch or prepare dinner; whether they will be able to read the newspaper or watch the television shows they want to; and so on. In other words, people are engaged in time management from the moment they wake up until they go to sleep. Even sleeping is a timed event, ending when one awakens to the sound of an alarm ringing or a radio playing or a roommate or spouse saying, "It's time to get up." Smartwatches or phones can measure and report REM and non-REM sleep so not just the number of hours is measured but the quality of sleep.

## Perceptions of Time across Cultures

As mentioned earlier in the chapter, individuals perceive time differently owing to many factors. A widely held concept in anthropology is that time perceptions are strongly influenced by culture. The person most associated with studying how culture influences the way people think about time is E. T. Hall, author of *The Silent Language*. The three anthropological models of time—linear-separable, circular-traditional, and procedural-traditional—were introduced by Hall (1959) and further delineated by Robert Graham (1981) and Alma Owen (1991). These models define time in the context of various activities, life stages, or time of the year. By doing this, the models illustrate what time means to different cultural groups and the ways in which they process and structure time.

### Linear-Separable Model of Time

Where are the ways forward? Most Western European cultures view of time as linear. This is the dominant worldview of business and commerce so timetables, deadlines, and schedules are important. Promotion up the chain of command is an example of linear thinking. Linear-separable time processing is related to economic time. An investment in time today is expected to have a payoff in the future. Long-term planning is accepted as normal in the linear-separable model. Most North Americans think long-term planning or goal setting would be for 5–25 years. For example, a job interviewer may ask a college student, "Where do you see yourself in five years?"

This model also treats the past, present, and future as distinct entities that are broken down into units. Thus, in linear-separable time orientations, stories, steps, and procedures are usually told in chronological order.

Speed of preparation is valued, so time-saving products such as frozen entrees, boxed macaroni and cheese, and canned soups are accepted.

As mentioned earlier, time can be measured in a variety of ways ranging from clocks to calendars. Appointments are kept on time. Furthermore, it is assumed that the future will bring better things. The linear-separable model represents an optimistic point of view because improvements are expected over time.

## Procedural-Traditional Model of Time

The procedural-traditional perception is very different from the linear-separable model. Individuals with a procedural perception consider the actual steps, event, or procedure to be more important than the time spent in the activity. Being prompt is not as critical as doing things correctly or when conditions are right. Several tribes of American Indians and Alaskan Eskimos subscribe to a procedural perception of time. *Procedural time processing is characterized by staying with a task until it is completed no matter how much time it takes.*

Scientists looking for cures and people who quilt or do other arts and crafts may subscribe to procedural-traditional models of time. They are focused on taking the right steps and finding a solution or making a product regardless of how long it takes. Another example of this is putting together a jigsaw puzzle with 500 or 1,000 pieces; the puzzle solvers will happily spend hours over several days on this activity. There is no deadline or end point other than finishing the puzzle however long it takes. This would be the same with finishing crossword puzzles.

There are hundreds of ways to streamline your day. Here are some.

1. Get help. For example, a stone flew up from the road and hit the windshield of a new car. The owner was dismayed at the dent which was right in his line of vision. The insurance adjuster told him whom to call and a technician came to his house within hours and patched the windshield so that the chip could no longer be seen. This service was free and efficient, and the car owner was amazed.

2. Use your human energy effectively. Study or do difficult reports during your peak energy time, usually 10 or 11 A.M. for most people.

3. Buy gift cards. Shop online.

4. Use in-store or online with purchase wrapping services.

5. Buy prepared or delivered to your door food.

6. Send free greeting cards online. Share photos directly online with family and friends or through networks.

7. Reduce walking and searching by having basics, such as tissues, clocks, scissors, pens, paper, and cleaning supplies, in most rooms. This technique is especially important in two-story or three-story houses.

8. Use automatic bill paying and direct deposit.

9. Buy movie and theater tickets or order food to pick up in advance.

10. Start earlier and shop early when stores are not crowded. Home supply stores say their slowest time is Sunday morning. A corollary to this is to ask for the earliest appointment at the dentist or doctor; you are less likely to be bumped by emergencies that occur during the day.

11. Double recipes, eat half, freeze the rest. Share with family and neighbors.

12. Buy multiples of nonperishables like paper products, soap, cleaning supplies, shampoo, toothpaste, and detergent.

### Circular-Traditional Model of Time

A circular or cyclical perception emphasizes the repetitive nature of time; this model assumes that today will be much like yesterday, and tomorrow will be more of the same. Time follows a rhythmic pattern with regular beginnings and ends, but without discrete units of past, present, and future. In the circular perception, things may move forward or may remain the same. The circular perception is often associated with poverty because life for the poor, regardless of country, may change little from day to day. People living in primitive or agricultural-subsistence cultures may also subscribe to the circular perception, as they may be born, live, raise their families, and die on the same land as did their grandparents. Time is not saved or spent; it just is, and life is lived day by day.

---

**CRITICAL THINKING**

#### A Weekend Mindset

If you are mostly linear and very task-oriented you might want to consider how to slow it down and get into a weekend mindset which has components of the circular-traditional model of time. Read the following and react,

> "Its important to remember that the benefits of the vacation mindset spring from your mental-state not from what you're doing. Some people managed to attain a vacation mindset while doing their usual chores, slowing their pace, staying focused in the present and noticing sensory stimuli. Some play upbeat or reflective music." Others avoid or lessen social media (have you tried that?).

Source: Shellenbarger, S. (April 10, 2019). Making a weekend more weekend-like. *The Wall Street Journal*, A 12.

## Some Effects of Cultural Differences

None of these models of time perception is good or bad; they simply illustrate cultural differences that affect managerial and consumption behavior. It is also important to note that many countries use a combination of the models or include cultural groups that subscribe more to one model than another. As the critical thinking exercise showed weekend time use may be circular-traditional whereas weekdays may be linear.

Companies that market products internationally are aware of these cultural differences. Take the example of washing clothes. North Americans like large-capacity machines that wash clothes fast, whereas frequent, small loads that take an hour or more of washing time are acceptable, even desirable, in other countries. Also because of aesthetics, tradition, and types of clothing and activities, differences exist in appearance of washing machines, their placement in the house, and the washing procedures.

Here are a few examples (Jordan & Karp, 2003):

- In China: Aesthetics are important because many families keep washers in living areas owing to space limitations; color preferences are gray or green, and there needs to be a grease removal cycle to remove grease stains caused by bicycle-riding.

- In Brazil: Washers are white with transparent lids; they are raised on four legs so that consumers can wash underneath the machine; soaking is a tradition so there is a soak cycle as part of the main cycle; small loads and more frequent loads are the tradition.

- In India: Appliances have wheels for easy moving; washers are not isolated; they have a position of pride in the home, and there is a sari (delicate) cycle to wash women's wraparound fabrics.

- In England: Combined washers and dryers are common, and they are typically placed in the kitchen near the other appliances and the sink rather than in a separate room or behind closed doors.

Let us go back to the discussion of time use across cultures. In Western cultures, all three models exist, although the linear-separable model is dominant. Guy Claxton, an English psychologist specializing in the structure of the human mind and the author of *Hare Brain Tortoise Mind*, says that the Western hurry-up methods have their drawbacks because slow ways of knowing exist and are useful:

The individuals and societies of the West have rather lost touch with the value of contemplation. Only active thinking is regarded as productive. Sitting gazing absently at your office wall or out of the classroom window is not of value. Yet many of those whom our society admires as icons of creativity and wisdom have spent much of their time doing nothing. Einstein, it is said, would frequently be found in his office at Princeton staring into space. The Dalai Lama spends hours each day in meditation. Even that paragon of penetrating insight, Sherlock Holmes, is described by his creator as entering a meditative state "with dreamy vacant expression in his eyes" (1997, p. 4).

Latin America provides an example of how perceptions of time can affect consumption behavior. Latin Americans generally view time as less concrete and less subject to scheduling than viewed by North Americans. Consequently, appointments and meetings rarely start at the scheduled time. Since eating fast in an impersonal setting is not valued in Latin America, fast-food outlets popular in the United States and Great Britain, such as Kentucky Fried Chicken, McDonald's, and Wimpy, had difficulty penetrating Latin American markets (Penteado, 1981), although this is changing. Convenience foods such as boxed cereals sell well in North America because quick breakfasts that save time are highly valued. They are less successful in unhurried cultures where a warm breakfast may be more desired or lingering over coffee or tea.

In circular perception, the concept of the future is vague. Typically, Asians think of longer time spans than thought of by North Americans. This perception leads to a different sense of urgency. In Asian countries, businesses are planned for the long run over several decades rather than for the short term. On the other hand, the Japanese have been very receptive to many American–European time-saving convenience goods and fast-food restaurants. The 7–11 convenience store chain is headquartered in Japan.

Research studies have tried to establish the validity and monitor the cultural changes in the three types of time perceptions. A study of 48 East and Southeast Asian students (men and women from Thailand, Japan, and Malaysia) attending a large Midwestern university found that procedural processing was most frequently used by them, followed by circular processing, and linear processing was rarely used. In contrast, linear processing was apparently the most used by U.S. students, followed by procedural processing, and then by circular processing (Lindquist et al., 1993). The U.S. students were more likely to view time as a valuable and limited commodity—something to be scheduled—whereas the Asian students were more concerned with the task itself rather than time.

Naturally, people with different time perspectives may find it difficult to understand each other. Often, people from the United States who become restless when made to wait are viewed as rude by people from non-Western cultures. Conversely, people who are always in a hurry may think cultures that are slower and less orderly are behind the times.

To be effective in international business and education, one must be sensitive and adjust to the dominant time orientation and the connected behaviors (slower or later mealtimes, for example), priorities, and hierarchies. Network Theory is an academic discipline that applies to many science and human behavioral fields but for the purposes here the emphasis is on how your social position within a culture affects your power, beliefs, and behaviors. For example, a person's position in a network affects the amount of influence he or she has and we often make errors based on opinions of our friends or colleagues. A leader in this research is Stanford University economist Matthew O. Jackson whose books include *Social and Economic Networks* and *The Human Network*. The latter was reviewed in a newspaper column. "How one person treats another involves looking beyond the relationships to the network in which they are embedded. Mr. Jackson observes. 'Yet as technology enables us to choose our relationships from a much larger pool…'" (as reported by Oren Cass (April 3, 2019) in Like Goes with Like, *The Wall Street Journal,* A15). Focus on the phrase "choose our relationships from a much larger pool"—how in the long run will enlarged networks affect time orientations and differences among groups?

## Biological Time Patterns

Cultural perceptions of time use provide insight into how different groups of people perceive time. Another important aspect of time is how individuals perceive time. Each person has an internal clock that tells her or him when to wake, go to sleep, and eat. **Circadian rhythms** are the daily rhythmic activity cycles, based on 24-hour intervals, that humans experience. The word "circadian" comes from the Latin words *circa* (about) and *dies* (day). Before birth, babies are exposed to these daily rhythms from their mother's eating and sleeping patterns.

Jet lag and the disorientation caused by changing work shifts are examples of how humans react when their rhythms are disturbed. In the case of jet lag, people experience psychological dislocation and disruption of bodily rhythms caused by high-speed travel across several time zones in an airplane. Their sleeping and eating patterns are thrown off. Changing work shifts have been found to be a stressor for individuals and families.

# Quantitative and Qualitative Time Measures

Perceptions have to do with people's estimations of time, but time can also be measured in units. **Quantitative time measures** refer to the number, kind, and duration (e.g., minutes, hours, day) of activities that occur at specific points in time (Goldsmith, 1990). A quantitative time researcher would be interested in how many minutes a day an individual spends in bill paying, food preparation, shopping, eating, driving, grooming, playing, childcare, elder care, and working. Most of the quantitative time-use data are gathered in four ways:

1. In the *self-report* or *diary method*, individuals record their own time-use data on a form provided by the researcher.

2. In the *recall method*, individuals are asked to think back (recall) and explain in detail a previous day's activities to an interviewer in person, or over the telephone, or by self-report on a form provided by the researcher.

3. In the *observation method*, a trained researcher observes and records the precise way, duration, and sequencing of an individual's activities. This method has been used extensively in anthropology and child development.

4. The *self-observational control-signaling method* is rarely used for collecting data on household time use but is used extensively in business management studies.

In this latter method, subjects are asked to record their time use at a given signal, such as when a bell sounds, a telephone rings, or a light flashes. Permission would be gained by management and human subjects or human resources committees. The method incorporates a self-report, but the reports in the control-signaling method are required at random times and are less routine and less time-consuming for the subject than are the lengthy ongoing daily self-reports. Because the signals occur sporadically and the subject responds immediately, some researchers conclude that the control-signaling method produces more accurate data than do the other methods.

Using a combination of methods with built-in cross-checks is generally considered to be the best way to obtain accurate data. Examples of extensive quantitative household time-use studies are the 1967–1968 Walker–Telling study of 1,296 families in Syracuse, New York, and the 11-state spin-off studies (Walker, 1983; Walker & Woods, 1976). These studies used 24-hour recalls as told to interviewers and diaries. Among other things, the New York study established that the presence of young children in the home dramatically increased the amount of household work. In 1994, in another time-use study, Allen Martin and Margaret Sanik reported that women spent more time in household work if there was a young child or a teenager in the household and that men contributed more time to household production as they aged.

In *The Second Shift*, sociologist Arlie Hochschild (1989) wrote that many employed women work at a job during the day and go home and work until bedtime at household chores and childcare—in other words, women work two jobs. Through interviews and observations, she found that in some marriages where the husband earned more, he was justified doing less housework because he contributed more monetarily; she also found marriages where the wife earned more, felt guilty, and therefore did more housework. Hochschild concluded that rarely is housework evenly divided between working parents and that there is a gap between their ideals and the reality of their busy lives.

In her follow-up book, *The Time Bind*, Hochschild explored further the alternating between home and work lives. She says that "the more attached we are to the world of work, the more its deadlines, its cycles, its pauses and interruptions shape our lives, and the more family time is forced to accommodate to the pressures of work" (1997, p. 45). Today, Hochschild and many sociologists continue this precedent setting work on the emotions involved in work and home life.

**Qualitative time measurement** investigates the meaning or significance of time use as well as how individuals feel about their time use—that is, the satisfaction it generates. It also accounts for whom they are spending time. Consider the following comment by the Duke of Windsor, who abdicated the British throne to marry an American divorcée in 1937. "You know what my day was today?" asked the former king, "I got up late and then I went with the Duchess and watched her buy a hat" (Menkes, 1987). This quote calls to mind another, the 1970 movie *Alfie* with a theme song that asked, "What's It All About?" Feelings about everyday time use relate heavily to a search for life purpose.

Thomas J. DeLong in his book *Flying Without A Net* says we need to change fear into paths for success and that three central fears and anxieties drive dysfunctional behaviors. These are:

- Lack of purpose and direction

- Sense of isolation and abandonment, being disconnected

- Feeling of insignificance (e.g., "Do I matter?") (2011, p.42)

> ## CRITICAL THINKING
>
> ### Who Cares About Your Time?
>
> When students are walking to and from class they are often on their phones. To whom are they talking? Conversations may be about where they have been and where they are going and hopefully what they are learning. On a daily or weekly basis who do you communicate with about what you are doing? Are these the same people as a year ago?

The "with whom" part of how time is spent is important because daily life is not defined solely by what we do, but also by whom we are with or with whom we are communicating. According to an exhibit on "The Time of Law" at the Gulbenkian Museum in Lisbon, Portugal, "Awareness of time is a construction of individual personality and human solidarity." Mihaly Csikszentmihalyi (1997) estimates that people spend roughly equal amounts of time in three social contexts:

1. Among strangers, co-workers, fellow students. This is "public" space where one's actions are evaluated by others and where one competes for resources.

2. Among family and friends. This is a place of kinship, special bonds, and home.

3. In solitude. Time spent alone.

In technological societies, more time is spent alone than was common in tribal societies, where being alone was often considered dangerous. Many people are uncomfortable being alone, but it is important to learn to tolerate solitude or else the quality of our lives is bound to suffer (Csikszentmihalyi, 1997). The popularity of Zooms, chat rooms, blogs, and texting may be partially explained by this need to connect with others even when one is alone physically.

Is she alone? Not really.

Prior to the 1970s, nearly all time-use measurement was quantitative. Since then, several studies have used qualitative measures as well as a combination of quantitative and qualitative measures. The increased use of qualitative measures is a response to the growing recognition that simply knowing how many minutes are spent washing dishes or diapering a baby does not provide as meaningful time-use data as knowing how persons performing the task feel or how they interact with others involved in the task. Asking qualitative questions also lets the researcher know how the individual feels; thus, the burden of interpretation is no longer on the researcher where obvious bias or perceptual errors could occur.

## Demands, Sequencing, and Standards

Three concepts introduced earlier in this book—demands, sequencing, and standards—are an integral part of the discussion of time from a managerial perspective. Since time is a limited resource, individuals have to make decisions about how to allocate their time. Demands, sequencing, and standards affect these decisions.

### Demands

As lives become more complicated, increasing demands are placed on time.

Demands are events or goals that necessitate or motivate action. For example, schools demand attendance, workplaces demand a certain number of hours of work, parents demand a safe neighborhood for their children, the children's coach demands that they spend time practicing, and citizens demand fair government.

Many of these demands may not be met, but they are goals or ideals worth striving for. One would assume that saving time is the main reason why people buy and use appliances, but research shows that conventional appliances do not always reduce time demands. In the United States, the difference in time spent on cooking between women who use a microwave oven and those who do not is just four minutes (Robinson & Milkie, 1997). Experiments are always underway to create appliances and computer-aided systems that will more effectively save time and at the same time serve families as well or better than before.

Demands on time within families and organizations may conflict. One child may want the parents to attend her school play while a sibling wants them to come to his soccer game. At work, employees find several tasks competing for their attention. Stretching limited resources, including time, to meet conflicting demands is a dilemma all people experience. Families with young children or disabled family members may face even greater demands on their time. Teenagers and dependent elderly may put high emotional demands on the family, and meeting those demands takes time.

Unfortunately, demands are often the strongest when resources are the weakest, as in the case of young married couples who are trying to set up a household, have children, and become established in their careers—all at the same time. Time demands are also high for families trying to balance more established careers and home responsibilities. According to John Robinson of the University of Maryland and Geoffrey Godbey of Pennsylvania State University, Americans have about 40 hours of leisure time a week now versus 35 hours in 1964.

> "It just doesn't feel like it," Robinson said. "They perceive that they have less and are more rushed." The thief is perception; people are losing time only in their minds, but the perception feels more real than the reality. Too, that leisure time tends to come in shreds rather than blocks.
>
> (Werland, 2000, p. D6)

Besides demands external to the person, there are internal demands as well. All individuals have a **tempo**, meaning a time pattern or pace that they feel comfortable with. One person may be described as "high energy, always on the go, or hyper," whereas another is described as "slow, thoughtful, and deliberate." Successful organizations thrive on having members with both types of temperament.

Sometimes the demand for time is uneven and difficult to manage, and tradition plays a part. For example, bicycle stores may be empty during weekdays but crowded on Saturdays with children and parents. Outdoor volleyball courts, tennis courts, and golf courses are usually overbooked on weekends. Thus, demand can range from none to excessive and can be irregular as well. When shopping, consumers try to gauge when demand will be low, lines short, and stores not crowded. Sara says she and her husband, Karl, always grocery-shop on Sunday mornings because it is so peaceful. As these examples illustrate, the concept of demand can be applied to time as well as to other constructs and contexts, such as shopping demands and energy demands. In the United States, Sundays have turned into popular times to browse and shop in person and online. This transformation started around 1900 when libraries and ballparks remained open on Sundays. By the mid-1960s most stores and restaurants were open on Sundays, although a few national fast-food chains continue to be closed on Sundays and most stores and restaurants offer reduced hours.

## Sequencing

Each of us gets to choose our sequence, our pacing, and our path of growth. A **sequence** is when one event or step follows another in a series or an arrangement.

Examples of sequences are sharpening a pencil before writing with it, unlocking a door before entering a house, or making an appointment before going to the dentist. Individuals' daily lives are filled with many such sequences. Sequencing refers to the order of activities in time, as in a series of events. Sequencing may be simple or complex. In a simple sequence, one person performs one task. A complicated sequencing plan involves many people and many tasks. Obviously, a large family with children at different ages will have more trouble completing tasks and holding to a set sequence than a person living alone will.

Malcolm Gladwell (2000), author of *The Tipping Point,* says we are at heart gradualists, people who like sequences, schedules, and regular routines, but at the same time, the routines and expectations can be shaken up when something new arrives on the scene.

---

### CRITICAL THINKING

**Fast Change**

In Gladwell's book he says, "It is that the best way to understand the emergence of fashion trends, the ebb and flow of crime waves, or, for that matter, the transformation of unknown books into bestsellers, or the rise of teenage smoking, or the phenomena of word of mouth, or any number of the other mysterious changes that mark everyday life is to think of them as epidemics. Ideas and products and message and behaviors spread just like viruses do" (p. 7). Can you think of an idea, product, message, or behavior that took off rapidly? Why do you think it did?

---

Schedules, which are sets of time-bounded activities, are made up of two mental processes: sequencing and time-tagging. **Time-tagging** is a mental estimation of the sequences that should take place, the approximate amount of time required for each activity in the sequence, and the starting and ending times for each activity (Avery & Stafford, 1991). Repeatedly following the same sequences with the same start and end points leads to procedural routines where the person no longer thinks about the individual steps in the sequence. Remember learning how to drive a car or use a computer? At first, you were slow and had to think carefully about each step. In time, you became faster and the sequence felt more natural. Schedules and sequences can be mental or they can be written, as in a schedule of college classes or a program of forthcoming events.

As mentioned earlier, many individuals and families feel overwhelmed by demands on their time—they are living in a time of drought, in a barren land with little relief. They feel short of time because of the phenomenon of multitasking, which is becoming more and more the norm. As described in Chapter 6, tasks can be divided into three main categories: interdependent, dovetailed, and overlapped. In *interdependent* activities, one task must be completed before the next task can begin. *Multitasking* is the same as dovetailing.

An example of an interdependent activity is mailing a letter. The letter has to be written and the envelope stamped and addressed before mailing. Doing two or more activities at once is called *multitasking*. A person may, for example, fold laundry and watch television at the same time. In fact, people are so used to having the radio or the television playing in the background that they do not consider these as competing activities. Many dull, repetitive activities lend themselves to dovetailing. The one drawback to multitasking is that if you do too many activities at one time, the end results may be less satisfactory than desired. A meal can be burned, a deadline missed, or a message misinterpreted if a person is trying to do too much at once.

*Overlapping* involves giving intermittent attention to two or more activities until they are completed. For example, a parent might put a baby to bed, and then read while partly listening to check whether the baby is falling asleep. On any given day, people use all three types of sequencing. Along this same line of thought, Claxton warns that

> *There is an old Polish saying, "Sleep faster; we need the pillows," which reminds us that there are some activities which just will not be rushed. They take the time that they take. If you are late for a meeting, you can hurry. If the roast potatoes are slow to brown, you can turn up the oven. But if you try to speed up the baking of meringues, they burn. If you are impatient with the mayonnaise and add the oil too quickly, it curdles. If you start tugging with frustration on a tangled fishing line, the knot just becomes tighter.*
>
> *(1997, p. 1)*

Individuals may favor a certain type of sequencing based on his or her style, pace, or tempo. Most people go through a certain sequence of events when they first awaken in the morning. They perform routine activities such as putting on a bathrobe, going to the bathroom, washing their face, combing their hair, checking their messages, watching the morning news programs or reading the newspaper, dressing, and eating breakfast. As the day progresses, they move into more complicated sequencing involving dovetailing and overlapping activities. At bedtime, they revert to a more habitual sequencing mode, essentially reversing the morning routine with a snack, brushing teeth, going to the bathroom, undressing, watching television, and going to sleep.

Successful managers understand their recurring patterns and how they need to manage their time to be effective. They may have to break their normal sequence if they want to move ahead. If they are achievers, it means that they want to accomplish things, but sometimes this is at the expense of having enough personal interaction. If this is a weak spot, the manager will have to make time to visit with others, stroll around the offices and factories, and go to the water cooler or break room. As a counterpoint to this, a manager who is totally people-oriented or news-oriented (wanting to know what is going on) may have difficulty settling down to tasks and will have to arrange his or her time accordingly to move projects along.

Another way to discuss the impact of personality on time use is to categorize people as mainly polychronic or mainly monochronic. **Polychronic** refers to liking to do several things at once, whereas **monochronic** refers to preferring to focus on one activity at a time, such as reading or watching a football game on television. The monochronic person dislikes being distracted from the activity at hand, and this has been the subject of many television situation comedy episodes. For example, on *Everybody Loves Raymond*, several plot lines revolve around Raymond or his father or brother being disturbed by Raymond's wife or mother while the men are trying to watch sports on television. An example of a polychronic or multitasking person is someone who pages through a magazine while talking on a cell phone and carrying on a conversation with the person next to him.

A **routine** is a habitual way of doing things that saves time and energy for other activities. Routines and habits provide stability to our lives. Young children thrive on routines at home and in preschool. Learning logical ways of sequencing activities is part of the socialization process. Some of us need more routine than others. The roots of this need probably stem from childhood socialization patterns, personality, and temperament. Remember that, as was said earlier, goals should be made part of your everyday routine. Are you moving positively toward your goal achievement or moving farther away? If more relaxation time is a goal, consider the words of wife and mother Joann Gardner, 36, of Brooklyn, New York:

> *"I would feel guilty about doing anything for myself," says Gardner, a stay-at-home mother and a former freelance television producer. But last spring she picked up a novel she'd received for Christmas and liberated herself. Now, at least three times a week, she snuggles guilt-free under the covers in the middle of the day and savors a book for an hour while 19-month-old Rainer naps "I do laundry on weekends now, when my hus-band can watch our son," says Gardner who squeezes in more chores during Rainer's nap time on those days she doesn't read or nap herself. "The breaks keep me sane," she says. "I'm not on my last nerve all the time."*
>
> *(Jackson, 2003, p. 216)*

## Standards

A standard is an acknowledged measure of comparison or a criterion. The notion of standards incorporates the concept of value. It can be said that people have a certain set of standards, meaning that they conduct their lives in a particular way. Standards serve as guides or measures of human behavior. As discussed earlier, a more detailed definition of standards by DeMerchant (1993) describes them as quantitative and/or qualitative criteria, or measures of values and goals, that reconcile resources with demands and affect how certain tasks or activities are completed. Standards are used in a variety of fields including education, biology, and sustainability (Dietz & Grabs, 2021).

---

**Suggested Activity**

*Write a list of your routines. Which ones do you have? This could include morning rituals, bedtime rituals, driving routes, parking spaces, classroom seats, or mealtime preferences, to name only a few. Are your routines similar or dissimilar to the way you were raised?*

*What differences have you noticed between your routines and those of your roommates or friends? Discuss with others what you have written. What does throw you off your routine?*

---

Author Matthew O. Jackson (2019) says that your social position determines your power, beliefs, and behaviors. Do you agree? Standards are related to social position and relevant to this chapter on managing time because in today's fast-moving world, individuals and families often do not have enough time or energy to meet the standards they aspire to—in keeping their homes clean, exercising regularly, eating appropriately, meeting family needs, and accomplishing work. An article about daily time use in rural households in India reported that women, including pregnant women, worked an average of 14–16 hours per day (Singal et al., 1993). Their hours were split between a variety of jobs in the home, and farm and livestock management. Clearly, maintaining standards in all areas under these conditions is difficult.

Standards have both quantitative and qualitative aspects. Quantity refers to a measurable amount. Quality refers to a degree or grade of excellence, the essential character or nature of something. Quantitatively, a teacher may set a standard of grading 50 math papers an hour. Qualitatively, a person may want food prepared to a certain standard of nutrition, taste, and attractiveness.

Conflict arises in homes and organizations when people have different standards. For example, if a teacher expects to grade 50 math papers an hour, an intern assigned to the teacher who can grade only five papers an hour will fall below expectations. In a restaurant, if food is not prepared to the expected standard, a customer may send it back to the kitchen. In a home, some family members may be perfectly happy living in a mess that other family members cannot tolerate. One of the virtues of living on a college campus is the opportunity to experience the many different ways people can live and the different standards they have.

Standards of quality and quantity form the criteria for action. Demands lead to an alteration of standards. Students cramming for a test will not have time to cook dinner or go to movies with friends. Preparing for the test demands all their time and attention, so household work and friends may have to wait.

The more complex the lifestyle and the greater the number of people involved, the more regular the standards are if everyone involved is going to survive and thrive. The military is an example: Beds must be made a certain way, and rooms are inspected. Everyone wears uniforms. When 1,000 service people must be fed in one hour, food lines must move efficiently. Because of the vast numbers of people and the complexity and seriousness of their tasks, there is little room for individual choices or variations in standards.

---

### Suggested Activity

If you had a choice between earning more money at your current job and working fewer hours at your current job, which would you choose? In a survey conducted at the University of Connecticut ("The Tomorrow Trap," 1999), most workers chose more money, and men were more likely than women to choose "more money." So, we have a paradox: most American workers say they want more time with their immediate family, but they also want to earn the extra money that comes from longer hours. What do you think about this? Does it have to be time versus money? What are the alternatives? Discuss in groups.

---

## SUMMARY

This chapter focused on time and time management. Time is a limited, elastic, nonrenewable, and scarce resource. It has value. Time has been the subject of much philosophical debate from ancient to modern times such as in Malcolm Gladwell's *The Tipping Point* where he speculates on why some changes occur rapidly, why some ideas or products spread like an epidemic while others gradually evolve. For example, voice-enabled devices (such as Amazon Echo and Alexa devices) are in one in four U.S. homes and 40 percent of homes have more than one. The devices do not always get along and take homeowner's time to set up, adjust, and use them.

Time perceptions vary from individual to individual and within and between cultures; personality and preference also come into play. Network Theory indicates with larger shared network pools given technological advances and increased interactivity internationally that in the long run our time perceptions may change especially in business and organizational settings. The ABC method of time prioritizing is a useful way of managing time, as is the concept that daily time use should be related to goals sought,

Both quantitative time measures (i.e., those using units such as seconds, minutes, hours, and days) and qualitative time measures (feelings about time use) provide useful information for managing households and businesses. Time-use data have many practical applications to the home, the marketplace, and the work world. Studies show that Tuesday is the most productive day of the week.

Happiness is highest on Saturdays and Sundays with over 50 percent of Americans reporting a lot of happiness and enjoyment without much stress or worry. This drops to 46 percent on a typical Monday, according to the Gallup organization. News of imminent troubles can affect these percentages. Perceptions of time vary by a number of factors discussed in this chapter.

Demands, standards, and sequencing lead to the application of time management to work and other activities. Too little time and too much responsibility increase stress, the subject of Chapter 11. The next chapter will examine the complexity arising from trying to balance work and family life.

## KEY TERMS

circadian rhythms
communication multitasking
discretionary time
drift time
focus groups
monochronic
nondiscretionary time

Network Theory
perception
polychronic
qualitative time
    measurement
quantitative time measures
routine

sequence
tempo
time
time displacement
time management
time perception
time-tagging

## REVIEW QUESTIONS

1. Malcolm Gladwell, the author of *The Tipping Point,* says, "We are all, at heart, gradual-ists, our expectations set by the steady passage of time. But the world of the Tipping Point is a place where the unexpected becomes expected, where radical change is more than possibility" (pp. 13–14). What does he mean by this in the context of the chapter?

2. Couples often come home from work very tired and then begin the dinner and evening routines. What are solutions or ways of thinking and acting to make this transition easier?

3. What is the balance in your life between discretionary and nondiscretionary time? Which do you have more of? Often holidays and summers offer drift time. Is this true in your case? If so, do you enjoy drift time? What do you do differently?

4. What is your opinion of the quotation from David Elkind about today's hurried child? Are children overscheduled?

5. According to Mihaly Csikszentmihalyi in *Finding Flow,* people spend roughly equal amounts of daytime in three social contexts (i.e., with strangers or co-workers/students, with family and friends, and alone). Is your time similarly spent? If you could change your time, use in any way, what would you change? Explain your answers.

## REFERENCES

Ashbourne, L., & Daly, K. (2010). Parents and adolescents making time choices: Choosing a relation-ship. *Journal of Family Issues, 31*(11), 1419–1441.

Avery, R., & Stafford, K. (1991). Toward a scheduling congruity theory of family resource manage-ment. *Lifestyles: Family and Economic Issues, 12*(4), 327.

*BBC News Report.* British children among laziest. Retrieved March 15, 2008, from http://newsvote. bbc.co.uk. First published May 9, 2006.

Berry, L. (1990, February). Market to the perception. *American Demographics, 12,* pp. 30–33.

Bianchi, S. (2000, November). Maternal employment and time with children: Dramatic change or surprising conti- nuity? *Demography, 37*(4), 401–414.

Boss, S. (2000, September 25). On the clock, all the time. *Christian Science Monitor,* pp. 11, 16.

Clark, D. (1999, June 21). Managing the mountain. *The Wall Street Journal,* p. R4.

Claxton, G. (1997). *Hare brain tortoise mind.* New York: Norton.

Crossen, C. (2003, November 5). Daylight saving time pitted farmers against the "idle" city folks. *The Wall Street Journal,* p. B1.

Csikszentmihalyi, M. (1997). *Finding flow.* New York: Basic Books.

Delong, T. (2011). *Flying without a net.* Boston: Harvard Business Review Press.

DeMerchant, E. (1993). Standards: An analysis of definitions, frameworks and implications. *Proceedings of the Eastern Regional Home Management—Family Economics Conference*, Blacksburg, VA.

Dietz, T., & Grabs, J. (2021, February 16, online). Additionality and implementation gaps in voluntary sustainability standards. *New Political Economy*.

Elkind, D. (1988). *The hurried child*. Reading, MA: Addison-Wesley.

Felbus, M. (April 12, 2019). Keeping the peace, Alexa devices have to learn to get along. *USA Today*, p. 3 B.

Garfield, S. (February 3–4, 2018). We can't stop watching the clock. *The Wall Street Journal*, p. C7.

Gladwell, M. (2000). *The tipping point*. Boston: Little, Brown and Company.

Gerson, S., & Gerson, S. (2012). *Technical communication processes and product*. Upper Saddle River, NJ: Pear- son.

Godbey, G., & Graefe, A. (1993, April). Rapid growth in rushin' Americans. *American Demographics*, pp. 26–27.

Goforth, C. (2002, November 20). Most people do more on Tuesday. *Tallahassee Democrat*, p. 5E.

Goldsmith, E. (1990). The effect of women's employment on quantitative and qualitative time-use measurements: A review and synthesis. *Home Economics Forum, 4*(2), 18–20.

Graham, R. (1981). The role of perception in consumer research. *Journal of Consumer Research, 7*, 335–342.

Greene, K. (2003, June 9). How to survive the first year. *The Wall Street Journal*, pp. R1, R4.

Greene, K. (2008, September 22). Baby boomers delay retirement. *The Wall Street Journal*, p. A4.

Hall, E. T. (1959). *The silent language*. New York: Fawcett World Library.

Hochschild, A. (1989). *The second shift*. New York: Viking.

Hochschild, A. (1997). *The time bind*. New York: Henry Holt.

Jackson, M. (2003, September). Stopping the clock/creating sacred time. *Real Simple*, pp. 212–217.

Jackson, M. (2019). *The human network*. New York: Pantheon.

Jordan, M., & Karp, J. (2003, December 9). Machines for the masses. *The Wall Street Journal*, pp. A19–A20.

Kaufman, C., & Lane, P. (1993). Role overload and the perception of time pressure. In D. Thompson (Ed.), *Marketing and Education: Partners in Progress* (pp. 25–30). Proceedings of the Atlantic Marketing Association, Orlando, FL.

Koncius, J. (March 3, 2021). How the pandemic has changed the way we see and use our home – maybe forever. *The Washington Post*, At Home newsletter.

L'Abate, L., & Harel, T. (1993). Deriving, developing, and expanding a theory of developmental competence from resource exchange theory. In U. Foa, J. Converse, K. Tornblom, & E. Foa (Eds.), *Resource Theory: Explorations and Applications* (pp. 233–269). San Diego: Academic Press.

Lakein, A. (1973). *How to get control of your time and your life*. New York: New American Library.

Lakein, A. (1998). *Give me a moment and I'll change your life: Tools for moment management*. New York: McMeel Publishing.

Lindquist, J., Tacoma, S., & Lane, P. (1993). What is time: An exploratory extension toward the far east. In M. Levy & D. Grewal (Eds.), *Developments in Marketing Science* (Vol. 16, pp. 186–189). *Proceedings of the Annual Conference of the Academy of Marketing Science*, Miami, FL.

Martin, A., & Sanik, M. (1994). Determinants of married men's and women's time spent in household production in 1985. *Proceedings of the 1994 Conference of the Eastern Family Economics and Resource Management Association* (pp. 1–17). Pittsburgh, PA.

Mattingly, M., & Bianchi, S. (2003, March). Gender differences in the quantity and quality of free time: The U.S. experience. *Social Forces, 81*(3), 999–1030.

Menkes, S. (1987). *The Windsor style*. Topsfield, MA: Salem House.

Mintz, S. (2000, June 22). How juice went from stone age to ice age. *The Wall Street Journal*, p. A22.

Mutz, D., Roberts, D., & Van Vuuren, D. (1993, February). Reconsidering the displacement hypothesis. *Communication Research, 20*(1), 51–75.

Owen, A. (1991). Time and time again: Implications of time perception theory. *Lifestyle: Family and Economic Issues, 12*(4), 345–359.

Penteado, J. (1981, May 25). U.S. fast foods move slowly. *Advertising Age*, p. S-8.

Robinson, J., & Milkie, M. (1997). Dances with dust bunnies: Housecleaning in America. *American Demographics, 19,* 40.

Senge, P. (1999). *The dance of change.* New York: Doubleday.

Shellenbarger, S. (2002, September 26). Making time to veg: Parents find their kids need life balance as well. *The Wall Street Journal,* p. D1.

Singal, S., Srinivasan, K., & Jindal, R. (1993). Women's work status and their time use pattern in rural households of Haryana. *Journal of Consumer Studies and Home Economics, 17,* 99–104.

Taylor, C. (2003, May). Balancing act. *Smart Money,* pp. 77–83.

Taylor, F. (1911). *The principles of scientific management.* New York: Harper & Brothers.

The tomorrow trap. (1999, December 17). *The Wall Street Journal,* p. W16.

Walker, K. (1983). An interstate urban/rural comparison of families' time use: Introduction. *Home Economics Research Journal, 12*(2), 119–121.

Walker, K., & Woods, M. (1976). *Time use: A measure of household production of family goods and services.* Washington, DC: American Home Economics Association.

Welcome to the 36-hour day (January 30, 2007). Retrieved March 7, 2008, from http://www.emarketer.com/Articles.

Werland, R. (2000, January 11). Pressed for time? *Tallahassee Democrat,* pp. D1, D6.

Zaslow, J. (2006, August 10). Hoarders vs. deleters: How you handle your email inbox says a lot about you. *The Wall Street Journal,* p. D1.

# Managing Work and Family

DOI: 10.4324/9781003166740-10

… Unemployment claims hit a 50-year low in the United States prior to the Covid-19 pandemic.
… U.S. student loan debt is higher than credit card debt. Student loan debt is over three trillion dollars.

This chapter explores the domains of work and family life and the spillover between them. We all have concerns about how to manage our school or work life and our personal life. The aim is not only to achieve balance but also to increase fulfillment. Our daily moods fluctuate. "We may start mornings feeling pretty hopeful (at least once the caffeine kicks in), but our outlook often slumps in the afternoon before rebounding in the evening" (Brobaw, 2018, p. A15).

## CASE STUDY

### Out of Africa: Working Remotely

Work can be enjoyable and turning it off is not so easy. During a three-week trip to Africa, Steve Swasey of Netflix said he logged in and made work decisions in Africa. He says he doesn't mind working while he is traveling because he is away a lot. However, "sometimes my wife is not so sure. I've been known to hide away on the balcony of a condo in the early hours, when she's sleeping."

*Source: Shellenbarger, S. (2011, July 20). Unlimited vacation, but can you take it.* The Wall Street Journal, *p. D3.*

## CASE STUDY

### Dr. Jane Goodall, Famous Scientist, and Conservationist, Advice on Leading a Full Life

The Covid-19 pandemic found Dr. Goodall, age 86, at home in her childhood home in Bournemouth, England, spending a lot of time on Zoom living away from her usual home in Tanzania, Africa. Her case is presented here as a reminder of how locations change and as an example of an incredible life and contribution.

*Goodall first began to fulfill her dream of living among African wildlife, when, at 22, she voyaged to Nairobi aboard a boat from London. There, she met paleontologist Louis Leakey, who hired her to work as his assistant and eventually sent her to Tanzania's Gombe Stream National Park, where she began her work with chimpanzees.*

*Goodall's observations disproved major beliefs about human uniqueness, including that we're the only species capable of using and making tools and that we're the only ones who have personalities and emotions.*

She married twice and has one son.

*Source: Florsheim, L. (2021, March 15). Jane Goodall's Advice on how to lead a full life.* The Wall Street Journal.

We seek success and the right blend of activities. "Not only is work harder to measure but it's also harder to define success," says Homa Bahrami, a senior lecturer in Organizational Behavior and Industrial Relations at UC Berkeley's Haas School of Business. She says,

> *"The work is intangible or invisible, and a lot of work gets done in teams so it's difficult to pinpoint individual productivity." She says information-age employees measure their accomplishment in net worth, company reputation, networks of relationships, and the products and services they're associated with—elements that are more perceived and subjective than that field of corn, which either is or isn't plowed.*

> *(Sandberg, 2008, p. B1)*

We do not want to waste time in unsatisfying activities such as participating in an all-day work meeting or retreat with no obvious outcomes. Being productive and successful at work has an enormous impact on a person's self-esteem. Ryan explains how his performance review at work went poorly:

> *I walked into my boss's office for my performance review. I was nervous. My yearly bonus rides on a successful review, and my ego cannot handle too much abuse. "Have a seat," said my boss. He pointed to the chair on the other side of his desk. I tried to assess whether my boss was in a good or bad mood. That information would tell me a lot about whether this meeting would be easy or painful. His face looked somber and serious. Not good. My boss said, "Obviously, this meeting is to talk about your performance evaluation. Generally speaking, your performance over the past twelve months has been acceptable. There are some aspects that need improvement."*

> *(Fisher & Shapiro, 2005, pp. 116–117)*

Ryan says that is when his heart started beating rapidly. He barely heard the positive points because he focused on the criticisms, which included his lack of follow–through, not being available, and spending too much time with his family. His boss suggested that Ryan take his cell phone when going out to pick up his kids. It was a very hard message to hear. Ryan was angry.

Notice how Ryan's boss crossed the line between work and family life. There is no question that the boundaries between work and personal life are blurring. Robert Reich, former U.S. Secretary of Labor, says:

> *In the old days, we might have taken work home in a briefcase and then late at night maybe gone through it and done whatever needed to be done. Now we turn on the computer. And everything we do during the day is right in front of us. All the connections, all the people, all the problems, and all the projects are going 24 hours a day. It's not just the computer. It's the pager, the cell phone, the voicemail and the instant messaging.*

> *(Blumenstein, 2001, p. R15)*

Another way of saying this is that for many of us work and life have been squashed into one. "It can be daunting," acknowledges Erich Dierdorff, a management professor at DePaul University. He adds, "If there's already all these demands placed on you, even moving the needle a little bit on your time management skills is going to have a much larger impact, " Dr. Dierdorff says,

> *If not now, When? You don't have to be a hyper-detail-oriented, Type A personality to add boundaries to your day and streamline your schedule, Dr. Dierdorff says. Start with the basics, like learning to give priority to tasks that are important.*

> *(Feintzeig, 2021)*

## Introduction to Work and Family Research

Throughout this chapter there will be many research study results, but here are a few standouts to get us started. Bianchi and Milkie (2010) in a review of work–family research organized the family perspective into six topics:

1. Gender, time, and the division of labor in the home

2. Paid work

3. Maternal employment and child outcomes

4. Work–family conflict

5. Work and family issues and health

6. Work–family policy

One can add to this paternal employment and child outcomes, the effects of unemployment, and the many research studies from the perspective of employers, business management, and the organizational behavior side.

Family research may be specialized to certain groups like Hispanic families or African American families or military families. For example, even in peacetime family separation is an issue for military families. Over 2 million citizens serve on active duty or in the U.S. military reserve making it the largest government employer. Walmart is the largest civilian U.S. employer with 1.5 million employees followed by Amazon with 1.3 million.

> ### CRITICAL THINKING
>
> In what ways would long-term separation be a stressor for military families?

One of the difficulties in discussing work and family research is the complexity arising from combining the two major domains of everyday life. A study found that smaller organizations/employers often created more innovative nurturing environments than did larger employers (MacDermid et al., 2001). The reasoning is that smaller employers are closer to their employees and understand their needs better. They were more likely to be flexible to allow for personal or family business.

The focus of this chapter is on the resource management problems and solutions associated with balancing work and family or personal life roles. Since statistics indicate that most college graduates will marry and work full-time, the problems of combining work and family are not just societal issues but personal issues of significance for the readers of this chapter.

To give perspective, if one were to believe media outpourings, one might think that the "superwoman" and "superman" model of working and loving is a new phenomenon. It is not. People have been combining several roles for centuries. They have worked split shifts, served in the military, or in some other way worked a variety of hours or jobs or in more than one location, at the same time trying to raise a family and have a personal life. Individuals may be friends, siblings, parents, children, workers, employers, caregivers, neighbors, students, teachers, and volunteers; indeed they may play many more roles, depending on choices and circumstances. Perhaps of all these roles, work and family stand out as the most important ones to an individual's self-image and are the most demanding of her or his time.

CRITICAL THINKING

If your parents or grandparents were asked, "How successful are you at balancing your work and family life?" What would their responses be?

## Overview of Work and Family

We play roles all the time (right now you are being a student) and we want fulfilling ones. According to the book *Beyond Reason*, a fulfilling role has the following qualities:

1. *It has a clear purpose,* whether it is something big like tackling global warming or small like taking ten minutes to relax or exercise.

2. *It is personally meaningful.* This could be problem solving or helping children.

3. *It is not a pretense.* This is not about acting; this is about your life and what you want to do.

The last factor, "not a pretense," means to keep it real. A fulfilling role is one you choose to play, whether it is as a mother or father or president of an organization or being on a board of directors. Roles can be temporary or long-lasting, or conventional, provided by society or the office, or self-defined.

Adults spend most of their time sleeping (one-third of our lives); at home, alone or with families or friends; or at work. When Sigmund Freud was asked his recipe for happiness, his short answer was "work and love."

*Work can interfere with family and family can interfere with work.* With the rapid influx of women into the labor force, more awareness of work–family conflicts has ensued; there has been a shift in the public's perception of the interchange between work and family.

More and more families are feeling pressured for time and stressed from coping with conflicting work and family demands. In response, employers wanting the most satisfied and productive workers possible are re-examining childcare and elder care policies and providing flextime and other schedule changes to accommodate family needs.

**There are several facts, figures, and research findings about the work and family interchange. For instance,**

- Different generations of workers appear to react differently to similar working conditions with some groups working around the clock while others place a heavier emphasis on nesting, family, and community. They all work hard but in their own way, some requiring more flexibility and say in their schedule.

- In the United States, women on average earn less than men, but the earnings gap is closing.

- Most U.S. teenagers have jobs before they graduate from high school.

- Families with two earners, one parent, or young children are likely to experience work–family conflict and job tension.

- Spousal support has a positive relationship with a job commitment.

- The problems of combining work and family are worldwide concerns that will become increasingly important as more nations become industrialized and crowded causing more competition for resources.

- Commuter marriages (large distances, two separate households) are more common than one would think.

For over a decade a married couple has had the situation where she works as a professor in the South and he is a professor in the Midwest, they met in Ohio but she needed to go elsewhere for a job. They are older, do not have children from the marriage, and plan to retire together in one location in a few years. More extreme commuter marriages involve partners living in different countries for reasons of education, an award such as a Fulbright, corporate placement, or military service. Shared goals and purpose and constant communication are essential for making these situations work.

## Work and Family Conflicts

At the center of the work and family debate is the concern that a person who is heavily involved in one domain (work or family) may not be psychologically or physically available for the other. This can be referred to as **involvement balance.** Related to this are issues of:

1. Stress

2. Turnover or retirement intentions

3. Absenteeism

4. Substance abuse

Work and family conflict may arise when a person is torn between work and family demands, and frustration and dissatisfaction develop. It may also arise when spouses, coworkers, employers, and children differ over how work and family time should be divided.

Stress is another factor to consider. Korean researchers Cho et al. (2004) found that dual-earner families in Seoul reported far more time pressure than reported by households with full-time housewives.

### CASE STUDY

#### Overload

*Overwork went straight to Douglas Heddings' back. The founder of Heddings Property Group in New York City, Heddings has suffered from chronic stress-related back pain for more than a decade. Even as he recuperated from spine surgery, the pace didn't let up. His inbox filled at the rate of 50 emails per hour. The back problem "has a great deal to do with the fact that I feel I have to be on call 24/7," Heddings says. "This is not good for my mental and physical well-being." Researchers agree. Frequent long hours can increase stress and touch off a host of health hazards, including insomnia and high blood pressure. Poor decision-making starts to creep in.*

*Source: Robinson, J. (2011, March 22). Don't melt down. Entrepreneur. Retrieved from www.entrepreneur.com/article/printthis/219311.html.*

As one way to manage work and family demands, more couples are choosing to have children later in life. Baby boom women married late, delayed childbearing, and spaced their babies farther apart. Although some parents choose not to work outside the home when their children are young, the general trend is toward increased employment participation for mothers of infants and young children. In a classic study, Voydanoff (1989) identified several job demands that are related to work–family conflict:

- Role ambiguity (doubt or uncertainty)
- Role conflict
- Intellectual or physical effort
- Rapid change
- Pressures for quality work
- Pressure to work hard and fast
- Heavy workload

A Families and Work Institute study found that "many U.S. workers may be working too hard, leading to more mistakes on the job, neglected personal relationships, and higher health-care costs" ("Study: Many U.S. Employees Feel Overworked," 2001). Given the effects of the pandemic, the Institute emphasized one kind word "flexibility" regarding how employers can help employees manage (Kim et al., 2020).

Work pressures and constant travel strain personal and family relations. A top executive at a large retail warehouse chain said that her first trip to China was exciting but when it became four trips a year it was a strain because she had a two-year-old daughter and as a single parent she had to make extensive caregiving arrangements plus she really missed her daughter.

In an answer to the question of who would be the most time-pressured person, Susan Roxburgh's research found that the answer tis the affluent, parents, caregivers, and people in high-demand, low-control jobs (2002). In *To Love and Work: A Systemic Interlocking of Family, Workplace, and Career*, David Ulrich and Harry Dunne describe a therapy session with a busy executive who "glancing at his watch as he sat down for his first and only interview, announced that he could take one hour to decide whether or not to divorce his wife" (1986, p. 129). These authors also say that many workers treat the home as a "pit stop," or a refueling place, for the main purpose in life: getting ahead at work. Spouses and children are virtually ignored in the "pit stop" approach to home and family life.

### CRITICAL THINKING

Have you ever used your apartment, dorm room, or house as a "pit stop" or noticed that your parents did? Are clothes strewn everywhere and dirty dishes piled in the sink and on the counter? What happens when the home is simply for refueling?

## Benefits of Work and Spillover to Families

Work can allow a person to move toward goals through greater responsibility, learning new skills, and achieving a higher position. Work can benefit families and be a source of pride. Friedman and Greenhaus report in *Work and Family—Allies or Enemies?* (2000) that

- Individuals who earn a high income have healthier children and are more satisfied with childcare.

- They have greater autonomy on the job.

- They engage in networking and have family-supportive employers.

Most employees are in the labor force primarily because they or their family needs the money and secondarily because they need to use their skills and feel like they are contributing and progressing. Bonuses, promotions, praise, awards, and raises are the other benefits of work that can increase self-esteem. In addition, several studies indicate that performing the multiple roles of worker, spouse, and parent is positively related to women's physical and mental health (Voydanoff, 1989).

Benefits are also an important part of employed work that spills over into personal life. Health insurance is the most expensive and fundamental benefit. Other types include dental insurance, life insurance, retirement plans, and reimbursement for moving, travel, and training/educational expenses. The total benefits package can increase your total compensation by 30 percent or more, so although employees tend to focus on salary, they should pay close attention to benefits packages and what they offer. They should also manage the benefits by updating coverage to suit changing personal or family needs.

Another positive aspect of work is that many people enjoy it, at least certain aspects of it. For both men and women, there is even the possibility of passion (defined as personal intensity) in work expressed in experiences and emotions. According to Richard Chang (2001), a passion plan at work begins from the heart and then progresses to:

1. Discovering core passions

2. Clarifying purpose

3. Defining actions

4. Performing with passion

5. Spreading excitement

6. Staying the course

Sharing the excitement of learning and working together.

Chang says that organizations are driven and defined by their collective passions. For example, a publishing house can be driven by a love of books and literature. If fashion designers do not care about customers, how can they design apparel and accessories that excite the customer enough to want to buy? If an individual is energized or inspired by work, wouldn't it make sense that the emotion would spill over in a positive way to home and family life?

The preponderance of research literature focuses on the negative aspects of balancing work and family; but it would be irresponsible not to emphasize the benefits as well. Many people are happiest being busy in both realms. The problems arise when the roles become overwhelming. Solutions to this from a family management point of view are addressed next.

## Resolving Work and Family Conflicts

**Individuals or families may find the following approaches helpful in reducing work–family conflict:**

1. Manage the conflict so that different ideas, opinions, and approaches are brought out for discussion.

2. Resolve the conflict before it becomes too disruptive.

3. Cultivate a sense of humor and thus create an atmosphere of mutual support.

4. Take some time off—a day, a long weekend, or more. Schedule a vacation, having something to look forward to can take the pressure off day to daytime stress.

5. The pandemic transformed the way work was done, with more employers giving employees the opportunity to work remotely. They included the largest tech companies, such as Facebook, Twitter, and Google. The employees should make sure how homes are set up that can help work from home (**WFH**) to succeed. A way to reduce work-family conflict is to free WFH spaces from personal items such as household receipts, bills, paperwork, and homework not related to paid work. Too much mixing of these things results in misplaced papers and lost time while organizing.

The first option on the list is a preventive strategy, and the second can be used when conflict already exists and needs to be addressed immediately. The second strategy comes into play when the conflict interferes with family members' ability to get their work done and threatens the security and the functioning of the family as a whole and individual family members. The third strategy involves using humor as a coping skill. When family–work conflicts first emerged, everyone was quite serious about the issue, but as we've gotten more used to the conflicts as a society, some humor has emerged in the form of cartoons, online videos, billboards, magazine articles, novels, television shows and advertisements, and in-home banter. Much of the humor comes from taking situations more lightly, realizing you can't control the national economy or the universe, and accepting that mistakes happen. Humor can be a form of affection and a symbol of understanding that heals the conflict or at least soothes it. Taking vacations will be discussed later in this chapter. Working remotely keeps growing.

It is not unusual for individuals and families to hope that time conflicts will go away (e.g., things will be better next week when my report is finished or the accounts are in), but they seldom do. If the conflict builds to a crisis, the persons involved examine the cause of the frustration and discuss solutions. Conflict usually arises from one or more of the following:

- Disputes over money or about time use.

- Disputes over work involvement.

- Disputes over values, what is important.

An additional stressor on family–work conflict is when there is severe economic hardship. A national survey analysis of working Americans found that economic hardship was associated with higher family–work conflict and that this pattern was stronger among men (Schieman & Young, 2011, p. 46).

**From a family management perspective, the way work–family conflicts are resolved depends on the answers to the following questions:**

1. How strong is the individual's involvement in work? As mentioned earlier, this is called involvement balance.

2. How flexible is the work situation? Studies show time and again that flexible scheduling is associated with increased family cohesion, more balance, and less conflict.

3. Are there better ways to meet children's and spouse's needs?

Obviously, compromise is one solution to a couple's or a family's work–family conflicts. In **compromise** each person makes concessions, giving in a little to gain a valued settlement or outcome (e.g., harmony, an intact functioning family). Accommodation is another solution wherein the needs of each person are accommodated or adjusted to as best they can be.

As work–family time conflicts can be a lifelong battle and work and family demands change over time, the people involved should not rush the process. Once they agree on when to leave for work in the morning, for example, each person should regularly check to see whether the agreement is still working or whether a new schedule is needed.

## Unemployment and the Family

The number of Americans filing for unemployment hit a 50-year low in 2019 and began to rise during the Covid-19 pandemic according to the U.S. Dept. of Labor. Much of what is happening (during and post-pandemic) is a rearranging of where the jobs are and how many of them can be done remotely.

When economic times are bad, work becomes a scarce commodity and people are more willing to make compromises. Prior to the pandemic, economic recovery or expansion was happening in several countries including the United States.

In economic theory, *an unemployment rate of 5 or less is considered desirable,* and an unemployment rate of 10 percent or more is considered an indicator of depression. During the Great Depression of the 1930s, unemployment went over 10 percent and since then there have been places in the country (e.g., when a plant closes) that have experienced unemployment rates of over 10 percent. In other nations of the world, 15 percent or more unemployment is not unusual. Each country has its own way of defining what is normal when it comes to unemployment.

Although this chapter so far has focused on the problems of combining work and family life, there are problems associated with not having enough work, being underemployed, and being unemployed. What happens to the work and family interchange when a breadwinner suddenly is out of work? Going from eight hours of work per day to zero requires an adjustment of time and ego as well as an adjustment by the family to the loss of income and benefits. Most of the studies on unemployment were done in the Great Depression and focused on men. Since the recession of the 1980s, the downsizing of companies in the 1990s, and the 2006–2010 recession, studies investigate the effects of unemployment on both men and women. During the 2006–2010 recession, housing prices dropped or steadied, foreclosures went up, and retirement investment plans went down in value (in some cases plummeting to half their former value) spurring more people to stay employed longer or change their investing strategy. In recent years, house sales and home repairs rose and home mortgage rates were low. Many people were regrouping to find new areas of employment.

---

### CRITICAL THINKING

#### Anticipating Change

React (agree or disagree):

President John F. Kennedy once said, "The time to repair the roof is when the sun is shining," By this he meant, one has to fix a potential problem before it gets out of hand.

---

When people are on social assistance (welfare) and getting ready to re-enter the job market they experience stress, economic hardship, and even trauma. A resource is **SNAP** which stands for the Supplemental Nutrition Assistance Program, an American federal assistance program formerly known as the Food Stamp Program. A Canadian study found that mothers who are re-entering the workforce experienced time crunch, overload, and work–family conflict (Gazso, 2007). This study illustrated that low-income workers have even more trouble balancing work and family concerns than experienced by higher-income workers because they have less flexibility and fewer resources to fall back on. Quality childcare and dependable transportation are issues.

Larson, Wilson, and Beley (1994) found that stress stemming from job insecurity is related to marital and family dysfunction and a host of family problems. Unemployment is a crisis event affecting all aspects of a person's and a family's life including resource management and social support systems. In a study of 216 unemployed women in Louisiana, the researchers found that the women sought and successfully obtained assistance from relatives and friends (Retherford et al., 1989). The women's parents were especially helpful in providing emotional support. Overall, the way people react to unemployment depends on the length of the unemployment period, the circumstances surrounding the unemployment, and the potential for future employment, as well as the strength of the family support systems and financial status of the unemployed person. Suggestions for helping partners/spouses find jobs include

- Letting the unemployed spouse guide the pace of the job search. There will be days of totally unproductive time; resist asking about the search daily.
- Listening to the spouse: Where do they really want to work? What do they want to do?
- Talking about your workplace, keeping the conversation going.
- Doing things (nonwork-related) to show that you care.

When unemployment rises nationally, workers cut back on sick days, and as a result, absenteeism goes down during economic hard times. People worry that if they are not at their desks, they are more vulnerable to layoffs. The policy of having sick days is being re-considered especially with the changing environment of working remotely.

Owing to changes in the U.S. economy, increasing numbers of blue-collar workers in the steel, automotive, rubber, textile, apparel, and electronic industries have been vulnerable to extended unemployment, permanent job loss, or re-employment at lower wage and benefits levels (Smith & Price, 1992). A study of women workers who lost their jobs in textile and apparel plants in Georgia provides insight into how the loss of work affects families. The researchers found that the stage in the family life cycle and the demands of combining productive work and family responsibilities contributed to the women's experience of unemployment and their labor market participation (Smith & Price, 1992). For example, one woman in the study observed:

> It's kind of nice, really, being at home with children. I spent 20 years working and my mother-in-law raised the kids because I had to work. My husband likes it too. He likes me cooking for him, being at home when he comes home and not running around trying to clean and cook and take care of the children. (p. 67)

Another participant in the study reacted differently:

> After you've worked all this time and paid for things, you feel guilty, like you're not doing your part. It's hard to get used to not carrying your own weight. You worry about emergencies if you've only got one insurance carrier, lose a sense of security. I miss being independent. When we go on vacation I would put my own portion in the pot. It's really a change—I've learned to be dependent. I guess I've learned who was in charge. Just giving up the independence [from] bringing home a good salary was something. (p. 69)

## Social Support and Work and Family

As the previous quotations indicate, the interchange between work and family involves many issues. Both men and women experience work–family conflict. Frone (2000) asserted that men and women suffer poor health from work stress effects. Many studies have shown that marriage usually has a positive effect on the physical and mental health of the couple. Children of married parents also experience better health than children of single parents. Marriage seems to improve health for all involved (Koball et al., 2010).

Perrewe and Carlson (2002) found that social support played a greater role for women than for men in reducing family-interference-with-work conflict.

> Social support is at the core of the work-family interchange. We need to know more about what types of social support (at the workplace and at home) are the most effective, what works best. Again, it appears that values come into play. What does the employee value?
>
> (Goldsmith, 2007, p. 164)

Generally, far more is known about the effects of work on family than vice versa. Ulrich and Dunne (1986) observed that many of the ways that people react to work, employers, and coworkers are based on early childhood experiences, especially relationships with parents and siblings. The boss may serve as a parent figure, and how the employee responds to that boss may have a lot to do with how she or he perceives authority. Loyalty to parents and the family unit may spill over into loyalty to the firm. Relationships between coworkers may be a reliving of the childhood give and take between brothers and sisters.

Going beyond childhood experiences into the present day, it is acknowledged that marital satisfaction and family responsibilities affect work performance and a person's motivation to work. Thus, severe personal or family problems affect work performance. Someone going through a difficult divorce or having problems with children may talk about his or her problems at work and be distracted from the tasks at hand. Many employers including colleges and universities offer **Employee Assistance Programs (EAPs)** to help workers and families with emotional, financial, and legal difficulties, and problems such as alcoholism and drug abuse. For example, more than 97 percent of the nation's largest companies (AT&T, DuPont, McDonnell Douglas, and General Motors, to name a few) offer EAPs but few take advantage of them. Not knowing about them is one reason another is the possible stigma attached although confidentiality is assured (Hoyt, 2017).

Americans generally rate their life satisfaction quite high: 78 percent rate their satisfaction at 4 or 5 on a 5-point scale but engaged workers (those who identify with their work and actively promote company objectives) are more likely to say a 5 than a 4 ("Gallup Study Finds," 2003). The kinds of statements that the Gallup Organization uses to reach these conclusions include "I have gotten the important things I want in my life" and "The conditions of my life are excellent." Among the actively disengaged employees, 51 percent reported that they behaved poorly at home during the past month, whereas only 18 percent of engaged employees reported this. According to the Gallup study, divorced people are slightly more likely to be actively disengaged.

Countries around the world have various cultural norms and family-supportive policies. For example, The Netherlands is a nation "with a strong cultural norm of mothers staying at home or working limited hours. Although this argument holds for many countries, what sets The Netherlands apart from other European countries is that this norm is largely realized" (Mills & Täht, 2010, p. 861). This means that the preference and behavior of Dutch mothers is to stay home and not work at all or to work part-time.

## Family-Supportive Workplace Policies

EAPs are one example of the increased commitment of work organizations to provide family-supportive policies and practices. Other solutions, programs, or changes that support more family–work balance include:

- A compressed workweek (e.g., working 4 days a week at 10 hours per day vs. 5 days a week at 8 hours per day). The state of Utah tried this but then went back to a five-day workweek. Some universities and businesses close at noon on Fridays or have a policy of being closed on Fridays in the summer. The four-day work week nationwide is currently under debate.

- Part-time hours or alternative work schedules. Studies show that perceived control (such as of schedules) increases perceived balance (Tausig & Fenwick, 2001).

- Job sharing.

- Tuition reimbursement.

- Self-employment, which is becoming an increasingly popular option. Men who are self-employed report greater job satisfaction and more job-to-home spillover when there are small children in the family.

- Married, self-employed women report less negative spillover from job to home, greater job satisfaction, and less job burnout (Hundley, 2001).

- Access to outside services. For example, help for workers in finding (and in some cases paying for) childcare and elder care.

- On-site seminars on topics ranging from identity theft to stress prevention to better writing skills or off-site in Zoom meetings.

- Mentoring programs.

- Wellness programs. These might include on-site fitness centers, free on-site health checkups, exercise classes, low-cost flu shots.

- Flexible hours. Let employees make up their own schedules within a range of acceptable hours. "Regardless of the source of the flexibility, the need is clear. Everyone concerned needs to cut families a little slack up front, to avoid tearing the delicate fabric of family life" (Shellenbarger, 1999, p. B1).

- WFH and telecommuting which is a catchall word for working from anywhere, most likely from home. This is a popular alternative to physical headquarters 8-to-5.

Like a growing number of people, Shannon Bryant long dreamed of working from home. Stuck in traffic commuting for more than an hour a day, wishing for more personal time, she hated "feeling like I was in the rat race," says Ms. Bryant, a healthcare consultant. But she hadn't a clue how to ask her boss for a change. She found help in an unexpected place: The Internet. On a friend's advice, she searched websites on job flexibility and found a template for a telecommuting proposal to hand to her boss. After some homework and preparation, she presented the proposal and won approval. She's now seven weeks into her new work-at-home setup, and it's going well (Shellenbarger, 2003, February 13, p. D1). The following are more ways to enrich work–family balance:

- Achievement awards. These should go beyond plaques and into usable items such as movie passes, restaurant vouchers, gift cards, company stock, designated parking spaces, and bonuses. An influencer, leader, or manager has reward power and should use it (Goldsmith, 2015).

- Dry-cleaning services, food shops, low-cost cafeterias, after-school care and childcare centers on-site, and free dinner for those working late delivered to the office. As economies slowed worldwide, many firms cut back on these extras, but as economies pick up and employee happiness and retention move to the forefront the perks return. Also, certain younger industries such as high-tech ones tend to offer these perks more than older industries do. **Perks** (a shortened version of the word **perquisites**) can misfire if they are unevenly distributed, if popular ones are discontinued, and if staffers would rather have raises than perks. Perks are social experiments, and the wise manager keeps abreast of which perks are favored.

- Drop-in centers. These mini offices (satellite offices) in the suburbs allow employees to avoid the commute into the city every weekday. Another option is free shuttle buses or vans from satellite offices or shopping center parking lots to downtown.

- On-site educational services or online webinars. Examples are free or subsidized classes such as certificate programs or Master of Business Administration classes for employees with bachelor's degrees who are moving into management positions and aiming to get higher degrees.

How successful are these methods? Companies report that they help lower absentee rates and improve employee retention, especially in highly mobile fields, such as technology. Policies, programs, and services that relieve stress such as dress-down or casual Fridays should diminish absenteeism. Ideally, employees should have input into what options are offered. Consistency within companies and across companies would also be helpful for employees who transfer or change jobs.

## Family and Medical Leave Act (FMLA)

In recognition of the difficulty of combining work and family, many nations and companies have developed specific policies regarding employee leave for personal, family, or health reasons. As previously mentioned, policies vary greatly by country and by employer. Many countries offer paid leave for mothers and more than a dozen offer paid paternity leave for a couple of weeks or up to 14 months in Sweden. In 2000, 12.4 percent of eligible Swedish fathers took leave and that percentage nearly doubled in 2010.

### Henrik

*One of Henrik Holgersson's friends laughed in his face when he told him he was going to spend the better part of 2011 as a stay-at-home dad. "What kind of a man are you?" the friend asked Holgersson, who works for an event management company. But just about everyone else was positive. His employer and coworkers patted him on the back and wished him luck. Holgersson took out 240 days of parental leave paid for by the government while his girlfriend, Jenny Karsson, went back to her job as a real estate agent, after eight months at home with their son, Arvid. "To take care of Arvid is a real fatherly thing to do. I think that's very masculine," said Holgersson, 34, gently rocking his 1-year-old son's stroller on a walk around the block near his apartment in Sweden.*

*Source: Nordstrom, L. (2011, October 25). Swedish dads swap work for childcare. Associated Press, Tallahassee Democrat, p. 4.*

In the United States, in 1993 President Bill Clinton signed the Family and Medical Leave Act (FMLA), which allows workers at companies with more than 50 employees to take up to 12 workweeks of *unpaid leave* to care for newborns and newly adopted children or to care for ill family members or themselves. So, if you are an eligible employee, you are entitled to 12 weeks of leave for certain family and medical reasons during a 12-month period. Can an employee be fired if he or she takes FMLA leave? No, it is unlawful for an employer to interfere with or restrain or deny the exercise of any right provided under the Act. However, it should be noted that many U.S. workplaces, such as retail shops, grooming salons, and architecture and consulting firms, have fewer than five employees; so, many employees are not covered by FMLA. About 60 percent of the U.S. workforce is eligible for leave under FMLA, but few take it, mainly because it is unpaid.

Prospective parents who meet the qualifications set out in the Act no longer have to be concerned about whether they will be allowed to be away from work before, during, and after the birth of their child (leave) or whether they will have a job to come back to (job security). Adoption and foster care are covered as well as the illness of a child, spouse, or parent. More details of the Act are given in Table 10.1.

Many employers had policies in place long before the passage of FMLA. In a 1993 survey of 524 companies, 7 out of 10 respondents said they already offered leave to employees for adoption, family illness, or childbirth, and that costs of such policies were insignificant ("Most Small Businesses Appear Prepared to Cope with New Family Leave Rules," 1993). The *Wall Street Journal* article that reported the survey quoted one employer's comments:

*As far as we're concerned, it's not a problem, says Bill Parsons, president of Palmer Johnson Inc. The Sturgeon Bay, Wis., boat builder already grants family leave to its 350 employees. "In an era where companies are competing for employees, the enlightened companies have already thought about how to handle and treat employees with respect," he adds.*

("Most Small Businesses," 1993)

Table 10.1  The Essence of Family and Medical Leave Act of 1993

The Family and Medical Leave Act applies to all public agencies, including state, local, and federal employers, local education agencies (schools), and private-sector employers employing 50 or more employees in 20 or more workweeks in the current or preceding calendar year within a 75-mile radius.

- Covered employers must grant an eligible employee up to a total of 12 workweeks of unpaid leave during any 12-month period for the birth of a child or placement of a child for adoption or foster care, for the care of a seriously ill child, spouse, or parent, or in the case of his or her own serious illness.

- Employers have to continue health care coverage for the employee during the leave.

- Employers have to guarantee that employees will return to either the same job or a comparable position.

- Employers can refuse to reinstate certain highly paid "key" employees after their leave. Such employees are defined as the highest paid 10 percent of the workforce and whose leave would cause economic harm to the employer.

- Employers can exempt employees who have not worked for at least one year and who have not worked for at least 1,250 hours, or 25 hours a week, in the previous 12 months.

- A doctor's certification has to be obtained to verify a serious illness. Employers may require a second medical opinion.

- Employers can substitute an employee's accrued paid leave (such as sick or annual leave) for any part of the 12-week period of family leave.

- Under some circumstances, employees may take the leave intermittently, by taking leave in blocks of time or reducing their normal weekly or daily work schedule.

- Employers are permitted to require an employee taking intermittent leave for planned medical treatments to transfer temporarily to an equivalent alternative position.

Source: Goldsmith, E. (1993). Family leave: Changing needs of the world's workers. United Nations, Occasional Paper Series, No. 7, p. 6.

## The Meaning of Work and Leisure

The next part of this chapter explores the meaning of work and leisure and its managerial implications. **Work** is effort expended to produce or accomplish something or activity that is rewarded, usually with pay. **Effort** is exertion or the use of energy to do something (Goldsmith, 1993). Because so many hours are spent in work, it makes a tremendous difference to one's overall sense of contentment and growth. Thomas Carlyle, a 19th-century British historian and essayist, wrote, "Blessed is he who has found his work; let him ask no other blessedness." A fascinating study by Roehling, Roehling, and Moen (2001) explored the concept of company loyalty and how it fits into the work and family debate. They found that flextime policies have an almost universal employee loyalty payoff and that childcare policies help as well. Even more important is the existence of an employee-friendly atmosphere. Employees appreciate supervisors who are sensitive to work–family conflicts.

*The average workweek today is about 30 percent shorter than it was over a hundred years ago.* Around 1900, a six-day workweek was common. In 1938, President Franklin D. Roosevelt signed the Fair Labor Standards Act, which established a 44-hour workweek, which was reduced to 40 hours by 1941. A generation ago, the conventional wisdom among economists was that America was turning into an "affluent society," in which ever more efficient technology would produce an abundance of wealth requiring less and less labor. This did not happen for a variety of reasons, but the end result is that U.S. workers are working more at this point in American history than was predicted. The four-day workweek is still elusive. Choice of occupations has increased significantly. In 1850, the U.S. Census listed 322 job titles; today there are over 31,000.

> *The fact hit home for me when I returned to the U.S. in 1996 after a decade abroad. I began to notice that not one of the other seven people in my office left their desks at lunchtime, the way folks used to. the Bureau of Labor statistics reports that since 1985 paid vacation time has declined, and so has the average time that workers take off sick. Not surprisingly, more than one-third of the people in the FWI survey said that they often or very often feel used up at the end of the workday.*
>
> *(Hunter, 1999, p. 38)*

## Feeling Overworked

Even if working at home, an employee can feel overwhelmed by the endless Zoom meetings and reports that are due. Explain your story. Do you feel overworked? The typical American spends 15 percent of his or her life at the office (or another way of saying this is in paid work) so what happens during that time greatly affects health and relationships with coworkers as well as with family and friends.

> *Traditionally, researchers have focused on the ways in which different labor affects the body, investigating the hazards associated with activities such as coal mining, truck driving and professional football. In recent years, however it has become clear that even seemingly safe workplaces can negatively influence well-being. This is largely because jobs don't just take a physical toll—they also exact a mental price*
>
> *(Lehrer, 2011, p. C22).*

Nonstandard work schedules can result in greater relationship dissatisfaction—an example of the spillover from work to home. Working overtime not only brings in extra money but also extra stress in an already overwhelmed family. It happens in many jobs that working evenings and weekends is not compensated with money. The employee is expected to show up to award dinners, to take guests around, to go to parties and events. These extra duties may sound pleasurable but after an eight-hour workday with commuting on top and taking time away from family and friends, these are not fun. One woman did not get home until 10:30 after a Thursday evening event and said she could not do it anymore.

Notice the body language of this overworked employee.

Sometimes a person really is working too many hours and other times they simply feel overworked because it is not just about quantity but also about intensity. According to a report by Galinsky, Kim, and Bond titled "Feeling Overworked: When Work Becomes Too Much,"

> Feeling overworked is a psychological state that has the potential to affect attitudes, behavior, social relationships, and health both on and off the job. Information from our focus groups suggested that feeling overworked is often an acute condition, which may largely subside once work demands decrease, rather than a chronic condition—though for some employees it is clearly an ever-present feeling.
>
> (2001, p. 6)

As may be expected, employees with poorer-quality jobs and less control express the most dissatisfaction. Is it possible to improve the workplace or organizational culture?

### CRITICAL THINKING

#### Organizational Culture

*According to John Arnold and Ray Randall et al. (2016, p. 592), "Organizational culture may be crucial to an organization's performance but it is also difficult to understand and change." Why is it so difficult for organizations to change? If you were a director or manager, what would you do? In Work Psychology. UK: Pearson.*

The kinds of things that lead to poorer jobs include less job autonomy, more wasted time, fewer learning opportunities, the lack of affordable health insurance, and less job security. Less-supportive workplaces, characterized by inadequate materials and equipment, inadequate support from people at work, inadequate flexibility to manage work and family responsibilities, and lack of respect, also add up to feeling overworked and unappreciated. Overworked employees reported more work–life conflict, loss of sleep, higher levels of stress, poorer coping skills, less successful personal relationships, and health problems and were more likely to neglect themselves than were workers who said they were generally not feeling overworked.

**What are the implications for employers? Several categories of concern include**

- workplace safety
- job performance
- retention (keeping workers)
- health care costs

**Work psychology** is a field of study and practice that "concerns all aspects of human behavior, thoughts, feelings and experiences concerning work" (Arnold et al., 2016, p. 16). Within it, there are important themes of diversity, gender, fostering pleasant work environments, and improving fairness in pay, training, and opportunities for advancement. An extensive study titled "Staying Ahead of the Curve 2003: The AARP Working in Retirement Study" (2003) of workers ages 45–74 found that they most wanted

1. A friendly work environment
2. A chance to use skills and talents
3. A chance to do something worthwhile

4. Respect from coworkers

5. The opportunity to learn something new

The main conclusion is that workers 45 and older treasure their work as a way to connect with others and to contribute to society, and they have practical concerns—such as making money.

## Work Ethic

**Work ethic** is the degree of dedication or commitment to work. Americans pride themselves (as do other nations) on having a strong work ethic. The *Journal of Business Ethics* has articles on work ethic studies across several nations and groups such as an article on Islamic values and work ethic from data gathered in Pakistan (Haq et al., 2019).

**Commitment** refers to the degree to which an individual identifies with and is involved in a particular activity or organization (Goldsmith, 1993). Work ethic is alive, well, and even flourishing in the United States (Brokaw, 1999). Here are the typical hours worked by various populations, according to a report from Bright Horizons Family Solutions in Watertown, Massachusetts,

- United States' employees average 1,966 hours a year.

- Japan's employees average 1,899 hours a year.

- England's employees average 1,731 hours a year.

- Sweden's employees average 1,552 hours a year.

- Norway's employees average 1,399 hours a year.

Work ethic is part of an individual's value orientation and, hence, is linked to managerial behavior. Individuals who adhere to a strong work ethic appear to be more polite, responsible, and conservative; they also tend to resist social change and be rigid (Furnham, 1987; Tang & Tung, 1988). Predictability, discipline, and order are also associated with a strong work ethic (Feather, 1984).

Workplaces can capitalize on the work ethic by investing in their employees by offering training and travel opportunities and in so doing investing in the company and the company's future. Work ethic is an internal motivator but the employer can infuse new energy into it. Here are some options:

- Tech seminars or as previously mentioned webinars or online conferences

- College courses onsite or online

- Industry-specific training or certificates

- Continuing education classes

## CASE STUDY

### Driven Professionals

*Driven professionals possess tunnel vision when it comes to getting jobs done with all due speed and effectiveness. They're very impatient with any obstacle or anyone who gets in the way of reaching the desired outcome. One doctor admitted that he became frustrated with those who got in the way of his crossing things off his list—who prevented him from finishing a task when he wanted to do it or assembling the resources necessary to purchase state-of-the-art medical technology. This was also true when he was home and his young children didn't achieve what he felt they should achieve …*

Source: DeLong, T. J. (2011). *Flying without a net. Boston, MA: Harvard Business Review Press.*

The concept of work ethic has been redefined based on the switch to the knowledge economy. The new workplace requires specific skills (often online-related) and a great deal of employee discretion. Some workplaces allow the use of cellphones or IPads at work, others do not and some allow the employer to look in on the use of office computers. If too much time is spent on personal messaging, then the employee, who is informed of this potential practice ahead of time, is talked with and adjustments made. Many employees would find this too constrictive and would look for a more flexible workplace.

Many organizations reward employees who interpret and respond to change, including the unpredictable moods and actions of other people. Thus, discipline remains an important attribute, but to strive to learn, to conquer new problems, and to find solutions are more likely to generate success than mere dutiful drudge work. "The knowledge economy gives us not only the opportunity but also the obligation to reunite work with independent thinking, self-expression, and even joy" (Postrel, 1998, p. A10). Even Scott Adams, the creator of the comic strip "Dilbert," which pokes fun at the workplace, says, "I'm not at all sad about the state of work right now. I think people are generally happier than they've been in a long time" (Stafford, 1998, p. 2E).

As work ethic is based on values, adherence or nonadherence to a work ethic is a form of self-expression and definition. People develop a work ethic or not depending on what they feel is important and if it is of a driven nature then inborn temperament plays a role as well. Educators and parents influence the development of work ethic in children by rewarding work performance. The overall culture, the economy, and work environments further contribute to the development and the sustenance of a work ethic.

## Workaholism and Vacations

**Workaholism** refers to the inability to stop thinking about work and doing work, and the feeling that work is always the most pleasurable part of life. Work satisfies the need to be recognized and approved of in a way that the other realms of life cannot satisfy.

### CASE STUDY

#### 'Game of Thrones' Music Maestro

Ramin Djawadi is the award-winning composer behind "Game of Thrones" and "Iron Man." When asked: "To what do you credit your success?" He said:

*Hard work. That kind of goes hand-in-hand with what I like about my job – I really love what I do. I've always wanted to do it, so it makes long hours and hard work a lot easier. I work every day, including Saturdays and Sundays – I would say every day is a Monday for me – and I just really like to work hard, which I always do…It's very difficult, especially now that I have little twins. With kids, it makes it even harder. One of the things I did is that I built a studio at home so I could work at home a lot.*

*Source: Susannah Hutcheon (April 16, 2019). Meet the "Game of Thrones" music maestro. USA Today, 4B.*

Most workers are simply people who enjoy doing hard work and as the case study of Ramin Djawadi shows they make adjustments as children come along.

True workaholics may have trouble sleeping, relaxing, going on vacation, or spending time alone or with their children and spouse. Here is an example:

*Publishing consultant Aaron Sigmond and his wife recently went to the Hudson Valley in upstate New York for a 10-day vacation. After a grueling work schedule, the couple needed time to regenerate and commune with the breezy Catskill Mountains, the lulling flow of the Hudson River and the gently sprawling fields of nearby farms. The only problem: They couldn't stand it. Four days before the vacation ended, they left the Victorian house they had rented. "The peace and quiet and solitude just wore on me," says Mr. Sigmond. "It was just the most stressful vacation ever."*

*(Sandberg, 2003, p. B1)*

In an essay, the author Mark Kingwell says,

*The values of work are still dominant in far too much of life; indeed, these values have exercised their own kind of linguistic genius, creating a host of phrases, terms, and labels that bolster, rather than challenge, the dominance of work …'Don't fire me! I don't want to be out of work!' Work looms larger than ever …*

*(July 2011, "The language of work," Harper's Magazine, p. 19).*

Twelve percent of American workers never take vacations, and the United States does not have a nationally mandated vacation policy for workers. U.S. workers effectively give back over $21 billion a year to their employers by not taking vacations (Sandberg, 2003). Some blame it on capitalism, materialism, competition, worry about job security, and upward mobility. Vacations can seem like a step backward for workaholics: they feel they will fall behind. Others find work stress to be predictable, even enjoyable; vacations involve a lot of unknowns. During tough economic times, some fear that if they leave for a vacation their job won't be there when they return and this fear sometimes becomes a reality.

## CASE STUDY

### Jared

Jared was an engineer who had worked for a firm for 15 years as a project manager. He went on a family vacation for a week and on his return was met at the front door of the office building where he was employed and told he was fired and to return at 4 P.M. and a box of his belongings would be brought to him. He had no warning. He

> was not allowed to go to his office to clean out his desk or to say goodbye to cow-orkers. It was a shock. He drove around and finally went to a coffee shop where he spent the day before returning for his box which had family photos and a few odds and ends. He found out later that others had been let go in the week that he was gone. The firm gave him two months severance pay and it took him four months to find another job. Jared has since changed jobs two times and has not found a job as much as he liked the first one.

In terms of Freud's definition of happiness as a combination of work and love, the constant workaholic may be neglecting the "love" side of life in favor of the "work" side. One myth about workaholics is that they are the most productive workers in a home or in an organization. This is usually not true because workaholics are addicted to work, not necessarily to goal attainment. They lack organization, and their energy is not channeled properly. Workaholics often suffer from fatigue and stress and may experience health problems from a lack of exercise and rest. They also lack a sense of balance, and this deficiency may spill over into a failure to understand why other employees or family members do not also work constantly.

In short, workaholics may be difficult to live with at home or at the office. A hard worker is different from a workaholic. A hard worker realizes that work is just one part of life, tolerates others' mistakes and her or his own, stays on top of work schedules, cares about others, and can choose to stop working—such as taking lunch breaks without worrying.

Gerson (2010) says we need flexible families as well as flexible workplaces to function smoothly. Workaholics truly need flexible families and understanding about their need for over-achievement and their inability to stop thinking about work (DeLong, 2011). As a remedy for tunnel vision as a form of workaholism, Thomas DeLong recommends seeking a range of experiences, looking within organizations for numerous opportunities for learning and growth, volunteering, and talking with others. The answer is not to isolate but to reach out.

The case study about Jared reinforces that taking a vacation may be taking a chance but this is a rare occurrence and, of course, the layoffs were about to happen in his company, his vacation had nothing to do with it. More and more companies are redefining their vacation policies and realizing the value of vacations. As an example, Netflix, a streaming business, with 800 employees near the beginning was offering three to five weeks off a year. Netflix has since grown to over 9,400 employees. The Motley Fool, a financial services company, was offering four weeks on average. Traditionally, employees had to work at a company for six months before they were given a paid vacation but a growing number of employers are offering "no vacation" or "open-ended time off" policies that leave it up to the employee or employer to agree on how much vacation is right. There is also more variance in when the employee can take a vacation. Some employees find this liberating while others would like more structure. What would be your preference?

## The Three Ps: Procrastination, Parkinson's Law, and Pareto's Principle

In contrast to a workaholic who constantly works or thinks about work, a **procrastinator** puts off work and postpones decisions. Procrastinators are difficult to work with because they seldom finish tasks on time and consequently often disappoint their coworkers and employers. They are difficult to live with too because they often forget or fail to meet family obligations.

Everyone procrastinates now and then, but procrastination is excessive when it is pervasive across all arenas of life. When this happens, procrastination is more than a bad habit—it has become a lifestyle. Procrastination is a way to escape responsibility and resist the structure of growing up. It may be related to a fear developed in early childhood or to an unresolved conflict.

Sometimes, a person procrastinates because he or she really does not want to do whatever is required. A child who dislikes playing the piano will delay practicing. A child who continually avoids practicing may be signaling that he is no longer interested. In that case, perhaps the piano lessons should stop and another activity or free time be substituted. Someone who constantly procrastinates on work assignments may be in the wrong job and would be happier elsewhere.

Some individuals (e.g., students putting off studying for a test and pulling an all-night cramming session) say they like the feeling of rushing to meet deadlines and the excitement of the last-minute push; they insist that they perform best when living on the edge. This approach may work for them some of the time, but what if others are relying on them for information (e.g., a team report for a class), there is a family crisis, or they become ill the night before an assignment is due? Procrastination can be overcome if the procrastinators are willing to change by rearranging their approach to assignments and rewarding themselves for planning ahead and being on time.

Another concept related to the organization of work is called "Parkinson's law." In 1957, the English historian C. Northcote Parkinson studied the Royal Navy and found that the more people hired, the more work they created, without necessarily increasing the organization's output. His observation led to the formulation of **Parkinson's law,** which states that a job expands to fill the time available to accomplish the task. This law illustrates the elasticity of time and work.

Parkinson's law is evident in people who have a lot of time on their hands. They may take all day to mail a letter or to go grocery shopping. They stretch a routine task that could be completed in half an hour into an all-day expedition.

The third P of working and its organization is the Pareto principle. Vilfredo Pareto, a 19th-century Italian economist and sociologist, discovered that in any series of elements to be controlled, a selected small fraction of the elements always accounts for a large fraction of effectiveness. The **Pareto principle**, also known as the 80–20 rule, states that 20 percent of the time expended usually produces 80 percent of the results, while 80 percent of the time expended produces only 20 percent of the results. According to this principle, the bulk of an individual's time is wasted in low-productivity activities. The solution to this phenomenon is to recognize that it exists and focus more of one's attention on the activities and relationships that matter and put less time and energy into things that do not.

## Workforce Trends

There are many trends in the workplace. One stressor is underemployment wherein the individual takes employment beneath their level of education and experience. Another stressor is recent college graduates struggling to pay back student loan debt. Total U.S. student loan debt exceeded credit card debt and runs over $3 trillion.

In the workplace, another trend is *sustainability* which may refer to policies and practices with lasting value or to going green: introducing environmentally friendly policies such as car pooling and recycling. It refers to providing lasting quality impact. In sustainable organizations, the management takes the leadership position that home, work, and community would benefit from green policies and incentives. It reflects their ethics as a company. A payoff can be that being green helps bolster recruitment efforts and provides an environmentally friendly/healthy workplace. A specific example is NRG Systems, a Vermont company, which offered a $1,000 bonus each year to employees who bought a Toyota Prius. Of the 85 employees, 26 purchased a car the first year (Spors, 2008). Other companies are switching to electric vehicles for work use such as trucks for hauling.

Another trend is simply *more people working more than one job* in a variety of settings or *working longer hours*. A person may be an administrative assistant by day and a waitress on nights and weekends. The average full-time job, although officially 40 hours, is in reality about 47 hours per week, according to Juliet B. Schor's book *The Overworked American* (1991), and can go to the extreme of 60 hours or more. Workers also report long commutes, chirping cell phones, never-ending emails or twitters, and lost weekends. The "lost weekends" concept (time spent reading reports, grading papers, answering emails, etc.) illustrates the blurring of the distinction between work and leisure.

Another trend is that *the workforce is aging* as the baby boomers move forward through life. The Age Discrimination Act of 1967 protects most workers ages 40 and older from discrimination in the workplace.

A worldwide trend is a *redefinition of work space*, whether at home or in more traditional workplaces. The move is away from individual offices and cubicles into shared spaces and shared computers (many on wheeled tables), workstations, and so forth. It's all about mobility. "People are working in a variety of different settings. They're moving constantly, both within the office and outside the office" (Powers, 1998, p. 21). An early experimenter with reducing office space was Anderson Worldwide, which reduced the office-to-employee ratio from 1:1 to 1:5.3 in its San Francisco office, thus saving on the cost of rent, furnishings, and utilities. As more and more companies scatter their employees around the globe, they will be relying more on technology to bring people together rather than on a physical space.

*Mobility* is also evidenced by people moving from job to job, and therefore from location to location, more often today than in the past, according to Phyllis Moen of Cornell University. She says that "The lock-step template of American life is obsolete This has enormous consequences for policy, employers, communities, families, and individual lives" (Powers, 1998, p. 14). For young people, job hopping is very common. A typical American holds 8.6 different jobs between the ages of 18 and 32, with most changes occurring before the age of 27, according to the Bureau of Labor Statistics. The point at which a worker on the rise becomes a worker who's consigned to history is coming earlier in people's careers, usually around age 44, according to the Bureau of Labor Statistics. To avoid plateauing, workers are encouraged to try new projects, mentor younger workers, take assignments abroad, and/or get fresh training so as to keep their careers lively, interesting, and challenging.

In the United States and in other developed countries, the workforce is "graying," meaning more workers are getting older. By 2015, older workers (55 and up) will account for 20 percent of the workforce. Studies show that older workers are actively engaged in constructing their work lives and their identities as workers (Work, Life, and Social Class, 2004). People's careers are no longer linear with a distinct beginning and ending. Rather, they are unpredictable and involve many phases in and out of employment or with different employers.

Another trend is **downshifting**: opting for a simpler life, usually less pay, less stress, more time, in a more personally satisfying occupation. Basically, in downshifting, a person decides that more is not always better. The individual's reduced income is offset by a more frugal lifestyle. Obviously, downshifting is not for everyone. Someone whose self-worth is measured by status and money would have a hard time turning his or her back on a large income. So, who should consider downshifting? Not those who truly love their career and enjoy consuming to the hilt:

> But others, like Jacque Blix, just feel trapped in that world. For years, an unhappy Ms. Blix couldn't leave the AT&T marketing job that brought her a good salary and the status of succeeding in a non-traditional role for women. "I felt if I took less money I'd be taking a step backward and denying my potential as a human being," she says. Eventually, she and her husband, David Heitmiller, a corporate product manager, did downshift, saving 30% of their income over three years to finance their corporate exits. They tell their tale in their book, Getting a Life. "We saw that we could live with less income and still be happy," she says.
>
> (Lancaster, 1998, p. B1)

## Home-Based Work and Telecommuting

As has been discussed already in this chapter, it is hard to ignore the growing WFH trend. Home-based work and the increase in the amount of telecommuting is also called telework or mobile work. It is a work arrangement in which employees do not have to be in a central workplace such as an office building on a specific schedule or they may only have to come into the office for in-person meetings one to three days a week. Estimates vary as to the number of telecommuters there and a potential source for figures is the U.S. Bureau of Labor Statistics and for federal employees a source is the United States Office of Personnel Management. Rather than exact numbers, the point to remember is telecommuting is a growing trend and it reduces organizational, space, and transit costs, saves energy and fuel, and enhances work–life balance. Technological advances have made telecommuting more feasible and efficient.

Telecommuting may be through an employer or may be through self-employment; and, as stated earlier, there is a rise in the number of self-employed. The term "home-based work" in some ways is outdated because so much of work is done at airports, on commuter trains, and in all kinds of locations. This section refers to work done outside of a traditional office or workplace.

### CASE STUDY

#### Sophia

Sophia is 49 years old and a public relations manager with clients. She works out of her home to save money on renting an office space. Since she and her husband are empty nesters their home has extra space for home offices, but she prefers to go out. So every weekday she takes her laptop and heads for Panera's, a restaurant that provides free wi-fi and an atmosphere that she likes. Sophia knows a lot of the regular diners and the staff. She gets coffee and something to eat and settles into her favorite spot and stays there for hours. She writes, meets clients, responds to radio interviews, nearly everything and she says this way she is around other people which she likes and doesn't have to worry about giving directions to her house or cleaning it up.

The information age, with its emphasis on online information and communication, has made it possible for more people to work from many locations, but this trend is not without its problems.

Work meetings can take place anywhere.

> *It didn't take Tony Bono long to figure out he had a problem with telecommuting: "My mailman was scared of me," he says. A new job assignment had led him to start working from his Cherry Hill, N.J. home. But Mr. Bono soon grew so lonely that he found himself waiting for the mailman each day and racing to greet him: "Hey! Hi, Tom, how are you doing? Want to come in and have a drink?" Mr. Bono recalls saying. He wasn't surprised when the postman started avoiding him. It's an ironic twist on corporate America's march toward telecommuting: A small but significant number of foot soldiers dislike the trend.*
>
> (Shellenbarger, 2006, p. D1)

The mail person manages his or her time too. The sooner the mail is delivered the sooner he or she can return the truck and go home.

Working from home has implications for interpersonal relations including family relations and involves management considerations such as the arranging of childcare and the allocation of time, technology, money, and space (Tausig & Fenwick, 2001). Researchers have found that for women the overwhelming reason given for working from home is the ability to take care of young children while earning an income. Another reason is the difficulty of finding outside employment has forced many people to be creative. A nine-state study concluded that

> *Demands imposed through the complexity of the family were related to increased intrusions by means of telephone calls and space conflicts, illustrating that homebased workers and their families must learn to manage the realities of overlapping tasks. Resources can undoubtedly mediate these intrusions if the family can afford a separate office or workspace for the business, or a phone line dedicated exclusively to the business, but when financial resources do not allow additions such as these, the throughput process of the home-based worker and his or her family becomes even more important.*
>
> (Fitzgerald & Winter, 2001, p. 88)

So having enough space is a key factor in success. Another factor is time management.

Methods such as the dovetailing and overlapping of activities described earlier in this book come into play as home-based workers juggle their work and family responsibilities. Owen, Carsky, and Dolan provide this insight into home-based work:

> Even the choice of a home-based occupation over a market job may reflect a commitment or priority by the worker to meeting the needs of the family, especially when family demands are high, such as when young children are present. The degree to which home-based workers can control the various aspects of time may influence the satisfaction derived from the work and from the family/work interface.
>
> (1992, p. 136)

The stereotype of a home-based business is a female-owned enterprise such as a childcare center. But that is inaccurate; a survey revealed that 59 percent of home-based workers are male. The typical person is about 44 years old, married, and employed in a white-collar profession such as marketing, sales, or technology—for example, software engineering. Kathryn Stafford, a professor at Ohio State University who worked on a study with Barbara Rowe of Purdue and George Haynes of Montana State, said: "We found that most home-based workers are men performing traditional work in fields like sales and construction" (DeLisser & Morse, 1999). They also found that home-based business owners were better educated and more affluent than the rest of the population. A further finding was that 88 percent of home-based owners sell most of their products or services within their state or an hour's drive from their homes. For example, in Ohio, home-based work contributes more to the state's personal income rolls than farming does.

In the late 1990s, 30 million Americans were working from home at least some of the time, the highest share being among those ages 18–29 (Allen & Moorman, 1997) and the trend continues. Are home-based businesses the nirvana people hoped for? It saves on commuting time and saves on renting office or warehouse space but in some cases, other problems surface.

> Many home-office workers feel as though they're working in a vacuum. They feel isolated and struggle with a perception that they're not quite "legit." They lament the loss of support staff, employer-provided educational opportunities, health insurance, pension plans, and paid vacation time. They scramble to find suitable places to meet with clients. Those who run businesses also run the risks of running into zoning and IRS audits.
>
> (Allen & Moorman, 1997, p. 57)

So, start-ups and home-based businesses, like the other trends, have their pluses and minuses. The next few decades will determine how these trends play out; which continue, which don't; and in what ways they will be altered as people search for new options. Notice the number of people who get out of their homes and take a laptop to Starbucks or another coffee shop and set up for several hours as a way to get around others and get different atmosphere. Some people work better with a "buzz" around them than total silence.

One switch is the inclusion of more office space and built-in desks in new home construction, although it should be noted that wireless communication affects home space in other ways.

> The bedroom will become the new frontier of multitasking, as growth in wireless technology allows work to expand into once-sacred domains of the home. Homes with wireless networks will grow to nine million in the coming year Mark Chernis takes his laptop to bed—a habit he says brings him and his wife closer. In the past, they had to go to separate rooms wired for Internet use to go online after hours. "It used to be,

*'Good night, Honey, I'll see you later.' And I'd get this sad face from her," Mr. Chernis says. Now, he and his wife retire together "and she falls asleep on my shoulder while I'm working on my laptop," says Mr. Chernis, president of Princeton Review. Similarly, if his wife wakes up in the night, she grabs a laptop they keep by their bed and browses the Internet.*

*(Shellenbarger, 2003, December, p. D1)*

## Volunteer Work: Donating Time

So far, this chapter has focused on paid work. Another type of work that requires time, energy, and commitment is **volunteer work**, or work that does not generate pay. *About half of all Americans volunteer each year in the nonprofit sector.* This compares to about 13 percent in Germany and 19 percent in France. Regarding charitable donations, Germany leads the group, followed by the United States, and France ("Review & Outlook," 1999). Canadians volunteer in large numbers, especially in community service.

People perform volunteer work for several reasons, but one of the most important is their sense of social consciousness. They want to contribute to their family's well-being (e.g., by volunteering for Boy Scouts or Girl Scouts, coaching, or the PTA) or to contribute to others and to the community. Many of the volunteers are stay-at-home mothers or fathers who head school committees and run large volunteer organizations and boards. These experiences and contacts are useful to them when they re-enter the workforce.

Volunteer work also provides a sense of self-worth and self-esteem and heightened social and leadership skills. It is of enormous economic value to society. It provides social cohesion and solidarity. Recognizing the worth to the community, some businesses and government agencies allow workers to take time off to perform volunteer work such as tutoring or helping with school events. They may actively build partnerships. Volunteerism used to conjure up the image of a kindly lady volunteering at the hospital or through her garden club. Today, volunteers come from all ages, races, and income levels.

High schools and universities are offering courses and credit for volunteer service. The courses teach students how to work as volunteers and managers of organizations that have goals other than making a profit. For example, Donald Tobias and Stephen Watson teach such a course at Cornell University. The goal of their course is to introduce students to the management practices and principles in the public sector and nonprofit organizations.

*"At Cornell we aren't just turning out students who will be actively involved in careers," Tobias says, "We also are helping to produce people who will be citizens in their communities. Many of our students may become members of boards of directors for not-for-profit organizations, so they need to know how those organizations work and how to think strategically about management decisions and strategies based on the mission of the organization."*

*(Mackin, 1998, p. 10)*

## Managing Work and Leisure

Earlier in this chapter under the section titled "Workaholism and Vacations," the subject of vacations was introduced because workaholics have a difficult time taking vacations, but the subject of leisure is much bigger than simply vacations. **Leisure** is defined as freedom from time-consuming activities, tasks, duties, or responsibilities. As seen in the last chapter, studies show that we have more leisure time today than in the past, but it does not feel like it. How does one get in the relaxation or leisure zone? Read the case study.

**Being in the Zone**

*By mile 10 of my first half marathon, the persistent, frigid drizzle had forced my fingers into a clenched C shape. The thrill of running alongside thousands of people after weeks of solo training had mellowed into a quiet, somewhat dull drive toward the finish line. Then, without warning or conscious effort, my body started moving faster. The hard pavement felt like a supportive mattress. A sense of elegance freed me from my clumsy body. I was – there is no other way to put it – at one with the cityscape around me. I was in the zone.*

Source: Jessica Wapner (April 11, 2019). Being in the zone is great. but how do you get there? Washington Post, p. 13.

What Jessica could have been experiencing is a "second wind" whereby initial energy is followed by a lull and renewed in a second spurt of energy related to how our muscles react to extreme exercise. In Chapter 1 in Figure 1.2 we had Maslow's Hierarchy of Needs, Abraham Maslow, a psychologist, was also the first academic to write about what he called 'peak experiences' moments of elation that come from pushing ourselves in challenging tasks (Wapner, 2019). This concept was pursued further by Mikaly Csikszentmihalyi with his concept of being in "the flow" which is a highly focused mental state explained in his book *Flow: The Psychology of Optimal Experience* (1990). He is a leader in positive psychology. **Time bursts** occur when an individual concentrates for 15–20 minutes on a task with no outside interruptions and no use of the Internet or mobile phones or daydreaming (Goldsmith, 2020). Harnessing time bursts, putting them to use, can lead to a lot of work (paid work, volunteer work, housework, creative work) being done in a short time. After this level of intensity could follow a need for change such as moving around or a short break and then perhaps, a second wind, a second time burst, will ensue.

Leisure time is interspersed throughout people's lives (such as reading, going to plays and school events, jogging, text-messaging, or spending time with family and friends) and is formally designated as vacation time. The amount of time typically designated for vacations varies considerably by country. As previously noted, the United States does not have required vacation laws.

Is it possible to have too much leisure? What amount of vacation per year do you think is the right amount? Universities vary in their policies about when they are shut down. A typical time is between Christmas and New Year, and

U.S. colleges close for the whole of Thanksgiving week in November. What do you think of these policies? If you live in a country other than the United States, what are typical days that your university is shut down for holidays and/or vacation time?

*By almost every measure, Europeans do work less and relax more than Americans. According to data from the Organization for Economic Co-operation and Development, Americans work 25 percent more hours each year than*

> the Norwegians or the Dutch. The average retirement age for European men is 60.5, and it's even lower for European women. Our vacations are pathetically short by comparison: The average U.S. worker takes 16 days for vacation each year, less than half that typically taken by the Germans (35 days), the French (37 days) or the Italians (42 days) …For most Americans, work is a rock-solid source of life happiness. Happy people work more hours each week than unhappy people do and work more in their free time as well.
>
> (Brooks, 2007)

Why is there a difference between countries? Labor experts say powerful unions, especially in Europe, have negotiated hard for more vacation time and have enjoyed political support as time off has become intertwined with economics.

Though it is a matter of intense debate, some European governments argue that the combination of more holiday time and a shorter workweek translates into more jobs. U.S. workers, on the other hand, have focused more on pay increases and WFH. "We've got a cultural problem with leisure time," says Herbert Rappaport, a professor at Temple University. "We are an overworked, overtired, underpleasured culture" (Sandberg, 2003, p. B1).

Weekends are usually times of increased leisure. Studies indicate that men have more leisure time for themselves and spend less time on weekend household chores than women do. Interests and hobbies garner the maximum weekend leisure activity time for both men and women; playing with children comes second. In a study of 1,404 men and 1,623 women, researchers found that men were more likely than women to respond to overload by cutting back (Higgins et al., 2010).

In *The Harried Leisure Class* (1970), Linder argues that high hourly earnings make time so precious that many people cannot afford the time it takes to enjoy life on a daily basis and are forced to eat meals on the run, cut short the foreplay of lovemaking, attend short religious services, and browse or glance at books rather than read them. For example, Neil, a college professor, says he reads movie and book reviews but rarely has time to see a movie or read a book cover to cover. By reading reviews, Neil can still converse with his colleagues. He is not distressed by his busy lifestyle and says that at this stage in his life he really values work over leisure. He spends most of his time in work-related pursuits most of which he finds stimulating and pleasurable.

In view of such approaches to work and leisure, what part does leisure play in human life? People must answer this question for themselves. One person's idea of leisure is sewing; another prefers to play tennis or paddleboard. Leisure was once mostly associated with social or recreational activities (e.g., snowmobiling, boating, swimming), but it now includes relaxation and meditation as well as more lively pursuits. In its broadest context, *leisure is a state of mind*. Not everyone has the time or the resources to go elsewhere to enjoy recreation and leisure. Thus, there is a growing worldwide recognition of the need to provide leisure facilities such as parks and fitness trails in crowded urban areas.

## SUMMARY

The advice is set boundaries, take control of work and life—easier said than done especially when working remotely. Workplaces are re-inventing themselves. Some say investing in their employees is a way of investing in their company and the future. Several ideas were given of how workplaces can do this with cost-effective solutions that re-spark the work ethic in all of us.

The fundamental message of this chapter is that work and family are two of the most important domains in our lives. We try to figure out ways to balance these domains or roles and find fulfillment. Flexible families and workplaces ease the balancing act. If an individual is so heavily involved in one domain that it impedes the other, it is called involvement balance.

This chapter emphasized the importance of social support meaning the support of family, friends, and cow-orkers, in combating work stress and finding a life balance. It also focused on the problems of managing work and family life roles and provided solutions to work–family conflicts. The positive aspects of work were explored along with the stressors associated with it.

In the United States and other developed nations, the workforce is "graying," meaning the proportion of older workers in the total workforce is higher. Employers and governments are re-examining childcare, elder care, vacation, and family medical leave policies to accommodate employees' needs.

Many countries offer paid leave for personal and family reasons. More than a dozen countries offer paid paternity leave with Sweden being one of the leaders in offering substantial time off for childcare. The U.S. Family and Medical Leave Act of 1993 is an example of a national work–life policy for men and women. About 60 percent of the U.S. workforce is eligible to benefit from it; but because it offers unpaid leave, fewer than one would expect take it.

The three Ps—procrastination, Parkinson's law, and Pareto's principle—are important to understanding the organization of time, work, and personal or family life. This understanding includes the internal motivator of the work ethic, the phenomena of workaholism, and the harnessing of the power of time bursts. Today's workforce includes more women and members of minority groups as well as more home-based workers. Telecommuting can have its drawbacks including an increased sense of isolation. Social media reduces isolation.

Americans have surpassed the Japanese in an average number of work hours. Researchers have found that the benefits to the employer of having work–life-friendly policies are increased company loyalty and employee retention.

Not all work is paid; volunteer work and creative activity are important parts of many people's lives. Just as work is changing, so is leisure. Indeed the amount of leisure is increasing, but it does not feel like it to many people. Legally required vacation days vary worldwide. The United States does not have legally required vacation days, but they exist in Finland, Sweden, Australia, Colombia, and Japan, to name a few. About 12 percent of American workers never take vacations. Too little time off and too much responsibility can lead to stress, the subject of the next chapter.

## KEY TERMS

| | | |
|---|---|---|
| commitment | leisure | telecommuting |
| compromise | Pareto principle | time bursts |
| downshifting | Parkinson's law | volunteer work |
| effort | perquisites (Perks) | work |
| Employment Assistance Programs (EAPs) | procrastination | workaholism |
| | SNAP (Supplemental Nutrition Assistance Program) | work ethic |
| flextime | | WFH (work from home) |
| involvement behavior | | work psychology |

## REVIEW QUESTIONS

1. How do you envision your future workplace/office? Will there be more flexibility and telecommuting? What other perks do you see? Do you anticipate a change from the standard forty-hour workweek?

2. List three ways individuals and families can help resolve work–family conflict. Which one do you think is most effective?

3. The Russian playwright Chekhov said that life and work are inseparable. Our work is not in competition with our lives—it is merely one part of life. And in the end, we will be remembered for what we did with our lives and how we lived it. Do you agree or disagree? Explain your answer.

4. What is the difference between a hard worker (as in the composer Ramin Djawadi case study) and true workaholism? Do you know any workaholics? Are there consequences to not stopping thinking about work or taking a vacation or break?

5. What is your definition of leisure? Why would 12 percent of the American workforce never take vacations?

## REFERENCES

AARP. (2003). *Staying ahead of the curve 2003*: The AARP Working in Retirement Study. Retrieved March 31, 2004, from http://research.aarp.org/econ/multiwork_2003.html.

Allen, K., & Moorman, G. (1997, October). Leaving home: The emigration of home office workers. *American Demographics, 19*, 57.

Arnold, J., Randall, R., et al. (2016). *Work psychology.* UK: Pearson.

Bianchi, S., & Milkie, M. (2010, June). Work & family research in the first decade of the 21st decade. *Journal of Marriage and Family, 72*(3), 705–725.

Blumenstein, R. (2001, September 10). Is there a downside to being connected all the time? *The Wall Street Journal*, p. R15.

Brobaw, E. (January 10, 2018), Hacking the clock. *The Wall Street Journal*, A15.

Brokaw, T. (1999, May–June). The way we worked. *Modern Maturity*, pp. 42–43, 49.

Brooks, A. (2007, June 20). Happy for the work. *The Wall Street Journal*, p. A16.

Chang, R. (2001). *The passion plan at work.* San Francisco: Jossey-Bass.

Cho, H., Lee, K., Lee, Y., Kim, O., & Kim, Y. (2004). A study of time pressure and life satisfaction of Koreans. *Research and practitioner's paper abstracts* (p. 41), XXth International Federation of Home Economics Congress, Kyoto, Japan.

Csikszentmihalyi, M. (1990). *Flow: The psychology of optimal experience.* New York: Harper & Row.

DeLisser, E., & Morse, D. (1999, May 18). Enterprise. *The Wall Street Journal*, p. B24.

DeLong, T. (2011). *Flying without a net.* Boston, MA: Harvard Business Review Press.

Feather, N. (1984). Protestant ethic, conservatism, and values. *Journal of Personality and Social Psychology, 45*(5), 1132–1141.

Feintzeig, R. (March 7, 2021). Time management tricks to take back control of your calendar. *The Wall Street Journal*. 8 pm ET online.

Fisher, R., & Shapiro, D. (2005). *Beyond reason: Using emotions as you negotiate.* New York: Viking.

Fitzgerald, M., & Winter, M. (2001). The intrusiveness of home-based work on family life. *Journal of Family and Economic Issues, 22*(10), 75–92.

Friedman, S. D., & Greenhaus, J. H. (2000). *Work and family—Allies or enemies.* New York: Oxford University Press.

Frone, M. (2000). Work-family conflict and employee psychiatric disorders: The national comorbidity survey. *Journal of Applied Psychology, 85*, 888–895.

Furnham, F. (1987). Work-related beliefs and human values. *Personality and Individual Differences,* *8*(5), 627–637.

Galinsky, E., Kim, S., & Bond, J. (2001). *Feeling overworked: When work becomes too much.* New York: Families and Work Institute.

Gallup study finds that misery at work is likely to cause unhappiness at home. (2003, June 23). Retrieved December 1, 2003, from http//gmj.gallup.com/home.aspx.

Gazso, A. (2007, December). Balancing expectations for employability and family responsibilities while on social assistance: Low-income mothers' experiences in three Canadian provinces. *Family Relations, 56,* 454–466.

Gerson, K. (2010). *The unfinished revolution: How a new generation is reshaping family, work and gender in America.* New York: Oxford University Press.

Goldsmith, E. (1993). Family leave: The changing needs of the world's workers. *Occasional Paper Series,* No. 7, International Year of the Family, Vienna, United Nations.

Goldsmith, E. (2007). Stress, fatigue, and social support in the work and family context. *Journal of Loss and Trauma, 12,* 155–169.

Goldsmith, E. (2015). *Social influence and sustainable consumption.* Cham: Springer.

Goldsmith, E. (2020). *Time bursts.* White Paper by author.

Haq, I., Rahman, Z., & De Clercq, D. (2019). Explaining helping behavior in the workplace: The interactive effect of family-to-work conflict and Islamic work ethic. *Journal of Business Ethics, 155*(4), pp. 1167–1177.

Higgins, C., Duxbury, L., & Lyons, S. (August 2010). Coping with overload and stress: Men and women in dual-earner families. *Journal of Marriage and Family, 72,* 847–859.

Hoyt, A. (2017, August 22,). Why hardly anyone uses employee assistance programs. *HowStaffWorks.*

Hundley, G. (2001). Domestic division of labor and self/organizationally employed differences in job attitudes and earnings. *Journal of Family and Economic Issues, 22*(2), 121–139.

Hunter, M. (1999, May–June). Work, work, work, work! *Modern Maturity,* pp. 36–41.

Kim, S., Galinsky, E., & Pal, I. (2020, April). One kind word: Flexibility in the time of Covid-19. *Families and Work Institute.*

Kingwell, M. (July 2011). The language of work. *Harper's Magazine,* p. 19.

Koball, H., Moiduddin, E., Goesling, B., & Besculides, M. (2010). What do we know about the link between marriage and health. *Journal of Family Issues, 21*(8), 1019–1040.

Lancaster, H. (1998, January 20). "Downshifters" find more balance in life by shrinking careers. *The Wall Street Journal,* p. B1.

Larson, J., Wilson, S., & Beley, R. (1994). The impact of job insecurity on marital and family relationships. *Family Relations, 43,* 138–143.

Lehrer, J. (2011, August 20–21). Your co-workers might be killing you. *The Wall Street Journal,* p. C22.

Linder, S. (1970). *The harried leisure class.* New York: Columbia University Press.

MacDermid, S., Hertzog, J., Kensinger, K., & Zipp, J. (2001). The role of organizational size and industry in job quality and work-family relationships. *Journal of Family and Economic Issues, 22*(2), 191–216.

Mackin, J. (1998, Summer). Learning to be an effective volunteer. *Human Ecology Forum,* pp. 10–14.

Mills, M., & Täht, K. (2010, August). Nonstandard work schedules and partnership quality: Quantitative and qualitative findings. *Journal of Marriage and Family, 72,* 860–875.

Most small businesses appear prepared to cope with new family-leave rules. (1993, February 8). *The Wall Street Journal,* pp. B1–B2.

Owen, A., Carsky, M., & Dolan, E. (1992). Home-based employment: Historical and current consideration. *Journal of Family and Economic Issues, 13*(2), 121–138.

Perrewe, P., & Carlson, D. (2002). Do men and women benefit from social support equally? Results from a field examination within the work and family context. In D. L. Nelson & R. J. Burke (Eds.), *Gender, Work Stress, and Health: Current Research Issues* (pp. 101–114). Washington, DC: APA Books.

Postrel, V. (1998, September 4). The work ethic, redefined. *The Wall Street Journal,* p. A10.

Powers, M. (1998, Spring). The new template of American life. *Human Ecology Forum,* pp. 13–32.

Retherford, P., Hildreth, G., & Goldsmith, E. (1989). Social support and resource management of unemployed women. In E. Goldsmith (Ed.), *Work and Family: Theory, Research, and Applications*. Newbury Park, CA: Sage.

Review & outlook: A Christmas story (1999, December 17). *The Wall Street Journal*, p. W17.

Roehling, P., Roehling, M., & Moen, P. (2001). The relationship between work-life policies and practices and employee loyalty: A life course perspective. *Journal of Family and Economic Issues, 22*(2), 141–170.

Roxburgh, S. (2002). Racing through life: The distribution of time pressures by roles and role resources among full- time workers. *Journal of Family and Economic Issues, 23*, 121–145.

Sandberg, J. (2003, July 30). Sun, beach, sand—I think I'd rather be back in the office. *The Wall Street Journal*, p. B1.

Sandberg, J. (2008, February 19). A modern conundrum: When work's invisible, so are its satisfactions. *The Wall Street Journal*, p. B1.

Schieman, S., & Young, M. (2011). Economic hardship and family-to-work conflict: The importance of gender and work conditions. *Journal of Family and Economic Issues, 32*(1). 46–61.

Schor, J. (1991). *The overworked American*. New York: Basic Books.

Shellenbarger, S. (1999, May 12). New research helps families to assess flaws in work plans. *The Wall Street Journal*, p. B1.

Shellenbarger, S. (2003, February 13). If you'd rather work in pajamas, here are ways to talk the boss into flex-time. *The Wall Street Journal*, p. D1.

Shellenbarger, S. (2003, December 18). Polish your resume, emailing in bed, a peek at next year's work-life trends. *The Wall Street Journal*, p. D1.

Shellenbarger, S. (2006, August 24). When working at home doesn't work: How companies comfort telecommuters. *The Wall Street Journal*, p. D1.

Shellenbarger, S. (2011, July 20). Unlimited vacation, but can you take it. *The Wall Street Journal*, p. D3.

Smith, S., & Price, S. (1992). Women and plant closings: Unemployment, re-employment, and job training enrollment following dislocation. *Journal of Family and Economic Issues, 13*(1), 45–72.

Spors, K. (2008, February 26). Workers get incentives to live greener. *The Wall Street Journal*, p. B12.

Stafford, D. (1998, October 28). New "Dilbert" book chronicles "Joy of Work." *Tallahassee*.

Study: Many U.S. employees feel overworked. (2001, May 16). Retrieved August 8, 2001, from www.cnn.com/2001/CAREER/trends/05/16/work.study/index/html.

Tang, T., & Tung, Y. (1988). *Some demographic correlates of the Protestant work ethic*. Tulsa, OK: Southwestern Psychological Association (ERIC Document Reproduction No. ED 300 702).

Tausig, M., & Fenwick, R. (2001). Unbinding time: Alternate work schedules and work-life balance. *Journal of Family and Economic Issues, 22*(2), 101–119.

Ulrich, D., & Dunne, H. (1986). *To love and work: A systemic interlocking of family, workplace, and career*. New York: Brunner/Mazel.

Voydanoff, P. (1989). Work and family: A review and expanded conceptualization. In E. Goldsmith (Ed.), *Work and Family: Theory, Research, and Applications*. Newbury Park, CA: Sage.

Wapner, J. (April 11, 2019). Being in the zone is great. But how do you get there? *Washington Post*, p. 13.

*Work, life, and social class: A life-span perspective* (2004, Fall/Winter). Wellesley College, MA: Wellesley Centers for Women.

Chapter **11**

# Managing Stress and Fatigue

## MAIN TOPICS

Theoretical Frameworks

Stress Research

Crises and Adaptation to Stress

    Planning and Organizing

    Outsourcing

    Decision-Making and Stress

    Psychological Hardiness and Resilience

    Theory of Adaptive Range

    The Body's Response to Stress

    Diet, Exercise, and Stress

Stress Management

    Type A and Type B Personalities

    Techniques for Reducing Stress

    Job Stress

    Burnout

    Nonevents and Virtual Events

DOI: 10.4324/9781003166740-11

## DID YOU KNOW THAT...?

Burnout problems are increasing in different ways.
Children experience stress just as adults do

## CASE STUDY

### A Carefree Hour

*When Karen Haley sidles up to the bar near her husband, she asks for the bill right away and does a mental check of the time. There's no room for endless banter, dessert or even a bathroom break. They need to go their separate ways – one to day care and preschool, and the other to elementary school – for the 6 p.m. pickup of their three young children. "We have time for a beer and 30 minutes of conversation," says Ms. Haley, 39, an Indianapolis non-profit executive. "It's kind of a ticking clock." Mini-dates are the more practical cousin of a Saturday night out.*

*Source: Alina Dizik (May 9, 2018). Overbooked parents try mini-dates. The Wall Street Journal, A 9.*

After the mini–date in the case study could follow the evening routine as in the next case study. After some sleep, then the morning routine. Americans are working more and sleeping less according to the American Time Use Survey by the U.S. Labor Department. The average amount of time Americans spent sleeping fell by five minutes to eight hours and 30 minutes and time spent working went up for men. "Men's increased work hours signal that a healthier job market is stemming a tide of labor-force dropouts" (Cheney, 2017).

## CASE STUDY

### Hot Buttons

*"Families tell us there are two times of the day that are their hot buttons: getting ready for school and the evening with all their kids' homework and cooking dinner," says Scott Thomas, national director for architecture at builder Pulte-Group Inc. Since laundry rooms are too small and most people use the back entry to their homes, "we've created the drop zone," says Mr. Thomas. The drop zone is being brought into older homes, too. Washington, D.C., real-estate agent Laura McCaffrey says she finds herself increasingly building them*

> *into mud rooms, hall closets or basement walls. "A place to actually put stuff is a much more sought-after area," she says. "A closet with a pole and hangers won't do."*
>
> Source: Mitra Kalita, S. (2011, November 2). Blueprint for a New American home. The Wall Street Journal, p. D1.

Coping with stressful times of the day is one of the most difficult things that families do. The case study shows that home builders and realtors are responding to their needs.

Here is another coping example, this one focusing on the spillover from family to work:

It is a huge challenge to focus on work when something major happens in your personal life. Even under normal circumstances, employees struggle to balance personal and work responsibilities. When personal demands skyrocket, that delicate balance can collapse, whether the cause is happy—such as planning a wedding or preparing for the birth of a child—or not, such as a family illness. At times, focusing on work can feel nearly impossible. Some strategies can help: Planning, organizing, and compartmentalizing, say career advisors. (White, 2006, p. B8)

Following on the last chapter, this quote shows the interchange of work and family life and provides solutions in the form of strategies for dealing with stress, the subject of this chapter along with fatigue management.

The word "stress" has many definitions, but for the purposes of this book, **stress** refers to the body's reaction to a demand, or a physical or an emotional situation that causes imbalance. It can get in the way of managing responsibilities even simple tasks. Stress affects:

- How you feel

- How you behave

- How you think

- How you decide

*Stress usually involves a state of tension. It is considered a process rather than an end state.* A process implies that changes occur over time and across different situations.

Stress may be related to anxiety, fatigue, burnout, and decreased satisfaction with personal and work lives. It may also be linked to higher rates of absenteeism, quitting, and moving; poorer physical and mental health; and lower rates of commitment to jobs and relationships.

Stress is as natural as breathing but learning how to strategically handle stress is something we all have to do. Diverse family forms, more work demands, care of the chronically ill and disabled, and other pressures on individuals and families stretch human resiliency as far as it can go.

Managing stress, fatigue, and sleep is the subject of this chapter. Rapid information transfer is just one example of the many stresses encountered in today's world. Fatigue, a concept covered extensively in early management books and courses, has re-emerged as a significant management/wellness problem. People are not getting enough rest and relaxation. They spend their weekends running around, getting ready for the next workweek. There is just too much to accomplish in too little time. In addition to examining the effects of stress on families and society, this chapter will offer suggestions on ways to manage stress and fatigue.

---

**CRITICAL THINKING**

How do you define stress? What causes stress to you? Think about what affects you emotionally and physically. What would you like to do differently? Do you believe that happiness comes from within and making peace with the past is part of that?

---

## Theoretical Frameworks

There are several useful frameworks for understanding how stress affects individuals and families. The *Process of Social Stress Theory* says that a broad array of conditions combine over time to create a process of stress. The three main domains of stress are:

1. Sources of stress

2. Mediators of stress

3. Manifestations of stress (physical, mental, relational)

A way to diminish stress is to have social support (as resources) to fall back on when times get hard or when changes are occurring too rapidly. As individuals and as families "we need to prepare ourselves for the possibility that sometimes big changes follow from small events, and that sometimes these changes can happen very quickly" (Gladwell, 2000, p. 11).

*Family ecology theory* emphasizes how the family interacts with the environment. Major sources of stress are factors outside the family like epidemics, crime, work demands, and foul weather. People are far more sensitive to the environment than they are aware. The stress literature tends to emphasize relational stressors, but environmental stressors are equally important. Noise, pollution, poor lighting and ventilation, crowding, isolation, vibration, lack of adequate parking, static, litter, car fumes, and poorly insulated and designed homes, factories, and offices are all examples of environmental stressors.

---

**CRITICAL THINKING**

### Crowding Causes Stress

Is the area you live in increasing or decreasing in population? Crowding causes stress. It can be temporary such as at a street fair or parade or it can be permanent and building like in crowded cities and metropolitan areas around the globe. In the United States, two Texas metropolitan areas are growing at a faster pace—Dallas-Ft. Worth-Arlington and Houston—The Woodlands—Sugarland (each gained over a million people in less than ten years), and they are followed by Orlando and the Phoenix area. Another form of stress is when places are decreasing in population or popularity causing house prices to drop such as in Greenwich, Connecticut (bedroom community to New York City). To be a **metro area** it has more than 50,000 people according to the Office of Management and Budget.

*School and work are particularly stressful because these environments are central to most people's lives, and they view their self-worth in terms of their success or failure in these areas. Ray, a university vice president, has an office overlooking a construction site. He says the pounding starts at 8 A.M. and goes constantly until 5 P.M., and this is the prognosis for the next two years. He is stressed. How can he talk with people or write reports under these conditions? The pounding starting at 8 a.m. is a trigger or event and if it does not start until 8:15 Ray waits for it.*

## CRITICAL THINKING

Pauline used to work in advertising for the local newspaper. Now, she has another full-time job, but her son's school keeps asking her to handle the advertising for their annual holiday bazaar. She wants to say no. Should she? What are her options?

Technology can lead to more stress or stress relief.

Source: Creative Eye/MIRA.com

In *family systems theory*, the family is viewed as a system where each member influences the others. As in any system, boundaries need to be set.

People exhibit stress in lots of ways: replying angrily to a child, experiencing road rage, and showing impatience to service providers. Daily hassles that build up stress include annoying practical problems, disappointments, disagreements, and family and financial concerns (Garrison et al., 1994). Contributing to these everyday stresses are the new technologies and constant streams of information. For example, owing to instant messaging, messages that once took weeks to arrive are now immediate and require instant responses. The pressure to respond and participate is enormous.

Clutter is a source of a great deal of stress. So, getting rid of mental as well as physical clutter is a de-stressor. According to the federal government's National Institute for Occupational Safety and Health (NIOSH), more than half the workers in the United States view their job as a major stressor. Although this is a U.S. study, the author of this book would like to point out that students and faculty around the world have said that managing stress and fatigue is a significant problem in their lives and that this chapter and the one on time management are their favorites. Too much stress is not just a North American problem; it is a world-wide problem. No wonder people dream of a carefree mountain or coastal vacation.

## Stress Research

A person who is stressed experiences several stages or levels of stress. For example, getting ready to give a speech involves many stages: preparation, writing, rehearsal, and delivering the speech. Stress may occur at any or all of these stages.

It will be stated several times in this chapter that stress is inevitable. Although there seems to be more stress today than ever before, stress is timeless. It exists in all societies no matter how primitive. In fact, the potential for stress exists whenever one person interacts with another or with the environment. An approaching hurricane or tornado is stressful, and so is an approaching belligerent ex-boyfriend or ex-girlfriend.

As these examples suggest, stress may occur when a person feels threatened or scared. When the potential for harm is high or people feel they lack the resources to reduce the threat, stress increases. **Stressors** are situations or events that cause stress such as a missed plane or bus.

Stressors can be categorized as internal (self-generated), relational, or environmental. Here is a list of potential stressors; check off all that has happened to you in the last five years.

Starting a Job _____

Quitting a Job _____

Addition of a Family Member _____

Loss of a Family Member _____

Engagement or Wedding _____

Sudden Unexpected Change _____

Moving _____

Ongoing Family Conflict _____

Disappointing Event _____

Roommate or Family Hassles _____

Graduation from High School or College _____

School Problems _____

Caring for a Family Member _____

Significant Illness (self or someone close) _____

Stress can have positive or negative causes and is culturally and personally defined. What is stressful in India may not be considered stressful in the United States and vice versa. Individuals vary in their reactions to stress, too. What is acutely stressful for one person may not affect another at all.

Stress also varies in degree from everyday, normal stress, such as minor disagreements with roommates or family members, to more prolonged serious stress that can lead to troublesome symptoms. Telltale signs of stress, besides those already mentioned, include social isolation and sudden changes in appearance such as disheveled clothing and significant weight gain or loss.

Stress can be explained within the context of *systems theory* because stress comes from a variety of sources (inputs) and has a variety of outcomes (outputs). As it is a process, stress is generally considered a through-put, but stress can also be an input as it enters the system, or an output because one person's actions may cause stress in another person. For example, worrying is a process that is stress-producing. The cause of the worry may be an outside stressor that is input to the system. What the worrier finally decides to do may transfer the stress to another person. For example, the retiring chairperson of a committee may gleefully pass on a thick file of past committee business and procedures to the incoming chairperson and in so doing pass the stress on to the other person.

There is evidence of gender differences in reacting to stress. Men's blood pressure rises more sharply in response to stress than women's. But women react to more stressors and a greater variety of them; they report feeling stress more often, perhaps because they see daily life with a wider scope (Adler et al., 1999).

## Crises and Adaptation to Stress

**Crises**, which are events that require changes in normal patterns of behavior, often cause stress. Getting a flat tire while driving to work is a crisis. The driver must deviate from her normal pattern and fix the tire. How the driver reacts to the crisis will depend on many factors—the time, her expertise at changing tires, whether she has a spare tire or not, how far she is from a service station, and so forth. Another example is when Kevin fell and broke his leg. In the hospital emergency room next to his bed a monitor kept loudly beeping to the point that he had a panic attack.

He pleaded with the nurse to turn off the monitor which was malfunctioning and she did. Then, he relaxed and laid back in his bed.

Several researchers have developed models and scales that illustrate how individuals and families adapt to crises. These models and scales show the systematic interaction of crises, resources, pileup, and adaptation. **Stress overload, pileup, or spillover** refers to the cumulative effect of many stresses building up at one time. An upset employee might say, "I can't take it anymore, I quit!" On the home front, stress spillover may take a different sort of mode.

---

### CASE STUDY

#### Stress Spillover in Couples

*The term "stress spillover" refers to when stress from external sources leaches into a relationship. In an ongoing longitudinal study of 300 couples in the first five years of marriage, researchers at the dating site eHarmony, found that relationship satisfaction declines when an individual talks about a bad event with a partner who is not supportive. And the couple is more likely to argue the next day. If the parent is supportive, the study found, relationship satisfaction stays steady and the couple is less likely to argue. Gian Conzaga, psychologist and senior director of research and development for eHarmony in Santa Monica, Calif., says, "If your normal response to your partner is to not be supportive, over 20 years that will become a really big problem." On the other hand, sharing a good event with your partner makes you happier in the relationship, regardless of the partner's reaction...*

*Source: Berstein, E. (2011, October 4). Putting the honey back in "honey, I'm home." The Wall Street Journal, p. D4.*

Using the rating scale in Table 11.1, individuals can determine how much stress they have experienced in the past year. The originators of the scale, Holmes and Rahe, claim that substantial stress pileup can increase the incidence of illness. Note that the highest stressor event is the death of a spouse (100 points) and the lowest stressor event on the scale is a minor violation of the law (11 points). Scores of 100–200 are normal, but scores over 300 are considered high and indicative of trouble ahead.

**Table 11.1** Social Readjustment Rating Scale: The Stress of Adjusting to Change

| Events | Scale of Impact | Events | Scale of Impact |
|---|---|---|---|
| Death of spouse | 100 | Son or daughter leaving home | 29 |
| Divorce | 73 | Trouble with in-laws | 29 |
| Marital separation | 65 | Outstanding personal achievement | 28 |
| Jail term | 63 | Spouse begins or stops work | 26 |
| Death of close family member | 63 | Begin or end school | 26 |
| Personal injury or illness | 53 | Change in living conditions | 25 |
| Marriage | 50 | Revision of personal habits | 24 |
| Fired at work | 47 | Trouble with boss | 23 |
| Marital reconciliation | 45 | Change in work hours or conditions | 20 |
| Retirement | 45 | Change in residence | 20 |
| Change in health of family member | 44 | Change in schools | 20 |
| Pregnancy | 40 | Change in recreation | 20 |
| Sex difficulties | 39 | Change in church activities | 19 |
| Gain of a new family member | 39 | Change in social activities | 19 |
| Business readjustment | 39 | Mortgage or loan less than $10,000 | 17 |
| Change in the financial state | 38 | Change in sleeping habits | 16 |

*(Continued)*

| Events | Scale of Impact | Events | Scale of Impact |
|---|---|---|---|
| Death of a close friend | 37 | Change in number of family get-togethers | 15 |
| Change to a different line of work | 36 | Change in eating habits | 15 |
| Change in number of arguments with spouse | 35 | Vacation | 13 |
| Mortgage over $10,000 | 31 | Christmas | 12 |
| Foreclosure of mortgage or loan | 30 | Minor violations of the law | 11 |
| Change in responsibilities at work | 29 | | |

Life change is stressful. To determine how much stress you have experienced from life changes in the last year, add up the points for each of the events listed that you have experienced in the last year. Then refer to the following chart to determine how serious your condition is. For example, if you get married, get pregnant, buy a house, take a vacation, and celebrate Christmas, your total would be 50 + 40 + 31 + 13 + 12 = 146.

| Life Change Score | Chance of Illness in Next Year |
|---|---|
| 0–150 | 37% |
| 150–300 | 51% |
| 300+ | 80% |

Scores of 100–200 are common; 300-plus is high.

Source: Holmes, T. H., & Rahe, R. H. (1967, August). The social readjustment rating scale. *Journal of Psychosomatic Research*. Reprinted with permission from Elsevier.

As the Holmes and Rahe scale illustrates, stress levels can rise as a result of one major life change or from a series of small changes. Fixing a flat tire on the way to work may not be a big problem by itself, but as the day unfolds if the driver loses her keys, fights with her boss, and forgets an important meeting, stress pileup can occur. The individual may feel she cannot handle any more stress. Likewise, families experience a stress pileup: too many conflicting appointments and too many demands on time, energy, emotions, and money will cause stress to build up to the point where the family cannot cope.

*"When an aversive event is unpredictable, it is more upsetting and distressing than one that is predictable," says Prof. Richard McNally. "The 1986 shuttle explosion was pretty jarring, but for people who remember Challenger the loss of Columbia is similar enough to be less shocking." Even dissimilar stressors can produce habituation. "When a lot of bad things happen you just can't react as intensely," Prof. Prigerson says. "Some sort of adaptation kicks in." Predictability, too, can lead to habituation. The human nervous system has evolved to pay selective attention to novel and surprising stimuli and to ignore expected and repeating ones, the better to conserve finite processing resources.*

*(Begley, 2003, p. B1)*

David Dollahite (1991) developed the ABCD-XYZ Resource Management Model of Crisis/Stress. His model emphasizes how individual and family decision-making, adaptive coping, and management behavior can be activated to reduce the impact of crisis/stress situations. As shown in Figure 11.1, his model has seven key parts:

**A** Stressor event or situation, the stimulus that forces some response

**B** Coping resources

**C** Definition of the situation

**D** Demands of the situation

**X** Crisis or stress

**Y** Cognitive coping and management

**Z** Adaptive behavior, which entails growth and change and leads to a better fit between the environment and the person or family

An oval surrounding ABCD-XYZ places individuals and families within their historical, economic, techno-logical, cultural, legal, political, religious, and natural environmental contexts. Health (mental and physical), values, heredity, and development (stage of life cycle) form other important contexts. Mostly what this model shows is a systems approach to stress: one area affects another. Stress and stressors cannot be studied in isolation; they are part of an interactive system involving individuals and families in a larger environmental context.

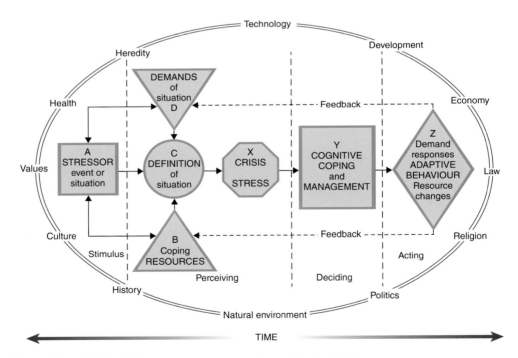

**Figure 11.1** ABCD-XYZ resource management model of crisis/stress.

Source: Dollahite, D. C. (1991). Family resource management and family stress theories: Toward a conceptual integration. *Journal of Family and Economic Issues, 12*(4), 265, with kind permission from Springer Science + Business Media.

## Planning and Organizing

This section ties closely to Chapter 6 on Planning, Implementing, and Evaluating and Chapter 9 on Managing Time. Stress reactions can be diminished by

- Planning and organizing daily activities by making lists and segmenting your day. Try to focus either on work or on personal life, but not on both at the same time. If under extreme stress, reschedule appointments and push back deadlines.

- Using the ABC method of time management described in Chapter 9. Reset priorities: Decide what is most critical to accomplish which are the A-level activities, goal-oriented, and relegate C-level activities to another day or in the evening.

- Realizing the need to set a new agenda or develop a new plan.

- Calling on a trusted friend to talk through a personal crisis.

- Finding a way to release emotions so that they don't distract you. Here is an example of developing a new plan:

> *Mr. Davila had to ratchet up his organizational skills. In the past year, he has spent about 25% of his typical workday helping his elderly parents. They evacuated to Texas right before the storm hit. The ensuing flood destroyed about 70% of their home, Mr. Davila estimates. His sister also lives in New Orleans and had to deal with rebuilding her own heavily damaged home after the flood. Responsibility for their parents fell primarily to Mr. Davila. His tasks included helping them sell what remained of their home, finding them new housing in Atlanta, and helping them secure a loan for the new home… At the same time, his clients depend on him and he didn't want to let them down. His solution: Hyperorganization.*
>
> *(White, 2006, p. B8)*

His hyperorganization involved writing out a plan for the next day at the end of each day. At night when he was home, he made a list of calls that needed to be made to help his parents. He created spreadsheets with phone numbers and names. So, the evening became family time and during the day he dealt with work issues.

## Outsourcing

One way to adapt to stress is to try to reduce it. To lessen stress, Americans increasingly are outsourcing traditional homemaking and childcare functions, a trend driven by three factors: more women working, an older population, and a larger middle class. **Outsourcing** is defined as paying someone else to do one's work.

> *Outsourcing is a logical extension of David Ricardo's 1817 theory of **comparative advantage**. Individuals, no less companies, do best when they focus on activities in which they can add the most value, and outsource other activities to specialists. And since housework has traditionally not been counted as an economic activity, the impact on the economy of extending outsourcing into the huge household-services sector will be massive.*
>
> *(Sheth & Sisodia, 1999)*

The potential benefits of outsourcing include generating more employment and higher tax revenues, putting more individual effort into higher work productivity, and investing remaining time into hobbies or other preferred activities. The following are some examples of activities and tasks that are being outsourced:

- Meal preparation/cooking: increased use of restaurants, home delivery, takeout, personal chefs, and prepared foods from supermarkets.

- Childcare, elder care (including home-based nursing), and pet care including pet walking or in-house care.

- Shopping: personal shoppers, buying over the Internet, using services that will pick up and deliver—such as for shoe repair, firewood, dry-cleaning, videos, and mailing packages (in short, less in-person shopping).

- Yard work, pool cleaning, interior design, and home improvements.

- Organizing. Personal service companies who rearrange closets, clean garages, or wait for the refrigerator or air conditioning repair person are on the rise (in the latter case much of that is done online rather than having a person come to the house or office).

Contrary to popular belief, it is not the rich who are driving up the demand for these services (they already have them), but the time-starved middle class who are taking outsourcing to new heights. The hesitation to outsource has eased as more people have extra income and place a higher value on their personal time. Do they want to spend it cleaning the house or mowing the lawn? Or would they prefer to pay for these services and spend their time doing something else? How much they outsource has a great deal to do with their comfort level with the idea, a subject to be explored next.

## Comfort Zones and Internal and External Stress

Stress is present in all human relationships and activities and only becomes harmful when there is a resource imbalance and rebounding is thwarted. Stress reduction is a means of restoring balance in lives. As mentioned in Chapter 2, in systems terminology the return to balance is called homeostasis. When a system becomes unbalanced, the homeostasis mechanism is triggered, and an attempt is made to reach a comfort zone. A **comfort zone** is a combination of habit and everyday expectations mixed with an appropriate amount of adventure and novelty. It represents that space in which the level of stress feels right for the individual—the quantity of work is enough to make life interesting but is not so burdensome as to produce discomfort or other undesirable effects. However, if one wants to get ahead socially or in a profession, often one moves out of one's comfort zone by meeting new people and going to new places. For example, when moving into a new neighborhood you can wait for the neighbors to introduce themselves or you can greet them when you see them.

Professionally, you may have to go to meetings, conferences, or training in other cities. In short, a comfort zone is a good thing, the way the lives of most of us are arranged; but taken to the extreme it can be limiting. For example, a student from a small town in Vermont graduated with a degree in chemistry from Dartmouth. He was accepted into graduate school at the University of Chicago; this means getting out of his New England rural/small town comfort zone. He is excited about the program and the city, and a little worried; but he is going forward.

Families and organizations have comfort zones just as individuals do. For example, a sudden drop in the stock market may shake the comfort zones of Wall Street brokerage firms as well as those of families who have invested in the stock market. The passage of stress from Wall Street to the family and individual level is an example of the **domino effect**. Another example of the domino effect is the impact that a company president's personal problems may have on the entire organization. The anxiety at the top may rumble downward through the organization, leading to a long list of workplace problems: diminished worker satisfaction, decreased productivity, subgroup conflict, misuse of authority, role confusion, scapegoating, and substance abuse (Ulrich & Dunne, 1986). In situations such as this, where stress is brought on from outside the individual, people are said to be experiencing **external stress**.

## External stress may come from any of the following three kinds of experiences:

1. *Acute major stress* resulting from a recent event, such as a car accident, job loss, moving, or death of a loved one.

2. *Ongoing, role-related stress* caused by chronic difficulties in one's work or family roles.

3. *Lifetime trauma stress* resulting from having undergone severe trauma, such as early-childhood loss of one or both parents or exposure to calamitous strains such as wartime or natural disasters.

In contrast, **internal stress** originates in one's own mind and body. An ambitious person may bring on internal stress by setting too high a standard for achievement (e.g., expecting to win every award, title, or promotion). Or a person may be stressed about her or his body image or lack of friends. Adolescents are particularly sensitive about their physical appearance (McLellan et al., 1992).

Everyone tries to balance internal and external stresses. Some stress is necessary to drive behavior—to get individuals out of bed in the morning and get them going. In this sense, stress serves as a motivator. Too much stress can be debilitating, however, and leads to immobilization.

## Hans Selye: Founder of Stress Research

Despite the long-standing fascination with stress, it was not until the last century that a scientific explanation for stress and its effects on the body was developed. Hans Selye (1907–1982), a biology professor at the University of Montreal, is called the father or founder of stress research especially biological stress. His interest began in medical school. He pointed out that everyone lives with some degree of stress all the time and that complete freedom from stress is death. Perhaps his greatest contribution was in showing that there are two types of stress: harmful stress— called **distress**—and beneficial stress—called **eustress** (from the Greek word *eu*, meaning good, as in euphoria). A person who gets on an airplane and feels sick with fear and anxiety is distressed. A fellow passenger feeling a sense of adventure and excitement is experiencing eustress. Both people are in the same situation, but they react differently. As this example illustrates, to understand the stress reaction, one must consider the person involved and not just the situation or crisis. The example also shows that not all stress is upsetting or damaging.

As Selye (1976) wrote, normal activities, such as a game of tennis or a passionate kiss, can produce stress without causing conspicuous damage. A woman manager says, "I oversee over 500 volunteers where I work. My day is filled with complaints, but when I solve issues one at a time, I get a buzz from the results. That's when stress is energizing" (Arnott, 2002). Another way to think of good stress is to call it "challenge stress." Challenge stress is related to a lot of endeavors, from public speaking to participating in races. This kind of stress leads to things employees or participants value—such as money, skills, fame, or promotion.

Selye studied the body's adaptive response to stress and reported that the stress syndrome is fundamental to virtually all higher forms of animals. He developed a comprehensive theory of the body's adaptive processes, based on a three-stage general adaptation syndrome. He was also the first scientist to identify the main organs and hormones involved in the stress response. His concept of stress led to new avenues of research in degenerative diseases, including coronary thrombosis, brain hemorrhage, hardening of the arteries, high blood pressure, kidney failure, arthritis, peptic ulcers, and cancer.

His experiments led him to theorize that to eliminate stress and individuals' adaptive reactions would be to eliminate all change, including growth, development, and maturation. Without stress human lives would be at complete rest—rather boring, to say the least.

Selye was often asked what could be done to reduce distress. He advised individuals to watch for signs that they were becoming too keyed up. On a personal note, he said that he tried to forget immediately everything that was unimportant because trying to remember too many things is a major source of psychological stress.

## Decision-Making and Stress

Selye's conscious decision to forget unnecessary information was one method he used to reduce stress. Delegating work or decisions to others is another way to reduce stress. For example, using the services of travel agents or travel search engines to arrange trips or book online can reduce stress for a frequent traveler. In efficient households, chores are often delegated to the spouse and children. A third way to reduce stress is to postpone decisions when there is no hurry. Most good decisions are not made in a hurry. Taking the time to think out all the alternatives and identify the best use of resources leads to sounder decisions. In addition, individuals, employees, and families can use many other methods to reduce stress. As an example, Toffler (1970) observed:

> I have seen a woman sociologist, just returned from a crowded, highly stimulating professional conference, sit down in a restaurant and absolutely refuse to make any decisions whatever about her meal. "What would you like?" her husband asked. "You decide for me," she replied. When pressed to choose between specific alternatives, she still explicitly refused, insisting angrily that she lacked the "energy" to make the decision.
>
> (p. 324)

In an employment situation, a way to reduce stress is to surround oneself with competent workers. Consider how carefully a newly elected president, prime minister, or governor selects the members of the cabinet. A navy admiral expressed his thoughts on the importance of employee selection:

> If you have the capability to do this, surround yourself with competent, capable people. I found that if I have people that are working for me of this caliber, that makes my job much easier you try to get the best performer you can get—the best qualified, the best experienced. It gives you confidence in what they are doing and that it's going to be correct.
>
> (Quick et al., 1990, p. 55)

How to react to stress is a decision involving conscious problem solving. Because stress permeates all aspects of individual and family life, everyone needs to master these problem solving skills: Sound decision-making leads to improved lifestyles and a sense of well-being. As Chapter 8 pointed out, potential stressors for individuals and families include poverty, lack of adequate housing, and disabling conditions. Each of these stressors provides ample opportunity for decision-making.

Using data from the National Survey of American Life, researchers Karen Lincoln and David Chae (2010) found that social stressors that occur inside the home such as financial strain as well as those experienced outside the home such as unfair treatment had negative consequences for marital quality and psychological distress. Further, they found that African Americans especially experience mental health consequences from unfair treatment and financial strain.

Listening to music is a stress reducer.

## Psychological Hardiness and Resilience

Hardy individuals tend to have an internal locus of control, meaning they feel responsible for their own lives and most of what happens to them. For example, when Debra, a 35-year-old bride, learned the morning of her wedding day that the dry cleaners had ruined her "going away dress," she quickly drove to the nearest clothes store, grabbed half a dozen dresses in her size, tried them on, and bought one. Was it what she had planned? No. Was she stressed? Yes.

Was she calm? Yes, according to store clerks who waited on her. They reported that she bought a dress in less than ten minutes and left happy. Debra exhibited a personality characteristic called psychological hardiness. In looking back, she said, "I was so happy to be getting married, nothing was going to bring me down." **Psychological hardiness** describes people who have a sense of control over their lives; are committed to self, work, relationships, and other values; and do not fear change. Such people may suffer fewer health consequences from crises or traumas. Allied to this is **psychological resilience** defined as the capacity to handle severe stressors including traumatic events. It might also be referred to as mental toughness. Scales have been developed to measure it. Certain professions such as police officers have been studied regarding psychological resilience (van der Meulen et al., 2019).

Debra's experience with the ruined dress was a **nonnormative stressor event.** These events are unanticipated experiences that place a person or a family in a state of instability and require creative effort to remedy. **Normative stressor events** are anticipated, predictable developmental changes that occur at certain life intervals. For most college students, registering for classes is a normative stressor event. Flunking out of school is a nonnormative stressor event.

Some people are extremely resilient when faced with either type of stressor event. People who are likely to be resistant to stress have a disposition composed of the three Cs: commitment, control, and challenge (Kobasa, 1982). They have a sense of purpose, are committed to their work and their families, rely on others, and know that others count on them.

Psychologically hardy people realize that stress and challenge are normal parts of life and that they have the resources to deal with them. Individuals who perceive less stress and express more hardiness report significantly greater work–life satisfaction (Nowack, 1991).

## Theory of Adaptive Range

Someone once jokingly said that the only person who really welcomes change is a wet baby. But the theory of adaptive range suggests that some level of change is vital to everyone's health and well-being, although too much unwanted change can be damaging. As mentioned earlier, everyone's life includes a comfort zone in which certain things and relationships do not change.

Consider the example of James, a 40-year-old male who has gone through a series of relationships and has been divorced twice. He likes to travel, eat different foods, visit with friends, and see the latest movies. If something new is happening, he is there. He wears "in" clothing and has the latest exercise equipment. He is highly intellectual and easily bored. On the surface, he looks like the epitome of change and adventure, but in a later interview James reveals that he has had the same job and house for 15 years and has a 10-year-old Irish setter he loves.

The moral of this story is that most people opt for stability and consistency in certain areas of their lives and opt for change or novelty in others. James opts for stability in his work and home, but wants a change in his appearance, entertainment, and relationships. As a footnote to this story, James says he is tired of dating and is looking for a stable, lasting relationship. Is this believable? Is he ready for a change?

Before exploring further about personality and ways to manage and accommodate change and stress, an examination of how the body responds to stress is necessary because stress has as its base a physiological response.

## The Body's Response to Stress

Does the daily grind set your teeth on edge? Do you wake up with a sore jaw or aching teeth or worse? You may have habits such as grinding your teeth that can escalate into a pain in the temporomandibular joint, or TMJ, which joins the jaw to the skull. Thus, stress from a messy breakup or financial crisis can affect how you sleep and how you feel when you wake up in the morning. In the case of TMJ, the most common treatment is wearing a night guard that makes grinding more difficult. Some patients are still clenching or grinding their teeth during the day and that will involve other appliances, treatments, physical therapy, and even the realigning of computer keyboards and monitors so that the person holds his or her chin and jaw differently. Related to this, Amanda had been a patient of the same dentist for many years. In August he checked her teeth and everything was okay except for one cavity filling scheduled for October. When she came back in October he exclaimed, "There is a hole in the inside of your cheek, you are literally chewing yourself up, what is wrong?" Amanda was under extreme work stress and this cheek chewing had to stop. The dentist prescribed medicine and they both talked about techniques to reduce stress. When she came for a check-up in December the hole was gone. She and the dentist were relieved.

**Pain in TMJ and Amanda's situation are two examples of what happens to a person's body when he or she experiences extreme stress. The usual order is:**

- *First an alarm reaction* takes place. The alarm response begins when the brain perceives a threat to the sense of equilibrium. Something is not right. A loud siren, a sudden clap of thunder, or any other such disturbance serves as an alarm signal. After the brain is alerted, a chain of events ensues as both hormones and nerves bring about a state of readiness. In 1932, Walter Cannon of Harvard Medical School coined the phrase **"fight or flight syndrome"** to refer to this alerted condition of the body as it quickly prepares for physical battle or energetic flight to escape the situation. A threatened or alerted person will experience some or all of the following physical actions:

- Pupils of the eyes widen.

- Muscles tense.

- Heart races or pounds.

- Hearing sharpens.

- Breathing quickens.

- Hair stands on end.

- Hands feel clammy.

- Mouth becomes dry.

These actions, when synchronized, provide support for the emergency physical response if needed. In the meantime, the brain is trying to process how to react next.

*Second comes resistance.* In this stage, the body adapts to the demand. If a woman driving a car hears a siren, she will become alert to a threat and try to find the source of the noise. If the siren is coming from an ambulance behind her, she will pull over to let it pass. After the ambulance goes by, her body will relax and return to normal. Stress can be an energizer. For instance, people go to adventure movies and car races that give them a quick, but safe, brush with stress. Each person needs stimulation to survive. Staying in a safe, comfortable job for 20 years is one way to keep stress and stimulation low. Changing jobs or applying for a promotion increases stress and provides stimulation.

*Third is the exhaustion stage.* Once the danger and the excitement have passed, the body may feel tired and possibly susceptible to various illnesses. A family as well as an individual can reach the stage of exhaustion, leaving family members susceptible to various disorders and feelings of discontent or restlessness. For example, a family may feel let down, exhausted, or bored after a busy holiday season. Or, a student may experience let down when finals end and he or she returns home.

## Diet, Exercise, and Stress

Stress research and theory have generally focused on the negative aspects of stress (or distress). Because people are eager to reduce these negative aspects, they invest in the many stress-reducing products and regimens offered in the marketplace. Consumers should remember the cautionary phrase *caveat emptor*, meaning "may the buyer beware." Walking is a free and effective stress reducer.

Before investing any money in a miracle vitamin or food, consumers should know that the best nutritional preparation for stress is a balanced and varied diet as part of a lifestyle that includes regular exercise. No known singular food, vitamin supplement, or herbal remedy will eliminate stress, so don't buy into those claims. During stress, all three energy fuels—-carbohydrates, fat, and protein—are depleted. Individuals who eat well to obtain the nutrients needed and engage in regular exercise will be better prepared to withstand the impact of unavoidable stress than individuals with poor diets and low fitness levels.

Exercise is recommended as a necessary part of a health-promoting lifestyle and helps increase the ability to concentrate and perform tasks. Moderate exercise can combat excessive weight gain and has been shown to reduce stress because it raises the level of beta-endorphins, chemicals in the brain associated with pain relief, which has a positive effect on mood and behavior.

Innumerable research studies have been conducted on the beneficial effects of exercise in reducing stress. A study of scale development by Chang, Brown, and Nitzke (2008) found that increased physical activity and reduced dietary fat intake behavior impacted stress management in low-income mothers. According to the American Heart Association (AHA), only 1 in 10 Americans follows a consistent exercise program. The AHA says that even 10 minutes a day is beneficial. For the average healthy adult to maintain health and reduce the risk of chronic disease, he or she should exercise five days each week for 30 minutes each day (at moderate intensity) according to updated guidelines from the AHA and the American College of Sports Medicine. They suggest that the person do 8–10 strength-training exercises, with 8–12 repetitions of each exercise, twice a week. Moderate intensity means working hard enough to raise the heart rate and break a sweat yet being able to carry on a conversation.

## CASE STUDY

### Fast Lunches

*Time-pressed executives are ordering something new for lunch—fine dining at the speed of a drive-through window. In cities from New York and Chicago to Dallas and San Francisco, many white-tablecloth establishments are catering to their booked-solid clientele with a formal lunch that takes 30 minutes, from ordering through dessert. It's not exactly fast food. But the format does bring a new level of efficiency to a business ritual that otherwise can go on for an hour or more... Chris Tamblyn, a general manager for Internet service provider Level 3 Communications, Inc. says it helps him persuade customers to commit to a lunch meeting when he tells them it's the 30-minute lunch at Il Forrnaio, a chain of upscale Italian restaurant.*

*Source: Dizik, A. (2011, June 8). Restaurants Court Diners with no time to spare: Soup to pastry in 30 minutes, hold the chitchat. The Wall Street Journal, p. D1.*

## Stress Management

Beyond managing diet and exercise, what else can a person do to reduce the effects of stress? It appears that adults, as well as children, need time out meaning time to sort things out and reflect, relax, and do something to take the mind off of the current activity.

If a person wants to be innovative, creative, and find solutions they need to set boundaries. Other stress-reducing methods include:

- Restructuring work or reducing work demands
- Knowing when to shut down by cleaning off a desk, turning off phones and laptops
- Limiting checking email to twice or four times a day or whatever would be a reduction
- If you work at home, having a daily ritual that indicates the end of work, shutting lights off or closing a door, walking away.
- Getting more rest and relaxation
- Outsourcing (as discussed earlier)
- Meditating and deep breathing

- Doing massage, yoga, exercise

- Seeking social support

- Scaling back on service and volunteer work

Evidence suggests that stress relief and social support can prolong life. For example, in one study melanoma patients who received six weeks of structured group support suffered only half as many recurrences as suffered by their peers (Cowley et al., 1999). In another study, patients with early breast or prostate cancer who attended stress management groups lived significantly longer than equally ill patients who were not in groups (Elias, 1998).

---

### CASE STUDY

#### Jalecia

"I can't tell you how much I want to get off this Board of Directors," said Jalecia. "It has been way more work than I expected and we meet in person or online several times a month. I had to fly to Washington, DC a lot. Next month is the end of the two-year appointment and that is it." You could hear the weariness in her voice. She was trying to balance the Board with a family and full-time job in a state quite distant from Washington. This was a service appointment with no pay that her employer wanted her to take for networking purposes.

---

Often a combined approach is best. Individuals must determine the stress management techniques that work best for them. (Additional techniques will be discussed in the next section.) People with stress problems may seek individual treatment from a psychiatrist, psychologist, or physician, or they may join a support group or counseling workshop. These groups and workshops are usually offered at mental health clinics, hospitals, and universities in their wellness programs or through workplace Employee Assistance Programs (EAPs) discussed in the last chapter. Treatments or visits may last from half a day to several days. Who attends stress management programs? Men and women are almost equally likely to feel stress, but women are almost twice as likely to seek help (Waldrop, 1993). According to Cotton (1990), three categories of individuals tend to seek assistance with stress management:

1. People who are not experiencing any particular difficulty with stress but are generally health-conscious. They are interested in the preventive aspects of stress.

2. People who are distressed, anxious, or depressed. A distressed person is facing many ongoing stresses or hassles.

3. People with medical problems related to stress. These people are often Type A and may be referred by their physician. Read on for further information on Type A and Type B personalities.

### Type A and Type B Personalities

Researchers have established linkages among stress, illness, and certain types of personalities. One schema separates people into two groups of personalities:

- **Type A persons** are characterized by excessively striving behavior, high job involvement, impatience, competitiveness, desire for control and power, aggressiveness, and hostility. They may set for themselves high–performance standards. **Perfectionism** can be driven by different underlying motives such as being highly self-critical (Arnold et al., 2016, p. 420), Perfectionism can push people to do their best which is good but taken to extremes can lead to burnout and high anxiety.

- **Type B persons** are more relaxed, easygoing, reflective, and cooperative They may be **psychologically flexible** meaning using "thinking strategies that allow them to focus on actions (i.e. doing their job) while at the same time recognizing and accepting in a non-judgmental way the events going on in their mind – such as fear, worry and anxiety – are unhelpful thoughts" (Arnold et al., 2016, p. 421). They take a mindful approach. **Satisficing** is about accepting when things are good enough. A Type B person may reflect that their work or school report or paper is finished and accepted, maybe not perfect, but good enough.

Each person has a unique personality as discussed earlier in the book, but one way to generally categorize personalities is as either Type A or Type B. You lean more one way than the other. Each type reacts differently to stress. The Type B personality is usually calm and collected, and such persons are rarely stressed.

Angela was described by her friends as "cool as a cucumber." Ask your friends how they would categorize you. Type B's are patient; their pace is relaxed. They experience stress but are more likely to internalize it, and sometimes they can shrug it off.

The Type A personality is often impatient, wants things to happen quickly, and such persons become angry when things slow down. So, Type As do not handle stress well. On the other hand, they do not internalize it. Everyone around them will know they are stressed and they let some of the stress out by talking about it. The strength of interpersonal relationships will help them through stressful times. In a study of German business managers comprising Type A and Type B personalities, it was found that Type A personalities had greater perceived levels of stress, lower job satisfaction, and poorer physical and mental health than did Type B personalities (Kirkcaldy et al., 2001).

Time urgency refers to the feeling that there is not enough time to do everything. It leads to impatience, tension, restlessness, preoccupation (e.g., inattentiveness to others), and rapid eating and talking. Hostility means evaluating people, events, or situations negatively and being suspicious, distrustful, aggressive, and competitive. Type A personalities rarely leave the office; a suggested remedy is to encourage Type As to take lunch breaks and walks and get more of a life outside the office.

Type Bs are characterized by an absence of the habits and traits associated with Type As. They lack a sense of time urgency and its accompanying impatience. Type Bs wait in line better than Type As; they can relax without guilt, are more cooperative with others, and take a break when fatigued. They are more likely to recognize signs of stress within themselves and to take time for fun. Type Bs have goals and ambitions, but they have a confident style that allows them to wait for things to happen. Psychological flexibility has been shown in research studies to enable people to have good mental health and strong work performance (Arnold et al., 2016, p. 421).

Several studies have linked Type A behavior to an increased rate of heart attacks and other diseases, but counter-studies indicate that the factors are more complex. Thus, there is no agreement on the health risks associated with Types A and B behavior. Similarly, the origins of Types A and B behavior are uncertain. It has been suggested that the Type A behavior pattern is established at birth as part of inborn temperament and is accentuated through childhood if the parents are high achievers and impose high standards on their children. In summary, although there are some discrepancies and research continues on this topic, researchers agree that stressors are experienced differently by different types of people and that coping responses vary by dominant personality type.

## Techniques for Reducing Stress

Anxiety about chasing the future as well as dealing with the present often adds to stress. The question is what to do about it. Here is insight about goals and happiness.

> *Even when people achieve their goals, the payoff for which they endured all the stress, anxiety, and health repercussions that result from overworking is fleeting. Dan Gilbert at Harvard has shown that we are terrible at predicting what will or will not make us happy. We often overestimate the happiness something will bring us. Just like a cat who chases a toy but loses interest as soon as he catches it, when we finally get what we want – receiving a big end-of-year bonus, finding the perfect job, or even winning the lottery – we often find that we are not as happy as we thought we would be.*
>
> (Seppala, 2016, p. 22)

Coping strategies to reduce everyday stress that is not chronic or disease-related can be divided into two types:

1. problem-focused coping and
2. emotion-focused coping (Lazarus, 1991).

Problem-focused coping attempts to alter the actual relationships and change behaviors or environments. Emotion-focused coping concentrates on regulating the emotional distress caused by harm or threat. Someone could do this by avoiding thoughts of the stressor, replacing negative thoughts with positive, denying, or distancing. Positive thinking is used more by Type As than Type Bs as a coping strategy (Havlovic & Keenan, 1991). Emotion-focused coping requires a change in thinking or interpreting and a change in acting. *Moderate stress can be relieved by first determining the cause of stress*, then removing the stressor or moving out of the stressful environment, and, lastly employing techniques that change the response to stress.

## Specific techniques to help manage stress include the following:

- Identify the most helpful people in your life. Who is pulling for you?
- Manage smartphone technology to your advantage.
  - Try apps with soothing music.
- Organize time to allow for enjoyment, relaxation, fun, hobbies, and exercise.
- Complete tasks that have been started. There is more evidence building that multitasking doesn't work.
- Acknowledge and celebrate your own uniqueness and successes. Comparing with others can be a trap.
- Cultivate a sense of humor.
- Indulge yourself. Solitude works especially for those with demanding families. It is not just about being physically alone, but also about having only yourself on the agenda. An example is commuters on trains, buses, and airplanes pulling inside themselves and decompressing. They enjoy the commute, listening to favorite music, reading, watching television and movies, and thinking their own thoughts.
  - *If you need to get something done in a hurry like packing for a trip, try the time burst technique mentioned in Chapter 10, 15–20-minute sessions of extreme concentration and focus to complete a task or activity, followed by a release, a break, a change.*
- Find quiet environments and build family and friendship bonds. A study by Karen Grewen of the School of Medicine at the University of North Carolina, Chapel Hill, found that a brief hug and ten minutes of handholding with a romantic partner greatly reduced the harmful physical effects of stress (Elias, 2003).

- Keep things in perspective. Stay flexible. "Ultimately, it's how you spend your days—not your downtime—that matters" (Spencer, 2003, p. D1). The new thinking is to deal with stress when it happens by changing how you react to it rather than waiting for vacations, the spa, or yoga classes (although they help).

- Develop a positive attitude. Realize that one person cannot change everything. Much stress comes not from stressors but from perceptions of situations. Ask yourself the following questions:

  1. What is true progress? What is it that I want?

  2. What satisfaction level do I have? Am I mostly content?

  3. How much am I learning? They say that more is learned from failure than success. Consider the following quote:

  > We believe, value, choose, and know unconsciously as well as consciously. The way we perceive reality is strongly influenced by unconsciously held beliefs. The phenomena of denial and resistance in psychotherapy illustrate how thoroughly one tends not to see things threatening to deeply held images conflicting with deeply held beliefs.
  >
  > (Harman, 1998, p. 15)

### A study by pollsters Roper Starch Worldwide revealed that when stressed

- Twenty-three percent of men and 15 percent of women take a day off from work.

- Nineteen percent of men and 36 percent of women buy clothing.

- Fifteen percent of men and 26 percent of women eat a special dessert.

These techniques and study results may be useful, but how does a busy person find the time to relax? Consider the opening paragraph of an article on stress that appeared in *Parents* magazine:

> "We all know what we need to do about stress," says Alice, a legal secretary and the single mother of two young children. "We need to be good to ourselves, exercise regularly, eat well, get plenty of rest, and allow enough time for pleasure." Then she laughs and adds, "In other words, what we all really need is two weeks at a spa, complete with daily massage. Then when we return, we need a full-time maid, cook, and chauffeur."
>
> (Levine, 1990, p. 68)

As this quotation makes clear, reducing stress is more easily said than done. It is one thing to describe successful techniques for reducing stress; it is another, to fit them into an already busy life.

## Job Stress

**Job stress** is the harmful physical and emotional responses that occur when the demands of the job do not fit the worker. The demands may be beyond the capabilities and training of the employee or their manager. A 2021 report by the Society for Human Resource Management in Alexandria, Virginia found in a survey of U.S. workers that 84 percent agree that poorly trained managers created unnecessary stress and work.

The workplace is calling out for a change. Can we work together to find solutions? Proper training and experienced managers help.

Job stress can lead to poor health, injury, and even death. For many years, the Japanese have been aware of the severe consequences of too much work. Their word **karoshi** means death by overwork. Japanese researchers have found a link between long hours, heart disease, and high blood pressure coupled with an unhealthy lifestyle including no exercise, poor diet, and few medical visits to increase strain and anxiety.

**Extreme work** is a term referring to jobs that require 60-plus workweek hours as well as jobs that require a lot of travel and a 24/7 on-call schedule. Working 16.5 hours with lunch at the desk would be considered extreme work and is in evidence in seasonal jobs such as working during a Legislative Session in a state Capitol building. When asked about only having four hours to sleep, given commuting time and getting ready time, Freda said "It's my job, what I signed on for." If this pace kept up for more than three months one would expect health consequences and pushback. She uses weekends to recover and looks forward to an ocean cruise when the Session ends.

> *Extreme jobs are taking their toll on the health and emotional well-being of men and women. Even though a majority of people in these jobs say they love the challenge and adrenaline rush they get from them, they also suffer more ailments, such as high blood pressure and anxiety, as well as relationship problems with spouses and children they have hardly any time for.*

> *(Hymowitz, 2007, p. R8)*

Challenges are different from stress. Challenge energizes people and motivates them to learn new skills. When a challenge is met, the reactions are satisfying and relaxing. Thus, challenge is a natural and healthy part of productive work. Job stress, however, results when job demands are not met, usually because of excessive workloads: constant criticism, no end results, and only a sense of exhaustion and failure. Employees need to feel they are winning and succeeding and, if not, the expectations or the game plan needs to be redefined.

During a downward economy, job stress goes up because there are fewer jobs and less job security. Also, there are fewer workers for the tasks to be accomplished. When employees leave or retire, their positions are not filled.

Most workers report job stress, and often those lowest in the organization experience the most stress because they have the least control over their work and must answer to a long line of bosses. Waiting for signatures or approvals are stressors. Not surprisingly, those higher up in organizations report the least stress.

Karen Nussbaum, executive director of the Women's Bureau in the United States Department of Labor, says,

> *I think of stress and working parents in two issues—time and work. When you are a parent who works outside the home—which is the case for more than 50 percent of all mothers of preschoolers—you have less time and more worry. And the combination results in high stress.*

> *(Levine, 1990, p. 68)*

As Chapter 10 observed, stress is an inevitable result of work–family time conflicts. Travel associated with work can be a stressor. More than 8 in 10 business travelers say that work travel is stressful (Fisher, 1998). Travel is hardest

- On workers with young families. In one study, six in ten married travelers said they experienced stress when missing family milestones, such as a birthday or a wedding anniversary, or a child's sporting event (Fisher, 1998).

- At night. Traveling workers especially miss their children at bedtime.

- On spouses who are left behind. The burden of household work and childcare falls on them.

- When piles of work are waiting for the worker upon return from travel.

- When things go wrong. Canceled flights, lost luggage, or reservation difficulties create stress.

On the other hand, *the most enthusiastic travelers are those between the ages of 18 and 34.* They enjoy seeing new places. Almost 70 percent say that overnight business travel makes them feel important, and 68 percent say that trips provide a needed break from home and regular life (Fisher, 1998). Josiah, age 28 with a Bachelor's and Master's degree working in Washington, DC, told the author of this book he loves to travel with his job taking him to his home state of Ohio where he can see family and friends and all over the country. Thus, travel can produce distress or eustress. A lot of the reaction has to do with the traveler's lifestyle, age, career stage, and other criteria—such as the location of the travel destination and the meaning of the travel to their job success.

## CRITICAL THINKING

Darby set as her main career goal an all-expense-paid international trip by her retail company. When it finally happened, she realized she had to set a new goal. What are some of her options? If your job could send you anywhere in the world, what would your first choice be?

Typically, work and work-related activities, transportation to and from work, and preparation activities take up over 40 hours a week. Boredom, overload, role ambiguity, underutilization of talent or skills, poor job design, lack of advancement, shift work, low pay, transfers, miscommunications, difficult bosses, too many meetings, high job turnover, poor labor-management relations, lack of control, and incompetence all contribute to job stress.

Negative consequences or effects of stress may include anxiety, being accident-prone, lower productivity, and a host of other physical, mental, and behavioral problems.

Although work produces stress, remember that according to Hans Selye, not all stress is bad. Work provides a purpose for living and provides challenges. According to Selye (1974), work is a biological necessity:

> *[The] principal aim should not be to avoid work but to find the kind of occupation which for you is play. The best way to avoid harmful stress is to select an environment which is in line with your innate preferences—to find an activity which you like and respect.*
>
> (p. 85)

Further, he said, one of the worst stressors is continuous leisure from enforced retirement or solitary confinement. The person wonders what to do when there is a lack of schedule, rewards, goals, and demands. Earlier, Benjamin Franklin expressed this same sentiment when he said, "There is nothing wrong with retirement as long as one doesn't allow it to interfere with one's work."

Another way of looking at work and stress is that *the workplace may serve as a haven from the stress*, disappointment, and problems encountered in home and family life. It may be a relief to go to an office where everyone is polite, well-groomed, and courteous, if, for example, there are constant fights at home or a family member is an abusive alcoholic. A more popular image of the home, however, is as a place where the wounds inflicted in "that jungle out there" can be soothed (Ulrich & Dunne, 1986). As these examples indicate, asking people where they work and what they do is not enough. Professionals interested in helping families should ascertain whether work is a haven, a stressor, or a mixture of both for individual family members. They can also help individuals find ways to transition from the career–life balance the person has to the career–life balance the person wants.

## Burnout

Special attention has been placed on various professions including the tasks and work environments of trainee physicians (a high-risk group for lack of sleep and stress) to reduce their burnout (Zhou & Panagioti, 2020). Professors and government workers say they experience burnout from too many online webinars and Zoom meetings which are often back-to-back from Tuesday to Thursday. On National Public Radio on their *Talk of the Nation* show a discussion of burnout took place which included the following comments:

> People who are suffering from burnout tend to describe the sensation in metaphors of emptiness—they're a dry teapot over a high flame, a drained battery that can no longer hold its charge. Thirteen years, three books, and dozens of papers into his profession, Barry Farber, a professor at Columbia Teachers College and trained psychotherapist, realized he was feeling this way. Unfortunately, he was well acquainted with the symptoms. He was a burnout researcher himself... He'd just completed a book about burnout among teachers, a subject he'd once considered exceptionally urgent. "Yet even as I was writing," he says, "I had this sense that I really wanted to finish it so that I could go on to something else. I felt somewhat bored, and somewhat depleted. I'd said all I wanted to say." He ponders this point. "I guess," he says, "I lost the sense that it was important."
>
> (Senior, March 15, 2008)

New projects or careers may seem perfect in the beginning. This is the honeymoon stage when everything is wonderful. Employees are enthusiastic, with all sorts of hopes and expectations: Life is under way. They would rather work than do anything else. This is a recipe for **burnout**, a state of physical, emotional, and mental exhaustion caused by unrealistic goals and aspirations, and long hours. Burnout is a common feeling in society; young and old experience it.

Drive and idealism are good things, but if a hardworking perfectionist or a self-motivating achiever hits obstacles, frustration or failure may result. This stage is called the "awakening," the realization that early expectations might have been unrealistic, and it may lead to what the American Psychological Association calls **brownout** (a predecessor to burnout). In this stage, fatigue and irritability show up; eating and sleeping patterns may be disturbed; cynicism and indecision set in; and unless something or someone steps in to halt the downward spiral, burnout may result. The onset may be slow and the result of role conflict (being pulled in too many directions), role ambiguity (unclear expectations), or role overload (the inability to say "no," taking on too much responsibility).

Mental symptoms can include feelings of frustration, isolation, hopelessness, cynicism, apathy, failure, despair, detachment, and powerlessness. Every day is as bad as the last one. Stressed people know the end is in sight and feel some degree of control, whereas true burnouts do not see the end of their troubles. For example, holidays and vacations are eagerly looked forward to when someone is stressed or even-keeled. A burned-out person knows time off won't help much, if at all.

Physical symptoms may include aches in the neck, head, or back, or just a general lack of energy. The word "burnout" is associated with being worn out from doing too much work. Originally, "burnout" was used in the aerospace industry to describe the termination of rocket or jet-engine operations because of insufficient fuel. In resource management, burnout refers to emotional or physical exhaustion brought about by unrelieved stress. This all-inclusive definition shows that burnout can come from many sources.

Potential job burnout can result from fatigue, or frustration with a cause, a way of life, or a relationship that has failed to produce the expected reward, such as a politician losing an election. The president of an organization can experience burnout. A stockbroker described being on a country club board of directors for 15 years; when he had finally had enough of hearing complaints from members and being thwarted when he tried to introduce new ways of doing things, he quit when his term was over. Looking back, he is much relieved to have left that position, which was voluntary, yet caused a lot of stress.

In the 1970s, "burnout" was first associated with teachers, social workers, and others who worked in jobs involving considerable responsibility for the welfare of others. These jobs tended to have high turnover rates because workers were said to burn out after so many years on the job. In the 1980s, "burnout" was used to refer to just about anybody who was tired at the end of the day.

During that decade, Charles Maslach (1982) published the Maslach Burnout Inventory, which defined burnout as the subjective experience of emotional exhaustion, depersonalization, and reduced personal accomplishment resulting from the continuous caring for needy clients in human-service professions.

Today, burnout refers to both everyday and long-term exhaustion. Regardless of how the word is used, the phenomenon should not be ignored. If burnout is acute, a person may have a breakdown in health, may not be able to continue performing at the expected pace, and may become discouraged and drop out of a profession, when what he or she really needs is a break, a chance for retraining, and perhaps a better job–environment–person fit. Here are some other ways to combat job burnout:

- Be realistic about expectations, aspirations, and goals. Get in touch with yourself and what you really want, remember what felt good in the past, rebuild your inner resources.

- Clarify the job description with a supervisor. Maybe you need a new description or a transfer.

- Rest and relax; do not take work home with you (mentally or physically, learn to turn it off).

- Create balance in your life with other activities, groups, hobbies, and exercise.

- Avoid isolation: Closeness brings new insights, and it is hard to be agitated and depressed when surrounded by people and pets that you love. Confide in others outside the immediate workplace.

- Take time off, a long vacation, or a leave of absence.

- Ask for something different to do, take on a new project or set of responsibilities, and get out of the rut.

Burnout can happen in friendships, caregiving, and marital relationships, too. Distance, vacations, a new setting, or a renewed commitment may all help reduce relationship burnout. The importance of vacations was introduced in the last chapter, but here are another study's results to consider:

> Of 12,000 middle-aged men at risk for coronary disease, researchers found those who failed to take vacations had a higher risk of death from any cause, but particularly from heart disease, than those who took regular vacations. The results were controlled for education, income and the possibility that some of the men's health was too poor to take vacations Researchers say good vacations have a power that extends beyond the time you're away.
>
> (Shellenbarger, 2003, March 27, p. D1)

Burnout is generally regarded as a negative exhibited in depersonalization and emotional exhaustion. It can have negative consequences, for example, when employee burnout spills over into poor customer service (Shoshan & Sonnentag, 2019). But, like stress, burnout has its positive side. Burnout can be a signal for change. Viewed in this way, burnout can be a functional, positive developmental experience, rather than a dysfunctional, negative one. In 1997, Christina Maslach, a professor of psychology at the University of California, Berkeley, and coauthor of the book *The Truth about Burnout* concluded that

> *Most people think burnout is caused by work overload But while having too much to do can cause stress, it doesn't necessarily cause burnout. People will work long, hard hours willingly and happily if they love what they are doing, or if they can see it is making a difference Respect helps, too.*

> *(Smith, 1997, p. 11D)*

## Nonevents and Virtual Events

Most of the stressors covered so far have been caused by events like working too hard and too long or reactions to events. An interesting line of research has focused on the stress caused by nonevents—specific occurrences in people's lives that they look forward to and make plans around but that fail to materialize. Examples of nonevents are canceled weddings (these may be more stressful than divorces), postponed vacations, or not being invited to a follow-up job interview or an important social gathering. According to John Eckenrode of Cornell University,

> *We know that unanticipated negative events are more stressful than anticipated ones. With an anticipated event, you can do some preparatory coping. You know it's going to happen and you can mobilize your resources. Things that just hit you out of the blue, on the other hand, are more stressful because you don't know they're coming. And when you've invested a lot of emotional buildup in whatever it is you're looking forward to, the effects can be huge.*

> *(Powers, 1995, p. 6)*

Eckenrode says that many times people's plans are thwarted by others or something in the environment that is beyond an individual's control. He speculates that stress from nonevents is just part of life, that disappointment is as normal an occurrence as the good things that happen.

Working can be a pain in the neck.

CRITICAL THINKING

Have you ever experienced a nonevent? What was it? Gloria described a fund-raising party for the animal shelter, which cost $150 a ticket, as a nonevent: hardly anyone showed up, it was disorganized, and the food was mediocre. She said she knew it was for a good cause but it was disappointing. What are the odds she will go next year or recommend it to friends?

Related to this topic are **virtual events** (online events that may feature webinars and webcasts, could be a tradeshow or conference) that may or may not charge a fee or provide anything tangible. Stressors may involve getting professionally dressed and ready, having a spot in the home or workplace appropriate for filming or being filmed, and keeping pets and children quiet. Mishaps or mistakes happen. Perhaps you remember on YouTube the Texas attorney telling a judge "I am not a cat." The video court hearing went worldwide including translations in Japanese.

## Parents, Children, Stress, Burnout

The parent–child relationship can lead to stress for all concerned. There are many research studies on this subject including specialized topics such as how parental stress affects children with epilepsy or ADHD (attention deficit hyperactivity disorder). There is a Parenting Stress Index to measure parental stress with children 12 years or younger.

The parent–child relationship is one topic, another is to look at children as individuals and the variety of environments, situations, and health issues that may affect their stress or burnout levels. As an overarching comment, *children are as vulnerable to stress and burnout as are adults*. Hurried schedules and meals affect children as well as parents. Experts think childhood stress is increasing (Adler et al., 1999).

> As adults, we are usually busy as parents and workers and often feel stressed and experience burn-out at times, but would you ever think that children can experience stress too? Most of us probably think that childhood is a time when children are carefree, having no worries or responsibilities; yet, studies tell us that many children experience stress and have similar symptoms as those of adults. Like adults, children often have bad feelings and have difficulty handling their stress. Unlike adults, children do not have the means or the skills to understand or manage their stress in appropriate ways. Children must depend upon us to help them.
>
> (Ruffin, 2001, p. 1)

For parents, the stresses of child-rearing may begin as soon as the newborn infant arrives home from the hospital. One study of parents of infants three to five months old identified several stressors. Fussy behavior ranks near the top of the list.

A study by researchers Bronte-Tinkew et al. (2011) found that policies should be aimed at decreasing parental stress especially for fathers living in poor families. They also found that the more engaged fathers are with their children the less likely they are to report aggravation and stress.

A study found that the Americans most likely to be stressed out are women between the ages of 30 and 44 because they tend to be working mothers with young children (Waldrop, 1993). And at midlife, a major source of stress for the women surveyed was the return of adult children to the home for economic reasons and concerns about their children succeeding out in the world. Another study found that single parents and their adolescents are under potentially significant amounts of stress owing to family structure and developmental factors, such as the adolescents' movement toward independence (Houser et al., 1993). Countless studies reported extreme stress experienced by mothers caring for their home-schooled children during the Covid-19 pandemic.

A study of divorced fathers revealed that they too are stressed and sometimes backed off from childcare as a way to lessen stress in their lives. They essentially gave childcare and the daily hassles to the mother and took on breadwinning as their major role (DeGarmo et al., 2008). Of course, this is not true of all divorced fathers many of whom have sole custody or joint custody, but one of the main findings was that the more engaged and involved fathers experienced the greater levels of daily stress.

## Stress Warning Signs in Children

Stressed children give off many warning signs: poor appetite, excessive crying, headaches, and stomachaches, withdrawal, clinging behavior, hyperactivity, moodiness, and sleep problems. Children can experience stress from homesickness, parental divorce, and problems with family, friends, community, and school. In young children, possible signs of stress include bed-wetting, crying spells, tattling, hitting, kicking, thumb sucking, grinding teeth, fingernail biting, baby talk, and accident proneness. Parents and caregivers need to observe changes in behavior such as these. Younger children cannot articulate what is wrong. The general message is that it is all right to feel angry and disappointed, and with older children, management alternatives can be suggested or discussed, solutions sought. Calming techniques are helpful.

Competition for grades and activities produces stress. Jen, who transferred from a school 200 miles away, did not get picked for the varsity cheerleading team. She said she cried for weeks and could hardly face the kids at the new school. She never went to a football game in high school. She never felt she was given a fair chance. She said the places on the team were all predetermined for young women whom everyone had known for years rather than being filled based on athletic ability.

Barbara Howard, a pediatrician at Johns Hopkins, says a quarter of her patients are there for stress-related problems. She says, "They'll come in with abdominal pain, urinary frequency, headaches... a whole variety of complaints which could be mistaken for medical problems and often are" (Adler et al., 1999, p. 63). In addition,

> Parents are frequently wrong about the sources of stress in their children's lives, according to surveys by Georgia Witkin of Mount Sinai Medical School; they think children worry most about friendships and popularity, but they're actually fretting about the grown-ups. "The biggest concern," she says, "was that the parents are going to be sick, or angry, or they're going to divorce." And "often and somewhat surprisingly," says Giedd [Jay Giedd of the National Institutes of Health], "children have very global worries"—wars, environmental issues, and crime, the same things adults worry about.
>
> (Adler et al., 1999, p. 63)

Furthermore, researchers report, "Children who were neglected by their parents or raised in orphanages tend to have higher levels of stress hormones and may be 'hot reactors' later in life. As adults, they may feel empty or bored when on edge" (Adler et al., 1999, p. 60). On the other hand, according to Megan Gunnar of the University of Minnesota, children raised in secure, loving homes learn to modulate stress reactions.

Children can experience stress and overload from competitive, win-lose, rule-bound situations just as adults can. Consequently, the nature and outcomes of highly structured, competitive team sports can be childhood stressors. It is generally agreed that this type of sports activity is too stressful for very young children. To help children through these and other stressful situations, parents should be sensitive to any change overload, responsibility overload, or emotional overload their children may be experiencing.

In *The Hurried Child*, David Elkind, professor of child development at Tufts University, says that today's children are pressured to grow up too fast. He gives this example of responsibility overload:

> *Janet is ten years old but has many adult responsibilities. In addition to taking care of her clothes and room, she must prepare breakfast for herself and her younger sister and make sure that they get off to school on time. (Her mother leaves for work an hour before Janet needs to get to school.) When she gets home, she has to do some housecleaning, defrost some meat for dinner, and make sure her sister is all right. When her mother gets home, Janet listens patiently to her mother's description of the "creeps" at work who never leave her alone and who are always making cracks or passes. After Janet helps prepare dinner, her mother says, "Honey, will you do the dishes? I'm just too tired," and Janet barely has time to do some homework.*
>
> (Elkind, 1988, p. 150)

Janet is stressed not only from the work she does but also from the amount of responsibility placed on her shoulders at such a young age. In many one-parent and dual-career families today, children are required to take substantial responsibility for housework and childcare. How much is too much is a question worth thinking about.

Elkind points out that not only are homes more stressful today, but schools are also more stressful. Besides the usual competition for grades and in sports, children today are exposed to more threats and violence in schools than ever before.

Like adults, children can learn to moderate stress by following the techniques described earlier in the chapter—eating a balanced diet, engaging in regular exercise, enjoying free time, and being with people with whom they are comfortable. Elkind says that children can suffer from chronic stress, usually brought on by significant life changes, which can be reduced by reassurance and attention from parents and teachers. Parents and caregivers need to instill confidence in children and provide security. One idea is to say, "Try this out on your own first, but if you need help, let me know and I'll be there."

## College Students and Stress

It is generally assumed that the teen years are stressful and that the transition period from high school to college is exciting yet highly stressful. College students, most of whom are in their teens and 20s, are living in or emerging from a stressful life period. Boredom and school burnout are often the stressors during the high school years.

---

### CRITICAL THINKING

#### College Visits

High school students may size up which college to attend is by visiting them ahead of time, perhaps with their parents which may or may not include a specialized campus orientation tour. Did you go on college visits? How was the experience? Did the visits reduce stress and anxiety? Have you been a college tour guide or worked in the Visitor Center or know someone who has?

---

By college age, many of the boredom and burnout problems get replaced by renewed enthusiasm for education because of the new setting and the opportunity to specialize although some students report a sophomore slump, a slower period after the initial high of being a freshman. College seniors can express regret at graduation time and concern about missing the university environment and friends while others say they are tired of college life and ready to get out and earn a living and pay back their student loans or look forward to going on to graduate school. What do you anticipate your reaction will be to graduating?

### Ben

Ben, a 21-year-old college student, is studying hard for an exam. He might do well to give his brain a break.

> Just what he does during that break will determine how helpful that pause will be, a growing body of research shows. A stroll in the park could do wonders, for instance, while downing coffee could leave him just as stressed and depleted as before the break. And, sometimes forcing oneself to simply power through mental fatigue can be more effective than pausing. Like a muscle, our brains appear to get fatigued after working for sustained periods of time, particularly if we have to concentrate intensely or deal with a repetitive task, says Michael Posner, an emeritus professor at the University of Oregon who studies attention.
>
> Source: Wang, S. S. (2011, August 30). Coffee break? Walk in the park? Why unwinding is hard. The Wall Street Journal, p. D1.

College students are usually dedicated and in school by choice—they enjoy school for the most part and want to keep learning. They have career ambitions and life goals. But for all the pluses, the college years also have some negatives—stressors in the forms of relationships, grades, and emotional and physical problems. Uncertainty about what lies ahead is an ever-present stressor. Other causes of stress include major losses through divorce or separation, which have increased in recent years; having two working parents (which gives teens less time with parents); and higher and earlier exposure to drugs, sex, the ill-effects of gambling, and violence.

### Clare Unhappy, Switches Schools

This is a true story. Clare was the youngest of three sisters. The older two went out of state to a famous university and were very happy. Clare visited and planned to follow but one year into the same university she was unhappy with her roommate and classes. It felt like a failure at first. She transferred to the large state university in her hometown where she thrived. When you think about it, would it be unusual for all three sisters to think and react alike?

Ranjita Misra (2000) found that time management behaviors had a great buffering effect in reducing stress and that female undergraduate students were better than male students at time management. However, women had higher academic stress and anxiety. Males seemed better at using leisure and sports as stress reducer. In the Misra study, freshmen and sophomores reported more stress and higher anxiety levels than juniors and seniors.

### CRITICAL THINKING

What year in college are you? Have you observed that beginning students are more stressed than seniors? What sort of stresses are seniors experiencing?

According to another study, the top academic stressors for college students were tests and finals, and the top personal stressor was intimate relationships (Murphy & Archer, 1996). Another study found that the most psychological distress was experienced in freshman year and that it declined over the next four years (Sher et al., 1996). In response to this, many colleges and universities have put more effort in recent years into offering freshman orientation programs, specialized seminars, and living/learning dormitories for freshmen only.

For certain individuals, mild test anxiety has been found to motivate and facilitate performance. But test anxiety is more commonly associated with negative motivation and poor test performance (Hill & Wigfield, 1984). One study of undergraduate college students tried to determine whether test anxiety could be significantly reduced through regular relaxation exercises or physical exercises (Topp, 1989). The students were divided into three groups: a nonmeditative relaxation exercise group, an aerobics dance group, and a control group who did not meet during the seven-week study. Both the relaxation exercise group and the aerobics dance students (who increased in fitness also) reported a significant decline in test anxiety; the control group did not experience any change in test anxiety. The results from this study suggest that exercise reduces test anxiety, so a student suffering from it should consider incorporating exercise into his or her life. Another stressor for college students is meeting deadlines—deadlines for term papers, for projects, for club reports, for registering for classes, and so on. Time management techniques, including prioritizing, allocating time as best as one can, checking progress, and keeping a calendar or list, should help with the problem of meeting deadlines.

Not all college students are in their late teens or early 20s. More and more people over age 25 are returning to school after serving in the armed services, raising a family, or being engaged in some other work or family activities that caused them to postpone entering or finishing college. In addition to the college life stressors already mentioned, older students have problems involved with combining family life with student life, doubts about their ability to compete with younger students, more complicated financial situations, and other concerns about mixing a more mature lifestyle with the demands of college life.

All college students, regardless of age or life stage, undergo a change in their usual lifestyle. And as explained previously, change is stressful. As going to college is a new experience and the people and the environment are new, it is not surprising to find many students feeling and acting shy (Greenberg, 1983). Making new friends, talking with professors and advisers, using the services of counselors in the student counseling center and dormitories, and attending stress management workshops should help reduce stress along with following many of the solutions covered in this chapter.

## Fatigue

College students experience fatigue as well as stress. Irregular hours, studying for final exams, and weekend parties all contribute to fatigue. Chronic fatigue leads to impaired memory and response time. **Fatigue** refers to a lack of energy or motivation and a strong desire to stop, rest, or sleep. This feeling can come from mental or physical exertion, work, or play.

*Fatigue may either be related to stress or have nothing to do with it.* For example, at night you may be tired from a long day of activity and feel fatigued, but you are not necessarily stressed or tense. Short-term fatigue can be easily remedied with some rest, but long-term, chronic fatigue is more serious. Closely linked to fatigue are weariness, tiredness, exhaustion, and lethargy. We think of yawning as associated with fatigue or sleepiness. But, is it?

## CRITICAL THINKING

### Yawning

Read the following and see how you respond.

*Have you ever thought about yawning, for instance? Yawning is a surprisingly powerful act. Just because you read the word 'yawning' in the previous two sentences—and the two additional 'yawns' in this sentence—a good number of you will probably yawn within the next few minutes. Even as I'm writing this, I've yawned twice. If you're reading this in a public place, and you've just yawned, chances are a good proportion of everyone who saw you yawn is now yawning too...*

Source: Gladwell, M. (2000). *The tipping point* (pp. 9–10). Boston: Little, Brown and Company.

Causes of fatigue can be emotional as well as physical or a combination of the two. Physical symptoms are extreme; generally, a fatigued person simply feels tired. Fatigue is a normal part of daily life, but sometimes a person is more keenly aware of it than at other times. Fatigue can sneak up on an individual or build up to a point where the individual cannot function well. It can also be dangerous, as when someone falls asleep at the wheel. Because of this potential danger, individuals need to recognize personal fatigue sensations and do something about them.

Fatigue comes from many sources, such as sleep disturbances, sleep apnea, a variety of diseases including heart and lung diseases, pregnancy, depression, anxiety, and grief. As Chapter 10 emphasized, the demands and conflicts arising from trying to achieve too much in the work and family realms can result in fatigue. A survey of 666 male and female clerical and professional employees revealed that fatigue levels were similar at home and at work. One male professional penciled in the following comment at the end of the survey: "Going home is just exchanging one set of problems for another." The study also revealed that professional women experienced significantly more fatigue and role overload than did professional men (Goldsmith, 1989).

These findings have implications for those interested in personal and family management. What is happening in offices and homes that produces so much fatigue? And why are researchers finding that home and family life is just another stressor rather than a reliever of stress and fatigue?

## The Body and Fatigue

MRI scans of fatigued brains look very much like brains of people who are fast asleep. There is a point at which the body is not performing well, a person is simply too tired to think straight. Like stress, fatigue originates as a physiological response, and it comes from both internal and external sources. Regardless of where the fatigue originates, it is always felt as a subjective sensation by the person (Atkinson, 1985). Certainly, a person should consult a physician if fatigue is extreme and unexplained in origin. The physician will want to know whether the level of fatigue is constant throughout the day or whether there is any pattern.

Fatigue begins at an unconscious, microscopic level and progresses through stages until the person thinks, "I'm tired." At the final stage, the person experiences fatigue as a sensation (Atkinson, 1985). Because the mind is included at this level, psychological factors such as boredom, depression, and being upset are combined with the physiological ones that cause fatigue.

## Systems Theory: Sleep, Energy, and Fatigue

Systems theory is relevant to the discussion of fatigue because fatigue is a sign of energy imbalance: too much energy is being expended and not enough is being conserved. One way to look at energy is to envision an energy pool with an imbalance of energy boosters (inputs) and energy drainers (outputs). The energy pool is depleted when there are more energy drainers (bad habits, overwork, mental strain, illness, and occupational hazards) than energy boosters (nutrition, exercise, good sleep, pleasure, and mastery).

### Sleep

Getting a good night's sleep is restorative because sleep is a prime time when systems restore themselves so they are less reactive to the negative impacts of stress. Sleep is not a passive activity because insufficient sleep is recognized as an essential component of health and safety—we do not want drowsy drivers on the road.

Individuals ages 15–19 sleep more hours a day on average than older individuals. Sleep time tends to decrease with age until age 65 when it starts increasing. The Bureau of Labor Statistics American Time Use Survey collects data on sleep times. They report that the teenagers sleep considerably more on weekends than during weekdays showing less consistency in sleep patterns than older adults do. On average, Americans aged 15 and over sleep 8 hours and 30 minutes a day.

*Sleep absolutely affects health,* says Julian Thayer of the National Institute on Aging (Elias, 2003, p. 7D). The immune system seems to tune up at night, adding natural killer cells to fight off disease. "There's preliminary evidence that the strength of the immune system actually influences the quality of sleep in addition to being affected by it," says Michael Irwin of the UCLA Neuropsychiatric Institute (Elias, 2003, p. 7D).

Sleep, a critical energy booster, is vital to maintaining well-being and enthusiasm for life. It plays a major role in preparing the body and brain for an alert, productive, and psychologically and physiologically healthy tomorrow (Maas, 1998). Even though everyone needs sleep, sometimes the amount and timing are difficult to control. For example, falling asleep after a stimulating day may be difficult even though you are very tired. Another time, you may feel drowsy, even though you want to stay alert, such as in an afternoon class. Have you ever heard the expression, "I need to sleep on it"? It turns out that people all over the world say some version of it, and it has been proven to have some substance.

### CASE STUDY

#### Katie

"I get a lot less sleep [than I need]—less than six hours a night," says Katie Danziger, whose New York City-based company, nomie baby, sells parent-sanity-saving washable car seat covers and stroller blankets. Like many overloaded entrepreneurs, Danziger doesn't get any exercise. Instead, she turns all her time over to nomie baby and her three kids. If you don't take care of yourself, you can't take care of your business. But that bit of common sense usually gets trampled by overload and its partner, stress. Stop for a second? Not possible. Delegate? It would take too long to explain the how-tos to a staffer. Take a break to refuel? Too much to do. Shut off the BlackBerry at night? Might miss a sale. Entrepreneurs are, of course, an action-oriented bunch by definition.

Source: Robinson, J. (2011, April 11). Don't melt down. Entrepreneur. http://www.entrepreneur.com/article/printthis/219311.html.

Child eyes stressed mom.

*Sleep researchers have found that sleep influences "complex cognitive procedural thinking".*
*(Stickgold et al., 2004, p. 58)*

*Each waking moment bombards your brain with scores of sensations, thoughts, and feelings. If your brain tried to store them all as memories, you might experience terminal overload and be able to remember nothing. Undoubtedly, you're editing out some impressions as they hit you during the day. But sleep also seems to help.*
*(Stickgold et al., 2004, p. 60)*

As noted in Chapter 10, humans spend about one-third of their lives sleeping. A century ago nine hours per day was the norm. Recent studies indicate that the average married mom gets 6.7 hours. According to the Centers for Disease Control and Prevention (cdc.gov) about one-quarter of the U.S. population reports not getting enough sleep now and then and about 10 percent report chronic insomnia. Sleep is necessary for two reasons:

- To restore energy levels
- To help the body regulate and synchronize itself

Sleep provides rhythm to life (Goldsmith, 2007). Most people go to sleep and awake about the same time every day. While asleep, humans go through certain cycles of light and deep slumber. Figure 11.2 illustrates the rhythmic nature of typical sleep patterns.

There are two kinds of sleep: REM and NREM sleep. **REM, or rapid eye movement sleep,** occurs when the sleeper is in a light sleep; most dreams happen during REM. **NREM, or non-rapid eye movement sleep,** occurs when the sleeper is in an inactive, deep slumber. Through the night, the sleeper goes back and forth between REM and NREM sleep. Apps and smartphones can monitor the amount of REM sleep.

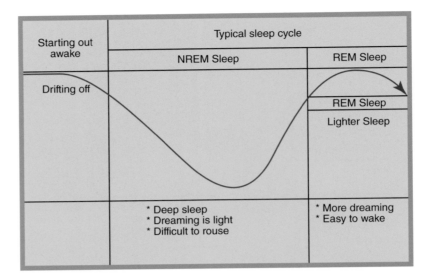

Figure 11.2 Typical sleep cycle.

Source: Based on National Center on Sleep Disorders Research.

Woman using smart phone.

**Insomnia** is the perception or complaint of inadequate or poor-quality sleep because of one or more of the following:

- Difficulty falling asleep

- Waking up frequently during the night with difficulty returning to sleep

- Waking up too early in the morning

- Unrefreshing sleep

When people are deprived of sleep for a long time or do not get the right balance of REM and NREM sleep, they can feel fatigued and irritable, and their abilities to make decisions and to concentrate diminish. This is why fatigue and insomnia are integral parts of the study of resource management.

Appropriate levels of sleep and rest are resources. For example, many athletes experience some form of precompetition stress that may result in insomnia during the night before their competition. This sleep withdrawal, even though temporary, has a negative influence on performance. Sleeping poorly impairs the ability to remember and learn.

---

### Suggested Activity

Plot your sleep pattern for three days on a graph. Mark when you go to sleep and when you wake up; include nighttime sleep and daytime naps. Do you see a pattern? Does doing an activity like this make you more conscious of your sleep patterns? Were you more likely to go to sleep earlier at night and get up earlier than normal?

---

According to the National Center on Sleep Disorders Research, preschool children (ages three to five) should get between 10 and 12 hours of sleep including naps. Older children need less; those between the ages of 6 and 12 need about nine hours of sleep a night. Teenagers need about eight to nine hours. Parents can help children sleep better by limiting drinks loaded with caffeine before bed, setting routines, and allowing time for children to unwind before bedtime. Caffeine may stay in the body for up to 12 hours, so caffeine consumption should stop around noon depending on the individual because reactions vary. Here is the caffeine content (milligrams per eight ounces) of several popular drinks:

- Coffee, 110 (approximate, varies by type of coffee)
- Mountain Dew, 37
- Coca-Cola, 23
- Arizona green tea, 7.5

Other disturbers of sleep are alcohol and drugs. Alcohol not only sedates but also disturbs normal sleep patterns.

Sleep problems are more prevalent in older people. As people age, natural changes in circadian rhythms and medications affect sleep patterns. Other things affecting sleep are the need to use the bathroom more often at night, physical pain from arthritis, coughing, nighttime heartburn, headaches, and depression.

Circadian rhythms are triggered by nighttime darkness, which releases a surge of melatonin leading to sleep; the dawn triggers awakening (Stickgold et al., 2004). Electric light (artificial illumination) appears to disrupt this natural pattern. Older people often feel sleepy early in the evening, and this can lead to falling asleep at 8 P.M. and waking at 4 A.M. Daytime exposure to natural light appears to help a person sleep better:

*For Mrs. Homer, it worked. The increased exposure to light "made a difference," she says. It also helped her realize how much time she was spending indoors in dimly lit rooms. Since then, she's kept up the exposure to light by visiting a park across the street from her high-rise a few times a week. "I didn't go into that deep dream sleep before, and I'm dreaming now."*

*(Greene, 2002, p. R10)*

Table 11.2 Sleep Hygiene Suggestions

The promotion of regular sleep is known as **sleep hygiene** according to the Centers for Disease Control and Prevention. Here are the recommendations for improving sleep from the National Sleep Foundation.

1. Go to bed at the same time each night and rise at the same time each morning.
2. Make sure your bedroom is a quiet, dark, and relaxing environment, which is neither too hot nor too cold.
3. Make sure your bed is comfortable and use it only for sleeping and not for other activities, such as reading, watching TV, or listening to music. Remove all TVs, computers, and other "gadgets" from the bedroom. This advice depends on the individual, most young adults sleep with their mobile device within reach and would be anxious if it was in another room.
4. Physical activity may help promote sleep, but not within a few hours of bedtime.
5. Avoid large meals before bedtime.

Source: Retrieved November 3, 2011, from http://www.cdc.gov/sleep/about_sleep/sleep_hygiene.htm.

There are sleep disorder clinics accredited by the American Sleep Disorders Association. Clinic staff study sleep patterns and help people suffering from chronic insomnia. Among the discoveries of these clinics is that stress and anxiety can affect the length and quality of sleep.

Work schedules can also influence sleep patterns and insomnia. For example, studies have shown that shift workers get three hours less sleep than people who work a normal daytime schedule, and up to 90 percent of shift workers report sleep disturbances (Atkinson, 1985). Irregular and rotating shifts (e.g., working nights one week, days the next) play havoc not only with the individual's health and sleep patterns but also with family schedules. Sometimes a family may see shifts as an asset; for example, shifts may allow someone to be home with the children always. On the negative side, however, husband and wife working on different shifts may rarely see each other. More intimate, face-to-face communication may be replaced with hurried phone calls and written messages.

According to James Maas (1998), two primary rules to follow are to establish a regular sleep pattern and get enough nightly sleep. Another rule suggested by the National Sleep Foundation is to make the bed a sleep- and sex-only zone. For someone experiencing sleep problems, desks, clutter, and computers and other reminders of work should probably be in another room beside the bedroom. See these suggestions and more in Table 11.2. Finally, keep following the latest scientific discoveries on sleep. So far, we know that sleep makes a person demonstrably smarter and appreciably healthier; it is an important part of a long and healthy life.

## Energy and Alertness

Clearly, getting adequate rest and sleep is an energy booster. An energetic person has the capacity to take on a job or an activity and complete it to the best of her or his ability. There are many types of energy boosters. In addition, some individuals seem to be born with more energy than others. Research is incomplete as to why this difference exists. Another little-understood energy phenomenon is how people re-energize themselves during the day.

Many people at one time subscribed to the drain theory, which asserted that individuals wake with a certain level of energy in the morning. As the day wears on, each activity takes away some of that energy until by nightfall the energy is depleted and the person sleeps. Then, according to the theory, sleep restores the person, and the pattern repeats the next day. The problem with the drain theory is that not all people are highly energized on first waking up, and during the day such things as food, exercise, and excitement refuel people. Each person has typical energy rhythms or patterns during the day, which can be altered by events. We experience ups and downs in alertness over the course of the day, even when our nighttime sleep is adequate. Alertness is quite strong around 10 and 11 A.M., which makes this a good time to take classes and tests. It dips at midafternoon, goes up again around 6 P.M., and then starts to fall until bedtime.

## Fatigue Management

The purpose of this book is not just to describe life management problems (e.g., people do not get enough sleep or rest), but to also present possible solutions.

Systems theory asserts that system parts are interconnected: If one part of the system is affected, other parts are affected, too. The subjects of sleep, energy, and fatigue are so interlaced that it is difficult to discuss one without discussing the others. To cope with fatigue problems, an individual needs to examine each part of the system, including diet, exercise, sleep, activity, and relationships. It could be that outside help is needed. **Cognitive behavioral therapy**—talk therapy that helps you change patterns of behavior and thinking—may calm or lessen system-wide inflammation and other problems.

What are other solutions to managing energy and fatigue better? First, an individual should be able to recognize his or her sleep patterns and fatigue signs and assign time and energy accordingly. In other words, it is up to the individual to self-monitor. Successful people rarely go blindly into a new activity; they first think about how much of their time and energy will be required. Second, when fatigue is imminent, the individual should try to cope with it by napping or sleeping, relaxing, eating properly, changing activity, or adopting whatever combination of these activities works best. As mentioned earlier, daily exposure to natural light, keeping a regular schedule, and avoiding all stimulants such as coffee, tea, and soft drinks containing caffeine at least two hours (some would say 6–12 hours) prior to going to bed will help improve sleep.

And, most of all, people should take time to sleep: It is important to their daily functioning and there is a threat to public safety when people are sleepy at the wheel or when operating machinery. A 2020 Subaru Outback car measures visual fatigue and alerts the driver ("you are getting sleepy."). So, technological advances will aid us in fatigue management.

## Chronic Fatigue Syndrome

According to the Centers for Disease Control and Prevention (cdc.gov) **chronic fatigue syndrome** (CFS) also referred to more simply as Fatigue Syndrome is a debilitating and complex disorder characterized by profound fatigue that is not improved by bed rest and can be worsened by physical or mental activity. The CDC says that the symptoms affect several body systems and may include weakness, muscle pain, impaired memory and/or mental concentration, and insomnia, which can result in reduced participation in daily activities. The number of people with CFS is difficult to measure because it tends to be underreported or misdiagnosed, or associated with other diseases such as diabetes or thyroid disorders. Sometimes there are flu-like symptoms. It is a public health concern because of missed days at school and work. Chronic fatigue is a contentious topic: It is not clear what causes the disease or even whether it is one disease or many; research is still under way. It may be a long-acting viral infection, a form of allergy, or something entirely different.

Patients with extreme chronic fatigue cannot work and have little energy for anything. People with chronic fatigue exhibit a variety of symptoms. The CDC defined the syndrome in 1988 and it has identified the main symptoms as chills or low-grade fever, sore throat, tender lymph nodes, muscle pain, muscle weakness, extreme fatigue, headaches, joint pain (without swelling), neurological problems (confusion, memory loss, visual disturbances), sleep disorders, and the sudden onset of symptoms (Cowley, 1990).

In addition to these symptoms, chronic fatigue differs from ordinary fatigue brought on by overexertion in several respects. In chronic fatigue

- Rest is not restorative.
- Minimal physical activity can bring on significant "exhausterbations" (S. Straus, personal communication, August 24, 1989).

Chronic fatigue is long-lasting and affects children as well as adults. A good night's sleep or a leisurely vacation will not help true chronic fatigue. It appears that lifestyle changes such as regular exercise like yoga and tai chi, stress and time management, a healthy diet, and, in some cases, medication supervised by a physician will help relieve symptoms.

## SUMMARY

Causes, reactions, and solutions to stress and fatigue were addressed in this chapter. Stress is normal, even useful but too long and too much can have negative consequences for relationships and one's own sense of well-being. It is a physical reaction to emotional or physical situations or demands. Planning, organizing, compartmentalizing, and outsourcing can all help in the management of stress.

When individuals experience excessive stress and fatigue, they question their life choices and they need to reevaluate their time use and commitments. They wonder whether it is necessary to hurry all the time. And are they really achieving more by hurrying? A fundamental question is in the rush, are families being shortchanged? "Extreme work" is a term that describes 60 hours or more of work per week and 24/7 access plus excessive travel. The Japanese have the word "karoshi" which means death by overwork.

Police score high on scales measuring psychological resilience, the capacity to handle severe stressors.

This chapter has largely been based on theories such as the Theory of Adaptive Range, the Process of Social Stress Theory, and Systems Theory and on research from psychology and the health and wellness fields. An important point is that moderate levels of stress and fatigue are a normal part of life.

Hans Selye was a major contributor to stress research. Among other things, he differentiated between two types of stress: distress (harmful) and eustress (beneficial).

Stress originates from two sources: internal and external. Stressor events can be normative (expected) or nonnormative (unanticipated). The body's response to stress and the fight or flight syndrome are important to understanding how stress works. An individual's personality and emotional state play significant roles in the evaluation of and reaction to stress. Type A and Type B personalities react differently to stress.

The meaning of burnout has changed over the years, but long-term exhaustion is serious and should not be ignored. The steps leading up to burnout and possible solutions to burnout were described in this chapter. Brownout is a predecessor to burnout. Prolonged fatigue, irritability, frustration, and neck, head, or backache are all signals of burnout. Trainee physicians score high in stress and burnout.

Although stress exists throughout the life cycle, childhood stress and the stress college students experience are particularly troubling. David Elkind has observed that children today may be pushed to grow up too fast and assume adult responsibilities at an early age.

Energy boosters can have a restorative effect on persons suffering from fatigue, so can sleep. Sleep researchers have distinguished rapid eye movement sleep from non-rapid eye movement sleep. Ordinary fatigue can be reduced by sleep and rest. Children need different amounts of sleep depending on their ages. A century ago nine hours of sleep a night was normal; now Americans ages 15 and older average 8 hours and 30 minutes according to the Average Time Use Survey conducted by the Bureau of Labor Statistics, and one-third of them get by on six or less.

Far more research is needed on the complex interplay among energy, fatigue, sleep, personality, and stress. Individuals can strive to maintain a balance of activity, rest, and energy; acquire the skills to understand themselves; and enjoy each other more. The next chapter covers another potential stressor and relaxer—the environment.

## KEY TERMS

brownout
burnout
chronic fatigue syndrome
   (fatigue syndrome)
cognitive behavioral
   therapy
comfort zone
comparative advantage
crises
distress
domino effect
eustress
external stress
extreme work fatigue

fight or flight syndrome
insomnia
internal stress
job stress
*karoshi*
metro area
nonnormative
   stressor events
non-rapid eye
   movement (NREM)
sleep
normative stressor
   events
outsourcing

perfectionism
psychologically flexible
psychological hardiness
psychological resilience
rapid eye movement (REM)
sleep satisficing
sleep hygiene
stress
stressors
stress overload, pileup,
   spillover
Type A person
Type B person
virtual events

## REVIEW QUESTIONS

1. **Are you mostly a Type A or Type B personality?** A book editor explained that he was Type B on the outside and Type A on the inside. How could this be? Do you know someone who appears to be one type of personality, but is the other type? Explain.

2. David Elkind observed that children are growing up too fast; they are pushed into too many activities and adult responsibilities. Do you agree or disagree? Explain your answer.

3. What happens to the body during each of the three stages of the stress reaction?

4. How could perfectionism have a good side? What may be a benefit?

5. Describe the drain theory of human energy and explain why it is inadequate.

## REFERENCES

Adler, J., Kalb, C., & Rogers, A. (1999, June 14). Stress. *Newsweek*, pp. 56–69.

Arnold, J., Randall, R. et al. (2016). *Work psychology, 6th edition*. UK: Pearson.

Arnott, N. (2002, November/December). Got stress? Don't worry. *Weight Watchers Magazine*, pp. 64–67.

Atkinson, H. (1985). *Women and fatigue*. New York: Putnam.

Begley, S. (2003, February 7). How humans react when bad things occur again and again. *The Wall Street Journal*, p. B1.

Bronte-Tinkew, J., Horowitz, A., & Carrano, J. (2011). Aggravation and stress in parenting: Associations with co- parenting and father engagement among resident fathers. *Journal of Family Issues, 31*(4), 525–555.

Chang, M., Brown, R., & Nitzke, S. (2008). Scale development: Factors affecting diet, exercise, and stress management. *BMC Public Health, 8*, 76.

Cheney, S. (June 28, 2017). More work, less sleep for Americans in 2016. *The Wall Street Journal*, p. A3.

Cotton, D. (1990). *Stress management*. New York: Brunner/Mazel.

Cowley, G. (1990, November 12). Chronic fatigue syndrome. *Newsweek*, pp. 62–70.

Cowley, G., Underwood, A., & Kalb, C. (1999, June 14). Stress busters: What works. *Newsweek*, p. 60.

DeGarmo, D., Patras, J., & Eap, S. (2008, January). Social support for divorced fathers' parenting: Testing a stress-buffering model. *Family Relations, 57*(1), 35–48.

Dollahite, D. (1991). Family resource management and family stress theories: Toward a conceptual integration. *Lifestyles: Family and Economic Issues, 12*(4), 361–377.

Elias, M. (1998, March 26). Antistress groups seem to support cancer survival. *USA Today*, p. D1.

Elias, M. (2003, March 10). Study: Hugging warms the heart, and also may protect it. *USA Today*, p. 7D.

Elkind, D. (1988). *The hurried child*. Reading, MA: Addison-Wesley.

Fisher, C. (1998, June). Business on the road. *American Demographics, 20*, 44–47, 54.

Garrison, M., Malia, J., Norem, R., & Hira, T. (1994). Developing a daily hassles inventory. *Proceedings of the 1994 Conference of the Eastern Family Economics and Management Association* (pp. 18–43). Pittsburgh, PA: Re source.

Gladwell, M. (2000). *The tipping point*. Boston, MA: Little, Brown and Company.

Goldsmith, E. (1989). Role overload: Professional men vs. professional women. *Proceedings of the Southeastern Regional Association of Family Economics—Home Management Annual Meeting*.

Goldsmith, E. (2007). Stress, fatigue, and social support in the work and family context. *Journal of Loss and Trauma, 12*, 155–169.

Greenberg, J. (1983). *Comprehensive stress management*. Dubuque, IA: Brown.

Greene, K. (2002, November 11). Aging well. *The Wall Street Journal*, p. R10.

Harman, W. (1998). *Global mind change*. San Francisco: Berrett-Koehler.

Havlovic, S., & Keenan, J. (1991). Coping with work stress. In P. Perrewe (Ed.), *Job Stress*. Corte Madera, CA: Select Press.

Hill, K., & Wigfield, A. (1984). Test anxiety: A major educational problem and what can be done about it. *Elementary School Journal, 85*, 106–126.

Houser, R., Daniels, J., D'Andrea, M., & Konstam, V. (1993). A systemic behaviorally based technique for resolving conflict between adolescents and their single parents. *Family Behavior Therapy, 15*(3), 17–31.

Kirkcaldy, B., Shephard, R., & Furnham, A. (2001). The influence of type A behavior and locus of control upon job satisfaction and occupational health. *Personality and Individual Differences, 33*(8), 1361–1371.

Kobasa, S. (1982). The hardy personality: Toward a psychology of stress and health. In J. Suls & G. Sanders (Eds.), *Social Psychology and Illness*. Hillsdale, NJ: Erlbaum.

Lazarus, R. (1991). Psychological stress in the workplace. In P. Perrewe (Ed.), *Job Stress* (pp. 1–13). Corte Madera, CA: Select Press.

Levine, K. (1990, May). Coping with stress. *Parents,* pp. 68–70.

Lincoln, K., & Chae, D. (2010). Stress, marital satisfaction, and psychological distress among African Americans. *Journal of Family Issues, 31*(8), 1081–1105.

Maas, J. (1998). *Power sleep.* New York: Villard.

Maslach, C. (1982). *Burnout: The cost of caring.* Englewood Cliffs, NJ: Prentice-Hall.

McLellan, T., Bragg, A., & Cacciola, J. (1992). *Escape from anxiety & stress.* New York: Chelsea House.

Misra, R. (2000). College students' academic stress and its relation to their anxiety, time management, and leisure satisfaction. *American Journal of Health Studies.*

Murphy, M., & Archer, J. (1996, January/February). Stressors on the college campus. *Journal of College Student Development, 37*(1), 20–27.

Nowack, K. M. (1991). Psychological predictors of health status. *Work and Stress, 5*(2), 117–131.

Powers, M. (1995, Fall). Dashed expectations. *Human Ecology Forum,* pp. 5–7.

Quick, J., Nelson, D., & Quick, J. (1990). *Stress and challenge at the top.* New York: Wiley.

Ruffin, N. (2001, June). *Children and stress: Caring strategies to guide children.* Blacksburg, VA: Virginia Tech University publication #350–054.

Selye, H. (1974). *Stress without distress.* New York: New American Library.

Selye, H. (1976). *The stress of life.* New York: McGraw-Hill.

Senior, J. (March 15, 2008). Excerpt: Can't get no satisfaction. *NPR Talk of the Nation Transcript.*

Seppala, E. (2016). *The happiness track.* New York: Harper & Row.

Shellenbarger, S. (2003, March 27). Slackers, rejoice: Research touts the benefits of skipping out on work. *The Wall Street Journal,* p. D1.

Sher, K., Wood, P., & Gotham, H. (1996, January/February). The course of psychological distress in college: A prospective high-risk study. *Journal of College Student Development, 37,* 42–50.

Sheth, J., & Sisodia, R. (1999, June 28). Outsourcing comes home. *The Wall Street Journal,* p. A26.

Shoshan, H. N., & Sonnentag, S. (2019). *The effects of employee burnout on customers: An experimental approach.* Oxford: Taylor& Francis.

Smith, C. (1997, December 24). A mismatch in the workplace sparks employee burnout. *Tallahassee Democrat,* p. 11D.

Spencer, J. (2003, March 11). Are you stressed out yet? *The Wall Street Journal,* p. D1.

Stickgold, R., Winkelman, J., & Wehrwein, P. (2004, January 19). You will start to feel very sleepy. *Newsweek,* pp. 58, 60.

Toffler, A. (1970). *Future shock.* New York: Random House.

Topp, R. (1989). Effect of relaxation or exercise on undergraduate test anxiety. *Perceptual and Motor Skills, 69,* 335–341.

Ulrich, D., & Dunne, H. (1986). *To love and work.* New York: Brunner/Mazel.

van der Meulen, E., van Veldhoven, J. P. M., & van der Velden, Peter G. (2019). Stability of psychological resilience of police officers: A three-wave latent class analysis. *Personality and Individual Differences, 144,* 120–124.

Waldrop, J. (1993, September). Josie and the pussy cats beat stress. *American Demographics, 15*(9), 17.

White, E. (2006, August 22). Staying focused on work when life gets in the way. *The Wall Street Journal,* p. B8.

Zhou, A., & Panagioti, M. (2020, August 18). Factors associated with burnout and stress in trainee physicians: A systematic review and meta-analysis, *JAMA Network Open.*

Chapter **12**

# Managing Environmental Resources

DOI: 10.4324/9781003166740-12

... More land is being conserved for family farms, forests, community gardens, dog parks, and trails.

... Buildings consume about 40 percent of all material resources in the United States and worldwide.

**CASE STUDY**

### Human Behavior and Environments

Jeremiah, a bakery worker, said when he put a $1 bill in a tip jar on the counter, others were more likely to do the same. Here follows an example that has implications for environmental behavior and everything else we do as social beings.

> *Social psychology studies have long shown that we generally use other people's behavior as a guide for how we ourselves should behave. An empty tip jar, or one filled with pennies, is likely to lead people not to tip or to tip very little, while a jar filled with signs of generous tipping makes customers feel that this is the norm they are supposed to follow.*
>
> *Source: Dan Ariely (2019, April 27–28). A remedy for big talkers in meetings. The Wall Street Journal, C5.*

If a neighbor puts solar panels on their roof, are other neighbors likely to follow? The opening case study from Dan Ariely of Duke University would indicate the answer is yes. This chapter puts environmentalism into the context of individual, family, and household behavior and how they are changing (read the Case Study about the clean-living generation).

**CASE STUDY**

### The Clean-Living Generation

Do you relate to the following?

> *They drink less alcohol, eat more vegetables, cut back on meat, meditate often, enjoy knitting and make their own pour-over coffee. Meet the "clean lifers," the young adults who revel in dodging the indulgence of their elders. "In terms of living an objectively healthy lifestyle, this group is inspiring the older generations," says Sam Calagione, chief executive and founder of Dogfish Head Craft Brewery Inc. Many young adults, having grown up during the recession, pursue healthful living as a way to find balance pursue healthful living as a way to find balance amid the global uncertainty that continues today.*
>
> *Source: Ellen Byron (2018, March 13). The clean-living generation. The Wall Street Journal, A9).*

Bike lanes, micro wind turbines, electric buses, autonomous (self-driving) cars, and more efficient water and waste collection systems—will lead to greener cities and lifestyles. This chapter shifts from a focus on self and individual worries about stress and fatigue to family ecosystems—the interaction between families and their environments. We return to issues introduced earlier in the book about home environments and the future pressing needs of cities as their populations grow. Due to inflation economic ups and downs, and environmental concerns in the United States, the average new house size which peaked in 2007 at 2,521 sq. ft. shrunk in 2010 to 2,377 sq. ft. and rose to 2,600 sq. ft. in the United States and 2,200 sq. ft. in Canada in 2022. From a historical perspective, the average U.S. house size in 1950 was 983 sq. ft. Worldwide the sizes and configurations of homes are shifting along with improving techniques and practices regarding energy and water use (Abeliotis et al., 2010; Berkholz et al., 2010). Homes are one of the types of buildings, which consider the overall impact on material resources of all types of buildings including high rises.

> *Buildings consume about forty percent of all material resources in the U.S. and worldwide. The primary materials used are wood, glass, concrete, and steel with every other imaginable material playing a role in building finishes and systems. Material selection is driven by four factors:*

- Cost

- Availability of labor

- Regulatory requirements, and

- Design Aesthetics

Cost of commodity materials are driven by worldwide demand and change on a daily basis
*(Goldsmith, 2015, p. 160)*

Steve Jobs of Apple fame said innovation is the ability to see change as an opportunity, not a threat. Wayne Gretzky, the hockey great, said, "I skate to where the puck is going to be, not where it has been." In this spirit we move forward, how can we have a better planet, better homes, and healthier families? Increased environmental awareness as it impacts individuals, families, and households is offered to the reader along with solutions for households. We do not stop with simply listing problems; everyday solutions are given. Here is an example:

Preventing energy waste has become a household preoccupation in the era of nearly $4-a-gallon gas and rising prices for everything from airline tickets to milk. Whether motivated by environmental impulses or a desire to reduce utility bills, many Americans are researching ways to create a more energy-efficient home. (Hodges, 2008, p. D1)

## Sustainability and Sustainable Behavior

Children are never too young to learn about sustainability and develop eco-friendly habits. Energy-efficient choices can save families about a third of their energy bill without sacrificing comfort. We want to make sustainable choices for our children and grandchildren. As **stewards** of the earth, we have a responsibility that extends beyond our immediate family circle.

> ***Sustainable behavior*** *is a multi-dimensional concept that includes behaviors such as conservation of natural resources through efficient use, recycling, purchase and use of green products and other behaviors that preserve the natural environment including air and water quality. One means of promoting these desirable behaviors is the use of social influence, that is, the influence that people have over other people. Social influence is how one person or group affects another's opinions, attitudes, emotions, or behaviors.*
> *(Goldsmith, 2015, p. 3)*

**Sustainability** is about conscious design and the consideration of the impact consumption choices make on the environment given finite resources. It involves ethics, ecology, and estimations of system life expectancies. A widely used definition comes from the Brundtland Report (1987) which states that sustainability is about "meeting the needs of the present without compromising the ability of future generations to meet their own needs." This report set forth a coherent set of principles and forms the bedrock of many disciplines. Some of the concepts include intergenerational justice and the three legs of sustainability:

- social

- economic, and

- environmental

Depending on the discipline one of these aspects is emphasized. In this chapter, we are mostly talking about the environmental side with applications to the social unit of the family. The cost savings discussed and worldwide impact touch on economics. To give perspective, a trend reported during the last recession was that

> despite a weak economy, more U.S. land is being voluntarily conserved as urban parks, family farms, forests, gardens and farmers' markets—a total of 10 million new acres since 2005, says a report out today. 'Even when times are tough, people want to take care of their home—the places they see every day,'

says Rand Wentworth, president of the Land Trust Alliance, a conservation group (Koch, November 16, 2011, p. 7).

**Resource education** brings current and potential sustainability problems to the forefront for discussion and resolution. It goes beyond sensitizing people to giving them the tools and information to act for sustainable development.

The goal is **sustainable development**—a form of growth wherein societal needs, present, and future, are met. Sustainable development requires the input and cooperation of all segments of society, producers as well as consumers. Toward this end, more careful decisions at every level are being made about the products and services brought into and used in the home.

Airplanes have high decibel levels and heavy impacts on the carbon imprint.

The impact on the land, air, and sea from the consumption of goods and resources is known as the **ecological footprint**. To explain further, the ecological footprint is the

> *amount of biologically productive land and sea area required for the support either of an individual's current lifestyle or the consumption patterns of a particular population. It should include the area required to absorb and render harmless the corresponding waste*

*(dolceta.eu, November 10, 2011)*

More specifically, the **carbon footprint** has to do with measuring and reducing the environmental impact of carbon emissions resulting from activities such as the use of fuel to transport goods or for travel.

> *A new concept is entering the consumer lexicon: the carbon footprint. First came organic. Then came fair trade. Now makers of everything from milk to jackets to cars are starting to tally up the carbon footprints of their products. That's the amount of carbon dioxide and other greenhouse gases that get coughed into the air when the goods are made, shipped and stored, and then used by consumers.*

*(Ball, 2008, p. R1)*

As the quote indicates, almost anything can be measured for the carbon footprint, and nations are rated on carbon dioxide emissions from fossil fuel consumption, in annual tons per capita. Table 12.1 shows the top four nations/areas on carbon dioxide emissions from fuel combustion, according to the International Energy Agency.

Once carbon footprint is measured, the next issue is how to label products about carbon footprint or being green in general. These labels are known as eco-labels.

Here is a practical environmental-impact example that households face—milk consumption and choice of packaging or bottling. "The dairy industry doesn't plan to put carbon-footprint labels on milk cartons, says Rick Naczi, an executive vice president 'for Dairy Management. 'It's something that would be very, very difficult to make understandable to consumers," he says. (Ball, 2008, p. R4) Currently, more people are drinking milk from non-dairy sources and are asking for glass milk bottles that are returnable, behavior harkening back to the home milk bottle delivery in the 1940s and 1950s. Perhaps you have seen glass milk bottles on front porches in old movies and television shows or you are in the practice of returning glass milk bottles to stores.

An Australian study (D'Souza et al., 2007) found that label dissatisfaction with green products was higher in older and middle-aged respondents. Within this group of respondents, there was some disagreement about the accuracy of labels and about the ease of understanding them. The United States does not have an

Table 12.1  Top Nations/Areas on Carbon Dioxide Emissions from Fuel Combustion

| Country | |
|---|---|
| China | 9 481 |
| USA | 4 888 |
| European Union | 3 956 |
| India | 2 299 |

Source: International Energy Agency, 2018

agreed-upon government eco-label across many lines of products, but government-sponsored eco-labels are available in over 20 countries including Canada, Australia, Japan, and Sweden.

College campuses are experiencing a renewed interest in going "green." More colleges are making sustainability programs a high priority, putting more resources into energy conservation efforts, and setting goals to reduce carbon emissions, according to survey results released by the National Wildlife Federation. Given the popularity of all things *green*, that is not surprising (Carlson, 2008). Here is an example, at Florida State University there is an administrative position called the Director of FSU Sustainable Campus. In 2019, FSU changed to all-electric buses with a savings of $10 million a year in fuel and maintenance costs (as reported in the May 2019 issue of *Florida Trend*).

## CRITICAL THINKING

What is your campus doing about recycling, food waste, green transportation, bicycles, cleaner air, energy use, compact fluorescent light bulbs, and other green adjustments? Do you agree or disagree that today's college-aged students are the greenest generation? Explain.

This chapter also touches on economic development. In the language of economics, the environment is considered a **natural capital**, a good to protect. Decisions are being made that are consistent with economic growth and environmental protection. According to Harris (2002), all nations seek economic development, but only in the last 40 years have they considered the impact that growth has on the environment. In many nations, the concept of environmental protection is even more recent than that.

Reducing what is sent to landfills is a goal. In the United States, the recycling rate has doubled during the last 20 years and recycling bins at the household level have made it easier. Recycling efforts are increasing worldwide.

In this chapter, the *3-Rs solution—reducing, reusing, and recycling*—will be highlighted. It is increasingly being accepted worldwide as a means of combating the negative effects on the environment. There is also a growing recognition of the total product life cycle—from the resources used to make the product, through its

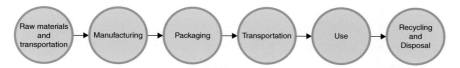

Figure 12.1 Life cycle assessments (LCA).

actual use, until its final disposal. The study of the life cycle of household products involves not only the material resources involved in their manufacture, distribution, and disposal, including energy and water use but also the human resources involved (Lee & Jepson, 2021; Uitdenbogerd et al., 1998). The term for this is **life cycle assessment** (LCA). LCA manufacturers are finding ways to reduce pollution and waste (see Figure 12.1). To summarize, environmental problems are intertwined with human behaviors.

Sigmund Freud, the founder of psychoanalysis, best known for his theories about the psyche (the mind) and social interaction, also made observations about humans in environmental contexts. In *Civilization and Its Discontents* (1930), Freud wrote that as civilizations become increasingly complex and modern, humans must renounce their innate selves. We must think about things greater than our immediate surroundings.

The difficulty may be in change resistance. For example, in some Scottish supermarkets, shoppers were accustomed to using store bags that were free, but now they are asked to pay a small charge for store bags or to bring their reusable bags from home. Each grocery store chain around the world is addressing the bag issue—most have found it useful to offer their own bags and to offer incentives for those customers bringing bags from home. During the Covid-19 response, some stores did not allow customers to bring shopping bags from home. Most changed this policy in 2021 so that bringing reusable tote bags from home was once again encouraged.

## CRITICAL THINKING

Does your grocery store encourage the use of bags from home or charge for in-store bags? How do shoppers in your area feel about plastic bags? Is there legislation or are there store policies that prohibit the use of plastic or paper bags?

*As world population continues to grow, and economic activity expands at an even faster rate, sustainability will become both more important and more difficult to achieve. This is the major challenge of the twenty-first century, and both economic and ecological understanding will be needed to formulate global, national, and local responses.*

(Harris, 2002, p. 439)

Thinking about others and the future of the planet is this chapter's theme. The management process takes place within an environmental context as illustrated in Figure 12.2. Building on the chapters on resources and managing human resources, time, stress, and fatigue, this chapter gives practical examples about how to manage the environment, particularly the near environment that directly affects individuals and families. The resource chapters share the philosophy that the way individuals and families allocate resources has an impact on the state of the environment and global well-being. Certainly, decisions and actions at the household level collectively affect not only the present state of the world but also the world that is to come. Even one simple behavioral change, such as carpooling, using cold water when laundering, or recycling bags, affects the environment.

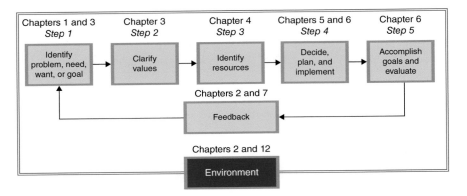

Figure 12.2 **The management process model.**

The present state of the environment is a result of developments and changes in the past as well as of current conditions. According to the best estimates, the human species, *Homo sapiens*, is 200,000–250,000 years old (the earliest skeletons come from Africa), and the earth is over 4.5 billion years old (Gould, 1989). The latest fossil evidence of early humans suggests 300,000 years. Phrasing it poetically, Gould says that in terms of the age of the earth, humanity arose just yesterday as a small twig on one branch of a flourishing tree. The realization of our minor place in earth's history gives us a sense of the magnitude of our responsibility to preserve what we have inherited. We are just beginning to understand both the limits and the potential of our planet and our role. What separates us from previous generations is this greater awareness of the benefits and limits of our environment. The importance of the choices individuals and families make regarding the environment is enormous and social influence has a tremendous effect on recycling and consumption behaviors (Goldsmith & Goldsmith, 2011).

## The Ecosystem and Environmentalism

A house is a system of interrelated parts, so the systems approach used throughout this book is particularly appropriate when discussing environmentalism. Systems are composed of living and nonliving things. Living systems (e.g., plants, animals, societies) are open systems that react to feedback. They can exist only in certain environments. Any change in the environment, such as a change in public health, the temperature, air pressure, hydration, oxygen, or radiation outside a relatively narrow range, produces stress to which living systems must adjust. Under severe stress or deprivation, they cannot survive or thrive. Homes were put to the test during the Covid-19 pandemic and the aftermath, and in this regard see the Critical Thinking exercise.

---

### CRITICAL THINKING

#### Homes Rethought

Reflect on how homes are changing and the recent acceleration in home design and function.

*In normal times, new trends in home design and home decorating bubble up simply because its time for something different. A few years of bold color and homeowners start painting things gray. After enough minimalism, a hunger for plaids and florals comes roaring back. But this time last year, a cultural experiment began that changed our relationships with houses and condos and apartments around the world. Suddenly, constantly, we were inside them. So much of public life – work, school, exercise shopping, dining and (virtually) socializing – began happening entirely within the walls of homes, at least for those able to do so. Architects and interior designers say that after 12 months of varying degrees of lockdown, people are discovering what does and doesn't work in their homes and becoming more confident about acting on it. They're realizing how familiar spaces can serve them better.*

Source: Melissa Rayworth (Associated Press, March 30, 2021). "Out of frustration come brilliant ideas: A homebound year has meant rethinking our rooms," *Tallahassee Democrat*, p. 1D.

As discussed in Chapter 2, the family ecosystem is the subsystem of human ecology that emphasizes the interactions between families and environments. Ecology is the study of how living things relate to their natural environment (Naar, 1990). An **ecosystem** is the subsystem of ecology that emphasizes the relationship between organisms and their environment. Organisms are living things—plants or animals. The place where an organism lives is its **habitat**.

The external conditions that surround and influence the life of an organism, an individual, a family, or a population constitute its environment (Naar, 1990). According to Gould (1998), beyond these basic definitions, there is a certain mystery to the balance of life:

> *We do not yet know the rules of the composition for ecosystems. We do not even know if rules exist in the usual sense. I am tempted, therefore, to close with the famous words that D'Arcy Thompson wrote to signify our ignorance of the microscopic world* (Growth and Form, *1942 edition*). *We are not quite so uninformed about the rules of composition for ecosystems, but what a stark challenge and what an inspiration to go forth: "We have come to the edge of a world of which we have no experience, and where all our preconceptions must be recast." (p. 404)*

Concern for the environment is called **environmentalism**. It can be found at all levels, from the individual— including activists like Rachel Carson—to the family to community organizations to government and industry. Furthermore, the levels overlap. For example, individuals can work through institutions by banding together, boycotting products or companies, writing letters, and voting for appropriate candidates. They can positively affect what industry produces, by buying only "green" (environmentally friendly) products. However, it should be pointed out that

> *Most consumers lack the scientific background to understand many environmental issues and few have relevant previous experience to guide them in assessing the relative environmental merits of market-place alternatives. Thus, the potential for consumer fraud and deception is great.*
>
> *(Cude, 1993, p. 207)*

A major emphasis of environmentalism is how to retain existing environmental resources. These resources can be divided into two types: social and physical. **Social environmental resources** include an array of societies, economic and political groups, and community organizations. In each of these, people are united in a common cause, such as saving the manatees, or in a more general concern, such as reducing global warming. **Global warming** is caused when carbon dioxide and other greenhouse gases collect in the air and trap solar heat reflected from the earth; over time, it can alter the earth's temperature, sea level, and storm systems (Pinchon, 1990). As an example, ocean temperatures have risen 1.4 degrees since 1970.

Air emissions are potential problems.

Carbon dioxide is released into the atmosphere by the burning of fuels, such as coal and oil; and the natural process of carbon dioxide recycling gets impeded by the destruction of forests.

**Physical environmental resources** include natural tangible (e.g., trees, soil, and ocean) and less tangible (e.g., air, sound, and light) surroundings. The latter part of this chapter will explore physical environmental management problems in the home and suggest eco-friendly practices.

**Eco-consciousness** refers to the thoughts and actions given to protecting and sustaining the environment. **Conservation** is the act or process of preserving and protecting natural environments from loss or depletion. Individuals and families who are eco-conscious discuss environmental issues, recycle, conserve, reduce energy consumption and waste, buy "green" products, and support environmental causes and groups. The degree of eco-consciousness varies, as shown on the continuum in Figure 12.3.

## Problem Recognition

Conversations can be difficult about environmental issues such as **climate change** which includes global warming and the resulting shifts in weather patterns. It is estimated that 15 percent of Americans are climate change deniers. Differences among members in their ecological interests and practices may be a source of conflict in families. One family member may walk around the house turning on the lights, whether required or not, while another follows carefully turning off the lights. Eventually, one of them is going to become irritated with the other's behavior.

Problem solving begins with the recognition that there is a problem to be solved. **Problem recognition** occurs when an individual or a family perceives a significant difference between the lifestyle practiced and

Figure 12.3 Continuum of environmental activism.

some desired or ideal lifestyle. The discrepancy must be large enough to push the individual to action. For example, Shannon and Dan enjoy fishing. One Saturday they go to a nearby lake and see a sign that says the fish in the lake are contaminated by high levels of mercury. Disappointed because they cannot fish, they recognize that water contamination is a problem affecting their choices and lifestyles. Shannon and Dan did not create the problem, but now they realize they are affected by it. What alternative courses of action do they have? They can quit fishing, go to another lake, or join others in an attempt to clean up the lake.

A problem can arise in one of two ways: need recognition and opportunity recognition. In **need recognition**, the person realizes how much he or she needs a certain product, service, or condition. In **opportunity recognition**, the individual realizes that she or he may have limited or no access to a product, service, or condition. For example, suppose the price of gasoline soared to over $15 a gallon—this propels need recognition. Those of us without electric cars need gasoline, but who could afford it? Now, suppose a gasoline shortage forces gasoline stations to close for a few days—this is an example of opportunity recognition. Drivers cannot purchase gasoline even if they want to, a situation that has occurred in the United States and other countries. Many environmental problems involve both need and opportunity recognition. Objects in the environment can trigger a need or opportunity recognition and reaction and alter the pursuit of goals.

## Suggested Activities

1. Where do you place yourself on the eco-consciousness continuum? Explain your answer and discuss in groups. Where do most students develop eco-consciousness—at home, at school, in organizations?

2. Have you celebrated Earth Day (the annual global event on April 22 supporting environmental protection)? Have you planted trees or participated in some other activities in honor of Earth Day first held on April 22, 1970? Do you plan to do something on the next Earth Day?

Communication plays a large part in the recognition of environmental problems. The sign warned Shannon and Dan not to eat the fish they caught. The federal government communicates environmental information through news releases, press conferences, warnings, and legislation. Social media and television communicate environmental news. Families communicate news about environmental conditions and behavior. Parents model littering or recycling behaviors for their children.

Once an environmental problem has been recognized, the individuals involved engage in an information search to resolve it. Information has been dubbed the ultimate **renewable resource** (meaning that it is essentially unlimited) because new technologies are constantly being devised to transmit, collect, store, process, package, and display it (Elkington et al., 1988). Through the Internet, environmental disasters such as oil spills are immediately reported. This is one of the reasons why environmental awareness is greater now than ever before.

Marshall McLuhan (1962), who coined the phrase "the medium is the message," said that the spread of electronic communications technology has established a global network. As individuals become more globally connected, they naturally become more globally aware. An example of the importance of global communications was the International Whaling Commission's decision, supported by the United States, to place a moratorium on commercial whale harvesting (Bohlen, 1990). Reports on the plight of the whales undoubtedly played a part in the decision.

## Biodegradability

**Biodegradability** is defined as the capability of the material to decompose over time from biological activity; more specifically it is a substance's ability to be broken down by microorganisms such as bacteria and fungi. Germs are microorganisms that can cause illness but they are also a normal part of life (see Critical Thinking exercise)

There are biodegradable detergents and products. A **detergent** is any substance or preparation containing soap and/or surfactants for washing and cleaning purposes. A paper straw biodegrades much faster than a plastic straw (in fact, some would say they never biodegrade), hence the reduction in the use of plastic straws.

---

### CRITICAL THINKING

#### Germaphobe Alert

React to the following. "Here's a germaphobe alert: There are likely more bacterial cells in and on you right now (39 trillion, on average) than there are actual human cells (around 30 trillion). Most of them are harmless, or even good for you, but some are pernicious. One in six Americans, for instance, comes down with an illness from food-borne microorganisms each year, according to the Centers for Disease Control. So how do we avoid harmful bacteria? There are some basic rules to observe: Wash your hands frequently when touching surfaces and before handling or eating food. Cook food to proper temperatures and store leftovers properly…The *five-second rule*: Many people believe that a piece of food dropped on the floor is safe to eat if you pick it up quickly. The idea is that bacteria don't have time to transfer in under five seconds. But that's plenty of time for nasty bacteria to 'leap' onto a piece of food."

Source: Paul Dawson and Brian Sheldon (2018, November 10–11). The myths of microbe-fighting *The Wall Street Journal*, C5.

---

### Biodiversity

*Species extinction or depletion is caused mainly by the loss of habitat*—and that loss is nearly always caused by human encroachment. As humans use more resources (land and water), fewer resources are available for other life forms. **Biological diversity** (or more simply **biodiversity**) is a multidimensional concept encompassing the variety and variability among living organisms and the ecological complexities in which they occur. The term includes different ecosystems and species and their relative abundance. In Chapter 4, *utility* was defined as the usefulness, value, or worth of a resource.

For a substance or idea to be considered a resource (something useful for achieving an end purpose or goal), it must first be recognized as having current or potential utility. For example, at one time, uranium was considered a worthless, silvery white metal. Now it is used in scientific research and as a nuclear fuel. One of the reasons animals, minerals, plants, and habitats must be protected is that their potential use and their role in the total ecosystem may not be fully understood yet. Scientists have identified/named 1.7 million species (this includes bacteria, fungi, nematodes, plants, animals, and insects) out of at least 8 million or more. They are developing an easy-to-use, publicly accessible database on every species. This century will reveal how many species are on Mars.

CRITICAL THINKING

**United Nations Report on Biodiversity**

*Scientists say nature is in more trouble now than at any other time in human history, with extinction looming over 1 million species of plants and animals. That's the key finding of the United Nations first comprehensive report on biodiversity. The report was released Monday and says species are being lost at a rate tens or hundreds of times faster than in the past. More than a half a million species on land lack sufficient habitat for long-term survival and are likely to go extinct, maybe within decades. The oceans are not better off. Researchers say the problem traces back to humanity but it's not to late to fix it.*

Source: "The latest report: Nature's worst shape in history," *The Associated Press*, May 6, 2019, 6:35 a.m. ET.

Many difficult decisions lie ahead as to which species will be saved and which will not. These decisions are part of a branch of study called environmental ethics. **Ethics** are systems of morals, principles, values, or good conduct. No discussion of environmentalism would be complete without considering the ethical issues involved. Each person decides what is the right course of action in personal situations as well as in the broader societal context. As E. O. Wilson, Harvard University biologist, said, "I suppose it will all come down to a decision of ethics—how we value the natural worlds in which we evolved and now, increasingly, how we regard our status as individuals" (1988, p. 16).

## Individual and Family Decision-Making

Individuals and families are taking on a greater share of responsibility for their environment and are relying less on larger institutions. Many people realize that government or business alone cannot be depended on to solve all the environmental ills that exist. The problems are too widespread to be remedied by one group. Furthermore, the boundaries of the problems are often difficult to discern. For example, consumption and disposal practices of individuals and families, as well as those of businesses and industry, contribute to the **waste stream** (all garbage or trash produced). This blurring of the boundaries between the traditionally defined roles of the public sector and the private sector is a growing trend.

One of the most difficult aspects of environmentalism is determining what is a real, acute problem or shortage and what is not. Media sources often give out conflicting messages about the severity of a problem or the best solutions. Now, more than ever before, critical thinking skills are needed to evaluate environmental information. Crosschecking the information by looking at several different reliable sources is one way of arriving at the truth of a situation.

Environmental decision-making by individuals is complicated enough, considering the range of values, resources, goals, and decision-making steps involved. Environmental decision-making in families is complicated. Family members may differ in their recycling behavior or use of hot water.

Sometimes one family member takes on the role of an environmentalist and sets the rules, turns down the thermostat, and turns off the lights when not in use. With so much environmental education taking place in schools, it is not unusual to find a school-aged child rather than a parent taking on this role. Children may be better informed about environmental issues than are their parents; and, with their youthful optimism, they are willing to try new ways of managing household waste or adjusting consumption patterns.

Water pollution has undesirable effects.

Can you think of an environmental or beneficial activity you participated in as a child? Was it at home, at school, or in a club or organization? Did you pick up litter? Did your family adopt a pet from a shelter? Describe the activity and your memory of it.

## Incorporating Agriculture into Communities

People have had backyard or kitchen gardens for centuries, but there is a trend toward "back to nature" or "back to the farm" with growing edible food in school and community gardens. Did your school have one? Did you participate in planting and maintaining the garden? Here are ways of incorporating agriculture into suburbia or smaller places such as towns and parks within cities:

1. Setting aside land for a farm, orchard, or vineyard. The land could be managed by farmers, landscape crews, or other salaried workers, perhaps started by a builder of a large housing development.

2. Community gardens which are tilled, ready to plant, with rules and rental fees usually. In some cases, a class or cooperative is involved with meetings and a market is formed for selling produce or plants or providing to charitable organizations.

3. Open areas with fruit and nut trees or berry bushes, lettuce, and other simple-to-grow vegetables available to residents in an area. Children like to pick their own farms, apple orchards, and corn mazes.

4. Offering fresh food box home delivery once a week in season or pick-up boxes at a farm.

CASE STUDY

### Farms Instead of Golf Courses

More people are spending time outdoors and golf has made a comeback Just as interior space of homes is being rethought, land use is being re-considered. The following case study is one idea among many.

A 2,300-acre development outside Charlottesville, Virginia, has apple orchards and cattle pastures.

> Used to be, developers built high-end suburban communities around golf greens. The hot amenity now? Salad greens Forget multimillion-dollar recreation centers—"our amenities are watching the cows graze and the leaves change," says Joe Barnes, development principal for Bundoran Farm The trend has its roots in the growing distaste for prototypical suburban sprawl: mile after mile of look-alike homes broken up by the occasional park. The sustainability movement, with its emphasis on conservation, preservation and local food production has helped, too.

> Source: Simon, S. (2011, September 12). An apple tree grows in Suburbia. The Wall Street Journal, p. R3.

To put this into the family resource management context, within the same family (as mentioned previously) there may be vast differences in types, styles, and levels of environmental awareness. Differences are even more evident between families and between communities. Some communities have active gardening programs others have recycling programs making it easier for people to participate. *Ease and convenience are significant factors in the success of conservation or agricultural programs.*

It does not have to be gardens per se. Developers are catching on with master-planned communities featuring nature belts for walks and using materials and landscaping that require less upkeep. Some U.S. communities in the West and Southwest where water is scarce have banned traditional lawns in favor of more easily maintained native landscapes and areas for agricultural production. Elsa Fuss, a mother of two who was looking at a development southwest of Denver that featured a 4-H livestock ranch and hundreds of acres of community gardens, said, "I know my kids will know computers, technology—all those things they're growing up with I also want them to know working with their hands" (Simon, 2011, R3).

**Green building** is about the relationship of a house and its occupants with the environment; it involves eco-friendly design and processes. Conservation of energy, water, and land is encouraged. The National Association of Home Builders estimates that more than half of its members incorporate green features such as eco-friendly finishes, formaldehyde-free cabinet components, flooring from sustainable sources, and efficient appliances when they build (Johnston & Gibson, 2008). From the consumer side, research indicates that "greens" like living with other "greens." In other words, a homeowner does not want to have the only house on the block with solar panels or a tankless water heater; he or she wants like-minded neighbors. They are looking for "green" communities.

> *Officials of Pardee Homes, a Los Angeles-based unit of timber-giant Weyerhauser Co., say that over the past year they have also opened two green subdivisions in San Diego after seeing the demand for savings on energy bills. By using fluorescent lighting and tankless water heaters, they say, they have been able to achieve energy savings of as much as 75% compared with conventional homes. They add that local environmental groups helped persuade them to take land-preservation measures such as replanting trees and plants.*
> (Carlton, 2003, p. B1)

## Environmental Problems and Solutions

The remainder of this chapter is divided into five parts: water, energy, noise, waste and recycling, and air quality. Each part describes the problems and presents solutions applicable to individuals, families, and households. To keep the chapter a manageable length, many important topics, including ocean pollution, ozone depletion, desertification, deforestation, and loss of soil, had to be omitted. All of these are important avenues for future study and research. Many of them overlap. For example, desertification refers to the increase in dry, barren land that supports little or no vegetation. This happens for many reasons, including the loss of soil, overpopulation, overgrazing, deforestation, and overcultivation.

Common to all environmental problems is the widespread increase in pollution. **Pollution** is a general term referring to undesirable changes in physical, chemical, or biological characteristics of air, land, or water that can harm the health, activities, or survival of living organisms. It can be thought of as contamination of a resource, a reduction of quality or usefulness (Harris, 2002). The information that follows is as accurate as possible, but it is up to the reader to keep abreast of the latest developments in the ever-changing field of environmentalism.

## Water Quality and Availability

Clean, safe drinking water for all is the goal. In most U.S. communities, the sources of drinking water include rivers, lakes, streams, ponds, reservoirs, springs, and wells. The Environmental Protection Agency (EPA) prescribes regulations to limit the amount of certain contaminants in public water systems. The Food and Drug Administration (FDA) regulates contaminants in bottled water. Drinking water including bottled water is reasonably expected to contain some contaminants. The reason is that as water travels to the surface it dissolves certain materials and picks up other substances from animal or human activity. Contaminant categories include:

1. Microbial contaminants such as viruses and bacteria

2. Inorganic contaminants such as salts and minerals

3. Pesticides and herbicides from a variety of sources from households to agriculture

4. Organic chemical contaminants including synthetic and volatile organic chemicals

5. Radioactive contaminants which can occur naturally or from oil or gas production and mining activities.

After water is pumped to the surface, U.S. cities may add disinfectants and fluoride for dental health. Adding fluoride is debatable and is not a standard practice around the world. In some cases, well water passes

Water contamination limits choices.

Source: © Elizabeth Goldsmith.

through activated carbon filter units or sand filtration systems to remove certain chemicals before entering the public water supply.

Worldwide, the *two main problems associated with water are shortages and pollution.* Since 1900 there has been a sixfold increase in worldwide water use. About one-fifth of the earth's population does not have safe drinking water. The Gates Foundation has made safe drinking water a priority worldwide. The primary concern is that water is safe and the secondary concerns are the aesthetics of color, taste, and odor. "With rising per capita incomes and growing populations, human consumption of water is rising while the demands for water for agriculture, manufacturing, recreation, and the environment also are increasing" (Libecap, 2010, p. 10).

The Environmental Protection Agency (EPA) requires all drinking water suppliers to provide an annual quality statement. These reports are available at epa.gov or from your local utility. According to the EPA, approximately 50,000 water contaminants have been identified, and more than 100 of these are regulated in the United States. All contaminants are potentially hazardous to human health. Lead is of particular concern for small children and pregnant women. To lessen exposure to lead when water is stagnant inside pipes for several hours flush taps for 30 seconds to 2 minutes before using it for drinking or cooking.

Households with private wells need to get their water supplies tested periodically. If a contaminant is found, the report will include how much was found and whether the level exceeds health standards. About 10–20 percent of Americans draw their water from private wells. In this case, samples of water can be tested at certified laboratories. The cooperative extension service can inform residents about testing services available. The EPA's safe drinking water hotline is 1-800-426-4791 for information on state-certified testing laboratories.

Because of the fear of water contaminants, water-purifying businesses ranging from legitimate to quasi-legitimate are thriving. Each year, U.S. residents spend over a billion dollars on home-based purifying equipment and water filtration services. In addition, consumers spend billions on bottled water, some brands of which are unregulated and less pure than tap water. Before investing in any equipment or services, consumers should first have their water checked by legitimate testing services that are not selling a product. Consumers can also check with their local Better Business Bureau or consumer protection agency to see whether there are any recorded complaints against the company from whom they are considering buying equipment or services.

Contamination of drinking water is not the only water-related issue. There are many others, including the following:

- *Drinking water:* Supply and conservation, treatment, and health considerations.
- *Groundwater:* Availability and depletion, quality and contamination, consequences to public health, detection, and monitoring.
- *Seawater:* Quality and quantity; preservation of sea life.
- *Water for agricultural use:* Conservation and supply.
- *Water for industrial use:* Supply and pollutants.
- *Water for household use:* Supply and quality, conservation, and water-efficient products.

Because this book is concerned primarily with individual and family management practices, this discussion will focus on drinking water and household water use.

DAILY RESIDENTIAL INDOOR WATER USE (before conversation measures)

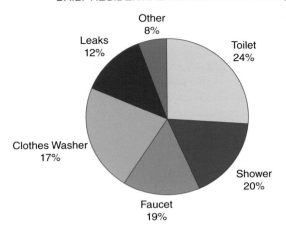

- If all U.S households installed water-saving features, water use would decrease by 30%. This would save an estimated 5.4 billion gallons of water per day, resulting in daily dollar-volume savings of $11.3 million or more than $4 billion per year.

- The largest daily user of water in the home is the toilet. By replacing this one product with a high-efficiency toilet(HET) you can greatly reduce a home's total water use.

Figure 12.4 Daily residential indoor water use.

Source: American Water Works Association Research Foundation, "Residential End Uses of Water." Their motto is "Manage Every Drop." Another source is the Environmental Protection Agency.

## Water Consumption and Shortage

To survive, first we need air and then we need water. "Due to the global challenge of water insecurity, desalination capacity in the world has grown in recent decades" (Lee & Jepson, 2021). **Water insecurity** (meaning lack of water availability) is most likely in places with low rainfall and inadequate water distribution sources and systems. Worldwide, safe drinking water is inadequate for millions of people. Water is also needed for sanitation and nearly all forms of production and consumption to support life including wildlife.

Each person on average in developed nations uses about 80–100 gallons of water per day. The typical U.S. household uses 5,300 gallons of water a month. More than half of this usage happens in the bathroom with toilets using the most (see Figure 12.4). Washing machines also use a substantial amount of the total. One way to conserve is to have energy-efficient, low-water-use washing machines. Leaks can waste 12 percent.

Given that the bathroom is the main source of water use, in 1994 the Federal Energy Policy Act restricted all new household faucets and showerheads to 2.5 gallons per minute. The Act also restricted toilets, limiting flush capacity to 1.6 gallons compared to a standard of 4 gallons in the 1970s. Some toilets average 4–6 gallons per flush. Newer toilets offer push control dual-flush for heavier or lighter use.

In the kitchen, most people are surprised to learn that dishwashers use less water (about 50 percent less) than washing and rinsing dishes by hand.

Water used to be cheap, clean, and abundant, but in many metropolitan areas and in the dry Southwest including west Texas, Arizona, New Mexico, and southern California, water has become a limited resource. As a result, many areas are regulating water use through rules and legislation. During shortages, cities have ordinances governing when cars can be washed or sprinklers used. In households, 20–62 percent of their total water use could be on outdoor areas such as lawns and pools. So, if homeowners want to conserve water and cut their water bills, they should examine both indoor and outdoor water use.

Piped water polluting a lake.

## Practical Ways to Reduce Household Water Use

Most homeowners cannot afford to replace their toilets, and this is certainly not practical for renters. Nevertheless, there are many low-cost or free ways to save water:

- Have a rain barrel that collects water from the roof that can be used for lawns and gardens.

  - Do not leave the water running while doing dishes, brushing teeth, or shaving.

  - Run full loads in the washing machine and dishwasher.

  - Match the water level to the size and type of laundry load. Use cold water.

  - Install low-flow shower heads. They mix air into the water flow to increase the water pressure. A 10-minute shower under a water-efficient shower head will save five gallons of water over a bath and save over $150 a year on energy used to heat water.

  - Fix leaky faucets. A slow drip from a single faucet adds up to 170 gallons of water loss per month.

  - Landscape with native plants that do not require additional watering.

  - Use only the necessary amount of water for cooking and rinsing food.

  - Water the lawn and garden early in the morning to avoid losing too much water to evaporation in the heat of the day. Watering cans use less water than hoses. Cover soil with compost or mulch to reduce evaporation.

  - Use buckets of water to wash the car rather than running water continuously from a hose or go to a commercial self-service car wash which is built to be water-efficient.

This list could go on, but these suggestions provide a starting point. Desalination research provides hope for a plentiful water supply in the long term. Desalinated seawater is the main source of water currently used in nations like Malta, an island nation in the Mediterranean Sea. Another solution is to grow crops that require less water. Currently, the world's human population continues to grow while the supply of freshwater remains constant. Cities are concentrating on these solutions:

1. Reducing unwanted chemical usage.

2. Reducing pollution.

3. Initiating recycling programs.

4. Building and monitoring efficient water distribution systems.

Learning how to conserve and apportion water will be one of the greatest management problems of the 21st century. Though the United States ranks sixth among water-rich nations in the world, it ranks third in water consumption and waste. As water becomes scarcer, its perceived value as a resource will increase. Learning to conserve now will begin a lifelong habit that will lead to saved money and a healthier environment.

## Energy

**CASE STUDY**

### Are Tiny Houses the Way to Go?

Would smaller houses save energy? They would if constructed and used properly. Read about this 280 square foot house built by Norwich University (in Vermont) students.

> The front of the house features a broader opening, with a kitchen and room for a sofa and table. The roof slopes down toward the back of the house, which includes a bathroom with a washer and dryer and a walk-in shower, and a bedroom with room for a queen-size bed and full closet. Energy efficiency is a key part of the project, with a tight building envelope, cellulose-insulated walls, triple-glaze windows and a high-efficiency heat pump and ventilation system. The installation of solar panels would make the build net-zero in terms of energy efficiency.
>
> Source: Stephen Mills (2019, May 6). Tiny house solves big problems. Tallahassee Democrat, 4B.

The main problems associated with energy are energy production, energy wastage, and pollution from the use of fossil fuels. **Fossil fuels** are the remains of dead vegetation, such as coal, oil, and natural gas, which can be burned to release energy (Naar, 1990). Fuel is used to provide physical comfort and mechanical power (Elkins et al., 1992).

Because electricity is the main form of energy used in today's homes, the emphasis in this section is on electricity with a few introductory comments here about the value of natural gas as an alternative for household use. Home owners using natural gas appliances have unlimited hot water, faster clothes drying time, more precision if using a chef-quality range, and an alternative to burning logs in wood stoves or fireplaces. It is economical in that it uses one-third less electricity, reduces personal carbon footsteps, and some cities offer rebates as incentives to use natural gas.

Historically, usable energy was most often produced by burning wood or a natural fuel such as coal or oil. One of the mistakes in North America's past was "cut-out and get-out forestry." Newer approaches involve replanting. Today, electricity is produced (or generated) from coal using generators driven by steam, from other fossil fuels such as oil and natural gas, from solar farms, from nuclear fuel and wind turbines.

Solar farms help the environment.

Hydroelectric power, which comes from generators turned by falling water, is another source of energy. Dwindling fossil fuels and concern over potential accidental radioactive discharges from nuclear power plants have led to efforts to find alternative sources of electrical energy. Among the alternatives under consideration are solar batteries, geothermal power stations, nuclear–fusion reactors, and magnetohydro–dynamic generators. Whatever the source of power, electrical energy is generated at a central point (e.g., a dam, an energy, or production plant) and then transmitted to delivery points or substations from where it is distributed to consumers. Figure 12.5 gives an ecosystem view of energy plants. The impacts of energy plants on society and the economy are noted in Figure 12.6.

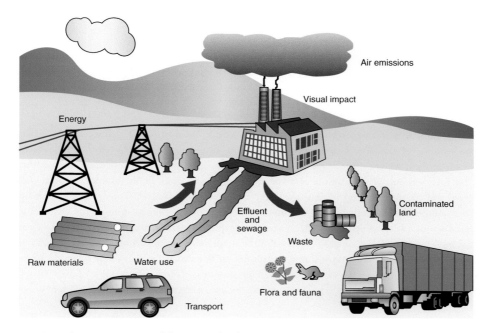

Figure 12.5 The environmental framework of an energy plant. This illustrates the interconnectedness of various factors in the energy plant environment.

Source: Welsh Development Agency.

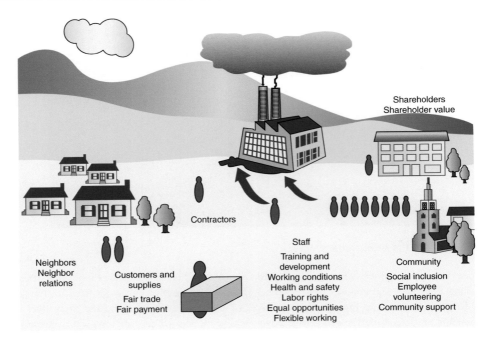

**Figure 12.6** The socioeconomic framework of an energy plant. This illustrates the people and policy aspects of energy plant environmental management.

Source: Welsh Development Agency.

### Energy Audits and Research

**Energy audits**, which are assessments of a home's energy efficiency, can range from free do-it-yourself audits with instructions over the Internet to inspections by paid professionals who can spend up to three hours scrutinizing a house including the attic and basement. Local utility companies or city or county utility offices may provide free or low-cost home energy audits.

An energy audit is performed by a specialist who makes a "walk-through" inspection of the interior and the exterior of a home. Upon completion of the inspection or shortly afterward, homeowners receive an analysis of what they can do to improve the energy efficiency of their homes. Auditors focus on determining where a house loses heat in winter and cool air in summer, and they identify appliances and heating/cooling systems that have better efficiency levels. College graduates who have studied resource management have been hired to work as home energy auditors for city and county government and utility companies, and as energy educators, researchers, and policy makers in state and national governments. For example, "because of the main environmental impact of the laundry process on energy consumption, the sustainability of laundering has also been of interest to researchers at the U.S. Department of Energy (DOE) almost since its inception" (Hustvedt, 2011, p. 228). There are 17 DOE National Laboratories that conduct research on a variety of subjects including home energy use and combating climate change.

Home energy use has gotten more complex with technology advancements such as charging smartphones. A century ago, a typical home may have had one electrical socket per room capable of delivering 100 watts of power; typical homes today have at least 4 per room and as many as 12–16 electrical outlets, and a typical home is wired to provide 12,000 or even more watts. On a late summer afternoon, a large house may consume over 4,000 watts of electricity (Crossen, 2001). The reasons for this growth include

- Larger houses. As mentioned earlier in the chapter, the size of the average U.S. home is 2,600 sq. ft. and 2,200 in Canada. In some parts of each country, huge houses are the norm. For example, in Aspen, Colorado, it is 15,000 square feet and in Boulder, Colorado, it is 6,000 square feet. To gain a perspective on this, the average South Korean family lives in a 1,200-square-foot apartment.

- More and larger appliances.

- The popularity of electronic devices and entertainment equipment.

- More air-conditioning. What was once thought of as a luxury is now standard. One way people save on air-conditioning costs is to limit the ac to one room of the house such as the master bedroom.

An incredible amount of energy is lost from such simple things as drafts.

> The U.S. Department of Energy's office of Energy Efficiency and Renewable Energy (EERE) estimates that draft reduction within a home can lower energy costs anywhere from 5% to 30% annually. Meanwhile, according to Department of Energy data provided by the U.S. Green Building Council, homes account for 21% of U.S. carbon dioxide emissions. And claiming a green home remodel makes for great bragging rights.
>
> (Hodges, 2008, p. D1)

Energy-efficient windows and window treatments can reduce loss from drafts. Depending on the climate and the home's insulation, for a 1,900-square-foot single-family detached home with an average of 2.7 occupants, about 50 percent of energy goes to space heating and cooling, 15 percent to hot water, 14 percent to appliances, 11 percent to lighting, and the rest to a variety of things including clocks, televisions, radios, and computers. So, the best way to cut energy bills is to alter heating and cooling, have energy-efficient appliances, and remove drafts. By improving insulation, weather stripping, and making a few alterations in a home (e.g., shutting drapes and doors, adding overhangs, adding storm windows), homeowners can save money and energy.

Children learn what comes into the house.

KWH and share of the total in U.S. households

| End Use | Billions KWH | Share of Total |
|---|---|---|
| Space cooling | 214 | 15 percent |
| Space heating | 207 | 14 percent |
| Water heating | 174 | 12 percent |
| Lighting | 91 | 6 percent |
| Refrigeration | 87 | 6 percent |
| Televisions (& related equipment) | 62 | 4 percent |
| Clothes dryer | 60 | 4 percent |
| Computers (& related equipment) | 26 | 2 percent |
| Furnace fans & boiler | 25 | 2 percent |
| Freezers | 20 | 1 percent |
| Cooking | 16 | 1 percent |
| Dishwashers | 7 | 1 percent |
| Other uses* | 460 | 31 percent |

*Includes small electric devices, exterior lights, pool heaters, backup generators, does not include electric vehicle charging.

Note: Some of the percentages were rounded up.
Source: U.S. Energy Information Administration, *Annual Energy Outlook* for 2019.

Besides windows, another source of heat loss is through cracks in walls and doors. Sometimes the homeowner will not notice these hairline cracks, but trained specialists can detect them using high-tech devices like infrared scanners. Specialists can also suggest how much home repairs will cost and where to get help.

Here are the sources of air leaks in homes, according to the U.S. Department of Energy:

| | |
|---|---|
| • Floors, walls, and ceilings | 31 percent |
| • Ducts | 15 percent |
| • Fireplaces | 14 percent |
| • Plumbing penetrations | 13 percent |
| • Doors | 11 percent |
| • Windows | 10 percent |
| • Fans and vents | 4 percent |
| • Electric outlets | 2 percent |

Several states charge different prices for energy use at different times of the day. The idea is to spread out the energy use by making people pay higher prices during periods of peak demand.

When Florida's summer heat gets blistering, Lamar Faulkner used to simply turn down the thermostat to keep his three-bedroom home near Pensacola comfortably cool. Now, he turns it up a few degrees. The reason: Mr. Faulkner's utility charges a premium—as much as five times the standard rate—to use electricity during summer afternoons when demand is greatest. (Gavin, 2002, p. D1)

## Practical Ways to Reduce Household Energy Use

Conducting an energy audit is a good way to find out about a specific home's energy use. This section provides several energy-saving ideas applicable to most homes.

---

**CRITICAL THINKING**

Curious fact: According to the U.S. Energy Information Administration, the state using the most energy per capita is Louisiana and the state using the least is Hawaii. Given the coverage so far do you have any guesses about why this is true?

---

Because air leaks are a major problem, insulation is an important way to reduce energy loss. Insulation comes in three forms: rigid panels or sheets of insulation; blankets, batts, or rolls (composed of fiberglass or rock wool); and blown insulation (rock wool, fiberglass, cellulose, or polyurethane foam). The higher the **R-value** (R stands for resistance), the higher the insulation properties. Insulation with an R-30 rating provides a better heat-flow barrier than one rated R-10. A better rating comes with a higher price. Another solution is double- or triple-glazed windows to reduce heat loss or heat gain. Storm windows or in the Case Study of tiny houses the conventional windows are usually triple-glazed. Weather stripping around windows and doors will also seal leaks. Window awnings will reduce heat gain in summer, and drawn, insulated drapes will reduce heat loss in winter.

The **site** is the location or situation of a house. **Orientation** is the location or situation of the house relative to points on a compass. In selecting the site and the orientation of the house, the homeowner and builder should take the natural environment into account. Warmth and shelter can be enhanced if environmental factors, such as hills, trees, winds, water, and the sun, are considered. The climate will determine the best site and orientation for a house. In states with hot climates, houses should have few windows on the west side to avoid the afternoon sun. What you do not want is huge sliding glass doors and balconies or patios on this side. In states with predominantly cold climates, houses should have few windows on the north side to reduce the cold drafts.

Landscaping affects heat loss and heat gain. **Deciduous trees**, such as oaks and maples that lose their leaves in the winter are good choices. Their leaves will shield the house in the summer but let the sunshine through in the winter. Trees and bushes can also serve as wind barriers.

According to the Department of Energy, the average U.S. household spends more than $1,000 each year to run household appliances and indoor lights. The following suggestions can reduce this amount considerably:

- Choose Energy Star light fixtures that use 70 percent to 90 percent less energy and distribute light more efficiently. Some last 15–25 years longer than traditional light fixtures.

- Look for an Energy Star certification on appliances—this means they are the most efficient in their class.

- Install a new, computerized thermostat that is ENERGY STAR-qualified. A programmable thermostat turns heating and cooling systems on and off at preprogrammed intervals.

- Clean or replace filters on furnaces regularly. Have an annual maintenance check of heating and cooling systems.

- Install tankless water heaters or turn the thermostat down on tank water heaters. Each 10-degree reduction cuts water-heating energy bills by 3–5 percent. However, to get dishes clean in a dishwasher, the water heater should not be set below 140°F (Fahrenheit), unless the dishwasher has its own water-heating system.

- When drying clothes, dry similar clothes together because lightweight synthetics dry much more quickly than thick robes or bath towels. Dry two or more loads in a row to take advantage of the residual heat.

- Keep the temperature setting in the refrigerator between 38°F and 42°F and the freezer between 0°F and 5°F. If the refrigerator and freezer are kept 10 degrees colder than this, energy consumption can increase by as much as 25 percent. Clean refrigerator coils at least once a year. A filled refrigerator or freezer is more energy-efficient than an empty or partially filled one.

- Use small appliances when possible because they require less energy than large ones. Microwave ovens and toaster ovens use less energy than conventional ovens. Coffeemakers, hair dryers, irons, and toasters do not consume much energy overall; they draw a lot of power but are in use for short periods of time. Because refrigerators and freezers run constantly, they use far more energy than other kitchen appliances do.

- Type of refrigerator matters. Refrigerators with freezers on top are 20 percent more efficient than side by side but this varies by manufacturer and style.

- Keep the refrigerator door open for a short time rather than opening and closing it frequently, which wastes more energy. Most of the cold air rushes out of the refrigerator as soon as it is opened.

- Replace old, inefficient appliances with efficient models. A refrigerator more than 10 years old uses twice the energy of a new one.

### CASE STUDY

#### Recycling Refrigerators

Aiden asks how do I recycle an old refrigerator when replacing it with a new Energy Star model? If your refrigerator is pre-1993 then you should recycle it because the refrigerant and insulation in older refrigerators may contain chlorofluorocarbons (CFCs) which are known to deplete the ozone layer. Not to mention using too much energy. The answers are: (1) Ask the retailer to recycle old ones properly, (2) Check with your Energy Office or local Electric Utility, (3) Ask about Municipal Pick-Up of Appliances, (4) Talk to a local scrap metal recycler. And, Aiden, be careful if the refrigerator is left outside, children playing can get trapped inside and suffocate, remove door or follow other safety measures.

- Check the energy efficiency of wood-burning stoves and fireplaces and ones using gas. A fireproof insert draft proofs wood-burning fireplaces and results in 8 percent less wasted heat. When buying a house or renting an apartment or house make sure the fireplace and heating/ac are safe, energy-efficient, and clean. Follow instructions for proper use.

- Clean the dryer's lint screen after each use. Run full loads in the dishwasher and clothes washer rather than running small loads more often. Periodically clean the dryer exhaust vent (from the dryer to the outside).

- Heating water accounts for 95 percent of the energy consumed for washing in the clothes washer. Save money and energy by washing in cold water, unless the clothes require hot or warm water, and always use a cold water rinse.

The ENERGY STAR label (noted in the previous list of energy-saving tips) is the national symbol for energy efficiency developed by the EPA and supported by the U.S. Department of Energy to help consumers select low-energy appliances. Appliances, and heating and cooling products that earn the ENERGY STAR label exceed the minimum federal standards for energy efficiency. Consumers should look for the Energy-Guide label (see Figure 12.7 for an example). Also, in cooperation with the EPA and the DOE, most computer and television manufacturers have joined the ENERGY STAR program that promotes the design of equipment that use less energy when turned on and off. The ENERGY STAR program is a work in progress; for example, more stringent standards went into effect for clothes washers in 2007.

Reducing the amount of energy used by appliances is helpful, but it is a myth that turning off lights and the television is the best way to conserve energy in the home; in fact, these consume a small portion of the home's electricity (Merline, 1988). Even small savings help, however, and consumers can reduce home energy consumption by

- Installing dimmer switches.

- Lighting areas for specific needs.

- Installing fluorescent lights or compact fluorescent lights (CFLs), which last longer and use significantly less energy than incandescent lights do.

Figure 12.7  The Energy Star or Energy Guide appliance label from a program run by the U.S. EPA.

- Using light colors on ceilings, walls, floors, and furniture because they reflect light and brighten a room.

- Replacing old lamps with new, more efficient ones. Dusting light bulbs and tubes increases light output and reduces the risk of potential pollutants.

- Turning off lights and electronics when not in use.

- Checking Energy-Guide or ENERGY STAR label before buying.

These suggestions can help, but it is important to remember that the greatest savings come from turning the thermostat down to 60°F in winter and turning it up to 80°F in the summer or turning it off altogether and opening the windows in pleasant weather.

Energy company records reveal that energy use varies widely even in neighborhoods where houses are the same size and style. Efficient appliances and lighting and the management of human behavior (e.g., shutting windows when the air conditioner is on) can substantially affect the energy use in the home.

In the future, there will be more total home automation systems. South Korea is a leading country in innovations for home technology for everyday household tasks. They use cell phones to manage everything from gas valves to washing machines. Locate energy-efficient builders, remodelers, and incentives in your area and Energy Star certified homes.

## CASE STUDY

### Recycling Cellphones

Eva asks, "What do I do with my old cellphone, there is no market for it?" She knows she should recycle cell phones, cell phone batteries, and other accessories. The answer is they may contain valuable resources—all of which took energy to extract and manufacture. Eva can go to cellphone stores and big box retailers who will take back old equipment and recycle them properly. Source: EPAs e-Cycling website (see Old Computers – Earth 911).

## Noise

Finding peace in nature is one way to reduce noise (internal and external). Jenny Odell author of *How to Do Nothing: Resisting the Attention Economy* says that birdwatching is her favorite slow-down activity. We are taught in school and by our parents to take a break and gaze out the window, looking at the land, the sea, and the sky is a relief from too much on-screen activity. Nature restores. A 12-year-old boy who lived on a mountain farm summed it up this way "I like that we live in a forest yet can go in the car to get anything we want."

Getting away from the noise is a pursuit yet we know less about noise pollution than about water and energy conservation. Noise pollution is less easy to delineate because people are not billed for the use of noise, and each person is a producer as well as a consumer of noise. Noise is simply any unwanted sound. It could come from tennis balls bouncing on public tennis courts across from your house or from airplanes flying overhead. Noise pollution can have harmful impacts on human or animal life which is why Disney does not shoot off fireworks at midnight at the Animal Kingdom in Orlando. Poor urban planning (and park planning) can add to noise pollution. It can be more than a nuisance it can produce serious psychological stress.

The intensity, or loudness, of sound is the amount of acoustic energy transmitted through the air; it is measured in **decibels (dB)**. The lowest sound humans can hear is 1 dB. An average home on a quiet street has a dB level of 50 (Pearson, 1989). A noisy office, a preschool classroom, or an alarm clock can be as loud as 80 dB. Sounds above 85 dB can cause hearing loss. A rock concert or being honked at on the street clocks in at about 115 dB. At 120 dB the hearer experiences discomfort or pain; a jet taking off is about 140 dB. Household appliances range from 60 to 90 dB, with the food disposal being the noisiest at over 90 dB. Too much noise can be annoying, besides being harmful, making it difficult to concentrate or relax.

Homes, offices, and other environments should strive to maintain a comfortable amount of noise. Research shows that people feel uneasy if they are deprived of environmental stimulation (i.e., too little sound, movement, or light) for too long. Too little sound may make a person feel uncomfortable or lonely. To counteract this effect, music is piped into elevators, grocery stores, and dentists' offices. Many people go to sleep better with the hum of a fan or the drone of music in the background. Some people sleep best with an open door from their bedroom to the main part of the house or apartment and prefer an open floor plan.

Too much noise is a more common problem than too little. Noise from loud neighbors, ringing phones, barking dogs, and screaming children can become an intolerable burden. Often it is not the noise itself that is irritating or harmful, but the continuing nature of noise or the combination of noises (e.g., the noise of the vacuum cleaner, the blender, the television, and fighting children slamming doors occurring at the same time). Poorly constructed buildings add to the noise level. Insulation and absorbing surfaces such as carpet, cork, or acoustical tiles can reduce noise. On common walls between apartments, brick, earth, and concrete reduce noise better than wood or aluminum siding. Soft, porous surfaces absorb sound, and hard, smooth surfaces reflect sound. A solution while on airplanes or working in a noisy office is to use noise-canceling headphones.

### Practical Ways to Reduce Noise

**Noise reduction** is the process of removing or reducing noise from a signal or source. The following suggestions will help reduce noise in the home:

- Find housing away from noisy traffic, airports, schools, and factories.

- Plant barrier trees and hedges to reduce noise. High walls and earth mounds also cut noise.

- Place bedrooms in quieter parts of the house. Put the garage on the noisy side of the site.

- Buy "quiet" appliances—these have more insulation.

- Turn down sounds on electronic devices.

- Draw heavy drapes and close blinds to shut out neighborhood noise.

- Weather strip windows and doors to prevent outside noise from entering the home. Inside the house, solid-core doors will reduce noise between rooms.

  - On a busy street, use triple-pane windows. A six-story hotel and condominium combination put heavy paned windows on the street side and regular windows on the other sides. If you were buying a condominium this is the kind of information you would want to know along with the amount of insulation between floors so you would not hear people walking above you or moving furniture. Plumbing matters too, would you hear every toilet flush and showers running in neighboring units? What about slamming doors? Another concern is who is below you. If it is a restaurant, you will not want that noise or those cooking fumes in your unit. Oscar reported hearing loud patrons and smelling restaurant fumes at his house from several blocks away so it doesn't have to be an apartment situation to be annoying.

As the world becomes more crowded, noise pollution will become a greater management problem than it currently is. Finding a quiet, peaceful place is becoming more difficult. Decreasing noise is a way to de-stress life. Another way to reduce stress is to add sounds that are soothing and pleasant. The rustle of trees, the singing of birds, and the sound of ocean waves are soothing to many people. Bringing more of these natural sounds into one's life and removing some of the irritating, mechanical ones may increase a person's overall sense of well-being.

## CASE STUDY

### Sell, Trade, or Recycle Electronics and Appliances

*One of the key trademarks of the "Kon Mari" method is to start by clearing out everything unwanted and unused. Think about how much tech junk you have – that drawer full of dusty cellphones, charging cable chaos and old earphones you haven't touched since you used them with your '80s Walkman. Pile them up, sort them and then sell, trade or recycle them....If you have a gadget bound for the trash heap, do the planet a favor and recycle it instead. Best Buy is one of the nation's largest retail recyclers of used electronics and appliances, and takes all kinds of used tech, regardless of where you bought it, how old it is or who made it. That's huge because, by 2021, the annual ewaste total is predicted to surpass 60 million tons – the equivalent of 12 million elephants (or 321 Golden Gate Bridges).*

*Source: Jennifer Jolly (2019, April 29). Spring cleaning extends to a declutter of gadgets. USA Today, p. 3B.*

## Waste and Recycling

The average American receives 41 pounds of mail (most of it unwanted) annually which wastes 100 million trees. According to the EPA, during the past 40 years the amount of waste (paper and otherwise) each person creates has almost doubled from 2.7 to 4.4 pounds per day. The most effective way to reverse this trend is to prevent waste in the first place, also known as source reduction. **Source reduction** refers to any change in the design, manufacture, purchase, or use of materials or products, including packaging, to reduce the amount or toxicity before they become municipal solid waste. Many retailers have stopped sending print catalogs in the mail. Another way is to reuse products or materials. Reuse centers include Goodwill and Salvation Army and specialized programs for building mate-rials or unneeded school materials. Manufacturing has changed too so that since 1977 the weight of a 2-liter plastic soft-drink bottle has been reduced from 68 grams to 51 grams. That represents 250 million less pounds of plastic per year going into the waste stream.

**Municipal solid waste** (MSW), also known as trash or garbage, is a worldwide problem as the population grows and more people gravitate toward cities. MSWs include products, packaging, grass clippings, furniture, clothing, bottles, food scraps, newspapers, appliances, paint and kerosene, and batteries. Historically, landfills were cheap and readily available, but vacant land is no longer cheap and is becoming increasingly scarce around cities. Suburbs have sprung up where landfills used to be. Americans throw away more than 50 billion food and drink cans every year. **Municipal landfills** collect household garbage and in the United States, these are predominantly regulated by state and local governments. Some things such as unused prescription medication and other medical waste should not be put into landfills. Consumers should take advantage of pharmaceutical take-back programs or household hazardous waste collection programs.

Composting is on the upswing. It consists of decomposing organic waste such as food scraps (fruit and vegetables, not meat or poultry) and yard trimmings with microorganisms (mainly bacteria and fungi) to produce a humus-like substance that can be used in gardening and landscaping.

The skyrocketing cost of land, coupled with concern about environmental pollution, has led to the exploration of new methods of waste disposal. Possible avenues include burying waste, burning it, recycling it, or not producing so much of it. Combining all four methods is called **integrated waste management**. In this system, waste products are sorted, recyclable items are reused, and the rest are burned cleanly in a furnace that also produces steam to generate electricity. Only the remaining ash goes to the landfill.

According to the EPA, the breakdown of U.S. garbage is as follows:

| | |
|---|---|
| Paper and paperboard | 38.6 percent |
| Yard waste | 12.8 percent |
| Food waste | 10.1 percent |
| Plastics | 9.9 percent |
| Metals | 7.7 percent |
| Glass | 5.5 percent |
| Wood | 5.3 percent |
| Other (rubber, leather, textiles, etc.) | 10.0 percent |

Recycling is popular and has gone mainstream, so recycling bins at work and at home are common. The EPA estimates that 52 percent of all paper, 31 percent of all plastic soft-drink bottles, 45 percent of all aluminum beer and soft-drink cans, 63 percent of all steel packing, and 67 percent of all major appliances are now recycled. Examples of recycling include the following:

- *Plastic:* Used for fiberfill for pillows, decks, flowerpots, paintbrush bristles, fence posts, insulation, and docks. For example, according to the American Plastics Council, U.S. households recycle over 1.4 billion pounds of plastic bottles each year.

- *Paper:* Used for game boards, puzzles, stationery, newspapers, toilet paper, paper towels, egg cartons, boxes, books, and tickets.

- *Glass:* Used for bottles, street paving, tiles, and bricks.

- *Aluminum:* Used for cans, lawn furniture, window frames, and car parts.

## *Practical Ways to Reduce Waste*

### Households can adopt the 3-Rs solution to the waste problem:

1. *Reducing.* Avoid buying products with excessive packaging; use a coffee mug at work (avoid using Styrofoam cups); buy in bulk (fewer packages); use lunch boxes instead of paper or plastic bags; and buy recycled paper products.

2. *Reusing.* Use both sides of sheets of paper; reuse old envelopes for messages and lists; reuse gift bags, wrapping paper and ribbons; and reuse cardboard boxes and glass jars. Take paper to shredding services.

3. *Recycling.* Take recycling materials to recycling centers. Hand down clothes from child to child; alter and reuse existing clothes; and donate used clothing to charities. Refinish, sell, or donate old furniture. Recycling is a series of activities.

These three methods involve management. Each requires time, energy, and commitment; decision plans must be made and carried out. Children can be taught the value of waste reduction in their families and in schools, or in organizations such as Scouts. Starting small and local makes the most sense for children. They can see the results of picking up litter in their playground and neighborhood. At home, children can separate waste into the appropriate recycling boxes and can help their parents take the trash to community recycling bins. Children enjoy being part of a community effort, and parents can model good-citizenship habits for the future. The fundamental message to children should be that each person can make a difference in the health of the environment.

## Air Quality

To be more environmentally friendly buy green, source goods and services that are local and sustainable. "Green procurement reduces waste, lowers greenhouse emissions, and conserves energy. Look specifically for products that are sustainably manufactured, do not contain toxic materials, and are made from renewable materials and/or otherwise can be recycled. Be discouraged by climate change if you must (and you must) but know that one small person -and one small business can make a difference" (Strauss, 2019). The author Charles Dickens said, "A very little key will open a very heavy door."

For statistics on indoor air pollution and outdoor air quality around the world consult the World Health Organization. The United Nations estimates that air pollution kills nearly 7 million people each year.

In the U.S. The Clean Air Act provides the principal framework for national, state, and local efforts to protect air quality. Clean air is given a high priority in the list of environmental concerns. The pollutants that lead to deteriorating air quality come from many sources, not from a single source. Air quality is threatened by too much ozone, airborne particles, sulfur dioxide, lead, nitrogen oxides, and carbon monoxide. Natural sources like windblown dust, debris from fires, and volcanic eruptions pollute. More than half of the nation's air pollution comes from mobile sources such as cars, trucks, motorcycles, airplanes, trains, buses, and boats. Stationary sources such as factories, dry cleaners, homes, and oil refineries also pollute the air.

Under the Clean Air Act, EPA established air quality standards to protect public health and the environment.

### The EPA has set national standards for six principal air pollutants:

* carbon monoxide

* ozone

* lead

* nitrogen dioxide

* particulate matter

* sulfur dioxide

Go to epa.gov to find out conditions where you live. Statistics show that national average air quality continues to improve as emissions decline.

Many companies advertise "green" pest control but consumers should be leery of claims because even though well-intentioned it is difficult for pesticides and application methods to be totally safe. Some products are better than others and directions should be followed carefully. Reducing harmful sprays and run-off into streams, lakes, and oceans are problems that scientists are trying to solve. Soil and water pollution contributes to many health and ecological problems, such as decreased quality of aquatic life and vegetation damage.

Air pollution is sometimes worse indoors than outdoors, particularly where buildings are tightly constructed or sealed to save energy or where they have poor ventilation systems. Sick-building syndrome is caused by the presence of pollutants in the air compounded by inadequate ventilation systems. Harmful indoor pollutants may come from building materials, furnishings, space heaters, gas ranges, wood preservatives, aerosols, and cleaning agents.

More than 90 percent of air pollution deaths occur in developing countries. Eighty percent of these deaths are caused by indoor air pollution; many poor people lack access to clean fuel and burn dung and wood for cooking and heating (Vo, 1998).

### In the United States, the top 10 indoor air pollutants according to the American Lung Association are

1. Secondhand smoke—smoking, radon, and secondhand smoke are the leading causes of lung cancer.

2. Biological contaminants—including bacteria, viruses, animal dander, dust mites, cockroach parts, pollen, molds, and fungi. These are usually inhaled alone or by attaching themselves to dust that is then inhaled.

3. Particulates—including solid particles and liquid droplets such as dirt, dust, and smoke.

4. Household products—including cleansers, personal-care products, and paint.

5. **Carbon monoxide** (CO)—an odorless and colorless gas, a product of the combustion of fossil fuels and burning wood. It is a leading cause of accidental poisoning in the United States. It is fatal at very high concentrations. Symptoms include headaches, dizziness, disorientation, nausea, and fatigue. Average CO concentrations have decreased substantially over the years according to the EPA. Many states require new homes to have a carbon monoxide monitor. Common sources are faulty furnaces, gas appliances, fireplaces, car exhaust, water heaters, and barbecue grills, but other sources are culprits as well:

    One June day three years ago Thad Dohrn turned on the air conditioner in his three-bedroom house in Ames, Iowa, for the first time that summer. The next morning his wife Stephanie complained of a headache. As he walked to the bathroom to check on her, he passed out. He came to, but then Stephanie passed out. "She came to and we walked outside. I was crying on the phone to our neighbors and was all confused," says Mr. Dohrn, now an associate athletic director at Columbia University in New York. Mr. and Mrs. Dohrn were taken to the hospital and diagnosed with carbon monoxide poisoning. The cause: A mechanical malfunction caused the air conditioner and the heat to be on simultaneously. The system didn't have proper ventilation either. And the Dohrns didn't have a carbon monoxide monitor. (Petersen, 2002, p. D1)

6. **Radon**—a naturally occurring gaseous by-product of radioactive decay of uranium in the earth— can enter a house through holes and cracks in the foundation, through cinder blocks, or through loose-fitting pipes, floor drains, or pumps. Concentrations are likely to be largest in the basements of buildings. The EPA estimates that between 10,000 and 40,000 lung cancer deaths a year in the United States are caused by radon ("Radon: The Problem No One Wants to Face," 1989). The U.S. Geological Survey has compiled a series of geologic radon potential assessments for the United States in cooperation with the EPA, so potential homeowners can go to epa.gov for maps showing where radon is highest. Basically, it is highest in the Midwest, Pennsylvania, and mountainous areas, and lowest in the Southeast and along the West Coast. State environmental protection departments provide lists of approved contractors able to make radon-reducing modifications. A radon level of four picocuries per liter or more is considered dangerous. Modifications can easily run to several thousand dollars per home, so it is wise to have a home inspection made before home purchase so that the current owner or builder will repair the home, and the cost of repair will not be passed on to the new buyer.

7. Volatile organic compounds (VOCs)—the "new smell" from carpets, wood cabinets, plastics, etc. One of the most common VOCs is formaldehyde.

8. Pesticides.

9. Lead—found in paint and lead pipes. Before 1978, most homes used lead-based paint.

10. Asbestos—microscopic mineral fibers that are flexible, durable, and do not burn.

## Practical Ways to Reduce Air Pollution

Air quality varies widely. The air quality index ranges from a low of 0 to a high of 500. Air quality from 0 to 49 is considered good; 300 and above is hazardous (Carpenter, 1989). Runners, construction workers, gardeners, children, and anyone else who is outdoors a lot need to be especially mindful of changes in air quality. Elderly people or younger persons with certain health conditions should beware also. These suggestions can help improve air quality:

- Use roll-on or solid deodorants; liquid or "spritz" pump sprays for deodorants or hair sprays are recommended over the use of aerosols because chemicals from aerosols contribute to smog.

- Keep the car engine tuned. Carpool and use public transportation and bicycles when possible. Reduce the number of trips you take in a car.

- Do not smoke. Encourage the designation of smoking areas outside of businesses and eliminate indoor smoking completely. Disney World in Florida banned smoking anywhere on the property in 2019 and forward.

- Air out houses and workplaces. Open windows at least once a week. Avoid burning leaves and trash so when you open windows it is best to determine first the outside conditions.

- Clean heater and air conditioner filters regularly. Use an air conditioner or dehumidifier to maintain an indoor relative humidity of below 65 percent.

- When building or remodeling a house, use safe building materials and installation methods. For example, paint with brushes and rollers instead of sprayers. Beware of asbestos and mold. Tile, insulation, and wallboard may need replacing by trained professionals.

- Put green plants in homes and workplaces. Certain types of green plants are particularly effective in filtering out indoor air pollutants. Negatives can be mold and insects so some U.K. and U.S. workplaces have banned office plants.

People who incorporate several of these suggestions into their daily life management are practicing **positive ecology**. By shifting to less-harmful energy sources, thinking more holistically, and being a "green" consumer including using eco-friendly cleaning products, individuals can help create a healthier home environment. Individuals should ask themselves, "What can I do to improve air quality, reduce pollution, and keep my family healthy?" "Health is the single most important indicator of the overall well-being of a society" (Carr & Springer, 2010, p. 743). Indoor environments directly affect the health and comfort of humans (Ma et al., 2021).

## SUMMARY

Conversations about climate change can be difficult. Appreciate the opportunity to consider different points of view. The road to a better planet requires consistency, patience, science, and kindness

The emphasis here is on the individual, family, and household behavior—problems and solutions. Reuse, reduce, and recycle when you can. Buy wisely. Seek peace and quiet where you can. It is important to reduce energy loss in the home with space cooling and heating taking the most energy and to reduce water use foremost in the bathroom, laundry, and kitchen. Sustainable behavior is a multidimensional concept that includes behaviors such as the conservation of natural resources through efficient use. Resource knowledge, practice, and education are subsets of family resource management. Marie Kondo's organizing principles (clearing out everything unwanted and unused) places her methods within the context of reducing and recycling.

The chapter covered environmental issues such as the degree of ecological footprint, sustainability, and provided practical suggestions for specific environmental problems relating to air, water, waste, noise, and energy. Noise is any unwanted sound. Words of warning were given about carbon monoxide, asbestos, mold, recycling refrigerators, and radon.

Centralized large groups of people require centralized services and regulations about garbage, water, energy, housing, and transportation. The trend of bringing agriculture to the neighborhood, household, and community level was discussed. More U.S. land is being conserved for family farms, gardens, and parks including dog parks and walking trails. "Green" building is about the relationship of a house and its occupants to the environment. It is a process of design and construction. Most builders are incorporating "green" features such as energy-efficient appliances, solar panels, and eco-friendly finishes in the homes they build. Energy audits are encouraged.

Life cycle assessments (LCA) are often conducted to evaluate environmental impact.

Although people rely to a degree on government, environmental organizations, workplaces, and universities for solutions, ultimately, they must look within for answers. As the actor, Beau Bridges said, "All the talk about how the environment is being ruined means nothing unless you're doing something about it in your own home." Families need to consider the environmental messages and values they are passing down to their children. If the days of limitless clean air and water, low-cost energy, and abundant peaceful, quiet environments are gone, what will be put in their place? Future generations should view the 21st century as a turning point toward more positive ecology.

## KEY TERMS

biodegradability
biodiversity
carbon footprint
carbon monoxide
climate change
conservation
decibels (dB)
deciduous trees
detergent
eco-consciousness
ecological footprint
ecosystem
energy audit
environmentalism ethics
fossil fuels
global warming

green building
habitat
integrated waste
    management
life cycle assessment (LCA)
municipal landfills
municipal solid waste
natural capital
need recognition
noise reduction
opportunity recognition
orientation
physical environmental
    resources
pollution
positive ecology

problem recognition
radon
renewable resources
resource education
R-value
site
social environmental
    resources
source reduction
stewards (stewardship)
sustainable behavior
sustainability
sustainable development
waste stream
water insecurity

## REVIEW QUESTIONS

1. How does the Three R's solution—reduce, reuse, and recycle—fit homes? Give practical examples.

2. Comment on the following statement by E. O. Wilson: "I suppose it will all come down to a decision of ethics—how we value the natural worlds in which we evolved and now, increasingly, how we regard our status as individuals." Do you agree or disagree? Include an explanation of the term "ethics" in your answer.

3. The author Pearl S. Buck said that "It is good to know our universe. What is new is only new to us." Explain what she might have meant by this and include sustainability in your answer.

4. Species are going extinct at an unprecedented rate. Give three reasons why you should care.

5. Near the end of the chapter, the term "positive ecology" was defined. Give an example of how you practice positive ecology or perhaps are inspired to after reading this chapter.

## REFERENCES

Abeliotis, K., Koniari, C., & Sardianou, E. (2010). The profile of the green consumer in Greece. *International Journal of Consumer Studies, 34*, 153–160.

Ball, J. (2008, October 6). Six products, six carbon footprints. *The Wall Street Journal*, p. R1.

Berkholz, P., Stamminger, R., Wnuk, G., Owens, J., & Bernado, S. (2010). Manual dishwashing habits. *International Journal of Consumer Studies, 34*, 235–242.

Bohlen, C. (1990). Report from the State Department. *EPA Journal, 16*(4), 15–16.

Brundtland Report. (1987). *World commission on environment and development (WCED). Our common futures.* Oxford: University Press.

Carlson, S. (2008, September 5). Colleges get greener in operations, but teaching sustainability declines. *The Chronicle of Higher Education*, p. A25.

Carlton, J. (2003, February 5). Home, green home: Builders embrace environmental goals. *The Wall Street Journal*, pp. B1, B8.

Carpenter, B. (1989, June 12). The newest health hazard: Breathing. *U.S. News and World Report*.

Crossen, C. (2001, August 16). How much power do you use? *The Wall Street Journal*, p. B1.

Cude, B. (1993). Consumer perceptions of environmental marketing claims: An exploratory study. *Journal of Consumer Studies and Home Economics, 12*, 207–225.

D'Souza, C., Taghian, M., Lamb, P., & Peretiako, R. (2007). Green decisions: Demographics and consumer understanding of environmental labels. *International Journal of Consumer Studies, 31*, 371–376.

Elkington, J., Burke, T., & Hailes, J. (1988). *Green pages: The business of saving the world.* London: Routledge.

Elkins, P., Hillman, M., & Hutchison, R. (1992). *Green economics.* New York: Doubleday.

Freud, S. (1961). *Civilization and its discontents* (J. Strachey, Trans.). New York: Norton. (Original work published 1930).

Gavin, R. (2002, August 22). Cut your electric bill: Do laundry at 3 A.M. *The Wall Street Journal*, p. D1.

Goldsmith, D. S. (2015) Sustainably managing resources in the built environment. Chapter 9 in *Social Influence and Sustainable Consumption* (pp. 155–169). Switzerland: Springer

Goldsmith, E. B. (2015). *Social influence and sustainable consumption.* Switzerland: Springer.

Goldsmith, E., & Goldsmith, R. (January 2011). Social influence and sustainability in households. *International Journal of Consumer Studies, 35*, 117–121.

Gould, S. J. (1989). *Wonderful life.* New York: Norton.

Gould, S. J. (1998). *Leonardo's mountain of clams and the diet of worms: Essays on natural history.* New York: Harmony Books.

Harris, J. (2002). *Environmental and natural resources economics: A contemporary approach.* Boston: Houghton Mifflin.

Hodges, J. (2008, September 18). A quest for an energy-efficient house. *The Wall Street Journal,* p. D1.

Hustvedt, G. (2011). Review of laundry energy efficiency studies conducted at the US Department of Energy. *International Journal of Consumer Studies, 35,* 228–236.

Johnston, D., & Gibson, S. (2008). *Green from the ground up: Sustainable, healthy and energy-efficient home construction.* Newtown, CT: Taunton Press.

Koch, W. (November 16, 2011). More U.S. land conserved as gardens, farms. *Tallahassee Democrat,* p. 7.

Lee, K., & Jepson, W. (2021). Environmental impact of desalination: A systematic review of life cycle assessment. *Desalination, 509,* Abstract.

Libecap, G. (2010). The economic institutions of water. *NBER Reporter,* Number 4, 10–13.

Ma, N., Aviv, D., Guo, H., & Braham, W. (January 2021). Measuring the right factors: A review of variables and models for thermal comfort and indoor air quality. *Renewable and Sustainable Energy Reviews, 135,* Abstract.

McLuhan, M. (1962). *The Gutenberg galaxy.* Toronto: University of Toronto Press.

Merline, J. W. (1988, August). Energy smarts. *Consumers' Research,* p. 38.

Naar, J. (1990). *Design for a livable planet.* New York: Harper & Row.

Odell, J. (2020). *How to do nothing: Resisting the attention economy.* New York: Penguin Random House.

Pearson, D. (1989). *The natural house.* New York: Simon & Schuster.

Petersen, A. (2002, October 17). New laws require home gas detectors. *The Wall Street Journal,* p. D1.

Pinchon, N. (1990, November 10). What causes global warming. *Knight-Ridder Tribune News,* p. 37.

Radon: The problem no one wants to face. (1989, October). *Consumer Reports,* 623–625.

Simon, S. (September 12, 2011). An apple tree grows in suburbia. *The Wall Street Journal,* p. R3.

Strauss, S. (April 18, 2019). Small-business changes can add up. *USA Today,* p. 4B.

Uitdenbogerd, D., Brouwer, N., & Groot-Marcus, J. (1998). Domestic energy saving potentials for food and textiles: An empirical study. A Report from Wageningen Agricultural University, Holland.

Vo, M. (1998, November 6). A look at the world by the numbers. *The Christian Science Monitor,* pp. 8–9.

Wilson, E. O. (1988). The current state of biological diversity. In E. O. Wilson (Ed.), *Biodiversity.* Washington, DC: National Academy Press.

Chapter **13**

# Managing Finances

**MAIN TOPICS**

Financial Management and Security

Family Economics: Avoiding Economic Fallout, Building Toward the Future

    The Business Cycle and Inflation

    Individuals and Families as Producers and Consumers

Income, Taxes, Net Worth, Budgets, and Saving

    Managing Credit and Reducing Debt

    Banking, Investments, and Insurance

    Financial Literacy, Children, and Families

    Saving for College

    College Students, Starting Out

Retirement and Financial Planning

    Financial Planning and Financial Counseling

Further Family Economic Issues

    The Gender Gap, Earnings Gap, and the Glass Ceiling

    Wealth and Poverty

DOI: 10.4324/9781003166740-13

... Income volatility is widespread with one-third of American households experiencing it.
... Inflation hit a 40 year high recently.
... The middle class in Asia will make up the majority of 2030 consumer spending.

## CASE STUDY

### Teens Put Off Getting Their Licenses and Buying Cars

*If teenagers are any guide, Americans' love affair with the automobile may no longer be something car makers can bank on. The percentage of teens with a driver's license has tumbled in the last few decades and more young people are delaying purchasing their first car – if buying one at all say analysts, generational experts and car industry executives. About a quarter of 16-year-olds had a driver's license in 2017, a sharp decline from nearly half in 1983, according to an analysis of licensing data by transportation researcher Michael Sivak.*

A case in point in the photo caption accompanying the article the above quote came from said "June Metzler with her father David, outside their home in Culver City, Calif, is 16 years old but sees no urgency in getting her driver's license."

Source: Adrienne Roberts (2019, April 20–21). Driving?
The kids are over it. The Wall Street Journal, B1.

This chapter provides an overview of personal and family finance with an emphasis on the planning aspects. As the case study shows consumer behavior is changing and with that comes changes in how we spend our money. What was once a rite of passage at sixteen having a driver's license and owning a car is no longer the norm. In fact, owning a car is coming into question and more couples are making do with one car versus several. Using mass transportation is more in vogue and walking and leasing cars or ride-sharing, Note the growth of Uber, Lyft Inc., and other transportation network services that match passengers with nearby drivers.

### Suggested Activity: Money Quotes to Ponder

Great quotes stimulate thinking especially about something so ordinary and every day as the need for money. React to these quotes by checking agree or disagree:

Agree      Disagree

_____      _____ An investment in knowledge pays the best interest (Benjamin Franklin)

_____      _____ I will tell you the secret to getting rich on Wall Street. You try to be greedy when others are fearful. And you try to be fearful when others are greedy (Warren Buffett).

_____      _____ Frugality includes all the other virtues (Cicero).

_____     _____ Money often costs too much (Ralph Waldo Emerson).

_____     _____ It's how you deal with failure that determines how you achieve success (David Feherty)

_____     _____ Everyday is a bank account, and time is our currency. No one is rich, no one is poor, we've got 24 hours each (Christopher Rice).

Did any of the quotes in the Suggested Activity make you smile or nod your head? The timely opening Case Study sets the pace for a discussion of how to manage the financial side of life. One way to do this is to have a clear vision of financial goals, what to save for and then the intricacies of your financial life, follow encompassing needs, careers, education, and retirement plans. Goals may include

- building a nest egg or emergency fund

- saving enough for you to further your education or to send kids to college

- buying a house you can afford

- making sure you have health insurance and funds set aside for retirement

- evolving at work or school, reskilling, changing jobs or majors, moving into management

A case in point, 35-year-old Parker, a government employee, said the only way I'm going to make more money is to move into management. The purpose of this chapter is to get you thinking about your financial plans and to better understand the goals, spending practices, and saving habits of others. Listening and observing others financial behavior are vital. It is an important subject to study because making informed decisions can provide stability and opportunity for individuals and families across many generations.

The best way is to get started _now_. There is a saying that if you wait until you can afford to have children you will never have them. Starting on financial management is much the same way. There is no better time than the present. It takes time and energy to get started, and people close to you should be aware that you are engaged in the process.

We cannot leave this introductory section without making a comment about the evolving economy and most especially the **digital revolution** which involves digital electronics and the worldwide greater access to information. The ways people are spending and saving money are changing along with careers and employment affecting all sorts of roles from blue-collar factory laborers to white-collar tech professionals. **Reskilling** means changing up through education, training, experience to meet the demands of the digital revolution.

## Suggested Activity

_How money is spent is a significant part of financial management. Have you, a friend, or a member of your family joined a gym, fitness center, or tennis or golf club and not used the facilities to the fullest extent? Discuss, in groups, the expense of joining and maintaining memberships and services offered. What was worth or not worth the expense? Are recreational facilities on your campus or in your apartment complex free? One fitness club offered a four-month membership for $209 that could be renewed—do you think this is a good value? Why?_

In married couples, both the husband and the wife should be actively involved in financial planning. This chapter builds on the previous ones which indicate that today fewer people in certain age groups are married and family size is smaller than in the past. For example,

> *Just over half of Americans age 55 to 64 live in married couple households, down from two-thirds of 55-to 64-year-olds in 1980, according to a recent report from the National Academy on an Aging Society. The report states: "Boomers' higher rates of divorce and separation, and lower rates of marriage, mean that fewer today belong to married-couple households, and more may experience greater financial hardship as a result."*
>
> *(Ruffenach, 2008, p. R8)*

What about singles starting out and suddenly on their own? Read the case study about the turnaround of Sonia.

---

**CASE STUDY**

### Sonia

*Sonia Lewis knew she had a problem when she couldn't afford nachos. Forced to turn down a friend's invitation to dinner because her bank account was overdrawn yet again – something that happened so frequently she called herself the "Overdrawn Queen" – Lewis realized just how much trouble she was in. Her grandmother, who'd been her "financial security blanket," had recently died. And her unexpected death forced Lewis to accept reality: Nobody was left to bail her out if she couldn't pay her bills. "If you fail with money or if you win with money, it's going to be on you," she remembers thinking.*

The article her story appeared in goes on to say that she signed up for a budgeting class taught at a local church and sold possessions she didn't need. She reduced her student loan debt and got on the plus side of her finances. She started a company called the Student Loan Doctor. Her top tips are (1) know your numbers (2) research loan forgiveness and (3) think about long-term housing.

*Source: Kaitlin Mulhere (2019, May). She went from "Overdraft Queen" to professional debt coach. Money, pp. 5–6.*

In the Case Study, Sonia went to classes at a local church to improve her financial knowledge. Regarding financial literacy it has been shown that educational efforts definitely increase the financial knowledge of both men and women (Goldsmith & Goldsmith, 2006). **Financial literacy** courses emphasizing sets of knowledge and skills to help individuals make informed effective use of their financial resources are on the upswing at the high school and college levels and community centers in many countries around the world.

The financial industries are changing to keep up with modern times. Many of the leaders in the banking and financial industries are women including Jelena McWilliams, Former Chairman of the FDIC (Federal Deposit Insurance Corporation). Financial industries provide customers with more online services and also have banks that don't look so much like traditional banks, some even have cafes. Capital One Café in downtown Boston has a doorman and a greeter and low-cost coffee (Peet's), long tables with chairs, and the motto "Banking reimagined."

Financial planning, part of the financial industry to be discussed later in this chapter, is not limited to individuals and married couples; friends and whole families too can become involved in planning. For example, in the Reddick family there are three sisters who are going to hike down the Grand Canyon together a year from now. Reservations have to be made that far in advance if a stay in the small lodge at the bottom of the Canyon is included. Each sister is setting aside money for the expense of flying in and out of Arizona and for hiking/lodging expenses. They are excited. It is a family plan that includes all three sisters getting into better shape to make the hike.

## CRITICAL THINKING

Is there something special you are saving for? If not now, can you envision something in the future you will be saving for? What is it? How much money will you need? How are you saving money? Will a gift take care of part or all of it?

Solutions and outcomes need to be factored in, at the same time realizing that in all plans there needs to be flexibility. Assume that not everything will work out. Tumbling financial markets from 2007 to 2011 and more recent ups and downs in the stock market make this readily apparent to investors, who during the recession saw their retirement or college savings substantially and dramatically reduced. So another realization is that we can plan, but we are part of a greater economic system that we cannot control. Controlling finances is one of the most important and practical aspects of management. And, we do have control over our personal finances at least to some extent. In a downturn or upturn, decisions have to be made even if the decision is to stay put. Control is an important concept because debt needs to be handled yet people are wasting money on purchases, services, or memberships they do not use (see Suggested Activity). Here is a specific example:

> For more than a year, Rachel Hulin paid $90 a month for a gym membership. She used it maybe four times in all—for a per-visit rate of roughly $315. "I felt sort of like an idiot," says the 24-year-old photographer. "I think I signed up for it to try to make myself go." Ms. Hulin later dropped her membership and joined another, less-expensive gym at $55 a month. But she admits she hasn't "gone in a while" there either.
>
> (Silverman, 2003, p. D1)

This particular area of consumption, gym membership, illustrates hope over reason. A three-year study of about 8,000 members showed that the average user paid $17 per workout even when a $10-per-use policy existed; most lost over $700 over the life of their gym contract (Silverman, 2003, p. D1). Other areas where self-control is a particular problem include buying over the Internet and from television shopping shows or infomercials.

Many industries, businesses, and the media take advantage of self-control issues. Can you name a few businesses or industries doing this? Where do they advertise? They are motivated to increase profits, whereas consumers want to fulfill needs at a reasonable price and at the same time build and conserve wealth. If you have ever felt confused about a purchase (should I or shouldn't I?) this is why.

Although this chapter begins with theory and the state of the economy, it moves quickly to the dollars-and-cents issues involved in money management. It covers poverty and wealth, credit, the gender gap, and the glass ceiling.

This chapter is placed near the end of the book because it builds on many of the principles discussed earlier, such as values, attitudes, goals, resources, and decision making. To reiterate, values are principles that guide behavior, and goals are end results that require action. Thrift, for example, is a value affecting financial management, and saving for a car is an example of a financial goal. Signing contracts for a gym membership but rarely going to the gym or going to warehouse stores and later throwing out half of the fruits, vegetables, and bakery products bought are examples of the gap that exists between values (ideals) and behavior.

Attitudes are concepts that express feelings in regard to some idea, person, object, event, situation, or relationship. They play an important role in consumption because individuals have innumerable consumer attitudes (e.g., preferring a particular brand, store, or product over another). One attitude shift is that people in the United States are beginning retirement planning at an earlier age, the average age being 32.

Decision making is choosing between two or more alternatives. All people must make financial decisions, but their choices are limited by how much money they have. Money is a material resource, but how a person chooses to spend it is a human resource. Financial plans are an integral part of management information systems and decision support systems.

Space limitations prevent an exhaustive examination of personal and family finance, a topic to which whole courses and thousands of books are devoted. Instead, this chapter provides an introduction to financial planning and related economic and lifestyle issues by focusing on families as producers and consumers and examining such concerns as what individuals and families do with their money and how they save for retirement.

## Financial Management and Security

**Financial management** is the science or practice of managing money or other assets. Financial management requires systematic and disciplined thought and action. Saving money rather than spending it, for instance, requires self-discipline and control, the ability to set goals, and a willingness to put future needs before current needs.

In the time management chapter, we discussed asking the question, "Is this the best use of my time right now?" A corollary appropriate to this chapter says, before buying anything, ask, "Is this the best purchase for me at this moment?" This question alone will keep you away from accumulating unnecessary debt. Being debt-free is a goal. Using cash and debit cards for purchases will set a person in the right direction.

### The Tauntons

*After Teresa and Mark Taunton short sold their $535,000 four-bedroom dream home in Celebration, Florida, at the end of the real estate meltdown in 2011, buying another house was the last thing on their minds." It makes you feel you could somehow end up in the same position," says Teresa, 57, describing the anxiety the couple experienced after selling their house for less than what they owed the bank. "We were just so leery of everything. But in late February, five years after they were officially allowed to make another home purchase, they closed on a modest ranch house for less than half the price of their former Orlando-area unit and just minutes away. "We were really tired of renting," Teresa says, Of their new house, she adds, 'It's comfortable. It's home."*

*Source: Paul Davidson (2019, May 1). The American dream is making a comeback. USA Today, B1.*

Security means freedom from risk, danger, anxiety, or doubt. Consider the doubts the Tauntons had in the Case Study about buying a house again. Adding the word "security" to "financial" provides another layer to the overarching concept of financial management.

> **Financial security** *is the ability to meet day-to-day obligations while planning, saving, and investing to achieve future financial goals such as education, retirement, home ownership, and small business startup. By building assets and managing debt, households are better able to contribute to the economic vitality of their communities.*
>
> *(Lawrence et al., 2008, p. 61)*

The procedures followed at each stage of financial management must be methodological, sound, and planned for in advance to the maximum extent possible. Essentially, financial plans are works in progress; they need to be revised when necessary. For example, an attorney said that he thought estate plans and wills should be updated every five years because laws and family circumstances change.

In systems terminology, financial management is a transformation process involving the identification of financial goals; collection of information; analysis of resources; decisions about whether to spend, invest, or save; and evaluation of decisions. Management takes the perspective that money, like any other resource, can be controlled and used to achieve goals. As Figure 13.1 shows, the financial management process can be divided into three phases: planning, action, and postplanning.

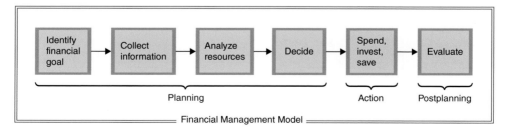

Figure 13.1 Financial management model.

During the planning stage, individuals begin by defining their financial goals. They then identify potential financial opportunities and determine what information and funds are needed to take advantage of these opportunities. Once they have analyzed their resources and decided how to use them, they can proceed to the action stage, where they save, invest, or spend their money.

In this phase, a **budget**, or a spending plan or guide, can be helpful by providing a visible means of controlling money. More coverage on budgets and examples is coming up. At the end of the process, as in any other management process, the decisions and their outcomes are evaluated. Throughout, money and other financial assets are treated as tools that can be used to enhance life and provide for growth and security.

## Family Economics: Avoiding Economic Fallout, Building Toward the Future

Approaching finances as a family—married-couple or single-parent—may involve the following questions:

Should I buy a new car or a used one or should I lease a car?

Can I afford to go to graduate school?

What happens if I lose my job?

When will we be able to retire?

What do I do if the child support payments are late?

How will I pay off my student loans?

What will my daughter's wedding cost?

All these questions are financial concerns. People who are financially pinched cut back in several ways, and children add another layer to financial worry. One of the greatest fears is losing a home and this fear became a reality from 2007 to 2011 for countless families when the rate of short sales (see The Tauntons Case Study) and foreclosures skyrocketed. Sometimes it was cheaper to walk away than to try and keep up with the mortgage payments. In regard to foreclosures, each state has a different version of the foreclosure process and usually courts and judges are involved and the result affects a homeowner's credit rating and ability to buy a new house for several years. College students often remember what it was like going through a recession while they were growing up and it has affected how they feel about renting vs. owning, about debt, and about other forms of money management.

### The Business Cycle and Inflation

Since individuals and families live in an economic system, they are not immune to the changes in the economy. Some of the main indicators of the economy include

- Personal spending
- Home sales including new and existing homes
- The consumer price index
- Unemployment rate
- Gross domestic product

Each of these will be described in the following paragraphs.

**CRITICAL THINKING**

When it comes to personal spending certain items are on the untouchable list such as a particular kind of cereal, hair shampoo, smart phones, toilet paper, orange juice, or a daily cup of gourmet coffee. In a survey by the National Retail Federation a specific type of coffee is on the untouchable list for one out of six consumers and it used to be for one out of seven. Do you have a particular brand of coffee or other drink that is non-negotiable? If so, what is it?

When the economy is down, corporations lay off thousands of workers, and governments do not replace with new hires those who move or retire, making the job market tighter. If the main or sole breadwinner is unemployed, the family suffers. When this book went to press, the U.S. unemployment rate was hovering around 3 percent which is low. The rate varies by state and by local area, for example, if the main employer such as a factory shuts down the unemployment rate is much higher and the community impacts are severely felt. An unemployment rate of 10 percent or more is considered an indicator of severe economic problems. A rate under 5 percent is desirable. During boom times and in high-growth areas, the unemployment rate can be as low as 2 percent. Describing a period of unemployment and giving perspective, a Northwestern University Kellogg School of Management professor said:

> The newspaper says the banking industry will lose 100,000 jobs this year. That's 100,000 middle-class people who thought they were going to be in control of their lives. Manhattan is filled with 40-year-olds out of work, deep in debt and overextended on their apartments. They never thought it would happen to them.
>
> (Adler, 1992, p. 22)

The key phrases here are "people who thought they were going to be in control of their lives" and "they never thought it would happen to them." In 2012, another 100,000 from the banking industry were laid off and the response was the same—people don't think it will be them. A human resources officer of a university explained it this way:

> A budget cut in labor means that some people will be laid off even if they are doing a very good and dependable job. One of the hardest things I ever had to do was call 52 employees in one by one and tell them they were being laid off and over and over again they would ask 'what have I done wrong' and the answer was nothing.

The unexpectedness of unemployment makes it difficult to adjust to and manage. In an analysis of activities that occupy household members' time when they are unable to find work as a result of an economic downturn, the researchers found that roughly 30–40 percent of the "extra" nonworking hours were spent in working in the home such as more cooking and more home repair. Searching for another job took about 1 percent of the extra hours and the unemployed used more than 20 percent of their lost work hours for extra sleep. Also, according to this analysis of the American Time Use Survey from the Bureau of Labor Statistics some 6 percent of the foregone work hours went to childcare (Belsie, 2011). Being unemployed definitely affects the work–family balance.

CRITICAL THINKING

**Brian**

Brian, age 36, was suddenly fired from his job in Los Angeles. His rent was close to $5,000 a month so it wasn't long before his savings were depleted. Unemployment benefits were only going to last a few more weeks. He tried to get a job quickly in Los Angeles but nothing was working out and he considered moving back to his college town in the South where living expenses were much cheaper. The problem was he was used to the fast-paced, urban life and felt going back to his college town be a step back. Brian was asking his friends for advice. What would you tell him?

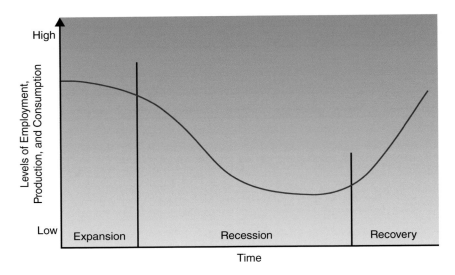

**Figure 13.2** The business cycle. The economy goes through various stages over time. The stages are cyclical and affect the levels of employment, production, and consumption.

To illustrate the ups and downs of the economy, the business cycle is made up of three main parts as shown in Figure 13.2.

1. **Recession:** A moderate and temporary decline in the economy.

2. **Recovery:** A hopeful stage when things are looking better, consumer buying and confidence are up, production is up, employment is up, retail sales improve, and new homes are being built. As this book went to press, the United States was in this stage.

3. **Expansion:** Prosperity, high growth, an active economy, and high employment rates.

In the 20th century, the world struggled through several economic crises, most notably the Great Depression, which peaked in the United States in 1933. In the 1990s there were boom times, called the "expansion phase." In the early 2000s, economic hard times returned in the form of a recession followed by a period of recovery and then another recession from 2007 to 2011 (with the lowest point at 2009) followed by ups and downs, signaling a recovery.

Many factors play into which part of the business cycle a nation's economy can be characterized as. One of the main factors is **inflation**, which means rising prices. U.S. inflation had been around 2 percent for many years which is considered a low inflation rate and it spiked upward in 2022. During times of economic uncertainty, people pull back on their discretionary spending including using less gasoline and eating out less. Another factor is that middle-class global spending is shifting. In 2009 most of the worldwide middle-class consumer spending was concentrated in North America, Europe, and the Asia Pacific. In 2030 this is predicted to take a great shift so that the middle class in the Asia Pacific will make up the majority of consumer spending according to the Organization for Economic Cooperation and Development (OCED). This is reflective of the estimated high growth in the size and spending power of the middle classes in India and China and nearby countries.

Inflation indicates the general way prices are going, but individual categories of products or services may be going up or down in a way significantly different from the general inflation rate. For example, televisions have gone down significantly in price relative to other costs. *Two areas rising significantly in cost are college tuition and health care.* The average college senior is in debt to the tune of $30,000 (2020 estimate varies widely by university and individual student) at graduation. College debt, although increasing, is not a new problem as evidenced in Joe's situation described next.

> *That's a problem Joe Palazzolo would love to have. Palazzolo, 25, graduated on Mother's Day from Rutgers University with a master's degree in public policy and student loans exceeding $116,000. His payment will average $800 a month. It could have been worse: Because of his top grades, Rutgers paid Palazzolo's tuition for his final year of graduate school. At a time when his friends are thinking about buying their first homes, he's looking for roommates to share a three bedroom house so he can limit his rent to $600 a month.*
>
> (Block, 2006, p. A1)

Home sales were listed above as an economic indicator. Low mortgage rates stimulate home building, the reselling of existing homes, and the refinancing of existing mortgages. When the housing market is up or down many side industries are affected. Spin-offs include sales in landscaping, insurance, appliances, swimming pools, cabinets, furnishings, hardware, building supplies, and financial products.

CRITICAL THINKING

Do you have student loans? Do you know how much you will owe when you graduated? Do you know students with huge loan debt? What is their plan to pay it back?

The main measure of inflation in the United States is the **consumer price index (CPI)** computed and reported each month by the Bureau of Labor Statistics (BLS). Economic assistants gather price information from selected stores, supermarkets, doctors' offices, rental units, and the like. Each month, about 80,000 prices are recorded in 87 urban areas. By collecting price data on a clearly defined market basket of products, the BLS can measure changes in prices. The CPI is used in formulating fiscal and monetary policy and in adjusting wages, salaries, and payments such as Social Security. For many retirees, the only raise they get is when Congress votes to increase their monthly Social Security checks owing to inflation.

## Individuals and Families as Producers and Consumers

Within the movement of the general economy, individuals and families play important roles as producers and consumers. Consumption choices include what food to eat, what clothes to wear, where to shop, and where to bank. Consumption decisions affect the present and future standard of living of an individual or family. An individual's or family's **level of living** is a measure of the goods and services affordable and available to them. **Standard of living** is what an individual or a family aspires to. On the production side, families produce children and transform raw products into finished products through such activities as woodworking, gardening, cooking, and sewing. In addition, families produce, process, manage, and provide a variety of other goods and services (e.g., childcare, elder care, home maintenance, transportation, health care, and education for family members). Financial well-being is part of overall well-being embracing health, education, caring, spiritual, and other needs (Goldsmith, 2015).

Households are both labor-intensive and highly productive. Household production is not included in the **gross domestic product (GDP)**, which is the total market value of all goods and services produced by a nation during a specified period, usually a year. For example, tomatoes canned at home, though used the same way as factory-canned tomatoes, are not counted in the GDP. Similarly, an individual's work in completing his or her income tax forms is not counted in the GDP, whereas the services provided by an accounting firm doing someone's income taxes is included. Thus, although individuals and families are significant producing units, their home-based production is not counted in the U.S. GDP. Several reasons have been given for this omission; the most logical is that household production is difficult to measure accurately. The GDP is reported quarterly and in the first quarter of 2019, it was 3.2 percent according to the Bureau of Economic Analysis. The value of this measure for the individual or consumer is not to memorize the exact percentage but to have a perception of whether the GDP is going up or down at a significant rate. For example, it was 1.9 percent in the first quarter of 2011 in the United States and in India it has been 6.2 percent in recent years.

## Income, Taxes, Net Worth, Budgets, and Saving

Just as GDP is a measure of a nation's well-being, income is one of the main measures of a family's financial well-being. **Income** is the amount of money or its equivalent received during a period of time. The main source of income for most people is their salary. Other sources are dividends from investments and savings accounts, gifts, and so on. There are several different kinds of income:

- **Discretionary income**: Income regulated by one's own discretion or judgment.

- **Disposable income**: The amount of take-home pay left after all deductions are made for benefits, taxes, contributions, and so on.

- **Gross income**: All income received that is not legally exempt from taxes.

- **Psychic income**: One's perception or feelings about income; the satisfaction derived from income.

- **Real income**: Income measured in prices at a certain time, reflecting the buying power of current dollars.

Take special note of psychic income. When helping individuals and families formulate budgets or financial plans, it is important to know not only how much money they have to work with, but also how they feel about money in general. What one person regards as very little money, another may consider a fortune. An accurate assessment of people's income or lifestyle requires some knowledge of not only their actual income but also how they perceive money and how strongly they feel the need to maintain an adequate level of living.

A personal tax levied on individuals or families on the basis of income received is called **income tax**. In 1913, the Sixteenth Amendment to the U.S. Constitution was ratified, making the personal income tax constitutional. On average, one-third of the typical U.S. family's income goes to paying federal, state, and local taxes. **Taxes** are compulsory levies that are an important source of government revenue. Taxes help cover government expenses and, in the case of income tax, help redistribute income and wealth. In 1789, Benjamin Franklin wrote that "in this world nothing is certain but death and taxes." After taxes, typically the remainder of a family's money goes first to housing, then transportation, then food, and then down the list to health/personal care, recreation, clothing, insurance, and other needs. The distribution of money varies greatly by the amount of income (e.g., the lower the income, the higher proportion spent on food), savings, and other investments.

Financial records for income tax purposes should be kept for three years, occasionally for five if there had been a problem in the past. Records to keep permanently include birth and marriage certificates, divorce papers, military records, bankruptcy filings, adoption papers, wills, and Social Security data. It should be noted that the federal government keeps a running record of Social Security earnings and one can access one's own data at any time.

**Net worth** is determined by subtracting what is owed **(liabilities)** from what is owned **(assets)**. To give a historical perspective, household assets have increased seven times in the last century. We may not feel better off, but we are. Estimation of net worth is considered the best measure of one's material wealth. It is important to estimate net worth because it shows where a person stands financially. A net worth estimate and yearly earnings calculation should be made at least once a year. Most often people do this at tax time in April in the United States

Figure 13.3 provides a sample form that can be used for computing net worth. Notice the wide variety of assets: actual cash on hand and money in checking and savings accounts; investments such as certificates of deposit, stocks, bonds, and mutual funds; real estate, which includes one's house and any other real estate owned; pension benefits to which an individual is entitled; retirement accounts, such as employer-sponsored 401(k) and 403(b) plans and Individual Retirement Accounts (IRAs); the value of a business; personal property such as jewelry, furniture, and appliances; and any automobiles owned. Liabilities include the mortgage on one's home, the balance owed on installment loans, such as on a car or refrigerator, the balance owed on credit cards, unpaid bills, and any taxes owed.

| Assets | |
|---|---|
| Cash on hand | $ |
| Checking accounts | $ |
| Savings accounts | $ |
| Money market funds | $ |
| Cash management accounts | $ |
| Certificates of deposits | $ |
| Stocks, bonds (market value)* | $ |
| Mutual funds | $ |
| Real estate (market value) | $ |
| Employer-sponsored retirement plans | $ |
| IRAS | $ |
| Vested company benefits | $ |
| Annuities (one-time investments paid upon retirement) | $ |
| Personal property** (market value) | $ |
| Automobiles (market value) | $ |
| Estate and trust values | $ |
| Cash value of whole life insurance | $ |
| Business venture values | $ |
| Debts owed to you | $ |
| Other | $ |
| | |
| *Total assets* | $ |
| | |
| Liabilities | |
| Loans (college, home, auto) | $ |
| Unpaid bills | $ |
| Personal debts (to friends, family) | $ |
| Other | $ |
| | |
| *Total liabilities* | $ |
| | |
| *Net worth* (total assets - total liabilities) | $ |

* Market value means what the asset would be worth if it were sold immediately.
** This category includes nearly anything with a resale value, such as clothing, furniture, books, bicycles, computers, jewelry, televisions, and appliances.

**Figure 13.3** Net worth statement. Net worth is calculated by subtracting liabilities (what is owed) from assets (what is owned).

The net worth statement of Jacob Sawyer, a junior in college, appears in Table 13.1. Jacob has some money in his checking and savings accounts, a car, and various items of personal property, most notably a computer. Jacob also has a number of liabilities, including his college loan, an outstanding balance on his credit card, and parking tickets he has not paid.

When Jacob's liabilities are subtracted from his assets, the result is −$2,817.83. Jacob has a negative net worth—he owes more than his assets are worth. Negative net worth is not unusual for someone at Jacob's life stage. College students and new college graduates often have college loans outstanding and might incur other financial obligations from moving and setting up a new lifestyle. As they begin to work full-time and their earnings increase, they are able to pay off their debts, and their negative net worth gradually declines;

Table 13.1 Jacob Sawyer's Net Worth Statement

| Assets | |
| --- | --- |
| Cash on hand | $ 40.00 |
| Checking account | 465.02 |
| Savings account | 807.15 |
| Personal property | |
| Cellphone | 100.00 |
| Bicycle | 125.00 |
| Laptop computer | 1,000.00 |
| Clothes and books | 250.00 |
| Automobile (12-year-old car) | 3,500.00 |
| Total assets | $6,287.17 |
| **Liabilities** | |
| College loan | $8,655.00 |
| Unpaid bills | |
| Balance on credit cards | 300.00 |
| Personal debts | |
| Loan from roommate | 110.00 |
| Other (parking tickets) | 40.00 |
| Total liabilities | $9,105.00 |
| Net worth | -$2,817.83 |

and then they begin to accumulate assets. Specific advice on how college students can manage their money is included in an upcoming section.

Whereas a net worth statement reveals current financial status, a budget helps individuals and families plan ahead and clarify their values and goals. As explained earlier, a budget is a spending plan. *A budget should serve as a guide*—one that the budgeter controls. It should be flexible and not put a straitjacket on spending. Many expenses, such as money spent on food, clothing, and entertainment, are **variable expenses**, whereas others are **fixed expenses**, such as rent, cellphone plan, and car payments.

If budgets are too rigid, they will not allow for unexpected or variable expenses, such as medical or dental bills or the costs of home maintenance. For example, replacing a leaking roof or a faulty furnace for $5,000 is an expense that must be met but cannot be budgeted for in advance except in the most general way.

Typically, budgets are based on monthly average spending patterns. Income is compared to outflow. The main source of income is wages and salaries. Housing expenditures (including utilities) take away the largest share. *So, begin each budget by looking first at rent or home mortgage payments.* Other large expenses include transportation (car payments and gasoline/maintenance), student loan debt payments, food, and credit/store card payments. When this book went to press the largest loans (liabilities) in the United States were in this order:

1. Mortgage payments

2. Student loans

3. Credit card debt

### When individuals are having a hard time meeting monthly expenses they can:

- Borrow more money or delay debt repayment

- Make more money (increase income).

- Reduce expenses (outflow).

- Sell something, downsize.

- Do a combination of all four.

One way to prepare for unexpected expenses is to budget a certain amount to be saved each month. The goal of saving is to build funds in a risk-free manner. Saving is what makes future spending or investing possible. How much should an individual or family save? The answer depends on their present lifestyle, responsibilities, and goals and on the lifestyle they desire.

*People in the United States and Canada save on average about 4 to 7 percent of their income, a rate that has been rising in recent years.* The "on average" means some people are spending more than they make (they are in debt) and, of course, there are others who save consistently. To get ahead or to save for something, such as the down payment on a house, individuals should strive to save 10–20 percent. Some lenders require a 20 percent down payment. In dual-earner couples, some live on one salary and save the other. Students may return home after graduation and live with their parents or siblings and save a considerable amount of money before they launch out on their own.

One way to approach saving is to have a goal of building an **emergency fund** (also called a contingency fund) of three to six months' income. Opinions vary on the length of time. Author and television personality Suze Orman suggests eight months' expenses in savings because the time it takes to find a job is getting longer. Estimates by the Bureau of Labor Statistics reveal that the average out-of-work person takes five to eight months to find a job. An emergency fund is used to tide people over until income begins again, so the amount should be enough to take care of life basics such as rent and food.

To build savings, young professionals should save regularly, even if in small amounts, to enable them to accomplish short- and long-term goals such as the purchase of a car or home. Figure 13.4 lists the goals of John, a recent college graduate, as a way to show how goals and finances are linked. Spaces are provided for you to write in your own financial goals—short-term, medium-term, and long-term.

Table 13.2 shows the budget of a young married couple, Matt and Samantha Kirby. As a young couple starting out, their sources of income and types of expenses are fairly limited. Their salaries are their biggest source of income, and their house and child care for their two-year-old daughter are their largest expenses. Notice that Matt and Samantha's budget does not leave any money for emergencies. They say they'll be able to start saving more in six months when Samantha finishes her training program at the bank and receives a substantial increase in salary and Matt finishes law school. In the meantime, they hope no emergencies arise.

| Financial Goals | John's Goals* | Your Goals |
|---|---|---|
| Short Term (0–3 years) | | |
| Goal 1: | Move across country | _____ |
| Goal 2: | Begin full-time job | _____ |
| Goal 3: | Find a roommate, rent an apartment | _____ |
| Medium Term (3–7 years) | | |
| Goal 1: | Establish him self in film business | _____ |
| Goal 2: | Buy new car | _____ |
| Goal 3: | Save money | _____ |
| Long Term (7–10 years) | | |
| Goal 1: | Start own production company | _____ |
| Goal 2: | Settle down, buy a house | _____ |
| Goal 3: | Marry, start a family | _____ |

* John is 23 years old. He recently graduated from a four-year university with a major in film studies. He plans to move to California and get into the film industry (behind the camera). He graduated debt-free, but has few possessions except a laptop, some furniture, and a used car. He has contacts in California for jobs and for roommates.

Figure 13.4 Financial goals by time.

Table 13.2 Monthly Budget for Matt and Samantha Kirby
Monthly savings (or losses) are determined by subtracting estimated monthly expenses from monthly income

| Income | |
|---|---|
| Salaries | |
| Samantha (part-time management trainee at bank) | $ 2,102.74 |
| Matt (part-time job while attending law school) | 850.00 |
| Dividends | 22.00 |
| Money gifts, scholarships (Matt's scholarship for law school) | 1000.00 |
| Other (Samantha writes a weekly column on financial management for a newspaper) | 100.00 |
| Total income | $ 4,074.74 |
| **Expenses** | |
| Mortgage payment on modest house | $ 874.88 |
| Food | 450.00 |
| Child care (part-time, for Kristin, their daughter) | 500.00 |
| Tuition/books | 255.00 |

(Continued)

| Expenses | |
|---|---|
| Gasoline/transportation | |
| Bus fare for Samantha | 26.00 |
| Parking at the university for Matt | 30.00 |
| Gasoline | 75.00 |
| Utilities (gas, electric, water, cable) | 150.00 |
| Cell phone | 160.00 |
| Insurance (life, car, home—Samantha's employer pays for health insurance) | 300.00 |
| Clothing and personal care (haircuts, cosmetics) | 150.00 |
| Credit card payments | 50.00 |
| Entertainment | 40.00 |
| Loans | |
| College (Samantha) | 190.00 |
| College (Matt) | 120.00 |
| Automobile | 239.85 |
| Personal spending | 120.00 |
| Miscellaneous | 35.00 |
| Total expenses | $ 3,765.73 |
| Total savings | $ 309.01 |

As this photo shows, think enduring and long-range when it comes to financial planning.

In drawing up your own budget, checking account and credit card statements can help you obtain an accurate account of your money flow.

Because expenses fluctuate from month to month, averaging several months' expenses will help you obtain a more accurate picture of typical monthly expenditures. Once individuals or families figure out their net worth and their typical monthly expenditures, they can create a six-month or one-year spending plan. By reviewing their net worth statement and monthly expenditures, people may be able to find places where they can spend less and save more.

## Managing Credit and Reducing Debt

The use of credit has plusses and minuses. An easy way to overspend is to use credit indiscriminately. A high level of individual and family debt has a long-term impact on the family economy and on that of nations. In recent years in the United States, the debt rate has gone down as people responded to the recession by saving more and spending less and paying down existing debt. A rebound in the housing market was experienced in the years 2015 and up so there was a leveling out and recently new surges of building and remodeling.

**Credit**, time allowed for payment, has been around for a long time. Credit means that an individual owes a certain amount of money, at a certain time each month, to a specific creditor at a certain rate. Failure to pay on time the recommended amount may result in penalties or fees.

**Debit cards** also known as cash cards are computerized banking transactions, they remove money directly from your account and are often used to pay for groceries and other everyday items. You are spending your own funds rather than borrowing additional money as you would when using a credit card. Prepaid debit cards are worth a certain amount of money, for example, $500. The advantages are that they do not require a credit history and it is nearly impossible to incur an overdraft or rack up debt. The main disadvantages are the fees and lack of consumer protection. Younger people use debit cards more than older people so debit cards are becoming more established as a normal part of the money management process.

> Many colleges have tightened rules on credit-card marketing on campus in order to discourage students from racking up huge amounts of debt. Now another kind of card is being pushed on campus—with its own set of issues. This fall, financial-services companies are focusing more of their campus marketing on "pre-paid debit cards," which work like standard debit cards except that they aren't linked to a traditional checking account. Among the issuers aggressively marketing their cards this year: U.S. Bancorp and Wal-Mart Stores Inc. The cards typically carry hefty fees and offer fewer consumer protections than credit cards. Fees are often charged when the card is activated, when it is used at an ATM and even when there's a lack of activity.
>
> *(Pilon, 2008, p. D1)*

Some universities, as examples Tulane University, the University of South Carolina, and Georgia Institute of Technology, forbid credit card companies from soliciting on-campus.

> When Laura Palazzolo, of New Hyde Park, N.Y., entered New York University this fall, she says she was bombarded with offers for debit cards from area banks handing out fliers on campus. She hopes to avoid using plastic too much. "I'm really trying to be careful," says Ms. Palazzolo, 18. "It's a little overwhelming when [companies] target you because you're a freshman." For now, she's using a student checking account she set up through her parents' bank that comes with a debit card.
>
> *(Pilon, 2008, p. D2)*

Debt follows a person through life. If you packed up your car in Virginia and drove across the country nonstop to Seattle, your credit rating and any information about outstanding parking or traffic tickets would get there before you arrive: with the Internet, financial records and status are instantaneous.

> ## CRITICAL THINKING
>
> Does your campus allow credit card or prepaid debit card solicitation on campus? Is it done during orientation or at student events or through the mail or email?

A credit card authorizes the holder to buy something in advance of paying for it. Using credit instead of cash makes shopping more convenient and reduces the risk of loss or theft associated with carrying large amounts of cash.

Credit card confidence varies by life stage. One study found that 20–24 year olds were less confident about their abilities to resist temptations and therefore had more trouble managing credit. Those in later adulthood and old age (61–85) were less worried about their debt and more easily resisted the temptation to overspend (Thums et al., 2008).

*Managing student loan debt and credit are two of the biggest management problems* individuals and families face. From a financial point of view, one of the problems is that interest on credit card payments is usually higher than what individuals earn on their investments. The following suggestions can help reduce the chances of credit mismanagement:

- Have only one or two cards, at most three. The typical bankrupt individual has 20 or more cards.

- Pay off credit cards on time in full each month to avoid interest charges. Only 36 percent of cardholders do this.

- Know what the agreement says; seek cards with the lowest annual percentage rate (APR) and no additional fees. The average yearly rate of interest paid over the life of credit or a loan is called the **annual percentage rate**.

- If a card has a teaser rate (a very low introductory level APR), use it but get rid of it when the rate goes up. Teaser rates are offered to college students; and when they graduate, the rates go up. The companies know from experience that most students will continue using the cards.

- Check credit card statements carefully against receipts. Do not allow the unauthorized use of a credit card number.

- Keep a list of credit card purchases as they occur, similar to the check stubs in a checkbook.

- Keep a list of credit card numbers in a safe place, lest they are lost or stolen, along with a list of toll-free numbers of credit card companies to notify in case cards are lost.

- If you are in debt, get out. First, pay off the credit cards with the highest APR.

Psychologically, it may help to pay off the card with the smallest amount owed first or to consolidate several small debts into one. Most people can handle 10–15 percent of take-home pay being used up for monthly consumer credit obligations; 20 percent or more puts consumers in a danger zone.

- Inform creditors if bills cannot be paid. Most will work with consumers to arrange payback plans.

- Contact a credit counseling service such as the National Foundation for Credit Counseling (nfcc.org) or the Consolidated Credit Counseling Services if the debt is out of control. They can help negotiate a lower rate or repayment schedule.

- Delete all spam e-mail regarding getting you out of debt.

Under the **Fair Credit Reporting Act**, you have the right to receive a copy of your credit report. **Credit bureaus**, reporting agencies that collect, store, and sell financial information, offer credit reports to consumers for free. The three main credit reporting centers are

- Equifax, econsumer.equifax.com

- Trans Union Corporation, transunion.com

- Experian, experian.com

Credit reports are used by institutions to determine your creditworthiness before they offer you a loan, a mortgage, a credit card, or a job. The institution (e.g., bank, store, or employer) pays a fee for the credit report. If a prospective consumer has a high **FICO score**, a numeric value assigned to credit habits, and credit history invented by Fair, Isaac and Company (FICO) in 1956 (the range is 300–850), a lender may offer a lower mortgage rate. A consumer in the high range can also ask for a lower interest rate on credit cards. As an example, a credit score of 720 may qualify you for a credit card rate of 9.6 percent versus 18 percent for someone with a score of 600. The person with the 720 score could save $86 in annual interest for every $1,000 in the balance. A score below 500 puts a consumer in the sub-lender or sub-prime category. A median score is 623. A score of 750 or above is considered very high.

---

### CRITICAL THINKING

#### Amy, Sergei, and Daughter Kristen

Parents in their 70s named Amy and Sergei wanted to put their 52-year-old daughter Kristen on their bank account. They thought they could do this over the phone but were told by the bank all three of them had to come in person to the bank and they would need to bring two pieces of identification each. Sergei who is mostly house-bound was incensed but complied. Why did the bank insist on seeing all three family members in person?

---

How do potential employers find out about your credit score? The way it starts is that on job application forms there is a box to mark off, giving employers the right to conduct background checks. Applicants can refuse to mark it, but the interview process might stop right there. Would you hire someone who did not check that box when dozens of other applicants checked it? Potential employers associate a good credit report with trustworthiness and reliability, and they value these characteristics whether or not the job involves handling money. What they are looking for in a prospective employee is not necessarily that he or she is debt-free, but that his or her debt is managed properly (i.e., show a record of steady payments).

A good FICO score can be established in a number of ways, including opening checking and savings accounts; paying bills, including rent, promptly; and opening a charge account with a store and promptly

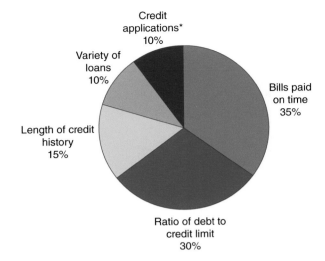

Figure 13.5 Factors influencing FICO scores.

*Open and close accounts with care.

remitting the monthly balance due. Potential lenders who are considering whether to extend credit or not also look at several factors, including owning a recent model cellphone and keeping it charged (shows dependability and accessibility), owning a laptop or iPad or similar tablet device and using it regularly, residential and job stability, education, income, and home ownership. If someone does not have an active cellphone or other digital devices what does this say about a person? There have been studies that show owning a cellphone and keeping up monthly payments for services (or in some way keeping it active along with personal computer use) correlates well with a high FICO score.

Regardless of the criteria used, the **Equal Credit Opportunity Act** prevents a lender from discriminating against a person in any aspect of a credit transaction because of race, sex, age, color, marital status, or other related factors.

Deciding how much credit to use and when to pay cash is part of the overall management problem of controlling money. The first step toward solving this problem is to define an attainable goal. Examples of specific financial goals include saving for a down payment on a house, or for college expenses, remodeling, a vacation, or additional investments and retirement. Once a financial goal is established and a plan drawn up, progress toward the goal should be reviewed to evaluate how well the financial planning is working.

## Banking, Investments, and Insurance

Saving and investing can take many forms. For example, cash can be put in interest-bearing checking accounts, savings accounts, money market accounts, and low-risk, longer-term savings instruments. Regardless of the type of account, the goal is to maximize the earnings from the investment of cash and to avoid fees, payments, and extra charges. **Liquidity**, the speed and ease of retrieving cash or turning another type of investment into cash, is another important consideration.

Checking accounts from banks and share accounts from credit unions allow the holder to transfer funds from the account to pay for goods and services. Banks commonly charge a fee for this convenience in per-check charges or monthly service fees, but they may also pay interest on the money in the account.

A savings account, also called a passbook account, typically pays higher interest than a checking account. A money market account pays an even higher rate of interest, and some offer check-writing privileges. These accounts are commonly called "NOW" (negotiable order of withdrawal) accounts and cash management accounts. Other low-risk possibilities for cash include government savings bonds and certificates of deposit (CDs). These typically pay higher interest than checking, savings, and money market accounts.

**Investment** is the commitment of capital to the achievement of long-term goals or objectives. Most people invest to build wealth and secure a comfortable future. It is important to invest because of rising prices; and because people are living longer, their money has to stretch further. Investing is a process that involves planning, money, information, time, and an understanding of risk, the possibility of experiencing suffering, loss, danger, or harm. In financial risk it is the chance of loss of money or opportunity.

Investment and insurance decisions rest not only on economic conditions, personal income, and life stage but also on one's ability to handle risk. Some investors are more conservative (less likely to take risks) than others. As one ages, usually one gravitates to more conservative, dividend-paying investments because if money is lost, the person does not have as much time to earn the income to bounce back again as does a younger person. However, even in retirement, some growth should be built in to keep up with inflation.

**Diversification** means having a mix of investments as a way to spread risk across several categories. Another basic principle is that the earlier an individual starts to invest, the longer time period the investment will have to grow. Youth is on the investor's side.

Several chapters would be needed to discuss the pros and cons of the different kinds of investments available. For the purposes of this chapter, the focus will be on the subject of investing and the most common types of investments.

- *Stocks* represent ownership in a company (e.g., Uber, Microsoft, IBM, Coca-Cola, Apple). There are thousands of stocks from which to choose. Usually the best strategy is to buy good stocks and hold on to them.

    *"People want to do something, which is why they tend to over-trade," says Clifford Asness, managing principal of New York hedge-fund manager AQR Capital Management. "But the object of the market is not to entertain us. You should stay diversified, pay low fees, relax and get on with the rest of your life.*
    *(Clements, 2003, October 8, p. D1)*

- *Bonds* are investments in which a person lends money to an organization such as the government or a corporation. Examples of U.S. Treasury Department bonds are I Bonds and Series EE Bonds. Information about them can be obtained from savingsbonds.gov. Generally, bonds are considered more conservative (safer) investments than stocks, but less liquid. Maturity dates run from a month to 30 years. Interest or dividends are distributions of money that governments or corporations pay to bondholders (some stocks also pay dividends). Usually, dividends on bonds are paid twice a year and are a source of income.

- *Mutual funds* are groups of stocks, bonds, or other securities managed by an investment company. Their chief benefits are diversification and professional management.

- *Real estate* includes real estate directly (such as a primary residence or a lot owned) or indirectly owned (such as in a partnership or a Real Estate Investment Trust, commonly known as a REIT).

- *Other forms of investment* include Individual Retirement Accounts (IRAs), employer-sponsored retirement plans, precious metals (i.e., gold, silver), gems, and collectibles.

Before starting to invest, a person should have ample cash for daily and monthly expenses, an emergency fund set aside, paid-off credit cards, and insurance. Usually, people start with secure investments such as money market funds, certificates of deposit, U.S. Savings Bonds, retirement plans at work, U.S. Treasury Securities, and savings accounts. Then, after some of these are owned, they move up the investment ladder to other categories offering more income and growth. The last category to consider is a speculative investment where more risk is prevalent.

*The purpose of insurance is to protect people and financial assets.* It provides peace of mind. A sound financial plan includes protection from major risks (e.g., auto accidents, natural disasters, health problems) that can threaten financial security. **Insurance** is a financial arrangement in which people pay premiums (payments) to an insurance company that reimburses them in the event of loss or injury. Usually, the most costly and the most important form of insurance is health insurance. Most employers offer health insurance as part of their benefits package. This may change if government policy changes.

Other types of insurance include property, liability, automobile, disability, life, and long-term care insurance. Usually, group policies (insurance company contracts sold through organizations such as professional associations or alumni groups) are less expensive than individual policies. Decisions about insurance depend on how much protection is needed, how much you can afford, and how much is given by employers. Insurance coverage should be appropriate to an individual's or a family's life stage, needs, and goals.

A full course in personal finance or family financial analysis will cover many of the terms and concepts introduced in this chapter at a deeper level. Financial well-being is critical to a person's overall sense of well-being and success. Learning to manage money is a lifelong process, which begins in childhood. *People between the ages of 45 and 54 have the highest median income of any age group,* but they also have the highest expenses, because they may have children in college while they are also saving for their own retirement. Over their life span, individuals and couples have to re-evaluate, update, and renegotiate their goals and spending and investing plans many times. For example, experts suggest that financial plans, in general, and, specifically, insurance policies and retirement accounts should be examined each year to determine whether they still meet the individual's and family's needs.

## Financial Literacy, Children, and Families

*Financial literacy* defined earlier (knowledge and understanding of financial concepts and risks)" is an international concern. From financial literacy research, the conclusion can be drawn that

> *one is financially literate when one has the skills to explain and predict the relationships between concepts, e.g., the relation between savings and investments, between risks and returns, between average annual return and inflation etc. The OECD (Organization for Economic Co-operation and Development) definition of financial literacy implies that consumers have the motivation and confidence to apply financial knowledge.*
>
> *(Durband et al., 2019, p. 19)*

At one time, the financial unit in high school family and consumer sciences (FCS) classes was as simple as looking at budgets and doing checkbook exercises" (Franklin, 2007, p. 17). Current financial units in FCS (in all 50 states) and economics classes go way beyond this to build financial literacy skills. Unfortunately not every high school has FCS and economics classes. In a Texas study parents said they would be willing to pay extra property taxes for the implementation of financial literacy education (Davis & Durband, 2008). The U.S. Department of Treasury is leading financial education efforts and promoting financial literacy testing nationwide. There is not only interest in improving the financial literacy of children but also that of adults (Eccles et al., 2010; Eccles et al., 2011; Hanna, 2011; Mayer et al., 2011).

As adolescence is a time of significant change, it is a good time to establish values and skills in money management. A study of middle schoolers found they were highly status-conscious, which was linked to self-image and identity, but they had little understanding of how much effort, financial outlay, and cost to family relationships earning a lot of money might take (Beutler et al., 2008). The word "relationships" has been explored in innumerable family relations and family economics studies. Relationship satisfaction refers to an individual's feelings and thoughts about another person in a marriage or partnership. Research shows that a partner's spending behavior does indeed influence relationships (Britt et al., 2008). Students, at various levels, are interested in this social side of finances as well as in the changes economics brings to family finance.

> *"For too long we have thought that economics is what they do at MIT and not what you do when you make day-to-day decisions,"* says Robert Duvall, president and chief executive of the National Council on Economic Education, a New York-based organization that provides training and educational resources for teachers.
>
> *"Every high-school graduate should have a course in economics because you need that skill set in this complicated world."* Today's teens need financial education more than their parents did at their same age, says Carrie Schwab Pomerantz, senior vice president and chief strategist for consumer education at Charles Schwab Corp. That's because kids today are less likely than previous generations to ever receive a pension and more likely to graduate with credit-card debt and student loans.
>
> *(Mincer, 2007, p. R7)*

Raising children is costly too, one of the most expensive things anyone does. The estimate by the U.S. Department of Agriculture (USDA) is $233,610 to raise a child from birth through age 17 for middle-income families with two children. This is projected to rise in a current young child's life to $284,570 over time given the inflation of 2.2 percent (Lino, 2017) Lower-income families on average spend less. It is more expensive to raise urban rather than rural children. The outlay per child is reduced with each additional child, perhaps out of necessity, perhaps because bedrooms can be shared, clothes and toys handed down, and so on. Without a doubt, the costs of rearing and educating children add to the financial strain on families. The top three most expensive child-raising expenses are:

- Housing 29 percent

- Food 18 percent

- Child care/education 16 percent

The other categories include clothing, transportation, health care, and miscellaneous. The **Consumer Expenditure Survey** (CE) program in the Bureau of Labor Statistics (BLS) provides data on expenditures, income, and demographic characteristics of U.S. consumers. The program regularly releases data reports on the cost of raising children and about income, and expenditures for all age groups. The term BLS prefers to use is consumer unit. The USDA assumes that when people have children they will move into larger homes. Their calculations assume that for each child, a family adds 100–150 square feet of living space (the size of a typical bedroom). A way to save here is to go against the tide, that is, to not increase housing size or to live in a less expensive place, or at least to get a refinance at a lower mortgage rate. As food comes next, there are thousands of ways to save money. A simple trick is to use search engines on the Internet and type in the word "discount" and see what happens. For large families, other ideas are to join warehouse clubs, or shop in supercenters, or buy in bulk at sales, or use food delivery services that have sales.

Transportation includes the purchase and finance charges of vehicles, repair and fuel expenses, and insurance. The value of new cars drops by as much as 40 percent in the first two years of ownership, so the advice is to avoid buying a new car, consider a relatively new model coming off a one-to-three-year lease, and use the Internet to comparison shop prices of vehicles and insurance. Much of the expense of health care comes from health insurance premiums, so it pays to shop around.

Child-rearing expenses are highest in the urban West, followed by the urban Northeast, the urban South, and the urban Midwest. Housing costs contribute greatly to differences between regions, as do costs of child care and education.

The study of children and money involves more than estimating how much it costs to raise them. Children are not passive consumers. From the first time they spit out strained peas, they are letting their parents know their preferences.

Parents respond by buying what their children like, and later the children themselves collectively spend billions of dollars a year on smartphones, electronics, cosmetics, toys, snacks, candy, gifts, athletic events and equipment, musical recordings and instruments, and other goods and services. They also influence their parents' expenditures on nearly all family-related purchases, including housing, cars, computers, vacations, breakfast cereals, pets, and restaurant meals. Half of all U.S. households have pets and spend an average of over $500 a year on pet care with a dog in the first year costing over $1,000. The cost depends on the type, number, age, and health status of the animals. Pet insurance is available.

As part of the socialization process, children learn much of their spending behavior from their parents. For example, a study of elementary schoolchildren found that mothers who were restrictive and warm in relationships with their children were also more likely to use communication messages that promoted monitoring and control of children's consumption activities.

Although adorable, pets can be more expensive than expected.

Most children are ready to receive an allowance or handle a small amount of money as soon as they understand the concept of time. Readiness to handle money varies greatly from child to child, but usually comes around the age of 7 or 8. Understanding time is important because it enables children to wait for Saturday (a traditional day for handing out allowances). If they can wait for Saturday, then they will understand about waiting for money and parceling it out after they receive it. One method of training children for the responsibilities of adulthood is to encourage them to save part of their allowance, but again children's ability to do this varies with age and maturity. The younger the child, the more likely he or she will spend money quickly rather than save it for bigger items. The average 9-year-old will probably not be interested in saving for college—it is too far away.

Children need to learn that money is a tool—something they can use to get what they want. Along the way to disciplined money management, children will make mistakes, such as buying toys that fall apart or fail to live up to their expectations. Making dissatisfying or disappointing expenditures is part of the learning process. Both the mistakes and the successes of money management experiences in childhood will prepare children for the bigger expenses ahead.

## Saving for College

There are many ways to save for college and options, programs, and tax deductions are changing all the time. Tax-advantaged college savings vehicles include Roth IRAs, 529 plans, and Coverdell Education Savings Accounts. There are also state savings plans for college education and federal financial-aid programs and university offerings such as scholarships. Universities are exploring new ways to pay for tuition back after graduation. Some with too many in-coming freshers are offering students money to delay their first year in order to better balance enrollment surges.

Another alternative is setting up a trust fund or investing dollars in children's names. The income will be taxed to them at a lower rate than it is to parents. The rate changes at age 14. Scholarships are available—from state and private sources—based on need, grades, and other merit-based achievements. While a student is in college, the HOPE Scholarship, Bright Futures, and the Lifetime Credit programs reduce taxes. Each state names its state-based program differently. The HOPE scholarship is available to college students in Georgia. A study of students who had had the scholarship and lost it (because their Grade Point Average dropped below 3.0) found that the students were particularly financially vulnerable and subject to higher levels of debt and maladaptive financial management practices (Goetz et al., 2008). A conclusion was that students who struggle academically may also struggle with financial management.

Students nearing graduation and owing loans should talk to college financial-aid experts, accountants, or financial planners about the best way to pay back the loans. Many students set up a payment program whereby they are loan-free in 10 years.

The subject of student loan debt is debated by presidential candidates and new solutions are being proposed. There is a trickle-down effect on the economy when graduates cannot buy houses or other large purchases because a significant portion of their income is going to paying back student loans.

As a concluding comment, research studies reveal that people often regret that they did not get more education.

A college education is one of the best investments anyone can make.

## College Students, Starting Out

The college years are critical for developing financial skills. The bottom line is to stay out of debt and save and invest as much as you can. One of your most valuable assets is your earning power and going to college will increase that earning power. Anything you can do to increase your salary early in your career is a booster too. While in school or soon after graduation look for internships, certifications, and improving skills and credentials which was explained earlier as reskilling.

Young professionals and college students today are managing far more money, possessions, and credit than their parents did at a similar age. College students have favorable attitudes toward credit cards as useful tools for managing money (Xiao et al., 1995) and use debit cards extensively Starting out may be hampered by credit card debt and student loans. Most graduates expect to be comfortably well-off in time.

## CRITICAL THINKING

Do you expect to be a millionaire? At what age? Since the main determinant will be income/salary, what is the usual yearly salary in the profession you are training for?

A multi-year study at the University of Arizona revealed that as seniors more students declared themselves financially independent or at least less dependent on their parents than during their freshmen year. Regardless of the year in school, their parents provide valuable influence through an ongoing conversation about finances. The study found that there are three main financial styles of college students:

Drifters (30 percent in this category) characterized as the least accepting of parents' styles; exploring, but not committed to a personal style, average in knowledge, worst behaviors.

Followers (39 percent in this category) characterized as most accepting of parents' styles, most unconcerned about developing personal style, had better knowledge and behaviors than drifters.

Adapted from National Endowment for Financial Education Digest, November/December 2011, page 2.

Pathfinders (31 percent in this category) characterized as low in accepting parents' styles, most committed to personal style, and best in knowledge and behaviors (see Figure 13.6)

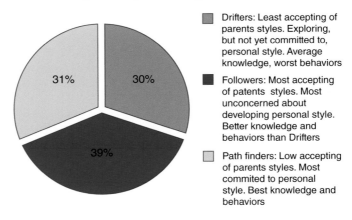

Figure 13.6 Financial management styles of college students.

> ### CRITICAL THINKING
>
> Which of these three styles describes you the best? Explain why.

Being in college brings with it new levels of freedom. Students should beware of falling into a habit of debt that can follow them for years. As mentioned earlier, a bad credit record can hurt when searching for a job. After graduation, build a nest egg or emergency fund and keep it in a totally safe place like a bank or savings account.

Many of the money management principles already covered in this chapter apply to college students, but, to reiterate, here are some tips for setting up a budget and maintaining a good credit record:

- Make a list of predictable monthly expenses and income. Ask yourself, how much money do I really need?

- Set aside money for savings and emergencies.

- Keep track of everything you spend. It helps you stick to your budget. Save receipts.

- Pay all bills on time—from the cell phone to your credit card bill. Immediately open bills on arrival. They usually arrive about 15 days before they are due. Use automatic payment systems and direct deposit whenever possible.

- If you are in financial trouble, address it immediately; call creditors, and contact your parents. If services are turned off or creditors are calling, consider contacting the counseling center at your university. The counseling center can provide access to free or reduced-fee credit assistance.

- Do not gamble or have a gambling app on your smartphone. Studies reveal that having a gambling app and using it frequently is a sign to lenders that you are a poor credit risk. Access to such data is becoming pervasive and with it regulation and privacy issues abound.

Students can increase their financial literacy and economize by

- Taking personal finance courses. Studies show that formal instruction in personal finance increases men's and women's investment knowledge and closes the knowledge gap between genders on this subject (Goldsmith & Goldsmith, 2006).

- Living on less (e.g., sharing an apartment or house, eating out less).

- Working more hours. While in college, according to the Bureau of Labor Statistics, most students work.

- Joining co-op programs or getting paid internships.

- Applying for financial aid and loans. A popular option is the federally sponsored lending program known as Stafford loans.

- Living at home while going to school or after graduation, and during the summers between semesters, thereby reducing living expenses.

- Attending cost-effective community colleges and state universities and regardless of college or university type, applying for scholarships, fellowships, and work–study opportunities.

Given the high cost of college education, many parents and students might question whether it is worth it. From a financial perspective, the answer is yes. According to U.S. Department of Commerce data, education does provide an economic return in that most degrees beyond high school will result in substantially higher income in a lifetime for individuals.

## Retirement and Financial Planning

When a person retires, everything changes or nearly everything if the individual stays in the same house or in the same community, even then the cost of living rises and spending patterns change. One of the biggest decisions anyone ever makes is when to retire and once retired, how to manage daily life and finances. The time, psychological, sociological, and financial effects are enormous. One woman said she couldn't stop working because she would miss the office atmosphere so much—someone to talk with on a daily basis. The critical planning years are five to ten years before retirement when a realistic estimation can be made of how much it will cost to live and how much income per month from various sources is likely.

Certain career fields, such as entertainment and professional sports, mean that retirement (securing money) decisions have to be made fast. A staggering statistic is that 78 percent of NFL players either go bankrupt or are under financial stress within two years of retirement (Langone, 2019).

Retirement planning advice comes in many forms including online blogs and news columns (see the Case Study on Social Security) and takes on the form of rules of thumb or steps to follow. The rules are usually about how much to save and when to start, how to allocate retirement investments, and how to safely draw down retirement savings.

The accuracy of the steps to follow and the rules of thumb are debatable and the main problem is that one size does not fit all. A lower-income person would need to save much more proportionate to income than a higher-income person if getting by is the goal. In a study of university employees, the researchers found that male respondents with higher levels of education were more aware of retirement rules of thumb than females or men with lower levels of education (Mayer et al., 2011).

### CASE STUDY

#### Social Security

A number of changes have been suggested to secure Social Security's future such as increasing the age for partial or full benefits or changing the cap. "The full benefit age is 66 years and 2 months for those born in 1955. It will rise gradually to 67 for those born in 1960 or later. But could the full retirement age rise to 70 to help a broken system? A change in 1956 allowed women to collect benefits as early as age 62. In 1961, amendments made men eligible also at age 62. But if you collect early, you get a reduced benefit. If you start your retirement benefits at 62, your monthly check is reduced by about 30 percent. One favorite fix proposed for the Social Security shortfall is raising the income threshold on which the tax applies. For 2019, that is $132,9000. So earnings above that amount are not subject to the Social Security tax, which is 6.2 percent for employees. Employers kick in a matching 6.2 percent.

*Source: Michelle Singletary (2019, May 13). In search of a simple fix for social security. The Washington Post.*

Until recently, North Americans were retiring progressively earlier. There is a movement called **FIRE** (which stands for financial independence and retiring early) that relies on heavy savings during the working years. In general, the trend toward early retirement has flattened out. Some say it's poised to reverse, leaving many working later in life. A Wells Fargo survey found that one-quarter of middle-class Americans say they will work until at least age 80 to live comfortably in retirement. From a human behavioral standpoint, there is a lot of anxiety about when to retire and estimating what the outcomes might be.

With the massive baby boom generation (born 1946–1964) entering or already in retirement, the question of how long they'll stay at their jobs is looming larger or will they work part-time as part of the **gig economy**? Gig economy refers to extra paid work or employment, temporary or seasonal, interim or consulting. Anyone at any age can be part of the gig economy but it is especially appealing for older adults hoping to make extra money. They have the flexibility to work at different hours.

## CRITICAL THINKING

### Professional Athletes

Consider this special planning need. Professional athletes have a much shorter time span than average workers to save for retirement.

*The staggering statistic that 78% of NFL players either go bankrupt or are under financial stress within two years of retirement...Staying financially healthy as you get older comes from following the same core principles, whether you're running for a first down or climbing the management ranks at a corporate job.*

Source: Alix Langone (2019, May). What Prof Athletes Can Teach Us About Retirement. *Money*, p. 60.

According to Catherine Collinson of the Transamerica Center

*Planning not to retire is simply not a viable retirement strategy. Planning to work past age 65 is an important opportunity to continue earning income, save more and help alleviate a retirement savings shortfall, however, it's important that workers be proactive in setting a retirement savings goal, saving and investing for retirement, and having a backup plan if they are forced to retire sooner than expected.*

*(Mont, 2011)*

More and more retirees are choosing to work part-time rather than bow out of the labor force altogether. In a survey, 71 percent of those approaching retirement said they planned to work in some fashion later in life, preferring the idea of alternating between work and leisure (Ruffenach, 2008). The main reason to continue working is to afford big health care bills, which is a concern for many. Because they want to earn more money, some seniors fall victim to financial scams (read about Barbara in the Case Study).

## CASE STUDY

### Barbara Stops Billing Error

Here is a potential problem. With over 50 million Americans aged 62 and older, they are prime targets for financial exploitation by persons they know and trust and by strangers. Financial exploitation has been called "the crime of the 21st century."

Sometimes the exploitation is on purpose, sometimes it is by error. Barbara, age 92, got a bill suddenly for $3,000 for her usual medical treatments which were low-cost and paid for by her insurance. She called the office on Monday and was told not to pay the bill and they would investigate and turned out it was a billing error. If she didn't have the presence of mind to do this, she would have written a check and sent it. Her family was involved in supporting her following up on the unexpected bill. "A key factor in some cases of elder financial exploitation is a mild cognitive impairment which can diminish an older adult's ability to make sound financial decisions." In her case, Barbara could handle it. Suggested steps to lessen billing errors and scams:

1. Awareness and prevention

2. Planning ahead for financial well-being and possibility of diminished financial capacity

3. Reporting and early intervention that results in loss prevention.

4. Talking over finances with reliable adult children or siblings or trusted financial professionals such as CPAs (Certified Public Accountants) and elder care attorneys.

*Source: "Money Smart for Older Adults. Participant/Resource Guide" (June 2013), co-sponsored by the Consumer Financial Protection Bureau and FDIC (Federal Deposit Insurance Corporation). Barbara's story is a real-life example with the name changed for anonymity.*

A factor affecting when to retire is the availability and affordability of health care and health insurance. In the United States, a government-sponsored health insurance program known as **Medicare** starts at age 65. Only one-third of the surveyed baby boomers could correctly identify that Medicare eligibility starts at age 65 (Ruffenach, 2008). So, a planning issue is gathering all the information necessary to make informed decisions. For example, in rare situations Medicare can start earlier.

Another decision is whether to buy **long-term–care insurance**, policies that provide benefits for a range of services not covered by regular health insurance or Medicare. Typical coverage includes extended stays in long-term care facilities and the costs of assisted living in one's own home. The younger the person, the more affordable the rates are. Most people look into long-term–care insurance in their 50s or 60s. As premiums for long-term–care insurance are high, not everyone can afford them.

People in their 60s realize that retirement can last 20 to 40 years, so investment growth is still important. Retirement assets should earn above the inflation rate. It is also the time to create an estate plan and make sure wills are current. Another thing to think about is how much income will be needed in retirement. Options should be explored with financial professionals. The kinds of mistakes that potential retirees make include

- Guessing, not knowing how much money they have

- Thinking they will work forever

- Taking a loan against their 401(k) or 403(b) retirement plans

- Not getting full benefits, in particular, not providing for health insurance

- Not knowing tax advantages and strategies

- Underestimating how much money they will need

The potential solutions include

- Talking with friends, family, and financial professionals about plans

- Formulating a plan and investing time and energy in it

- Learning more about finances

- Considering retirement benefits besides salary

- Joining employer retirement plans; it is rarely too late

- Getting vested where you work (meaning putting in enough years to qualify for employer-sponsored retirement plans)

- Creating a backup plan of where to work and live

- Saving as much as possible and investing securely

Financially strapped retirees may turn to their children for help. Often what happens is that their children are getting older too but can't retire because they are helping out mom or dad.

Rae Mauro, a 66-year-old research analyst from Valencia, Calif., opted not to retire because she needed the salary to pay for a nursing attendant for her 87-year-old mother, who suffers from Alzheimer's. Ms. Mauro says she gets little help from her siblings. (Higgins, 2003, p. D1)

If children are called on to help aging parents, there are a number of strategies to consider, including

- Buying something from parents (i.e., jewelry, real estate) or helping them to sell something such as a piece of property or a car. Make sure they are using their points, paybacks, or gift cards from their credit card accounts.

- Taking a tax deduction. If a person is paying more than half of a parent's support, he or she can claim the parent as a dependent on tax returns (see a tax consultant or accountant about this because rules change depending on parent's income).

- Keeping separate accounts. Have parents sign a power of attorney form that gives the child power to handle their finances if they become ill or incapacitated.

- Taking advantage of reverse mortgages, which allow homeowners aged 62 or older to receive a loan against their home, which is repaid with interest when the borrower sells the house, moves, or dies. This results in a smaller inheritance for children, which some retirees will resist.

In all these strategies sensitivity should be used because control is very much an issue when it comes to financial management and this is a lifelong concept. It is difficult for parents to give up financial control or to trust that their children know what is best; and, as the previous example of Rae Mauro shows, siblings may not agree on what is best. In the following example, it should be noted that the homeowner still has to pay property taxes and homeowner's insurance so reverse mortgages may not be the best solution for elders who have too much money wrapped up in their house. All costs and benefits have to be considered.

> *Convincing parents also takes patience. Stephen George Rozich of Laguna Niquel, Calif., says it took years to persuade his mother to do a reverse mortgage on her $80,000 Colorado home The one Mr. Rozich arranged for his mother paid her about $300 a month in extra cash and gave her a credit line of roughly $14,000.*
>
> (Higgins, 2003, p. D2)

Financial planning for retirement can begin at any age, but many individuals wait until they are in their 40s to become serious about it. A study of current financial planning research in Australia, Canada, the United Kingdom, and the United States showed that most of it was on estate distribution analysis, pension alternatives, and tax optimization (Fagan & Brayman, 2011). Although people tend to think of retirement planning as being for themselves and their spouse, it can also involve providing for the financial needs of dependent aging parents. Individuals who provide or anticipate providing financial assistance to their parent or parents while also providing financial support to children are known as the **sandwich generation**.

As mentioned earlier, types of investments include employer-sponsored retirement plans and Individual Retirement Accounts (IRAs). Before investing elsewhere, individuals should consider putting available funds into tax-sheltered plans to the maximum allowed. In so doing, income tax will be reduced and wealth grows tax-free. For example,

- Most employers offer 401(k) or 403(b) plans. If $200 a month is put into a tax-sheltered account at 9 percent interest, the return is $73,327 in 15 years.

- If an employer does not offer such a plan, alternatives are to open an Individual Retirement Account, or SEP or Keogh if self-employed. If $2,000 a year at 9 percent is invested in these types of accounts, the end result is $102,320 in 20 years.

Money can be automatically deducted from every paycheck toward a retirement plan, or monthly payments can be arranged from a bank account. As the examples show, the growth of a retirement fund depends on the amount invested, how often, and for how long. It also depends on how the fund is invested. More and more, individuals are having to make decisions about how their particular retirement fund is invested.

To determine retirement needs, individuals themselves or human resource personnel at places of employment or financial planners can run financial information through software programs. The information needed includes a person's age, salary, employer-sponsored retirement plans or IRAs, SEPs or Keoghs, other investments, number of years employed, the percentage of salary being saved, projected retirement age, and the future income the person would like to have. Based on the analysis of this information, a person may choose to save more, change investments, or work longer or participate in the gig economy.

There are many variables, including the ups and downs in the economy and one's health, that will affect final retirement income; and calculations are at best estimates. The farther the person is away from actual retirement, the less accurate are the estimates. Individuals and their families should be open to agility, a shift in ability, goals, and needs. Altering lifestyles as the need comes up.

Once someone has reached age 65, there is a 49 percent chance of reaching age 86 for men and age 89 for women. On average, at age 65 a man can expect to live to be 82 and a woman, 85. People tend to underestimate how long they will live. Part of retirement planning is estimating Social Security income (note the details given in Case Study on Social Security and in Figure 13.7).

Personal retirement savings may run out, but Social Security continues (hence, the name). Since the **Social Security Act** became law in the United States in 1935, Social Security has been one of the main sources of expected income for those reaching their retirement. Other sources of income include employer-sponsored retirement plans, savings and investments, and money from part-time jobs and various types of IRAs. As might be expected, the higher the income of the retiree, the lower his or her reliance on Social Security. Although Social Security was designed to be a supplement to the retired person's savings and pensions, for many it is the sole or main source of income.

| Year of Birth | Full Retirement Age |
|---|---|
| 1937 or earlier | 65 |
| 1938 | 65 and 2 months |
| 1939 | 65 and 4 months |
| 1940 | 65 and 6 months |
| 1941 | 65 and 8 months |
| 1942 | 65 and 10 months |
| 1943–1954 | 66 |
| 1955 | 66 and 2 months |
| 1956 | 66 and 4 months |
| 1957 | 66 and 6 months |
| 1958 | 66 and 8 months |
| 1959 | 66 and 10 months |
| 1960 and later | 67 |

Figure 13.7 Retirement ages for full social security.

Figure 13.7 shows what age a person has to be to receive full Social Security. The earliest age to receive a partial benefit is 62. Once a person begins receiving early benefits, the reduction is permanent in terms of the person's own benefit as well as those of their spouse and children. This is especially important if a person's spouse is considerably younger and will depend on the benefits of the person who is retiring.

What do most people do? *Almost 70 percent of retirees take Social Security before age 65* (Clements, 2003, April 23, p. D1). Women have a greater life expectancy, yet they are more likely than men to opt for early retirement.

> *"I think they're making a mistake," says Henry Hebeler, author of "J. K. Lasser's Your Winning Retirement Plan" and founder of a Web site devoted to retirement issues (analyzenow.com). "When you talk to people who are in their 80s, they'd give anything to have a bigger Social Security check."*
> *(Clements, 2003, April 23, p. D1)*

To find out how your Social Security is adding up go to ssa.gov, visit the Social Security Office locally, or call (800) 772-1213. The website provides a calculator to estimate potential benefits, given different retirement ages.

As has been mentioned, people become eligible for a reduced level of Social Security retirement benefits at age 62. In certain cases, Social Security benefits can begin earlier for disabled employees and survivors. So, an important decision people in their 60s must make is whether to retire early at 62 or keep working to obtain full benefits. Affecting this decision is Medicare, the United States' basic health insurance program for people 65 or older. Medicare has two main parts: hospital insurance and medical insurance, which helps pay for doctor visits and home health visits. In the United States, the Social Security and Medicare programs are closely linked, but each has its own rules. People who retire at 62 will have to get health insurance on their own; this is commonly referred to as Medigap insurance—filling the gap until age 65 when Medicare starts. In some cases, a former employer will extend health insurance until age 65 or offer it at a reduced rate to encourage employees to retire early. The Medicare drug benefit started in 2006 and offers extra help to people on limited incomes.

> **Suggested Activity**
>
> *See Figure 13.6 and look up at what age you can retire for a full Social Security benefit. In the total class or in groups discuss the fairness of the sliding scale. Also discuss the pros and cons of retiring with partial benefits at age 62.*

## Financial Planning and Counseling

Retirement planning is only one aspect of the broader category called financial planning and there is also financial counseling. Starting financial planning early in life will give you a head start. It should not be done in isolation as mentioned previously involve others in the process including trained financial advisors. Diversify investments which spreads the risk across various categories.

A survey of Consumer Finances datasets showed that a greater proportion of households are using financial planners (Hanna, 2011). **Financial counseling** is distinct from planning, it entails changing financial behaviors and outcomes such as getting out of debt, dealing with significant lifestyle changes and creditors, or habits like gambling and compulsive spending (Durband et al., 2019). It usually involves a series of steps to getting financial matters back on track. Financial counseling is available through workplace programs, credit unions, organizations like the National Foundation for Credit Counseling, banks, military bases, universities, and financial counselors in private practices.

This chapter has provided basic information on the economy and financial management. Although the terms do not change rapidly, the figures and policies are subject to change owing to inflation and such other things as tax codes and federal college loan programs. Individuals and families have to stay alert and find the latest information. An avalanche of material is available to help investors track the status of their funds. Financial advice for a price is also readily available through magazines, newspapers, and in-person services. According to a study by the Roper organization, when U.S. residents want financial advice, they are most likely to turn to friends and relatives, then to their bank officer, lawyer and accountant, financial planner, real estate broker, and stockbroker.

A successful retirement requires careful financial planning.

During the last 30 years, there has been a shift away from the face-to-face consumer–adviser interaction toward more technology-based information exchange. A study by Jinkook Lee (2002) found that phone, mail, and computer technology were all used. Depending on the demographic and on the product and service, there were different consumer preferences. For example, face-to-face interaction was preferred when obtaining mortgages but it was far less important when obtaining credit cards. Generally speaking, younger, more educated and affluent consumers are more open to using technology to gain answers and less insistent on face-to-face interactions.

Before investing in the services of a financial planner or other finance professional, a potential customer should check credentials and see whether any complaints are on file with the Better Business Bureau or the state Office of Consumer Affairs. Under the National Securities Markets Improvement Act of 1996, the Securities and Exchange Commission regulates financial advisers managing more than $25 million in assets.

With corporate scandals and other exposés of financial mismanagement in the housing and banking industries, closer scrutiny of mortgage lenders, and investment managers and advisers is in place. However, given the wide range of services offered, it is difficult for any government agency to keep on top of fraud and quasi-legal doings.

A **financial planner** (also known as a financial advisor) looks at an individual's or a family's total financial picture and helps that person or family develop a plan to achieve goals. Over 300,000 people in the United States call themselves financial planners or advisors, so it is important to choose wisely. To do this ask friends, coworkers, and family members for recommendations and find out the advisor's or planner's credentials. Table 13.3 lists a few questions you might ask a financial planner. One of the best feelings is finding someone who immediately gets who you are and where you want to go. The best-known credential is Certified Financial Planner (CFP). A person with a CFP has passed rigorous examinations and been approved by the International Board of Standards and Practices for Certified Financial Planners. Financial planners may be fee-only (so much per hour to set up a budget, develop financial plans, or give advice), commission-only, or based on a combination of fee and commission. The choice depends on consumers' needs and circumstances, such as whether they want a long-term relationship or a one-time consultation.

Table 13.3  Questions to Ask Before Engaging a Financial Planner or Advisor[a]

1. What experience do you have?
2. What are your qualifications?
3. What services do you offer?
4. What is your approach to financial planning?
5. Will I be working with you or with a team? Who are the others?
6. How will I pay for services?
7. How much do you usually charge?
8. Have you ever been publicly disciplined for unlawful or unethical action in your professional career?
9. Can you put everything agreed upon in writing? (This would be a written agreement that outlines the services and fees.)

[a]This list of questions was adapted from a presentation made by Bruce Ogier, CFP, on October 23, 2008, in the Family Financial Analysis class at Florida State University. It should be noted that some stockbrokers use the term advisor or account executive and their main function (buying and selling stocks and bonds, for example) may not offer the full range of services associated with the term financial planner. The job of the client is to hire the right planner or advisor for the services desired and many individuals have several advisors to meet different needs.

Successful financial planning requires a conscious effort. Joseph Coughlin, founder and director of the Massachusetts Institute of Technology AgeLab, was interviewed about working with financial planners toward retirement:

> *A financial plan is only a means to an end, Coughlin says, and that end is a retirement filled with vitality and independence. A good plan will provide you with the ability to execute on your retirement plans, not just save for them.*
>
> *(Myers, 2008, p. S5)*

## Further Family Economic Issues

This last section of the chapter explores various economic issues impacting on the family, ending with wealth and poverty.

### The Gender Gap, Earnings Gap, and the Glass Ceiling

The **gender gap** is the difference in earnings between men and women employed full-time outside the home. In the 1970s women earned approximately 60 percent of what men earned. By 2022, the gender gap had narrowed considerably. Less of a gender gap exists between men and women at younger ages than there is for older generations. There is debate as to why the gender gap still exists and how to encourage more women to be leaders in politics and in the workplace, to rise to the top to better salaries and visibility. One reason may be that women, on average, work fewer years than men. This affects their lifelong earnings and retirement savings. Women, on average, work 32 years compared to 44 years for men before retiring. Women's caregiving responsibilities are the primary reason why they work fewer years and sometimes it is their preference. At retirement, women's median income is only 58 percent of that of men's (Ruffenach, 2008). Since these numbers keep changing sources to consult for the latest information are the U.S. Census Bureau, the U.S. Bureau of Labor Statistics, and similar government entities in other countries.

As women move up the corporate or government ladder, they often hit an invisible barrier that stops them from moving further. They can see the positions at the top that they want, but they cannot reach them. This phenomenon is known as the **glass ceiling**. In the engineering and construction industries, they call this the concrete ceiling. Studies are being conducted to determine why gender barriers exist and where they tend to be found. Generally, it is assumed that women want to move ahead and that corporations and other employers, for a variety of reasons, have imposed barriers impeding their advance. A highly engaged leader encourages collaboration and the sharing of ideas with all employees and says, "Let's Go."

The glass ceiling may be caused by more than the barriers imposed by employers. One study found that the barriers might be at least partially imposed by the women themselves in that they have lower salary expectations even before they enter the job market.

Researchers have found that parents, especially fathers, have a strong positive impact on their daughters' career expectations (Hoffman et al., 1992). Other studies indicate that schools may not provide as many opportunities for success for girls as they do for boys. Thus, supportive families and schools are important to the goal setting and potential career success of women students. Because the gender gap is closing and the glass ceiling appears to be shattering (i.e., more women are moving up and commanding higher salaries and better titles), women's employment issues are rapidly changing. More studies will clarify the values, attitudes, and behaviors involved with these issues.

## Wealth and Poverty

**Wealth** is the state of being rich and having a high net worth. The way to wealth is to be debt-free by practicing frugality and owning assets such as businesses, houses, cars, and investments outright. Examples of frugality include going without extras, living in a less expensive house than one can afford, and driving a less expensive car. In short, the way to becoming wealthy is to live as if you are not wealthy, according to Thomas Standley and William Danko (1998), authors of *The Millionaire Next Door*. Their research on millionaires revealed a more modest lifestyle than one would expect. They found that wealth takes sacrifice, discipline, and hard work. Many of the wealthy are in what may be considered unglamorous enterprises such as wall-board manufacturing and they drive modest family-style vehicles. They are usually married with children and own stocks, bonds, and real estate, and have other financial assets. The authors' main point is that to be wealthy means *living within one's means*, choosing an occupation well, being satisfied, building net worth, and keeping aware of changes worldwide. Read the following case study about NFL's Andrew Hawkins and cars.

### CASE STUDY

#### Andrew Hawkins

> By the time he'd reached his second year in the NFL, Andrew Hawkins was surrounded by Lamborghinis, Ferraris, and Bentleys. Now was the moment, he decided to buy himself a new car. Nothing too flashy, though. Maybe a Mercedes or an Audi. Whatever it was would be an upgrade from the used 2005 Chevy Impala he'd bought in college. During a practice break at a Cincinnati Bengals training facility in 2012, he was scrolling through car models on his phone when Mike Brown, the billionaire owner of the Bengals, pulled into the parking lot. He was driving a Chevy Impala nearly identical to Hawkins's, but Brown's didn't even have the CD player. "It was a wake-up call for me," Hawkins, who retired from the NFL in 2017, tells MONEY…"I thought, This is the richest guy in the entire city – he's a billionaire. If he's got my car, I'm good."
>
> Source: Langone, A. (2019, May). What pro athletes can teach us about retirement. Money.com, 60.

Most people, of course, are not wealthy, and they are not living debt-free. As Chapter 8 explained, *poverty* is the state of being poor and lacking adequate means to provide for basic material needs and comforts. In the United States, about 20 percent of American children live in families with annual incomes below the federal poverty line. Poor children are at risk for physical, cognitive, and socioeconomic problems.

The United Nations Department of Public Information keeps statistics on the world's poor. Africa is the continent with the largest number of people living in extreme poverty, followed by Asia. According to the World Bank 767 million people still live on less than $1.90 a day, and the majority are women and children residing in rural areas. Children under five suffer the most from malnutrition due to their young developing bodies being less resilient to the effects of living without clean water, regular food, and health care. Changes in wealth affect eating patterns. For example, wealthier consumers in China and India are eating more meat. According to the U.S. Department of Agriculture, American consumers eat 222.2 pounds worth of red meat and poultry per year, and the consumption is far less in India and in China, but this is changing upward.

Although the U.S. economy is generally better off than most countries, poverty is still widespread, especially in manufacturing and rural areas where the economic engine has slowed down. Poverty is a serious problem because poverty in childhood can have lifelong repercussions:

> Poverty is the roadblock to educational progress of many disadvantaged youth. Poor teenagers are four times more likely than nonpoor teens to have below average basic academic skills. More than half of the 15 to 18-year-olds from families with incomes below poverty had reading and math skills that placed them in the bottom 20 percent of all teens.
>
> (Leidenfrost, 1993, p. 5)

*Poverty can be either a temporary or a chronic state of living.* If people are unemployed for a few months, they will experience a temporary decline in income, but if they have saved for a rainy day, their lifestyle will not be severely affected immediately. Likewise, college students may live at or below the poverty level, but this is a temporary state that will be remedied when they get their first full-time job. The mindset of a person who is experiencing temporary poverty is different from that of a person or family immersed in permanent poverty.

Because the study of management focuses on control and planning, educators and family facilitators need to be sensitized to the fact that not everyone has equal access to resources or the equal ability to use them. According to Rettig, Rossman, and Hogan (1992),

> People who are poor must devote their financial resources to meet basic needs. They have minimal freedom to allocate money, time, or human energy for other than immediate uses and have little to give toward planning for future needs. Families and individuals with lower levels of living have less freedom to decide, little control over resource access, fewer opportunities for human resource development, and their use of material resources is significantly diminished. Families can be "poor," not only in material resources, but also in human resources of imagination, initiative, self-discipline, and the ability to seek alternatives. (p. 35)

*Most people in the United States, 50–70 percent, are in the middle class and derive their income largely from earnings—* that is, wages or salaries from occupations. Wealthier people generally derive a considerable proportion of their income from investments; the higher the income, the higher the portion from investments tends to be. So wealth is not the same as income. A person who earns a great deal of money but spends it all each year is not wealthy; he or she is just living high, according to Standley and Danko.

From a management standpoint, the goals of a middle-class family may be to educate the children and have a secure lifestyle rather than to accumulate vast wealth. The very wealthy, who have an abundance of money, property, and investments, spend a great deal of time trying to retain their fortunes so that they can pass on their money to their descendants. With the exception of highly successful athletes, business tycoons, entrepreneurs, and actors, most of the very wealthy have acquired their fortunes over a long period of time or through inheritance.

## SUMMARY

Handling finances is a lifelong pursuit requiring management skills. A comprehensive picture of consumers is provided by the Consumer Expenditure Survey (CE) from the Bureau of Labor Statistics. CE is a collection of information on the buying habits of U.S. consumers. The data from this provides an overall picture of income levels and how people are allocating money.

Individuals and families make decisions within the overall movement of the economy. The ever-evolving economy is driven in part by the digital revolution which is changing how people make, spend, invest, protect, and use money and get information. Since adjusting to economic realities is an ongoing process with motivation and confidence being key factors, most individuals are responding by getting reskilled, paying off debt, saving more, readjusting their financial plans, and spending and investing more carefully. They are consulting with tax advisors, financial counselors, and financial planners more than in the past.

More college graduates are changing the way they plan to manage money (for e.g., renting more than owning, at least at first) once they graduate, some are returning home to live with their parents. The financial management styles of college students in one study were categorized as drifters, followers, or pathfinders.

A consumer's lifestyle refers to the ways he or she chooses to spend time, money, and energy including deciding where to live and how to make a living. Self-control and knowledge are keys to successful financial management, which is a transformation process involving three phases: planning, action, and postplanning. Handling money is one of the most common management skills, but also one of the most difficult. Setting up a budget and determining net worth are two ways to get an idea of a person's financial status.

The goal of financial management is to maximize net worth and life satisfaction and to attain and maintain a comfortable lifestyle. A lifestyle refers to how individuals choose to spend time and money and how their values, attitudes, and tastes are reflected in consumption and production.

Values and goals influence the way finances are managed, and a gap exists between values (ideals) and actual behavior. Savings and investments are important aspects of financial management. Saving for children's college education is an example of a long-range goal of many families. Not everyone has the luxury of planning for the future, however; low-income families must devote their financial resources to meeting basic daily needs.

Taxes make up the largest expenditure for the typical family in the United States—it spends about one-third of its income on taxes—followed by housing and household expenses, and transportation. The largest average debt is for mortgages, then student loans, and then credit cards.

Many families, especially those with children, struggle to stay ahead. Individuals and families need to understand how expansion, recession, recovery, inflation, and mortgage rates affect them. The last chapter of this book focuses on the future including projected changes in demographics, space exploration, the economy, the environment, and technology, and summarizes the subjects of rational choice, managerial judgment, values, and decision making.

## KEY TERMS

| | | |
|---|---|---|
| annual percentage rate (APR) | diversification | fixed expenses |
| assets | emergency fund | gender gap |
| budget | Equal Credit Opportunity Act | gig economy |
| Consumer Expenditure Survey (CE) | Fair Credit Reporting Act | glass ceiling |
| consumer price index (CPI) | FICO score | gross domestic product (GDP) |
| credit | Financial literacy | gross income |
| credit bureaus | financial management | income |
| credit cards | financial planners (advisors) | income tax |
| discretionary income | financial security | inflation |
| disposable income | FIRE (financial independence retiring early) | insurance |
| | | investment |
| | | level of living |

| | | |
|---|---|---|
| liabilities | psychic income | Social Security Act |
| liquidity | real income | standard of living |
| long-term care insurance | recession | taxes |
| Medicare | reskilling | variable expenses |
| net worth | sandwich generation | wealth |

## REVIEW QUESTIONS

1. Regarding the effects of unemployment or the process of interviewing read the following and react. "Every time I thought I was being rejected from something good. I was actually being redirected to something better" (author Steve Maraboli). Do you agree or disagree? Explain your answer.

2. What is a FICO score? What is its range, and what is a good one? How does a FICO score affect a person's future financial choices?

3. Authors Standley and Danko say that to be wealthy means living within one's means and choosing an occupation well. What do you think of this advice?

4. What are some of your fixed and variable expenses? Do you have a monthly budget or estimation of income and outflow?

5. Why do nearly 70 percent of retirees take Social Security before reaching their full retirement? What are the pros and cons of this decision?

## REFERENCES

Adler, J. (1992, January 13). Down in the dumps. *Newsweek,* pp. 18–22.

Belsie, L. (2011, November). *Time use during recessions.* Cambridge, MA: The NBER Digest.

Beutler, I., Beutler, L., & McCoy, J. K. (2008). Money aspirations about living well: Middle school student perceptions. *Financial Counseling and Planning, 19*(1), 44–60.

Block, S. (2006, June 12). In debt before you start. *USA Today,* p. A1.

Britt, S., Grable, J., Goff, B., & White, M. (2008). The influence of perceived spending behaviors on relationship satisfaction. *Financial Counseling and Planning, 19*(1), 31–43.

Clements, J. (2003, April 23). Why it pays to delay: Too many retirees start collecting social security early. *The Wall Street Journal,* p. D1.

Clements, J. (2003, October 8). Why the rising market is a bummer: Practically everything's overpriced. *The Wall Street Journal,* p. D1.

Davis, K., & Durband, K. (2008). Valuing the implementation of financial literacy education. *Financial Counseling and Planning, 19*(1), 20–30.

Durband, D., Law, R., & Mazzolini, A. (Eds.). (2019). *Financial counseling.* Switzerland: Springer.

Eccles, D. W., Ward, P., & Goldsmith, E. (2010, November). The relationship between household wealth and house- holders' personal financial and investing practices. *Proceedings of the Association of Financial Planning and Counseling Annual Meeting,* Denver, CO.

Eccles, D. W., Ward, P., & Goldsmith, E. (2011, April). How do we make financial education policy work? How research on personal finance practices associated with wealth accumulation can enhance the effectiveness of financial education programs. *Proceedings of the Annual Conference of the American Council on Consumer Interests,* Atlanta, GA.

Fagan, B., & Brayman, S. (2011). Financial planning literature survey. *Journal of Personal Finance, 10*(1), 109– 140.

Franklin, I. (2007). Expanded financial literacy unit helps students make wise choices. *Journal of Family & Consumer Sciences, 99*(1), 17–18.

Goetz, J., Mimura, Y., Desai, M., & Cude, B. (2008). HOPE or no-HOPE: Merit based college scholarship status and financial behaviors among college students. *Financial Counseling and Planning, 19*(1), 12–19.

Goldsmith, E. (2015). *Social influence and sustainable consumption.* Switzerland: Springer.

Goldsmith, E. (2016). *Consumer economics: issues and behaviors, 3rd edition.* Oxford: Routledge.

Goldsmith, R., & Goldsmith, E. (2006). The effects of investment education on gender differences in financial knowledge. *Journal of Personal Finance, 5*(2), 55–69.

Hanna, S. (2011). The demand for financial planning services. *Journal of Personal Finance, 10*(1), 36–62.

Higgins, M. (2003, April 23). How to shield your wallet from your parents' woes. *The Wall Street Journal*, pp. D1– D2.

Hoffman, J., Goldsmith, E., & Hofacker, C. (1992). The influence of parents on female business students' salary and work hour expectations. *Journal of Employment Counseling, 29*(1), 79–83.

Langone, A. (May 2019). What pro athletes can teach us about retirement. *Money.com*, 58–63.

Lawrence, F., Lyons, A., & Gorham, E. (2008). Family economics research priorities set. *Financial Counseling and Planning, 19*(1), 61–62.

Lee, J. (2002). A key to marketing financial services: The right mix of products, services, channels and customers. *Journal of Services Marketing, 16*(3), 238–256.

Leidenfrost, N. (1993, Fall). Poverty in the United States: Characteristics and theories. *Journal of Home Economics, 85*(3), 3–10.

Lino, M. (2017). *The cost of raising a child.* USDA Report.

Mayer, R., Zick, C., & Glaittli, K. (2011). Public awareness of retirement planning rules of thumb. *Journal of Personal Finance, 10*(1), 12–35.

Mincer, J. (2007, July 9). Teach the children. *The Wall Street Journal*, p. R7.

Mont, J. (June 8, 2011). 5 retirement mistakes that will haunt you. *Focus on Lifelong Investing Online*, Yahoo.

Myers, R. (2008, October 4–5). Five tips for working with your financial planner. *The Wall Street Journal*, P. S5.

Pilon, M. (2008, September 11). The new card: Prepaid debit. *The Wall Street Journal*, pp. D1–D2.

Rettig, K., Rossman, M., & Hogan, J. (1992). Educating for family resource management. In M. Arcus, J. Schvaneveldt, & J. Moss (Eds.), *Handbook of Family Life Education* (Vol. 2). Beverly Hills, CA: Sage.

Ruffenach, G. (2008, September 1–14). Measuring your retirement IQ. *The Wall Street Journal*, p. R8.

Silverman, R. (2003, July 16). Why you waste so much money. *The Wall Street Journal*, p. D1.

Standley, T., & Danko, W. (1998). *The millionaire next door.* New York: Pocket books.

Thums, S., Newman, B., & Xiao, J. (2008). Credit card debt reduction and developmental stages of the lifespan. *Journal of Personal Finance, 6*(2&3), 86–107.

Xiao, J., Noring, F., & Anderson, J. (1995). College students' attitudes towards credit cards. *Journal of Consumer Studies and Home Economics, 19*, 155–174.

# 14

# Managing Tomorrow

## DID YOU KNOW THAT...?

… SmartFarms have self-driving tractors and drones to fly over forests and crops.
… 38 million Americans live alone.

This final chapter prepares you and your family to face the challenges that lie ahead, as well as to put these in the context of living your life fully and with as few regrets as possible. Novelist F. Scott Fitzgerald wrote,

DOI: 10.4324/9781003166740-14

"Suddenly she realized that what she was regretting was not the lost past but the lost futures, not what had not been but what would never be." In many ways, this is a deep-thinking chapter about how you envision the future and your place in it. Inventor Henry Ford said, "Thinking is the hardest work there is, which is the probable reason so few engage in it." On the practical side, we'll cover the latest leadership and management practices necessary for maintaining a competitive edge and building a better functioning planet.

This chapter builds on the previous ones and offers a window into the future. Noted Harvard professor E. O. Wilson said, "It is exquisitely human to search for wholeness and richness of experience." What future richness is in store for all of us? Probably greater mobility and more use of technology to ease our lives and communication. But, we can also expect a more crowded planet. The worldwide population is expected to rise to 9 billion by 2050.

Here are some projections for newborns. In 2018, more than 3.78 million babies were born in the United States and 16 million in China. The U.S. birthrate hit a 32-year low in 2018—this represented a 2 percent drop from the year before and a falling below replacing current population levels. The findings come as younger people push off marriage and start families later in life as reported in *USA Today*, March 16, 2019. Thirty-eight million Americans live alone.

## Technology and Innovation

Before proceeding further, it should be cautioned that speculating about the future and possible explanations are not without risks especially when it comes to health and social issues like marriage, divorce, and childbirth. In his 1899 novel *When the Sleeper Wakes,* H. G. Wells predicted color television and supersonic aircraft, but he made the less-than-successful prediction that hypnotism would replace conventional anesthetics in medicine. Likewise, Jules Verne, in *Twenty Thousand Leagues under the Sea,* published in 1870, was visionary regarding the development of submarines, but missed on his prediction that automated baby-feeding machines would take care of the rising world population. The human touch is irreplaceable.

### As we proceed through the 21st century we will experience

- Increasing urbanization.

- Increasing globalization and higher education levels.

- The continued rising and falling of national economies.

- Increasing strain on natural resources and the creation of new solutions such as self-driving cars and tractors.

The greatest leaps in energy and consumption demands will come from India and China where populations are expected to grow by 25 percent in the next few decades. Consider this:

> While housing bubbles around the world have burst, China's market has been seen as different because its surge in home building has been driven less by financial leverage than by real demand from a rapidly urbanizing population. Anywhere from 15 million to 20 million people move to Chinese cities each year.
>
> (Batson, 2008, p. A6)

Currently, more than 80 percent of the world's people live in developing countries living on less than $10 a day and nearly half are children or teenagers. Population growth has slowed in the richest countries which are aging. More rapid growth is happening in low to middle-income per capita countries, and these economies will supply needed workers and demand for products and services.

Poverty is a relative term: what is considered poverty in Australia, Western Europe, Japan, South Korea, the United States, and Canada would not be considered poverty in a developing country. As we proceed, the concept of proper living standards will be redefined. People's expectations of what constitutes "the good life" will undergo a vast change in the 21st century. How do you compare city and national economies where $15 an hour is the minimum wage in San Francisco, California, compared to $2 a day in Haiti—both in North America. Certainly cost of living varies greatly in these two locations but does it merit that difference in wages? **Income inequality** exists within nations and between nations.

The challenge will be in meeting everyone's needs while preserving the environment and being mindful of policies that affect future generations within and across borders. The concern over climate change was addressed at the Kyoto Summit held in Japan in 1997. An outcome was the Kyoto Protocol, which was ratified in 2008 by many countries around the world. Nearly everyone agrees that something has to be done about global warming, but the concern countries have is about how much it will cost to implement the suggested steps to reduce greenhouse gas emissions. As countries prosper and share resources, the need for international cooperation expands.

Where people once burned wood and oil for heating and cooking, they now turn to electricity to run their refrigerators and heat pumps. Bicycles are being replaced by motor scooters and cars, which bring with them not only more mobility and employment opportunities but also more pollution and congestion. Therefore, more fuel-efficient and less-polluting cars and mass transportation are needed.

As economies develop, homes increase in size and technology. The United States has 4 percent of the world's population but uses about 25 percent of the world's energy.

Soaring business activity and increased urbanization strain energy systems and water supplies. Less-developed countries are urbanizing at a faster rate as compared to wealthier areas; so, although the whole world is becoming more urban, the transformation is not experienced evenly across the world. More thought is being given to increasing conservation, expanding and diversifying energy and water supplies, and improving home and workplace energy efficiency.

Besides environmental issues, what else can we expect to come? For one thing, people are demanding more **transparency**, which means openness in revealing information about the operations of companies, organizations, institutions, and governments. As economies develop, people live longer, work longer, become more literate, and demand better working conditions including **onboarding** experiences integrating new employees into organizations and cultures (see the Case Study)

### CASE STUDY

### New School/New Job

Emma, age 21, anticipating her first full time job related to the following.

*Most of us remember our first day at a new school. Stomach in knots, we meandered down an unfamiliar hallway with a schedule in hand, trying not to trip on a book bag or walk into a locker. Years later, we transferred these emotions to the work world, where we showed up for a job transition not knowing what to expect or what to do. It is well known in management circles that a high-quality onboarding experience is an important factor in employee effectiveness and morale. In fact, Society for Human Resources Management research indicates that employees who participate in a structured onboarding program are 58% more likely to stay with their organizations after three years.*

Source: Peter A. Gudmundsson (2019, May 30 10:41 a.m.).
How to adjust to a new job. U.S. News Money.

Improved health and technology will lead to a better life for us all.

Source: Phototake NYC.

Expect more emphasis in higher education on providing experiences that develop students' knowledge of leadership and ability to demonstrate leadership skills in their campus, career, and worldwide communities. Also expect growth in literacy worldwide with the sharpest leaps in the world literacy rate of women. Reading documents is still problematic even in developed countries, including in the United States where about one-third of the population has below-basic or basic document literacy, which can cause problems personally and in the workplace. There is still a long way to go when it comes to literacy—financial or otherwise. According to the United Nations, globally about 800 million adults are illiterate, meaning they cannot read.

Regarding everyday life, we will continue to see adjustments and advances in food, apparel, and housing (Sullivan et al., 2011). For example, global alcohol consumption keeps falling. New jobs must be created and new institutions will emerge. *The family will endure* as it always has, but its form will continue to alter.

## CRITICAL THINKING

How do you think families will change? Describe different family forms that you know.

Families will engage in more management activities than ever before because the increasingly complex world in which they live will offer them so many choices such as an explosion of choices in health care, education, and other services. Other predictions include

- More personalized electronics
- More use of social online networks

- New forms of financial transactions
- More smart sensors in homes, in schools and other buildings, on bridges, streets, and in harbors.
- More forms of artificial intelligence (intelligence demonstrated by machines).

## Visionary Leadership and Managerial Judgment

Values, decision-making, goals, and resources work together to form the basis of a holistic construct called managerial judgment. **Managerial judgment**, defined as the ability to make decisions and accept change for the betterment of self and humankind, is this chapter's theme. Individuals, families, communities, and countries are encouraged to think about what may happen in future so they can better prepare themselves and make smarter choices. *The ultimate goal of the manager today is the creation of a better tomorrow.* As explained throughout this book, management takes a proactive approach, meaning that through reasoning, determination, and decision-making, worthwhile changes can be implemented.

### CASE STUDY

#### Mike's Determination on the Field and Off

*Mike McEnany knew from a very early age that he could overcome pretty much any obstacle through sheer determination. He was a standout lineman for his high school football team, but at 180 pounds he was considered far too small for a major college program. Undaunted, McEnany drove from his home in Florida to Mississippi State University seeking, against formidable odds, to make the team on the basis of a walk-on tryout. He graduated as one of the team's leading tacklers. It was the same kind of passion that drove McEnany to build his own roofing company, based in Tampa, while still in his mid-twenties. Today he heads one of Florida's largest contractors, with more than 100 employees.*

*Source: Slack, C. (2011). Real needs: Real solutions. Merrill Lunch Advisor, p. 17.*

As the case study shows, one's basic personality translates from one domain to another. Management needs more **leaders** (experts, authorities, facilitators, and guides) who participate in communities, as contributors to scientific, social, or economic advances, and by so doing employ others and improve human lives. "Leadership is not about personality; it's about practice" (Kouzes & Posner, 2002, p. 13). It involves making a difference for the public good in an active, purposeful, diverse, team-oriented, broad-based, and ethical way. Leaders in the newest sense operate in a connective way. They bring resources together and get information flowing, rather than operate in a hierarchical fashion (top-down management). They don't take "no" for an answer, *Gen Z (in their teen years and early twenties when this book went to press) are very concerned about the society around them and they are a powerful generation when it comes to issues like immigration, climate change, and gender equality* (Howland, 2019).

**There is no doubt that visionary leaders will emerge from Gen Z and the Millennials before them. Visionary leaders look to the future by:**

1. Supporting global trade and the exchange of ideas,

2. Facilitating the dissemination of new technologies and sound management and environmental practices, and

3. Contributing to safety in the workplace and in schools, to the development of useful products and services, and to advances in health care, transportation, and education.

Building leadership potential is a goal of family resource management. Leaders recognize problems and seek to solve them. Visionary leaders also understand that they themselves and those they lead may have different decision-making styles. In Chapter 2 we discussed that satisficing refers to picking the first good alternative that presents itself so that a **satisficer** tends to make a decision and sticks with it. An alternative to this is a **maximizer**, a person who wants to be certain they have made the right choice and therefore is less likely to fully commit to a decision and in so doing may be less happy in their everyday lives (Sparks et al., 2011). Maximizers spend a lot of time searching for information and confirmation and may fret or obsess about choices. There are low-level maximizers and high-level maximizers who may cause themselves a lot of worry and grief. Finding the right choice or making the right decision can be a never-ending process and for those leaders facing deadlines, the maximizers in the group can cause a lot of frustration. Research is underway to understand better how satisficers and maximizers operate in groups including within families.

> **CRITICAL THINKING**
>
> Are you primarily a satisficer or a maximizer? Can you give an example of both types of decision-making style in your own life or that of a friend?

The chapter now turns to the specifics of household innovations and then moves to a discussion of the challenges involved in managing information and innovation overload. It concludes with an examination of possible changes in family life and the global community, with an emphasis on demographic shifts and environmentalism.

## Household Innovations

Certainly, life was poorer and harder before the arrival of many of the technological advances of the late 19th and 20th century. One innovator was 27-year-old Alexander Graham Bell who set out to invent a "talking telegraph" in 1875. His telephone is light-years away from the smart phones of today but he set the pace. An invention underway is "smart" slippers for seniors with the idea that the slippers could read and report a medical problem or accident. It was found that slippers are more likely to be worn around the house than jewelry such as medical alert bracelets or necklaces, but more importantly than the slippers per se is this notion of several monitors or options instead of just one. A rethinking of the function of households is taking place. Households include everything that exists or takes place within a house or apartment.

To go back in time again, consider the state of the American home before 1940. Most of the U.S. population still lived on farms, less than one-third of the homes had electric lights, and only one-tenth had a flush toilet. A sample of home economics alumnae from 1939 to 1959 who lived in home management houses on college campuses revealed what it was like to live in a congregate situation during those years. The alumnae concluded that communication, cooperation, and tolerance were necessary for group living and management (Tifft et al., 2011).

CASE STUDY

## CASE STUDY

### Then and Now

Today's students in family resource management come from a wide variety of backgrounds and most likely take lecture and discussion courses either online or in person. It is enlightening to read how their predecessors experienced living in home management houses from 1939 to 1959:

> Two residents moved into the house from family farms. They felt the residence course was likely more fun for these girls than it was for students who had already experienced living on campus. Another, reared on a farm, reported she was not used to buying so much food. Her self-sufficient family raised their vegetables and butchered their own chickens and cattle. One of the residents who came from a family farm felt others had more social experiences than she did because of being isolated on the farm. Living in the house did not interfere with relationships outside the house. Boyfriends were welcome, visiting often. One interviewee remembers that her future husband was a good potato peeler. "It seems to me, Bud spent lots of time on a stool on the back porch, peeling potatoes"… [During World War II] Social interactions increased when soldiers and sailors arrived for training courses in radio and engineering and moved into residence halls adjacent to the home management houses. While planning a pheasant hunt, several soldiers made a deal with house residents that if they were successful, the women would cook the dinner. Both hunting and dining were successful.

> Source: Tifft, K., Fletcher, J., & Junk, V. W. (2011).
> Home management house: Reflections of alumnae.
> Journal of Family and Consumer Sciences, 103(2), 18.

Current households rely so much more on food bought and prepared outside the home that it is difficult to picture the home and campus life depicted in the case study. Today's homes function at such a higher level. As has been stated many times in this book, the number of households is growing but the number of inhabitants per household is decreasing. There are more singles living alone or single–parent families, which is affecting the needs of the households and, in turn, the demand for household innovations. But, interestingly enough there is a return back to the farm, back to farmer's markets, and buying produce grown locally. It could be said that in reality, things haven't changed all that much except that they have accelerated and involve advanced technologies.

Given that people's housing needs change and that products try to keep pace, what can be predicted for future homes? Undeniably there will be more connectivity. Today, toddlers have computer toys. Whereas some current college students remember when their families got their first laptops or a time when all adults in the household had their own laptops, others will not remember a time when computers were not part of their home life. A study indicated that attitudinal beliefs are extremely important in determining the use of a home computer (Brown et al., 2006). The researchers found that if computer use is considered so natural as to be a habit, then the decision to have them at home would be consciously made. Today, more college students are taking online classes and whole degree programs online.

Regarding smartphones and home products with microprocessors, there will be more handheld devices for various functions beyond the remote devices already commonplace. Because handheld devices are easily mislaid and clutter up homes, the trend will be to consolidate devices and functions into multipurpose devices or central controllers such as smartphones. The push is on to make them more multi-functional, smaller, and affordable. A question families face is at what age to give their children smartphones and what type and degree of access. Parents may limit the use to conversations between family members and known friends.

Inside homes, lighting and temperature controls will be particularly sophisticated. Houses can be divided into temperature zones that can be individually programmed to deliver heating and cooling during the times of day when the zones are used. Homeowners can set the temperatures for the zones using touch-screen computers or handheld voice controls that are linked to a central computer and to sensors in each zone. Temperatures will be held within a smaller range than with the old-fashioned thermostats, which conventionally allowed temperatures to vary within a six-degree range. You have probably experienced sensor-lighting in public bathrooms or classrooms that go on when you enter and off when you leave. We will see more of this technology in homes. The most effective home automation systems will support both centralized and distributed control and communication standards

## CRITICAL THINKING

Would you be interested in having more remote-controlled appliances and electronics? Why or why not? Is it more likely someone would forego the homemade casserole to warm up a store-bought frozen meal or pizza in the microwave oven?

Appliances, cars, televisions, telephones, and computers will continue to get smarter. The electronics industry is challenged to keep products simple enough to operate and to figure out how to provide for repairs, replacements, and recycling.

These developments in home automation are linked to consumers, who have to decide which innovations to adopt and which to turn down. Consumers will also have to shop around for the best prices and decide how to install a system. They may have to adapt their schedules to incorporate the technology, especially in the initial phases.

This section has focused on home automation, but automation is already all around us in stores, workplaces, and financial institutions. Computers and the Internet revolutionized the kind of work that could be done from home, and this trend will continue. Wireless connections have made it easier not to be tied to a desk. The trend toward shopping, working, and conducting business from the home raises several questions. One of them is how to remember all the passwords and codes. In the future, there will be one code for everything, making it far easier than it is presently.

Researchers continue to study how working from home affects family relations and time management; they are concerned that as people stay at home more, they will feel isolated.

As an earlier chapter indicated, human contact is desirable. People seek out others and want face-to-face contact and experience the sights and sounds of life. Meetings and major sporting events sell out even though they can be watched for free on computers through life-streaming, television, or smartphones.

In the home, other developments will include the more efficient use of energy. For example, better insulation materials will create a thermal shell so tightly closed that buildings can be heated or cooled with a smaller-capacity pump. Insulated ducts and improved insulation for windows will reduce air leakage by as much as 50 percent. The supply of electricity will also be more efficient owing to advances in *superconductivity*—the conduction of electricity with almost no power loss. Electricity will also be conserved by the use of compact fluorescent lights (CFLs) and E- lamps that will last far longer than present models.

All in all, tomorrow's homes will be more energy-efficient, adaptable, affordable, and supportive of individuals' and families' lifestyles. The race is on between companies to be the top suppliers of the new home systems and products.

## Adopting Innovations and Applying Technology

General definitions and lists of concepts are helpful as we delve further. **Technology** is defined as the application of the scientific method and materials to achieve objectives; another definition is knowledge systematically applied to useful purposes. In the book titled *The Future* by former Vice President Al Gore (2013) and in the *Innovation Explosion*, several terms and definitions are included (Quinn et al., 1997): Gore lists six crucial choices (on pp. xiv–xv, abbreviated here) that confront us:

1. The emergence of a deeply interconnected global economy

2. The emergence of a planet-wise electronic communications grid

3. The emergence of a completely new balance of political, economic, and military power in the world that is radically different.

4. The emergence of rapid unsustainable growth.

5. The emergence of a revolutionary new set of powerful biological, biochemical, genetic, and materials science technologies.

6. The emergence of a radically new relationship between the aggregate power of human civilization and the Earth's ecological systems.

Here are useful definitions (from Quinn, Baruch, & Zien) that have stood the test of time,

Have you used or seen one of these?

- **Invention or discovery** involves the initial observation of a new phenomenon (discovery) or provides the initial verification that a problem can be solved (invention).

- **Innovation** consists of the social and managerial processes through which solutions are first translated into social use in a given culture. "Technological innovation involves a novel combination of art, science, or craft employed to create the goods or services used by society" (p. 3).

- **Diffusion** spreads approved innovations more broadly within an enterprise or society" (p. 3).

- **System understanding**, basically "know-how," involves understanding the interrelationship and rates of influences among key variables. "Some people may possess advanced skills but lack system understanding. They can perform selected tasks well but do not fully understand how their actions affect other elements of the organization or how to improve the total entity's effectiveness" (p. 2).

- **Intellect** means knowing or understanding, the capacity to create knowledge, the capability for rational or highly developed use of intelligence. "It includes (1) cognitive knowledge (or know what), (2) advanced skills, (3) system understanding, (4) motivated creativity, discovery or invention, and (5) intuition and synthesis" (perception and the ability to put information together), and the capacity to understand or predict relationships (p. 3).

Individuals considering a new technology or product will first become aware that it is available; then they will search for information, evaluate the information, and perhaps try out the product (e.g., test-driving a new car) to decide whether they like it or not. Once consumers decide to adopt a new product, they move into the application phase, when they actually use the product. Even when consumers adopt a new technology, however, they do not necessarily use it to the fullest extent possible. For example, even though modern kitchens are more technologically advanced than ever before and meal preparation is easier, more meals are eaten out today than in the past. It is easier to eat out or pick something up than to make something and clean up afterward.

Decision-making in the marketplace.

Not everyone can be an innovator even if they want to because the latest thing may not be available or affordable. According to William Gibson, a science fiction writer, "The future is already here—it's just unevenly distributed." For example, broadband Internet access first took off in South Korea, then in Canada, and then in the United States. Also, computer adoption depends on having high levels of education in the labor force.

> In general, rich countries are on the technology frontier and rely on research and development to achieve further improvements in technical efficiency. Low-income countries, in contrast, have the option of adopting technologies already developed elsewhere. Yet not much is known about the process by which new technologies spread from one country to the others.
>
> *(Watson, 2001, p. 1)*

Government, industry, universities, and individual inventors contribute to the development of technology. Novel approaches to problem solving are necessary. Increasing observational skills is one direction this is taking. A **paradigm shift** refers to a situation where an individual or a team tackles a problem with radically innovative solutions rather than taking a gradual step-by-step approach. As the pace of change accelerates, more paradigm shifts will be needed.

Accompanying these rapid advances in technology is a counterbalancing concern for the quality of the environment. As described in Chapter 12, a growing concept in the global industry is clean technologies, including processes and products that preserve the environment and do not pollute. Several countries, most notably Japan, the United States, Australia, Canada, and many European countries including Germany and Malta, have given priority to the development of such technologies.

## The 5S Management Concept

As noted near the beginning of the book, family resource management borrows heavily from other disciplines especially from business management with a focus on streamlining tasks also known as work simplification. And, as you know, this book focuses a great deal on organization. To add to the mix of theory and practice already presented such as the Marie Kondo method, KonMari, on organizing, there is a managerial concept called 5S. It is derived from a list of five Japanese words which when loosely translated into English become five words beginning with the letter "S." The 5S concept has emerged in the business management and the manufacturing world as an organizational tool applied to the appearance and function of everything from plant floors to cubicles. Sometimes a sixth element is added being safety.

> The 5S principles can be applied to individual and family life and the home. The five Ss refer to
> **S**ort: *Order items and activities*
> **S**traighten: *Arrange*
> **S**hine: *After the task is done, clean and restore areas*
> **S**tandardize: *Consistent methods save time*
> **S**ustain: *Maintain, reduce waste, evaluate*

The idea is that less clutter enhances productivity and that aesthetics matter. Designated places for things eliminate the need to hunt, thus saving time. As an example, in reconfigured hospitals, doctors and nurses put stethoscopes in a drawer marked "stethoscope" rather than placing them on hooks or leaving them on desktops. In the media world with 24-hour news networks, shared desks have made this concept important too; each person is expected to keep his or her desk neat because someone on the next shift will be using it. Jay Scovie, an employee of a company that makes solar panels and copy machines, was subject to the 5S mandate at his workplace as explained below:

> That means companies like Kyocera Corp., Mr. Scovie's employer, are patrolling to make sure that workers don't, for example, put knickknacks on file cabinets. To impress visitors, the company wants everything to be clean and neat. Meanwhile, doctors in Seattle are relearning where to stick their stethoscopes. And output from the printer at Toro Co., a Bloomington, Minn., lawn mower maker, is sorted daily and tossed weekly. Sweaters can't hang on the backs of chairs, personal items can't be stowed underneath desks and the only decorations allowed on cabinets are official company plaques or certificates.
>
> (Jargon, 2008, pp. A1, A15)

The 5S philosophy spills over into the home by providing a way to organize and utilize spaces so that everything has its place. It also implies a need for more storage such as closets and drawers and organizing systems with the intent to improve efficiency by eliminating waste and improving flow. Since homes are shared spaces, the 5S method makes sense as a way to upgrade efficiency and provide a more pleasing sleek appearance. In reformatting a home, some of the organizing questions are

- What should be kept?

- Where should it be kept? Tools and materials should be kept at the point of use.

- How often is it used? Is it daily, weekly, seasonal, or annual use?

- Is it in good working condition or does it need to be replaced?

Answering these questions is the beginning of a decision-making process about the use and appearance of homes. In many homes, the least used objects are on the highest shelves of kitchen cabinets or stuck in the back of cabinets or on the top shelves of closets or in garages, basements, or attics. As the world becomes more crowded, updating and the efficient use of space will become more and more critical.

With 5S the emphasis is on how we live and work *now* versus how we used to live and work. A lot of clutter in homes is from our past lives (some reassuring and deserving a place) rather than from our current lives and needs. Families are dynamic and changing. The following quote is another example of the crossover between workplace and home-based methods of organizing:

*John Boze, coordinator of the hospital's spine clinic and a professed clutterbug, said it took a while to get the hang of organizing the piles of paperwork on his desk and sorting them into bins. His workspace has improved, he says, but he can't seem to make those skills portable. "My girlfriend says I need to 5S my desk at home. She says it looks like I'm building a nest."*

*(Jargon, 2008, p. A 15)*

## CRITICAL THINKING

Do you have a space in your home that looks like you are building a nest? What do you think of the 5S concept? Do you notice a trend toward more streamlined homes or toward more clutter? What makes it easier to keep homes organized? Can some individuality be lost in the 5S concept, whether at home or at the workplace?

## Information and Innovation Overload

"Humanity is the species forced by its basic nature to make moral choices and seek fulfillment in a changing world by any means it devises" (Wilson, 2002, p. xxii). As families master new technologies, they must cope with a host of new data, moral dilemmas, and information. As someone becomes more skilled in a task it requires less thought and energy.

*Studies of the brain have shown that the pattern of activity associated with an action changes as skill increases, with fewer brain regions involved. Talent has similar effects. Highly intelligent individuals need less effort to solve the same problems, as indicated by both pupil and brain activity. A general* **'law of least effort'** *applies to cognitive as well as physical exertion. The law asserts that if there are several ways of achieving the same goal, people will eventually gravitate to the least demanding course of action*

*(Kahneman, 2011, p. 35)*

When consumers are bombarded with too much data and information, they may not be able to process all of it or they may employ the law of least effort. They may also, as described in Chapter 7, experience overload.

The information superhighway that is envisioned for the near future may contribute to information overload. Among other things, the information superhighway is expected to include more television channels. How many television channels can an individual care about? Will more variety lead to more creative programming or will the slots be given over to endless rebroadcasts of a handful of movies and TV shows?

Rapid advances in technology are also leading to **innovation overload**. One of the ways to reduce innovation overload is to reduce the amount of risk the individual perceives. As noted earlier in this text, information is one way to reduce a person's perception of risk. The more one knows about a product or service, the less risk is involved. Another way to reduce overload is to accept that the phenomenon exists. Consumers need to decide how much overload they can successfully handle and adopt new products at a pace that feels comfortable to them. Why go to five different coffee shops if the one near your house feels comfortable and familiar?

Innovations should provide clear-cut benefits to consumers. Before adopting an innovation, potential consumers should ask themselves, "Will this product or service make my life better?"

## Family, Home, and Global Change

One might wonder what will happen to individuals and families in the midst of all these changes. What does the future hold for families? The good news is that people are living longer and healthier lives. Chapter 8, on managing human needs gave many statistics along these lines. To review, the greatest concentration of people is in Asia. China is the most populous country, followed by India and the United States.

In the last several years fertility and marriage rates have declined in the United States Singles and nontraditional families are more accepted as the norm. Ethnic minority families have a strong presence in the United States and will probably comprise over 50 percent of the population in 2050.

The recession in the United States brought attention to the conservation of resources including finances especially for ethnic minority families (Behnke et al., 2010). This type of research finding falls under the broader category of **conservation of resources theory**. During tough times, economic or otherwise, people become more resourceful. By conserving what they have and becoming self-enterprising, people feel more in control. They say, "this is something I can do." An example is that more companies were started including 565,000 a month in 2010 in the United States than had started in the previous 15 years according to the Kauffman Foundation, the largest foundation devoted to entrepreneurism (Slomski, 2011). The Kauffman Foundation reports this trend continues with more than a half million people in the United States starting a business every month but with the added comment that most of them need better financing to start, grow, and sustain their company. Rethinking the future, entrepreneurship and innovation exist within economic realities.

Most of the world's population resides in cities (straining natural resources such as clean air and water), and the trend is toward increased urbanization. Perhaps the only concrete thing one can say about the future is that change is inevitable. From an individual's standpoint, a change may be welcome, as in a pay raise, or threatening, as in a job loss. Change upsets the status quo, disturbing those who are wedded to the known and experienced. Here is an example. Theme parks, such as Disneyland in Anaheim, California and Disney World in Orlando, Florida, and others around the world, have to decide what rides and decorations to keep and which ones to retire and replace. Purists who have visited the parks often since their youth dislike any change or alteration, whereas newcomers do not have these preconceived notions of how the theme park should look and function. The parks have to balance the needs of returning customers with the needs of newcomers. So does the world.

Similarly, families have to decide which holiday traditions to uphold and which ones to change. Martha, an 80-year-old great grandmother, said as the holiday season approached, "You know, with the economy as tight as it is, I think this year I might not send checks to all the relatives, especially those I don't see, who never write or call." After the holiday season, her daughter donated her old artificial tree to Goodwill with the notion that she would get a real tree or do something else in the coming year.

Changing holiday traditions is one symbol of families moving on, another is actually physically moving. Moving can be a source of stimulation, adventure or stress, or all of these combined. Fourteen percent of the U.S. population moves each year according to Census data. The pluses and minuses are described by a corporate spouse, who says, after living in four states,

> I admit that I haven't always given Amy's considerations as much thought as they deserve, nor did we talk about her concerns as much as we should have. For me, selfishly, a job transfer is the start of a new adventure, something exciting and fresh after so many years seeing the same old sights and driving the same old roads.
>
> (Opdyke, 2004, p. D1)

Pride in shared accomplishment.

In the United States, newer homes have more bathrooms and bedrooms and fewer decks, fireplaces, and basements according to the National Home Builders (NHB) "The Home of the Future" report. They also say that gas is the predominant heating fuel, followed by electricity and oil. Vinyl used to be the main exterior wall material but that is being replaced by fiber cement. Preference of wall materials and interiors vary considerably by area of the country and around the world. Ceiling heights in new homes have gone from eight feet to nine feet and storage spaces and closets are being reconfigured. Other preferences are emerging, including more demand for planned communities with sidewalks, jogging trails, and more shared outdoor space.

The NHB report differentiates between demands in average homes versus those in upscale homes. The demand among both the groups is high in the category of "green," meaning more desire for energy-efficient appliances and mechanical equipment and water and energy conservation features. Homeowners are interested in protecting natural capital and in seeking reliable and affordable energy.

## Quality of Life and Well-Being

Updating home design and function is just part of a very large concept called quality of life and well-being. Urbanization, crowding, economic growth, environmentalism, and the accelerated pace of living are transforming where and how we live. Accelerated pace is part of a larger concept called the **acceleration effect**, which means that each unit of saved time is more valuable than the last unit. Thus, time and privacy are becoming more valuable.

> ### CRITICAL THINKING
>
> Do you agree or disagree that time and privacy are becoming more valued? Some would say privacy is less valued given Gen Z and Millennials heavy use of the Internet and social media. Explain your reaction and give an example of time and privacy. An example.

Technology allows families to make better use of their time. For example, instant messaging requires far less time and fewer physical steps than mailing a letter. When one looks nationwide and worldwide, access to technology (telephones, computers, databases, publications) is not distributed evenly; moreover, nor will it be in the near future. The large gap between the haves and the have-nots is related to the **quality of life**, defined as the level of satisfaction with one's relationships and surroundings. Another definition of quality of life is simply one's well-being. One of the goals of management is to provide the ways and means to improve the quality of life for individuals and families.

A commonly used measure of the quality of life is a country's gross domestic product (GDP), a measure of a nation's total output of goods and services, which was discussed earlier in the book. It was introduced in the 1930s and quickly became the standard-bearer of statistical indicators. The United Nations ranks countries by GDP. Realizing that economic data provide only one measure of the quality of life, the United Nations and other organizations assembled another indicator, the human development index (HDI), which measures overall progress, in 174 countries, based on the following dimensions: life expectancy (long and healthy life), adult literacy rate and education level, and GDP per capita (and a decent standard of living) The economists who met to formulate the HDI sought to evaluate development not only by economic advances but also by improvements in well-being. See Table 14.1 for the top-ranked HDI countries. Norway has been at the top for over a decade.

Table 14.1 Very High Human Development

| HDI Rank | Human Development Index (HDI) value* |
|---|---|
| 1. Norway | 0.957 |
| 2. Switzerland | 0.957 |
| 3. Australia | 0.944 |
| 4. Ireland | 0.938 |
| 5. Germany | 0.936 |
| 6. Iceland | 0.935 |
| 7. Hong Kong | 0.933 |
| 8. Sweden | 0.933 |
| 9. Singapore | 0,932 |
| 10. Netherlands | 0.931 |
| 11. Denmark | 0.929 |
| 12. Canada | 0.926 |
| 13 United States | 0.924 |
| 14. United Kingdom | 0.922 |
| 15. Finland | 0.920 |
| 16. New Zealand | 0.917 |
| 17. Belgium | 0.916 |
| 18. Liechtenstein | 0.916 |
| 19. Japan | 0.909 |
| 20. Austria | 0.908 |

The 2022 Report is similar.

Source: The United Nations,*The 2018 Report was released September. 14, 2018, and calculates HDI values based on 2017 estimates. Note that the HDI numbers are very close.

**Well-being** refers to the health and happiness of the total person, involving body, mind, and spirit, and includes measures of life expectancy, health, and education. There are many dimensions to the concept of well-being. The four conventionally discussed dimensions are economic well-being, physical well-being, social well-being, and emotional well-being:

- *Economic well-being* has to do with the degree of economic adequacy or security individuals and families have.

- *Physical well-being* has to do with the body and its needs. Keeping healthy and safe, eating right, getting enough sleep, and managing stress are all subtopics within this category.

- *"Social well-being* is the social space of the family as a group, whereas psychological well-being is the emotional space of an individual in the family. It is concerned with the social needs of the family played out in daily interactions in interpersonal relationships within the family groups and with the larger community, including the workplace" (McGregor & Goldsmith, 1998, p. 4).

- *Emotional well-being* has to do with the emotions (feelings) of an individual.

Although well-being sounds like a pleasant-enough topic (you may be amused by the Case Study about wellness and travel), problems arise when the different types of well-being come into conflict within the individual and between individuals.

*We all start off with dreams for our life—what we want to be, what we want to do, where we want to do it. But in marriage, the dreams of two partners collide and sometimes they ricochet in random directions.*

*(Opdyke, 2004, p. D1)*

## CASE STUDY

### Wellness and Travel

*When did the word wellness begin popping up everywhere? Was it three years ago? Five? All of a sudden, it was a huge topic of discussion. People didn't want to take trips just to go somewhere new anymore, they wanted to holistically rejuvenate their bodies and spirits, whether during a camping trip deep in nature, a forest-bathing session, or a head-to-toe detox at a renowned destination spa. For some, lying by the pool with a margarita felt too much like a guilty pleasure. Still, I find wellness to be a slightly nebulous word. What I think we're really talking about when we talk about wellness is reflection and self-improvement. For me, travel helps facilitate the conversation I'm always having with myself about how to be a better person and live a richer life, plain and simple.*

*Source: Jacqueline Gifford, Editor (2019, June),*
*Letter from the editor. Travel & Leisure, p. 16.*

Recently, three other dimensions of well-being have emerged as topics in the literature and in everyday life. They are

- *Environmental well-being.* This has to do with the level of environmental quality.

- *Political well-being.* This has to do with a person's internal sense of power, autonomy, and freedom, not necessarily involvement in politics.

- *Spiritual well-being.* Broadly and individually defined, spiritual well-being may include hope, faith, peace, joy in living, enlightenment, connectedness, and purpose. A poll summarized that

> *Findings suggest that a majority of Americans consistently reported that the American Dream (for themselves and their family) is more about spiritual happiness than material goods. However, the size of this majority is decreasing. Most Americans believe that working hard is the most important element for getting ahead in the United States*
>
> (Hanson & Zogby, 2011, p. 570).

A fundamental question to be addressed is which dimensions are most critical to a specific person's sense of well- being? For example, a person may value economic well-being over social well-being. He or she may take the raise and promotion and move the family far away from other family members and friends. Regarding economic well-being, it is evident that some people are content with very little of a material nature, whereas others need all the trappings of success.

## Multiculturalism

A more expansive worldview has helped to foster a movement or philosophy called **multiculturalism**, which means the expression by cultural and ethnic groups of their heritage. It refers to a society that allows for and, in fact, encourages a combination of several distinct cultures. Some countries have formal multiculturalism policies and government offices designated to advocate for the preservation of cultures usually within the larger society. Examples of countries with official multiculturalism policies are Canada and Australia.

Multiculturalism is about attitudes and attempts to retain the uniqueness of different groups rather than letting them be subsumed into the greater society. It is a move away from the homogenization of the world, an attempt to hang on to the past and to take the best parts of it into the future. A related concept is empowerment, encouraging individuals to express themselves, their ethnicity, and culture.

Some advocates of multiculturalism see it purely as tolerance. Others want to go beyond the theoretical and apply multiculturalism to government programs, schools, universities, churches, other institutions. The basic idea is that each ethnic group's culture should be acknowledged and preserved.

In the United States in languages, Spanish is second to English so that if one answers a survey online or on the phone often one is asked if they want to respond in English or Spanish. This would vary by region in the United States reflecting the composition of the local population.

Because Canada has two official languages (French and English), it is one of the world leaders in multicultural research and government policy. As more nations embrace a model of multiculturalism, programs involving sociocultural integration and cultural retention will become more important. The main goals of such programs are to bolster cultural identity and self-esteem while promoting intergroup respect. Rather than being divisive, multiculturalism and ethnic diversity can be a source of national strength and identity. Ethnicity is a part of a society's cultural environment. Recognition of the differences as well as the commonalities among groups of people is part of the more complex view of the world that we have today.

## Sustainability, Environment, and Consumption

This chapter has already introduced the concept of environment within the context of technological advances. The crowding of our planet and its misuse has led to many environmental problems, but it has also led to new paths in sustainability education and cooperation (Dewhurst & Pendergast, 2011).

"The central problem of the 21st century is how to raise the poor to a decent standard of living worldwide while preserving as much of the rest of life as possible" (Wilson, 2002). Government, the private sector (including individuals and families), and science and technology have to come together to find solutions. What is particularly interesting about environmental problems is that they are not confined to national borders. Birds, bats, and insects fly over invisible national boundaries all the time, so nations have to cooperate when it comes to fostering biological diversity.

Also, one has to take into account the different philosophical approaches to life regarding what matters. For example, many people have the idea that more is better. As a result of this outlook, store shelves in some countries are crowded with essentially duplicate products, confusing consumers and making it difficult to shop in the store. At the same time, in other parts of the world, people are starving. To even talk about consumption in terms of countries is becoming outmoded because in food markets around the world, consumers can find bok choy from Shanghai, tuna from Portugal, pasta from Italy, bananas from Costa Rica, and vanilla beans from Madagascar.

*Lifestyle* was defined earlier in the book as a sense of a style or a pattern of living that reflects the attitudes, values, and resources of individuals and families. To add to this concept is the term **lifestylist** which refers to someone who helps create a particular lifestyle, such as someone who designs the interior of a home or an advertisement that would appeal to a young family or a 40-year-old bachelor, or a retired couple with a dog. Products, art, and accessories can contribute to this vision of a lifestyle.

The desire to accumulate material things is giving way to a redefined quality of life in which better does not necessarily mean more. Smaller, well-designed energy-efficient homes with recycling features are in vogue in many communities and nations. Social influence theory indicates that what others think and say has a tremendous effect on whether one chooses to be "green" or not (Goldsmith, 2015; Goldsmith & Goldsmith, 2011).

The state of family finance and time will continue to be contributing factors in consumption decisions. *"Consumers these days are on a mission. They want to quickly locate a product, evaluate it, pay and get out"* (Yin, 2004, p. 13). The change from wanting to own all to owning only what is needed is an example of a paradigm shift.

Technology has been blamed for many environmental ills, but it also holds the key to solutions. Technology can be used to achieve long-term ecological balance. "Education for sustainability requires an understanding

Family — what fundamentally matters.

of the interconnections and interdependence of humans and the environment. Opportunities to teach in this way must be revisited… " (Dewhurst & Pendergast, 2011, p. 575). Many more examples of human impact on the environment could be cited but now the chapter turns the focus to the subject of technology's ability to increase the world's food supply.

## Health Care and the Food Supply

Going forward, we need better food supplies, cleaner water, and better health care. Infant and maternal health care concerns persist as well as concerns about elder care. A few trends or innovations to watch for include

- Home health monitors (the Japanese already have toilets that take readings of urine content and send the readings indicating illness directly to the family's doctor).

- Further understanding of weight control and aging.

- Increased food supply, fewer acres needed to produce more abundant crops.

- Continued improvement in technology and an increased understanding of the human genetic code.

- Accelerated medical advances.

In the 18th century, Thomas Malthus predicted that the world's population would outgrow the food supply. Malthus, however, did not anticipate the advances in agriculture that have enabled the world population to reach its current level. SmartFarms have drones that fly over forests and crops to communicate with robots embedded in harvesting equipment on the ground. There will be sensors on livestock and in field crops and forest lands linked to the cloud where big data is transformed into useful information about watering, feeding, and management decisions.

Scientific research may someday ensure an expanded food supply by allowing foods to be grown in space stations and on other planets. In the 21st century, people may live on a self-sustaining moon base or on Mars. Consequently, when discussing future management problems and possibilities for individuals and families, one should keep in mind that soon there will be life not only on earth but also, possibly, in outer space. it is anticipated that by 2030 we'll put humans on the Moon or Mars, maybe even sooner. Indoor plumbing, airplanes, electric lights, and computers have shown that anything is possible. Ideas and inventions become everyday realities.

## SUMMARY

This chapter examined conservation of resources theory and trends and research on well-being, technology, families, households, consumption, income inequality, leadership, lifestyles, and the environment. Each area of study presents its own challenges and opportunities for managerial judgment. Change starts with the individual clarifying values and goals, making decisions, and culminating in using resources to reach solutions.

Decision makers include those who are primarily satisficers (tending to make quick decisions) or maximizers (those who want to be certain and have trouble committing to courses of action). Sometimes people follow the "law of least effort" meaning taking the least demanding path and others are stretching their imaginations to find the most comprehensive and sustainable life courses. Time and effort are costs that have to be figured into the balance of benefits and costs of decisions. Regardless of decision-making style, planning and self-responsibility are the hallmarks of forward-looking management.

Information and innovation overload and the acceleration of life present challenges that management can help with. This chapter introduced the 5S management concept which was derived from business management and manufacturing and applied to individual, family, and home life where organization is needed. The five Ss stands for sort, straighten, shine, standardize, and sustain.

Like any academic discipline, resource management has a history, a present, and a future. This chapter on the future concludes this book, which started with an overview of management, including its theoretical bases and history, progressed through chapters on specific concepts, and then applied those concepts to households and managing human resources, time, stress and fatigue, the environment, and finances. Given this coverage, it is fitting to end this chapter and the book with a look back and a look forward.

The past century was extraordinarily rich in innovation and scientific progress. There has never been a century like it, and the present century will be even greater. In the future, anything is possible. Human innovation has no limits. This book has introduced various problems related to individuals, families, and their micro-environments. Through planning, using technology wisely, and managing resources and outcomes much can be done to resolve issues and dilemmas. A key concept is that the ultimate goal of the manager today is a better tomorrow.

## KEY TERMS

acceleration effects
conservation of resources
    theory
diffusion
income inequality
innovation overload
intellect
invention

law of least effort
leaders
lifestylist
managerial judgment
maximizers
multiculturalism
onboarding
paradigm shift

quality of life
satisficers
superconductivity
system understanding
technology
transparency
well-being

## REVIEW QUESTIONS

1. What issues are GenZers tackling? Why are they an important generation influencing things to come?

2. What does the science fiction writer William Gibson mean when he says, "the future is already here—it's just unevenly distributed"? Explain your answer and give an example.

3. How can individuals and families cope with information and innovation overloads?

4. What does conservation of resources theory mean?

5. What is an example of determination in this chapter? Why is determination an important personality trait in times of constrained resources?

## REFERENCES

Batson, A. (2008, October 24). China aids home buyers to curb impact of slump. *The Wall Street Journal*, p. A6.

Behnke, A., MacDermid, S., Anderson, J., & Weiss, H. (2010). Ethnic variations in the connection between work- induced separation and turnover intent. *Journal of Family Issues, 31*(5), 626–655.

Brown, S., Venkatesh, V., & Bala, H. (2006). Household technology use: Integrating household life cycle and the model of adoption of technology in households. *The Information Society, 22,* 205–218.

Dewhurst, Y., & Pendergast, D. (2011). Teacher perceptions of the contribution of home economics to sustainable development education: A cross-cultural view. *International Journal of Consumer Studies, 35*, 569–577.

Goldsmith, E. (2015). *Social influence and sustainable consumption.* Switzerland: Springer.

Goldsmith, E., & Goldsmith, R. (2011). Social influence and sustainability in households. *International Journal of Consumer Studies, 35*, 117–121.

Gore, A. (2013). *The future.* New York: Random House.

Hanson, S., & Zogby, J. (2011). The polls-trends: Attitudes about the American dream. *Public Opinion Quarterly, 74*(3), 570–584.

Howland, D. (April 9, 2019). Gen Z favors Vans, Lululemon and Amazon. *Retail Dive,* 2/3.

Jargon, J. (2008, October 27). Neatness counts at Kyocera and at others in the 5S club. *The Wall Street Journal*, pp. A1, A15.

Kahneman, D. (2011). *Thinking, fast and slow.* New York: Farrar, Straus and Giroux.

Kondo, M. (2011). *The life-changing magic of tidying up.* New York: Ten Speed Press.

Kouzes, J., & Posner, B. (2002). *The leadership challenge* (3rd ed.). San Francisco: Jossey-Bass.

McGregor, S., & Goldsmith, E. (1998). Expanding our understanding of quality of life, standard of living, and well-being. *Journal of Family and Consumer Sciences, 90*(2), 2–6, 22.

Opdyke, J. (2004, January 7). The cost of a mobile marriage. *The Wall Street Journal*, p. D1.

Quinn, J. B., Baruch, J., & Zien, K. (1997). *Innovation explosion.* New York: Simon & Schuster.

Slomski, A. (2011, Winter). Investing in themselves. *Merrill Lynch Advisor*, 14–17.

Sparks, E., Ehrlinger, J., & Eibach, R. (2011). Failing to commit: Maximizers avoid commitment in a way that con- tributes to reduced satisfaction. *Personality and Individual Differences, 52*, 72–77.

Sullivan, P., Collier, B., & Goldsmith, E. (2011). Merchandising's evolving role in family and consumer sciences. *Journal of Family and Consumer Sciences, 103*(2), 59–64.

Tifft, K., Fletcher, J., & Junk, V. (2011). Home management house: Reflections of alumnae. *Journal of Family and Consumer Sciences, 103*(2), 17–22.

Watson, N. (2001, July). How technology spreads. *The NBER Digest*. Retrieved March 21, 2004, from http://www.nber.org/digest/jul01/w8130.html

Wilson, E. O. (2002). *The future of life.* New York: Vintage.

Yin, S. (2004, January). Chronic shoppers. *American Demographics*, p. 13.

# Glossary

## A

**Absolute values**   Extreme, definitive values that are inflexible.

**Abstract symbols**   Ideas rather than objects, unseen.

**Acceleration effect**   Quickening of life's pace so that each unit of time saved is more valuable than the last unit.

**Accommodation**   An agreement reached by accepting the point of view of another person.

**Actively acquired information**   Information the individual actively looks for, such as fashion coverage in magazines, or news on television or the Internet.

**Actuating**   Putting plans into effect, action, or motion.

**Adaptability (adaptive)**   The ability to cope with change, to make the necessary adjustments.

**Adjusting**   Checking a plan or an activity and making appropriate changes.

**Advocate or expert channels**   Experts in a field or people with a cause who are likely to contact receivers through letters, speeches, television, or the Internet. They have a message.

**Affective domain**   Value meanings derived from feelings.

**Africa rising**   Term used to describe Africa's growing middle class, rapidly spreading technologies, and rising incomes.

**Annual Percentage Rate (APR)**   Rate of interest paid over the life of credit or a loan.

**Anticipation**   Expectations and anxieties surrounding decisions.

**Artifacts**   Type, placement, or rearrangement of objects around a person.

**Assessment**   The gathering of information about results.

**Assets**   What a person owns, for example a house, car, or investments.

**Attitudes**   Concepts that may express values, serve as a means of evaluation, or demonstrate feelings in regard to some idea, person, object, event, situation, or relationship.

**Autonomic**   Family decision-making style in which an equal number of decisions are made by each spouse.

## B

**Behavior**   What people actually do, how they act.

**Best practices**   Methods and techniques to ensure quality.

**Biodegradability**   The capability of a material to decompose over time as a result of biological activity. More specifically, it can be a substance's ability to be broken down into microorganisms.

**Biological diversity or Biodiversity**    The variety and variability among living organisms and the ecological complexities in which they occur.

**Blended families**    Families that include children from previous relationships or marriages, also called stepfamilies, or reconstituted or combined families.

**Boomeranging**    Adult children returning to live in their parents' homes.

**Boundaries**    Limits or borders between systems.

**Boundary ambiguity**    Uncertainty about where the lines are, how daily life or work life should be arranged, and who should be invited to family and holiday events or meetings.

**Boundary management**    The establishment and maintenance of boundaries.

**Bounded rationality**    Individuals seek the maximum utility (satisfaction) from the decisions they make.

**Brainstorming**    Group communication technique in which members suggest many ideas no matter how seemingly ridiculous or strange. Afterward, the group examines each idea-separately to see whether it has merit.

**Brownout**    In brownout, fatigue and irritability appear; eating and sleeping patterns may be disturbed; cynicism and indecision may set in; and all this may lead to burnout.

**Budget**    A spending plan or guide.

**Burnout**    Emotional or physical exhaustion brought on by unrelieved stress.

## C

**Carbon footprint**    The impact of consumption and transportation on carbon emissions such as fuel used to transport goods or used in personal travel.

**Carbon monoxide**    An odorless, colorless gas that can cause death from accidental poisoning.

**Change**    To cause to be different, to alter, or to transform.

**Channel**    The medium or route through which a message travels from sender to receiver.

**Checking**    Determining whether actions are in compliance with standards and sequencing.

**Choice**    The act of selecting among alternatives.

**Chronic fatigue syndrome**    An affliction or disease exhibiting a variety of symptoms, including extreme long-lasting exhaustion.

**Circadian rhythms**    Daily rhythmic activity cycles, based on 24-hour intervals, that humans experience.

**Clarification**    The process of making clear, making easier to understand, or elaborating.

**Climate Change**    Includes global warming and weather pattern changes, water availability.

**Cocooning**    Remaining at home as a place of coziness, control, peace, insulation, and protection.

**Cognition**    The mental process or faculty by which knowledge is acquired.

**Cognitive Behavioral Therapy**    Talk therapy which helps you change patterns of behavior and thinking.

**Cognitive domain**    Value meanings derived from thinking about events, situations, people, and things.

**Cognitive psychology**    Scientific study of the mind (information processing) that explains human intelligence and how people think.

**Comfort zone**    A combination of habit and everyday expectations mixed with an appropriate amount of adventure and novelty, what feels comfortable to the individual.

**Commitment**    The degree to which an individual identifies with and is involved in a particular activity or organization.

**Communication**    The process of transmitting a message from a sender to a receiver.

**Communication multitasking**    Behavior of individuals and media companies when they engage in a variety of communication channels or forms at the same time, can lead to overload.

**Comparative advantage**   A theory that individuals, families, or companies do best when they focus on activities in which they can add the most value and outsource or delegate other activities.

**Compromise**   Process of resolving conflicts in which each person makes concessions, giving in a little to gain a valued settlement or outcome.

**Conflict**   A state of disagreement or disharmony.

**Conflict resolution**   Negotiations to remedy the conflict.

**Consensual decision making**   Process of reaching a mutual agreement equally acceptable to all individuals involved.

**Conservation**   The act or process of preserving and protecting natural environments from loss or depletion.

**Conservation of Resources Theory**   Thinking about and doing things to save and sustain resources.

**Constructive conflict**   A form of conflict or disagreement that focuses on the issue or the problem rather than on the other person's deficits.

**Consume**   To destroy, use, or expend.

**Consumer Expenditure Survey**   A U.S. Bureau of Labor Statistics data collection of consumer patterns.

**Consumer Price Index (CPI)**   A measure of price changes, which are collected by and reported by the Bureau of Labor Statistics. The CPI is the main measure of inflation in the United States.

**Contingency plans**   Backup or secondary plans to be used in case the first plan does not work out.

**Controlling**   Acting to check one's course of action.

**Creative thinking**   A novel approach to decisions, problems, and solutions.

**Creativity goals**   Productive of new things or new original or atypical ideas, striving, innovation.

**Credit**   Time allowed for repayment of money or goods that are borrowed; also refers to the amount of money borrowed.

**Credit bureau**   A reporting agency that collects, stores, and sells financial information.

**Crises**   Events that require changes in normal patterns of behavior.

**Critical listening**   Act of evaluating or challenging what is heard.

**Cultural values**   Generally held conceptualizations of what is right or wrong in a culture or what is preferred.

**Culture**   The sum of all socially transmitted behavior patterns, beliefs, arts, expectations, institutions, and all other products of human work and thought characteristic of a group, community, or population.

# D

**Data analytics**   Measurement of qualitative and quantitative data used to make decisions about possible outcomes.

**Debit cards**   (or cash cards) Provide computerized banking transactions straight from accounts.

**Decibel (dB)**   A measure of the loudness of sound.

**Decidophobia**   The fear of making decisions.

**Deciduous trees**   Trees that lose their leaves in winter.

**Decision making**   Choosing between two or more alternatives.

**Decision-making style**   The characteristic way that a person makes decisions.

**Decision plan**   A long, complicated decision process that includes a sequence of intentions.

**Decision rules**   Principles that guide decision making.

**Decisions**   Conclusions or judgments about some issue or matter.

**Decoding**   The process by which the receiver assigns meaning to the symbols sent by the sender, to convert from code into a plain memory.

**De facto decision making**   Process whereby decisions are made by a lack of dissent rather than by active assent.

**Demands**   Events or goals that require action.

**Demographics**   Data used to describe populations or subgroups.

**Demography**   The study of the characteristics of human populations that is, their size, growth, distribution, density, movement, and other vital statistics.

**Destination**   The receiver or audience in the process of communication.

**Destructive conflicts**   Interpersonal conflicts involving direct verbal attacks on another individual.

**Detergent**   Surfactant or mixture with cleansing properties.

**Diffusion**   Spreading of innovations including new ideas, products, services, and ways of doing things within an enterprise, organization, or society.

**Directional plans**   Progress along a linear path to a long-term goal fulfillment.

**Disability**   A long-term or a chronic condition medically defined as a physiological, anatomical, mental, or emotional impairment resulting from disease or illness, inherited or congenital defect, or traumas or other insults (including environmental) to mind or body.

**Discovery**   The initial observation of a new phenomenon.

**Discretionary income**   Income regulated by one's own discretion or judgment.

**Discretionary time**   The free time an individual can use any way she or he wants.

**Disposable income**   The amount of take-home pay left after all deductions are withheld for benefits, taxes, contributions, and so on.

**Distress**   Harmful stress.

**Diversification**   Having a mix of investments across several categories thus spreading risk and the opportunities for growth.

**Domi (plural domus)**   Latin term for house or home.

**Domino effect**   The passage of stress from one source to another.

**Dovetailing (multitasking)**   Situation occurring when two or more activities take place at the same time.

**Downshifting**   Opting for a simpler life usually less pay, less stress, and more time in a more personally satisfying occupation or lifestyle.

**Drift time**   Enjoyable, unscheduled time.

**Dual-career households**   Households in which spouses or partners have a long-term commitment to a planned series of jobs leading to desired career goals.

**Dual-income or dual-earner households**   Households in which spouses or partners have income-producing jobs.

## E

**Ecoconsciousness**   Thoughts and actions given to protecting and sustaining the environment.

**Ecological footprint**   Impact of the consumption and production of goods and services on the environment. The amount of biologically productive land and sea area required for the support of individuals or specific populations.

**Ecology**   The study of how living things relate to their natural environment.

**Economic security (insecurity) Having**   a stable income or resources to support a level of living.

**Economic well-being**   The degree to which individuals or families have economic or financial adequacy.

**Ecosystem**   The subsystem of human ecology that emphasizes the relationship between organisms and their environment.

**Effort**   Exertion or the use of energy to do something.

**Emergency fund**   Savings equal to three to six months' income.

**Empathetic listening**   Listening for feelings.

**Empathy**   The ability to recognize and identify another's feelings by putting oneself in that person's place.

**Employment Assistance Programs (EAPs)**   Employer-sponsored programs help workers and their families with emotional, work, financial, and legal difficulties.

**Emo-surveillance**   (emo stands for emotional) Refers to our ability to notice and read facial expressions and body language.

**Encoding**   The process of putting thought into symbolic form.

**Energy audit**   Assessment of a home's energy efficiency

**Entrepreneur**   Person who organizes, operates, and successfully manages a new enterprise.

**Entrepreneurship**   Process of creating new ideas, goods, services, procedures, and businesses by bringing together a unique package of resources to exploit, develop, or make use of an opportunity.

**Entropy**   A tendency toward disorder or randomness.

**Environment**   External conditions influencing the life of an organism or population.

**Environmentalism**   Concern for the environment.

**Equal Credit Opportunity Act**   Legislation that prohibits discrimination in any aspect of credit transaction against a person because of race, sex, age, color, marital status, or related factors.

**Equifinality**   The phenomenon in which different circumstances and opportunities may lead to similar outcomes.

**Ethics**   A system of morals, principles, values, or good conduct. Values underlie ethics.

**Eustress**   Beneficial stress.

**Evaluation**   The process of judging or examining the cost, value, or worth of a plan or decision based on such criteria as standards, demands, or goals.

**Expertise**   The ability to perform tasks successfully and dependably.

**External change**   A kind of change fostered by society or the outer environment.

**External noise**   Noise from the environment.

**External search**   The process of looking for new information from sources outside oneself.

**External stress**   Situations in which stress is brought on from outside the individual.

**Extreme work**   Describes jobs that require 60+ hours per week as well as jobs that require significant travel and a 24/7 call schedule.

**Extrinsic motivation**   Outside rewards or motivation.

**Extrinsic values**   Values that derive worth or meaning from someone or something else.

**Extroverts**   Overall types of character and response in which individuals are less interested in themselves and more interested in others, outgoing, fueled by being around other people.

## F

**Fair Credit Reporting Act**   Legislation mandating that individuals who are denied credit, insurance, or employment because of their credit report have the right to obtain a free copy of their report.

**Family**   Several definitions exist about families. The U.S. Census Bureau definition is a group of two or more persons (one of whom is a householder) who are related by birth, marriage, or adoption and reside together. A more open definition is two or more people who self-identify as a family and share resources.

**Family demography**   Study of the characteristics and numbers of families, noting changes in families and households.

**Family ecosystem**   A subsystem of human ecology that emphasizes the interactions between families and environments.

**Fatalism**   The feeling or acknowledgment that all events are shaped by fate.

**Fatigue**   Not having sufficient energy to carry on and the strong desire to stop, rest, or sleep.

**Feedback**   Information that returns to the system.

**Fertility rate**   Yearly number of births per 1,000 women of childbearing age.

**FICO score**   Numeric value assigned to credit habits such as bill paying on time and credit history.

**Fight or flight syndrome**   Alerted condition of the body as it quickly prepares for physical battle or energetic flight to escape the situation.

**Financial Counseling**   Changing financial behaviors and outcomes, includes changing habits such as gambling.

**Financial Literacy**   Knowledge and understanding of financial concepts, choices, and information.

**Financial management**   The science or practice of managing money or other assets.

**Financial planners (advisors)**   Professionals who help clients plan and manage their financial resources, including investments, based on goals. Advice can be sought on a specific topic or for a total plan.

**Financial security**   The ability to meet daily obligations while planning, saving, and investing to achieve future goals.

**FIRE Movement (Stands for Financially Independent Retire Early)**   Retiring earlier than conventional age by increasing income and savings and decreasing expenses.

**Fixed expenses**   Expenses in a budget for which the same amount is allocated each month, such as for rent or car payments.

**Flextime**   Variable hours for employees.

**Focus groups**   Selected groups of people who are questioned by a discussion leader or moderator about their views on different topics or products.

**Fossil fuels**   Remains of dead vegetation, such as coal, oil, and natural gases that can be burned to release energy.

**Functional limitation**   Hindrance or negative effect in the performance of household tasks or work activities.

**Futuristic Thinking Skills**   Ability to predict future events and trends that affect you.

# G

**Gender gap**   The difference in earnings between employed men and women.

**Genealogy**   An account of the descent of a person or family from an ancestor or ancestors.

**Genome maps**   Blueprints that researchers use to investigate the development of an individual animal or plant from fertilization to maturity.

**Gerontology**   The scientific study of the aging process.

**Gig economy**   Being part of an economic trend, working at an extra paid job or growing a side business.

**Green building**   The relationship of a house and its occupants with the greater environment, includes eco-friendly design and processes, concepts of sustainability.

**Glass ceiling**   Situation in which as women move up the career ladder they hit an invisible - barrier that stops them from moving further.

**Global warming**   Occurs when carbon dioxide and other gases collect in the air and trap solar heat reflected from the earth.

**Goal disengagement**   The letting go of goals or the redefinition of goals or end states.

**Goals**   End results that require action; the purpose toward which much behavior is directed.

**Goldsmith Model of Social Influence (see also Model of Social Influence)**   Systems diagram that begins with invention or innovation and follows steps with a feedback loop after evaluation.

**Gresham's law of planning**   Short-term concerns create priorities and deadlines that take managerial attention away from long-range concerns.

**Grit**   A combination of passion and perseverance.

**Gross domestic product (GDP)**   The total market value of all goods and services produced by a nation during a specified period, usually a year.

**Gross income**   All income received that is not legally exempt from taxes.

# H

**Habitat**   The place where an organism lives.

**Habits**   Repetitive, often unconscious, patterns of behavior.

**Habitual decision making**   Process of making choices out of habit without any additional information search.

**Handicap**   A disadvantage, interference, or barrier to what one wants to do, can be permanent or temporary.

**Happiness**   The degree to which one judges the overall quality of his or her life as favorable.

**Hatching**   Local area nesting, finding other places outside of the workplace or the home to spend time in.

**Homeostasis**   The tendency to maintain balance.

**Household**   All persons who occupy a housing unit such as a house, apartment, or single room.

**Householder**   The person (or one of the persons) who owns the home or in whose name it is rented.

**Household Pulse Survey**   Published by the U.S. Census Bureau to show the economic impacts of a specific situation such as household or consumer response to the Covid-19 pandemic.

**Human capital**   The sum total of human resources; all the capabilities, traits, and other resources that people use to achieve goals.

**Human ecology**   The study of how humans interact with their environment.

**Human resources**   The skills, talents, and abilities that people possess.

**Hypotheses**   Predictions about future occurrences.

# I

**I-messages**   Statements of fact about how an individual feels or thinks.

**Immigration**   The process in which people enter and settle in a country where they are not native.

**Implementing**   Putting decisions or plans into action.

**Income**   The amount of money or its equivalent received during a period of time.

**Income tax**   A personal tax levied on individuals or families on the basis of income received; in the United States, there are state and federal income taxes.

**Independent activities**   Activities that take place one at a time.

**Indirect channels**   Message communication forms such as radio, television, magazines, newspapers, and signs.

**Inflation**   Rising prices.

**Information anxiety**   The gap between what individuals think they understand and what they actually do understand.

**Information overload**   The uncomfortable state when individuals are exposed to too much information in too short a time.

**Innovation overload**   Consumer response to the accelerated pace of information, knowledge, and innovations.

**Inputs**   Whatever is brought into the system.

**Insomnia**   The perception or complaint of inadequate, interrupted, or poor-quality sleep.

**Insurance**   A financial arrangement in which people pay premiums to an insurance company that reimburses them in the event of loss or injury.

**Intangible resources**   Resources incapable of being touched, unseen, an example is intelligence.

**Integrated waste management**   A combination of methods used to reduce environmental pollution.

**Integrity**   Honest and consistent in principles, beliefs, and values.

**Intellect**   Knowing or understanding; the capacity to create knowledge; the capability for rational or highly developed use of intelligence.

**Interdependent activities**   Relationship between activities where one activity must be completed before another can take place.

**Interface**   The place or point where independent systems or diverse groups interact.

**Interference**   Anything that distorts or interrupts messages.

**Internal change**   Type of change that originates within the individual or the family and includes events or decisions that primarily affect family members.

**Internal noise**   Noise occurring in the sender's and receiver's minds, an example would be doubt.

**Internal search**   The process of looking within oneself for information for decisions.

**Internal stress**   Type of stress that originates in one's own mind and body.

**Interpersonal conflicts**   Actions by one person that interfere with the actions of another.

**Intrapersonal communication**   Inner voice, within the individual.

**Intrinsic motivation**   The underlying causes of and the internal need for competence and self-determination. The pleasure or value a person derives from the content of work or activity.

**Intrinsic values**   Values classified as ends in themselves, having internal meanings.

**Introverts**   Overall types of character or response in which individuals tend to think of themselves first and rely on inner-directed thoughts.

**Intuition**   The sense or feeling of knowing what to do without going through the rational process.

**Invention**   Process that provides the initial verification that a problem can be solved.

**Investment**   Commitment of capital to the achievement of long-term goals or objectives.

**Involvement balance**   If a person is heavily involved in one domain (work, school, or family), he or she may be less available, psychologically or physically, for another domain.


## J

**Job stress**   The harmful physical and emotional responses that occur when the requirements of the job do not match the capabilities, resources, goals, or needs of the worker.


## K

**Karoshi Japanese**   term referring to death by overwork.

## L

**Law of least effort**   If there are several ways of achieving the same goal, people will gravitate to the least demanding course of action.

**Leaders**   Authorities, experts, facilitators, and guides who participate in community-action programs, families, and as contributors to scientific, social, or economic advances and in so doing improve human lives.

**Learning goals**   Emphasize the gaining of comprehension, taking steps to know more.

**Leisure**   Freedom from time-consuming activities, tasks, duties, or responsibilities.

**Level of living**   The measure of the goods and services affordable by and available to individuals or families.

**Leveraging**   Doing more with less, stretching resources.

**Liabilities**   Sum total of what a person owes.

**Life cycle assessment**   Process of determining the life cycle of household products includes not only material resources in their manufacture, distribution, and disposal but also includes energy use, and the human resources involved.

**Life management**   All decisions a person or family makes and the way their values, goals, and resource use affects their decision making, which includes all the goals, events, situations, and decisions that constitute a lifestyle.

**Lifestyle**   The characteristic way or pattern in which an individual conducts his or her life.

**Lifestyle management (life management)**   Encompasses all the decisions an individual or family makes that impacts how they live.

**Life stylist**   Someone who creates or re-creates a particular lifestyle such as found in advertisements or in real estate open houses or model homes.

**Liquidity**   The speed and ease of retrieving cash or turning another type of investment into cash.

**Listening**   Hearing what is said and observing the actions communicated.

**Long-term-care insurance**   Policies that provide benefits for a range of services not covered by regular health insurance or Medicare, mostly obtained to help in the elder years.

**Low involvement**   Information that does not necessitate much thinking about or attention.

## M

**Macroenvironment**   The environment that surrounds and encompasses the microenvironment.

**Management**   The process of using resources to achieve goals. It involves thinking, action, and results.

**Management process**   The procedures involved in management thinking, action, and results.

**Management style**   A characteristic way of making decisions and acting.

**Management tools**   Measuring devices, techniques, or instruments that are used to arrive at decisions and plans of action.

**Managerial judgment**   The ability to accept and work with change for the betterment of self and humankind.

**Material resources**   Tangible resources; natural phenomena, such as fertile soil, petroleum, and rivers, and human-made items, such as buildings, money, and computers.

**Maximizers**   Individuals who want to be certain they have made the right choices and therefore are less likely to fully commit to decisions.

**Market share**   How much of the market someone or some company/group has (example, Amazon).

**Median age**   The measure of central tendency. In population statistics, the median is the value separating the higher half from the lower half.

**Medicare**    The United States basic health insurance for people 65 or older.

**Message**    The total communication that is sent, listened to, and received.

**Message construction**    Structure of a message that determines where information should be placed in a message to have maximum impact, which includes how often information should be repeated in a message.

**Message content**    What a message says; strategies or information that may be used to communicate an idea or policy to receivers.

**Metro area**    More than 50,000 people.

**Microenvironment**    The environment that closely surrounds individuals and families.

**Mindfulness**    A way of thinking or philosophical stance using new techniques in time and stress management.

**Mobility**    Technical term for changing residences.

**Model of Social Influence**    (also called Goldsmith Model of Social Influence) A process beginning with invention or innovation leading to evaluation and a feedback loop with buzz or talk.

**Monochronic**    Preference to focus on one activity at a time.

**Morphogenic systems**    Systems adaptive to change and relatively open.

**Morphostatic systems**    Systems resistant to change, stable, and relatively closed.

**Mortality**    The technical term for death.

**Motivation**    Movement toward goals or other desired outcomes.

**Multiculturalism**    The mix of ethnic and cultural groups in which each is recognized and respected.

**Multifinality**    The phenomenon in which the same initial circumstances or conditions may lead to different conclusions or outcomes.

**Municipal landfills**    Area or site for the disposal of waste.

**Multitasking**    Doing several activities at once, same as dovetailing.

**Municipal waste**    Trash and garbage collected in a community or city.

**Murphy's Law**    If something can go wrong, it will.

## N

**Natural capital**    A good (something worthy) humans have to protect, such as the environment.

**Need recognition**    Realization of how much an individual needs a certain product, service, or condition.

**Needs**    Things that are required or necessary.

**Negative feedback**    Information put into the system that indicates that the system is deviating from its normal course and that corrective measures may be necessary if the desired steady state is to be maintained.

**Network Theory**    Indicates with larger shared networks future interactions and time perceptions will change especially for businesses and organizations.

**Net worth**    Amount determined by subtracting liabilities from assets.

**Neuroscience**    Scientific study of the nervous system including brain.

**Noise**    Any interference in the communication process that prevents the message from being heard correctly; unwanted sound.

**Noise reduction**    Process of lessening or removing noise from a signal or source.

**Nondiscretionary time**    The time that an individual cannot control totally.

**Noise reduction**    The process of removing or lessening noise or unwanted sounds.

**Nonnormative stressor events**    Unanticipated experiences that place a person or a family in a state of instability and require creative effort to remedy.

**Nonverbal symbols**    Anything other than words that is used in communication.

**Normative stressor events**   Anticipated, predictable developmental changes that occur at certain life intervals.

**Norms**   Rules that specify, delineate, encourage, and prohibit certain behaviors in certain situations.

**NREM (non-rapid eye movement)-sleep**   Kind of sleep that occurs when the sleeper is in an inactive, deep slumber.

## O

**On-boarding**   Activities and introductions to make new employees or group members feel welcome and involved.

**Opportunity cost**   The highest-valued alternative that must be sacrificed to satisfy a want or attain something.

**Opportunity recognition**   Realization by an individual that she or he may have limited or no access to a product, service, or condition.

**Optimism**   A tendency or a disposition to expect the best outcome or to think hopefully about a situation.

**Optimization**   Process of obtaining the best result.

**Orientation**   The location or situation of a house relative to points on a compass.

**Ostrich effect**   Avoiding painful or disagreeable news or information. For example, not wanting to know what is in a letter or some other form of communication.

**Outputs**   End results or products, leftovers, and waste.

**Outsourcing**   Paying someone else to do one's work.

**Overlapping activities**   Situation in which one gives intermittent attention to two or more activities until they are completed.

## P

**Pace**   Speed at which a person speaks or communicates, also can refer to speed of performance in other activities.

**Paradigm shift**   The process in which an individual or a team tackles a problem by jumping ahead to radically innovative solutions rather than taking a gradual step-by-step approach.

**Pareto's principle**   The principle stating that 20 percent of the time expended usually produces 80 percent of the results, whereas 80 percent of the time expended produces only 20 percent of the results.

**Parkinson's law**   The idea that a job expands to fill the time available to accomplish the task.

**Passively acquired information**   Information that one hears or sees but does not necessarily seek, such as billboard advertisements or broadcasted announcements in a store.

**Perception**   The process whereby sensory stimulation is translated into organized experience.

**Perfectionism**   Personality trait or inclination to strive for no errors or mistakes.

**Performance goals**   Emphasize outcomes or actions, usually external things that can be seen or measured such as sporting events performance.

**Perquisites (perks)**   Employer given extras like parking spaces, awards, services, food, and travel.

**Persistence**   A person's staying power; the personality trait of not giving up when faced with adversity.

**Personality**   The range of consistent characteristics or traits influencing behavior and cognition.

**Peter Principle**   Idea or concept that people are promoted beyond their level of competence.

**Physical environmental resources**   Natural surroundings.

**Plan**   A detailed schema, program, strategy, or method worked out beforehand for the accomplishment of a desired end result.

**Planning**   A series of decisions leading to action or to need or goal fulfillment.

**Pollution**   Undesirable changes in physical, chemical, or biological characteristics of air, land, or water that can harm the health, activities, or survival of living organisms.

**Polychronic**   Liking to do several things at once.

**Positive ecology**   Practice of thinking and acting in such a way as to reduce waste and pollution.

**Positive feedback**   Information put into the system that anticipates and promotes change.

**Postpurchase dissonance**   Situation in which after a purchasing decision, the buyer is likely to seek some reinforcement for the decision to reduce doubt or anxiety.

**Poverty**   The state of being poor and unable to provide for basic needs on a consistent basis.

**Prepurchase expectations**   Beliefs about the anticipated performance of a product or service.

**Private resources**   Those resources owned and/or controlled by an individual, family, or group.

**Proactive**   Characteristic of taking responsibility for one's own life. Proactive people accept responsibility for their own actions; they do not blame others or circumstances for their behavior.

**Probability**   The likelihood of a certain outcome.

**Problem recognition**   Perception by an individual or family of a significant difference between their lifestyle and some desired or ideal lifestyle.

**Problems**   Questions, dilemmas, or situations that need solving.

**Problem solving**   Making many decisions that lead to the resolution of a problem.

**Process**   A system of operations that work together to produce an end result.

**Procrastinator**   Someone who puts off work and postpones and delays decisions.

**Proxemics**   Distance between speakers.

**Psychic income**   One's perception or feelings about income; the satisfaction derived from income.

**Psychological hardiness**   The characteristic way of people who have a sense of control over their lives; they are committed to self, work, relationships, and other values and do not fear change.

**Psychologically flexible**   Open to change.

**Psychological resilience (flexibility)**   Capable of handling severe stressor events.

**Public resources**   Those resources that are owned and used by all the people in a locality or country.

## Q

**Qualitative time measurement**   Investigation into the meaning or significance of time use; that is, the satisfaction it generates.

**Quality of life**   The level of satisfaction with one's relationships and surroundings.

**Quantitative time measures**   The number, kind, and duration (e.g., minutes, hours, days) of activities that occur at specific points in time.

## R

**Radon**   A naturally occurring gaseous by-product of radioactive decay of uranium in the earth.

**Reactive**   Characteristic of being overly affected by outside forces or things said.

**Real income**   Income measured in prices at a certain time, reflecting the buying power of current dollars.

**Real-options thinking** Process of staying open, waiting and watching for the right opportunity.

**Receiving** Listening to the verbal messages and observing the nonverbal messages.

**Recession** A moderate and temporary decline in the economy.

**Reference groups** The people who influence an individual or provide guidance or advice.

**Reflective listening** Listening for feelings.

**Relative poverty** Having significantly less income and wealth than others in a member's society.

**Relative values** Values that are interpreted based on context.

**REM (rapid eye movement) sleep** Kind of sleep that occurs when the sleeper is in a light sleep; most dreams happen during REM.

**Renewable resources** Resources that are essentially unlimited, can be replaced.

**Resilience** The ability to overcome obstacles and to achieve positive outcomes after experiencing extreme difficulties.

**Resiliency** Ability to adapt.

**Reskilling** Changing up abilities through education, training, and experience.

**Resource allocation** Parceling out or planning to give resources where they are needed.

**Resource education** Bringing current and potential sustainability problems to the forefront for discussion and resolution.

**Resource forecasting** Planning or allocating resources for the future, observing trends such as population growth.

**Resource leveling** Techniques for discovering underuse or overuse and reallocating appropriately.

**Resource Management** Process of planning, scheduling, and allocating resources to maximize satisfaction, well-being, and efficiency.

**Resource stock** The sum of readily available resources an individual possesses.

**Resourcefulness** The ability to recognize and use resources effectively.

**Resources** Whatever is available to be used.

**Responses** The individual reactions that follow a message.

**Retirement** Withdrawal from full or primary employment or position or occupation.

**Risk** The possibility of pain, suffering, danger, harm, or loss from a decision; uncertainty.

**Risk aversion** Avoidance of risk.

**Routine** A habitual way of doing things such as accomplishing basic tasks that saves time and energy for other activities.

**R-value** The level of resistance in insulation materials.

## S

**Sandwich generation** Individuals who provide or anticipate providing financial support and caring for their parents while also providing financial support and caring for their children.

**Satisficers** People who make decisions and stick with them.

**Satisficing** Selecting the first acceptable alternative.

**Scanning** An action in which individuals or families read the world searching for signals or clues that have strategic implications.

**Scarcity** A shortage or insufficient amount of supply.

**Scheduling** Sets of time-bounded activities to be done in the future based on work to be done or goals.

**Screen time** Amount of time spent on devices such as laptops, iPads, televisions, smartphones, and video games.

**Self-care** Functions and reactions under human control, self-initiated and deliberate to improve conditions such as health.

**Self-monitoring** Individuals noticing and altering their own actions, language, and reactions based on people around them includes being attuned to others before speaking or reacting.

**Sending** Saying what one means to say, with an agreement between verbal and nonverbal messages.

**Sequence** A following of one thing after another in a series or an arrangement.

**Sequencing** Ordering of activities or events so that one follows another.

**Setting** The physical surroundings where messages are communicated.

**Site** The location or situation of a house.

**Sleep hygiene** The promotion of regular and improved sleep.

**Social channels** Communication between people, such as between friends, neighbors, and family members.

**Social environmental resources** People united in a common cause through an array of societies, economic and political groups, and community organizations.

**SNAP (Supplemental Nutrition Assistance Program)** U.S. program provides food help and information for usually low-income individuals and families, replacing what was known as food stamps.

**Social influence** How an individual or a group affects other's opinions, attitudes, emotions, or behaviors.

**Social networks** Broad term referring to communication connections between individuals and groups, some contain visible profiles or the exchange of personal information online.

**Social Security Act** Under this U.S. legislation, retired persons and selected others receive monthly stipends from the government.

**Socialization** The process by which people learn the rules of society or groups.

**Source** The sender or communicator.

**Source reduction** Any change in the design, manufacture, purchase, or use of materials or products, including packaging, to reduce the amount of toxicity before they become municipal solid waste.

**Spam** Unsolicited unwanted messages or junk mail on the Internet.

**Standard of living** What an individual or family aspires to.

**Standards** The quantitative and/or qualitative criteria reconciling resources with demands.

**Stepfamilies** Also called blended families, refer to families that include children from previous marriages or relationships, joining together.

**Stewardship** Responsibility to preserve the earth.

**Storyboarding** A planning technique used by advertisers and screenwriters to show the main scenes (in comic-strip style) of a commercial, news program, television show, or movie.

**Strategic plans** Type of plans using a directional approach including a search for information and a consideration of the best way to proceed.

**Strategy** A plan of action, a way of conducting and following through on operations.

**Stress** Response of the body to demands made on it.

**Stress overload or pileup** The cumulative effect of many stresses building up at one time.

**Stressors events** Situations or occurrences that cause stress.

**Subsystem** A part of a larger system.

**Success** Achievement of something desirable, can also elicit a feeling of achievement.

**Superconductivity** The conducting of electricity with almost no power loss.

**Supplemental Nutrition Assistance Program (SNAP)** U.S. program that replaces the Food Stamp Program, a resource for low-income individuals and families.

**Sustainability** The conscious design and the consideration of impacts that consumption choices make on the environment given finite resources. Also refers to what endures, what will last, and establishing systems and processes that support life including human life.

**Sustainable behavior**   Actions and behaviors that can be sustained, that are considerate of others and the environment. Can refer to the use of natural resources at the individual and household level.

**Sustainable development**   A form of growth wherein societal needs, present and future, are met.

**Symbols**   Things that suggest something else through association.

**Syncratic**   Families in which the husband and wife share equally in making most of the decisions.

**Synergize**   To produce a third alternative, a product of group thinking.

**System**   An integrated set of parts that function together for some end purpose or result.

**Systems theory**   A theory that emphasizes the interconnectedness and the interactions among different systems.

**Systems thinking**   How parts interact, connections.

**System understanding**   Know-how. The understanding of the interrelationship and pacing rates of influences among key variables.

## T

**Tangible resources**   Resources that are real, touchable, or capable of being appraised.

**Task saturation**   Situation in which people are doing so much that they cannot plan or lead effectively.

**Taxes**   Compulsory levies that are an important source of government revenue.

**Technology**   The application of the scientific method and materials to achieve objectives.

**Telecommuting**   Working from places other than conventional offices and other workspaces.

**Telemedicine (telehealth)**   Modern interface between doctors and patients, electronic sharing of information.

**Tempo**   A time patterning or pace that feels comfortable.

**Theory**   An organized system of ideas or beliefs that can be measured; a system of assumptions or principles.

**Throughputs**   The processing of inputs.

**Time**   A measured or measurable period.

**Time bursts**   Short, intense effort and concentration.

**Time displacement**   Time spent in one activity takes away from time spent in another activity.

**Time management**   The conscious control of time to fulfill needs and achieve goals.

**Time perception**   The awareness of the passage of time.

**Time-tagging**   How one estimates sequencing, the approximate amount of time required for each activity in a sequence, and the starting and ending times for each activity.

**Transfer payments**   Monies or services given for which the recipient does not directly pay.

**Transformations**   Transitions from one state to another.

**Transparency**   Openness in revealing information about the operations of companies, organizations, institutions, and government.

**Type A persons**   People characterized by excessively striving behavior, high job involvement, impatience, competitiveness, desire for control and power, aggressiveness, and hostility.

**Type B persons**   People characterized by relaxed, easygoing, reflective, and cooperative behavior.

## U

**Uncertainty**   The state or feeling of being in doubt.

**Unemployment**   Being out of work.

**Utility**   Value, work, applicability, productiveness, or, simply, usefulness of a resource.

## V

**Value chains**   In business, value chains are the glue that holds a business together, likewise, value chains are the glue that holds a family together. Examples of links in the value chains would be traditions and holiday celebrations, certain ways of doing things, shared goals, and identity.

**Value orientation**   An internally integrated value system.

**Values**   Principles that guide behavior.

**Variable expenses**   Expenses in a budget for which money can be spent in a range of amounts, for such goods or services as food, entertainment, or apparel.

**Verbal symbols**   Words people use.

**Virtual events**   Online, involves people interacting on the web (virtual environments) vs. in-person.

**Visible symbols**   Symbols that can be seen.

**Vision**   A statement that serves as an inspirational guide for the future.

**Vision board**   A drawing or illustration of a guide for the future.

**Vision boards**   Collages of images of drawings, pictures, quotations, inspirations.

**Volunteer work**   Kind of work that does not generate pay, usually performed outside the home.

## W

**Wants**   Things that are desired or wished for.

**Waste stream**   All garbage or trash produced.

**Water insecurity**   Lack of clean water availability.

**Wealth**   The state of being rich and having an abundance of material possessions and resources.

**Well-being**   A state of existence in which the individual, family, or society has a sense of security and physical, emotional, and financial health. "All is well."

**WFH (Work from home)**   As the term suggests, working from home could refer to any place that is not a conventional office or company headquarters, or workspace.

**Work**   Effort expended to produce or accomplish something, or activity that is rewarded, usually with pay.

**Workaholism**   The inability to stop thinking about work and doing work and the feeling that work is always the most pleasurable part of life.

**Work ethic**   The degree of dedication or commitment to work.

**Work from Home (WFH)**   Covers personal, family, and household impacts of home-based employment such as division of labor, time, and use of space.

**Work psychology**   Field of study and practice that covers most aspects of work behavior and experiences.

**Work simplification**   Improved, more efficient work methods in the home or in other settings.

## Y

**You-messages**   Statements that often ascribe blame or judge others.

## Z

**Zoomers (Gen Z)**   People born mid to late 1990s and into the 2010s.

# Index